SOCIAL PSYCHOLOGY

FOURTH EDITION

James W. Vander Zanden
OHIO STATE UNIVERSITY

RANDOM HOUSE NEW YORK

To my parents

Grateful acknowledgment is made for permission to reprint material from the following:

Figure 3.2: Reprinted with permission of The Free Press, a Division of Macmillan, Inc., from SOCIAL PSYCHOLOGY by Roger Brown. Copyright © 1965 by The Free Press.

Figure 3.3: From Benjamin Whorf, LANGUAGE, THOUGHT, AND REALITY. Copyright © 1956 by The MIT Press. Reprinted by permission.

Figure 4.2: From THE SEASONS OF A MAN'S LIFE, by Daniel J. Levinson et al. Copyright © 1978 by Daniel J. Levinson. Reprinted by permission of Alfred A. Knopf, Inc.

Quotes (pp. 225–226) and photo (p. 225): Excerpts abridged from pp. 73, 74, 76 and Fig. 2 (photo) The "Victim" (p. 17) in OBEDIENCE TO AUTHORITY by Stanley Milgram. Copyright © 1974 by Stanley Milgram.

Quotes (pp. 477–479): From Erickson, Frederick, "Gatekeeping and the Melting Pot: Interaction in Counseling Encounters," *Harvard Educational Review,* February 1975, 45, 1. Copyright © 1975 by the President and Fellows of Harvard College. All rights reserved.

Cover photographs:
Barbara Kirk/The Stock Market (family)
Stan-Pak/International Stock (business meeting)
Ellis Herwig/The Picture Cube (couple)

Fourth Edition
987654321
Copyright © 1977, 1981, 1984, 1987 by Random House, Inc.

Library of Congress Cataloging in Publication Data
Vander Zanden, James Wilfrid.
    Social psychology.

    Bibliography
    Includes index.
    1. Social psychology. I. Title.
HM251.V293   1987   302   86-3276
ISBN 0-394-35810-4

Manufactured in the United States of America

Text design: Glen Edelstein
Cover design: Celine Brandis
Line art: Vantage Art, Inc.

Preface

Preparing this new edition of *Social Psychology* has been a happy experience. I deem myself fortunate to be able to spend my working days studying, teaching, and writing about matters that I would otherwise pursue as a hobby. Indeed, what can be more intrinsically fascinating than a discipline that so immediately touches the human condition as does social psychology? It allows us to examine and understand human behavior—to learn what makes us tick. But even more, the insights we gain from social psychology are applicable as we go about our daily activities. With this knowledge, we can lead fuller, richer, and more fruitful lives. And more broadly, we have the opportunity to improve the human condition.

As I noted in the preface to the previous edition, I owe a personal debt to social psychology. My wife died some fifteen years ago, and in the intervening years my sons have grown into young manhood integrated into my work and the whole undertaking we know as social psychology. Although both sons are now in graduate-degree programs in computer science, they remark how valuable they continually find the insights they have gained from the discipline. They believe that it has broadened their horizons, increased their options in life, allowed them to develop greater self-assurance, and promoted their self-actualization. Social psychology has likewise been of immeasurable benefit to me in my life. And I hope that instructors and students will also find the study of social psychology a meaningful and enriching experience.

Each new edition of *Social Psychology* has allowed me to survey the literature in the discipline and to discern the waxing and waning of research interests. Some topics, such as attribution processes and altruism, have continued as dominant research themes. Others, such as self processes and interpersonal relationships, have gained in research activity in recent years. Still others, such as groups, leadership, conformity, and race relations, have witnessed a slackening in research interest. Overall, the most notable trend, among social psychologists from both psychological and sociological backgrounds, has been the shift from studying social behavior to studying the social mind. American social psychologists tend to be dominated by an individualistic orientation and to slight what goes on within and among people as they interact with one another. However, it is these latter matters that drew me to social psychology and that seem especially to intrigue students. Consequently, I have attempted to find a balance between social mind and social behavior concerns in this text.

However compelling its subject matter, a textbook, to be successful, must meet two criteria: First, it must provide the appropriate information; second, it must communicate the subject matter effectively. I attempt to achieve these ends in a number of ways:

The book aims to capture student interest: Most instructors of social psychology find it a stimulating field, and there is no reason why students should not experience the same enthusiasm and challenge. Therefore, in this text top priority is assigned to making social psychology come alive. One device for achieving this is the inclusion throughout of excerpts from student journals. In their journals, students record observations or events and interpret them according to social psychological concepts or principles. These journal entries, in which student teaches student, afford vivid and readable accounts of the human experience.

The text aims to provide a scientifically sound presentation: The reader is exposed to a wide sampling of social psychological theory and empirical research. The solid research foundations of the book are reflected in the lengthy bibliography at the back of the text. This new edition contains some 600 new references.

The text aims to be contemporary: Social psychology is shown in its relation to the world in which the instructor and the students live. Various contemporary social matters and problems are examined, including advertising, the use of power, company cultures, attracting a mate, successful marriages, the quality of intimate relationships, legislating good Samaritanism, social dilemmas, victimization, rape, sexism, and terrorism. Each chapter contains at least one new boxed insert.

The text aims for an interdisciplinary synthesis: Some chapters necessarily emphasize psychological interests and research; others sociological interests and research. Care has been taken, however, to weave this material into a meaningful and coherent whole.

The text aims to provide maximum flexibility in teaching: Clearly, there is not one "right" way to teach social psychology, and the material that is presented can be adapted to suit instructors' own teaching objectives and their students' needs. The chapters are sufficiently independent that they can be assigned in any order without posing problems for the students. In short, users of this text should feel free to make it serve their particular purposes. *Social Psychology* is meant to be a tool, your tool.

Columbus, Ohio   James W. Vander Zanden

Contents

1 INTRODUCTION 1
Early Roots: Psychology and Sociology 3
Social Psychological Theories 5
Methods of Social Psychological Study 17
Boxed Insert • A Marketing Fiasco 20
Ethical Considerations 28
Summary 31
Glossary 32

PART ONE INDIVIDUAL SOCIAL
BEHAVIOR 35

2 SOCIAL PERCEPTIONS AND
ATTRIBUTIONS 37
Boxed Insert • Other Perceptual Worlds 40
Impression Formation 41
*Boxed Insert • The Halo Effect: What Is
Beautiful Is Good—Or Is It? 48*
Attribution 53
Boxed Insert • Clues to Lying 54
Perception of the Situation 61
*Boxed Insert • The Importance of Social
Definitions: Who Is a Jew? 64*
Summary 68
Glossary 69

3 SOCIAL COMMUNICATION AND
LANGUAGE 71
*Boxed Insert • Helen Keller: The Significance
of Language 72*
The Nature of Symbols and Language 74
*Boxed Insert • Arranging Speaking Turns in
Conversation 80*
*Boxed Insert • Eye Contact and Civil
Inattention 84*
Boxed Insert • Attracting a Mate 88
Acquiring Language 92
Language and Thinking 98
Summary 103
Glossary 105

4 SOCIALIZATION AND
DEVELOPMENT 106
Preconditions for Socialization 107
*Boxed Insert • Socializing New Employees
Within the Company Culture 108*
Learning Processes 115
Boxed Insert • Learned Helplessness 118
Socialization Across the Life Span 131
Summary 139
Glossary 139

5 IDENTITIES AND THE SELF 141
The Self 142
Boxed Insert • Self-actualization 144
Boxed Insert • Self-awareness 148
Self-perception 154
*Boxed Insert • Putting Oneself at the Center
of Events 155*
Self-conceptions 157
Boxed Insert • Shyness 158
Summary 169
*Boxed Insert • Choking and Self-
handicapping Behaviors 170*
Glossary 171

6 ATTITUDES AND ATTITUDE
CHANGE 173
The Nature of Attitudes 173
*Boxed Insert • Measurement of Attitudes
176*
Organization of Attitudes 182
Boxed Insert • When Prophecy Fails 188
Boxed Insert • Reactance 190
Persuasion and Attitude Change 194
Boxed Insert • Successful Selling 195
*Boxed Insert • The Effectiveness of
Advertising 198*
Summary 203
Glossary 204

PART TWO INTERPERSONAL
SOCIAL BEHAVIOR 207

7 NORMS: SOCIAL ORDER AND
CONFORMITY 209
Effecting Social Order 210
*Boxed Insert • The Ethnomethodological
View of Social Order 212*
Conformity in Group Settings 218
Compliance in the Absence of External
Pressure 227
*Boxed Insert • Obedience to Orders: Issues
of Morality in Combat 228*
*Boxed Insert • Additional Situational
Factors Governing Conformity and
Compliance 233*
Summary 234
Glossary 235

8 ROLES 237
The Nature of Roles 238
Boxed Insert • From Devil to Saint 239
Self-presentation 249
Boxed Insert • Poker: Tells and Lies 250
*Boxed Insert • The Quality of Intimate
Relationships 258*
Summary 259
Glossary 260

9 RELATIONSHIPS AND
INTERPERSONAL ATTRACTION 262
Social Relationships 262
Boxed Insert • Sociometry 268
Attraction in the Dyad 269
*Boxed Insert • "My, It's a Small World!"
270*
Boxed Insert • Successful Marriages 282
*Boxed Insert • Self-disclosure and Trust
Within the Dyad 290*
Responses to Dissatisfaction in a Relationship
294
Summary 294
Glossary 295

10 ALTRUISM AND HELPING
BEHAVIOR 297
Positive Forms of Social Behavior 298
*Boxed Insert • Altruism and Sociobiology
302*
*Boxed Insert • Legislating Good
Samaritanism 314*
Notions of a Just World, Equity, and Equality
317
Summary 326
Glossary 327

11 AGGRESSION AND
CONFLICT 328
Aggression 329

Boxed Insert • Family Violence 330
Boxed Insert • Averting Rape 350
*Boxed Insert • Reactions to Victimization
352*
Conflict 354
*Boxed Insert • The Prisoner's Dilemma
Game 362*
Summary 365
Glossary 367

12 THE PHYSICAL ENVIRONMENT
AND INTERPERSONAL
BEHAVIOR 368
Territoriality 369
*Boxed Insert • Territoriality in the Ordering
of Slum Life 372*
Boxed Insert • Privacy 378
How People Handle Space 381
*Boxed Insert • The Social Significance of
Space 382*
*Boxed Insert • Architecture and Public
Places 388*
*Boxed Insert • Captivity: Hostages and Loss
of Privacy 390*
Summary 394
Glossary 395

PART THREE SOCIAL
BEHAVIOR IN GROUPS 397

13 GROUPS AND GROUP
BEHAVIOR 399
*Boxed Insert • Support Networks and Health
400*
Characteristics of Human Groups 400
Boxed Insert • "We" Versus "They" 406
Primary Groups and Secondary Groups
412
Reference Groups and Membership Groups
418
Boxed Insert • Social Dilemmas 426
Summary 430
Glossary 431

14 POWER AND INFLUENCE 433
The Nature of Power 433
Power as Process 439
Boxed Insert • Machiavellianism 422
Boxed Insert • The Use of Power 448
From Might to Right 449
Summary 457
Glossary 457

15 PREJUDICE AND RACISM 459
Intergroup Relations 460
Boxed Insert • Intergroup Marriage 464
Boxed Insert • Combatting Racism 468

Sources of Racial and Ethnic Antagonism
  480
*Boxed Insert • The Effects of School
  Desegregation   484*
Summary   491
Glossary   492

16   GENDER ROLES, IDENTITIES,
AND SEXUALITY   493
Gender Roles and Identities   494
*Boxed Insert • Facial Prominence in
  Pictures of Men and Women   498*
*Boxed Insert • An Ethnomethodological View
  of Gender   504*
*Boxed Insert • The Psychology of Sex
  Differences   510*
Sexism   518
*Boxed Insert • Excuses of a Male Chauvinist
  Husband   519*
Summary   525
Glossary   526

17   COLLECTIVE BEHAVIOR   528
Elements of Collective Behavior and Social
  Movements   529
Boxed Insert • Terrorism   534
Boxed Insert • Rumors   538
Boxed Insert • Religious Cults   542
Crowd Behavior   547
Social Problems   552
*Boxed Insert • Margarine: The Rise and Fall
  of a Social Problem   553*
*Boxed Insert • The Meek Don't Make It
  558*
Summary   561
Glossary   562

GLOSSARY   563

REFERENCES   573

AUTHOR INDEX   630

SUBJECT INDEX   641

1 INTRODUCTION

EARLY ROOTS: PSYCHOLOGY
    AND SOCIOLOGY
SOCIAL PSYCHOLOGICAL
    THEORIES
Behavioral Theory
Cognitive Theory
Gestalt and Field Theories
Social Exchange Theory
Symbolic Interactionism
Role Theory
Ethnomethodology
Theoretical Overview
METHODS OF SOCIAL
    PSYCHOLOGICAL STUDY
The Survey
The Experiment
Naturalistic Observation
ETHICAL CONSIDERATIONS

I was driving home over a back road when I came upon a guy driving a new Porsche. He was going 20 miles an hour under the speed limit. The road was winding and I could not pass him. So I said to myself, "What would it take to get me to speed up if I were driving that Porsche?" My answer was, "Tailgate him." I then moved my car close behind the Porsche, but it did not seem to have any effect. I evaluated my own act, and it seemed to me that I was gesturing in a way that would get my point across. So I thought, "This isn't working. I had better try something else. I'll drop back a little, and the first chance I get, I'll pass him." When I reached an open stretch of road that had no oncoming traffic, I accelerated and attempted to pass him. But the driver also speeded up so that I couldn't get by. Again I appraised the situation and concluded, "I had better push the accelerator to the floor." I did so, but the driver speeded up to prevent my overtaking him. Frustrated, I said to myself, "That guy is going to get both of us killed. I'll just drop back of him and not try to pass." I did so. At this point

1

the guy gave me the "finger" and raced off in the Porsche. From this example, one can see the operation of the selfhood process. As we engage in social behavior, we mentally evaluate its product. We become an audience to our own actions. We adopt a state of preparedness for certain kinds of responses from other people. We test our behavior on an ongoing basis and revise it. Consciousness allows us to reflect on our behavior and to modify it in accordance with our definition of the situation.

*   *   *

Yesterday a female companion and I were joyriding in my sports car. I had taken a piece of candy from my glove compartment and placed it in my mouth. My girlfriend asked me what color the candy was and to let her see what it looked like. I concealed the candy under my tongue, opened my mouth, and moved close to her with my mouth open. I then closed my mouth and moved back. I asked her whether or not she saw the candy. She said, "No." Then I asked her if she saw my tongue. She said, "Yes." I next asked her, "What color is my tongue?" She said, "I don't know. I was looking for the candy." This is an example of selective perception. She was trying to perceive the color of the candy by looking at the candy and the candy only. But if she had not been so selective in her viewing and had taken notice of the color that the candy had stained my tongue, she would have known the color of the candy itself.

*   *   *

I never really thought I had pretty legs. I felt they were too big at the knees, too fat at the thighs, and too small at the calves. Last Thursday I wore gym trunks while throwing a football with some fraternity guys. Later my boyfriend told me a lot of the guys thought I had really pretty shaped legs. Well, then, I looked at my legs, and thought, "Boy, my legs do look pretty good." So I tried wearing my gym trunks again today. A couple of my girlfriends told me I had pretty legs. Strange as it may seem, my legs have been looking better and better to me. Now I feel quite confident about them and want to show them off. This just goes to show how the responses others make toward us affect how we come to see ourselves. Our self-image arises out of the feedback others give us in the course of social interaction.*

*   *   *

In their journals, all these students were concerned with social interaction—interpersonal behavior—the subject matter of **social psychology**.† The late Gordon W. Allport (1968: 3),‡ a psychologist, regarded social psychology as a scientific "attempt to understand and explain how the thought, feeling, and behavior of individuals are influenced by the actual, imagined, or implied presence of

---

* These edited quotations from student journals, and others that appear throughout this book, are reproduced by permission of the students.

† Concepts in **boldface type** are defined in a Glossary at the end of each chapter and in the Glossary at the back of the book.

‡ A single year in parentheses refers to the work cited in the References section at the end of the book. The number that follows the date is the page number.

others." In sum, social psychology is the study of people—loving, hating, working, helping, trusting, fighting, communicating. It focuses on the entire drama of our daily lives, all of our activities in relation to one another. As such, it studies the trivial and the vital, the transient and the abiding, the joyful and the painful, the superficial and the visceral.

EARLY ROOTS: PSYCHOLOGY AND SOCIOLOGY

Although social psychology is an ancient discipline (some point to Plato or Aristotle as its founder), it was officially launched as a separate field in 1908. In that year the first two English-language textbooks appeared—William McDougall's *Introduction to Social Psychology* and E. A. Ross's *Social Psychology: An Outline and Source Book.* McDougall was a psychologist; Ross, a sociologist. In the intervening years social psychology has retained its interdisciplinary links to both psychology and sociology (Boutilier, Roed, and Svendsen, 1980; Pepitone, 1981).

Because social psychology draws from the storehouses of both sociological and psychological knowledge, many universities and colleges offer social psychology courses both in their sociology departments and in their psychology departments. Indeed, until relatively recently, psychologists and sociologists tended to go their independent ways. Psychologists traditionally focused on individuals and the social stimuli that impinge on them. In contrast, sociologists concerned themselves with the reciprocal relationship between the individual and society, stressing the part that social interaction plays within human life (Stryker, 1977, 1980; Stryker and Statham, 1985).

Within psychology—the science of behavior and mental processes—social psychology is distinguished from other subfields such as learning, perception, and motivation (Jones, 1985). While all psychologists study behavior—sometimes even the identical responses—they differ in their primary interest. Social psychologist Robert Zajonc provides us with the following analogy:

> The rat's response of "turning left in a T-maze" may be analyzed in terms of the number of reinforced trials that have been given to the animal (the psychology of learning); or in terms of the level of the animal's hunger (the psychology of motivation); or in terms of the physical properties of the right arm of the maze as opposed to those of the left arm (the psychology of perception). If all of the above variations—reinforcement, deprivation, and physical stimulation—are held constant, and if we observe the rat's responses of "turning left in the T-maze" when there happens to be one other rat in the right arm of the maze, we become social psychologists. (1967: 1)

Although at one time a minor field within psychology, social psychology has gained considerable stature during the past three decades.

Within sociology—generally viewed as the science of social organization (society) and group life—social psychology has long enjoyed a prominent place. Indeed, many sociologists find it difficult to draw a line of demarcation between the fields. Among sociologists with a symbolic-interactionist orientation, the

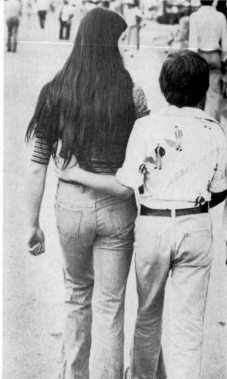

The Subject Matter of Social Psychology
Social psychologists study how the thoughts, feelings, and actions of people are influenced by other individuals. (Patrick Reddy)

overlap tends to be complete. Charles Horton Cooley (1864–1929), an influential early American sociologist and symbolic interactionist, placed the individual and society in a single frame of reference:

> A separate individual is an abstraction unknown to experience, and so likewise is society when regarded as something apart from individuals. The real thing is Human Life, which may be considered either in an individual aspect or in a social, that is to say a general, aspect; but is always, as a matter of fact, both individual and general. In other words, "society" and "individuals" do not denote separable phenomena, but are simply collective and distributive aspects of the same thing, the relation between them being like that between other expressions one of which denotes a group as a whole and the other the members of the group. (1902: 1–2)

In Europe, where social psychology never emerged as a separate specialty, leading sociologists such as Emile Durkheim (1858–1917), Max Weber (1864–1920), and Georg Simmel (1858–1918) dealt with social psychological matters as an integral part of their sociological studies.

Within the United States, social psychologists differ in their perception of the field. Some social psychologists, such as Edwin P. Hollander and R. G. Hunt (1971), view social psychology as a distinctive discipline—one that is not merely a mixture of bits and pieces from sociology and psychology, but a genuine fusion. Others, such as Zick Rubin (1973), view it not as a discipline like economics, history, sociology, and psychology, but as an "interdiscipline."

Whether social psychology is viewed as a qualitatively distinct discipline or as an interdiscipline, the overlap between sociology and psychology has contributed to a freshness in approach and has functioned as a stimulus to the further advancement of the frontiers of knowledge. Of course there are scholars who jealously seek to exclude rivals in neighboring sciences from what they view as "their" territory. Nevertheless, the prevailing attitude has increasingly become one of welcoming aid and collaboration from any qualified person, regardless of discipline. Each scientist can and should learn from the others.

SOCIAL PSYCHOLOGICAL THEORIES

Nothing is so practical as a good theory.

—Kurt Lewin

Theory is the net we weave to catch the world of observation so that we can explain, predict, and influence it (Deutsch and Krauss, 1965). Formulating a theory is a way of making sense out of a confused set of data through a symbolic construction by the human mind (Kaplan, 1964; Scarr, 1985). It allows us to bring together a multitude of facts in a meaningful manner so that we may comprehend them all at once. Consequently, theory is in part a summary of known facts and in part conjecture about the implications of such facts and the probable relationships that exist among them. Thus theory is a *tool*. More specifically, a theory performs a number of functions (Shaw and Costanzo, 1982).

First, it permits us to organize our observations and to deal meaningfully with information that would otherwise be chaotic and useless. Second, theory allows us to see relationships among facts and uncover implications that would not otherwise be evident in isolated bits and pieces of data. And third, it stimulates inquiry as we search for knowledge about many different and often puzzling aspects of our behavior.

Within social psychology, a number of differing theoretical traditions have emerged. This is hardly surprising, since the same behavior may be viewed from differing perspectives. Take, for example, the matter of eating. We could consider eating in terms of the experience of hunger that is alleviated by food; the stimulus that the sight or smell of food provides; the social meanings attributed to eating with friends or enemies; or the ways in which people fit their actions together to provide food or a particular meal. In this chapter we will examine several major approaches within contemporary social psychology. Since the various orientations will appear again in various parts of the book, we will limit ourselves to a brief description of each orientation.

Behavioral Theory

How an organism learns—acquires responses—has been the chief concern of a major and productive group of American psychologists whose approach is termed **behaviorism.** The behaviorist approach, which occupied the center stage in psychological work between 1920 and 1960, was initially set forth by John B. Watson (1914, 1919) and further developed and elaborated by such psychologists as Edward L. Thorndike (1907, 1931), Edward C. Tolman (1932), Edwin R. Guthrie (1935), Clark Hull (1943, 1952), and B. F. Skinner (1953, 1957, 1974). When Watson began his work early in this century, American psychology was preoccupied with topics like "mind," "image," and "consciousness." Watson rejected these concepts, labeling them "mystical," "mentalistic," and "subjective." Instead, he called for a totally objective psychology, one that would deal only with the observable activities of organisms—their "doings and sayings." Hence, Watson insisted that psychology should study how people in fact behave and that this could best be achieved by employing the experimental procedures of animal psychology.

Behaviorists have argued that introspection (observation of one's own perceptions and feelings) is unreliable and that psychologists should not concern themselves with internal or mental events. Instead behaviorists segment *behavior* into units called **responses** and they divide the *environment* into units called **stimuli.** Accordingly, behaviorism is also referred to as stimulus-response (or simply S-R) psychology.

Behaviorists assert that a particular stimulus and a particular response are "associated" with one another, producing a functional relationship or linkage between them. For example, a stimulus like one's friend coming into one's visual field elicits a response like a smile. This notion regarding the connection between stimuli and responses is a logical outcome of the behaviorists' downgrading of

Removing Barriers
By stripping away mystery and cant, social science can have a liberating effect. With knowledge, people can break down the barriers that lock individuals within unjust social arrangements. It offers us the opportunity to improve the human condition by helping us to achieve freedom, self-identity, and self-fulfillment. (Patrick Reddy)

inner mental considerations. It is not surprising, therefore, that extreme behaviorism is often termed a "black box" approach. Stimuli enter the "box" (the organism) only to come out as responses. The internal structures or mental processes that intervene between the stimulus and the response, since they are not directly observable, are minimized by traditional behaviorists.

Behaviorists stress the part that *reinforcement* plays in establishing and strengthening stimulus-response connections. Reinforcement refers to any event that strengthens the probability of a particular response. A good illustration of reinforcement procedures is provided by Benjamin Franklin. Two centuries ago a minister on a ship complained to Franklin that the sailors rarely attended prayer meetings. Franklin suggested that the minister take charge of passing out the daily ration of rum and that he dispense it immediately after the prayers. The minister did what Franklin recommended and "never were prayers more generally and more punctually attended" (Franklin, 1969). Chapter 4 will consider behaviorist theory at greater length.

Cognitive Theory

Man is a reasoning animal.

—Seneca,
Epistulae moralies ad Lucilium,
63 A.D.

Behaviorists view organisms as essentially *passive* receivers of stimuli. Indeed, early behaviorists viewed the brain as a kind of switchboard that merely routes the proper responses to incoming stimuli. In contrast, cognitive psychologists see the organism as an *active* agent in receiving, using, manipulating, and transforming information. They depict people as thinking, planning, problem solving, and decision making—as mentally manipulating images, symbols, and ideas. **Cognition** is a term referring to all the mental processes that transform sensory input in some meaningful fashion—that code, elaborate, store, retrieve, and appropriately use it.

In clear contradiction to behaviorist approaches, cognitive theorists believe that thoughts are causal factors in behavior. They criticize behaviorists for portraying individuals as robots who are mechanically programmed by environmental reinforcements. Instead, cognitive psychologists say that people are capable of intervening in the course of their affairs with conscious deliberation. They view people as able to make decisions that are rational in that the decisions are based on available information and an ability to process the information intelligently. Thus cognitive psychologists are interested in how we use information from our environment and our memories to make decisions about what to do. In recent years, the cognitive approach has displaced behaviorism as the leading focus of psychological work (Jones, 1985; Markus and Zajonc, 1985).

Among psychologically oriented social psychologists, interest in cognitive processes often blurs the boundary between social and nonsocial psychology (Jones, 1985). Given a researchable problem, they typically frame it in cognitive terms and ask how the situation, the stimuli, and the variables controlling the responses are represented in the minds of people. Hazel Markus and R. B. Zajonc (1985: 137) observe: "The result is that one can no longer view today's social psychology as the study of social behavior. It is more accurate to define it as the study of the social mind." A good illustration is *attribution theory,* which deals with the processes by which we impute causes to behavior (see Chapter 2).

Most of the critical questions of social cognition have to do with how we mentally represent social knowledge. The organism processes information in such a way that an image, symbol, or idea comes to stand for something else—for instance, an act, an object, an emotion, a sound, or an internal state. Information is processed by some type of internal or mental structure that receives and organizes it—what is termed a *cognitive* or *knowledge structure* (see Chapter 2). Such structures are organized stores of information (mental representations) that we have achieved as a result of prior information processing. They operate as frameworks for interpreting our current social experiences. These structures simplify perceptual inputs that would otherwise overwhelm us by their complexity. And they fill in where there is too little information, allowing us to make sense of an otherwise ambivalent situation. Thus cognitive structures help us to achieve some coherence in our environment, and they assist us in the construction of social reality. The memory system is assumed to contain countless knowledge structures (Markus and Zajonc, 1985).

Gestalt and Field Theories

The recent surge of interest in cognitive processes was influenced by the work of earlier Gestalt psychologists. Max Wertheimer (1880–1943) and two of his German co-workers, Wolfgang Köhler (1887–1967) and Kurt Koffka (1886–1941), are considered founders of the Gestalt movement (**Gestalt** is a German word meaning configuration or organization). The major emphasis of the Berlin Gestalt group was on the part-whole relationship, especially as it found expression within perceptual phenomena. The Gestalt psychologists emphasized that parts or elements do not exist in isolation; rather, they are organized into wholes. For instance, when we look at a building, we do not see lumber, shingles, bricks, glass, and other components—instead we see a house. Hence, the brain is said to process, organize, and interpret stimuli received from receptor organs; it relates an experience to other experiences in terms of some larger, more inclusive context.

The initial impetus to Gestalt psychology came in 1910, when Wertheimer discovered the *phi phenomenon*. The phi phenomenon involves the illusion of motion. If two lights blink on and off at a certain rate, they give the impression that the light is moving back and forth. The principle finds expression in motion pictures when stills are shown in rapid succession and in the apparent movement of neon-lighted arrows that seem to fly when lighted in succession. The experience of motion emerges from our organizing elements into wholes.

Gestalt theory provided an impetus to the work of Kurt Lewin (1890–1947) and his students. Although at one time a member of the Berlin Gestalt group, Lewin moved in sufficiently new directions for social psychologists to distinguish his field theory from Gestalt theory. Lewin's approach was based on the concept of **field** or **life space**. He felt that all psychological events, be they acting, thinking, dreaming, hoping, or whatever, are a function of life space—the person and the environment viewed as one constellation of interdependent forces (Deutsch, 1968). The life space consists of all past, present, and future events, since all three aspects of life can influence behavior in any single situation.

This emphasis on the relatedness of the individual and the environment constituted a major contribution to the field of psychology. Traditionally, psychologists had focused on the characteristics of individuals ("instincts," "heredity," "intelligence," "needs," and "habits") relatively independently of the situations in which the individuals operated. But according to Lewin, statements that do not take the situation into account are unacceptable. Lewin would rule out such observations as the following: "He is psychotic because of his heredity." "He became leader of the group because of his personality." "Her emotional outburst was due to hysteria." "Friends work together better than strangers" (Deutsch, 1968).

Lewin stressed that the understanding of behavior requires knowledge not only of a person's past experiences, present attitudes, and future expectations, but also of the immediate context or situation. John R. P. French (1944) inadvertently demonstrated this principle when he undertook an experiment designed to compare the behavior of organized and unorganized groups in a fear-provoking situation. While students were completing questionnaires in a locked room, the experimenter switched on a smoke machine that sent smoke curling under the door of the experiment room. Shortly thereafter, a fire siren was sounded. Unhappily for French, some students reacted in a disappointingly calm manner. In one group, a student said, "I smell smoke. Is there a fire?" while another serenely observed, "They probably want to test our psychological reactions." In another group, the first student to observe the smoke jumped up, shoved open the locked door, and knocked over the smoke machine. The response of subjects, then, depended on how they defined the *situation*—whether they saw the smoke as part of an experimental hoax or as caused by a real fire. The unexpected results of French's experiment demonstrate that social psychologists cannot interpret a subject's responses unless they have knowledge of the totality of psychological facts that exist in the person's life space at the time of the experiment.

Lewin's interest in life space led him to the study of group dynamics. One of his studies concerned behavior in various social climates (Lewin, Lippitt, and White, 1939). The research dealt with democratic and authoritarian leadership and the effects of such leadership on the productiveness and behavior of a group of boys. Authoritarian leadership was found to be accompanied by high levels of frustration and some degree of aggression toward the leader. When the leader was present, productivity was high; when he was absent, it was low. In contrast, democratic leadership was associated with greater individual happiness, more group-minded activity, greater productivity (especially in the leader's absence), and less aggressive displays. Studies such as this opened up important new ideas for social research and contributed to the growth of social psychology. Shortly before his death, Lewin was instrumental in developing what is now termed sensitivity training. The T-groups (training groups) that he set up were the first part of a movement later characterized by encounter groups.

Social Exchange Theory

Social exchange theory has roots within both psychology, identified with such psychologists as John W. Thibaut and Harold H. Kelley (1959), and sociology, identified with such sociologists as George C. Homans (1950, 1974) and Peter M. Blau (1964). However, the theory has gained popularity only over the past fifteen years, during which time publications in the area have grown exponentially (Beniger and Savory, 1981). The tradition represents an attempt to integrate the behaviorist theory that learning is brought about through reward and punishment with the principles of classical economics. According to this theory, people enter into exchange relationships because they derive rewards from doing so. Social exchange theorists broaden the economist's concept of exchange of

Social exchange theory

In my computer science class we have a good many tough assignments. One guy in class, Mike, seems to be quite bright and isn't at all reluctant to let everyone know that he's got the "smarts." In fact, he showboats all over the place, and he has succeeded in alienating a lot of us. By the end of the first week of classes, another guy, Dave, managed to take over the seat next to Mike. Dave made it a practice to "ego massage" Mike before classes, and soon Mike was letting Dave copy his homework. Well, the copying went on well into the third week. Then yesterday we got back our latest homework assignment, and Mike had five points taken off because he had allegedly copied the work from Dave. Mike was furious and told Dave to go see the instructor and own up. But Dave told Mike to take a "flying jump," and the relationship has now come to an end. Here is a good illustration of social exchange theory. Each individual got something from the relationship: Mike got an ego massage and Dave got homework. But when the cost got too high for Mike (and for Dave, had he owned up to his copying Mike's homework), the relationship blew apart.

commodities to include the exchange of social approval, love, gratitude, security, recognition, and so on. They broaden the behaviorist's theory of learning to include the process by which people satisfy one another's needs and by which they reward and punish one another.

In social exchange theory, people are viewed as being engaged in a sort of mental bookkeeping that involves a ledger of rewards, costs, and profits. *Rewards* are anything that human beings will incur costs to obtain. *Costs* are whatever human beings attempt to avoid. And *profits* are rewards less costs. Thus social behavior consists of an exchange of activity between at least two people that is perceived as being more or less rewarding or costly to one or the other. Such an activity (a job, a love affair, a marriage, a friendship) will continue only if it is profitable to both parties (relative to alternative activities). (See Chapter 9.) By way of illustration, let us assume that you and I are co-workers. I continually ask you for advice; you continually provide me with it. We are engaged in social exchange. I exchange my approval, recognition, and gratitude for your help. You exchange your help for my approval, recognition, and gratitude. Through this arrangement, we both derive important rewards. But we also experience costs: I suffer in self-esteem; you find that I interfere with your getting your work done. So long as we both find profit (reward minus cost) in the relationship, we are likely to continue it, just as in marketplace decisions. But unless each of us derives a certain minimum benefit, the interaction will cease, and no benefit will come to either of us.

In sum, social exchange theorists conceive of people as essentially rational beings. But they do not claim that individuals are always well informed or that

Social Exchange Theory
Viewed from the perspective of the social exchange
theory, the elderly suffer from a progressive erosion
of the resources that give them power. Consequently
they find that their bargaining position in society is
weakened. The distributive question of who gets
what, when, and how with respect to scarce goods
and services tends to be resolved in a manner unfavorable to the elderly. (Patrick Reddy)

the choices they make necessarily produce the best or wisest outcomes. The
theorists portray human life as a social endeavor because in most cases individuals can satisfy their needs only through or in cooperation with others. This fact
requires reciprocity among individuals and produces social interdependence.
However, all behavior involves costs. Consequently, people anticipate that their
actions will achieve rewards or reduce other costs. They are willing to commit
themselves to long-term relationships and to make continuing investments with
no immediate returns so long as they expect that they will eventually be able to
achieve more favorable outcomes.

While social exchange theorists do not necessarily consider themselves behaviorists, aspects of their formulations can be translated into behaviorist principles. Take the work of the noted behaviorist B. F. Skinner (Bredemeir, 1977).

In his experiments, Skinner wants a pigeon to engage in some behavior like the pecking of a dotted disk. For its part, the pigeon wants food. Under certain conditions, each party achieves his or her ends. Skinner of course emphasizes how he gets the pigeon to peck the dot. But it is equally true that Skinner is rewarded by the pigeon (the pigeon pecks the dot) only insofar as Skinner does what the pigeon requires him to do (provide a grain of food after each appropriate peck, maintain a dry and warm cage, protect the pigeon from cats, and the like).

In getting a pigeon to peck a dotted disk, Skinner has to "size up" the situation. He has to determine "what it will take" to get a pigeon to do what he desires— the "payoff" demanded by the bird. It costs Skinner something to "train" the bird (food, time, and energy). In essence we do much the same thing when we test the hypothesis that the car salesman will respond to a thousand dollars, twelve hundred dollars, and so on.

Social exchange theory has found various applications. One of the most note-worthy of these was undertaken by Robert Hamblin and his associates (1971) in the St. Louis school system. Using tokens (chips), candy, praise, and encouragement as reinforcement, the researchers got classroom nontalkers to talk, non-readers to read, and behavior problems to behave. Hence stimulus-response principles were employed to structure exchange relationships between teachers and their students.

Symbolic Interactionism

Symbolic interactionism as a distinct social psychological and sociological approach was developed primarily in the United States under the influence of the pragmatic philosophers, especially William James (1842–1910) and John Dewey (1859–1952). It was vigorously elaborated by such eminent sociologists as Charles Horton Cooley (1864–1929), George Herbert Mead (1863–1931), and William I. Thomas (1863–1947). Although there are a number of varieties of interactionist thought, Herbert Blumer (1969: 2) captures its essentials in three basic postulates: (1) "human beings act toward things on the basis of the meanings that the things have for them"; (2) "the meaning of such things is derived from, or arises out of, the social interaction that one has with one's fellows"; and (3) "these meanings are handled in, and modified through, an interpretative process used by the person in dealing with the things he encounters."

Symbolic interactionists point out that humans are social beings who live a group existence. Yet, in contrast with ants, bees, termites, and other social insects, human beings have little in the way of inborn, instinctive mechanisms by which to link themselves together and fashion their lives within communities and societies. Indeed, this has been the great merit of *Homo sapiens*. In the course of evolution, rather than developing highly specialized organic adaptations to particular environments (as in the case of the giraffe's long neck), the human organism has remained relatively generalized and able to adapt to quite different environments. *Homo sapiens* has made nonorganic or cultural adaptations through socially devised mechanisms.

Symbolic interactionists say that verbal and nonverbal symbols are the key to understanding human life. Symbols, especially language, permit us to carry on communication with one another (*inter*individual communication). They permit us to transmit knowledge, skills, ideas, and beliefs to one another. In this manner we establish a "commonness" so that both the sender and the receiver become "tuned" together for a particular message. Based on such shared information, we can go about the task of fitting our actions together.

Symbolic interactionists point out that meaning is not inherent in people and objects. Instead, meaning is assigned to people and objects by the perceiver. Thus individuals must *interpret* the world around them. Here again symbols play a vital part. Symbols permit us to carry on internal conversations with ourselves, functioning as important vehicles of thought (*intra*individual communication). Through the internal manipulation of symbols, we arrive at definitions of behavior and situations by attributing meaning to them.

Symbolic interactionists reject the notion that people automatically and mechanically react to given stimuli. Instead, they portray people as creatively constructing their actions in accordance with the meanings that the people attribute to a situation. Individuals are believed to rehearse their actions mentally before acting and then to function as audiences to their own actions.

Symbolic interactionists consider a certain amount of indeterminacy or unpredictability as inherent to human behavior because people must continually fashion meanings and devise ways to fit their actions together. As a consequence, much of human behavior has a tentative and developing quality: people map, test, devise, suspend, and revise their overt acts in response to the actions of others. According to this view, individuals negotiate interaction as they fit their lines of activity to the developing actions of others. Hence symbolic interactionists view institutions and groups as human-constructed realities. They do not consider institutions and groups to be etched in social granite for extended periods of time but rather to be dynamic, ongoing arrangements that undergo continuous evolution, negotiation, and reworking. They conceive of social life as process or becoming rather than as a static existence or fixed being. The treatment of the definition of the situation in Chapter 2, symbols in Chapter 3, the self in Chapter 5, social order in Chapter 7, and groups in Chapter 13 has been strongly influenced by the symbolic interactionist tradition.

Role Theory

Symbolic interaction theory and role theory share a number of elements in common (Stryker and Statham, 1985). Both focus on the subjective experiences and performances of people, particularly the definitions and meanings that people employ in achieving a group life. Both employ the theater as a social metaphor, giving a central place to the concept of role in their analyses (though some symbolic interactionists do not use the term on grounds that expectations for behavior are not fixed or structured patterns but emergent products of ongoing social interaction). And both depict society and self as "two sides of the same coin," contributing to the reciprocity of "society" and "the individual."

Role theory portrays social interaction in terms of actors who play their assigned parts in accordance with a script written by culture. Viewed in this

The Symbolic Expression of Inner States
According to symbolic interactionists, the task of the social psychologist is to try to experience the world as the other person experiences it (Blumer, 1969). (Patrick Reddy)

manner, role expectations are shared understandings that tell us what actions we can anticipate from one another as we go about our daily activities. By virtue of roles, we mentally classify people in terms of their common attributes, their common behavior, or the common reactions they elicit. In so doing, we collapse or telescope a range of behaviors into manageable bundles and come to specify who does what, when, and where. In sum, roles specify the social expectations that apply to the behavior of specific categories of people in particular situational contexts (for instance, doctors, students, uncles, elderly women, neighbors, shoppers). (See Chapter 8.)

Role expectations are grounded in values that are shared widely by the members of a community or society. They are the givens of interaction, since they are established (*institutionalized*) prior to interaction. Through learning in a social environment (*socialization*), rules for behavior are transmitted from one generation to the next. Individuals come to hold expectations for themselves and others because of the positions they occupy in an organized social environment, or *social structure* (a family, business, church, school, or neighborhood). As sociologists conceive of social structure, it consists of the interweaving of people's interactions and relationships in recurrent and stable ways. By virtue of social structure, we experience social life as orderly and patterned (Linton, 1936).

Some sociologists, like Sheldon Stryker (1980), seek to integrate symbolic interaction theory and role theory. They employ symbolic interactionism as a framework for analyzing social interaction and the social person. They use the concept of role to "build down" to the social person. In turn, role theory becomes a framework for handling social structure. It is used to "build up" from interaction to larger units of organized social life, particularly groups and institutions. The point where the two frameworks are joined is role. The concept serves to bridge social structure as conceived by role theory and the social person as conceived by symbolic interaction theory. The two approaches complement one another, allowing us to grasp the intertwining of "social structure" and "person."

Ethnomethodology

Over the past three decades, sociologist Harold Garfinkel and a number of his colleagues and students have evolved an approach to social phenomena that they term **ethnomethodology.** *Ethno,* borrowed from the Greek, means "people" or "folk" and is used in the formation of compound words like "ethnomedicine," "ethnobotany," and "ethnophysics." Such terms are commonly used by anthropologists to refer to a people's folk beliefs and practices. For instance, ethnomedicine has to do with the explanations that a particular people advance for illness and the remedies they employ. *Methodology* concerns procedures by which something is done or analyzed. Hence ethnomethodology in its most literal sense refers to the procedures (the rules and activities) that people employ in making social life and society intelligible and understandable to themselves (Garfinkel, 1974).

One of the early studies leading to the development of ethnomethodology was a jury research project in which Garfinkel had been involved. In the course of the study, he became curious about how jurors go about deciding the facts in a case and how they arrive at their interpretations of the law. From tapes of actual jury deliberations and interviews with jurors, Garfinkel found that jurors are concerned with such things as "adequate" accounts, "adequate" descriptions, and "adequate" evidence. Further, they wanted to be seen as behaving like "proper jurors." Jurors are active, story-constructing recipients of trial information (Devine and Ostrom, 1985).

Garfinkel examined the ways in which jurors go about determining what is "adequate" and what is "legal"—in brief, the everyday or folk methodology the jurors used in their deliberations. In sum, Garfinkel was not concerned with the facts or the laws involved in the specific cases. Rather, he was interested in the procedures the jurors themselves used for arriving at their interpretations of fact, for applying general rules to specific cases, and for justifying their actions.

The primary focus of ethnomethodology is on the practical, everyday activities of people, especially the methods they employ for producing and managing their affairs. It attempts to answer the question "How is the social activity done?" Ethnomethodologists seek to illuminate the commonplace, taken-for-granted activities that come to characterize everyday life—"the things that everybody already knows," which, although they influence behavior, go largely unexamined. At first glance, these phenomena are so "obvious" that we are blinded to the need for explaining them. In contrast to symbolic interactionists, who focus on social interaction per se (what occurs among and between individuals), ethnomethodologists emphasize the methods whereby each individual constructs interaction and an image of social life.

Ethnomethodologists say that to reveal people's underlying assumptions and procedures is to reveal the social world. They are particularly concerned with the way people manage to produce and sustain a sense of social order and structure—the process by which people go about "structuring" structure (how members of a society undertake to see, describe, and explain order in the world around them). Hence, in the illustration above, Garfinkel was concerned with the way jurors come to experience their deliberations as a part of the "legal system." The jurors fashion this reality not only to provide themselves with a sense of social order but also so that others might perceive them as "competent members of society." In this sense, then, the order that I as a person find in the world is not only "order for me," or even "order for you," but "order for us." The ethnomethodological view is considered in Chapter 7 and gender in Chapter 16.

Theoretical Overview

The details of these social psychological theories will become clearer as we encounter them in the chapters to come. Before proceeding, however, it might be well to pause and respond to the questions students often raise, namely, "Which theory is correct, which wrong?" and "Which theory is the best, which the worst?" In all candor, many social psychologists would answer that none of these theories is necessarily "correct," "wrong," "better," or "worse." They are simply tools—mental constructs that allow us to visualize (describe and analyze) something. By its nature, a theory limits the viewer's experience, presenting a tunnel perspective. But a good theory also extends the vision of what *is* seen, serving like a pair of binoculars. Thus *its degree of usefulness depends on what we are studying*.

Different theories draw our attention to differing aspects of the same phenomenon. In studying aggression, for instance, a behaviorist might focus on the learning experiences that reinforce aggressive behavior—on how parents, teachers, coaches, and others condition a subject to perform aggressive acts by the use of rewards. Cognitive psychologists might be interested in how people come to perceive, interpret, and think about given behaviors like aggression. Field-oriented social psychologists might concern themselves with the interplay between a person's characteristics and features of the person's situation that activate aggressive behavior. Social exchange theorists might focus on the social rewards that people gain by means of aggression. Symbolic interactionists might consider the social meanings that individuals assign to their acts as they contend against one another and then go about formulating their courses of action. Role theorists might be drawn to the social expectations that specify aggressive or nonaggressive behaviors. And ethnomethodologists might examine the methods people employ for arriving at their interpretations of aggression and for applying certain rules to specific acts of aggression.

Each approach, then, offers a somewhat different insight. Moreover, each theory provides a more effective approach, a better "fit," to *certain* kinds of data—*certain* aspects of behavior—than the other theories do. Consequently, each theory may have some merit and need not necessarily preclude the accuracy of some other theory in explaining given data or predicting given outcomes. Indeed, each theory is useful because it presents us with one piece of information in the exceedingly complex puzzle of human behavior.

METHODS OF SOCIAL PSYCHOLOGICAL STUDY

> *The investigator should have a robust faith—and yet not believe.*
> —Claude Bernard, *Introduction à la médecine expérimentale,* 1865

Science presupposes the existence of an empirical world; it rests on the assumption that a universe prevails apart from our experience of it. Since this universe has a real existence, it must be knowable. The task of science is to make the world intelligible to us. Scientists undertake to fathom and depict—to detect and establish—the *what is*. This, then, brings us to a consideration of the methods social psychologists, as social scientists, employ for depicting and analyzing behavior.

The Survey

Social psychologists are often interested in obtaining information about such matters as the extent of drug usage within a population, the impact of an advertising campaign, the incidence of abortion, political attitudes, the process whereby a new fad is diffused, or public reactions to an assassination. To do this calls for the employment of various quantitative methods—procedures for acquiring scientific knowledge that entail enumeration and measurement (data collected in numerical form).

Prominent in the social psychological arsenal of quantitative methods is the **social survey.** Survey data can be gathered in two basic ways. In the first, people are interviewed by a researcher who reads them questions from a prepared questionnaire. In the second, individuals receive a questionnaire in the mail, fill it out, and return it by mail.

Conducting a massive number of interviews or mailing a good many questionnaires, however, is exceedingly expensive and often also impractical. For this reason, social psychologists draw on small samples—that is, question relatively small numbers of people—to arrive at broad generalizations. Similarly, public opinion pollsters (such as those who work for Gallup, Harris, CBS, and NBC) employ a small sample of approximately 1,500 to tap the opinion of 230 million Americans within a small margin of error.

Although initially surprising, the success of this method is understandable. Consider, for example, a jar filled with 100,000 green and yellow marbles. We need not count all the marbles to know the proportion that is green or yellow. A sample of just 1,000 would allow us to estimate the ratio of green to yellow with great confidence, within a small margin of error, so long as each marble had an equal chance of being counted. Doctors proceed on the same assumption when they test our blood: Rather than draining all of it for testing, they take a small sample. When it comes to social behavior, however, the situation is not as simple as with marbles and blood. Accordingly, methodologists and statisticians have evolved various techniques for arriving at a representative sample (techniques that are usually taught only in more advanced courses). However, the results of surveys can be very inaccurate at times (see boxed insert, pp. 20–21).

While a social survey is often a major and complex undertaking, it need not always be so. The late Manford H. Kuhn (1960), for instance, devised a relatively simple questionnaire for identifying and measuring self-attitudes that can be used with small samples: the Twenty-Statements Test (TST). A single sheet of paper is headed with these instructions:

There are twenty numbered blanks on the page below. Please write twenty answers to the simple question "Who am I?" in the blanks. Just give twenty different answers to this question. Answer as if you were giving the answers to yourself, not to somebody else. Write the answers in the order that they occur to you. Don't worry about logic or "importance." Go along fairly fast, for time is limited.

The TST is probably the most widely used instrument in the study of self-conceptions. It has been employed in over one hundred reported research studies, and it achieved a measure of popular attention when it was administered to the early astronauts.

Children's answers to the "Who am I?" question tend to be scattered over a wide range and to focus on particular, individualistic aspects of their lives: "I boss too much," "I get mad at my sister," "I tattle on my sisters." As people mature, their self-conceptions tend to take the form of broad social categories: "I am a female," "I am twenty," "I attend church," "I have two parents," "I am attractive" (Kuhn, 1960; Mulford and Salisbury, 1964; Wellman, 1971).

Kuhn's "Who am I?" test is an *open-ended* questionnaire, in that it is designed to permit a free response; it does not limit an individual's response to answering precast answers. A *closed* or *structured* questionnaire—one in which responses are limited to stated alternatives—may also be employed. For instance, an individual may be asked to rate himself or herself on a five-point scale with regard to self-confidence: "very high," "high," "average," "low," "very low." In two studies—one by S. Frank Miyamoto and Stanford M. Dornbusch (1956), the other by Enrico Quarantelli and Joseph Cooper (1966)—the researchers used structured questionnaires for studying the same subject matter as Kuhn: self-conceptions. These studies revealed that our self-conceptions tend to reflect our assessments of the appraisals others make of us (see Chapter 5).

The Experiment

Far and away the most frequently used technique employed by social psychologists is the **experiment.** An experiment is a study in which the investigator manipulates one or more factors, termed independent variables, and measures other factors, termed dependent variables. The experiment constitutes the most effective method of testing a hypothesis that one variable (X) causally influences another variable (Y). The logic behind an experiment is this: If in the presence of a given variable certain changes occur in another variable, and if these changes do not occur in the absence of the given variable (all other or extraneous elements having been controlled so they do not intervene), then the changes must be due to the given variable.

In an experiment, investigators try to find out whether a relationship exists between two specific variables (X and Y). First, they systematically vary the first variable (X). Second, they observe the effects of such variation on the second variable (Y). We refer to the manipulated factor as the **independent variable** (X); it is independent of what the subject or subjects do. The independent variable is assumed to be the causal factor or determining condition in the relationship being studied. We call the factor that is affected—that occurs or changes as a result of such manipulation—the **dependent variable** (Y); it is usually some measure of the subject's or subjects' behavior. If, by way of illustration, students talk noisily when the teacher is out of the classroom but become quiet when he

A MARKETING FIASCO

Social research is a more complex undertaking than simply asking a few questions or making a few observations. Some years ago a brewery making two kinds of beer conducted a survey to find out people's beer preferences. It asked people known to favor its brand, "Do you drink the light or the regular?" To its astonishment, the firm discovered people reporting they preferred light over the regular by better than three to one. The truth of the matter was that for years the company, *in order to meet consumer demand,* had brewed nine times as much regular beer as light beer. It concluded that in asking people this question it in effect had asked, "Do you drink the kind of beer preferred by people of refinement and discriminating taste, or do you just drink the regular stuff?" What seemed to be a straightforward and simple question had in fact been "loaded" and produced biased results.

A misreading of marketing information also led the Coca-Cola Company to blunder. The firm thought it had a winner in April 1985 when it discontinued its ninety-nine-year-old product and brought out a new, sweeter Coke. In part, the formula change was designed to break what for several years had been Pepsi's biggest advantage in the market: its consistent ability to win taste tests against Coke. By July 1985, however, a consumer revolt forced the company to bring back the old, familiar flavor. When the firm initially announced its new formula, its executives had boasted that it was the surest move they had ever made. Research had revealed that people liked the new, sweeter formula better than they did the old. The company had spent about $4 million to taste-test the new soda pop on 190,000 consumers. Some were blind tests, without the emotion-laden brand name attached to them. Others asked, "What if this were a new Coke taste?" But the surveys never disclosed that the product being tested would replace the old Coke entirely.

In the first months after its introduction, the new Coke showed every sign of fulfilling its promise (Koten and Kilman, 1985). Shipments to Coke bottlers rose by the highest percentage in five years. The product was tried by a record number of people, and more than three quarters of those who tried it indicated they would be eager to buy it again. But then the mood of consumers changed. In June shipments fell 15 percent in some markets. And when in late June the company's researchers asked 900 consumers which Coke they liked better, 60 percent said the "old" and only 30 per-

---

or she enters, the change in the level of the classroom noise (the dependent variable) is caused by the teacher's presence (the independent variable) (Sanders, 1974).

The Laboratory Experiment

Most social psychological experiments take place in special laboratories, usually located in a university or a research institute, and hence are termed **laboratory**

cent the "new." By early July the company felt it was losing control of how the public perceived its product. A retired Seattle real estate investor had organized the Old Cola Drinkers of America, whose aim was to bring back the traditional drink. (It did not matter that the movement's founder expressed a preference for new Coke over old Coke in two blind tests.) Coca-Cola national headquarters was receiving more than 1,500 angry phone calls and a barrage of furious letters daily. On July 10, in one of the most stunning flip-flops in marketing history, Coke publicly apologized for scrapping the ninety-nine-year-old product and announced it would once again make it available—as "Coca-Cola Classic."

What the firm had failed to take into account when it changed the Coke formula was "brand loyalty" (Fisher, 1985). When a branded product has been around for a long time and is heavily promoted, it often picks up emotional freight: it becomes associated with a person's self-image and summons fond memories of days gone by. Many people felt that a symbol of American heritage should not have been tampered with. President Donald R. Keough of Coca-Cola admitted, "The passion for original Coke was something that just flat caught us by surprise. The simple fact is that all of the time and money and skill poured into consumer research on the new Coca-Cola could not measure or re-

veal the depth of emotional attachment to the original Coca-Cola felt by so many people" (Greenwald, 1985: 49). The firm conceded that its test marketing was flawed. Among other things, it had neglected to inform consumers that choosing the new Coke meant that they would never again be able to taste the original Coke. The company had also encountered difficulty in the mid-1950s when it first came out with 10-ounce, king-size bottles. Consumers were unhappy and said it did not taste the same as Coke in the traditional, green-hued 6½-ounce bottles. But the difference between the 1950s and the 1980s was that the firm never took the 6½-ounce size off the market.

Researchers find that the more closely a brand is bound to individuals' images of themselves, the more resistance there is likely to be to changing it (Fisher, 1985). The "I use this, this is me" principle applies to such things as cigarettes, perfume, and beer. For instance, Marlboro is the American market leader in the high-loyalty cigarette category: the Marlboro Man projects a macho image that many smokers like to associate themselves with. In the beer market, Budweiser is a high-loyalty market leader, tradition being a big part of its appeal. At the other extreme, with low loyalty, are products like cat litter, paper towels, and clothespins.

experiments. A laboratory allows the investigator to control conditions more carefully and to take measurements more precisely than is commonly possible in real-world settings. A good illustration of a laboratory experiment is one that was undertaken by Elliot Aronson and his associates and later meticulously detailed by them (Aronson and Mills, 1959; Aronson, Brewer, and Carlsmith, 1985). Aronson and his colleagues formulated the following *hypothesis* (a tentative guess, hunch, or proposition that can be tested to determine its validity):

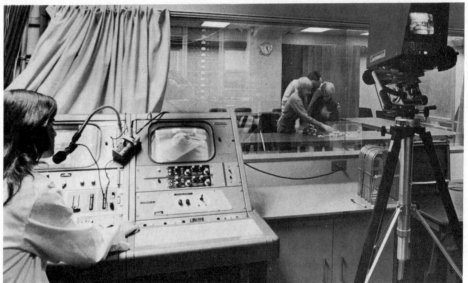

A Small-Group Laboratory

Small-group laboratories usually consist of two rooms. The rooms are separated by a one-way mirror, which permits observers in the control room to view subjects in the experimental room without themselves being observed (and thus impairing the spontaneous behavior of the subjects). Here one photo shows an observer viewing behavior from a control room. Viewed from the experimental room, shown in the other photo, the observer's window is simply a mirror. The televisionlike equipment is an added feature of this laboratory, which is at Ohio State University. In neighboring small rooms, subjects can individually, in isolation, view on a television screen behavior taking place in the experimental room. Such equipment might be used, for instance, to determine the relationship between the self-perceptions of subjects in the experimental room who are engaged in actual behavior and the perceptions other subjects who are observing form of them. Such equipment also enables researchers to videotape behavior being emitted in the experimental room. (Patrick Reddy)

individuals who undergo a severe initiation in order to be admitted to a group will find that group more attractive than they would find it if they were admitted with little or no initiation. This hypothesis was based on the commonplace observation that people who go through a good deal of trouble or pain to obtain something tend to value it more highly than those who acquire it with a minimum of effort.

The researchers recruited sixty-three college women as volunteers to participate in what was alleged to be a series of group discussions on the psychology of sex. This format, however, was merely a ruse. It provided a convenient method by which the researchers could make the subjects go through either a severe or a mild initiation so as to gain admittance to a group.

The young women were directed to report, one at a time, to the experimental room—the room in which the experiment was to be conducted—where they were met by a male experimenter. At this time, the experimenter explained to the subject that some people are shy and have difficulty discussing sex. He then asked the subject if she felt she would be able to discuss the topic freely. Invariably, the subject replied in the affirmative.

The women were randomly assigned to three experimental conditions: no initiation (the *control* condition), mild initiation, and severe initiation. Subjects in the control condition were told they could immediately join into the group discussion. Those in the mild or severe condition were informed they would first have to take a "screening" test. In the mild condition, the women were asked to read aloud five words that were related to sex but were not "obscene" (for example, "prostitute," "virgin," and "petting"). In the severe condition, each female subject was asked to read aloud to the male experimenter twelve obscene words and two vivid descriptions of sexual activity taken from contemporary novels.

After the subject had completed the reading (in both the mild and the severe conditions), she was told that she had performed satisfactorily and could join the group. But she was informed that for the first session she would be allowed only to listen to the group over earphones (supposedly to get the hang of what was going on). What each subject heard was a dull and banal discussion by three female undergraduates. The participants spoke dryly and haltingly on secondary sex behavior in animals, "inadvertently" contradicted themselves, mumbled, and hemmed and hawed.

At the close of the discussion, the experimenter returned and asked each subject to rate on a 15-point scale (0 being the worst rating; 15 being the most positive) the worth of the overheard discussion on seventeen dimensions. Following this, the subject was *debriefed*—that is, the nature and purpose of the experiment were explained to each woman. Debriefing is an important aspect of experimentation, because when it is done effectively it minimizes the negative effects that subjects may experience (Smith and Richardson, 1983; Sieber, 1983).

In the experiment, the independent variable had been the severity of initiation. The dependent variable was the rating given to the discussion by members of the group (the total score could vary between 0 and 255; $17 \times 15 = 255$). The average rating for subjects in the control condition was 167; for those in the mild condition, 171; and for those in the severe condition, 195. These results were interpreted as confirming the hypothesis. The subjects in the severe-initi-ation condition found the group considerably more attractive than did the sub-jects in the mild-initiation or no-initiation conditions. In turn, Aronson was able to relate this finding to an interpretation consistent with dissonance theory (see Chapter 6).

The Field Experiment

At times, a creative and imaginative researcher uses the "real world" as a labo-ratory; this is termed a **field experiment.** In this case, the researcher introduces the independent variable into a natural setting to determine its impact on be-havior. F. K. Heussenstamm (1971) provides us with a good illustration of this. He wanted to determine whether there is a relationship between having a Black Panther (a militant black organization) bumper sticker on your car and being cited for traffic violations. Fifteen student subjects, all of whom had had no traffic violations in the previous twelve months, were employed by Heussenstamm for the experiment. They affixed Black Panther bumper stickers to their cars.

By day four, one of the fifteen subjects had already been forced to drop out of the study because he had received three traffic-violation citations (the maxi-mum number allowed in the experiment). Three others received three citations each within the first week. Altogether, the participants received thirty-three citations in seventeen days. Heussenstamm accordingly concluded that a rela-tionship does exist between displaying a Black Panther bumper sticker and being arrested. This finding is of interest in clarifying the nature of power in America, especially as it comes into operation in confrontations between the white estab-lishment and black militants.

In comparison with laboratory experiments, field experiments offer a number of advantages (West and Gunn, 1978). First, they allow for the use of more representative subject populations than students enrolled in sociology or psy-chology courses. Second, greater certainty exists that the experimental situations are representative of those found in the real world. Third, it is possible to study under real-life conditions stressful events that it would be unethical to construct within laboratory settings. And fourth, field experiments minimize the problems of demand characteristics and experimenter effects (to be discussed below) that bias some laboratory experiments, since in field experiments the subjects are usually unaware that they are participating in an experiment.

Problems with Experimentation

Experiments, especially of the laboratory variety, offer substantial advantages over other techniques (Henshel, 1980; Berkowitz and Donnerstein, 1982). In-vestigators can control outside influences and arrive at causal relationships. But problems also plague experimental procedures. The possibility of systematic bias has posed particular difficulty. There are two principal kinds of bias that may intrude into social psychological experiments (Aronson and Carlsmith, 1968): bias arising from the demand characteristics of the experiment itself (Orne, 1962) and bias deriving from the unintentional influence of the experimenter (Rosenthal, 1966; Rosenthal and Rubin, 1978; Barnes and Rosenthal, 1985).

The bias associated with the **demand characteristics** of the experimental situation (cues that inadvertently guide and direct the responses of a subject) parallels the placebo problem in medical research. Subjects know that they are part of an experiment, that their behavior is being scrutinized, and that certain things are expected from them (Weber and Cook, 1972; Adair, 1984). "Good subjects" try to figure out the purpose of the research and then undertake to "help" the experimenter by confirming the hypothesis. "Faithful subjects" believe that a high degree of docility is required by research settings and that they should follow experimental instructions scrupulously. "Negativistic subjects" attempt to invalidate or sabotage the experiment. And "apprehensive subjects" worry about the adequacy of their performance and how the experimenter will evaluate their abilities or emotional adjustment. In any of these cases, extraneous considerations intervene to shape the responses of a subject and contaminate the experimental results (Carlston and Cohen, 1980; Carlopio et al., 1983).

Martin Orne (1962) was one of the first to point out that subjects participating in experimental studies tend to be unusually compliant. In one of his experiments, Orne had the subjects perform psychologically noxious, meaningless, and boring tasks over several hours. Despite the senseless nature of the behavior required of them, the subjects presumably interpreted the experiment as a test of their cooperation and took this fact into account in behaving in a compliant way.

The bias associated with **experimenter effects** has to do with distortions in experimental outcomes that result from the behavior or characteristics of the researcher. Some years ago, Robert Rosenthal (1966) reported on a number of rat experiments that he had undertaken with the assistance of student handlers. Rats performed better in carefully controlled tests if their handlers were told, falsely, that the rats had been especially bred for intelligence. The same kind of rats consistently turned in poor performances when the handlers had been told the rats were dull. Some social psychologists claim that in human experiments somewhat similar contaminating effects are produced by experimenters through subtle body movements, tone of voice, and facial cues (for instance, shifting posture, changing voice intonation while reading directions, or providing a fleeting glance at a critical juncture). Likewise, the age, sex, race, and social status of the researchers are thought to affect subjects and their responses (Barnes and Rosenthal, 1985).

Various techniques have been employed to minimize experimental bias. One procedure is to have an assistant who is unaware of the nature of the experiment's hypotheses deal with the subjects and collect the data. Of course, this is simply one precaution and not a guarantee of objectivity. (Like subjects, the "blind" experimenter may formulate his or her own hypothesis about the research and unknowingly bias the subjects.) Another procedure is to employ mechanical equipment, such as taped instructions. Yet these techniques often depersonalize the experiment and reduce the subjects' interest and motivation, merely substituting one type of bias for another. All of this points to the need for researchers to be alert to the problem of bias and to introduce appropriate measures within the specific context of their experimental situation to control it.

Naturalistic Observation

At times, researchers simply undertake an intensive observation and recording of people's behavior in a natural setting. The approach often entails **participant observation,** a procedure in which the researcher spends a good deal of time noticing, watching, and sometimes interacting with the people he or she is studying. Psychologists Leon Festinger, Henry W. Riecken, and Stanley Schachter (1956) used the participant-observation method to study the development of the belief system of a fanatical group and the subsequent modification of the group's beliefs when confirming evidence did not appear (see Chapter 6). Despite conscientious efforts to remain noncommitted, the researchers noted that the mere fact of their presence served to support the convictions of the group members. This is the major problem with participant observation: the presence of the observer may unintentionally but subtly modify the behavior of the subjects.

Perhaps the best-known sociological study employing participant observation is William Foote Whyte's *Street Corner Society* (1943). Whyte lived in a lower-class Italian neighborhood of Boston for three and one-half years. For eighteen months he lived with an Italian family so as to have an intimate view of family life and to establish contacts within the community. To be able to talk with the first-generation Italian immigrants, Whyte learned their language. He joined the second generation's activities. This included bowling, playing baseball, shooting pool, playing cards, eating and drinking, and otherwise "hanging out" with a group of young men who were known as "corner boys" and "the Norton gang."

One of the most important of Whyte's findings had to do with the impact of the Norton gang on its members' self-images. Frank, for instance, on the basis of general athletic ability should have been an excellent bowler (indeed, he had been a semiprofessional baseball player); but he performed poorly when he bowled with the gang. Alex was an outstanding bowler when he played "for the fun of it" on weekday evenings against the members of other groups; but on Saturday nights, when he played with the Norton gang, he would perform poorly. Why? Whyte discovered that both Frank and Alex ranked low in the Norton gang. For either Frank or Alex to have defeated Doc, Mike, or Danny, who made up the leading clique, would have been viewed as inappropriate. Bowling performance was related to the status the individual held within the group.

Harold Garfinkel (1964, 1967), a leading ethnomethodologist, has employed in his studies an interesting variation on personal-observation techniques—one that he terms **demonstration experiment.** This method entails introducing a "nasty surprise" in a situation or disturbing an interaction so as to reveal the underlying expectations of which we are normally unaware. Garfinkel disturbed others by simply not performing acts that they expected or by performing acts that they did not have reason to expect. And in one experiment he had his students behave toward their parents at home as though they, the students, were guests in the home rather than sons or daughters. The students' small acts of kindness and overall politeness were interpreted by their parents as displays of hostility, antagonism, or fatigue. Asking their parents whether they might look in the refrigerator for something to eat or asking permission to eat in the first

Naturalistic Observation

Much can be learned about human behavior by observing people in their natural habitats. The researcher attempts to capture the full richness and flavor of the human experience as it spontaneously occurs, not as it develops under experimental manipulation. (Patrick Reddy)

place generated parental confusion and surprise. Through such methods, Garfinkel seeks to reveal the "background understandings" that are taken for granted in commonplace conversations and incidents.

ETHICAL CONSIDERATIONS

Over the past two decades, a number of studies have generated heated debate regarding the ethics of the research. Among these studies have been the following:

☐ Stanley Milgram (1974), in studying obedience to authority, led subjects falsely to believe they were participating in a "learning study." In the course of the experiment, subjects were ordered to administer shocks to another person. The subjects believed the shocks to be of sufficient magnitude to injure or kill the person (see Chapter 7).

☐ Philip Zimbardo and his associates (Zimbardo, Haney, and Banks, 1973) set up a mock prison in the basement of the Stanford University psychology building. The "guards"—college students—subjected the "prisoners"—also college students—to such sadistic abuse that four of the ten "prisoners" developed fits of rage, crying, acute anxiety, and severe depression; a fifth developed a psychosomatic rash all over his body (see Chapter 11).

☐ Stephen G. West, Steven P. Gunn, and Paul Chernicky (1975) induced subjects to commit themselves to a lawbreaking, Watergate type of burglary (see Figure 1.1).

☐ Neil M. Malamuth, Maggie Heim, and Seymour Feshbach (1980) undertook to investigate individuals' sexual arousal when confronted with portrayals of sexual violence. They provided male and female students in two undergraduate psychology classes with booklets containing rape stories. Despite the later debriefing of the subjects after the experiment (when the researchers described its true nature), some psychologists have expressed concern that the women in the study may have become more worried about rape and limited their activities in a quest for safety (Sherif, 1980). Further, they question the effects such an experiment might have on young men who discover that they are aroused by a description of orgasm under cruelly violent circumstances (Malamuth, 1981).

Not surprisingly, many individuals have raised a variety of ethical questions about studies such as these. Indeed, the social psychologist Herbert C. Kelman (1967) insists that all research involving deception is morally wrong because deceit is dishonest. The psychologist Diana Baumrind (1964, 1985) agrees, contending that intentional deception in the research setting is unethical, imprudent, and unwarranted scientifically. And she maintains that even when subjects are debriefed, they gain a view of themselves as gullible and naive. This recognition invariably lowers their self-esteem and undermines their trust in scientific endeavor. Baumrind insists that concern for the rights of human beings is morally superior to freedom to seek knowledge and should take precedence over it.

An even more serious charge is that some experiments expose subjects to psychological trauma—even to physical, mental, and emotional impairment. Subjects may derive a devastating reflection of themselves as thieves, sadists, perverts, or potential murderers. And, as in the case of the rape study cited above, individuals may become fearful and alter their behavior. Minimally, many

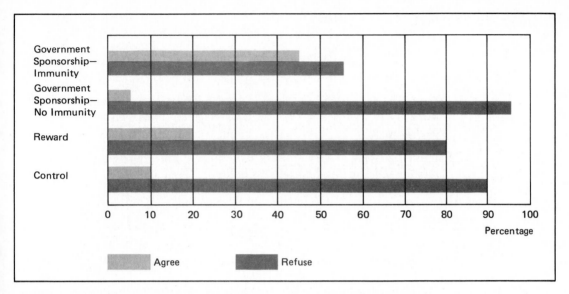

FIGURE 1.1 Commitment Rates of Subjects to a Watergate Type of Burglary
The experiment by Stephen G. West, Steven P. Gunn, and Paul Chernicky (1975)
was conducted in a field setting. The experimenters led the subjects to believe they
had an opportunity to participate in an illegal burglary. The rationale for the burglary was varied in accordance with the various explanations offered for the 1972
burglary of the Democratic Watergate headquarters. The eighty subjects were randomly assigned to one of four conditions: (1) the burglary was supposedly sponsored by an agency of the U.S. government, and the subject was warned that there
would be no immunity from prosecution if apprehended; (2) the same as condition
1 except the subject was guaranteed immunity from prosecution if apprehended;
(3) the purpose of the burglary was supposedly to obtain a copy of a design from
one advertising firm for use by another firm, and the subject was to receive $2,000;
(4) (the control condition) the subject was informed that the crime was being committed merely to determine whether the burglary plans designed by the experimenter would work, although nothing would be stolen. The compliance rates under
various conditions are shown in the graph.
(Adapted from S. G. West, S. P. Gunn, and P. Chernicky, "Ubiquitous Watergate: An Attributional Analysis," *Journal of Personality and Social Psychology* 32 [1975]: 55–65.)

experiments result in subjects' feeling embarrassed, guilty, or anxious about their
actions. Therefore, critics charge that experimenters who employ deception show
a lack of concern for their subjects' dignity and welfare.

Proponents of experimental procedures do not necessarily find these arguments convincing. Defenders of deceptive research argue that it is morally justified so long as the risks or costs to the subject are outweighed by the benefits
to humanity (Baron, 1981; Hunt, 1982c). For example, Elliot Aronson and J.
Merrill Carlsmith offer the following response to critics of experimental research:

Most experimental social psychologists are willing to assume this ethical burden,
feeling that, if using deception experiments is the only feasible way to uncover an

interesting fact, then the truths so uncovered are worth the lies told in the process so long as no harm befalls the subject. The experimenter can also take some comfort in the knowledge that in most cases, although the subject was not aware of the true purpose of the experiment, he at least knew that he was in an experiment. As such, he is aware of the fact that his relationship to the experiment is that of a subject. (1968: 35)

As for the anxiety that might be engendered, other social psychologists note that the ordinary testing of college students as part of the procedure for passing a course also generates anxiety—often substantially greater and more pervasive than that produced by experimental social psychologists (Rosenblatt and Miller, 1972).

In defense of his procedures, Stanley Milgram (1974) points out that a follow-up study revealed that participants felt positively about his study: 84 percent of the subjects stated they were glad to have participated in the experiment; 15 percent indicated neutral feelings; and only 1.3 percent indicated negative feelings. In addition, four-fifths of the subjects felt that more experiments of a similar sort should be carried out, and 74 percent indicated that they had learned something of personal importance from the study. Moreover, similar follow-up studies made after other such experiments have failed to demonstrate long-term negative consequences of the experimental manipulations (Clark and Word, 1974; Zimbardo, 1974).

Nonetheless, it should be recognized that experiments can have an impact on the subsequent behavior of subjects. Shalom H. Schwartz and Avi Gottlieb (1980*a,b,* 1981) followed up an earlier study that they had conducted in order to investigate this matter. In the earlier research they had attempted to determine whether or not subjects would attempt to assist another "subject" (in reality a confederate) who they had witnessed being attacked over closed-circuit television. Eighty-nine percent of the subjects had helped, either by directly trying to aid the victim or by calling the experimenter. When confronted with another bystander-intervention situation some six to ten months later, the subjects were less likely to help a seemingly distressed and injured victim than were control-group subjects. But subjects who were confronted with the situation eleven to twenty months later were more willing to provide the victim with assistance than were subjects in the control group. Schwartz and Gottlieb conclude that their original experiment had induced simultaneous cognitions in their subjects about the possible inauthenticity of need and generalized beliefs about the value of helping. With the passage of time, the former faded and the latter became more salient.

Some social psychologists say that role-enactment methods show great promise in meeting the criticisms directed at deception methods and even surpass them (Forward, Canter, and Kirsch, 1976; Geller, 1978). Like any simulation method, subjects are asked to participate in some kind of "as if" behavior. All the parties know the situation is not real, but they pretend otherwise for research purposes. On the basis of their role-playing behavior, subjects provide insights, estimates, intuitions, and introspections about themselves and others.

Critics remain skeptical of role-enactment procedures. Although recognizing that role-playing is an excellent method for *generating* hypotheses that then can be tested by alternative means, they question whether it is suitable for *testing* hypotheses about human behavior. They say that subjects have little direct awareness of their higher mental processes, especially under circumstances involving a high degree of emotion or motivation (Nisbett and Wilson, 1977*b;* West and Gunn, 1978; Cronkite, 1980; Hunt, 1982*c*).

What can we conclude about these matters? As Aronson and Carlsmith (1968) observe, social psychologists need to resolve their ethical dilemmas in a manner that avoids the extremes of (1) doing away with experimentation altogether and (2) failing to consider the rights and dignity of their subjects. In its ethical guidelines for research, the American Psychological Association (1982) emphasizes that the researcher must carry out his or her work in ways that respect the people who participate and that are in accordance with their dignity and welfare. Furthermore, it indicates that subjects should not be coerced to participate in an experiment and should have the freedom to drop out should they wish to do so. And finally, the experimenter should assume the responsibility for detecting and overcoming any undesirable consequences that may follow from an individual's participation in a study. Other major scientific associations, including the American Sociological Association, the American Anthropological Association, and the American Political Science Association, have also formulated codes of ethics for the protection of research participants.

Concern regarding the ethics of medical and behavioral research led Congress to enact the 1974 National Research Act. In response to this legislation, various federal agencies have established regulations governing the use of human subjects. Before a study can be undertaken, the project must be reviewed by an institutional review board (IRB). Institutional review boards are committees located at universities, research centers, and related institutions and are composed of researchers, administrators, and community representatives. The review process seeks to safeguard the subjects of government-supported research from risk to health and from deceit. Many social scientists felt that the regulations unnecessarily encumbered behavioral research and posed a threat to academic freedom and free inquiry. Whole lines of research were no longer possible (Hunt, 1982*c*). Consequently, in January 1981, the Department of Health and Human Services (DHHS) modified its earlier regulations and eliminated compulsory review for social and behavioral studies that pose little risk to the subjects and in which the subjects provide their informed consent. Further, incompletely informed consent was held acceptable if, in the view of the IRB, it involved "minimum risk to the subject" and if the research "could not practically be carried out" otherwise.

SUMMARY

1. Social psychology has roots in both sociology and psychology. This overlap has contributed to a freshness of approach and has been a stimulus to scientific advance.
2. Theory enables us to make sense out of a confused set of data. Furthermore, it allows us to go beyond our empirical data and seek implications and

relationships that are not evident in the datum taken by itself. And theory also stimulates inquiry.

3. Behavioral theories focus on how an organism acquires given responses (how it learns). These theories stress stimulus-response relationships.

4. Cognitive theorists depict people as thinking, planning, problem-solving, and decision-making organisms—as mental manipulators of images, symbols, and ideas.

5. Gestalt and field theorists are concerned with the relatedness of the individual and the environment—with all psychological events within a life space.

6. According to social exchange theory, social behavior consists of exchanges that are perceived to be rewarding or costly.

7. Symbolic interactionists concern themselves with how we come to define situations and fit our lines of action together by the use and manipulation of symbols.

8. Role theory portrays social interaction in terms of actors who play their assigned parts in accordance with a script written by culture. Role expectations are shared understandings that tell us what actions we can anticipate from one another as we go about our daily activities. By virtue of roles, we mentally classify people in terms of their common attributes, their common behavior, or the common reactions they elicit.

9. Ethnomethodologists are interested in the practical, everyday activities of people, especially the methods they employ for producing and managing their affairs. They seek to illuminate the commonplace, "taken-for-granted" activities that come to characterize life—"the things that everybody already knows," which, although they influence behavior, go largely unexamined.

10. Survey techniques involve the use of questionnaires and interviews.

11. The experiment constitutes the most effective method of testing a hypothesis that one variable causally influences another variable. The logic behind an experiment is the following: if in the presence of a given variable certain changes occur in another variable, and if these changes do not occur in the absence of the given variable, then all other things being equal, the changes must be due to the given variable.

12. Still another technique used by social scientists is naturalistic observation, in which people's behavior is observed and recorded as it occurs within a natural setting.

13. In designing and conducting research, social psychologists are faced with the task of balancing the value of the information gained from the research against concern for the rights and dignity of their subjects.

GLOSSARY

Behaviorism □ A psychological theory that is primarily concerned with the stimuli that impinge on an organism's sense organs and the responses that these stimuli elicit.

Cognition □ All the mental processes that transform sensory input in some meaningful fashion—that code it, store it, and appropriately retrieve it.

Demand characteristics □ Cues within the experimental situation that inadvertently guide and direct the responses of a subject.

Demonstration experiment □   A procedure for gathering data; the researcher introduces a "nasty surprise" or otherwise disturbs human interactions so as to reveal the underlying expectations of which we are normally unaware.

Dependent variable □   The factor that is affected in an experimental setting; that which occurs or changes as a result of manipulation of another factor (the independent variable).

Ethnomethodology □   The procedures (the rules and activities) that people employ in making social life and society intelligible and understandable to themselves.

Experiment □   A study in which the investigator manipulates or varies one or more variables (termed the independent variables) and measures other variables (termed the dependent variables).

Experimenter effects □   The distortions in experimental outcomes that result from the behavior or characteristics of the researcher.

Field (also termed **life space**) □   The person and the environment viewed as one constellation of interdependent forces.

Field experiment □   An experiment in which a researcher introduces an independent variable into a natural setting to determine its impact on behavior.

Gestalt □   A German word meaning configuration or organization. It suggests that the whole is greater than the sum of its parts; experience is viewed as organized and behavior as integrated.

Independent variable □   The factor that is manipulated in an experimental setting; the causal factor or determining condition in the relationship being studied.

Laboratory experiment □   An experiment in which specially constructed facilities are employed to facilitate determining the relationship between independent and dependent variables.

Life space □   See **field**.

Participant observation □   A procedure for gathering data whereby the researcher spends a good deal of time in a natural setting, noticing, watching, and at times interacting with the people he or she is studying.

Responses □   Behavior segmented into units.

Social exchange theory □   The view that people, as they enter into relationships with one another, are engaging in a sort of mental bookkeeping that involves a ledger of rewards, costs, and profits (rewards less costs).

Social psychology □   A scientific attempt to understand and explain how the thought, feeling, and behavior of individuals are influenced by the actual, imagined, or implied presence of others.

Social survey □   A method of research; the obtaining of quantitative data through interviews or mailed questionnaires.

Stimuli □   The environment divided into units.

Symbolic interactionism □   A social psychological theory that stresses the part verbal and nonverbal symbols play in interpersonal behavior.

Theory □   A way of making sense out of a confused set of data through a symbolic construction by the human mind; the net we weave to catch the world of observation.

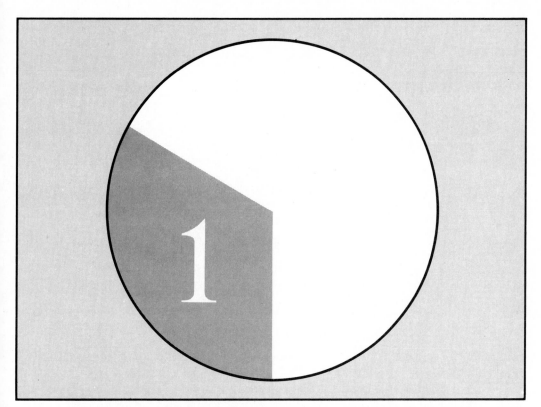

INDIVIDUAL SOCIAL
BEHAVIOR

2 SOCIAL PERCEPTIONS AND ATTRIBUTIONS

IMPRESSION FORMATION
  Categories and Schematic
    Processing
  Memory Processes in Social
    Perception
ATTRIBUTION
  Causality: Internal Versus
    External
  The Influence of Success and
    Failure

  Causality and Motivation
  Bias in Attribution Processes
  The Functions of Attributions
PERCEPTION OF THE
    SITUATION
  Definition of the Situation
  Shared Definitions of Situations

As you begin to study this chapter, you will find that someth ing peculiar will happen tothema ter ial. The struc tureof the wordsa ndsen ten ce swill notfol low thescriptt ow hichyo uar eac customed andy ouw ill be comecon fused. (As you begin to study this chapter, you will find that something peculiar will happen to the material. The structure of the words and sentences will not follow the script to which you are accustomed and you will become confused.)

    Your ability to derive information from your environment, interpret the information, and act upon it is not a simple matter. Indeed, you find yourself immersed in a world of sensation. But an awareness of sights, sounds, smells, tastes, and touches is of little value to you unless you can make sense of them. Thus you must give meaning to your sensations, a process termed **perception**. Consider that at this very moment you are primarily aware of the page in front of you

Perception
Perception is the mediating link between individuals and their environment. (Patrick Reddy)

and, most of all, of this sentence. But reflect. Are you not also seeing things below, above, and well to the sides of this page? What about the pressures on your skin, perhaps on the soles of your feet or on your elbows? Do you notice any noises or detect any odors? Clearly, you do not typically experience the world about you as a confusing mass of colors, noises, temperatures, and pressures. Rather, you see words and sentences, feel paper and cloth, hear voices and music, taste apples and candy, touch a dog and a friend. Your brain receives information from the senses and then organizes and interprets it. In this fashion your experiences take on meaning. Thus perception serves as the mediating link between you and your environment.

Because of perception, you transform outer stimuli into an inner system of meaning. The social philosopher Alfred Schutz observes:

> All our knowledge of the world, in common-sense as well as in scientific thinking, involves constructs, i.e., a set of abstractions, generalizations, formalizations, and idealizations specific to the respective level of thought organization. Strictly speak-

---

Money: A matter of social definition

It occurred to me today while writing a check for the dentist that the check in its own right was worthless as a commodity—a mere scrap of paper. Yet with this "scrap of paper" I was able to secure a relatively expensive service from a professional. Although the piece of paper did not possess any inherent commodity value, it nonetheless was defined in our society as a "check," as an instrument having value, and thus was accepted as a means of payment. It stood for "money" which was "in the bank." In truth, the "money" itself is worthless paper but had value only because people define it as having value. This point hit home during the recent inflationary period, when many people were fleeing from paper money into "hard money" (copper pennies, pre-1965 silver coins, gold double eagles), art, and antiques as a store of value. Many people do not define paper money as having the value of these other items.

---

ing, there are no such things as facts, pure and simple. All facts are from the outset facts selected from a universal context by the activities of our mind. They are, therefore, always interpreted facts. (1971: 5)

Perhaps an illustration would prove helpful in grasping the point Schutz makes. Some cloudless night, look up into the northern sky and find the seven stars that form the Big Dipper. Then try to discern in this combination of stars the image of a bear, a wagon, or a bushel. Most Americans find this exceedingly difficult—even impossible. Indeed, you will probably conclude that "it just looks like a dipper and that's all there is to it."

Other people have known this same group of stars by different names. To the ancient Syrians they were the Wild Boar; to the Hindus, the Seven Sages; to the Greeks, the Great Bear; to the Poles, the Heavenly Wagon; and to the Chinese, the Northern Bushel.

The interesting thing about all this is the influence that the assignment of such names (social constructs) has had on how people view this celestial configuration. From their writings it is clear that the ancient Greeks not only called these stars the Great Bear; when they looked into the northern heavens, they *saw* the figure of a bear. Nor does it really matter that there are some 203 other stars visible in the same constellation—Ursa Major—and that these stars offer the possibility of innumerable other combinations and configurations. In the case of the dipper, we single out seven specific stars. But we do not simply see seven stars: we see a "dipper." And for their part, the ancient Greeks saw a "bear." Not just culture but biological programming influence what we perceive. Thus other organisms see the world quite differently (see boxed insert).

OTHER PERCEPTUAL WORLDS

People only see what they are prepared to see.
　　—Ralph Waldo Emerson, *Journals,*
　　　　　　　　　　　　　　　　1863

The human biological organism makes perception possible, but it also sets limits on the perceptual process. As such, human beings are locked within a very special world, utterly different from that experienced by organisms with a different kind of perceptual apparatus. For instance, scientists have shown that insects like the honeybee are sensitive to ultraviolet light and live in a rich visual world different from that of human beings. By employing ultraviolet light (humans beings have yellow pigments in the lens of the eye to screen out ultraviolet light), these insects can sense the location of the sun even when it is hidden behind clouds. Further, they can see a tapestry of patterns on flowers and on their mates where human beings see only one or two colors (Webster, 1978).

By monitoring pigeons' heartbeats under various conditions, Melvin L. Kreithen and Thomas Eisner (1978) have demonstrated that pigeons can also see ultraviolet light patterns and images that are not visible to human beings. The researchers initially conditioned the pigeons to fear receiving an electric shock every time an image resembling a cross was flashed before them on a screen by means of normal light. Later, when the same image was produced with ultraviolet light and again shown to the pigeons, a similar agitated state was produced.

An accumulating body of evidence suggests that birds have a variety of sensory capabilities not available to human beings. They can feel changes in barometric pressure, are sensitive to geographic changes in the earth's magnetic field, can use the sun and the stars as compasses, can differentiate between airborne odors that characterize different regions, and can detect high-frequency noises (such as infrasounds produced by auroras and magnetic storms) that are undetectable to human beings. Such information is shedding new light on the puzzle of how birds navigate and follow certain migratory routes. For instance, scientists report that pigeons' heads contain traces of magnetite, an iron oxide that has magnetic properties. When coils are attached to their heads so as to produce magnetism different from the earth's magnetic field, pigeons have difficulty orienting themselves. And when they are placed in a chamber shielded from all magnetic radiation, pigeons flutter about aimlessly. Likewise, zoologists at Cornell University have shown that indigo buntings use star patterns in the night sky as navigational aids. When the birds are placed in chambers that simulate seasonal star patterns, the birds always try to take off in a northerly or southerly direction in accordance with the simulated season of the year (Webster, 1980). Findings regarding the perceptual worlds of other organisms highlight for us that *we experience the world not as it is but as we are.*

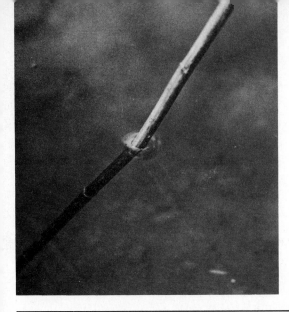

An Apparently Bent Stick
A one-to-one relationship does not necessarily hold between the physical world (a naturally occurring objective world) and our experience of it. Optical illusions provide a good illustration of this. Regardless of how often we have seen straight sticks in water, the stick still appears to be bent at an angle. This illusion is probably one of the oldest experienced by human beings. (Patrick Reddy)

IMPRESSION FORMATION

We live our lives not in isolation but in a social world. Consequently, we must gather and interpret information not only about objects and events but also about people. **Person perception** refers to those processes by which we come to know and think about others—their characteristics, qualities, and inner states. We construct images of others in ways that serve to stabilize, make predictable, and render manageable our view of social life. To the extent to which we attribute stable traits and enduring dispositions to other people, we feel that we are better able to understand their behavior and predict their future actions. And we use these notions to guide our interaction with them (Snyder and Uranowitz, 1978).

In our everyday lives, we confront two major questions about the people we encounter. What is this individual like? And why does this individual behave as he or she does? The first question has to do with *impression formation*. The second question has to do with how we explain and interpret the individual's behavior—the *attributions* we make regarding the causes of what a person says and does. In this section, we will examine the first question and in the next section, the second question.

Categories and Schematic Processing

One of the basic ways we process information about people and form impressions of them is through categories (Bargh and Pietromonaco, 1982; Pryor et al., 1983). A **category** is an abstract representation of conceptually related information. For instance, we commonly categorize people in terms of their roles (child, physician, husband, Hispanic, female) or their personalities (extroverted, surly, helpful, cheerful, talkative). We acquire many of our categories through socialization (see Chapter 4). But the human mind seems capable of forming categories of its own without outside help. Some evidence suggests that our minds are wired to extract from a group of related events the ingredients common to them and to file away incoming experiences in such a way that similarities overlap (Hunt, 1982a).

Categories afford many advantages. For one thing, they allow us to sort individuals into meaningful and manageable classes and assign labels to these classes (often by means of words). Life involves just too many items for us to be aware of each and every little detail. We like to solve problems quickly and easily. Categories enable us to simplify and generalize large quantities of information by "chunking" or "clustering" certain elements together. Thus categories assist us in finding our way about a world of highly diverse people.

Categories also provide us with a sense of order, constancy, and regularity in dealing with people. By pigeonholing individuals, we can relate our current encounters with them to past experiences. We are able to view a person as the same object despite a change in his or her mood and activities. And we can also treat two individuals that differ in some ways (for instance, two professors or two pedestrians) as equivalent—as the same kind of people. By virtue of categories we can minimize the disorder, chaos, and confusion that we would otherwise experience in our social interaction.

Prototypes

Social psychologists term categories that are mental structures for processing and organizing information **schemata** (singular, **schema**). Our memories of people—like those of other objects and events—are typically simplified yet highly structured reconstructions of our original perceptions. For the most part our memories are not lists of features or photolike reproductions. Instead, schemata are abstract mental frameworks—general knowledge structures—for interpreting information from the environment.

Many psychologists believe that all the contents of the mind are sorted into schemata (Goleman, 1985d). Viewed in this manner, thought is a road map through loosely connected schemata. Consider what happens when it is lunchtime and you are hungry. Attention to these facets of your experience activates various schemata—for instance, thoughts of nearby restaurants or what is in the refrigerator. If you then walk down the street with such schemata in mind, you will focus your attention on the restaurants and not on the other shops on the block; if you go to the refrigerator, you will look for cold cuts and not for the uncooked roast that you are planning for the Sunday dinner. Schemata shape the scope of our attention—what we will and will not notice.

In recent years, the concepts *prototype* and *implicit personality theories* have been used to describe the influences of schemata on person perception and memory. A **prototype** is a category that we mentally employ to represent a loose set of features that seem to belong together (Cantor and Mischel, 1979; Mischel, 1984). In like fashion, the term **implicit personality theories** implies that we commonly assume that a number of traits cluster to form an organized set of relationships (Schneider, 1973; Schneider and Blankmeyer, 1983). For instance, because of a prototype or an implicit personality theory, we tend to think of the "extrovert" or "used-car-salesman type" as a particular kind of person.

We employ prototypes or implicit personality theories as fuzzy guides in sizing up people. According to one view, when we perceive a person's traits or behavior, we match the incoming data against a set of mental prototypes (Schneider and Blankmeyer, 1983). If there is a good fit between the incoming data and a prototype model, we use the information associated with the model to fill in the gaps in our knowledge. The process allows us to make inferences about a person's characteristics and behavior beyond the information that is immediately available to us. Apparently, we arrive at such inferences spontaneously in order to make sense of the information we possess about people. And we store these inferences, as well as the information, in memory (Winter and Uleman, 1984). Of course in practice, the members of a category differ from one another in some details. Consequently, we must also make inferences about a person's novel attributes or behaviors and take these into account in fashioning our actions (Cohen, 1983).

Stereotypes can also be thought of as prototypes or implicit personality theories (Hamilton, 1979; Ashmore, 1981). **Stereotypes** are the unscientific and hence unreliable generalizations that we make about individuals by virtue of their membership in a group. When we encounter a member of some stereotyped group, we commonly infer that a cluster of traits applies to the person (Lord, Lepper, and Mackie, 1984). Thus knowing that a woman is pursuing a career and is a hard worker leads some individuals to assume that she is also competitive and unfeminine. Indeed, stereotypes influence the information we search for and attend to as well as how we label and store incoming information. In this respect stereotypes resemble superstition. Consider, for instance, the superstition that if a black cat crosses our path, some misfortune will befall us. The consequence of this superstition is that it makes black cats, *but only black cats,* highly visible. We hardly notice cats that are not black, since the superstition implies that they do not pose a danger to us. Indeed, the very logic of a superstitious belief discourages disconfirmation. We overlook the fact that misfortune sometimes occurs when a cat that is not black crosses our path; but when a black cat crosses our path, we find it easy to identify some instance of misfortune, no matter how slight or delayed in time. In like fashion, we may overlook hard-working career women who are "unaggressive" and "feminine." But it is otherwise with hard-working career women who appear to us as being "aggressive" and "unfeminine." They register!

Central Traits

Some forty years ago, the social psychologist Solomon Asch (1946) drew our attention to the fact that we form organized impressions of other people even after brief encounters. In a series of pioneering and influential studies, he demonstrated that we perceive an individual as having a set of interrelated traits that form an integrated personality structure. Asch gave subjects (college students) a list of characteristics of an unidentified person. Seven traits—intelligent, skillful, industrious, warm, determined, practical, and cautious—were listed. Another group of subjects was given the exact same list except that "cold" was substituted for "warm." Asch then had both groups describe the person by selecting from a

TABLE 2.1
Central Traits

Stimulus List 1	Stimulus List 2	Stimulus List 3	Stimulus List 4	Stimulus List 5
intelligent	intelligent	intelligent	intelligent	intelligent
skillful	skillful	skillful	skillful	skillful
industrious	industrious	industrious	industrious	industrious
warm	*cold*	*polite*	*blunt*	
determined	determined	determined	determined	determined
practical	practical	practical	practical	practical
cautious	cautious	cautious	cautious	cautious

	PERCENTAGE OF SUBJECTS CHOOSING A TRAIT AS CHARACTERISTIC OF THE UNKNOWN PERSON				
	Warm	Cold	Polite	Blunt	No Key Trait
generous	91%	8%	56%	58%	55%
wise	65	25	30	50	49
happy	90	34	75	65	71
good-natured	94	17	87	56	69
reliable	94	99	95	100	96
important	88	99	94	96	88

SOURCE: Adapted from S. Asch, "Forming Impressions of Personality," *Journal of Abnormal and Social Psychology*, Vol. 41 (1946), pp. 258–290.

different list, which contained pairs of opposite traits, the trait from each pair that they felt best characterized the individual.

Asch found that the portraits provided by the two groups were extremely different. Subjects who were told that the person was warm also assumed that the individual was generous, happy, and good-natured. In contrast, the cold person was depicted as stingy, unhappy, and unpopular. Thus one piece of information—whether the person was warm or cold—colored entire impressions.

In another version of the experiment, instead of warm or cold, Asch inserted "polite" or "blunt" in the list with the other six words. When the subjects chose characteristics from the list of opposite pairs of traits, the polite person was not depicted in a fashion appreciably different from the blunt person. (The results of both experiments are presented in Table 2.1.) Thus the warm-cold dimension constituted a stronger **central organizing trait** than the polite-blunt dimension—that is, it had a greater effect on overall evaluation. Asch concluded that different types of information about a person have different levels of importance in impression formation.

More recent studies have tended to confirm Asch's finding that we generally make inferences regarding traits about which we lack direct cues. The warm-cold variable appears to be an especially central trait when we are trying to evaluate another person's *sociability*. In other contexts, however, the warm-cold variable may be inconsequential. Of interest, bluntness, although not highly correlated with sociability, *is* highly correlated with honesty (Wishner, 1960). Bluntness *becomes* a central trait with respect to the honesty-dishonesty dimension; in this context, warmth becomes an irrelevant organizing trait. Certain traits, then, appear to be more *central* to one set than to others. Overall, research suggests that we infer favorable traits from one or more favorable stimulus traits and infer unfavorable traits from unfavorable stimulus traits (Warr and Knapper, 1968; Rosenberg and Olshan, 1970).

Summation and Averaging Models

It is not as yet clear what principle underlies the formation of an impression of another person when the information is complex. The two simplest models of impression formation are the *summation* (adding) and *averaging* models.

Perhaps an illustration of how these models are applied to a given situation will help us understand them. Take a case in which we already hold another person in high regard because the person possesses a certain trait. We then find that the person has another trait that we value in a positive manner. According to the *summation* model, each new piece of favorable trait information will *increase* the person's attractiveness to us; two items of favorable information will *always* produce a *more* favorable impression than one item. According to the *averaging* model, however, the new piece of favorable information will not have a favorable impact *unless* the characteristic has a higher value than the already known trait; and then its effect will be diluted. If the new-found trait is of equal value to the other, no change in the impression will occur. Moreover, if the trait is less highly valued than the already high average, it will *lower* the average and thus the person's overall attractiveness (a finding opposite to that provided by the summation model). A careful study of Table 2.2 should clarify the differing results produced by applying the two models.

Although considerable research evidence exists on this matter, it is not as definitive as we would like it to be (Ostrom and Davis, 1979). Norman Anderson, who has done a number of careful studies on the subject, has demonstrated that for the most part we average various traits in forming our impressions. He suggests, however, that a weighted-average model provides the best fit: we form an overall evaluation by averaging all bits of information, but we assign greater importance to highly positive or highly negative traits (Anderson, 1968). Thus as Asch noted, some traits are more central than others in fashioning our impressions of others.

Halo Effects

When we know that an individual has one trait, we assume he or she also possesses certain other traits. This is termed the **halo effect.** Hence we have a tendency to see a person who has one set of qualities that we like (or dislike) as being likable (or unlikable) in all other respects. Someone whom we judge to be pretty rather than ugly we are also likely to rate as cheerful rather than melancholy, smart rather than dull, nice rather than mean, and so on (Osgood, Suci, and Tannenbaum, 1957). (See boxed insert, pp. 48–50.)

The halo effect contributes to the blinding quality of love that we experience when we fall in love with someone with whom we are as yet relatively unfamiliar. Politicians attempt to capitalize on the halo effect when they appear warm and friendly but say little about the issues. Such deductions follow from the implicit

TABLE 2.2
A Comparison of Summation and Averaging Models of Impression Formation

WHERE NEW-FOUND TRAIT IS APPRAISED AS OF EQUAL VALUE TO PREVIOUSLY KNOWN TRAIT
Summation Model Trait 1. She is unselfish: +4 Trait 2. She is energetic: +4 Sum   +8
Averaging Model Trait 1. She is unselfish: +4 Trait 2. She is energetic: +4 Average $\frac{+8}{2}$ = +4
WHERE NEW-FOUND TRAIT IS APPRAISED AS OF HIGHER VALUE THAN PREVIOUSLY KNOWN TRAIT
Summation Model Trait 1. She is unselfish: +4 Trait 2. She is energetic: +6 Sum   +10
Averaging Model Trait 1. She is unselfish: +4 Trait 2. She is energetic: +6 Average $\frac{+10}{2}$ = +5
WHERE NEW-FOUND TRAIT IS APRAISED AS OF LOWER VALUE THAN PREVIOUSLY KNOWN TRAIT
Summation Model Trait 1. She is unselfish: +4 Trait 2. She is energetic: +2 Sum   +6
Averaging Model Trait 1. She is unselfish: +4 Trait 2. She is energetic: +2 Average $\frac{+6}{2}$ = +3

personality theory that "nice people tend to have nice attributes and less nice people have less nice attributes" (Nisbett and Wilson, 1977*a*).

Primacy Versus Recency Effect

Asch, as part of the study we discussed earlier, presented one group of subjects with a list of traits that became increasingly negative: intelligent, industrious, impulsive, critical, stubborn, and envious. He gave a second group the same list of traits, but in reverse order. The subjects formed differing impressions of the imaginary person, depending on whether they were first presented with the positive or the negative traits. A subject whose list began with favorable traits was more likely to form a favorable impression than one whose list began with unfavorable traits. Asch (1946) concluded that early information colors our perception of subsequent information—a concept termed the **primacy effect.**

In a study in which he portrayed a stranger named Jim to various groups of subjects, A. S. Luchins (1957*a,b*) similarly observed the dominance and durability of *initial* impressions. Where Jim was first depicted as introverted and later in the description as extroverted, the first description tended to prevail. When subjects first received the impression that Jim was extroverted and then later received an impression of him as introverted, they tended to view him as an extrovert.

In other types of settings, a **recency effect** operates—we tend to be most influenced by what we have *just* witnessed (McGuire, 1969; Jones and Welsch, 1971; Jones and Goethals, 1971). This tends to be the case when we are already familiar with a person and later acquire an array of new information about him or her. Further, the primacy effect may be reduced by warning subjects not to be misled by first impressions. And Luchins (1957*b*) found that when subjects are given contradictory descriptions of a person and the descriptions are separated by unrelated activities (the item of information that contradicts the first item is not given immediately following the first), the primacy effect is reduced—indeed, a recency effect occurs.

Processing Inconsistent Information

Research on person perception suggests that we tend to form and maintain impressions of other people that are relatively consistent. For the most part we have conceptions of which traits go together and which do not. This finding is reflected in such concepts as prototypes, implicit personality theories, stereotypes, central traits, the halo effect, and the primacy effect. The question that then arises is this: How can we form and maintain consistent impressions of people when the world presents us with a mixture of consistent and inconsistent information (Erber and Fiske, 1984)? We will address this question at greater length in Chapter 6, when we examine attitudes, and in Chapter 7, when we consider conformity. But let us take a preliminary look at the matter here.

There are a number of strategies that we can use to form and maintain consistent impressions of people in the face of mixed evidence. We can focus on the inconsistent information and attempt to assimilate it within our overall impression. Solomon Asch and Henri Zukier (1984) found that if subjects are presented with a pair of discordant personality traits such as "shy" and "courageous," they undertake to reconcile and integrate the traits. Taken in isolation, "shy" connotes reticence and withdrawal; "courageous," outgoingness. When we bring the two traits together in a person, the meanings are not weakened but rather modified. "Courageous" comes to imply more than usual personal determination, whereas "shyness" ceases to suggest weakness. We find it easy to imagine a person who acts bravely despite a strong reluctance to be conspicu-

THE HALO EFFECT: WHAT IS BEAUTIFUL IS GOOD— OR IS IT?

Aristotle once observed that "beauty is a greater recommendation than any letter of introduction." Social psychologists are finding that in many respects he was right. For the most part, their research suggests that the world is a more pleasant and satisfying place for attractive people because they typically enjoy decided social advantages (Reis et al., 1982). These effects are compatible with the stereotype that "what is beautiful is good" (Dion, Berscheid, and Walster, 1972).

Physical attractiveness is a characteristic that has a major impact on the impressions that we form of people (Deaux and Lewis, 1984). As unfair and unenlightened as it may seem, we tend to prefer attractive people over their less attractive peers. With the halo effect, we judge attractive individuals as having a larger number of socially desirable traits than unattractive individuals. Teachers expect attractive children to achieve higher school grades than unattractive children, and attractive children do so (Clifford and Walster, 1973). Further, the misdemeanors of good-looking children are judged as less serious than those of unattractive children (Dion, 1972); they are disciplined less severely (Berkowitz and Frodi, 1979); and people predict that they will have more successful careers (Dion, Berscheid, and Walster, 1972). In college, essays ostensibly written by attractive students receive higher grades than do the same essays when they are presumed to be written by homely students (Landy and Sigall, 1974). And attractive adults are thought to have happier marriages, better sex lives, higher status, and better mental health than their unattractive counterparts (Dion, Berscheid, and Walster, 1972; Dermer and Thiel, 1975; Cash et al., 1977). Even as newborns, the beautiful-is-good bias prevails, with physically attractive babies being judged smarter, more likable, and less troublesome than unattractive infants (Stephan and Langlois, 1984).

Likewise, jurors in mock rape trials are less likely to convict physically attractive defendants than they are to convict unattractive ones. When they convict attractive defendants, they go easier on them (Efran, 1974). For instance, in one study they meted out an average jail term of ten years to an attractive rapist versus nearly fourteen years for a homely one (Jacobson, 1981). But there are exceptions. Accused swindlers are seen as more dangerous and are given longer sentences when they are attractive (Sigall and Ostrove, 1975). However, the exception also proves the rule: Attractive individuals are viewed as being better at something (swindling) than are unattractive individuals, and for this reason they are deemed to pose a more serious threat to society (Webster and Driskell, 1983).

However, physical attractiveness may also work to a person's disadvantage, es-

What Is Beautiful Is Good—Or Is It?
Some American women attempt to
cultivate a highly stylized appearance
in accordance with traditional cultural
standards of beauty. Other women reject these standards as being plastic
and artificial, preferring instead a
more "natural look." The "what is
beautiful is good" research suggests
that the two groups of women may be
seeking to project different social images of themselves. (Patrick Reddy)

pecially if the person is a woman (Cash
and Janda, 1984). Attractive men and
women have a tendency to activate gender
stereotypes among their peers, with handsome men being perceived as more
masculine, and beautiful women as more
feminine, than their less attractive counterparts. These perceptions typically do
not work a hardship on men (Reis et al.,
1982). Indeed, they are an advantage. But
they do pose a disadvantage for women
who aspire to occupations in which ster-
eotypically masculine traits—including
being strong, independent, and decisive—
are thought to be necessary for success.
When it comes to jobs that clash with our
society's traditional gender roles (see
Chapter 16), attractive women tend to be
rated lower than less attractive women.
Thus less attractive women may have an
advantage over their more attractive peers
when seeking management positions—
traditionally a male preserve. Not surprisingly, several "dress for success" books
have made it to the best-seller list by advising women to get ahead in business by
wearing their hair short, using cosmetics
sparingly, and wearing conservative suits.
In brief, a sexist prescription holds: If a
woman hopes to advance in a man's world,
she had better not appear too feminine.
Box continues on next page.

The sociologists Murray Webster and James E. Driskell (1983) suggest that physical attractiveness frequently functions as a status cue. It activates widely shared cultural beliefs and practices much in the manner as do such status characteristics as race and sex. The advantages enjoyed by attractive individuals resemble some of the advantages that men traditionally have had in interacting with women, and whites in interacting with blacks. Although discrimination based on race or sex may be declining because of changes in laws and educational practice, discrimination based on attractiveness does not seem to be on the wane. Obese people in particular are the object of much prejudice. Negative attitudes seem to intensify during adolescence, particularly for females. However, obese people are increasingly "fighting back." They call for a revamping of cultural stereotypes that proclaim "large is ugly," and they insist that their needs and feelings be given at least as much consideration as those of other people.

ous—an individual who does not allow shyness to deter his or her action. By finding a fit between the dispositions, we undertake to see a person as a psychological unit. Thus the contradiction we encounter puzzles us and prompts us to look more deeply. We attempt to establish a coherent impression by looking for some sensible way to bring the characteristics together within a meaningful whole.

Another strategy for handling inconsistent impressions entails our ignoring inconsistent information (Hendrick, 1972; Erber and Fiske, 1984). We typically attend more closely to and remember better social information that is consistent with our expectations than we do information that is inconsistent with our expectations (Berman, Read, and Kenny, 1983). This approach seemingly affords the path of least resistance. Even so, we are ready to modify our judgments in light of new evidence under some circumstances. For instance, we may change our initial impressions of a person as we work with him or her on a task that has a prize associated with it. Under these circumstances, we are motivated by our stake in the outcome to give greater thought to a person's inconsistencies and to the new social information that we are receiving. In so doing, we may mull over the information and try to make sense of how it relates to the person's underlying nature. The conclusion we arrive at may be no more accurate than the initial impression, but it is nonetheless apt to be more thoughtful (Tetlock, 1983; Erber and Fiske, 1984).

Memory Processes in Social Perception

Perception does not occur in a vacuum. Instead, we bring to bear prior knowledge that we have structured and stored in our heads for the processing of new information about individuals. Consider a study undertaken more than thirty years ago by Gregory Razran (1950). He showed 150 men photographs of 30 young women, all strangers to them. He asked the men to rank each photograph on a 5-point scale that would indicate their overall liking for each woman and their assessment of her beauty, her character, her intelligence, her ambition, and her "entertainingness." Two months later, he again had the same group view the identical photographs, but this time each photograph had a surname attached to it. Some of the young women were provided with Jewish names, such as Finkelstein and Cohen. To other photographs, Razran affixed Irish surnames such as O'Shaughnessy and McGillicuddy; to still others, Italian surnames such as Valenti and Scadano; and finally to others, old American surnames such as Davis and Clark.

The surnames had a marked effect on the manner in which the men perceived the women. The addition of Jewish and Italian surnames resulted in a substantial drop in overall liking and a smaller drop in judgments of beauty and character. The falling in the likability of the "Jewish women" was twice as great as for the "Italians" and five times as great as for the "Irish." In contrast, the labels contributed to a rise in the ratings in ambition and intelligence for the women with Jewish surnames. Clearly, the labels (together with their associated cultural definitions) had a marked effect on the men's perceptions of the photographs and on their assessment of the young women. Indeed, the men "read into" the photographs aspects that jibed with their ethnic stereotypes.

The Nature of Memory

The Razran study demonstrates that we bring prior knowledge to bear in interpreting new information. This fact brings us to a consideration of memory. **Memory** refers to the retention of what has been experienced or learned and its activation when recollection occurs. Social life dictates that we be something more than creatures of the moment. Sustained patterns of interaction (social relationships) require us to retain information about others and mentally to retrieve this information as the situation requires. Without memory we would react to every event as if it were unique. And if we did not remember facts, we would be incapable of thinking or reasoning.

When we remember information, three things occur: (1) *encoding,* the process by which information is put into the memory system; (2) *storage,* the process by which information is retained until it is needed; and (3) *retrieval,* the process by which information is regathered when it is needed. These phases in information processing have been likened to a filing system (Higbee, 1977). Suppose you are an office clerk who has the task of filing a company's correspondence. You have a letter from a major customer suggesting a modification in a product manufactured by the firm. Under what category will you file the letter? Should you create a new category—"product suggestions"—or should you file the letter under the customer's name? How you encode the correspondence will have implications for where you store it and how you later go about retrieving it. When the boss instructs you to bring her the letter three months later, you will begin a search of the office filing cabinet. You may first look for the letter under the customer's name, next under "product suggestions," and so on until you locate it.

Now consider a memory illustration. At one time or another you very likely learned the names of the planets surrounding the sun. Try to recall their names. They are probably "in there," but for a variety of reasons you may be unable to retrieve the information upon demand. So what do you do? You proceed much in the fashion that the clerk did in retracing the letter. You may initiate the search by starting with the planet nearest the sun and then work outward in space. Or you may search for the "large" planets and then the "small" planets. Or you may employ idiosyncratic features to recall the planets, such as Jupiter has twelve satellites, Saturn has a series of thin, flat rings, Venus is the most brilliant planet, and so on (Houston, 1976). In so doing, you undertake to retrieve from storage the information you had previously encoded.

Memory processes have major implications for perception. For example, an accumulating body of research reveals that the encoding process involves the active selection of information. Individuals are sensitized to some stimuli more than to others. For instance, Claudia E. Cohen (1981) had two groups of subjects view a videotape of a woman and her husband carrying on a lively conversation while eating dinner and later while opening her birthday presents. One group was told that the woman was a waitress; the other group, that she was a librarian. On the basis of prior research, Cohen had established that Americans have contrasting stereotypes of women in the two occupations—for instance, they view waitresses as more likely to eat hamburgers, drink beer, enjoy pop music, and receive a nightgown as a gift, whereas they picture librarians as more likely to eat roast beef, drink wine, enjoy classical music, and receive a best-seller as a gift. Although the videotape contained equal numbers of "waitress" and "librarian" features, later testing revealed that the subjects selectively remembered those characteristics of the woman that fitted the prevailing stereotypes of her occupation.

Eyewitness Testimony

We not only selectively attend to information, which we then capture in memory. Our recollections of people and events also undergo alterations and distortions in memory. Research by Elizabeth F. Loftus (1979, 1984) shows how information given after an event can influence a person's later eyewitness testimony about the details of the event. She had subjects view a film of a traffic accident. She then had the subjects answer questions regarding the collision. Half of the subjects were asked about the cars "bumping" into one another; the other half were asked the same question but the word "smashed" was substituted for "bumped." Viewers who were asked the "smashed" question estimated that the cars had been traveling faster than did those who were asked the "bumped" question. And the former were more likely to "remember," erroneously, seeing broken glass following the accident. The difference in the phrasing of the questions continued to affect the answers the subjects gave to another set of questions one week later.

All this has implications for eyewitness testimony in court cases (Yarmey, 1979; Brigham et al., 1982). Frequently victims innocently fill in details they think they remember in order to tell a story that is plausible both to themselves and to their questioners. For instance, when Robert Buckhout showed subjects a film of a violent crime without showing the face of the attacker, 80 percent of the subjects nonetheless identified the "assailant" from a lineup of faces (Albin, 1981). In sum, our memories are fallible. At times we invent perceptions, even when we have no intention of doing so; indeed, we are often unaware that we have done so. We fill in the gaps in our knowledge by plausible constructions of what "must have" or "should have" happened to make sense of the scene. And matters are complicated by the questioning that a witness is likely to experience. First comes interrogation by the police and then by prosecution and defense attorneys in depositions before the trial. Family and friends likewise ask for information. Finally, months or even years later, a witness is expected to provide a judge and jury with testimony regarding even the smallest details. Of course matters become even more complicated when some individuals have a stake in deceiving a judge and jury, in cases where they confront monetary loss or imprisonment (see boxed insert, pp. 54–55.)

ATTRIBUTION

We not only form impressions of people in an attempt to determine what they are like. We also assess the causes and implications of what they say and do. If we are to carry on our activities and fit our actions to those of other people, we must extract meaning from the data that bombard our sense organs. In brief, we must draw conclusions about "what makes people tick," behaving as "intuitive psychologists" or "constructive thinkers." Social psychologists term these cognitive activities **attribution**—the processes by which we explain and interpret the events we encounter. As Fritz Heider (1958) points out, attribution allows us to organize the continuous stream of information we gain from the world into meaningful units. In this chapter, we will consider the attributions we make regarding the behavior of other people. In Chapter 5, in considering self-perception, we will treat the attributions we make regarding ourselves, our behavior, and our inner states.

Causality: Internal Versus External

One way that we make sense of our sensory inputs is through the notion of causality. **Causality** involves our attribution of a cause-and-effect relationship to two paired events that recur in succession. It is based on the expectation that when one event occurs, another event, one that ordinarily follows the first, will again follow it. The ability to appreciate that a cause must always precede an effect has proved of enormous survival value for human beings in the course of evolution. Young children show such versatility in grasping the notion of causality that some psychologists speculate we are biologically prewired in ways that expedite our understanding of cause-and-effect relationships (Pines, 1983). It seems that human beings are especially apt to seek the sources of events when they involve the actions of people (Heider, 1958; Schank and Abelson, 1977;

CLUES TO LYING

Situations constantly arise in which we would like to know whether or not a person is lying to us. Accordingly, we often scrutinize the person, looking for clues that may signal his or her deception. **Deception** entails any intentional verbal or nonverbal act that an individual performs in order to mislead another person. Social psychologists find that we are surprisingly inept at detecting lies. We are rarely accurate more than 60 percent of the time—a not particularly impressive figure, since guessing alone should enable us to achieve a 50 percent level of accuracy (Zuckerman, DePaulo, and Rosenthal, 1981). Even professionals whose work calls upon them to detect deception are often wrong (Goleman, 1985*f*). Customs inspectors are no better than ordinary college students at guessing which people are attempting to smuggle contraband. Police inspectors are no more successful in judging people lying about a mock crime than are students. And experienced federal law enforcement officers from the Secret Service and the criminal investigation divisions of the armed forces are no more adept at detecting deceit than are newly recruited officers.

Most of us expect that liars give themselves away through shifty eyes and nervous gestures. Common sense suggests that these behaviors stem from guilt associated with deceit or from emotional distress aroused by the prospect of being detected (Riggio and Friedman, 1983). But liars usually attempt to control their nervous movements so as to appear self-composed (Ekman, 1985). Even so, social psychologists have undertaken a search for physical signs that a deceitful person cannot suppress. In practice, lie detection is a dual task. It requires that the observer decide first, on the basis of deception cues,

Zajonc, 1980). This tendency is most pronounced when a person engages in unexpected behaviors (Hastie, 1984).

In everyday life, we typically distinguish between two types of causation—internal and external (Jones and Nisbett, 1971). **Internal causality** involves attributing responsibility for events to the personal qualities and traits of the individual. **External causality** involves attributing responsibility for events to environmental and situational circumstances that lie outside the individual.

The matter of internal and external causality is not of interest merely to social psychologists. It has a good deal to do with many contemporary issues and hence has immediate concern for all of us. For example, do children do poorly in school because they lack innate ability or motivation (internal causality), or because they are the victims of poor schools, inadequate teachers, racism, and poverty (external causality)? Do people become criminals because of inner psychological deficiencies, conflicts, and problems (internal causality), or because of their immersion in a social setting where social pressures, learning experiences, and

whether deception is occurring, and second, on the basis of leakage cues, which message or information is being concealed.

In attempting to discriminate truth from deception in our everyday interactions, we usually have access to a variety of cues, including words, tone of voice, and body movements. Overall, it seems that discriminations based on verbal cues are more accurate than those based on nonverbal cues (Krauss et al., 1981; DePaulo, Lanier, and Davis, 1983). For instance, liars often emit signs of anxiety—their utterances are higher pitched, slower, and more negative, and they make more grammatical errors and slips of the tongue. Also, they tend to distance themselves from their messages, using less immediate, less evaluatively extreme, and less personally involved speech forms (DePaulo et al., 1982). However, nonverbal cues may also be a giveaway. Generally people are more aware of and more practiced at controlling their facial behavior than other behaviors. Consequently, they are more likely to "leak" from the lower body than from the face (Ekman and Friesen, 1969). Deception is often associated with more fragmented bodily movements, reflecting a greater degree of arousal and greater difficulty in controlling it (Zuckerman et al., 1984).

Overall, the most reliable clues to lying are responses that a person makes automatically and that are thus subject to minimal control. The social psychologist Paul Ekman (1985) finds that telltale signs of emotional reaction are particularly useful clues, especially those associated with distress, fear, and anger. The signal for distress is a lifting of the inner part of the eyebrows. That for fear is the raising and pulling together of the eyebrows. And the clue for anger is the narrowing and tightening of the red margin of the lips. Smiles can also belie true feelings. A feigned smile tends to be asymmetrical, yielding a slightly lopsided expression. Yet there are no absolute clues to lying—only to the emotions that are likely to accompany it. Accordingly, it seems that most liars can fool most people most of the time.

poverty propel them into crime (external causality)? Should we hold the individual accountable for his or her behavior (internal causality), rewarding conformity and punishing deviance, or should we hold society responsible for human shortcomings (external causality), seeking to remedy unhealthy social conditions through social reform and directed social change?

Various studies (Duval and Wicklund, 1973; Storms, 1973; Goldberg, 1978; Watson, 1982) suggest that for the most part we tend to view internal factors as underlying *other* people's behavior. But we tend to stress the extent to which our *own* behavior is controlled by outside forces. We believe that we choose our actions to fit particular situational requirements, but we believe that others do what they do by virtue of their inherent personal traits, dispositions, and qualities. Social psychologist Lee Ross (1977) has coined the term **fundamental attribution error** to describe our tendency to overestimate the extent to which the actions of other people derive from their underlying dispositions or personality. Thus as "intuitive psychologists," we tend too often to be "nativists"—

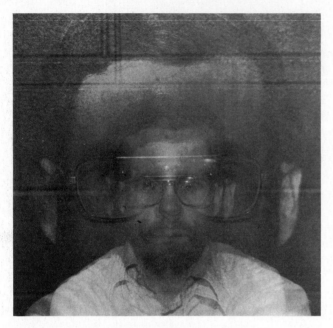

Attribution
There is more to a person than immediately meets the eye. From someone's overt actions we make inferences regarding his or her internal being. We make sense of the person's behavior by attributing causality to it. We commonly explain other people's behavior in terms of internal factors, but we tend to attribute our own behavior to external factors.
(Patrick Reddy)

proponents of stable individual differences—and too seldom "behaviorists"—proponents of situational influences.

A study by Richard E. Nisbett and his associates (1973) illustrates these points. The researchers asked Yale undergraduate students to write brief explanations of why they liked the girls they had dated most frequently in the past year and why they had chosen their majors. Next the students were asked to write brief paragraphs describing why their best friends liked the girls the friends had dated most regularly and why the friends had chosen their majors.

The results were then coded into two categories: internal causality ("I like warm people"; "I want a lot of money") and external causality ("She's a very warm person"; "Chemistry is a high-paying field"). When describing their own reasons for choosing girlfriends, the students listed external factors (properties of the girl) twice as often as internal factors (reasons associated with their own needs, interests, and characteristics). But when they gave their best friends' reasons for selecting girlfriends, the students cited external and internal factors about evenly. When explaining why they had chosen a specific major, they gave an almost equal number of external and internal reasons (seemingly, they saw themselves as selecting their majors with deliberation but as being "carried away" by women). But they attributed to their friends' selections of their majors almost four times as many reasons involving internal as external dispositions. Thus we tend to interpret the same behavior differently depending on whether it is our own or someone else's.

In part, these differences in attribution derive from our differing informational bases. We have knowledge about our own inner attitudes, dispositions, and inner states. But this information is normally not available to others. Accordingly, we focus our own attention on our environment rather than on our behavior, whereas our behavior is the focal point of other people's attention.

The Influence of Success and Failure

Not unexpectedly, social psychologists have shown that we attribute different sources to our successes than to our failures. A number of studies (Streufert and Streufert, 1969; Wortman, Costanzo, and Witt, 1973; Luginbuhl, Crowe, and Kahan, 1975; Weary, 1980) reveal that when we succeed at a task, we tend to attribute causality to ourselves; when we fail, to factors in the environment, the situation, or the actions of our opponents. Not surprisingly, teachers take causal credit for their students' successes but attribute their students' failures to low intelligence and poor motivation (Johnson, Feigenbaum, and Weiby, 1964; Beckman, 1970; Schopler and Layton, 1972).

Edward E. Jones and Richard E. Nisbett observe that when a student who is doing poorly in school discusses his or her problem with a faculty member, the two typically see the matter somewhat differently:

> The student, in attempting to understand and explain his inadequate performance, is usually able to point to environmental obstacles such as a particularly onerous course load, to temporary emotional stress . . . , or to a transitory confusion about life goals that is now resolved. The faculty adviser may nod and may wish to believe, but in his heart of hearts he usually disagrees. The adviser is convinced that the poor performance is due neither to the student's environment nor to transient emotional states. He believes instead that the failure is due to enduring qualities of the student—to lack of ability, to irremediable laziness, to neurotic ineptitude. (1971: 1)

Moreover, *when* people's performances go from good to bad or from bad to good makes a considerable difference in our attribution of causality. In a series of experiments, Jones and his associates (1968) had student subjects observe what appeared to be another student working at a series of difficult problems. In one condition, the student's performance increasingly improved: although the student missed a good many of the problems at the beginning of the test, he or she became more successful as the problem solving progressed. In another condition, the situation was reversed, and the student's performance deteriorated after an initial show of competence. In still another condition, the student's successful performances were randomly spaced. In all the conditions, however, the student was seen as correctly solving fifteen of the thirty problems.

Contrary to predictions, the performer who showed continual improvement was not consistently judged by the subjects to be the most able one. The subjects perceived the performer with the descending success rate as both more intelligent and likely to outperform those with ascending or random patterns. Moreover, subjects thought that the student whose performance had deteriorated had achieved more correct answers than was the case.

This research suggests that if we wish our professor or our employer to see us as intelligent, it is better to start with a bang and then let down rather than to begin slowly and finish spectacularly. It also provides bad news for late bloomers, for it supports the aphorism "First impressions are lasting impressions."

Causality and Motivation

Perhaps you have had the following experience. You have been watching a game involving your favorite basketball team. With three seconds left in the game and the score tied, a player on your team bursts toward the basket and suddenly propels the ball toward the hoop. As the buzzer sounds, the ball swishes through the net. Your team wins the game. Your friend, who has a low regard for your team, says, "Gee, were they *lucky.*" You indignantly respond: "Luck my eye! That was sheer *ability.*" "Naw," exclaims another friend. "Your guys were more psyched up. They put out more *effort.*" To which a third friend interjects: "Heck, it was an *easy* shot. Anyone could've made it." Four differing explanations were advanced for the same event: luck, ability, effort, and the difficulty of the task.

Bernard Weiner (1972, 1979) has built his approach to attribution on these four concepts. He points out that social psychologists have commonly assumed that when people make an internal attribution of causality, they are doing so in terms of inferences about personal *ability* (one's own or another person's intelligence, skill, resourcefulness, and so forth); in contrast, when people make an external attribution, they are assigning causality to *chance* factors. Weiner insists, however, that such assumptions are inadequate and even misleading, for they confuse an internal-external dimension with a stability-instability dimension (whether an occurrence is stable or unstable across various events). Thus Weiner proposes that attribution be considered in terms of a *stability* (stable-unstable) dimension and a *control* (internal-external) dimension. The addition of a dimension gives rise to four attributional factors: *effort* (internal and unstable); *ability* (internal and stable); *luck* (external and unstable); and *task difficulty* (external and stable). In other words, we can attribute a given outcome to our own or another individual's ability or effort, to sheer luck, or to the difficulty of the task.

Attribution along the control dimension (explanation in terms of internal or external factors) influences how we feel about our successes or failures. For instance, we experience a sense of pride in an accomplishment when we can locate the source of success within ourselves but of inadequacy when we attribute the failure to ourselves (Weiner and Kukla, 1970; Leventhal and Michaels, 1971; Riemer, 1975). On the other hand, attribution along the stability dimension influences our expectations that we will experience future success after an initial success and failure after an initial failure because we assume that conditions will remain stable across time (Weiner et al., 1972; McMahan, 1973; Fontaine, 1974).

Findings such as these have applications within many contexts. Take education. Educational psychologists find that when students attribute their successes to high ability, they are more likely to believe that future success is highly probable than if they attribute their success to other factors. In contrast, the attribution of an outcome to low ability makes future failure seem highly probable

(Nicholls, 1979). We find it much more devastating to think that we failed by virtue of low ability than that we failed because of bad luck, lack of effort, or task difficulty.

Evidence also suggests that both success and failure feed on themselves. Students who typically perform better than their peers tend to attribute their superior performances to high ability; consequently, they anticipate future success. When on occasion they encounter episodes of failure, they attribute their difficulties to bad luck or a lack of effort. However, those students who typically perform more poorly than their peers commonly attribute their successes to good luck or high effort and their failures to poor ability. High attainment breeds attributions that maintain a high self-concept, high academic motivation, and continued high attainment. But it is otherwise for those students with low attainment (Nicholls, 1979; Covington and Omelich, 1979; Forsyth and McMillan, 1981). Further, students who attribute their achievement to ability tend to prefer tasks in which competence determines the outcome. Conversely, students who attribute success to luck are likely to avoid ability tasks and to prefer games of chance (Fyans and Maehr, 1979).

Bias in Attribution Processes

Our discussion has shown that meaning does not inhere in people's behavior. Rather we *impute* meaning to what individuals say and do. The process is a subjective one, and it does not necessarily result in the same conclusions that would be reached by an objective observer or a social scientist. We have seen that our perceptual processes bias our interpretations of causality, success and failure, and motivation. Other factors also intrude upon perception. Such biases assume particular importance because we carry our attributions regarding people's behavior over into our later encounters with them. Hence the consequences of our attributions at any given time partially determine our attributions at a subsequent time (Lau, 1984). Indeed, as we will see in Chapter 15, we often manipulate or interpret our interaction with members of another race to make our expectancies regarding them seem true—a process termed the *self-fulfilling prophecy*.

Mood Biases

We tend to process incoming information in a way that is consistent with our current mood (Schwarz and Clore, 1983; Krantz and Rude, 1984; Zajonc, 1984). Both happiness and sadness direct our attention to either happy or sad kinds of information and color our evaluations of people. Likewise, such emotions as fear and disgust influence our judgments regarding other people's emotional states. We typically attribute to them feelings consistent with those that we feel (Schiffenbauer, 1974; Clark, Milberg, and Erber, 1984). And we find it easier to remember things that are congruent with our current mood (Forgas, Bower, and Krantz, 1984). Thus happy people are more likely to recall friendly, relaxed encounters with others, whereas sad people are more apt to recall unpleasant, tense happenings.

Self-Biases

A variety of biases are introduced by our self-images into the attributions we make regarding the behavior of other people. One of these is the **self-serving bias**—the tendency to interpret the outcomes of our behavior in ways that put ourselves in the best possible light (Snyder, Stephan, and Rosenfield, 1976; Lewicki, 1983, 1984). For instance, football coaches with losing records protect their self-esteem by attributing the consistently poor performance of their teams to external factors (Carver, DeGregorio, and Gillis, 1980). Another bias results from tendencies toward a **false consensus**—we overestimate the extent to which other people's thinking resembles our own (Fields and Schuman, 1976; Ross, Greene, and House, 1977; van der Pligt, 1984). This egocentric bias leads us to assume that other people hold opinions on current issues that more closely approximate our own attitudes than is really the case.

Societal Biases

Societal and cultural definitions also bear on attributional processes. A person's race, sex, and socioeconomic status influence the attributions we make regarding his or her behavior. For instance, when a middle-income or white person makes an application for unemployment benefits, we often attribute different causes to the behavior than when a working-class or black person makes the same application. Likewise, should a woman jog at night and be accosted and robbed by an assailant, we are more likely to blame the woman than we are to blame a man under similar circumstances—a phenomenon termed *blaming the victim* (Howard, 1984). We will have more to say on these matters in Chapter 11, when we consider rape and various rape myths.

The Functions of Attributions

Attributions fulfill a variety of functions (Kelley, 1971; Pittman and Pittman, 1980; Forsyth, 1980). First, they provide us with explanations for what takes place in our physical and social worlds. They permit us to approach life by means of the principle of determinism. Consequently, we can assume that events do not occur in a random or haphazard fashion but rather that they operate on a cause-and-effect basis. And we can conclude that certain regularities and recurrences characterize the universe—for instance, that day follows night and spring follows winter; that if we strike a match, fire results; and that when we smile, others typically take it as a friendly gesture.

Second, attributions permit us to predict various happenings. We can anticipate that traffic will flow primarily into the city in the morning and out of the city in the evening; that our social psychology class will meet on designated days, at a designated hour, and in a designated place; and that our friend will be happy to see us after an absence. When taken singularly or in combination, explanation and prediction enhance our feelings of control (Rothbaum, Weisz, and Snyder, 1982). The attribution process permits us to gain knowledge that we can apply to the management of ourselves and the environment. Such attributions are reassuring and promote self-confidence.

Third, attributions serve to protect, maintain, or extend various beliefs that we have about ourselves. An accumulating body of research suggests that we are more likely to attribute to ourselves positive than negative outcomes (Weary, 1980). As we noted earlier in the chapter, we tend to attribute successes to ourselves and failures to others, the situation, or various external factors. Many of these mechanisms function to protect or enhance our self-esteem.

And finally, attributions assist us in the formulation of our behavior (Riess et al., 1981). On the basis of our attributions, we present ourselves to others as certain kinds of people in hopes of gaining certain outcomes (see Chapter 8). For instance, we "dress up" for a job interview or a date in the expectation that the other party will view us in a favorable manner (the attribution that people look favorably on others in these settings if they wear "nice-looking" clothes). Consequently, attributions influence and assist us as we fashion our behavior and make our way about the physical and social worlds.

PERCEPTION OF THE SITUATION

> *It is the disposition of the thought that altereth the nature of the thing.*
> —John Lyly, *Euphues: The Anatomy of Wit*, 1597

We size up people and their behavior in order to anticipate what is likely to occur and to guide our actions in accord with these expectations. Thus far in the chapter we have examined what we as individuals bring to the process and especially the mental activities involved in social perception. Our understanding of human behavior can be further extended by looking at the social context or situation in which we behave (Argyle, Furnham, and Graham, 1981). Social psychologists view a **situation** as all the social factors that influence a person's experience or behavior at a given time and in a given place (Theodorson and Theodorson, 1969; Hewitt, 1976). It is at the intersection of time and space that we fashion our actions.

The situational context in which stimuli occur has consequences for their interpretation (Simpson and Ostrom, 1976; Messé et al., 1979; Alexander and Rudd, 1984). This is revealed in a study by N. G. Cline (1956). He presented subjects with outline drawings of three faces—one smiling, one glum, and one frowning—arranged in pairs. The judgments formed about each face depended in part on the face with which it was paired. Thus when paired with the glum face, the smiling face tended to be interpreted as dominant, vicious, gloating, and bullyish; but when paired with the frowning face, the smiling face was viewed as peaceful and peacemaking—as wanting to be helpful and friendly. Other research suggests that when people define us as being with friends who are attractive, they often view us as being more attractive than when we are by ourselves (Geiselman, Haight, and Kimata, 1984).

Defining Situations
In order to carry on social interaction—to fit our lines of action to those of others—we first need to arrive at shared definitions of the situation (shared "meanings"). (Patrick Reddy)

Definition of the Situation

Rightly to perceive a thing, in all the fullness of its qualities, is really to create it.

—C. E. Montague, *The Right Place*

Any one of multiple worlds—vastly different visions—may emerge, depending on which stimuli we "register," the linkages we make among these stimuli (the web or fabric we weave of them as we employ concepts), and our interpretations of the stimuli. A bank, for example, is a quite different social institution to student radicals, its shareholders, its officers, its employees, its depositors, loan seekers, and armed robbers. In the course of daily life, we fashion an "invisible world"—a world made up of various conceptions, such as our image of banking institutions. We actively forge reality as we communicate and interact with others—as we come to define banks as agents of oppression in our association with fellow radicals or as human benefactors in our association with fellow investors or bank officers.

Thus as we engage in social life, we find it necessary to arrive at a definition of the situation. A **definition of the situation** is the *meaning* we give to our immediate circumstances, the interpretation we make of the social factors that bear on us at a given time and in a given place. Thus as the sociologist W. I. Thomas (1937: 42) pointed out, "Preliminary to any self-determined act of behavior there is always a stage of examination and deliberation which we may call the definition of the situation."

Defining situations

I have been observing students taking lecture notes over the past several days. I had thought that students listen to a lecturer and individually decide what they should or should not take down. Yet I have noticed that a few students usually decide for the rest of the note takers what is and what is not important. When these "leaders" write down something in their notebooks, they "define" for the rest of the students that given material is significant. Others then likewise seem to follow suit. Indeed, not to take notes at such times is to be deviant—some sort of "dummy." We do not, it seems, independently experience the world. Rather we filter our perceptions through the social screens provided by others. Through the cues and clues we mutually afford one another, we interpret for one another which experiences are worthy of attention and which experiences are to be ignored. But we are not all equal in influence. Some individuals are pegged as "leaders."

Drawing on our storehouse of memories and recollections, we bring pertinent features of past experience to bear on present experience. In so doing, we arrive at meanings (as in the case of the banking institution). We engage in a process of self-indication (we "mentally" or "internally" note and assess things); we act in accordance with the way we interpret the flood of stimuli that we receive. We undertake to evolve some meaningful configuration in which various elements (like the banking institution) are seen as things to be desired or avoided, as obstacles to be overcome, as conditions we must accept, or as means to some end.

How we define situations has profound consequences for both ourselves and others. For instance, clinical psychologists find that our beliefs about how people are supposed to act when drinking influence our reactions to alcohol (Marlatt and Rohsenow, 1981). Men become more aggressive in laboratory situations when they believe that they are drinking vodka but in reality are only drinking tonic water. And they become less aggressive when they actually drink vodka but think they are consuming tonic water. By the same token, men typically become sexually aroused when they believe that they are drinking the real thing but in fact are not. Women also report feeling more aroused when they think they have been drinking alcohol, but curiously, a measure of their vaginal-blood flow reveals that alcohol actually causes them to become physically less aroused.

Sociologists point out that *if human beings define situations as real, they are real in their consequences* (Thomas, 1931: 189). For example, if we think of Jews, blacks, whites, or Chinese as having certain characteristics—whether these ideas are true or false—our definitions will influence our behavior. Strongly negative ideas have led to the tragedies of warfare and genocide (see boxed insert, pp. 64–65.)

THE IMPORTANCE OF SOCIAL DEFINITIONS: WHO IS A JEW?

The following is a transcript of a classroom discussion:

Instructor: Who is a Jew?

Student 1: It's a religion. It means you are a member of a religious group.

Instructor: You say it is a religion. I know a young woman by the name of Rebecca Cohen. Her parents are Jewish. Her brothers are Jewish. But she says she isn't Jewish. She's an atheist. She claims religion is a silly superstition. Is she a Jew?

Student 1: No, she's not Jewish. If she says she isn't, she isn't.

Instructor: You say she isn't Jewish. Last weekend she went to meet her boyfriend's parents, and his parents were horrified. They told their son they didn't want him going with a Jew. It would be even worse if he were to marry one. Rebecca insisted that she wasn't Jewish, but his parents were equally insistent that she was. Is she a Jew?

Student 2: Yes, I think she is a Jew. She is a Jew because her ancestors were Jews. She was born a Jew.

Instructor: Okay, let me give you another case. I know a young woman of Catholic background who married a Jewish fella and she converted to Orthodox Judaism. Her sons go to a Yeshiva [an Orthodox Jewish school]. Yet if you ask her about religious ideas she indicates that she believes in Divine Sci-

Or take the matter of belief in the existence of supernatural beings. Some people, for example, have a firm idea of what elves are like and what they do. Indeed, the notion of "little people" is a common one in folklore (for example, Irish mythology regarding leprechauns). If people believe in elves, they take elves into account in their behavior; they do things that they think will please the elves and avoid doing things that they think will displease them. (Something of this sort occurred with those of us who as children believed in Santa Claus. Around Christmas time we were careful to influence the appraisals that Santa would make of us.) Are elves, then, real? If by "real" is meant having physical existence, we must respond in the negative. But in a social sense, if people believe elves to be real, they are indeed very real. Definitions, then, are a critical element in social interaction.

Shared Definitions of Situations

For the most part we do not first see, and then define, we define first and then see. In the great blooming, buzzing confusion of the outer world we pick out what

ence—sort of a spiritual healing, self-awareness, self-realization cult. If you ask her if she is a Jew, she'll respond affirmatively. Is she a Jew?

Student 2: Yes, I'd say she is a Jew 'cause she says she is a Jew.

Instructor: Okay, let's think about that for a moment. If I told you I was black [the instructor is a brown-haired, blue-eyed, white-skinned male], would you believe me?

Student 2: [*Hesitates*] Yeah, I'd believe it. [*Pause*] Maybe deep down I wouldn't believe it, though. [*Giggles*]

Instructor: Now I'm getting confused. On the one hand, you say you determine whether a person is a Jew by asking them. But then you tell me you don't always believe people.

Student 3: A Jew is a person that is treated like a Jew.

Instructor: Okay, let's look at this definition. As I understand it, Senator Barry Goldwater's father was Jewish and his mother was Episcopalian. If Barry Goldwater had beaten President Johnson in the 1964 Presidential election, would Barry Goldwater have been America's first Jewish President?

Student 3: No, I don't think so. I don't think Goldwater is Jewish.

Instructor: Well, if Barry Goldwater had lived in Nazi Germany, would he have been identified as a Jew and gassed in a concentration camp?

Student 3: I guess so.

Instructor: What are we to make of all this? Who is a Jew? I think Jean-Paul Sartre put it best of all: "A Jew is a man whom other men call a Jew." It's a matter of social definition, what people believe to be the case and how they act. If people define situations as real [in this case, if they define one as a Jew], they are real in their consequences.

---

our culture has already defined for us, and we tend to perceive that which we have picked out in the form stereotyped for us by our culture.

—Walter Lippmann, *Public Opinion,* 1922

At bottom, human life consists of the acts of individuals—or more precisely, social (interhuman) acts. A **social act** is behavior that is oriented to or influenced by another person or persons (Theodorson and Theodorson, 1969: 4). Hence human association is a flowing and developing process in which our acts are organized, bent, redirected, and forged as we take others into account. Whatever we do—be it exchanging a greeting, making love, walking along a city street, playing Monopoly, or talking with a professor—we of necessity need to immerse ourselves in the world of others. In the process of taking others into account, we become aware of them, identify them, make an appraisal of them, attune ourselves to the meaning of their actions, and try to figure out what they have in mind and intend to do.

The activities of others, then, enter as positive factors in the formation of our own conduct. In the process, we may start or stop given lines of action; abandon

Shared definitions of the situation

If we are to mesh our actions with those of other people, we must have shared definitions of the situation. This point was driven home to me today by the following series of events. My boyfriend told me to meet him at the library after class. We always meet at "our" table, which is at the far end of the study room. After class I made my way over to the library. I caught sight of my "boyfriend" at "our" table wearing his green ski jacket. I was thinking about other matters as I walked over to the table. I came up behind my "boyfriend," put my arms around him, said "Hi, Sweetie," and reached around to kiss his cheek. As I did so, I encountered the astonished look of a boy wearing a coat that was the exact duplicate of that worn by my boyfriend. I was embarrassed and flustered, and simply muttered, "Sorry, I thought you were my boyfriend." Then I hightailed it out of the library. The warmth and affection that should have ensued had it been my boyfriend did not take place. My boyfriend—a smiling, easygoing, people-oriented guy—would have reciprocated my kiss. Things would have worked out with my boyfriend because we would have shared the same definition of the situation. They did not work out with the stranger because our definitions did not jibe.

The Social Act
Human life is a flowing and developing process in which we fit our actions to those of others by taking account of their actions toward us.
(Patrick Reddy)

Differing Definitions of the Situation
Meanings are not inherent in behavior but are attributed to them by individuals in interaction with one another. Consequently, behavior that many adults define as vandalism may be mandated by teenage peer groups. (Patrick Reddy)

or postpone others; revise, check, intensify, or transform still others. In exchanging a greeting, making love, or whatever, we must continuously *fit* our own line of activity in some fashion to the developing action of others. We need to organize, construct, and negotiate lines of conduct (Blumer, 1969: 108–113).

If we are mutually to fit together our lines of actions, we need agreed-upon meanings—*shared* definitions of situations. We require common understandings of life's activities—a blueprint or map that tells us in rather broad terms what we can expect of others and what others can expect of us. We term these shared cognitive (mental) maps, which provide us with guideposts and guidelines for social life, **culture.**

Definitions of situations arrived at on one occasion often hold for future occasions. The consistency with which we define a succession of situations derives from the fact that we generally view the world from the same perspective, one that we culturally share with our associates. We come to hold a common vocabulary of symbols and labels—standard terms and meanings—that permit the smooth flow of interaction (Denzin, 1970: 270).

This fact is highlighted where "usual" definitions of the situation are absent and where, instead, contrasting definitions prevail. Such is the case, for example, in a nudist camp. Within the nudist camp, the meanings attached to clothing by the society at large no longer prevail (Weinberg, 1965). Nonnudists assume—on the basis of traditional cultural definitions—that breakdowns of modesty in dress result in rampant sexual interest, promiscuity, embarrassment, jealousy, and shame. However, people within a nudist-camp setting subscribe to a variety of *shared* (countercultural) meanings that offset these consequences: they share the views that nudism and sexuality are unrelated and that there is nothing shameful about exposing the human body. New shared (countercultural) definitions of modesty prevail—not staring, not behaving suggestively, and not making erotic overtures. One nudist woman observed: "I got so mad because my husband wanted me to undress in front of other men that I just pulled my clothes right off, thinking everyone would look at me." She was amazed—even initially disappointed—when no one did.

Definitions of situations—"meanings"—are not some absolute, objectively inherent property of objects or circumstances; rather, they are fashioned in social interaction. And they are sustained through social interaction. In the nudist-camp situation, for instance, measures are taken to exclude single young men who come simply to "gape at the women."

SUMMARY

1. Perception is the mediating link between us and our environment. It is the process by which we give meaning to our sensations—to sights, sounds, smells, tastes, and touches. By virtue of perception, we transform outer stimuli into an inner system of meaning.

2. One of the basic ways we process information about people and form impressions of them is through categories. Categories afford many advantages. For one thing, they allow us to sort individuals into meaningful and manageable classes and assign labels to these classes. For another, they provide us with a sense of order, constancy, and regularity in dealing with people.

3. Social psychologists refer to categories that are mental structures for processing information as schemata. A schema is an abstract mental framework—a general knowledge structure—for interpreting information from the environment. In recent years the concepts prototype and implicit personality theories have been used to describe the influences of schemata on person perception and memory. Stereotypes are an example of prototypes or implicit personality theories.

4. When we enter the presence of others, we typically seek to understand them, or size them up. Important to this process are central organizing traits, summation and averaging of traits, halo effects, and primacy and recency effects.

5. Memory processes influence social perception. The encoding process of memory involves the active selection of information. But we not only selec-

tively attend to information that we then capture in memory. Our recollections of people and events also undergo alterations and distortions in memory.

6. In our daily lives, we are forced by our experiences to act as "intuitive psychologists" and judge the causes and implications of our own and other people's behavior. This derives from the fact that perception is not simply a process of sensation but also a process of interpretation. An important concept for making sense of the universe of sensation is our attribution of causality to the successive occurrence of two paired phenomena.

7. Various studies suggest that for the most part we tend to view internal factors as underlying other people's behavior but that we tend to stress the extent to which our own behavior is controlled by outside forces.

8. We attribute different sources to our successes than to our failures. When we succeed at a task, we tend to attribute causality to ourselves; when we fail, to factors in the environment, the situation, or the action of our opponents.

9. Attributions fulfill a variety of functions. First, they provide us with explanations for what takes place in our physical and social worlds. Second, they permit us to predict various happenings. Third, they serve to protect, maintain, or extend various beliefs that we have about ourselves. And finally, attributions assist us in the formulation of our behavior, especially in how we go about presenting ourselves to others.

10. The situational context in which stimuli occur has consequences for their interpretation. Any one of multiple worlds may emerge, depending on which stimuli we register, the linkages we make among these stimuli, and our interpretations of the stimuli. Thus as we engage in social life, we find it necessary to arrive at a definition of the situation.

11. If human beings define situations as real, they are real in their consequences.

12. If we are mutually to fit together our lines of action, we require agreed-upon meanings—shared cultural definitions of the situation.

GLOSSARY

Attribution □ The process by which we explain and interpret events that we encounter.

Category □ An abstract representation of conceptually related information.

Causality □ Our attribution of a cause-and-effect relationship to two paired phenomena that recur in succession.

Central organizing trait □ A characteristic that has a strong effect on our overall evaluation of a person.

Culture □ Shared cognitive (mental) maps that provide us with guideposts and guidelines for social life; shared recurrent definitions of given kinds of situations.

Deception □ Any intentional verbal or nonverbal act that an individual performs in order to mislead another person.

Definition of the situation □   The meaning we give to our immediate circumstances; the interpretation we make of the social factors that bear on us at a given time and in a given place.

External causality □   The attribution of responsibility for events to environmental and situational circumstances that lie outside the individual.

False consensus □   The tendency to overestimate the extent to which other people's thinking resembles our own.

Fundamental attribution error □   Our tendency to overestimate the extent to which the actions of other people derive from their underlying dispositions or personality.

Halo effect □   The assumption that when a person has one trait, he or she also possesses certain other traits.

Implicit personality theories □   We commonly assume that a number of traits cluster to form an organized set of relationships.

Internal causality □   The attribution of responsibility for events to the personal qualities and traits of the individual.

Memory □   The retention of what has been experienced or learned and its activation when recollection occurs.

Perception □   The process by which we give meaning to sensations.

Person perception □   The processes by which we come to know and think about others—their characteristics, qualities, and inner states.

Primacy effect □   The way in which early information colors our perception of subsequent information.

Prototype □   A category that we mentally employ to represent a loose set of features that seem to belong together.

Recency effect □   The tendency to be most influenced by what we have just witnessed.

Schemata (singular, **schema**) □   Abstract mental frameworks—general knowledge structures—for interpreting information from the environment.

Self-serving bias □   The tendency to interpret the outcomes of behavior in ways that put ourselves in the best possible light.

Situation □   All the social factors that influence a person's behavior or experience at a given time and in a given place.

Social act □   Behavior that is oriented to or influenced by another person or persons.

Stereotype □   The unscientific and hence unreliable generalizations that we make about individuals by virtue of their membership in a group.

3 SOCIAL COMMUNICATION AND LANGUAGE

THE NATURE OF SYMBOLS AND
   LANGUAGE
Symbols
Language
The Meaning of Meaning
Paralanguage
Body Language
Gender and the Communication
   Process

ACQUIRING LANGUAGE
Learning Theory
Nativist Theory
A Resolution of Divergent
   Theories
LANGUAGE AND THINKING
Language and Thought
The Linguistic Relativity Thesis
The Language as a Container of
   Thought Thesis

STOCKTON, Calif.—The worst possible fate befell two young masked robbers last night. They tried to hold up a party of thirty-six prominent, middle-aged women, but couldn't get anybody to believe they were for real.

One of the women actually grabbed the gun held by one of the youths.

"Why," she said, "that's not wood or plastic. It must be metal."

"Lady," pleaded the man, "I've been trying to tell you, it IS real. This is a holdup."

"Ah, you're putting me on," she replied cheerfully.

The robbers' moment of frustration came about 9:00 P.M. at the home of Mrs. Florence Tout . . . as she was entertaining at what is called a "hi-jinks" party.

Jokes and pranks filled the evening. Thus not one of the ladies turned a hair when the two men, clad in black, walked in.

"All right now, ladies, put your rings on the table," ordered the gunman [the women were prominent in Stockton social circles].

"What for?" one of the guests demanded.

"This is a stickup. I'm SERIOUS!" he cried.

All the ladies laughed.

HELEN KELLER: THE SIGNIFICANCE OF LANGUAGE

The most important day I remember in all my life is the one on which my teacher, Anne Mansfield Sullivan, came to me. I am filled with wonder when I consider the immeasurable contrast between the two lives which it connects. It was the third of March, 1887, three months before I was seven years old.

On the afternoon of that eventful day, I stood on the porch, dumb, expectant.... Have you ever been at sea in a dense fog, when it seemed as if a tangible white darkness shut you in, and the great ship, tense and anxious, groped her way toward the shore with plummet and sounding-line, and you waited with beating heart for something to happen? I was like that ship before my education began, only I was without compass or sounding-line, and had no way of knowing how near the harbour was....

I felt approaching footsteps. I stretched out my hand as I supposed to my mother. Someone took it, and I was caught up and held close in the arms of her who had come to reveal all things to me, and, more than all things else, to love me.

The morning after my teacher came she led me into her room and gave me a doll. The little blind children at the Perkins Institution had sent it and Laura Bridgman had dressed it; but I did not know this until afterward. When I had played with it a little while, Miss Sullivan slowly spelled into my hand the word "d-o-l-l." I was at once interested in this finger play and tried to imitate it. When I finally succeeded in making the letters correctly I was flushed with childish pleasure and pride. Running downstairs to my mother I held up my hand and made the letters for doll. I did not know that I was spelling a word or even that words existed; I was simply making my fingers go in monkey-like imitation. In the days that followed I learned to spell in this uncomprehending way a great many words, among them *pin, hat, cup* and a few verbs like *sit, stand* and *walk*. But my teacher had been with me several weeks before I understood that everything has a name.

One day, while I was playing with my new doll, Miss Sullivan put my big rag doll into my lap also, spelled "d-o-l-l" and tried to make me understand that "d-o-l-l" applied to both. Earlier in the day we had had a tussle over the words "m-u-g" and "w-a-t-e-r." Miss Sullivan had tried to impress it upon me that "m-u-g" is *mug* and that "w-a-t-e-r" is *water,* but I persisted in

One of them playfully shoved one of the men. He shoved her back.

As the ringing laughter continued, the men looked at each other, shrugged, and left empty-handed. (*San Francisco Examiner,* April 4, 1968)

Communication is central to social behavior. Where communication is ineffective—where a mutual understanding is not realized—joint action is blocked.

confounding the two. In despair she had dropped the subject for the time, only to renew it at the first opportunity. I became impatient at her repeated attempts and, seizing the new doll, I dashed it upon the floor. I was keenly delighted when I felt the fragments of the broken doll at my feet. Neither sorrow nor regret followed my passionate outburst. I had not loved the doll. In the still, dark world in which I lived there was no strong sentiment or tenderness. I felt my teacher sweep the fragments to one side of the hearth, and I had a sense of satisfaction that the cause of my discomfort was removed. She brought me my hat, and I knew I was going out into the warm sunshine. This thought, if a wordless sensation may be called a thought, made me hop and skip with pleasure.

We walked down the path to the well-house, attracted by the fragrance of the honeysuckle with which it was covered. Some one was drawing water and my teacher placed my hand under the spout. As the cool stream gushed over one hand she spelled into the other the word *water,* first slowly, then rapidly. I stood still, my whole attention fixed upon the motions of her fingers. Suddenly I felt a misty consciousness as of something forgotten—a thrill of returning thought; and somehow the mystery of language was revealed to me. I knew then that "w-a-t-e-r" meant the wonderful cool something that was flowing over my hand. That living word awakened my soul, gave it light, hope, joy, set it free! There were barriers still, it is true, but barriers that could in time be swept away.

I left the well-house eager to learn. Everything had a name, and each name gave birth to a new thought. As we returned to the house every object which I touched seemed to quiver with life. That was because I saw everything with the strange, new sight that had come to me. On entering the door I remembered the doll I had broken. I felt my way to the hearth and picked up the pieces. I tried vainly to put them together. Then my eyes filled with tears; for I realized what I had done, and for the first time I felt repentance and sorrow.

I learned a great many new words that day. I do not remember what they all were; but I do know that *mother, father, sister, teacher* were among them—words that were to make the world blossom for me, "like Aaron's rod, with flowers." It would have been difficult to find a happier child than I was as I lay in my crib at the close of that eventful day and lived over the joys it had brought me, and for the first time longed for a new day to come.

SOURCE: Helen Keller (1904), *The Story of My Life.* New York: Grosset & Dunlap. Pages 21–24.

This fact is highlighted in the above newspaper account. The holdup was botched because the parties failed to effect common definitions of the situation. They did not become "tuned" together and hence failed to synchronize their actions. **Communication** is the process by which people transmit information, ideas, attitudes, and emotions to one another. As such, communication is basic to the human condition.

THE NATURE OF SYMBOLS AND LANGUAGE

Most of us are familiar with the story of Helen Keller. Although born a perfectly healthy and normal child, very early in her life she was stricken with a severe illness that left her deaf and blind. In her autobiography, *The Story of My Life* (1904), Helen Keller tells that during her early years she remained imprisoned in her body, having at best only nebulous and uncertain links to the outside world. For all practical purposes her handicap had locked her within a highly private world. Since she was unable to see or hear, she could not acquire language or other symbolic means of communication in the manner of most children. Accordingly, she was excluded from the public world in which human beings link themselves together within those *interpersonal* networks that constitute human society. Later, through the skilled and patient teaching provided by Anne Mansfield Sullivan, Helen Keller learned the American Sign Language. In time, using a special Braille typewriter, she became an accomplished author.

The boxed insert (pp. 72–73) contains an excerpt from *The Story of My Life*. Here Helen Keller details how coming to learn language afforded her an understanding of an environment that until then had been virtually meaningless to her. She came to recognize that everything has a "name." In brief, she grasped the significance of words. Through the use of words—verbal "handles" for grouping perceptions into units—she could symbolically categorize and manipulate the events and objects in the world around her (see Chapter 2). This association between a verbal symbol and experience made it possible for her to use the symbol in the absence of experience. And since the symbols were *shared* with others, she could transfer her mental state to others by the use of words. Similarly, others could open their mental states to her.

Communication, then, is the primary means by which we link ourselves together within the larger human enterprise. As a result we live our lives largely within symbolic environments. Although various social insects (ants, bees, and termites) also aggregate in organized groups, their behavior seems to be principally integrated on a physiological and instinctive basis. Since we are largely lacking in such inborn mechanisms, symbolic communication has become the chief compensating mechanism by which we coordinate and structure our be-

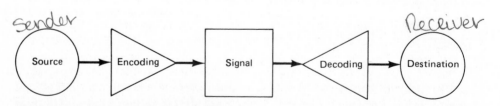

FIGURE 3.1 The Communication Process
One party (the source) encodes an idea by putting it in the form of a signal which the other party (the destination) decodes.

havior within groups and societies. In this sense, language was the "ticket" that admitted Helen Keller to social life and thus to full humanness.

Communication allows us to establish "commonness" with one another. A sender and a receiver become "tuned" together for a given message. This requires that one party *encode* a message by taking an idea and putting it in the form of a signal that can then be transmitted to the other party. Once coded and sent in signal form, the message becomes independent of the sender. The act of communication is completed when the other party (the designation) receives the signal and appropriately *decodes* it. Figure 3.1 provides a diagram of the communication process.

Forms of Symbols.

Symbols

We live in a world of symbols. A **symbol** is any object or event that has socially come to stand for something else. It is a sign that conveys meaning by virtue of some socially shared convention, some understanding between users. Symbols are arbitrary stand-ins for actual things. Although symbols stand for other things, they bear no necessary relationship to them. Thus, for example, the word "small" is larger than the word "big," and on this page the symbol "orange" appears just as black as the symbols "black" and "white" (DeVito, 1970).

Symbols take a good many forms. Spoken and written words are familiar examples. But we also communicate with objects: in most societies, masks, hair styles, clothing, body adornments, tattooing, ribbons, veils, medallions, or other devices serve to communicate the social status of the wearer and the gravity of an occasion. Colors often have symbolic connotations: in the Western world, "red" brings to mind anger (and Communism); "blue," emotional depression; "yellow," cowardice; "white," purity and innocence; "black," evil and mourning (although among blacks, there has been a recent trend to reverse the traditional symbolism by associating "black" with goodness and "white" with badness [Williams, Tucker, and Dunham, 1971]).

Gestures—social acts with symbolic significance—may similarly serve communicative purposes:

> Among the Wanyika, people meet by grasping hands and pressing their thumbs together; dwellers in the region of the Niger join their right hands and separate them with a pull so that a snapping noise is made by thumb and fingers. The handshake of the Arab seems to be a scuffle in which each tries to raise to his lips the hand of the other. . . . Polynesians stroke their own faces with the other person's hands. . . . In some Eskimo tribes . . . the courteous way of greeting a stranger is to lick one's own hands, draw them first over one's own face and then over that of a visitor. . . . Among the Polynesians, Malays, Burmese, Mongols, the Lapps, and others—a usual salute is that of smelling each other's cheeks. (Hiller, 1933: 101–119)

Some gestures have the same or similar meanings in several cultures. A good example is the side-to-side head motion meaning "No." However, some behaviors have a specific meaning in one culture but not in another. For instance, the

---

Symbol

In the dorm some of us have our girlfriends from out of town up for over the weekend. When we are in our room with our girl we put a conventional necktie on our doorknob to signal "Do not disturb—Occupied!" The necktie is a symbol that has a shared meaning among the guys in the dorm.

French gesture of putting one's fist around the tip of the nose and twisting it signifies that a person is drunk, but it is not a gesture employed in other cultures. And a gesture may have one meaning in one culture and a quite different meaning in another culture. Thus the thumbs-up gesture was employed by Roman emperors to spare the lives of gladiators in the Colosseum. It is now favored by American and Western European airline pilots, truck drivers, and others to mean "All right." But in Sardinia and northern Greece, it is an insulting gesture, paralleling the insulting middle-finger gesture of American society (Ekman, Friesen, and Bear, 1984).

 Symbols, then, are socially shared vehicles of human communication. Meaning is encoded in symbols, especially language. Symbols are critical to human social behavior because behavior is carried out in accordance with intended meanings. More particularly, they are the vehicles through which meanings come to be shared. As such, symbols permit human beings to fit their lines of action together, functioning as guides to what they say and do (Robinson, Balkwell, and Ward, 1980).

Language

"Speech," wrote Thomas Mann, "is civilization itself." Indeed, speech may well be our most distinctive feature as human beings. Leslie White, a cultural anthropologist, observes that

> without articulate speech we would have no *human* social organization. Families we might have, but this form of organization is not peculiar to man; it is not *per se, human.* But we would have no prohibitions of incest, no rules prescribing exogamy [outgroup marriage] and endogamy [ingroup marriage], polygamy or monogamy. . . . Without speech we would have no political, economic, ecclesiastic, or military organization; no codes of ethics; no laws; no science, theology, or literature. . . . Indeed, without articulate speech we would be all but toolless. . . . In short, without symbolic communication in some form, we would have no culture. "In the Word was the beginning" of culture—and its perpetuation also. (1949: 33–34)

Language is a socially structured system of sound patterns (words and sentences) with standardized meanings. Language is our principal vehicle for communication, finding expression in speech. Writing is secondary and developed

Symbols
Human beings employed a great many vehicles for transmitting messages to one
another. (Patrick Reddy)

3 properties of language

in imitation of the spoken word (DeVito, 1970). Language has a number of
distinctive properties (Gould, 1983). First, it is symbolic, enabling us to denote
abstract ideas and events distant in time and place. Second, it allows for innovation so that we may say things in new ways. And third, language is transmitted
culturally through socialization processes.

Language operates at two levels. At the *inter*individual level it permits us to
carry on communication with others. We find it possible to transmit to other
people information, ideas, attitudes, and emotions. At the *intra*individual level
it facilitates thinking. Words allow us to partition the world into manageable
units and domains of relevance. *Words* are verbal labels, in a sense "handles,"
that we apply to categories of objects, events, and people. As noted above, this
symbolic property of language lets us deal conceptually with things in another
time and place and frees us from a here-and-now world.

The Meaning of Meaning

Symbols have meaning. But philosophers and psychologists alike have had much
difficulty defining "meaning." One observer of the human condition notes that
"there is perhaps no more bewildering and controversial problem than 'the
meaning of meaning'" (Cassirer, 1944: 112). Some philosophers have employed

the term to refer to some sort of metaphysical "essence" that characterizes a thing. However, this is not the way most psychologists and sociologists use the word. Generally, social scientists conceive of **meaning** as the *relatedness* of something to all other events or objects with which it is associated in the experience of an individual or group (Kerckhoff, 1964: 418). It is the expression of all the information we have in our memory that is tied or bonded to the symbolic representation of something (Rubenstein, 1973: 31).

Social scientists find it helpful to distinguish between the denotative meaning and the connotative meaning of a word. The **denotative meaning** "points out" an object—it refers to certain specific properties or patterns of that object. The denotative meaning of the word "pig," for example, is "a four-legged, curly-tailed mammal covered with coarse bristles." But "pig" also has a **connotative meaning** which consists of the emotional and evaluative associations of this word. The connotative meaning of "pig" has judgmental overtones (however inaccurate)— dirty, greedy, coarse, gross, and brutish. Further, the word "pig" was employed during the late 1960s by some young people and political radicals as a highly charged derogatory term for a police officer. Misunderstandings often arise in human communication because of the different connotative meanings words have for different people. The words "capitalism," "Zionism," "love," "freedom," "independence," and "democracy" are good illustrations of this.

So as to identify connotative meanings of words more precisely, psychologist Charles Osgood (1962) has developed a form of measurement he terms the **semantic differential.** After analyzing many English words, Osgood found that connotative meanings primarily flow along three dimensions: an *evaluative* dimension (good–bad; pleasant–unpleasant; sacred–profane); a *potency* dimension (strong–weak; large–small; heavy–light); and an *activity* dimension (fast–slow; active–passive; sharp–dull). For instance, with the word "rosebud" we are likely to associate a connotative meaning of good, impotent, and passive on the three dimensions; in contrast, the word "quicksand" has associations of bad, strong, and passive. Other studies have found that these same dimensions (evaluation, potency, and activity) characterize connotative meanings in such diverse languages as Japanese, Finnish, and the Kannada dialect of India (Osgood, 1967; Osgood, May, and Miron, 1975). Although the same dimensions for connotative meanings are found in differing cultures, any *given* word may have different connotative meanings depending on the culture in question. For example, "rain" is a relatively unpleasant word for American college students; but for a Hopi Indian the word has pleasant associations because for the Hopi, rainfall is scarce and essential (Carroll, 1964).

Paralanguage

Paralanguage refers to the nonsemantic aspects of speech—the stress, pitch, and volume of speech by which we communicate expressive meaning. It has to do with *how* something is said, not with *what* is said. Tone of voice, pacing of speech, silent pauses, and extralinguistic sounds (such as sighs) constitute paralanguage (see the boxed insert on arranging speaking turns, pp. 80–82).

Paralanguage is what we are referring to when we say, "It wasn't what she said; it was the way she said it." Consider, for instance, the difference in the meaning of the response "You old so-and-so" under the following circumstances:

1. As an angry retort to "Hereafter you get home on time [husband to his wife]." (hostile intonation)
2. As a response to the sexual invitation "Let's spend the night together." (seductive intonation)
3. In recognition of a display of special ability or insight, such as, "See, you can solve the problem by placing a ladder against the beam above the window." (admiring, friendly compliment)
4. As a response to the suggestion "Let's call in sick tomorrow morning and play golf." (jocular, playful agreement)
5. As a response to an order from a status equal, such as, "Carry these boxes up to the third floor." (grudging assent)
6. As a response to a greeting—"Hey, Bill!"—in a chance encounter on the street with a friend one has not seen in some time. (pleased surprise)

Baby talk is a type of paralanguage (Caporael, 1981). While baby talk contains unique words (for example, "choo-choo" for train and "tum-tum" for stomach), it is truly distinctive in its paralinguistic features, especially its high pitch and exaggerated intonations. It has been documented in numerous languages from Gilyak and Comanche (the languages of small, isolated preliterate Old World and New World communities) to Arabic and Marathi (languages spoken by people with literary traditions). Most commonly, baby talk is directed toward infants, animals, and, under some circumstances, adults. Among adults, it is used to display mockery, irony, and sarcasm, but it is more commonly employed between intimate friends and lovers and by hospital staff to patients.

In one study, researchers examined the relationship between doctors' feelings as reflected in their speech and doctors' success in referring alcoholic patients for continued treatment (with "success" defined as the individual making and keeping an appointment at a clinic for alcoholics). This study revealed that the doctors' tone of voice was related to successful referral. An "angry" tone tended to be associated with ineffectiveness, since many alcoholic patients are especially sensitive to rejection. In contrast, a positive relationship existed between inferred anxiety and effectiveness in referral; alcoholics perceived "anxious" speech by the doctor as having a nervous quality revealing concern (Milmoe et al., 1967).

Body Language

> He that has eyes to see and ears to hear may convince himself that no mortal can keep a secret. If his lips are silent, he chatters with his fingertips; betrayal oozes out of him at every pore.
>
> —Sigmund Freud, "A Case of Hysteria," 1905

Body language (also termed **kinesics**) entails the nonverbal communication of meaning through physical movements and gestures. We tap our fingers to show

ARRANGING SPEAKING TURNS IN CONVERSATION

There was language in their very gesture.

—Shakespeare, *The Winter's Tale,* 1611

Consider how we navigate a crowded sidewalk. If we were to move like two sets of robots, each set maintaining its line of march, few if any of us would avoid bumping into others. However, through mutual glances and gestures we communicate with one another about our speed and direction of movement so as to minimize collisions. In effect, these glances and gestures serve as routing or crash-avoidance devices (see photo). Similarly, in crossing a street we often look at the motorist for cues that will give us personal assurances of safety. We in turn style our body gestures so as to provide easy evidence of our proposed course of movement.

Just as it is desirable to avoid collisions on the sidewalks and streets, it is desirable to avoid a good deal of simultaneous talking in conversations. Typically, we take turns in speaking and listening. We spend relatively little time in mutual silence or simultaneous talking, and very often the transitions from one speaker to another involve no perceptible speaker overlap or pause (Trimboli and Walker, 1982). But how do we manage to avoid verbally bumping into one another in our conversations? The answer to this question lies in the rules and signals involved in turn

taking. Let us consider a number of these (Duncan, 1972; Fast, 1970; Trimboli and Walker, 1984).

TURN-YIELDING SIGNALS

Turn-yielding signals involve a number of behavioral cues that we display either singly or simultaneously:

1. *Intonation.* The person speaking raises or lowers his or her voice as evidence of a terminal clause. An example would be raising the voice on "this" in the question, "Do you like this?"
2. *Paralingual drawl.* The final syllable or a stressed syllable of a terminal clause is uttered in a slow, drawn-out manner.
3. *Body motion.* If hand gesturing has been used during the speaking turn, it is ended; if not, the speaker's tensed hands are relaxed. If the speaker asks a question—for example, "What time is it?" or "Where are you going?"—the head comes up on *it* or on the *ing* in *going.* The speaker's eyes also tend to open wider with the last note of a question, as a signal for the other person to start his or her answer.
4. *Verbal clues.* The person speaking utters a stereotyped expression—"but uh" or "you know"—followed by a phrase: ". . . but uh, I guess that's just the way he is," or ". . . you know how it is."
5. *Syntax.* The person speaking completes a grammatical clause that involves a subject-predicate combination.

Navigating a Crowded Sidewalk
One way in which pedestrians accommodate themselves to one another so as to maintain a constant flow of traffic is by the so-called step-and-slide maneuver (Wolff, 1973). Two individuals typically do not (as might be expected) move completely out of each other's path so to avoid contact or bumping. Rather, they both cooperate to effect a "clean pass." Starting at about a distance of five feet, each slightly angles his or her body, turns the shoulder, and takes an almost imperceptible step to the side; hands are pulled inward or away to avoid hand-to-hand contact; bodies are twisted backward to maximize face-to-face distance. In this way, passing is executed with little or no body contact. (Don McCarthy)

ATTEMPT-SUPPRESSING SIGNALS

As the speaker, we exhibit cues that maintain our turn. For example, our voice maintains the same pitch, our head remains straight, our eyes remain unchanged, and our hands continue gesturing. Further, we

Box continues on next page.

fill the pauses with sounds such as "uh," "umm," or deliberately never finish a sentence by ending each utterance with "and . . ." or "but the umm. . . ."

BACK-CHANNEL COMMUNICATION

The listener cues us into the fact that she or he is not seeking a turn: some typical cues, for example, are using such signals as "mm-hmm" and "yeah"; nodding the head; completing the speaker's unfinished sentence; and restating in a few words an immediately preceding speaker's thought (Kraut, Lewis, and Swezey, 1982). The smile can also function as a type of back-channel communication (Brunner, 1979).

Such subtleties, such taken-for-granted mechanisms, facilitate communication. They make possible a back-and-forth exchange without the need of saying, "Are you finished? Now I will talk."

---

impatience. We shrug our shoulders to indicate indifference. We wink an eye to demonstrate intimacy. We lift an eyebrow in disbelief. We rub our noses or scratch our heads in puzzlement. We slap our forehead when we realize we've forgotten something. We shift uncomfortably in our chair. We extend a hand for a handshake. Through the motions of our bodies, limbs, faces, and eyes we communicate information about our feelings, attitudes and intentions.

Multichannel Communication

Intense looking may indicate either love or hostility (see the box on eye contact and civil inattention, pp. 84–86). A tense body posture may signal respectfulness or hostility. The meaning of such behaviors is usually clarified when we look at additional behavior channels. Thus we often impute love to an intense gaze, close distance, and relaxed posture (Schwarz, Foa, and Foa, 1983). Likewise, we frequently combine body language with verbal language and paralanguage. Indeed, on the basis of his research, psychologist Albert Mehrabian (1968) has devised a formula for the ratio by which the three ingredients are combined: the total impact of a message is 7 percent verbal, 38 percent vocal, and 55 percent facial. The kinesicist Raymond L. Birdwhistell also offers the "educated guess" that "no more than 30 to 35 percent of the social meaning of a conversation or an interaction is carried by its words" (1970: 197). Although they may disagree on the exact proportion of meaning they attribute to verbal and to nonverbal clues, most researchers conclude that nonverbal clues are typically the more salient (Argyle, Alkema, and Gilmour, 1971; Archer and Akert, 1977). Further, we tend to give greater weight to facial expression than to either verbal content or vocal intonation in interpreting a communication in which these elements seem contradictory (Bugental, Kaswan, and Love, 1970; DePaulo et al., 1978). This explains why English-dubbed foreign films so often seem flat: The gestures and expressions of the actors do not exactly match the spoken language. Of course, in real life, much depends on the situation, the kind of behavior being

Body Language
To which man is this young woman attracted? How has she sealed off the man on the left from interaction with her? How has she positioned herself so as to form an interaction enclosure with the man on the right? What does the body language of the man on the right convey regarding his response to the young woman? How has the man on the left sealed himself off from the woman? (Don McCarthy)

judged, and the availability of multiple channels of information (O'Sullivan et al., 1985).

Body Language, Liking, and Attitude Change

Mehrabian's (1968, 1972) research suggests that we use posture to indicate liking. The more positively we feel about people, the more we tend to lean toward them, the more time we spend looking them directly in the eyes, and the closer we stand to them. Hugh McGinley, Richard LeFevre, and Pat McGinley (1975) likewise find that communicators with open body positions achieve greater attitude change in others than do communicators with closed body positions. An open body position is one in which we hold our elbows away from our bodies, extend our hands and arms outward, hold our knees apart, stretch out our legs, and cross one ankle over the other knee. A closed body position is one in which we hold our elbows next to our bodies, cross our arms, press our knees together, place our feet together, and cross our legs at the knees or ankles.

EYE CONTACT AND CIVIL INATTENTION

Eye contact between people frequently functions as a channel of nonverbal communication. Depending on how people define the situation, it may signal an aggressive or dominating intent, as in a staredown; a sense of intimacy or close bonding, as among lovers; or a fervent call for assistance, as with a prisoner of war appearing before a television camera. Experimental evidence suggests that a mutual gaze is physiologically arousing and that this arousal accounts for the powerful impact of eye contact as a channel of communication. Of course gazes come in many variations. We can glare, gawk, ogle, or leer. We alter the symbolism of a gaze by tilting our head, widening or narrowing our eyes, or lowering or raising our eyebrows. For instance, we typically perceive the lowering of brows as more assertive and domineering than we do the raising of brows (Mazur et al., 1980).

Eye contact assumes considerable importance in public settings. We employ eye contact as a means for assessing strangers and defining their intentions. Consider our behavior on a city bus, a subway, or an elevator. For the most part, we do not value these forms of public transportation for their own sakes; we think of them simply as means of moving from one place to another. We are "exit-oriented": We get on to get off (Davis and Levine, 1967). Therefore, when we are within such contexts we usually aim to protect our own rights and to maintain a proper social distance from strangers. One way to achieve these outcomes is through **civil inattention:** We give others enough visual notice to signal to them that we recognize their presence but then quickly withdraw visual contact to show that we pose no threat to them. Since being close to another signals the possibility of an interaction, we need to emit a negating signal if we are to avoid interaction. We do so by cutting off eye contact, a maneuver of civil inattention Erving Goffman (1963: 84) dubs "a dimming of the lights." Thus despite the closeness of our bodies and our mutual vulnerability, little focused interaction occurs, few of us are accosted, and few friendships arise. We project cues to ensure that these things *do not take place* (Levine, Vinson, and Wood, 1973).

A social psychology student made the following observation when he violated the expectations associated with civil inattention:

I got on the elevator with three other guys. We each promptly positioned ourselves at the four corners—one corner for each of us. In this manner we maximized the physical distance between us. We averted eye contact by facing the elevator door and keeping our eyes fixed upon the lighted floor numbers.

To see what would happen, I twisted my upper torso and with a quick head turn and eye glance looked all three guys straight in the eye (I was standing in the corner by the elevator door). In-

Civil Inattention
Usually, little focused
interaction occurs
among passengers on
a public conveyance.
(Don McCarthy)

stantaneously, the guys' eyes shot up to the elevator ceiling; the reaction was simultaneous in all three; their eyes *darted* out of eye contact.

Frankly, I felt uneasy about having undertaken my little experiment; I immediately felt that I had made a sexual overture to the guys and my own aversion to homosexuality was activated. And I was also embarrassed because I thought the guys probably saw me as a "queer." When the elevator door opened, I took off like a bat out of hell.

Should we wish to initiate a conversation with a person with whom we are unacquainted, we signal our interest through a violation of the principle of civil inattention. If we are seated on a bus or at a cafeteria table, we may attempt "to break the ice" by following an initial look (the look associated with civil inattention) with an additional mutual look. The exchange of an additional look makes conversation much more likely (Cary, 1978a).

Different social contexts provide a different permissible looking time—the amount of time that we can hold another person's gaze without being rude, aggressive, or intimate (Fast, 1978). The permissible looking time is zero on an elevator; it is a little longer in a crowded subway or *Box continues on next page.*

bus; and it is still longer out on the street. Apparently greater leeway is permitted pedestrians "to look one another over." This is most apparent on college campuses, particularly among male and female students. Nonetheless, female students commonly defer to male students when men stare at them; they lower their heads and avert their gaze from the staring male, whereas men generally maintain a more direct gaze (Cary, 1978b). The eye game is not only a man-woman thing. Homosexuals often identify one another by means of extended eye contact, followed by a backward glance after a few paces. If the other reciprocates with a backward glance, a pickup is in the offing (Fast, 1978).

Not all people feel comfortable with the eye game. One way to deal with the problem is to take oneself out of the game altogether by wearing sunglasses. This permits the person to receive other people's eye clues without in turn sending any. Hollywood stars and celebrities have long appreciated the value of sunglasses in allowing them to ignore their fans without hurting their feelings. The glasses provide a sanctuary, although seldom a disguise. Indeed, sunglasses are likely to call attention to the wearer, especially in the absence of strong sunlight (Fast, 1978).

Body Language and Courtship

Albert Scheflen, a psychiatrist turned kinesicist, suggests that body language plays a critical part in courtship behavior (1965; Davis, 1970). He says that we exhibit a readiness to court by heightened muscle tone. We hold ourselves erect; we tighten up our legs and take the slouch out of our posture. Even our faces change: the jowliness and pouches under our eyes shrink; our eyes seem to brighten; our skin tends to become either flushed or pale.

As these changes occur, the woman or man may begin to exhibit what is called "preening behavior." A woman may stroke her hair, check her make-up, rearrange her clothes, or push her hair away from her face. A man may straighten his hair, tug at his tie, readjust his clothes, or pull up his socks. These are all signals that say, "I'm interested in you. Notice me. I'm an attractive person."

Courting couples exchange long looks and flirting glances; they cock their heads and roll their pelvises. A woman will tend to put her head to one side, slightly expose one thigh, place a hand on her hip, or protrude her breasts. She may slowly stroke her own wrist or present a palm. Scheflen observes that under ordinary circumstances American women rarely reveal their palms but that during courtship they are prone to do so—even smoking or covering a cough with a palm out (Davis, 1970). (See the boxed insert on attracting a mate, p. 88.)

Body Language and Status

Status and body language are closely associated with each other (Rosa and Mazur, 1979; Mazur et al., 1980; Givens, 1983; Edinger and Patterson, 1983). When a

Preening
The smoothing of one's hair during conversation with a person one wishes to attract is a form of body language.
(Don McCarthy)

person in authority talks to a subordinate, the lower-ranking person tends to listen intently with his or her eyes riveted to the superior. To look about would indicate disrespect. But when the subordinate is speaking, it is deemed appropriate for the boss to look around or gaze at his or her watch. All the while, high-status individuals typically claim more direct space with their bodies, talk more, and attempt more interruptions than do their low-status counterparts (Leffler, Gillespie, and Conaty, 1982). And people in submissive roles tend to crouch slightly and display self-protective stances (by, say, folding their arms or hugging themselves, crossing their legs, or reaching up and touching their throats). People in dominant roles typically use more expansive gestures (for example, by spreading their arms and legs and creating an air of opening).

A high-status person can take the liberty of patting a low-status person on the back or shoulder, a behavior not permitted a person of subordinate rank (simultaneously, the subordinate will stand pigeon-toed—a sign of submission—and the boss will toe out—a sign of dominance). And the high-status person takes the lead. If the high-status person remains standing, then the subordinate is also expected to remain standing. Only when the high-status person sits can the lower-status person feel free to do so. Moreover, the high-status person can drop by a subordinate's office without notice, but the subordinate must call for an appointment.

ATTRACTING A MATE

David Givens (1983) is a research anthropologist who has been termed "the Sherlock Holmes of courtship." He has investigated nonverbal communication among men and women at parties, singles bars, cafeterias, airports, and parks. Givens compares courtship with tennis and football—one part is natural ability and the other nine parts effort. Consequently, he contends that you can improve your fortunes in love by analyzing your behavior and cultivating the appropriate interpersonal signals.

The first step, Givens says, is to dress and present yourself in ways that tell potential mates what you are and are not. Your clothes and hair style can convey either "See me" or "Skip me." The second step is to show that you are approachable. Find your Romeo or Juliet and gaze a little longer than normal when looking at him or her, or cross-gaze by looking back and forth across the person's view without making eye contact. Preferably, bring the person into your zone of radiance, some 18 to 48 inches in front of you, where your cues have the greatest impact. If you receive smiles and eye blinks—as opposed to pursed lips and cold shoulders—begin a conversation. What you say is not particularly important. The key thing is to say something, and it does not have to be cerebral, cute, or witty.

Givens finds that when people show rapport with one another, they swivel their upper bodies toward each other and align their shoulders in parallel. They face one another squarely, lean slightly toward each other, and establish eye contact. Should they disagree, they unwittingly or unconsciously turn their bodies away from each other. Accordingly, Givens says that you should cultivate rapportful messages.

Givens suggests that a man should speak slowly. He should tilt his head to one side and nod as a woman makes her points. All the while, the man should lean forward, align his shoulders with the woman's, hold his face tipped slightly down toward the floor (Robert Redford style), and gaze upward into the woman's eyes. He should gaze three seconds at a time, then drop his eyes downward for three seconds before meeting the woman's eyes again. A woman should turn her body directly toward the man and lean slightly forward. She should afford an initial three-second eye-to-eye gaze and a hair preen. Then she should gaze down and synchronize into an alternating contact-gaze, downward-gaze pattern with the man. She should stand erect, relax her shoulders, and slightly arch her back. If the conversation sputters fitfully, if he has dead eyes, or if she fails to lean forward, Givens suggests you accept the inevitable and enjoy the food. But if you manage to cross the hurdle of the conversation phase, you are ready for phase three, the first touch. But he cautions that you should not grab. And once serious kissing starts, it is too late to ask, "Can't we just be friends?"

Difficulties in Deciphering Body Language

If, indeed, the motions, wiggles, and fidgets that accompany ordinary speech define inner psychological states, then we should be able to decipher body language. And some kinesicists have attempted to do just this (Birdwhistell, 1952, 1970). Yet what may initially appear to be an easy task has in fact proved to be exceedingly difficult. The resulting formulations have been shown to be rather imprecise (Dittmann and Llewellyn, 1969; Freedman et al., 1973; Ekman and Friesen, 1974; Zuckerman et al., 1975; Zuckerman et al., 1981; O'Sullivan et al., 1985). In a lengthy series of experiments, Robert Love (1972) tried unsuccessfully to establish a consistent relationship between body language and attitudes. He finally concluded that individuals display nonverbal patterns that correlate reliably with inner attitudes only when persons consciously undertake to convey a given message with body language. All of this suggests that as a field, kinesics is still very much in its infancy.

The Facial Expression of Emotion

There is, however, one aspect of body language that has been shown to be linked with certain inner states—the facial expression of emotion. Over a century ago Charles Darwin (1872) argued that the facial behaviors associated with emotion are universal to human beings, having been established in accordance with the principles of evolutionary theory. Other scientists have also sought a biological basis for various facial expressions. They note the important signaling functions that facial behaviors play in the social life of many animals (Chevalier-Skolnikoff, 1973; Hinde, 1974). For instance, apes and Old World monkeys typically lower their eyebrows to convey dominant or threatening intentions and raise their eyebrows to display submissive or receptive intentions (Keating et al., 1981). Further, researchers have observed that congenitally blind children show many of the same basic emotional patterns in their faces as sighted individuals (Fulcher, 1942; Charlesworth and Kreutzer, 1973).

Paul Ekman (1972, 1980) has concluded that there are certain constants across cultures in the connection between specific emotions and particular facial behaviors. He and his associates showed subjects from widely different cultures photographs of the faces of individuals that in Western societies are judged to display six basic emotions: happiness, sadness, anger, surprise, disgust, and fear. Ekman found that college-educated subjects in the United States, Brazil, Argentina, Chile, and Japan ascribed the same emotions to the same faces. Moreover, with the exception of their failure to discriminate fear from surprise, the isolated and preliterate Fore of New Guinea made similar distinctions. (Among the Fore, fearful events are almost always surprising—like the sudden appearance of a hostile member of another village or the unexpected meeting of a "ghost.")

Ekman takes this evidence as demonstrating that the central nervous system of human beings is genetically prewired for the facial expression of emotion. However, he does not rule out the importance of environment. Learning determines which circumstances will elicit a given emotional expression, and cultures formulate their own "display rules" that regulate the expression of emotion. Hence, as viewed by Ekman, the face is a crucial vehicle for the subjective

Multiple Channels of Communication
All of these photos were taken at a high school. In each photograph identify as many channels as you can by which messages are being telegraphed to one or more individuals. (Patrick Reddy)

expression of experience. It is the primary agency by which an individual's inner emotional life is made visually accessible to the world.

Gender and the Communication Process

Folklore has long attributed "female intuition" to women. According to this view, women are more adept than men in nonverbal communication. An accumulating body of research is providing some evidence in support of this popular belief (Hall, 1978). On the whole, psychologists find that women are more visually attentive to other people than are men. And women are better judges than men of the meanings behind voice tones, facial expressions, and body movements—the sorts of things people cannot or will not put into words.

One explanation for women's nonverbal advantage is that women are socially oppressed and hence must give greater attention to an accurate reading of the needs and demands of more powerful others. Another speculation is that the ability is genetic or prewired because nonverbal sensitivity on a mother's part might permit her to detect distress in her children or threatening signals from adults, thus enhancing the survival chances of her offspring. Still another explanation is that women in male-dominated societies usually find themselves watching and listening and might therefore develop greater nonverbal ability through sheer practice.

Sociologists also point out the maintenance of a conversation is somewhat problematic and requires the continual, turn-by-turn efforts of the participants. However, this does not mean that there is an equal distribution of work in a conversation. For instance, Pamela Fishman (1978) finds that a woman typically carries the greater burden in keeping a conversation moving with a man. She analyzed fifty-two hours of tapes made in the apartments of three middle-class couples between the ages of twenty-five and thirty-five. The women raised nearly twice as many topics of conversation as the men because many of the women's topics failed to elicit any response. In addition to exercising their right to inject new topics, men controlled topics by veto—they would refuse to become a full-fledged conversational participant. Both men and women regarded topics introduced by women as tentative, and many of these topics were quickly dropped. In contrast, topics introduced by men were seldom rejected and often resulted in a lengthy exchange. By failing to respond to women, men required the women to continually come up with potential topics for conversation until one was finally provided that the men found acceptable.

The tapes revealed that the women would resort to attention-getting devices when faced with the men's grunts or long silences. The women asked three times as many questions as did the men. A question does conversational "work" by ensuring a minimal interaction, a response from the other party. And more often than the men, the women would preface their remarks with comments like "D'ya know what?" and "This is interesting" and, as talk lagged, used the interjection "you know" with considerable frequency. Such phrases function as go-ahead signals that the other party may speak up and that what is said will be heeded. In sum, Fishman found that the people who do the routine maintenance work, the women, are not the same individuals who either control or necessarily benefit from the conversational process. Other research confirms this finding (Roger and Schumacher, 1983).

Men also account for the vast majority of the interruptions in a conversation. In cross-sex conversations in public places, over 90 percent of the interruptions are made by men. Even in more relaxed settings, men account for 75 percent of the interruptions (Zimmerman and West, 1975). Also, women's voices tend to be more "colorful" than those of men. They vary more in pitch, and women change pitch more frequently than men do. Speaking more tunefully may be a strategy for getting and holding attention, a strategy that women employ more often than men because they tend to be ignored more. In sum, gender differences in social power affect cross-sex conversations (Pfeiffer, 1985; Kollock, Blumstein, and Schwartz, 1985).

ACQUIRING LANGUAGE

We have been considering the nature of language. Let us now turn to the topic of how we acquire language. At about one year of age, the typical child shows signs of understanding some words and employs a few sounds to signify persons or objects. By eighteen months, the child generally has a repertoire of three to fifty words; by the age of two, the child is able to form simple two- and three-word sentences. By the age of four, most children have mastered the entire complex and abstract structure of the English language. In brief, within a mere four years, preschool children routinely have realized a stunning intellectual feat.

How is this remarkable accomplishment to be explained? Two quite different answers have been supplied to the question—one by social scientists who take a learning-theory approach, another by social scientists who take a nativist approach.

Learning Theory

The learning theory of language acquisition is closely identified with the formulations of Harvard psychologist B. F. Skinner. In his book, *Verbal Behavior* (1957), Skinner draws attention to several ways in which a speech response may arise in small children. First, there are *mand* responses—*mand* being a term Skinner coined, drawing it originally from such words as com*mand* and de*mand*. The mand response may start out as simply a babbling noise—a random utterance—but that noise results in the parent's providing a stimulus that satisfies the child's need. Thus, for example, the child may emit a sound that makes the parent think the child is asking for (*manding*) water. The parent accordingly provides the child with water and alleviates a drive state—thirst. Such a sequence, when repeated on several occasions, enhances the probability that "wa-wa," "water," or something like this will be uttered by the child whenever he or she is thirsty and wants water.

Second, Skinner suggests there are *tact* responses, a term suggested by con-tact. This response arises when the child is in actual contact with an object or

Development of Language Skills
Children soon discover that they can advance their mastery of the environment and affect their fate by becoming increasingly competent in language use. Language affords a child a crucial vehicle for communication with other people. (Jim Leeke)

event. In this case, the child may be babbling in the presence of water and may randomly utter a "wa-wa" sound. The parent in turn associates "wa-wa" with water (an association not as yet made by the child) and rewards the child. When the sequence is repeated, the child learns to make this response whenever he or she comes into contact with the relevant stimulus—in this case water.

Third, Skinner identifies *echoic* responses (*from echo*). The child *imitates* the sound that parents make in relation to a given stimulus. For example, the child may repeatedly hear his or her parents refer to a clear liquid as "water" and in turn may undertake to echo the response, producing "wa-wa." He or she is then rewarded by the parents (perhaps by a smile, a hug, or attention) for having made this particular utterance.

Underlying Skinner's approach to language acquisition is his theory that learning proceeds on the basis of reinforcement. He is interested in the stimuli that elicit given responses and the rewards or punishments that in turn maintain and strengthen these behaviors. Skinner believes that children learn grammatical constructions in much the same manner that they learn words. They learn specific sentence frames into which they substitute words by means of generalization. Hence a child may have learned the sentence "I want a cookie" through reinforcement. The child finds that he or she can substitute words to produce other sentences, for example, "I want milk," "I want the doll," and so on. In this manner, extensions of conditioning principles are employed to describe the ways in which phrases and sentences are acquired (Catania, 1979; Salzinger, 1979; Julia, 1983).

Learning theorists focus their attention on the ways mothers and fathers facilitate their children's acquisition of language. **Caretaker speech** is a good illustration of this. Caretaker speech differs from everyday speech in its simplified vocabulary; higher pitch; exaggerated intonation; short, simple sentences; and high proportion of questions and imperatives. As noted earlier in the chapter, speech with the first two characteristics is termed baby talk. When youngsters begin uttering meaningful, identifiable words (around twelve to fourteen months of age), their parents invariably speak **motherese**—a simplified, redundant, and highly grammatical form of language. Many of the features of motherese result from the process of trying to carry on a conversation with immature conversational partners (Snow, 1977). Mothers and fathers typically restrict their utterances to the present tense, to concrete nouns, and to comments on what the child is doing or experiencing (for example, statements as to what objects are called, what color they are, and where they are located).

Nativist Theory

Nativist theorists, closely identified with Noam Chomsky, a linguist at the Massachusetts Institute of Technology, vigorously dispute Skinner's learning-theory formulations. They argue that if a person had a vocabulary that was limited to one thousand words, was restricted to sentences of fifteen words or less, had limited choices among words, and could learn a new sentence every second, waking or sleeping, it nonetheless would take that person more than thirty years to learn all the possible sentences. Language consists not simply of words but also of sentences, and there is no limit to the number of sentences that can be formed. Thus Chomsky says that the essentially trial-and-error process depicted by learning theorists cannot account for a child's mastery of his or her language by age four or five. Even adults would be overwhelmed by the enormousness of what young children must learn in order to speak and communicate (Miller and Chomsky, 1963). Consider how formidable a foreign language such as Chinese or Russian appears to you. Indeed, the words we utter in speaking are more like one giant word than neat packages of words (because typically we do not pause between words but run them together). Yet most children acquire language with little difficulty.

Chomsky says that the key to language acquisition is not the learning of particular words or word arrangements but an inborn *language-generating mechanism*. He terms this mechanism the **language acquisition device (lad)**. This device provides nonverbal, intuitive rules—called by Chomsky *productive rules* or *transformational grammar*—which enable speakers to generate the infinite variety of sentences that they produce and to understand the infinite variety of sentences that they hear.

It is Chomsky's (1968, 1975) position that language is genetically programmed into the human brain—that human beings are "prewired" with neuronal circuits

Language Usage: Learned or Biologically Programmed?
Learning theorists argue that language is learned in the same fashion as is any other behavior. In contrast, nativist theorists contend that the human infant is biologically preadapted for the basic structure of language and merely has to learn the peculiarities of a particular language. (Patrick Reddy)

that predispose them to language. In support of this view, he cites data on what he refers to as *linguistic universals*. While the world's languages differ in their surface characteristics (*surface structure*), they have basic underlying similarities in their composition (*deep structure*). For example, all languages recognize a difference between vowels and consonants; all use syllables; all employ nouns, verbs, and objects; and all permit the user to ask questions, give commands, deny statements, and so on. These basic rules—the universal deep-structure characteristics of human languages—need not be learned; rather, in Chomsky's view, they constitute a sort of inborn prefabricated filing system to structure the words and phrases that make up human languages. All that is required is that the child reach an appropriate stage in maturation; his or her readiness or capacity to speak is then "released" by appropriate stimulation from other people who speak (Lenneberg, 1969). In sum, children's prewired language capabilities enable them to master any of the world's languages; they learn the particular language of their culture, however, by taking the verbal production of speakers in their environment as "data." Hence Chomsky does *not* claim that children are genetically endowed with specific languages (English, Japanese, or Arabic). Rather, he says that children possess an inborn capacity for generating grammar (the foundations of grammar being fundamentally similar among the world's languages).

A Resolution of Divergent Theories

What are we to make of these divergent theories regarding the acquisition of language? One way to approach the matter is to identify a basic difference between the theories advanced by Skinner and Chomsky. For his part, Skinner is *not* particularly concerned with what goes on inside the organism. For this reason, his theory is at times referred to as a "black box" approach: Stimuli basically enter the box at one end only to come out the other end as responses. Skinner does not believe that what goes on within the box is the fundamental concern of the psychologist; he is not interested in the mental processes that intervene between the stimulus and the response. According to Skinner, the task of psychology is to describe, predict, and control *observable* behavior. Chomsky, in contrast, concerns himself primarily with the black box. He is concerned with the genetic programming within the black box that is responsible for the underlying rules making for the *deep structure* of language.

The problem with both approaches is that each tends to neglect the very phenomena that interest the other. Both innate and learned aspects, however, play a part in the acquisition of language, so each approach provides only part of the picture.

Thus Skinner's learning-theory approach leaves much unexplained. Many common utterances of young children are hardly imitations of parental speech—for instance, "more high," "more wet," "no down," "all gone lettuce," "no drop mittens," and "not fix" (Braine, 1963). And children of deaf parents coo, fuss, and babble as much as other children, even though parents with normal hearing are much more likely to come to (and thus reinforce the speaking of) their child when he or she fusses. Hence the earliest development of human sound appears to be relatively independent of the amount, nature, or timing of the sounds made by parents. Furthermore, although deaf parents make sounds different from those heard in the community at large, language in their nondeaf children invariably begins to develop at the usual time and goes through the same phases as in other children (Lenneberg, 1969).

The research of psychologist and neurologist Eric H. Lenneberg reveals that a child's language milestones are closely associated with his or her motor milestones (see Table 3.1). Presumably this does not reflect any immediate, causal relation. Rather, Lenneberg suggests, language development, like motor development, is closely related to physical growth and development. Lenneberg insists that these developmental stages hold regardless of culture, a phenomenon he explains in these terms:

> Maturation may be characterized as a sequence of states. At each state, the growing organism is capable of accepting some specific input; this it breaks down and resynthesizes in such a way that it makes itself develop into a new state. This new state makes the organism sensitive to new and different types of input, whose acceptance transforms it to yet a further state, which opens the way to still different input, and so on. (Lenneberg, 1969: 641)

Thus Lenneberg portrays language acquisition as involving a continual interchange between the organism and its environment; indeed, the organism literally changes itself as it responds.

TABLE 3.1
Correlation of Motor and Language Development

AGE IN YEARS	MOTOR MILESTONES	LANGUAGE MILESTONES
0.5	Child sits using hands for support; engages in unilateral reaching	The child's cooing sounds change to babbling by introduction of sound containing consonants
1.0	Child stands; walks when held by one hand	Syllabic reduplication; the child displays signs of understanding some words; applies some sounds regularly to signify persons or objects (the child's first words)
1.5	Prehension and release fully developed; child's gait propulsive; creeps downstairs backward	The child has a repertoire of three to fifty words that are not joined in phrases; displays trains of sounds and intonation patterns resembling discourse; demonstrates good progress in understanding
2.0	Child runs (with falls); walks stairs with one foot forward only	The child has a repertoire of fifty words; two-word phrases are the most common; the child shows more interest in verbal communication; evidences no more babbling
2.5	Child jumps with both feet; stands on one foot for one second; can build a tower of six cubes	The child acquires new words every day; the child seems to understand virtually everything said to him or her, but still reveals many grammatical deviations
3.0	Child tiptoes 2.7 meters (8.9 feet); walks stairs with alternating feet; jumps 0.9 meter (3 feet)	The child possesses a vocabulary of some 1,000 words, about 80 percent of which are intelligible; the grammar of utterances reveals close approximation to colloquial adult speech; syntactic mistakes are fewer
4.5	Child jumps over rope; hops on one foot; walks on line	Language is well established; the child's grammatical anomalies are restricted to unusual constructions

SOURCE: Adapted from E. H. Lenneberg, "On Explaining Language," *Science*, Vol. 164 (1969), p. 636.

To say that a biological predisposition for the development of language is anchored in the operating characteristics of the human brain is not to deny the part that environmental factors play in language acquisition. Studies of children in orphanages or in socially deprived households reveal that significant differences exist between the language development of these children and that of children reared in normal middle-class homes with stimulus-rich environments. And as Roger W. Brown (1958: 193) has pointedly noted: "Man does not develop language if he grows up among animals or in isolation. Language is acquired by the human being born into a linguistic community."

Language acquisition, then, cannot be understood by examining genetic programming or learning factors in isolation from each other. Rather, complex *interactions* take place between biochemical processes, maturational factors, learning strategies, and the social environment (Blount, 1975; Nelson, 1977). A dynamic interplay occurs between all of these factors; no factor by itself can produce a language-using human being. Instead of asking which factor is the most important, we need to inquire as to the ongoing process by which the factors dynamically come together.

LANGUAGE AND THINKING

In everyday life, we employ the word "thinking" in a variety of contexts (Carroll, 1964: 75): "I am just thinking"; "What do you think about her?"; "I wish I had thought of that possibility myself"; "I think they'll come soon"; "I just couldn't think of his name"; "I was thinking about my childhood"; "I think she is mentally retarded"; "Think this through carefully." Common to these expressions is the notion that thinking is an unobservable process that takes place within our minds: we "reason," "conceive," "believe," "remember," "expect," "evaluate," "consider," "analyze," and "reflect." As employed by social psychologists, **thinking** generally refers to a process of mental manipulation of images, symbols, and ideas. Such mental activity allows us to "make something" out of our perceptions. We employ information from our environment and our memories to make decisions about what to say and do.

Language and Thought

A substantial portion of our thought is linguistic in nature. This idea finds expression in the term "inner speech"; in our daily lives we literally talk to ourselves. But to talk to ourselves implies language, a system of symbolic sound patterns. When you say to yourself, "I am going to school this morning," you encode a variety of objects and experiences: "I"—the material you; "am going to"—a process of moving the material you from one place to another; "school"—a place where given standardized activities transpire; "this morning"—a segment of time.

By classifying experiences into symbolic concepts (words), we can unscramble stimuli in a meaningful fashion. We link stimuli together and relate current sensations to past sets of perceptual organization and experience, as in the illustration above. Central to the thinking process is the ability to deal with things in other times and places; we are not limited to immediately present, here-and-now stimuli.

The important part language plays in the thinking process is vividly portrayed by Helen Keller in the excerpt from her autobiography provided earlier in the chapter. In this and her other writings, Helen Keller describes how the acquisition of words brought about an intellectual and emotional revolution in her life. Through language she became aware of herself and other people. At one point she writes (1938: 117): "When I found the meaning of 'I' and 'me' and found that I was something, I began to think. . . . Then, consciousness first existed for me." The memories she had of her first seven years were vague, and she was reluctant to apply the term "ideas" or "thoughts" to the products of her mental processes. Language enabled her to encode her experiences and to focus her

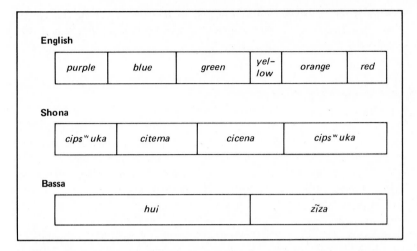

FIGURE 3.2 The Mappings of the Color Spectrum in Three Languages

Bassa makes a single major color cut: *hui* is for the blue-green end of the spectrum and *zīza* is for the red-orange end. Shona, in contrast, groups together the reds and purples (the two ends labeled *cips^w uka*) and recognizes two other groups that are approximately the blues and the greens-plus-yellows.

(SOURCE: Roger Brown, *Social Psychology* [New York: Free Press, 1965], p. 316.)

attention on the coded features. In so doing, she could manipulate images, symbols, and ideas—in brief, she could think.

Although much of our thinking takes place in language, it is possible to think without language. Some musicians claim that they "hear" the music they are composing before writing it down on paper or even before playing it on an instrument. Similarly, we can visualize a maneuver with an automobile, a series of tennis strokes, or a dance step—and these visualizations constitute mental activities that qualify as a nonlinguistic kind of thinking (Carroll, 1964: 76). And we represent spatial information diagrammatically or in maps. All of this suggests that knowledge has more than one form of representation and that some thought involves symbols different from those of language.

The Linguistic Relativity Thesis

The Arabs have some 6,000 different names for camels. The Hanunoo, a people of the Philippine Islands, have a name for each of ninety-two varieties of rice. And, as reflected in Figure 3.2, the color spectrum is mapped quite differently in English, Bassa (a Liberian language), and Shona (a Zimbabwean language). Does this mean that if we speak different languages we experience different social realities? Or put another way, does the language we speak control the manner in which we perceive and understand the world? Edward Sapir (1949) and his student Benjamin L. Whorf (1956) respond to these questions affirmatively. In what has become known as the **linguistic relativity thesis** (or the Whorfian hypothesis), Sapir and Whorf argue that thought is relative to the language in which it is conducted—that is, we organize the world and react to it in particular ways because of the linguistic system in our minds.

Sapir puts the matter in these terms:

> The "real world" is to a large extent unconsciously built up on the language habits of the group. No two languages are ever sufficiently similar to be considered as representing the same social reality. The worlds in which different societies live are distinct worlds, not merely the same worlds with different labels attached. (Sapir, 1949: 162)

Hence, according to Sapir, Whorf, and other proponents of the linguistic relativity thesis, we adopt the view of the world that is fashioned and portrayed by our language. Since our languages differ, our world views differ (see Figure 3.3). Proponents of this thesis argue that we selectively screen sensory data in terms of the way we are programmed by our language, so speakers of different languages will inhabit different sensory worlds. We admit some things while filtering out others; thus experience as it is perceived through one set of linguistically patterned sensory screens is quite different from experience perceived through another set (Hall, 1966).

Supporters of the Whorfian hypothesis cite the Navajo language, a language that stresses sharply defined categories, as a case in point (Kluckhohn and Leighton, 1946). It focuses on the minute distinctions that characterize activity. The Navajo emphasize verbs, as opposed to nouns or adjectives, and favor the concrete and particular, as opposed to abstractions. The word "rain" provides us with an illustration. White Anglo-Americans report their perception of the event in a variety of ways: "It has started to rain"; "It is raining"; "It has stopped raining." The Navajo, while able to convey the same ideas, do so by providing finer discriminations:

> To give only a few instances of the sorts of discrimination the Navaho must make before he reports his experiences: he uses one verb form if he himself is aware of the actual inception of the rain storm, another if he has reason to believe that the rain has been falling for some time in his locality before the occurrence struck his attention. One form must be employed if rain is general round about within the range of vision; another if, though it is raining about, the storm is plainly on the move. Similarly, the Navaho must invariably distinguish between the ceasing of rainfall (generally) and the stopping of rain in a particular vicinity because the rain clouds have been driven off by the wind. (Kluckhohn and Leighton, 1946: 194)

Proponents of the Whorfian hypothesis insist that these differences between the grammars of Navajo and English crystallize and perpetuate divergences in *manner of thinking* between the two peoples.

Few, if any, social psychologists challenge the Whorfian premise that the symbols (words) employed linguistically by a people reflect their chief cultural

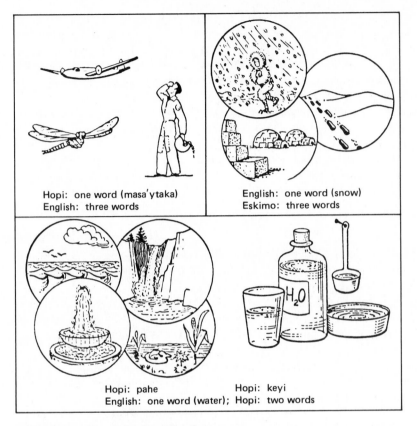

FIGURE 3.3 The Whorfian Thesis
Benjamin L. Whorf advances the hypothesis that the picture we have
of the universe shifts from tongue to tongue, that languages "slice
up" experiences differently. The Hopi Indians, for instance, have one
noun that covers every being or thing that flies (with the exception of
birds). The Hopi refer to an insect, an airplane, and an aviator by the
same word and find no difficulty in doing so. To American English
speakers, such a category seems too large and inclusive, as would
the American English category "snow" to an Eskimo. American English speakers employ the same word for falling-snow, snow-on-the-
ground, snow-packed-hard-like-ice, slushy-snow, and wind-driven-
flying-snow, quite different things in the world with which the Eskimos must contend. Likewise, Hopi speakers distinguish between
water placed in a container and water in other settings.
(SOURCE: Benjamin Lee Whorf, *Language, Thought, and Reality* [Cambridge,
Mass.: M.I.T. Press, 1956], p. 210.)

concerns—rice, snow, rain, or whatever. What is the subject of controversy,
however, is whether or not perceptual capabilities are altered by the acquisition
of language. Critics of the Whorfian hypothesis argue that a person, regardless
of his or her language community, can distinguish among the varieties of rice

that receive special labels in the Philippine Hanunoo community, even if the person cannot give the Hanunoo names. The same holds for the varieties of snow recognized by Eskimos or the fine points about rain itemized by Navajos.

For the most part, social psychologists take the view that "languages differ not so much as to what *can* be said in them, but rather as to what is *relatively easy to say in them*" (Hockett, 1954: 122). This more modest version of the thesis has come to be known as the *weak* Whorfian position (although Whorf himself never espoused it). For instance, it is easier to refer to "small brown grains of rice with dark brown spots" with one word, as among the Hanunoo, than with the array of words required in English.

The Language as a Container of Thought Thesis

According to the linguistic relativity thesis, language is the determinant of thought: language shapes thought by providing socially acquired concepts or categories into which people mentally sort their perceptual stimuli. The contrary view says that thought provides the concepts or categories that *then* find expression in language. Language is said to be merely the container of already established thought. Thus according to this latter position, thought takes place independently of language; language functions simply as a mode for conveying thought.

Research by psychologists Marc H. Bornstein, William Kessen, and Sally Weiskopf (1976; Bornstein and Marks, 1982) helps to clarify the view of those who hold that language is a container of thought. This work has shown that four-month-old infants partition the color spectrum into four basic hues: blue, green, yellow, and red. Thus *before* formal cultural training and *before* acquiring language, infants evidence a high degree of organization of the color world. This research suggests that the human organism distinguishes between the four hues and that such categorization *precedes* language; hence, language is said to be simply the container of preexisting thought.

The study made use of the phenomenon of *habituation*—if we repeatedly present the same stimulus to a baby, the baby will soon stop responding to it. When the infant no longer responds to a stimulus, a slightly different stimulus can be introduced. If the baby responds, it demonstrates that the child can distinguish the latter stimulus from the preceding one.

Bornstein and his associates employed a variety of hues (colors) in their study. The range of light wavelengths that are visible to humans extends from 400 to 700 millimicrons (the color spectrum). The blues and violets correspond to short wavelengths (near 400 millimicrons) and reds to long wavelengths (near 700 millimicrons).

The researchers discovered that the babies responded to differences in wavelengths as though they perceived *categories* of hue—blue, green, yellow, and red. For instance, the infants responded differently to two wavelengths selected from adjacent hue categories, such as "blue" at 480 millimicrons and "green" at 510 millimicrons. Hence, when the babies habituated to blue, they were then shown green, and they again became interested in the stimulus presentation. However, the babies did *not* respond differently to two wavelengths separated by the same physical distance (30 millimicrons) when selected from the "blue" category at 450 and 480 millimicrons. (They remained bored with the stimulus presentations.)

From this evidence Bornstein and his associates conclude that infants encounter the visual world with certain biases. Infants' mental representations are organized into color categories rather than exact wavelength codes (Bornstein, 1976). This is of considerable interest because color constitutes a *continuous* physical dimension; hues *grade* into one another on the color spectrum (for instance, "red" is not a sharply delimited entity but rather a zone to which we impute "thinghood"). The fact that babies "break up" the color spectrum suggests to Bornstein that babies are naturally endowed with the ability to discriminate color information in terms of preverbal categories:

> Anatomy and physiology give to the color spectrum a strong perceptual structure. Cultures may still arbitrarily overlay their own organization onto this built-in structure, but there are undoubtedly limitations to the roles of culture, experience, and learning in basic categorization. (Bornstein and Marks, 1982: 73)

Other researchers also find that a child's first words are names for preexisting cognitive categories (Lenneberg, 1967; Nelson, 1972; Zachry, 1978).

The linguistic relativity and the language-as-a-container-of-thought positions stand in sharp contrast. The one argues that speech shapes thought; the other that thought shapes speech. Yet many social psychologists believe that the two views are not mutually exclusive—that language and thought *interact* in such a manner that each reciprocally influences and shapes the other. The problem in some respects parallels the learning and nativist controversy surrounding the acquisition of language. The one position (speech shapes thought) emphasizes the role of learning factors; the other (thought shapes speech), the role of prewired hereditary factors. As with the language acquisition controversy, the issue is not so much a question of which ingredient is more important or prior to the other but a question of how language and thought interact to afford a given outcome. What we think affects what we say, and what we learn through verbal communication affects our thought.

SUMMARY

1. Communication is central to social behavior. Where communication is ineffective—where a mutual understanding is not realized—joint action is blocked. Communication is the primary means by which we link ourselves together within the larger human enterprise. As a result we live our lives largely within a symbolic environment.

2. Communication allows us to establish commonness with one another. A sender and a receiver become tuned together for a given message. This requires that one party encode a message by taking an idea and putting it in the form of a signal which can then be transmitted to the other party. Once coded and sent in signal form, the message becomes independent of the sender. The act of communication is completed when the other party

(the destination) receives the signal and appropriately decodes it.

3. We live in a world of symbols. A symbol is a sign that conveys meaning by virtue of some socially shared convention, some understanding between users. Symbols are arbitrary stand-ins for actual things. They take a good many forms. Spoken and written words are familiar examples. We also communicate with objects. Gestures serve communicative purposes too.

4. Language operates at two major levels: (1) it enables us to carry on communication with others—to transmit to other people information, ideas, attitudes, and emotions (*inter*individual communication); and (2) it facilitates thinking (*intra*individual communication). Language aids us in partitioning the world into manageable units and domains of relevance.

5. Meaning is the expression of all the information we have in our memory that is tied or bonded to the symbolic representation of something. Words have both a denotative and connotative meaning. Charles Osgood has developed a form of measurement—which he terms the semantic differential—for identifying the connotative meanings of words. He finds that connotative meanings primarily flow along three dimensions: an evaluative dimension, a potency dimension, and an activity dimension.

6. Paralanguage has to do with how something is said, not with what is said. Tone of voice, pacing of speech, silent pauses, and extralinguistic sounds constitute paralanguage.

7. Body language involves the motions of our bodies, limbs, faces, and eyes, through which we communicate information about our feelings, attitudes, and intentions. The formulations provided by kinesicists have proved to be imprecise. However, there is one aspect of body language that has been shown to be linked with inner states—the facial expression of emotion.

8. Women are more adept than men nonverbally, perhaps because of their disadvantaged position in society. Social power affects both the verbal and nonverbal aspects of conversation.

9. There is considerable controversy about the process of language acquisition. Learning theorists and nativist theorists each advance a different explanation of the process: learning theorists emphasize environmental factors, whereas nativist theorists stress genetic factors.

10. Language acquisition involves a continual interchange between the organism and its environment; the organism literally changes itself as it responds.

11. A substantial portion of our thought is linguistic in nature. By classifying experiences into symbolic concepts (words), we can unscramble stimuli in a meaningful fashion. We link stimuli together and relate current sensations to past sets of perceptual organization and experience. Central to the thinking process is the ability to deal with things in other times and places.

12. According to the linguistic relativity thesis, language is the determinant of thought: Language shapes thought by providing socially acquired concepts or categories into which people mentally sort their perceptual stimuli. The contrary view says that thought provides the concepts or categories which then find expression in language. Language is said to be merely the container of already established thought. Thus according to the latter position, thought

takes place independently of language; language functions simply as a mode for conveying thought.

13. The linguistic relativity and the language-as-a-container-of-thought positions stand in sharp contrast. The one argues that speech shapes thought; the other that thought shapes speech. Yet many social psychologists believe that the two views are not mutually exclusive—that language and thought interact in such a manner that each reciprocally influences and shapes the other. What we think affects what we say, and what we learn through verbal communication affects our thought.

GLOSSARY

Body language □   The nonverbal communication of meaning through physical movements and gestures.

Caretaker speech □   A systematically modified version of the language used with adults, with which parents address infants and young children. Caretaker speech differs from everyday speech in its simplified vocabulary; higher pitch; exaggerated intonation; short, simple sentences; and high proportion of questions and imperatives.

Civil inattention □   Giving others enough visual notice to signal to them that we recognize their presence, but then quickly withdrawing visual contact to show that we pose no threat to them.

Communication □   The process by which people transmit information, ideas, attitudes, and emotions to one another.

Connotative meaning □   The emotional and evaluative associations of a word.

Denotative meaning □   That part of the definition of a word that "points out" an object or event—that gives certain specific properties or patterns of the object or event.

Kinesics □   See **body language**.

Language □   A socially structured system of sound patterns with standardized meanings.

Language acquisition device (lad) □   According to Noam Chomsky, an inborn language-generating mechanism that all human beings possess. Chomsky believes that the human organism is genetically prewired for language usage.

Linguistic relativity thesis □   The theory that we adopt the view of the world that is fashioned and portrayed by our language; and since our languages differ, our world views differ.

Meaning □   The relatedness of something to all other events or objects with which is associated in the experience of an individual or group.

Motherese □   A simplified, redundant, and highly grammatical form of language employed by parents in communicating with young children.

Paralanguage □   The nonsemantic aspects of speech—the stress, pitch, and volume of speech by which we communicate expressive meaning.

Semantic differential □   A form of measurement developed by Charles Osgood for assessing the connotative meanings of words.

Symbol □   Any object or event that has come to stand for something else.

Thinking □   A process of mental manipulation of images, symbols, and ideas.

4 SOCIALIZATION AND DEVELOPMENT

PRECONDITIONS FOR
    SOCIALIZATION
  Genetic Endowment
  An Appropriate Environment
LEARNING PROCESSES
  Conditioning
  Observational Learning
  Cognitive Development
  Internalization

SOCIALIZATION ACROSS THE
    LIFE SPAN
  Role Transitions and
    Socialization
  The Life Stages of Men and
    Women

Once more let us consider the case of Helen Keller. As we noted in the previous chapter, deafness and blindness locked Helen Keller during her first seven years within a highly private world. Special training permitted her to compensate for her handicap and to gather and interpret information from the surrounding world through her remaining senses. Nonetheless, she was still excluded from the public world until language allowed her to become "tuned" together with others for the sending and receiving of messages. Communication linked her within the symbolic environment in which human beings live their lives. Yet to become fully human—a functioning social being—it was also necessary for Helen Keller to acquire the lifeways of her society. In brief, she had to undergo socialization.

Socialization is a broad concept that encompasses the entire process by which we develop, through interaction with other people, the ways of thinking, feeling, and acting that are essential for effective participation within society. It is the process by which a mere biological organism becomes transformed into a social being. We are not born human; we possess only the potential for becoming human. Compared with other organisms, we are remarkably "open" or "unfinished" beings. Thus our humanness is bestowed and sustained through social interaction. Socialization is a process that continues through life: An initiate is socialized within the League of Women Voters; a new patient within a hospital ward; a bride and groom within marriage; a senior citizen within a Golden Age Village; an upwardly mobile person within a new social class; a religious convert within a new religion; an accounting student within his or her profession; and a new employee within a corporation (see boxed insert, pp. 108–109).

PRECONDITIONS FOR SOCIALIZATION

Man is so educable an animal that it is difficult to distinguish between that part of his character which has been acquired through education and circumstance, and that which was in the original grain of his constitution.

—Francis Galton, *Inquiry into Human Faculty,* 1883

Socialization makes two fundamental contributions to human life. First, it provides the foundation for effective participation in society. As infants, we enter a society that is already an ongoing concern. Indeed not only are the society and its culture in operation when the infant arrives, but they continue in operation after the individual's death. Hence the human organism needs to be fitted and to fit itself into a social environment—to take on the ways of its society's people and to fashion a competence for controlling and shaping its own fate.

Second, socialization makes society possible. In the absence of socialization, society could not perpetuate itself beyond a single generation, and culture would be nonexistent. Through socialization, vast numbers of organisms—human beings—are able to fit their actions to the developing actions of others through shared definitions of the situation. Common understandings of life's activities provide a map telling us in broad terms what we can expect of others and what they can expect of us. These cultural guidelines—ready-made definitions of the situation—are what is transmitted through socialization.

In sum, the individual and society are twin-born. They are mutually dependent "on this unique process of psychic amalgamation whereby the sentiments and ideas of the culture are somehow joined to the capacities and needs of the organism" (Davis, 1949: 195). However, human socialization presupposes the existence of an appropriate genetic endowment and an appropriate environment. There is an old notion that each of us enters the world with a clean slate (*tabula rasa*) upon which parents and others inscribe the rules of social life. While the imagery is dramatic, it is nonetheless inaccurate. None of us is born with a clean slate. We have a double inheritance, one genetic and the other social (Rose, 1979). In the absence of either, humanness would not arise.

SOCIALIZING NEW EMPLOYEES WITHIN THE COMPANY CULTURE

Richard Pascale (1984), a private consultant and a lecturer at the Stanford Business School, has examined the ways in which well-managed firms like IBM, Procter & Gamble, and Morgan Guaranty Trust socialize new employees into their corporate cultures. He has identified seven steps. First, the company subjects prospective employees to a rigorous selection process. By grilling job applicants and telling them the bad side as well as the good, a firm prods the applicants to remove themselves from consideration if they do not feel they can "fit." For instance, Morgan Guaranty, a New York investment banking house, encourages applicants to discuss the demands of the job with their spouses, girlfriends, or boyfriends because new recruits sometimes work 100 hours a week.

Second, the company subjects new recruits to experiences that are calculated to shake them up and render them amenable to corporate values, beliefs, and behaviors. In some respects the procedures resemble military boot camps (Goffman, 1961a). Employees are expected to assume the hair styles, clothing fashions, and standardized articles that establish an organizational identity. At times employees must also perform self-effacing tasks. For instance, Procter & Gamble requires recent college graduates to color in a map of sales territories. (The message is, "You may have accomplished a good deal, but you are still in kindergarten as far as this organization is concerned.") And newcomers are given more work than they can possibly do. These practices leave individuals psychologically and emotionally receptive to the

Genetic Endowment

Just as he is overshadowed by us, so the chimpanzee overshadows all other animals. He has the ability to solve quite complex problems, he can use and make tools for a variety of purposes, his social structure and methods of communication with his fellows are elaborate, and he shows the beginnings of Self-awareness.

—Jane van Lawick-Goodall, *In the Shadow of Man*

The notion of talking animals strikes a responsive chord in most of us. As with the fictional account of Dr. Doolittle, who talked with the animals, social psychologists and the lay public alike have been fascinated with studies of "talking" apes. Over a half century ago, Luella Kellogg and Winthrop Kellogg (1933) raised an infant chimpanzee named Gua along with their son Donald. So far as possible, the Kelloggs treated the two infants in an identical manner. Both Gua and Donald

roles and identities demanded of them by the corporation.

Third, companies send the newly humbled recruits into the trenches, requiring them to master one of the areas that constitutes the core of the firm's business. Individuals are provided a field (for instance, finance) and given considerable, carefully monitored experience. Fourth, at each stage along the way, employees are evaluated. They are measured by their operating results and rewarded accordingly. For example, Procter & Gamble appraises managers on the basis of three factors crucial to a brand's success: building sales volume, building profit, and introducing planned change. At IBM, employees who violate a corporation norm—for instance, by handling subordinates too harshly—find themselves assigned to what is called "the penalty box" (usually, a fairly meaningless job at the same level but at a less desirable location). The penalty box lets employees know that they have erred but that they will be given another chance in the future.

Fifth, right from the beginning, the company seeks to instil its overarching value system. For instance, prior to its breakup, AT&T stressed an incredibly strong service ethic dedicated to guaranteeing phone service to customers through an emergency. Identification with this value allowed AT&T to demand of its employees a good many personal sacrifices. Sixth, the company fosters a folklore that affirms its entrenched values. Thus for over 100 years, AT&T cultivated a folklore captured by the photo of a nineteenth-century Bell System lineman fighting to keep the telephone lines open during a blizzard (Langley, 1984). Seventh, the company supplies its employees with role models— peers and superiors who are recognized as winners and who share the firm's exemplary traits. Protégés watch the role model write memos, make presentations, and handle problems, and then try to duplicate the characteristics and behavior. By socializing employees in these ways, a firm achieves order, continuity, and consistency.

learned to respond correctly to all sorts of vocal commands—indeed, at first, Gua responded more correctly to human commands than Donald did. When the Kelloggs would say, "Show me a bow-wow," Gua would point to a picture of a dog. But as Donald came to acquire language and employ speech, Gua was soon outdistanced. Despite patient teaching by the Kelloggs, the chimp never acquired a single human word.

In the 1940s, another husband-and-wife team, Cathy Hayes and Keith Hayes (1951), managed to teach a chimp named Viki to make sounds approximating the words "mama," "papa," and "cup." In her three years with the Hayeses, Viki learned to dust furniture; wash dishes; sharpen pencils; saw, hammer, and sandpaper furniture; and paste photographs into an album. In many respects the chimp functioned like a language-deficient child.

During the past three decades, a number of psychologists have picked up where the Kelloggs and the Hayeses left off and have taught more than twenty chimpanzees how to use various kinds of symbols. Reasoning that earlier attempts to teach chimps to talk had failed because of their inadequate vocal equipment, Allen Gardner and Beatrice Gardner (1971) hit upon a way to circumvent the chimpanzee's lack of a pharynx (the space above the voice box that changes shape to produce various sounds); they taught a chimp, Washoe, American Sign Language—the sign language of the deaf. Among Washoe's earliest words were "come-gimme," "more," "up," "sweet," "go," "hear-listen," "tickle," "toothbrush," "hurry," "out," and "funny." Later Washoe began to combine words into sentencelike strings such as "come-gimme sweet" and "out please." By the time the chimp was four, she could understand and express in sign language 160 words. Later, working with another psychologist, Rober Fouts, Washoe displayed the ability to fashion new terms. She invented the phrase "dirty monkey" for an annoying monkey, having previously used the word "dirty" to refer only to feces or soiled objects. In time the word "dirty" came to be a kind of swear word for Washoe. And she is said to have designated a watermelon as a "drink fruit" and a swan as a "water bird."

At Stanford University and later at private quarters, the developmental psychologist Penny Patterson trained a young gorilla, Koko, to use correctly over 500 words by the same sign language approach. Like Washoe, Koko is said to put together words she has learned so as to devise appropriate names for new objects: "finger bracelet" for a ring, "white tiger" for a zebra, and "eye hat" for a mask. Patterson (1985) says that the signs employed by Koko are quite similar to those that deaf children create. Koko "talks" to herself, to people, and to other animals. In 1983, Koko requested a cat by pulling two fingers across her cheeks to indicate whiskers (Zimmerman, 1985). She was given a pet cat, which she named All Ball. She would carry All Ball about, dress him in linen napkins, and play chase games with him. When All Ball would bite her, she would "say" he was "obnoxious." One night the cat wandered off and was killed by a car. Ten minutes after Patterson broke the news to the ape, Koko began weeping with the tearless, hooting cry of the lowland gorilla. Several days later Koko was asked if she wanted to talk about the cat. Koko signed "cry" by running her finger from each eye down her cheeks. Asked if she understood what had happened to All Ball, she signed, "Sleep cat."

Two other psychologists, Ann Premack and David Premack (1971), upon learning of the Gardners' success, initiated a program with a young chimpanzee, Sarah. They constructed a number of distinctly shaped and colored pieces of plastic, each signifying an English word. "Banana," for example, was represented by a pink plastic square, "give" by a green bow tie, "pail" by a red zigzag-like lightning bolt. Sarah has learned over 130 such words and can construct simple sentences such as "Ann give apple Sarah." She can also read and obey sentences like "Sarah insert apricot red dish," selecting the correct fruit and dish from among several possibilities.

While the Premacks were teaching Sarah, Duane M. Rumbaugh and his associates at the Yerkes Primate Research Center in Atlanta were working with Lana, another chimpanzee. Lana has been taught to converse with people through a computer language, called Yerkish in honor of the center's founder, Robert M. Yerkes. Lana communicates by means of a computerized keyboard—a console with 75 buttons, each bearing a distinctive geometric symbol (made up of tri-

Lana at Her Computer Console
If Lana attempts to command the operation of any of the automated food-dispensing devices in her room, the computer will accept and relay only messages that are correct Yerkish. For instance, if Lana pushes the word buttons in the following sequence, "Please, machine, give milk," an automated dispenser with a straw will fill with milk. If instead Lana says, "Please, machine, make milk," the computer rejects the sentence. (Duane M. Rumbaugh)

angles, circles, squares, or lines) that stands for a word. With time, Lana graduated from passive learning to inquiring about things that she wished to know—pressing buttons to ask "? what name-of this" (in the computerized language, the question mark precedes the question). The Yerkes researchers have also trained two chimps (Sherman and Austin) to communicate with one another from separate rooms via the consoles. For instance, each tells the other the location of food that the experimenter has hidden from him (Savage-Rumbaugh, 1979; Savage-Rumbaugh, Smith, and Lawson, 1980). However, the star performer has been Kanzi, a four-year-old pygmy chimpanzee (a rare ape species that is believed to be the one closest to human beings in genetic make-up). As an infant, Kanzi had played in the laboratory while researchers were teaching word symbols to his mother. To the amazement of researchers, Kanzi spontaneously began using several of the symbols at about age two, apparently having mastered them by observing. He identifies objects by name, comments on his actions, describes actions he desires to carry out, and responds correctly to the symbols used by others. Kanzi also understands some complex sentences that are spoken in

English. For example, if he is asked, "Will you get a diaper for your sister Mulika?" he will fetch one and take it to her (Eckholm, 1985a, 1985b).

In the course of this research with apes, psychologists have claimed to have taught chimps to combine words to describe new situations, to understand "if-then" concepts, to describe moods, to tell lies, to select and use words in syntactical order, to indicate desire, and to anticipate future events. However, Herbert S. Terrace (1979) has questioned many of these conclusions. He spent four years teaching sign language to a chimp named Nim Chimpsky. The chimp managed to learn some 125 words and picked up new words at the rate of about two per week. But Terrace asserts that the success of his own and related efforts can be explained as mere prompting on the part of the experimenters and as mistakes they have made in reporting their data. He claims that much of the apes' behavior is simply a product of drill and not much more remarkable than what a dog does in learning to sit or heel. And Terrace disputes the view that apes are themselves capable of stringing words together to form meaningful sentences, the essence of language. He suggests that the apes, rather than mastering American Sign Language, have merely learned a number of vocabulary items that they arrange in ways that approximate English word order. But the apes, he asserts, are themselves incapable of using grammar to generate sentences—to manipulate the sound code so as to compose a large number of novel but integrated and meaningful word combinations. To these charges, some psychologists reply that the critical matter is that the chimps nonetheless *do* succeed in communicating with one another and with human beings. And they say that it is conceited to claim that human beings are far removed from other animals—a view resembling the pre-Copernican certainty that Earth lies at the center of the universe.

Thomas Sebeok and Donna Jean Umiker-Sebeok (1980) of Indiana University also argue that the chimps in the American Sign Language studies only appear to be employing language. The animals may have learned nothing more than an association between some action or object and a particular gesture. They claim that human beings who observe the chimps' actions typically impute to them human meanings, a form of anthropomorphism in which human traits are ascribed to animals, plants, and natural events. As such, the Sebeoks assert, chimp language is simply an extreme case of the Clever Hans phenomenon.

Clever Hans was a German circus horse who at the turn of the twentieth century confounded scientists by his ability to solve mathematical problems put to him. In response to a problem, the horse would stomp his hoof the correct number of times. Later, carefully monitored experiments established that Clever Hans was not adept at mathematics but at reading human body language. From the unintentional cues of people about him—their stance, their hands, their facial expression, the size of their eye pupils, and their breathing patterns—Clever Hans determined when he was to stop tapping. In like manner, the critics of chimp studies say that the trainers are cuing the chimps rather than conversing with them.

Admittedly, these matters are at present quite confused. Indeed, about the time Terrace was downgrading the accomplishments of the chimps, University of Oklahoma researchers reported that Washoe had taught her seventeen-month-old adopted son, Louis, ten signs that he uses almost daily (including "hug," "drink," "food," "fruit," "come," "give me," "hot," and "that"). Perhaps the safest conclusion we can make at the present time is that, despite the notable achievements of various apes, nobody is yet likely to mistake the capabilities of any ape for those of a normal three-year-old child (Limber, 1977). Apes learn to deal with signs sluggishly and often only after being plied with bananas, cola, and M&Ms. In contrast, for human children learning is its own reward. They pick up words spontaneously (Gould, 1983). Indeed, deaf children individually develop on their own a languagelike system of signs that resembles spoken language (Goldin-Meadows and Feldman, 1977). Research shows that deaf children—like normal children—have a strong bias to communicate in languagelike ways (Goldin-Meadows and Mylander, 1983). All this suggests that there is a continuum of communicative ability ranging through various levels of sophistication. Although the skills exhibited by the chimps are clearly related to human skills, they are not equivalent to human skills. Chimps lack the level of communicative competence that characterizes the typical human being, and hence, when compared with human beings, they are inhibited and impeded in the development of thought processes. Clearly, for human socialization to occur, an appropriate genetic endowment is required.

An Appropriate Environment

> *Men are like plants; the goodness and flavour of the fruit proceeds from the peculiar soil and exposition in which they grow.*
>
> —Michel Guillaume Jean De Crèvecoeur, *Letters from an American Farmer,* 1782

Socialization also presupposes an appropriate environment. This fact is starkly illustrated by cases involving extremely isolated and deprived children. The sociologist Kingsley Davis (1949) has reported on two such cases. Both children had been born out of wedlock, and their mothers, because they were ashamed, had kept them secluded over a period of years. The children were given only enough attention to keep them alive. When discovered, each at about age six, they were extremely retarded, showing few if any human capabilities or responses.

In one case, that of Anna, the child could not talk, walk, or do anything that showed intelligence. In addition to being in an extremely emaciated and undernourished condition, she was completely apathetic, remaining immobile, expressionless, and indifferent to everything.

Anna was placed first in a county home and later in a school for retarded children, where she died of hemorrhagic jaundice at ten years of age. By the time of her death, she had learned to talk in phrases, walk, wash her hands, brush her teeth, dress herself (except for fastening her clothes), follow simple instructions, play with a doll, and engage in other human activities. Because of her early death, it is impossible to know how fully Anna might have developed. Further, Davis inferred from her development that she was somewhat deficient, or retarded, from the outset.

In the other case, that of Isabelle, the child's mother was a deaf mute. The two had spent most of their time together in a darkened room. Although at first medical specialists believed Isabelle to be both deaf and retarded, she was given prolonged and systematic training by experts at a Midwestern university. Within a week she made her first attempt at vocalization. As months passed, she went rapidly through each of the stages of social and cultural learning said to be typical of American children. By age fourteen, she had finished sixth grade and was rated by her teachers as a competent and well-adjusted student. Isabelle is reported to have completed high school, to have married, and to have had her own normal family.

Davis concludes his report on the two cases by observing,

> Isolation up to the age of six, with failure to acquire any form of speech and hence missing the whole world of cultural meaning, does not preclude the subsequent acquisition of these. . . . Most of the human behavior we regard as somehow given in the species does not occur apart from training and example by others. Most of the mental traits we think of as constituting the human mind are not present unless put there by communicative contact with others. (1949: 207–208)

More recently, Susan Curtiss (1977) has stirred renewed interest in deprivation cases with her report on Genie. In 1970, California authorities discovered Genie when her fifty-year-old mother ran away from her seventy-year-old husband after a violent quarrel and took the child with her. Genie was thirteen years old and had been isolated in a small room, rarely having contact with anyone. The social worker in the welfare office where Genie's mother applied for public assistance immediately took note of Genie's condition. She notified her supervisor, who called the police. Genie was hospitalized, and her parents were charged with willful abuse. However, on the day he was to appear in court, Genie's father committed suicide.

When Genie was admitted to the hospital, she was a malformed, incontinent, unsocialized, and malnourished youngster. On various maturity and attainment tests she scored as normal one-year-old children score. Psychologists, linguists, and neurologists at nearby UCLA designed a program to rehabilitate and educate Genie. In time, she began to use two phrases that she employed in a ritualized way as though they were single words: "stopit" and "nomore." Somewhat later she began to string two words together on her own, such as "big teeth," "little marble," and "two hand." However, unlike normal children, Genie never acquired the ability to ask questions, and her understanding of grammar remains limited. Four years after she began stringing words together, her speech remained slow and resembled a garbled telegram.

Psychologists and linguists are uncertain why Genie has failed to learn the kind of grammatical principles that underlie human language (Pines, 1981). Genetic factors do not appear to underlie her deficiencies. Nor can her difficulties be attributed to the absence of competent teachers. Since her discovery and until she reached the age of twenty, Genie enjoyed an enriched environment and the services of accomplished speech therapists. In 1978, Genie's mother was awarded legal guardianship of her daughter and filed suit against UCLA research-

O*perant conditioning*

A couple of days ago my four-year-old sister complained of a stomach ache, so I bought some Tums and gave her a few. Yesterday the same thing happened, and again I gave her some Tums. I guess she thought they tasted pretty good, because today she is faking another stomach ache. This is a good illustration of operant conditioning. The frequency of her behavior was changed according to the event that followed it. The candy reward served to reinforce the "stomach ache" behavior.

ers for subjecting Genie to "unreasonable and outrageous" testing, not for treatment, but to exploit Genie for personal and economic benefits. The damage suit brought to a halt research on Genie's development. One hypothesis that psychologists have advanced to account for Genie's language deficiencies is that there are critical periods in the development of language capabilities and that these periods cannot be successfully passed through once children enter puberty.

In sum, studies with chimpanzees and the cases of isolated and deprived children add up to this: *Both* an appropriate genetic endowment and an environment that provides learning possibilities are essential for producing a human personality. Human beings are not passive objects simply acted upon by internal genetic forces or external environmental forces (Rossi, 1984). Genetic and environmental factors interact and interpenetrate. As a result, the human organism modifies itself by responding. Learning is a good illustration of this principle, a matter to which we now turn our attention.

LEARNING PROCESSES

Learning is basic to the human condition. It enables the human organism to adapt itself to its environment. Accordingly, learning is not restricted to what takes place in formal education, but is an ongoing, lifetime process. By **learning** we mean a more or less permanent modification in an organism's behavior or capability that results from its experience in the environment. Learning occurs in three principal ways: (1) conditioning, (2) imitating the behavior of another, and (3) changing the cognitive structure by which we think about our environment. Let us consider each of these processes in turn.

Conditioning

As pointed out in Chapter 1, behavioral theory is concerned with the behavior of people—what they actually do and say. It describes the process whereby individuals, as a result of their experience, establish an association or linkage between two events. For instance, you very likely have formed an association between a hot stove and a painful, burning sensation; between attending class

Operant conditioning

One of my roommates has a problem of oversleeping his alarm in the morning. Some months ago he was using an ordinary Big Ben of the hand-wind variety. The alarm would go off in the morning but he would fail to wake up. So he bought an electric digital clock with a high piercing alarm sound. All went well for the first three or four days, and my roommate would wake up when his alarm went off. Then his old problem returned and, despite the piercing alarm sound, he would continue to sleep. The poor guy was extremely perturbed as he is a premed student and he was missing his morning classes. My roommate and I decided to see what we could do to help the guy. We secretly devised a plan based on operant conditioning procedures (in this case, an aversive stimulus). When the alarm clock went off in the morning, we promptly threw a glass of cold water in my sleeping roommate's face (no problem since his alarm invariably woke us up). We did this for three mornings. Then we stopped our practice. This was seven months ago. In the interval my roommate has experienced no more difficulty waking up at the sound of his alarm.

Behaviors of the Operant Variety
Among the behaviors teachers wish to establish among students is the practice of raising their hands and waiting to be called on before speaking aloud. This type of behavior is learned through operant conditioning. (Patrick Reddy)

Reciprocal Reinforcement
Much of human interaction is characterized by reciprocal reinforcement. Here the mother and infant are each reinforcing the other. The infant's behavior is reinforced by food and her mother's attention. The mother's behavior is reinforced by her child's smiles and coos. (Patrick Reddy)

and passing a course; and between showing up late and upsetting your friends. The process by which this association or linkage occurs is termed **conditioning**.

Conditioning has been the focus of much psychological research, particularly in the 1950s and 1960s. No psychologist is more closely identified with the behaviorist approach than B. F. Skinner. Indeed, it is hardly surprising that in a survey conducted in 1967 among heads of college psychology departments, Skinner was selected as the most influential American psychologist of this century. Much of Skinner's scientific reputation derives from his studies of **operant conditioning**—a type of learning in which behavior is altered in its strength by its consequences.

Operant conditioning is illustrated by Skinner's experiments with pigeons. Skinner places a hungry pigeon in an experimental chamber. He teaches the pigeon to make a full circle in about two to three minutes in the following way. The hungry bird struts about the chamber under Skinner's watchful eye. When

LEARNED HELPLESSNESS

Learning allows organisms to build on past experiences in coping with present experiences. In this manner, they attune themselves to the realities that they encounter in the world about them. But not all learning experiences promote effective adjustment. Over the past fifteen years, the psychologist Martin E. P. Seligman and his associates (Seligman, 1975; Garber and Seligman, 1980) have undertaken research which reveals that some organisms, when exposed to uncontrollable events, acquire a learned helplessness. **Learned helplessness** entails a generalized expectancy that events are independent of what one does. It is the notion that one's own actions and consequent events are not causally related. Once acquired, this attitude interferes with an organism's subsequent coping with later events that are controllable.

Seligman stumbled on learned helplessness while conducting experiments with dogs. In order to test facets of learning theory, Seligman would strap the animals in a harness and give them electric shocks. The dogs were then placed in a two-compartment shuttlebox, where they were supposed to learn that they could escape the shocks by jumping across the barrier separating the compartments. It is little wonder that animal lovers have vehemently upbraided Seligman for cruelty to dogs.

Seligman found that dogs who had not previously been exposed to shock quickly learned to jump the barrier. But it was otherwise with the dogs who had been exposed to shock under inescapable conditions. Rather than attempting to escape from the shocks, these latter dogs would at first run about the compartment and howl. But then they would settle down, passively whine, and simply submit to the shocks. Seligman concluded that the dogs

the pigeon makes a slight clockwise turn, Skinner instantly rewards it with a food pellet. Again the pigeon struts about, and when it makes another clockwise turn, Skinner repeats the procedure. When the bird has mastered making a full circle, Skinner reinforces the bird only when it moves in the opposite direction. Then he waits until it makes a clockwise circle followed by a counterclockwise circle. In about fifteen minutes, Skinner has conditioned the bird to do a perfect figure eight. Additionally, Skinner has taught pigeons to dance with one another and play Ping-Pong.

In these experiments, a pigeon's behavior is modified by its consequences. The pigeon turns in a particular direction and is rewarded with food. The food functions as a reinforcer. A **reinforcer** is any stimulus (environmental influence) that follows a response and increases the probability of its occurrence (Skinner, 1953). Skinner contends that much of life is structured by arranging reinforcing consequences, or payoffs. Businesses reward appropriate work behavior by giving employees salary increases. A man dating a woman whom he likes tries to ensure that she will go out with him again by showing her a good time. And a doctor must make certain that a patient feels benefited by an office visit in order to

had learned from their experiences in the harness that they could not affect events in their environment.

Various educational psychologists find remarkable parallels between the happenings with Seligman's dogs and the academic experiences of some schoolchildren (Dweck, 1975; Diener and Dweck, 1978; Weisz, 1981). These children give up when they encounter failure in achievement situations. They conclude that their academic outcomes are uncontrollable. Carol I. Diener and Carol S. Dweck (1978) have found an appreciable difference between "helpless" and "mastery-oriented" children in their approach toward failure. Helpless children tend to ruminate about the cause of their lack of success, viewing it as the product of uncontrollable factors. Consequently, they spend little time searching for new approaches for overcoming failure. In contrast, mastery-oriented students worry less about explaining their past errors and focus more on ways to overcome and surmount their difficul-

ties. In sum, helpless children develop defeatist attitudes. They come to underestimate the number of successes in their experiences and to overestimate the number of failures. And whereas mastery-oriented children expect their successes to continue, helpless children continue to anticipate the worst—failure (Diener and Dweck, 1980).

Dweck (1975) has experimentally undertaken to train helpless children to attribute their failures to a lack of effort rather than to a lack of ability. When the children learned to make attributions that stressed motivation rather than ability as the determinants of failure, they showed considerable improvement in their coping responses to failure. But another group of helpless children whom she provided merely with success experiences (such as those guaranteed by programmed instruction) continued to evidence despair and hopelessness when confronted with failure situations.

[handwritten margin notes: learned Helplessness / Chg attribution actions Ø just give success experienced.]

induce the patient to return for additional treatment. But reinforcement may also result in maladaptive behavior, including learned helplessness (see boxed insert).

Many of the principles of conditioning have found use in **behavior modification.** The approach applies the results of conditioning theory and experimental psychology to the problem of altering maladaptive behavior. The technique has been applied in classrooms in the form of "token economies." A token—a poker chip, a check mark, a star, a stamp, or a numerical rating—is used in a manner similar to money. The teacher specifies the behaviors that will be rewarded (reinforced), makes the receipt of a token contingent on behavior, and allows the exchange of the token for some desired object or activity. Most educators recommend that token reinforcement programs be used to "prime the pump," allowing natural reinforcers to take over after the desired behaviors are well established. Since tokens function as extrinsic rewards, the danger always exists that students will become "hooked" on mechanisms of extrinsic motivation, decreasing their intrinsic motivation.

*L*earning through modeling

I am quite upset as I write this. Over the past year I have been baby-sitting with Debbie, my neighbor's four-year-old daughter. The mother is about twenty years old, unmarried, lives alone except for Debbie, and clearly has more than she can handle emotionally or financially. When I have taken care of Debbie, it has disturbed me how violent she is with her dolls. I have seen her reprimand her "baby" by grabbing the doll by the arms or legs, swing the "baby" about, and pound the "baby's" head against the floor or a table. As she does it, she exclaims, "Bad baby, bad baby." Well, today while I was at school, a neighbor discovered that the mother is a child abuser and has been beating Debbie. The local authorities are now investigating the case. Debbie has been "learning" her mother's behavior toward children—I never realized that she was imitating what she herself had been experiencing. I now can see how patterns of child abuse can be transmitted from one generation to the next through socialization and child-rearing practices.

Observational Learning

Much human behavior is socially transmitted, either deliberately or inadvertently, through the examples provided by people whom we observe. Indeed, if we depended solely on direct experience for learning—exclusively on the rewarding and punishing consequences of behavior—most of us would not survive our formative years. Learning to cross a busy street in traffic is one of many behaviors best learned by following someone's example. We can avoid tedious, costly (even fatal), and haphazard trial-and-error experimentation by imitating the behavior of socially competent models. By observing others, we learn novel responses without necessarily having had the opportunity to make the responses ourselves (Bandura, 1969, 1973a, 1977).

Social psychologists refer to this process as **observational learning.** At times the terms *imitation, identification,* and *modeling* are used interchangeably with observational learning. All of these terms refer to the tendency for individuals to reproduce the actions, attitudes, or emotional responses displayed by real-life or symbolized models (Bandura and Walters, 1963). Theorists like Albert Bandura (1977) and Walter Mischel (1971, 1973), who stress the part that observational learning plays in human adaptation, are referred to as *social learning theorists*.

Bandura (1977), a psychologist whose research has contributed much to our understanding of these matters, suggests that modeling can influence the observer in three different ways. First, as we have noted, persons can acquire new patterns of behavior through observing others. Models need not, however, be

Modeling
Much human behavior is socially transmitted; this child has undoubtedly watched mothers giving babies their bottles. (Patrick Reddy)

presented in real-life forms. Symbolic or pictorial presentations—through magazines, books, movies, and television—function as highly influential model sources. Bandura and his associates find that children are as likely to imitate aggressive behavior if they witness it in a movie or an animated cartoon as they are if they witness it in a real-life situation (Bandura, Ross, and Ross, 1963). On the basis of his research, Bandura warns that even when aggressors are punished, they often teach children new forms of aggressive behavior. The children may later reenact the aggressive actions when the situation suits them.

A second major influence of modeling is that it may either strengthen or weaken previously learned inhibitions of behavior. Inhibitory effects result when the observer sees that the model experiences punishing consequences for some behavior. For example, teachers frequently punish one child in the presence of classmates and achieve a "spillover" effect—the other children are deterred by what they witness. Inhibition tends to become weaker when the model is rewarded for the behavior (disinhibition). For instance, students who witness other pupils successfully violating school rules are themselves more likely to follow suit.

And third, the actions of others may serve as social promptings (spurs or instigators) that facilitate or stimulate similar behavior in observers. This finds expression in *vicarious conditioning*—conditioning realized through imaginative participation in the experience of another. In one experiment, Bandura and an associate had subjects watch another person—supposedly another subject, but in reality a stooge—"display" a variety of pain responses to an "intense shock" following each sounding of a buzzer. Later the subjects displayed physiological evidence of emotional discomfort when the buzzer was sounded, despite the absence of the model and the fact that the subjects themselves never directly experienced the "shock" (Bandura and Rosenthal, 1966).

Social learning theorists emphasize that our capacity to employ symbols is critical to our ability to comprehend and deal with our environment (Bandura, 1977; Rosenthal and Zimmerman, 1978). Verbal and imagined symbols permit us to represent events, analyze our conscious experience, communicate with others, plan, create, imagine, and engage in foresightful action. Symbols are the foundation of reflective thought and enable us to solve problems without first having to enact all the various solutions. In fact, social learning theorists insist that stimuli and reinforcements exert little influence on our behavior unless we first represent them mentally and interpret them in a meaningful fashion (see Chapter 3).

Cognitive Development

> *Man's mind stretched to a new idea never goes back to its original dimensions.*
>
> —Oliver Wendell Holmes

Thus far in our consideration of various mechanisms of learning, we have examined processes that occur in essentially the same fashion over the life cycle of an individual—conditioning and observational learning. The changes that take place are gradual and continuous, without any abrupt transformations in form, so that learning builds upon itself. However, some students of child psychology argue that development does not occur in simply an additive or cumulative manner, one in which new bits of information are continually being acquired. Rather, they seek to identify various *stages* of development through which normal children pass. They say that each stage is marked by discontinuities or abrupt changes from the previous one. Viewed from this perspective, the kind of learning that takes place in a stage differs from that of the preceding stage. This is because the predominant mode for handling information—the cognitive or thinking structure—changes from one stage to the next. According to psychologists like Jean Piaget (1896–1980), who emphasize **cognitive stages in development,** all normal individuals pass through the same sequential periods in the growth or maturing of their ability to think (to gain knowledge and awareness of themselves and their environment).

For Piaget, the critical question in the study of development is how the child *adjusts* to the world in which he or she lives. His technique for observing, recording, and understanding the way a child thinks is to imagine himself inside the child's mind and to try to see the world as if through the child's eyes.

Piaget says that the thought of infants and children is not a miniature version of adult thought. It is qualitatively unique (different in kind). Thus when children comment that the sun follows them about when they go for a walk, that dreams come through the window, and that the name of the moon is the moon, they are not "illogical"; instead, children are operating from a different mental framework or set of rules for interpreting the world. Piaget terms such a mental framework or set of rules a scheme. A **scheme** is a cognitive structure that an individual evolves for dealing with a specific kind of situation in the environment.

Piaget conceives of the individual and the environment as engaged in an ongoing *interaction* that generates new perceptions of the world and new organizations of knowledge. A new experience interacts with the existing cognitive structure (scheme) and alters the structure, thereby making it more adequate. This modified structure in turn influences the individual's subsequent perceptions. These new perceptions are then incorporated within a more complex cognitive structure or scheme. In this manner, experience modifies scheme and scheme modifies experience (Cross, 1976).

As Piaget views this adjustive process, it consists of two basic processes: assimilation and accommodation. **Assimilation** is the process of taking in new information and interpreting it in such a fashion that the information conforms to an *existing* scheme. Piaget conceives of the process as one in which children typically stretch a scheme (a vision or model of the world) as far as possible to fit new observations. At times, however, the child encounters information that does not fit its current scheme of the world. The child must then refashion or reorganize the scheme so as to better fit the real world. In effect, children are required to invent increasingly better schemes to depict the world as they grow up. **Accommodation** is the process of changing a scheme to make it a better match to the world of reality. In accommodation, preceding structures become a part of later structures. Consequently, each stage in cognitive development witnesses the emergence of new organizational components, and each stage is in turn the starting point of the next stage.

A good illustration is provided by Piaget's research dealing with the conceptions that children develop regarding dreams. In response to questioning, one four-year-old said that she dreamed about a giant and explained, "Yes, I was scared, my tummy was shaking and I cried and told my mommy about the giant." Asked, "Was it a real giant or was it just pretend? Did the giant just seem to be there, or was it really there?" she answered, "It was really there but it left when I woke up. I saw its footprint on the floor" (Kohlberg and Gilligan, 1971: 1057).

In Piaget's view, this child's notions should not be dismissed as merely the product of a wild imagination. From a four-year-old's perspective, dreams are real. As she grows older, she will have new experiences that will lead her to question her scheme regarding dreams. For instance, she may discover that a "footprint" is not in fact on the floor. This observation will cause her to change her scheme regarding dreams so as to derive a better match with reality. She then will conclude that dreams are not real but rather fictional events. Additional experiences will result in new revisions of her conceptions. She will recognize that her dreams are not seen by others and still later that dreams are internal happenings. Finally, at about six to eight years of age, she will become aware that dreams are mental events that lack material existence.

As portrayed by Piaget, development proceeds from simplicity to complexity, from the pure egocentrism of the infant to the group perspective of the adult. In so doing, Piaget distinguishes four stages in the development of cognition or intelligence:

Sensorimotor Stage

birth – 18 mos. ①

The sensorimotor stage, from birth to the age of eighteen months, lays the basis for thought development. The child learns to identify critical features and some of the essential properties of the world he or she sees. Piaget terms the period "sensorimotor" because the primary developmental tasks confronting the child are concerned with the coordination of motor activities with sensory inputs.

In this stage of development children grasp the principle of *object permanence.* Piaget observed that when a child of four or five months is playing with a toy and the toy rolls out of sight behind another toy (although remaining within reach), the child does not look for the toy. The infant does not recognize that objects have an independent existence. This explains the delight infants take in playing peek-a-boo. When a mother removes her face from the child's view and then returns it, the child is surprised and pleased. If the child believed the object existed when it was not seen, the child would not be surprised and pleased at its reemergence and there would not be any point in the game. At about the age of eight months, the child grasps the fact of object constancy and will search for toys that disappear from view (Elkind, 1968). Thus in this stage, the child becomes able to differentiate between objects and experiences and to generalize about them—all of which lays the groundwork for later intellectual and emotional growth.

Stage of Preoperational Thought

18 mos – 7 yr. ②

The period called the stage of preoperational thought, from the age of eighteen months to the age of seven years, is characterized by the initiation of *symbolic* activity, particularly language. Initially children identify words and symbols with the objects they are intended to represent. Thus a child will become upset when someone steps on, say, a stone that it has designated as a frog.

But of even greater significance, symbols allow children to receive, transmit, and otherwise manipulate information about the world around them (Flavell, 1977). They gain the ability to absorb information conveyed to them by others. Conversely, they also become able to transmit information to others and in turn to receive corrective feedback from others as to the adequacy of their knowledge and skills. And they develop the ability to communicate internally with themselves—to symbolize, store, and think about their daily experiences.

Stage of Concrete Operations

7–11 yr. ③

The overriding characteristic of thinking throughout the stage of concrete operations, the period from seven to eleven years of age, is its increasing abstractness. Children come to master various logical operations, including arithmetic, class and set relationships, measurement, and conceptions of hierarchical structures. Probably the most investigated aspect of this stage has been the growing

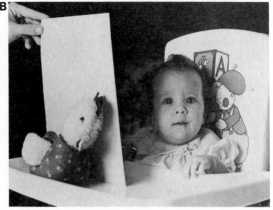

Evolution of the Child's Concept of Object Permanence

Jean Piaget found that the child of four months does not recognize that objects have an independent existence. If an object is removed from the child's vision but remains within the child's reach, the four-month-old will not pursue the object (photos *A* and *B*). Around eight months, however, the child will retrieve it. At about this age, the child grasps the principle that an object continues to exist even though it is out of sight: object permanence (photos *C*, *D*, and *E*). (Patrick Reddy)

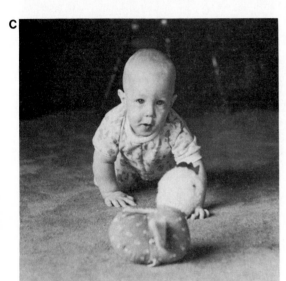

A   B   C

A Conservation Experiment
(*A*) Place two balls containing the same amount of clay in front of a four-year-old child and ask if the balls are the same size. Invariably the child responds affirmatively. (*B*) As the child watches, roll one of the balls into a long, sausagelike shape and again ask if the clay objects are the same size. (*C*) The child will now say that one of the clay objects is larger than the other. In the experiment depicted in the photographs above, the child indicated that the sausage-shaped clay is larger than the clay ball. Not until the child is several years older will he come to recognize that the two different shapes contain the same amount of clay (the principle of the conservation of quantity). (Patrick Reddy)

ability of children to "conserve" mass, weight, number, length, area, and volume. The preoperational child, for instance, cannot understand that when lemonade is poured from a full glass into a wider glass which the lemonade fills only halfway, the amount of lemonade remains unchanged. The child "centers" on only one aspect of reality at a time; he or she sees that the glass is half empty and concludes that there is less lemonade than previously. In the stage of concrete operations, the child comes to understand that the amount of lemonade remains the same. In so doing the child grasps the **principle of conservation**—the notion that the quantity of something stays the same despite changes in shape or position.

The Stage of Formal Operations
In the previous stage, the child's thought remained somewhat fixed on the concrete properties of objects and events in its environment. In the stage of formal operations, from eleven years on, the child becomes capable of dealing with even greater abstractness and can engage in hypothetical reasoning based on logic. Whereas a younger child confronted with the problem "If coal is white, snow is———" will insist that coal is black, the adolescent will respond that

snow is black. The adolescent has gained freedom from physical "givens" and can deal with hypothetical possibilities. In this phase, then, the child acquires the capacity for adult thought.

Some critics have faulted Piaget for linking his stages with particular age ranges. Piaget maintains, however, that the specific ages as such are not vital; it is the order of the stages that is important. Further, critics charge that Piaget gives insufficient attention to various cultural, social, and experiential factors in the development of thought. Development psychologists like Jerome Kagan (1971) and John H. Flavell (1978, 1982) argue that Piaget's portrayal of development as a series of stages provides an unrealistically rigid perspective. They say that human cognitive growth is too varied in developmental mechanisms, routes, and rates to be accurately depicted by an inflexible stage theory.

Researchers also find that Piaget underestimates the thinking capabilities of younger children (Brainerd, 1978, 1979). For instance, by altering the way a task is presented to youngsters, it is often possible to elicit from them concrete operational thought and, occasionally, even formal operational thought. Likewise, a child's culture makes a good deal of difference. Both striking similarities and marked differences are found in the performance of children from differing cultures on various cognitive tasks (Ashton, 1975; Dasen, 1977). But even if some particulars of Piaget's explanations are wrong, he has provided us with a new vision of children as active beings who fashion and shape their mental capabilities in the course of interacting with their environment.

Internalization

To make your children capable of honesty is the beginning of education.

—John Ruskin, *Time and Tide,* 1867

For young children, conformity to the expectations of others is largely a product of external controls. Standards for behavior—judgments of right and wrong, evaluations of good and bad, and assessments of desirable and undesirable—are foreign to the infant. Such standards may be part of his or her society's culture, but as yet the child does not know them. The birth of each generation subjects society to a recurrent "barbarian invasion." Accordingly, the members of society have a considerable stake in fashioning the child into "one of our kind" as expeditiously as possible. Hence they generally take great pains to shape the child within the "proper" cultural mold. Only in this manner can the child be transformed from a social liability into a social asset.

As the child grows older, an increasing proportion of behavior becomes independent of *external* control; to a considerable extent, he or she gradually comes to be governed by *internal* monitors. These internal monitors carry on many of the functions previously performed by the external controls (Aronfreed, 1969). In brief, **internalization** occurs—the process whereby an individual incorporates within his or her personality the standards of behavior prevalent

Learning appropriate moral values

When I was in kindergarten I made the mistake of being "too honest." My parents had stressed to me during my early years the importance of always telling the truth and not lying. On one occasion, which I still vividly remember, my parents were visiting with a neighbor lady who must have weighed at least 300 pounds. I commented that she was a fat lady. I had not intended to insult the woman. I was merely making an observation, and an honest observation at that. My parents were very upset and scolded me. I had to apologize to the lady. All of this highlights the fact that morality is not a simple matter. Much depends on the situation. Children must learn when it is and is not appropriate to tell the truth. Many times in life we are expected to tell "white lies."

within the larger society. Social control (external control) becomes *self*-control.

In most cases, internal control, or self-control, is simply a product of conditioning and modeling. Of special interest, however, is the emergence of what has been termed **conscience**—the internal operation of ethical or moral principles that control or inhibit the actions and thoughts of an individual. Violations of such principles commonly produce feelings of shame and guilt. Various studies show that children reared in Western societies become increasingly capable of rendering moral judgments consistent with prevailing social codes as they advance in age (Boehm, 1962; Kohlberg, 1963; Piaget, 1948). But their increasing internalization of moral standards (the acquisition of conscience) is *not* paralleled by an increase in behavior that conforms to societal rules (Blasi, 1980; Sears, Rau, and Alpert, 1965). This absence of congruence is not surprising. As we shall see in Chapter 6, a one-to-one relationship does not generally exist between states of mind and overt action; considerable discrepancy can occur between the two.

There is a difference of opinion among social psychologists as to how conscience formation proceeds. Social learning theorists like Bandura and Mischel say that children acquire moral standards in the same manner that they learn any other behavior. They have shown the effects that a model has on an observer's subsequent behavior (Bandura, 1965, 1977). Further, social learning theorists see behavior as variable and dependent on situational contexts. Thus depending on the circumstances, a person may steal an item or cheat on an examination in one situation and be scrupulously honest in another. This is hardly surprising, since most actions lead to positive consequences in some situations and not in others. Consequently, individuals develop highly discriminating and specific response patterns that do not generalize across all life situations (Mischel and Mischel, 1976).

Social learning theorists conceive of moral development as a cumulative process that builds upon itself gradually and continuously. In sharp contrast to this perspective, cognitive-developmental theorists like Piaget and Lawrence Kohlberg, a Harvard psychologist, say that moral development takes place in stages. A child's moral thinking is said to be shaped by the mode of thought—the stage of cognitive development—that currently characterizes the child. As a consequence, a child's morality in one stage of cognitive development differs appreciably from that of earlier and later stages.

Kohlberg (1969a,b, 1973, 1976, 1980, 1981) has expanded upon Piaget's stage approach. He claims that children pass through a sequence of six culturally universal and invariant stages in moral development. This requires that children move step by step through each of the stages, so that reaching any stage necessitates passing through the preceding series of stages. Moreover, each successive stage is considered to be morally superior to the preceding stages.

Kohlberg has gathered these data by asking subjects questions about hypothetical moral dilemmas. One of these stories has become famous as posing a particularly difficult dilemma:

> In Europe, a woman was near death from a special kind of cancer. There was one drug that the doctors thought might save her. It was a form of radium that a druggist in the same town had recently discovered. The drug was expensive to make, but the druggist was charging ten times what the drug cost him to make. He paid $200 for the radium and charged $2,000 for a small dose of the drug. The sick woman's husband, Heinz, went to everyone he knew to borrow money, but he could only get together about $1,000, which is half of what it cost. He told the druggist that his wife was dying, and asked him to sell it cheaper or let him pay later. But the druggist said, "No, I discovered the drug and I'm going to make money from it." Heinz got desperate and broke into the man's store to steal the drug for his wife. Should the husband have done that? (Kohlberg, 1963: 18–19)

On the basis of children's and adults' responses to dilemmas of this sort, Kohlberg has arrived at six stages in the development of moral judgment. He groups these stages into three major levels: the *preconventional level* (stages 1 and 2); the *conventional level* (stages 3 and 4); and the *postconventional level* (stages 5 and 6). Table 4.1 summarizes these levels and stages and provides the typical type of responses that subjects provide to the story of Heinz. Study the table carefully for a thorough understanding of Kohlberg's approach. Note that the stages are not based on whether the moral decision about Heinz is pro or con. Rather, Kohlberg is concerned with the style of reasoning the subject employs in reaching a decision.

Each of Kohlberg's levels reflects a different type of relationship between an individual and the society's rules. The preconventional level characterizes young children, some adolescents, and many criminals. At this level, the societal rules are external to the individual. At the conventional level, typical of most adolescents and adults, the individual has *internalized* the rules of the wider society. The postconventional level is estimated to be attained by less than 25 percent of all Americans. At this level, individuals *differentiate* between themselves and the rules of others, and define values for themselves in terms of rationally considered, self-chosen principles. Although differences exist among individuals, both in the order and in the rate they attain given levels, evidence seems to suggest that in Western nations the course of moral development does indeed

TABLE 4.1
Kohlberg's Stages in a Child's Moral Development

LEVEL ONE	PREMORAL	REACTIONS TO EXAMPLES OF THEFT OF DRUG
Stage 1	*Obedience and punishment orientation.* The child obeys rules to avoid punishment; "conscience" is the irrational fear of punishment.	Pro: Theft is justified because the drug did not cost much to produce. Con: Theft is condemned because the thief would get caught and go to jail.
Stage 2	*Naive hedonistic and instrumental orientation.* The child's action is motivated by a desire for reward or benefit. The rightness of the conduct is judged in terms of the extent to which a given action satisfies oneself.	Pro: Theft is justified because she needs the drug and he needs his wife's companionship. Con: Theft is condemned because his wife will probably die before he gets out of jail so it will not do him much good.
LEVEL TWO	MORALITY OF CONVENTIONAL ROLE CONFORMITY	
Stage 3	*"Good boy" morality.* The child is oriented toward seeking approval of others; consideration is given to needs and intentions of others.	Pro: Theft is justified because he is unselfish in looking after the needs of his wife. Con: Theft is condemned since he will feel bad thinking of how he brought dishonor on his family; his family will be ashamed of his act.
Stage 4	*Law and authority maintain morality.* The child is oriented toward "doing one's duty," respect for authority, and maintaining the social order.	Pro: Theft is justified because he would be responsible for his wife's death. Con: Theft is condemned because he is a lawbreaker.
LEVEL THREE	SELF-ACCEPTED MORAL PRINCIPLES	
Stage 5	*Morality of contract, individual rights, and democratically accepted law.* The child is concerned with balancing the rights of the individual and the protection of society.	Pro: Theft is justified because the law was not fashioned for situations in which an individual would forfeit a life by obeying the rules. Con: Theft is condemned because others may also have great need.
Stage 6	*Morality of individual principles of conscience.* The child is concerned about self-condemnation for violating his or her own principles. The child's own conscience is the guide, and that guide is based upon abstract, universal moral principles.	Pro: Theft is justified because he would not have lived up to the standards of his conscience if he allowed his wife to die. Con: Theft is condemned because he would not have lived up to the standards of his conscience if he had engaged in stealing.

SOURCES: Lawrence Kohlberg, "The Development of Children's Orientations Toward a Moral Order," *Vita Humana,* Vol. 6, 1963, pp. 11–33; and Kohlberg, *Stages in the Development of Moral Thought and Action* (New York: Holt, Rinehart and Winston, 1969).

tend to follow the sequence depicted by Kohlberg (Nisan and Kohlberg, 1982; Walker, 1982; Colby et al., 1983).

More recently, Kohlberg (1978) has revised a number of his formulations. At one point he seemed to have dropped his sixth stage, which some have criticized as culturally biased and Ivy League elitist. In his sixth stage, Kohlberg had undertaken to capture the ideal of brotherhood, equality, and community, which he found embodied in the philosophies of individuals like Rev. Martin Luther King, Jr. But at a symposium in the late 1970s, Kohlberg confided that he was having increasing difficulty locating stage-six persons: "Perhaps all the sixth-stage persons of the 1960s had been wiped out, perhaps they had regressed, or maybe it was all in my imagination in the first place" (quoted by Muson, 1979: 57). Even so, he has more recently posited yet another—a seventh—stage of development, which is more religious and transcendental in nature (Kohlberg, 1981).

The developmental psychologist Carol Gilligan (1982a,b), who worked with Kohlberg for more than a decade, contends that Kohlberg's moral dilemmas capture men's but not women's moral development. She finds that men and women have different moral domains. Men typically define moral problems in terms of rights and rules—the "justice approach." Women conceive of morality as an obligation to exercise care and to avoid hurt—the "responsibility approach." Men see autonomy and competition as central to life. Accordingly, they depict morality as a system of rules for taming aggression and adjudicating rights. Women deem relationships as central to life. Consequently, they think of morality as protecting the integrity of relationships and maintaining human bonding. In sum, Gilligan portrays men as separating themselves from others and pursuing independence in the course of their development. In contrast, she depicts women as attempting to achieve greater integration within the larger human enterprise. Gilligan's approach has given rise to considerable controversy, inviting additional research on these matters (Deaux, 1985).

SOCIALIZATION ACROSS THE LIFE SPAN

We often think of socialization as something that takes place during childhood and ends with adulthood. Yet as noted at the beginning of the chapter, socialization is a lifetime process. Indeed, within modern societies we expect people to acquire various skills in school, to recover from unhealthy patterns of behavior in mental hospitals, to undergo "resocialization" in prison rehabilitative programs, and to learn a firm's operating procedures in special seminars and conferences. Throughout life we move into and out of roles, all of which dictates an ongoing process of socialization.

Role Transitions and Socialization

Role socialization frequently entails three phases (Mortimer and Simmons, 1978). First, individuals fantasize about, experiment with, and try on the behaviors associated with a new role, what social psychologists term *anticipatory*

Socialization Occurs Across the Life Cycle Socialization is a continuous process that encompasses the entire life span. (Patrick Reddy)

socialization. For instance, children prepare themselves for adult roles of spouse and parent by "playing house." Likewise, as pointed out above, modern societies develop formal programs that allow individuals to try out roles in apprenticeship, intern, probationary, and rehabilitative programs. Second, once people assume a new role, they find that new situations compel them to alter, adapt, and remake various of their behaviors. For example, as individuals move from the single to the married state, they must fashion new interpersonal skills, since much of the marital role is hidden from children. And third, people find that as they move across the life span they must disengage or exit from certain roles. Rituals like graduation exercises, marriage, retirement parties, funerals, and other "rites of passage" are socially established mechanisms for easing some role transitions.

But moving into and out of roles may pose difficulties for individuals. The anthropologist Ruth Benedict (1938) notes that some roles do not build comfortably upon other roles and on occasion even conflict with earlier training. Role discontinuity often confronts children as they pass from childhood to adulthood. Whereas children are socialized to be nonresponsible, submissive, and sexually inactive, adults are expected to be responsible, dominant, and sexually active (Mortimer and Simmons, 1978). Irving Rosow (1974) claims that a somewhat similar discontinuity emerges again toward the end of the life cycle, in that the experiences of adulthood do not equip the elderly to occupy themselves during retirement.

The sociologist Orville G. Brim (1966) suggests that other factors also contribute to role discontinuity. The geographic and social mobility demanded by modern achievement-oriented societies interferes with stable career patterns. Exposure to multiple subcultures and countercultures complicates the effects of mobility by confronting people with an endless series of novel role demands. And much learning is rendered obsolete by rapid technological advances, shifts in gender norms, and new opportunities for women and minorities.

Brim also observes that the content of socialization differs at different stages of the life cycle. We learn different elements at different times and places in our lives. Thus socialization during adulthood differs in a variety of ways from that of childhood. First, society focuses chiefly on children's underlying values and motives, whereas in adulthood the primary focus falls on overt behavior. Second, childhood socialization is oriented toward the transmission of basic skills like toilet training and language competence, whereas adult socialization calls for the synthesis of a vast array of already learned responses. Third, childhood socialization emphasizes the idealistic aspects of morality, whereas adult socialization emphasizes realism (for example, children are taught not to lie, but later they learn that they are supposed to tell "white lies"). And fourth, early socialization places less emphasis than does adult socialization on mediating conflicting demands (for instance, some requirements of the spouse role conflict with those of the parental role and must be reconciled). Thus the content of socialization changes as individuals move through the life cycle.

The Life Stages of Men and Women

Popular interest in the periods and transitions that occur across the life span received considerable impetus from Gail Sheehy's best-selling book *Passages* (1976). In it, Sheehy views adult development as a succession of stages, a sort of stairway made up of discrete, steplike levels. Each stage poses problems that must be resolved before a person can successfully advance to the next stage. By passing from one stage to the next—*passages*—an individual acquires new strengths and evolves an *authentic identity.* Such an identity has many of the qualities that the psychologist Abraham Maslow equates with the self-actualized person (see Chapter 5). Sheehy's approach was influenced by the work of psychologist Daniel J. Levinson and his associates at Yale (1974, 1976, 1978).

The Male Life Cycle
The Yale researchers studied forty men in their mid-thirties to mid-forties (representing blue- and white-collar workers in industry, business executives, academic biologists, and novelists). They concluded that the primary task confront-

ing men throughout adulthood is one of building a workable life structure. Fashioning a life structure entails periodically making critical choices and deciding on and pursuing relevant goals. At these intervals, men must reappraise their current structure and create a new one that is more in keeping with their evolving circumstances. Thus the social world provides a powerful impetus to change and influences the course of a man's life structure across time. The stages identified by Levinson are depicted in Figure 4.1 and may be summarized as follows.

EARLY ADULT TRANSITION   Between seventeen and twenty-two years of age, men must move from an adolescent life structure to one of early adulthood. This transition involves modifying earlier relationships with family and friends and making choices for adult living. Major life events often include graduation from high school, moving out of the family home, entering college or the military, and graduating from college or completing military service.

ENTERING THE ADULT WORLD   Beginning in the early twenties and extending until the late twenties, men explore various life alternatives and make provisional commitments to adult roles and responsibilities. They must sample different kinds of relationships, keep choices about career and employment open, and begin assuming new responsibilities. Among the life events that assume major importance for many men are occupational choice, first job, marriage, and the birth of children.

THE AGE THIRTY TRANSITION   The years between ages twenty-eight and thirty-three constitute a transitional period during which men reexamine many of their earlier commitments. They reopen many questions about their choice of a marriage partner, a career, and life goals, often with painful consequences. A voice within the self says: "If I am to change my life—if there are things in it I want to modify or exclude, or things missing I want to add—I must now make a start, for soon it will be too late" (Levinson et al., 1978: 58).

SETTLING DOWN   Having usually made some firm choices in the previous phase about their career, family, and major relationships, men between the ages of thirty-three and forty seek to carve out a niche for themselves in society. They emphasize "making it" in the adult world and moving up the ladder of prestige and achievement in their career or profession.

Toward the end of the settling down period, typically between the ages of thirty-six and forty, men enter a distinctive phase that Levinson designates as "becoming one's own man." They often feel that no matter what they have accomplished, they lack sufficient independence. Whereas they may have looked to an older, more experienced person as a mentor, they now want to move out on their own. At this time they may try for a crucial promotion or some other critical form of recognition.

THE MID-LIFE TRANSITION   As men enter their early forties, they begin asking themselves: "What have I done with my life?" "What have I accomplished?" and "What do I still wish to accomplish?" Whereas they looked ahead at age thirty,

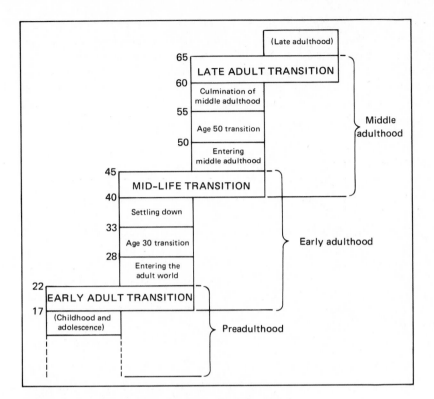

FIGURE 4.1 Periods in Adult Male Development
At periodic intervals across the life span, men must reappraise them-
selves and the goals that they are pursuing.
(SOURCE: Daniel J. Levinson et al., *The Seasons of a Man's Life* [New York:
Knopf, 1978], p. 57.)

they now look to both the past and the future, and attempt to appraise their
lives and the direction in which they are headed. Often they sense a gap between
"what I've got now" and "what it is I really want," which leads them to an interval
of soul searching.

MIDDLE ADULTHOOD RESTABILIZATION   At about age forty-five and for the next five
years, men tend to stabilize the patterns set down in the previous period. Sometimes this new life structure is initiated by a significant life event—a change in
job or career, a divorce or love affair, or a move to a new community. This phase
is not the last developmental period, but it is the last one that Levinson and his
associates have studied so far.

Other researchers (Gould, 1972, 1978; Vaillant and Vaillant, 1981) have studied additional periods in the male life cycle. For instance, the psychiatrist Roger
L. Gould finds that during the late forties men conclude that the die is pretty
well cast and that their fortunes for better or worse are more or less established.

Phases in Adult Male Development
As viewed by psychologist Daniel J.
Levinson and his associates, the
adult man is shaped by external social forces and his own inner career
clock. Each period of life is a new
part of his life structure. (Patrick
Reddy)

Accordingly, they begin to resign themselves to many of life's negative aspects. This adjustment carries over into their fifties. Men often mellow, becoming more accepting of themselves and of their spouses, children, and friends. No longer do most men experience the strong drive to succeed that characterized their early thirties. They recognize that life is time-bound, and they begin to come to terms with the fact that they too will die. Yet these thoughts are not particularly disturbing and permit them to search for a new serenity.

The Female Life Cycle

The stages in the female life cycle remain largely unexplored. Levinson has expanded his research to encompass women, but this work is still under way. Even so, an accumulating body of evidence demonstrates that the phases that apply to adult men do not necessarily apply to adult women. As we will see in Chapter 16, the way the world looks to men is not necessarily the way it looks to women. And the way men think about the world is not necessarily the way women think about it. Thus men and women often inhabit different social worlds, even though they occupy the same physical location. This fact is a consequence of somewhat differing life experiences for men and women.

One crucial difference between the adult experiences of men and women has to do with the gender roles assigned them by society, a matter that is explored at greater length in Chapter 16. Although women are entering the paid work force in increasing numbers, the legacy of traditional definitions and arrangements poses obstacles for them. Household and child-care responsibilities still fall primarily upon women. For instance, one study of American married couples found that even when wives have full-time jobs, they do most of the housework (Blumstein and Schwartz, 1983). Only 22 percent of the men, as opposed to 59 percent of the women, contribute eleven or more hours a week to household chores. The net result is that many women are compelled to carry dual responsibilities, and they experience role overload. Nor are professional women exempted. A recent survey of women who are physicians found that 75 percent of them are not able to share cooking, shopping, money management, and child-care duties with a spouse (Collins, 1982*b*).

The economist Lester C. Thurow (1981) points out that women confront a substantial career disadvantage should they have children. The years between ages twenty-five and thirty-five are the decade in the life span when men typically make it if they are going to do so. During this time, lawyers and accountants become partners in the top firms, business managers make it onto the "fast track," college professors secure tenure at good universities, and blue-collar workers find positions that generate high earnings and seniority. But it is also the decade when women are most likely to leave the labor force to have children. When they do, present procedures for achieving promotions and acquiring critical skills extract an enormous lifetime price from women.

Our society's gender practices often compel women to make a choice between a career and a family, although men typically are not confronted with this dilemma. Hence whereas 51 percent of women executives at top corporations are single, only 4 percent of their male counterparts are single; in addition, whereas 61 percent of the women are childless, only 3 percent of the men have no children (Hull, 1982; Fraker, 1984). In sum, the more successful a man is, the more likely it is that he will marry and have a family. But for women it is the other way around (Rubin, 1980).

Over 90 percent of all American women now work for pay at some point in their lives. This means that more women are entering or reentering the labor force, changing jobs, undertaking new careers, or returning to school. Simultaneously, growing numbers of women are rearing children as single parents. Numerous combinations of career, marriage, and childrearing present themselves to women, with respect to both timing and commitment. Many American women who are now in their forties and fifties stopped their schooling or work at the time they married or gave birth to their first child. They then remained in the home during most of the child-rearing years. When they undertake to return to the paid labor force, they often find themselves with obsolete skills or trained only in traditional "women's jobs"—such as teaching and social work—in which jobs are currently scarce. A decision to get a paid job may also complicate a woman's relationships with other family members. Her husband may feel threatened by the change. And the skills and traits valued in the domestic role—a sense of attractiveness, lovability, and dependency—run counter to the aggressive and actively self-promoting necessities of work and school (Mogul, 1979).

The "stock taking" that Levinson finds occurring among men in their early forties may take place earlier among women. Childless women in their thirties frequently confront a "last chance" dilemma with respect to motherhood. At about the same age, women who are full-time parents and homemakers find that their absorption with childrearing duties is decreasing, and they often contemplate what the future holds for them. And middle-aged women who are juggling child-care and work responsibilities increasingly reflect on their coming life pattern (Mogul, 1979).

There is also reason to question whether the phase of becoming one's own man that Levinson identifies for men applies to the careers of most women. During this phase, men seek to free themselves from a previously central male mentor—a sponsor in higher-level management who takes an interest in teaching and guiding a subordinate. In many instances, it means a close personal friendship and a willingness to use power and influence on behalf of the protégé's career. However, many women do not enter—or reenter—the work world until they are in their late thirties, and few of them have mentors, either male or female.

In sum, the life patterns of women are quite different from those of men. And given our contemporary family and work arrangements, the job and career opportunities afforded women are complicated by the social organization of child care. All this contributes to a decidedly different cast to the life cycle of women.

The Stage Approach Controversy

Although stage approaches draw our attention to the broad and orderly changes that occur across the life span, many sociologists and psychologists point out that they oversimplify adult life (Neugarten, 1979; Dannefer, 1984). In some respects, the timing of life events is becoming less regular as age loses some of its customary meanings. For instance, it is no longer unusual to encounter the twenty-eight-year-old mayor, the thirty-year-old college president, the thirty-five-year-old grandmother, the fifty-year-old retiree, the sixty-five-year-old new father, and the seventy-year-old student.

Futher, the sociologist Bernice L. Neugarten points out that the themes of life reported by adults of all ages are recurrent ones that do not typically follow a single, fixed order:

> [The themes of adulthood] do not in truth emerge at only given moments in life, each to be resolved and then put behind as if they were beads on a chain. Identity is made and remade; issues of intimacy and freedom and commitment to significant others, the pressures of time, the reformulation of life goals, stocktaking and reconciliation and acceptance of one's successes and failures—all of these preoccupy the young as well as the old. It is a truism, even though it sometimes goes unmentioned, that the psychological preoccupations of adults are recurrent. They appear and reappear in new forms over long periods of time. This being so, it is something of a distortion to describe adulthood as a series of discrete and neatly bounded stages, as if adult life were a staircase. (1979: 891)

Levinson, too, acknowledges that adults do not march in lock step through a series of stages. The pace and change in a person's life are influenced by a great many factors—war, a death in the family, poor health, a sudden windfall. Thus wide variations occur among people.

SUMMARY

1. We are not born human; we possess only the potential for becoming human. We become human through the process termed socialization.
2. Socialization helps us to understand two kinds of phenomena: (a) how a person becomes capable of participating in society and (b) how society is possible.
3. Studies with chimpanzees and the cases of Anna, Isabelle, and Genie reveal that *both* an appropriate genetic endowment and a favorable environment are essential for producing a human personality.
4. Learning is basic to the human condition; it enables the human organism to adapt itself to the environment. Learning occurs in three principal ways: (a) conditioning, (b) imitating the behavior of another, and (c) changing the cognitive structure by which we think about our environment.
5. Conditioning describes the process whereby individuals, as a result of their experience, establish an association or linkage between two events. Operant conditioning is a type of learning in which behavior is altered in its strength by its consequences.
6. Through observational learning, individuals can acquire new patterns of behavior, strengthen or weaken inhibitions of previously learned behavior, and realize vicarious conditioning.
7. Jean Piaget has popularized the view of cognitive stages in development. He outlines four stages in the development of intelligence: the sensorimotor stage; the stage of preoperational thought; the stage of concrete operations; and the stage of formal operations. Some critics have faulted Piaget for what they see as an unrealistically rigid perspective.
8. Children are born without social awareness. Through socialization, external controls become internal controls (self-control), and the child develops a conscience.
9. Socialization is a continuous, lifetime process. However, the content of socialization differs at different stages of the life cycle.
10. Life-cycle approaches undertake to identify the common elements in the human experience as individuals develop through the life span. The phases that apply to men do not necessarily apply to women. One crucial difference between the adult experiences of men and women has to do with the gender roles assigned them by society.

GLOSSARY

Accommodation □ In Piaget's theory, the process in cognitive development of changing a scheme (cognitive structure) to achieve a better match to the world of reality.

Assimilation □ In Piaget's theory, the process in cognitive development of taking in new information and interpreting it in such a manner that the information corresponds to a currently held scheme of the world.

Behavior modification □   The application of the results of conditioning theory and experimental psychology to the problem of altering maladaptive behaviors.

Cognitive stages in development □   Sequential periods in the growth or maturing of an individual's ability to think—to gain knowledge and awareness of the self and the environment.

Conditioning □   The process whereby individuals, as a result of their experience, establish an association or linkage between two events.

Conscience □   The internal operation of ethical or moral principles that control or inhibit the actions and thoughts of an individual.

Identification □   See **observational learning.**

Imitation □   See **observational learning.**

Internalization □   The process whereby an individual incorporates within his or her personality the standards of behavior prevalent within the larger society.

Learned helplessness □   The generalized expectancy that events are independent of what one does; the notion that one's own actions and consequent events are not causally related.

Learning □   A more or less permanent modification in an organism's behavior or capability that results from its experience in the environment.

Modeling □   See **observational learning.**

Observational learning □   The social transmission of behavior, either deliberately or inadvertently, through the examples provided by people whom we observe.

Operant conditioning □   A type of learning in which behavior is altered in its strength by its consequences.

Principle of conservation □   The notion that the quantity of something stays the same despite changes in shape or position.

Reinforcer □   Any stimulus that follows a response and increases the frequency or probability of its occurrence.

Scheme □   In Piaget's theory, a cognitive structure that an individual evolves for dealing with a specific kind of situation in the environment.

Socialization □   A process by which individuals develop, through interaction with other people, the ways of thinking, feeling, and acting that are essential for effective participation within society.

5 IDENTITIES AND THE SELF

THE SELF
  Controversy Surrounding the Self
  The Material Self
  The Social Self
  Selfhood as a Communicative
      Process
SELF-PERCEPTION
  Self-attribution
  Self-knowledge

SELF-CONCEPTIONS
  Cognitive Scripts About
      the Self
  Sources of Our Self-
      conceptions
  Self-esteem
  Self-conceptions and
      Behavior

To participate as effective members of society—to enter into sustained social interaction with others—we must establish who we are in social terms. Just as we must impute meaning to the people, objects, and events in the world around us, so we must also assign meaning to ourselves. In so doing, we establish our identities. In its simplest definition, **identity** is the answer we supply to the question, "Who am I?" Our identity consists of our sense of placement within the world and the meaning we attach to ourselves within the broader context of human life. It derives from the roles we play and the relationships we form (Thoits, 1983). In our everyday activities, we interact with others not so much on the basis of what we actually are as in terms of our conceptions of ourselves and of others. We act toward one another on the basis of who we think we are. As such, our identity leaves its signature on everything we do. Little wonder, then, that so many of us are preoccupied with and worry about our identity.

During the past fifty years or so there has been a shift in emphasis from making one's way in the world of work and business to finding oneself. The question increasingly posed for us is not What can I do? but Who can I be?

*E*stablishing identity: ol' alma mater

Prior to the opening of the new school year each fall, stores in the vicinity of college campuses across the nation stock up on items bearing the college's name and emblem—items such as notebooks, shirts, sweaters, jackets, caps, beer mugs, bracelets, rings, blankets, and bric-a-brac. And each year, without fail, incoming freshmen are eager buyers of such items, loading themselves up with "identity markers." Sophomores, in contrast, seem relatively immune to the fever, perhaps even looking down their noses at it somewhat contemptuously.

Freshmen for the most part are unsure of their identity as students at alma mater. They lack a secure anchorage in the educational and social life of the campus; as yet they are not "with it"—they are not integrated or fully accepted within campus life. To compensate and nail down their identity with alma mater, they display emblems that highlight such identity. They search for external marks of identification because they as yet lack genuine internal identifications.

Since sophomores are integrated within the college scene and have developed campus identities and loyalties, they feel a lesser need for special alma mater items. They viscerally know they are part of alma mater; they see the lavish and ostentatious display of college insignia as in bad taste—"kid stuff." In truth, the excessive vigor with which freshmen secure and display such emblems reveals not so much their loyalty to alma mater as their uncertain loyalty to it. As Shakespeare notes, "Methinks the lady doth protest too much."

When we have difficulty answering the question Who am I?—when we lack a set of ready definitions of ourselves—we experience varying degrees of anxiety (Klapp, 1969; Buss, 1980). Consider the sense of discomfort, alienation, and utter despair that is revealed in such commonly heard statements as "I just can't seem to find myself," "I'm so confused about myself," and "I don't seem to be able to get my life together." What is more, most of us try to be unique—to find differences between self and others (Snyder and Fromkin, 1980).

THE SELF

The consciousness of selfhood is the very core of our physical being. About it are gathered all the joys and all the miseries of life.

—James R. Angell, *Psychology*, 1908

The concept of the self is closely linked with that of identity. Indeed, some social scientists at times employ the two concepts in a roughly interchangeable manner. Others view identities as subunits of the global self (Burke, 1980). Actually, the

Developing and Clarifying Identity
According to Erik Erikson, adolescence presents young
people with the developmental task of synthesizing a variety of new roles and crystallizing their self-conceptions.
As he views the process, a certain amount of role confusion, turmoil, and uncertainty is inevitable. (Patrick Reddy)

theoretical concept of the self has a much longer tradition than that of identity,
being traceable to the work of William James (1842–1910), a nineteenth-century
philosopher and psychologist (1890). The concept of identity, in contrast, gained
prominence in the 1960s, especially with the popularization of the works of Erik
Erikson (1950, 1959).

The **self** is the individual as known to the individual in a socially determined
frame of reference (Murphy, 1947: 996; Newcomb, 1950: 328). It is an abstraction
that we develop about our attributes, capacities, and activities (Coopersmith,
1967). The self entails the conception we develop of our own behavior—the
system of concepts we employ in attempting to define ourselves (Gergen, 1971).
As such, it is the custodian of awareness. We experience ourselves as being
entities separate from other entities and as having continuity through time (being
the same person over time). The notion of the self provides us with a sense of
being a distinct, bounded, identifiable unit (Elliott, Rosenberg, and Wagner,
1984). Indeed, it is this very sense of selfhood that people with some severe
forms of mental illness (schizophrenia, for example) experience as lost; they feel
at sea in a flood of stimuli, since they lack a stable self-image and clear self-
boundaries—a clear sense of where they begin and end.

SELF-ACTUALIZATION

Within psychology, some theorists who posit a self, such as Abraham Maslow (1967, 1970) and Carl Rogers (1970), stress that self-realization or "actualization" constitutes a basic motive in human behavior. Some years ago, Maslow suggested that people have a hierarchy of needs ranging from the most basic, physiological needs to higher, more humane, creative ones. He claimed that it was necessary to satisfy needs lower on the hierarchy before the individual could begin satisfying the higher ones. The highest need, self-actualization, could be realized only after all the lower ones were satisfied.

Maslow advances the view that humankind is inherently good and that the ultimate goal of human effort is self-direction, growth, fulfillment, and happiness. He upbraids psychology for its "pessimistic, negative, and limited conception" of humanity. Rather than dwelling on human frailties, Maslow insists that psychology should explore human strengths.

Maslow, Rogers, and other humanistic psychologists reject both the behaviorist and the psychoanalytic views as being too mechanistic. Behaviorists are criticized for their hostility toward the concept of the self and for their view of people as objects buffeted about by *external* stimuli. Psychoanalysts are faulted for their image of an "iceberg self"—of personality as lying mostly beneath the surface of consciousness—and for their view of people as objects buffeted about by hidden *internal* stimuli. Against behaviorist and psychoanalytic theories, humanist psychologists counterpoise an optimistic perspective: They feel that people can move toward full individuality and actualization through conscious design.

Maslow studied the lives of important, famous figures from history whom he considered to be *self-actualizers*—Abraham Lincoln, Albert Einstein, Walt Whitman,

Controversy Surrounding the Self

Few concepts in the social sciences touch upon more significant issues, yet entail more ambiguities, than the concept of the self. Many social scientists, as well as philosophers, theologians, and humanists, consider it a critical concept. Others in the same fields think it a useless and misleading one (Yinger, 1965). Indeed, after 1910 the concept of the self was driven out of psychology by the onslaught of behaviorism, a school of thought identified with psychologist John Watson (1925). The behaviorists claimed that "consciousness" is neither a definable nor a usable concept, but merely another word for what used to be called the soul. They insisted that we only observe *activities* of human beings and that science should limit itself to that which can be directly observed. Thus behaviorists such as Watson sharply attacked what they termed "introspective psychology" and focused on conditioning and stimulus-response phenomena. More recent behaviorists, such as B. F. Skinner (1953), continue the battle against those who believe

Jane Addams, Eleanor Roosevelt, and Ludwig van Beethoven. From the facts about their lives, he constructed a composite picture of a self-actualized person:

1. They have a firm perception of reality.
2. They accept themselves and others for what they are.
3. They evidence considerable spontaneity in thought and behavior.
4. They are problem-centered rather than self-centered.
5. They have an air of detachment and a need for privacy.
6. They are autonomous and independent.
7. They resist enculturation and stereotyped behavior, although they are not deliberately unconventional.
8. They are sympathetic to the human condition and promote its welfare.
9. They establish deep, profound relationships with a few people rather than superficial bonds with many people.
10. They have a democratic world outlook.
11. They have a considerable fund of creativeness.
12. They transcend their environment rather than merely coping with it.
13. They have a high frequency of "peak experiences," marked by rapturous feelings of excitement, insight, and happiness.

The chief criticism directed at Maslow's formulation is the imprecision of his concepts; "self-actualization," for instance, lacks clear definition. Furthermore, he is not entirely clear on the criteria he employs for selecting his self-actualization persons. Generally, they are people Maslow likes. Conceivably, however, there are ways of actualizing oneself other than those of which Maslow approves. And although individuals like Lincoln and Eleanor Roosevelt, whom Maslow considers self-actualized, displayed great social compassion and did much to improve the human condition, their relationships with their children and spouses were in some respects unsatisfying and unhappy.

in the concept of the self, asserting that nothing is to be gained—and much lost—by positing a self as a factor in the study of behavior.

In 1943, Gordon W. Allport revived the concept of the self in psychologically oriented social psychology. This reawakened interest in the self has found reflection in Abraham Maslow's (1967, 1970) theory of motivation, which stresses the importance of optimal development, or "actualization," of the self (see boxed insert). Similarly, Carl Rogers emphasizes the key part self-acceptance plays in healthy personality functioning (1970). Many other contemporary psychologists are critical of the behaviorists' neglect of subjective experience (Buss, 1980; Wicklund, 1979; Wegner and Vallacher, 1980). They believe that the essential goal of our modern age should be to develop a sense of selfhood and of self-worth.

Within sociologically oriented social psychology, Charles Horton Cooley (1864–1929) and George Herbert Mead (1863–1931) have made pioneering contributions to our understanding of the self (Cooley, 1902, 1909; Mead, 1932,

1934, 1938). This work has been carried on by the present-day symbolic interactionists (Blumer, 1969; Rosenberg, 1979; Stryker, 1980). Interactionist sociologists stress the view that our humanness derives from the mutual impact we
have upon one another. Through our actions we reciprocally shape and reshape,
direct and redirect, and forge and reforge our social beings. Our identities—who
we are and what we are—are bestowed on us, sustained, and altered through the
process of social interaction (Blumstein, 1975). Other individuals are mirrors
that provide us with reflections—in the form of continuous judgments and assessments—of our worth, desirability, and merit. Indeed, interactionists say that
in large measure we hold the keys to one another's self-images through the
feedback provided by our behavior toward one another. In recent years, the
interactionist perspective has found its way increasingly into the work and
formulations of psychologically oriented social psychologists as well (Ellis and
Holmes, 1982; Stephenson and Wicklund, 1984; Hass, 1984).

The Material Self

> When I say "I," I mean a thing absolutely unique, not to be confused with any
> other.
>
> —Ugo Betti, *The Inquiry,* 1944–1945

One way in which an individual experiences herself or himself as an object is as
the "bodily me," the **material self.** We encounter ourselves as a stream of sensations from within the organism—from viscera, muscles, tendons, joints, and
other parts of the body. For the most part, we are only dimly aware of this
sensory stream; often we are totally unaware of it. But at certain times—in
moments of exhilaration during and after physical exercise or when experiencing
pleasure or pain—this sensory stream becomes highlighted in the consciousness.
In any event, each individual groups together various internally derived stimuli
(sensations or raw sense data) and treats them as the "bodily me." Allport offers
some vivid examples of stimuli "in" and "out" of the "bodily me":

> Think first of swallowing the saliva in your mouth, or do so. Then imagine expec-
> torating it into a tumbler and drinking it! What seemed natural and "mine" suddenly
> becomes disgusting and alien. Or picture yourself sucking blood from a prick in
> your finger; then imagine sucking blood from a bandage around your finger! What
> I perceive as belonging intimately to my body is warm and welcome; what I perceive
> as separate from my body becomes, in the twinkling of an eye, cold and foreign.
> (1955: 43)

Most Westerners designate an area midway between and slightly behind the
eyes as the location of the self (Claparède, 1924). Nonetheless, the "self" as the
word is used in the social sciences is not to be found somewhere in the body,
nor does the word refer to a corporeal body; the self lacks a physical existence.
Rather, the self is a concept—a mentally constructed image each individual has
regarding himself or herself. The self represents a way of thinking and speaking
about our experience rather than a physical thing or a psychic entity.

The Social Self Cooley/Mead.

We also experience the self as a social object. In attempting to understand this process, sociologist Charles Horton Cooley (1902) originated the concept of the "looking-glass self" (see boxed insert, pp. 148–149). He viewed the social self as arising through a process in which we imagine how we appear to others. Our ability to take the perspective of another person is a basic requirement of all social behavior (Hass, 1984).

George Herbert Mead (1932, 1934, 1938) later elaborated upon Cooley's ideas and contributed many insights of his own. Mead indicated that we achieve a sense of selfhood by acting toward ourselves in much the same manner in which we act toward other people. When we do so, we are said to be "taking the role of the other toward ourselves." In other words, we examine ourselves from the vantage point of another person's mind.

The phrase "taking the role of the other toward ourselves" does not mean that at some point we cease being ourselves. Rather, we assume a *dual* perspective: simultaneously, one is the *subject* doing the viewing and the *object* being viewed. In imagination, one steps out of oneself, so to speak, into the position of another and looks back upon the self from this standpoint—a reflexive process. Thus "taking the role of the other toward ourselves" is nothing more than responding to ourselves in the same way in which other people might respond to us: Just as they might become angry with us, so we become angry with ourselves; just as they might rebuke us, so we rebuke ourselves; just as they might argue with us, so we argue with ourselves; and so on.

Mead designates the subject aspect of the selfhood process the "I" and the object aspect the "Me." Consider the child who is being disciplined by a teacher. The child, guilty of some rule infraction, is told to stay after school. The child, about to complain, imagines the teacher's sentiment and realizes that to protest may simply result in an increase in the detention time. In this illustration, the child imagines the attitude of the teacher toward the child; the child is said to take the role of the teacher and to view herself or himself as an object or "me." It is the child as subject or "I" who decides that it would be unwise to complain. The use of the personal pronouns in the following inner statement by the child illustrates the object-subject dimensions: "The teacher will get even madder with *me* if *I* complain."

According to Mead, children typically pass through a number of stages in the development of the self. At first, in the play stage, children assume the role of one person at a time and attempt to enact the behavior associated with the role, such as mother, cowboy, police officer, or teacher. Very often the model is a **significant other**—a particular person who has considerable influence on our self-evaluation and our acceptance of given social norms. For instance, two-year-old children may examine a doll's undergarment, pretend to find it soiled, reprimand the doll, and take the doll to the bathroom. The children are proceeding from the perspective of a particular person—in this case, very likely the mother—and then responding to the situation as the mother would respond. By imitating their mothers, the children take over the attitudes of the mother toward given behaviors and toward themselves. They play the role of the child and then the

SELF-AWARENESS

A problem associated with selfhood is this: How can a person be both the subject that is doing the perceiving and the object that is being perceived? Charles Horton Cooley (1902) suggests that we accomplish this by assuming in imagination the stance of other people and then, in our mind's eye, looking at ourselves as we believe others see us—a phenomenon Cooley terms the **looking-glass self.**

Cooley suggests that the process has three principal elements. First, we imagine how we appear to other people; we gain a glimpse of ourselves as we would in a mirror. For instance, one may think of himself or herself as being sickly looking. Second, we imagine how others judge our appearance; one is aware that people typically think of a sickly looking person as unattractive. Third, we experience some sort of feeling such as pride or mortification; thinking of oneself as sickly looking would probably make one feel unhappy and embarrassed.

We are most aware of this process when we are concerned with the impression we are making on others. In making a speech before the class or in approaching a professor after class, for example, a person may have butterflies in the stomach. The individual wonders, "Am I coming across successfully?" or "Do I appear bright or stupid?" The looking-glass self is the means by which one carries on a self-evaluating conversation with the self.

Cooley's notion of taking the self as the object of one's own attention has been echoed in a more recent theory of self-awareness (Duval and Wicklund, 1972; Wicklund and Hormuth, 1981; Stephenson and Wicklund, 1983). This theory proposes a dichotomy between the objects of conscious attention. We can direct our attention outward toward the environment, or inward toward the self. **Self-awareness** is defined as attention focused inward. To the extent that our attention is centered upon the self, we are said to be more self-aware than when our attention is scattered or directed outward. Self-awareness is presumed to increase whenever we encounter a stimulus that reminds us of the self. Stimuli such as mirrors, cameras, tape recorders, TV monitors, or an audience lead us to focus attention on the self. Research suggests that when others attend to us, we become more intensely aware of the self (Scheier and Carver, 1977; Carver

role of the mother—alternating the object and subject ("me" and "I") perspectives. They imaginatively place themselves in their mothers' shoes and then respond as children to the words they uttered and the acts they displayed when they were taking the role of the mother.

In the play stage, children assume the role of only one other person at a time. All this changes in the game stage, as children broaden their perspective to encompass the points of view of many people at the same time. In a game such as football, all eleven roles are closely and tightly interwoven. If the play involves

**Shyness and Embarrass-
ment: The Selfhood Process**
To be shy and embarrassed is
to be self-aware. It is mentally
to step out of oneself into the
position of another, and to
look back upon oneself from
this vantage point. It is to feel
"self-conscious," as this girl
does. (Patrick Reddy)

and Scheier, 1978, 1981). Presumably, this heightened self-attention is what leads to our subsequent reaction—conformity, embarrassment, pride, or simple awareness of our salient characteristics.

According to self-awareness theory, when we focus on the self, we compare what we believe about ourselves with what we *wish* we were like. Thus if we fail to reach a goal, behave immorally, or act in a way that conflicts with our values, we experience a *within-self discrepancy*. This state is painful because we recognize our inadequacies. Under these circumstances, we attempt to live up to our ideals, redefine our personal standards, rationalize our behavior, or seek some distracting experience. (We turn off the switch of self-focus and throw on the switch of outer-focus.)

a sweep to the right, the end has to coordinate his or her behavior with that of the halfback, the quarterback, the tackle, and guard in a way quite different from that involved in a passing play. All the players must know the responses associated with the other positions and take these responses into account in devising their own behavior. The game entails a social situation that links people within a network of role relationships and a web of role demands. Consequently, games socialize and prepare children for cooperative, coordinated endeavors as group members.

Developing a Sense of Self
This ten-month-old child is developing a sense of being separate and distinct. He gives evidence of recognizing his reflection in the mirror. (Patrick Reddy)

In due course, individuals enlarge their perspective to encompass the community or society as a whole. No longer do they simply take the perspective of particular persons such as the mother or that of particular players in a game. They now gain a synthesized overview of the cultural workings of their community and view themselves from the perspective of the **generalized other.** They became capable of distilling and extracting from their experiences with a specific person or specific persons in a game those overriding elements that hold for all social life.

Clearly the self is an exceedingly important element, by which people are integrated within the larger fabric of social existence. It is the means by which people can make indications to themselves of things in their surroundings and guide their actions accordingly. Thus anything of which we are conscious is something that we are indicating to ourselves—the rain striking the window, the ringing doorbell, the smarting of our nostrils from cigarette smoke, the remark of a friend. **Self-indication** is a dynamic communicative process in which we internally note things, assess them, give them meaning, and entertain various actions on the basis of the meaning (Blumer, 1962: 181–183). In this manner, we transform the external world into an internal world. In sum, the self provides a bridge between the individual and the larger social order.

The looking-glass self

The part the looking-glass self plays in my life was illustrated last evening when I was driving home on the outer belt. Although I had just finished drinking a six pack, I wasn't "drunk." But I was feeling good and exceeding the speed limit. All of a sudden out of nowhere came a highway patrol car with its flashers on. I pulled over to the side of the road and an officer came up to my window. He asked for my driver's license and registration. I gave them to him and he went back to the patrol car to check them out. All the while I was thinking to myself, "I wonder if he thinks I'm drunk. I'd better keep cool, be polite, and not let him catch a whiff of my breath. Good thing I pitched those empties at the last rest area." A short while later, he came back to my car and instructed me to come with him and get in his car. I asked him, "What did I do?" He said, "You were going a little fast." I made certain to walk steadily and slowly. I kept wondering, "Will he give me a breathalyzer test?" I took particular pains not to breathe on or toward him, because I was certain my breath smelled like a brewery. He began to fill out a ticket form for speeding, telling me that he had clocked me doing 72 miles per hour. He said I had the option of appealing the ticket in court or waiving a court appearance and paying the ticket ($50) within one week. I was still worried about the beer, so I decided to seem compliant and cooperative. I said to myself, "I would be less likely to give a guy a ticket for drunkenness if he appeared subdued and nonbelligerent." In so doing, I took "the role of the other" and placed myself mentally in the officer's situation. I told him, "I didn't know I was going so fast and I'll take it easier in the future." He gave me a copy of the ticket, telling me, "Slow it down a little. Take care." And that was that.

The generalized other

Last evening a group of us went to see an X-rated movie. I had never seen one before. We had to wait in line along the sidewalk outside the theater. The theater is in the campus district, and I felt exceedingly uncomfortable. I was ashamed of what I believed other people would think of me if they saw me going to a porno movie. I worried that my professors or someone who knew my parents might observe me. This is a good example of the generalized other. Through socialization processes, I had come to take over the view of the larger society that porno movies are licentious and reveal lewd, carnal appetites—deviant sexuality. The conceptions I hold of the expectations others have of me tell me that if I am seen as watching porno movies, others will disapprove of me.

Roles and the Self

In order to play our own role successfully, we must know the requirements both of our role and of the other person's role. According to George Herbert Mead, in the course of translating the requirements of our role into action, we imagine ourselves in the role of the other person. This process of the self enables us to take into account the behavior of the other person when we fashion our reciprocal behavior. (Patrick Reddy)

Selfhood as a Communicative Process

> *Consciousness of self gives us the power to stand outside the rigid chain of stimulus and response, to pause, and by this pause to throw some weight on either side, to cast some decision about what the response will be.*

> —Rollo May, *Man's Search for Himself*

Mead was not only interested in the formation, content, and evaluation of the self (the "me" aspects). He also examined the part the self plays in perceiving, judging, and acting in the world (the "I" aspects). According to Mead, the key to the selfhood process is communication, especially language and gestures. Through gestures we present ourselves to others and they in turn present themselves to us. A gesture is any behavior that can be assigned some meaning by either an actor or an observer. Considered by itself, however, a gesture is an

Selfhood and Communication
Communication entails reciprocally shaping and fitting our gestures to the gestures of others so as to attain a mutuality of understanding. It is an ongoing interpretive process in which we test and revise our messages in accordance with the feedback others provide us with through their gestures. (Patrick Reddy)

incomplete act; it becomes complete only insofar as a viewer determines what it stands for. Put in still other terms, gestures involve us in a communication process, one in which "commonness" is achieved to the degree to which a sender and receiver become linked together through a similar reading of a message—that is, to the extent to which they come to understand each other (Turner, 1968*a;* Blumer, 1969).

In acting, we usually have in mind some interpretation for a gesture—whether the gesture is a vocal utterance, a shrug of the shoulders, a clenched fist, a deep sigh, a bowed head, a grin, or a flirtatious glance. We hope to signal something to another—to clue them in to what we are planning to do or to what we would have them do. To accomplish this, however, requires that we ourselves already associate an interpretation with a gesture; we must assign meaning to it. Thus we internally ask what sort of act would activate within ourselves a certain response: "What would it take to get me to respond in a given way?" In our mind's eye, so to speak, we address ourselves and respond to the address. We then continue the process by addressing ourselves anew, carrying on an inner conversation.

As we engage in a social act, we simultaneously evaluate the product of the act: "Did the act come off in a fashion that I would understand had it been directed to me by another?" In so doing, we adopt the stance of another and see ourselves as we imagine others hear or see us, becoming an audience to ourselves. In the process of acting we may also remake or modify our behavior so that it fits more closely the meaning we initially had intended it to have.

On the basis of our interpretation of our own acts, we adopt a state of *preparedness* for certain kinds of responses from another. If one of us comments on a professor's lecture, complains about a headache, takes hold of someone else's hand, or grimaces, we expect that the other person will in turn activate a range of responses that will fit with our expression in some accustomed fashion: that the person will agree or disagree with the comment, offer sympathy, settle her or his hand comfortably within ours, or cease certain behavior.

When the other person in turn engages in some act, this marks the beginning of another phase of the interaction process—one of *testing and revision*. The original actor recognizes the gesture as being either one for which he or she is prepared or one that falls outside the anticipated range. But this person's expectations regarding the other's act influence his or her perception of it—that is, human beings do not simply pick up a message; they also help shape it. If one expects sympathy from another person, one may overlook the faint note of sarcasm in the other's response; if a slight is anticipated, the sincerity of the expressed concern may be overlooked and the response interpreted as sarcasm. We respond, then, not so much to the acts of others as to our perceptions and interpretations of their acts—to the meaning their acts have for us (Turner, 1968*a*).

SELF-PERCEPTION

In Chapter 2 we considered perception, the process by which we gather and interpret information. We noted that perception permits us to sense the world around us and assign meaning to this sensory input. We examined person perception, the process by which we come to know and think about others—their characteristics, qualities, and inner states. Now we turn our attention to **self-perception**—the process by which we come to know and think about ourselves (the characteristics, qualities, and inner states that we attribute to ourselves). In the course of social interaction, we fashion conceptions of ourselves that stabilize, make predictable, and render manageable our view of ourselves. By attributing stable traits and enduring dispositions to ourselves, we feel we are better able to understand our behavior and chart our future actions. However, the ways in which we perceive ourselves are not necessarily the ways in which others see us—a point highlighted by the egocentric bias discussed in the boxed insert.

Men and women have pondered the nature of the self for a very long time. And for centuries philosophers and poets have contemplated the matter. Within the past several decades, a giant industry has emerged providing endless insights and advice through paperbacks, magazines, tape cassettes, human potential seminars, therapists, and gurus. We are encouraged to be true to ourselves, to get in touch with ourselves, to come to terms with ourselves, to improve ourselves, to transform ourselves, and to "actualize" ourselves. All this raises the question of what sources of information we call on when we perceive and think about the "self." How do we decide what we are like? There are two basic sources of information about ourselves (Andersen and Ross, 1984). One source is our overt behavior, from which we make inferences regarding the kind of people we are—self-attribution. Another source is our covert thoughts and feelings—self-

PUTTING ONESELF AT THE CENTER OF EVENTS

In our daily lives, we typically see ourselves at the center of events. This is what social psychologists term the **egocentric bias** (Greenwald, 1980; Zuckerman et al., 1983). In other words, we overperceive ourselves as the victims or targets of events that, in reality, are not directed toward us. For instance, when a professor singles out an especially good or poor exam for a few preliminary remarks before returning the papers to a class, you tend to overestimate the likelihood that one of the exams belongs to you (Fenigstein, 1984). In like fashion, you tend to overestimate the likelihood that you, rather than another person in a group, has been chosen to participate in an experimental demonstration. And if you are a lottery player, you sense that your ticket has a far greater probability of being selected a winner than it in fact has (Weinstein, 1980; Greenwald and Pratkanis, 1984).

The egocentric bias results in each of us experiencing life through a self-centered filter. This skewed view of reality influences our perception of events and our later recall of the events from memory. Thus Miron Zuckerman and his colleagues (1983) find that in group discussions we consistently exaggerate our own importance. We perceive ourselves as attracting more attention, as having a greater impact on others' opinions, and as being more often the object of other people's comments than is the case. The bias also shows up in memory. It is far easier to remember information if it somehow refers to oneself (Greenwald and Pratkanis, 1984). Accordingly, when we are asked to remember an event that occurred some years ago, we typically recall what happened to us much more readily than we remember the general events that occurred at the time. And we fabricate and rewrite memory to enhance our importance in the events, seeing ourselves as leading players in the drama (Goleman, 1984a). It seems that it is easier and more efficient to organize experience in terms of what happens to us than it is in any other format. In sum, the mind perceives and stores information in terms of the egocentric bias.

Among some individuals the egocentric bias is excessive, leading to a paranoid perception of the world. The mild, positive personalization of events is normal; but among paranoid individuals it becomes extreme and overgeneralized. Such individuals are rigid in their egocentricity, even in the face of convincing evidence that they are overdoing it. In contrast, the egocentric bias seems to diminish among depressed persons. Whereas nondepressed people commonly overestimate the credit due them in an undertaking, it is otherwise for those who are depressed. The self-enhancing bias of nondepressed individuals may provide them with an illusory "glow"; that feeling is somehow lost during a depression (Watson and Clark, 1984).

knowledge regarding our inner, private experiences. Let us examine each of these sources in turn beginning with self-attribution.

Self-attribution

In the course of our daily lives, we extract meaning from the data we receive from our sense organs regarding ourselves and arrive at innumerable inferences. Interestingly enough, we apparently use much the same kind of evidence and logic (attribution of causality) in forming conclusions about ourselves as we do in perceiving others. We come to know our own attitudes by inferring them from our overt behavior—from what we say and do. Thus we surmise our own attitudes in much the same fashion as we surmise the attitudes of others: We scrutinize situations for external cues and then make attributions regarding these cues (Bem, 1965, 1967, 1972; Kelley, 1967; Taylor, 1975). In sum, we infer our inner states from the same external cues that are available to outside observers.

For example, if someone asks you whether a friend of yours likes banana splits, you think over what the person usually gets at the ice cream parlor and what he or she says about desserts, and then answer, "Yes, (s)he gets banana splits quite often; (s)he must like banana splits."

Daryl Bem (1972) extends attribution theory (Chapter 2) to our perceptions of ourselves. Bem would argue that when someone asks you whether you like banana splits, you really do not know until you observe or recollect your own behavior and then say, in effect, "That's right. I do always seem to order banana splits, so I guess I must like them." Hence, according to Bem, we infer our own attitudes from scrutinizing situations that provide us with external clues to our internal states. We reach our conclusions on the basis of observations of our own overt behavior and the contexts in which it occurs.

Steven A. Kopel and Hal S. Arkowitz (1974) have provided experimental confirmation of Bem's self-perception theory. They administered three series of electric shocks to forty-five subjects. In the first series, the pretest, the researchers measured the pain and tolerance thresholds of each subject. For the second series of shocks, subjects were randomly assigned to one of three groups: in the first group, subjects were asked to role-play upset behaviors while receiving shocks; in the second, subjects were asked to role-play calm behaviors while receiving shocks; in the third (the control group), subjects were given no role-playing instructions regarding their behavior while receiving shocks. For the third and final series of shocks, none of the forty-five subjects received any role-playing instructions.

The researchers found that, relative to those in the control group, subjects who role-played calm behaviors during the second series of shocks responded less fearfully (they showed increased pain-tolerance thresholds between the first and third series); those who role-played upset behaviors responded more fearfully (they showed decreased pain-tolerance thresholds between the first and third series). Yet the pulse rates of the subjects, which were monitored during the series, were not affected by the role-playing manipulation. These findings suggest that the subjects inferred the painfulness of the shock from what they had said and done during role-playing, and not from their internal state.

Self-knowledge

We have seen that one way we come to know ourselves is through the inferences we make about ourselves—inferences that are based on our words and deeds. We also derive notions of what we are really like from self-knowledge regarding our covert thoughts and feelings. These subjective experiences are inherently private and become available to others only indirectly when we tell them what is going on "inside" us. Indeed, we believe that our private thoughts and feelings are more revealing and representative of us than are samples of our public behavior. Thus one study found that most of us think that other people can learn more about our essential nature through access to our private thoughts and feelings for a single day than they could by observing our overt behavior for several months (Andersen and Ross, 1984). This finding is hardly surprising. For one thing, we experience our thoughts and feelings as spontaneous expressions of the self, and typically beyond our will and ability to control. For another, we experience our thoughts and feelings as taking place "within us" and as mediating our "external" words and deeds. The existence of these private, inner experiences, and their seeming coherence and continuity, prompts us to conclude that there is an enduring self (Greenwald, 1980, 1982).

While people also infer their inner states from behavioral cues, under some circumstances their private thoughts and feelings overwhelm the external evidence. For instance, some individuals appear socially adept, yet they continue to perceive themselves as "socially incompetent" or "privately shy" (Zimbardo, 1977; Bandura, 1981). (See boxed insert on shyness, pp. 158–159.) In such cases, people's self-attributions contradict the evidence supplied by their behavior, presumably because their inner thoughts and feelings tell them otherwise. Thus our self-inferences derive from covert as well as from overt information.

It seems that in many cases information regarding people's inner states is more informative than information about their actual behavior. Research suggests that access to a person's thoughts and feelings in a particular situation tells us more about the individual's characteristics and attributes than does parallel information about his or her actions in the situation (Andersen, 1984). And when strangers gain information regarding someone's thoughts and feelings, they come to assess the person more the way the person assesses himself or herself. Thus, in our culture, when people wish to increase the intimacy of an encounter or deepen mutual understanding, they frequently reveal to another person certain of their inner thoughts and feelings.

SELF-CONCEPTIONS

> *Men can starve from a lack of self-realization as much as they can from a lack of bread.*
>
> —Richard Wright, *Native Son*, 1940

As we recurrently experience the world around us and people's appraisals of us, we evolve assessments of ourselves. We conceive of ourselves as dull or bright;

SHYNESS

Shyness is a kink in the soul, a special category, a dimension that opens out into solitude. Moreover, it is an inherent suffering, as if we had two epidermises and the one underneath rebelled and shrank back from life.

—Pablo Neruda

On the basis of surveys in eight countries involving over 6,000 people, Philip G. Zimbardo (1978) finds that an average of 80 percent of all individuals report that they are currently shy or had been shy at some period in their lives. Even some celebrities define themselves as shy, including Barbara Walters, England's Prince Charles, Terry Bradshaw, Fred Lynn, Catherine Deneuve, Carol Burnett, and Warren Beatty. Virtually all of us feel a little shy at one time or another, especially in face-to-face interaction with strangers and particularly with those of the opposite sex. Often we want to impress others, but the fear of failing places pressure on us.

Shyness involves a shrinking from human contact, an alienating force that often derives from a feeling of inferiority and a fear of taking risks. Zimbardo believes that shyness arises out of a person's social experiences. Indeed, about a quarter of all people who are shy as adults say that they were not shy as children. In contrast, a fair proportion of people who were shy as children seem to outgrow shyness as they enter adulthood. We should not conclude, however, that shyness is the reverse of sociability. Some shy people are introverts. But a goodly number are sociable; they wish to affiliate with others and they prefer being with others to remaining alone. Research reveals that shyness and sociability are separate personality factors (Cheek and Buss, 1981).

Zimbardo finds that shyness shortchanges people because it leads them to avoid other people and consequently cuts them off from the flow of life. It restricts freedom by creating a barrier for people in

personable or grouchy; responsible or irresponsible; lovable or unlovable; diligent or lazy; beautiful or ugly; logical or illogical; moral or immoral; and so on. In considering the crystallization of our identities, we find it useful to distinguish between self-images and self-conceptions (Turner, 1968b; Swann and Hill, 1982). A **self-image** is a mental picture or concept one has of oneself that is relatively temporary, subject to change from one social situation to another. One's **self-conception** is the more overriding view of oneself, a sense of self through time— "the real me," or "I myself as I really am." Neither self-images nor self-conceptions are necessarily sharp and clear, precisely formulated. Both, to one degree or another, tend to be somewhat vague. Nor is a self-conception simply a moving average or summation of our self-images. It tends to have a more independent and stable quality. At best the succession of self-images serves to *edit* rather than supplant our self-conceptions (Turner, 1968b). Accordingly, it is not surprising

achieving happiness and fulfilling their potential. Shy people are big losers—in school, in business, in love, in any arena where people meet their needs in the course of interaction with others. They are concerned with being negatively evaluated; they fear that if others knew them as they really are—their private selves—that their private selves would be found wanting and unacceptable. In one respect, the shy are too self-aware, too preoccupied with the adequacy of their own behavior. This diminishes their spontaneity—their ability to "let go"—and they fail to immerse themselves fully in the currents of ongoing social interaction. In fact, some individuals are so shy that they are reluctant even to apply for welfare, pick up unemployment checks, use clinic services, or check a book out of a library if they have to talk with somebody.

Zimbardo finds that shyness is often associated with low self-esteem, a lack of confidence in oneself and in one's relationships with others. If the problem is severe, he recommends that the individual receive professional assistance. In his experimental shyness clinic at Stanford University, Zimbardo and his associates try to teach shy individuals sets of skills by which they can successfully relate to other people. They help the shy learn such things as how to give and receive compliments and how to start, continue, and terminate a conversation. They emphasize improving body language, particularly making eye contact, smiling, being attentive, leaning forward, nodding, making sounds and gestures of approval, and so on. Since shy people often experience anxiety in new situations—palpitations, tremors, blushing, butterflies in the stomach, constricted breathing, and the like—they are taught techniques to manage anxiety, to relax, and mentally to rehearse appropriate (and rewarded) behavior. Some therapists also employ assertiveness training in role-playing contexts. Shy people act out situations that produce butterflies in the stomach—returning a defective item to a store, asking an employer for a raise, or calling someone for a date (Dullea, 1981).

that life-span research reveals that self-conceptions and related psychological structures remain stable over periods as long as thirty-five years (Costa and McCrae, 1980; Block, 1981).

Cognitive Scripts About the Self

Social psychologists are coming to recognize that the term "self-conception" is one of the most useful and integrative notions yet developed for understanding behavior. Our self-conceptions involve *schemata*—mental scripts or frames containing organized bodies of information in memory—by which we select and process information about ourselves (Markus, 1977; Smith, 1984). (See Chapter 2 for a discussion of schemata.) Schemata involving the self are termed **self-schemata** (singular, **self-schema**). Self-schemata allow us to bring to each new

Crystallizing Identities
As people continually assess us,
so we come to assess ourselves.
We come to fashion self-conceptions that have a somewhat independent and stable quality to
them. (Patrick Reddy)

situation of social interaction the cognitive generalizations about the self that we have evolved from past experience. These self-conceptions reflect the consistencies that we have discovered about our own social behavior—the patterns we have repeatedly observed in the course of our social interaction with others. From these observations, we generate mental frameworks that allow us to make inferences about the happenings in our interpersonal relationships. For instance, we employ self-schemata as reference points or cognitive prototypes against which we interpret incoming information about other individuals (Lewicki, 1984). Thus the notions we have regarding our own attitudes and behavior also function as standards for appraising what others say and do.

Once established, our self-conceptions serve as selective mechanisms that influence the information we attend to, how we structure it, how much importance we attach to it, and what we subsequently do with the information. As we accumulate particular types of experience, our self-conceptions become increasingly resistant to inconsistent or contradictory information, although they never become entirely invulnerable to it. The reason is that we interpret experience through our self-concept filters; we selectively perceive information (tune out information and tune in information) on the basis of the conceptions we have previously fashioned about ourselves. This fact may account for the persistence of incorrect body images among people who have gained or lost many pounds. It also influences our adjustment to a serious loss. If being a mother is a central element in a woman's self-schema, then the death of her only child destroys the schema and necessitates its replacement by a new schema. But should the same woman have a weak self-schema as a daughter, she may recover quite readily from the death of her own mother (Sobel, 1981).

Research by Hazel Markus (1977) reveals that individuals who define themselves as "independent" are more likely than individuals who do not characterize themselves in this manner to select self-descriptive trait adjectives that reflect independence (for instance, "individualistic," "ambitious," "adventurous," "self-confident," "outspoken," and the like). Further, they require shorter times to process independence-type words for self-descriptive purposes than other types of words, are able to supply a larger number of specific examples of independent behavior, believe themselves more likely to engage in future independent-type behaviors, and are resistant to information that implies that they are dependent. Markus finds a parallel pattern of results with dependent stimuli for individuals who define themselves as "dependent." In sum, it makes a difference how we think about ourselves.

Sources of Our Self-conceptions

It is thus with most of us; we are what other people say we are. We know ourselves chiefly by hearsay.

—Eric Hoffer, *The Passionate State of Mind,* 1954

By acting on the external world and changing it, he [the individual] at the same time changes his own nature.

—Karl Marx, *Das Kapital,* 1867

Central to much early theory and research within social psychology was the following postulate: Our self-conceptions arise from social interaction with other people, and in turn, our self-conceptions guide and influence our subsequent behavior. The writings of social psychologists like Charles Horton Cooley and George Herbert Mead, and of neo-Freudian psychiatrists like Harry Stack Sullivan (1947, 1953), are based on the view that we discover ourselves in the actions of others toward us. For example, retrospectively, we may ask the question, "Who am I?" In practice, however, the answer comes before the question (Yinger, 1965). From the moment of birth on, each of us is told: "You are a girl (boy)." "You are my daughter (son)." "You are Catholic (Protestant, Jewish, Muslim)." "You are black (white, Chinese, Chicano)." "You are a good girl (boy) and a full-fledged member of this group [entitled to all the rewards confirming these words]." Or "You are a bad girl (boy) and unacceptable to our group [with the point driven home by significant others through the penalties that they administer]."

Psychologist Monte D. Smith and his associates (1978) investigated adult academic expectations of children and children's self-concepts. They found that parents and teachers expect children from higher socioeconomic backgrounds

Self-appraisals as Reflected Appraisals
We map our self-images through the feedback others provide us. They tell us who we are and what we are. And to maximize favorable and positive feedback—to inflate our sense of self-worth—we attempt to conform with others' definitions of us. The result is often rather stereotyped behavior. (Patrick Reddy)

to excel academically, relative to socioeconomically disadvantaged youngsters. When children from high socioeconomic class homes experience academic failure, the discrepancy between adult expectations and child performance is comparatively large. The discrepancy between expectancy and performance results in lowered self-concepts. In contrast, children with disadvantaged backgrounds do not experience lowered self-concepts as a result of academic failure, since the discrepancy between adult expectancy and child performance is comparatively small.

According to the symbolic interactionist school of thought, our self-appraisals are reflected appraisals. Consequently, we are said to hold the keys to one another's identities. If we are accepted, approved, and liked for what we are, we tend to acquire attitudes of self-acceptance and self-respect. If others belittle, blame, and reject us, we are likely to develop unfavorable attitudes toward ourselves. S. Frank Miyamoto and Sanford M. Dornsbusch (1956) found support for these propositions in a study done among members of ten groups—two fraternities, two sororities, and six sociology classes. Each subject rated himself or herself on a 5-point scale for each of four characteristics: intelligence, self-confidence, physical attractiveness, and likableness. In turn, the students rated every other member of the group in terms of the same attributes. The researchers found that those students accorded high esteem by others reflected higher self-esteem than those poorly regarded by others.

Enrico L. Quarantelli and Joseph Cooper (1966) looked further into the question of self-appraisals in a study of 594 freshmen and 432 sophomores in the dental school of a Midwestern university. The students were provided with a 10-

point scale representing an arbitrary distance between a dental student and a dentist:

```
            1   2   3   4   5   6   7   8   9   10
Dental student |   |   |   |   |   |   |   |   |   |   Dentist
```

They were then asked to indicate where they placed themselves on the scale at the present time; where they thought their parents, classmates, upperclassmates, and friends placed them; and where they thought the members of the dental faculty currently saw them. In addition, the faculty members rated the students in terms of where they thought the students stood in their dental careers.

Among the Quarantelli–Cooper findings were the following:

1. Our self-conceptions are more closely related to our *perceptions* of how others rate us than to how others *actually* rate us. Thus the dental students' self-conceptions were more closely related to their perceptions of how the faculty rated them than to how the faculty did in fact rate them.

2. Those of us who have a high self-evaluation perceive others as having a higher rating of us than do those of us with a low self-evaluation. Thus dental students who felt their classmates had a high estimation of them had a higher self-rating than did dental students who felt their classmates had a low estimation of them.

3. Those of us who have a high self-evaluation anticipate a higher future self-rating than do those of us whose current self-evaluation is low. Freshman dental students who at the time of the study had a high self-evaluation anticipated a higher self-rating as sophomores than did freshman dental students with a low self-evaluation at the time of the study.

4. Those of us who have a high self-evaluation perceive the generalized other as having a higher rating of us than do those of us with a low self-evaluation. Thus dental students who felt that, in combination, the faculty and their parents, classmates, upperclassmen, and friends (the generalized other) had a high estimate of them in fact had a higher self-rating than those dental students who felt that these people had a low estimation of them.

Overall, the study reveals that it is the perceived response rather than the actual response of others that is the more important in the formation of self-conceptions. Other research supports this conclusion (Shrauger and Schoeneman, 1979; Rosenberg, 1979; Schafer and Keith, 1985).

The mirror metaphor (self-appraisals are reflected appraisals) captures something essential about the formation of our self-conceptions, but not everything. Consider Daryl Bem's self-perception theory that was discussed earlier in the chapter. Bem (1972) says that individuals infer their attitudes and inner states from the observations they make of their own behavior and the contexts in which it occurs. But Richard B. Felson (1981) points out that self-perceptions of the sort described by Bem require that individuals already possess standards or

Reflected appraisals

Today I went over to the gym for freshman basketball practice after missing three days of practice because of a viral infection. For some reason the guys assumed that I had been moved up to the varsity team and that was why I hadn't been around. As a result the guys were somewhat in awe of me and were seeing good points in my game that the coach has yet to see. Anyway, their comments made me feel very good, and as practice wore on I played better than I have ever done before. This just goes to show how our self-conceptions are "reflected appraisals." We gain our self-images on the basis of the feedback others give us about ourselves. And how we feel about ourselves (our self-image) affects our behavior.

criteria for interpreting what they observe. In large measure, people acquire such standards or criteria from others in the course of socialization. In brief, self-perception frequently entails applying cultural standards and group norms to oneself.

By way of illustration, consider individuals who have homosexual inclinations but who hide their preferences from others. In so doing, they avoid negative feedback (reflected appraisals). Nonetheless, they derive from American culture definitions as to what constitutes homosexuality and highly value-laden judgments regarding homosexuality. Using these definitions, persons may acquire a homosexual identity and an unfavorable self-appraisal without receiving direct communications about their homosexual preferences from others. Self-attributions and self-appraisals regarding mental illness may at times develop in a like manner.

Any number of social psychologists direct our attention to another matter (Goffman, 1959; Shrauger and Schoeneman, 1979; Felson, 1980, 1985). Considerable deception characterizes social life. We seek to manage the impressions we provide others in the course of daily interaction (see Chapter 8). Moreover, people are reluctant to evaluate others openly in face-to-face encounters, particularly if the assessments are negative or if the other party is not known well. Indeed, to tell an employer, supervisor, or teacher how one truthfully feels is typically believed to entail considerable risk. And individuals usually provide a close associate with unfavorable evaluations only when these are directly solicited and when the friend has already made some negative self-appraisal. In part, these barriers to open communication account for the popularity of sensitivity training sessions, in which individuals may find out what others really think about them.

Another factor also affects the information we receive from others in evolving our self-appraisals. Researchers find that many of our self-conceptions are highly resistant to change under naturally occurring conditions (Shrauger and Shoeneman, 1979). And clinicians often complain that they have considerable difficulty changing their patients' self-conceptions, even after months or years of intensive therapy (Wylie, 1979). One reason that our self-conceptions are so stable derives from the way we process information that we receive from others about ourselves. For instance, we are more likely to attend to and remember feedback that confirms rather than disconfirms our self-conceptions (Swann and Read, 1981*a*). Moreover, we tend to minimize and ignore social feedback that runs counter to our self-conceptions (Swann and Ely, 1984). And finally, we often actively cultivate behaviors in others that substantiate our self-conceptions (Swann and Read, 1981*b*; Fazio, Effrein, and Falender, 1981). For example, a man who thinks of himself as an intimidating figure may validate this conception by inducing others to cower and grovel in his presence. And individuals who conceive of themselves as unlovable often sustain this conception by causing lovers to reject them. Complicating matters even more, not all others are "equally significant" to us (Gecas, 1982; Hoelter, 1984).

All this highlights the fact that we are not passive beings acted upon by others so that we merely mirror their conceptions of us. We are *active* agents who shape our own beings in the course of continual interactive dialogue with our entire environment (Wrong, 1961, 1976; Franks and Marolla, 1976; Gecas and Schwalbe, 1983). We derive a sense of self not only from the reflected appraisals of others but also from the feedback we gain regarding our power and competence as we adapt to and cope with the world about us. Through interaction with others and through the effects we produce on our material environment, we gain a sense of our adequacy, energy, skill, and industry. We come to know ourselves and evaluate ourselves on the basis of our actions and their consequences, and from our accomplishments and the products of our efforts. Thus we are hardly at the mercy of our surroundings and the assessments of others. Indeed, conflict and crisis compel us to change. We make our own history—we evolve or develop—as we confront and master the requirements of life. In this sense we forge our self-conceptions as we actively and relentlessly pursue our various ends (Riegel, 1975*a*, 1975*b*, 1976).

Self-esteem

> *A man cannot be comfortable without his own approval.*
>
> Mark Twain, *What Is Man?* 1906

Self-esteem refers to the personal judgment we make of our own worth (Coopersmith, 1967). Indeed, self-esteem is such an important aspect of our self-conception that some social psychologists often employ the terms synonymously. A series of studies by Kenneth J. Gergen, a social psychologist, and his colleagues provides us with insights regarding various social factors that impinge upon our self-esteem.

Others' Judgments of Us
Our self-esteem is anchored primarily in our ongoing social relationships (Faunce, 1984). As such it tends to reflect the views that others hold of us.

Gergen (1965, 1972) had college women rate themselves on a large number of items designed to measure self-esteem. Several weeks later they were interviewed by a trainee in a large interviewing project; the interviewer was actually a confederate of Gergen's. The young women were informed that the trainee's major task was to learn to be honest and spontaneous as she engaged in the interviewing task. In the course of the interview, the young women were questioned about the same self-esteem indicators that had been on the the test administered earlier. The interviewer showed subtle signs of agreement whenever a student rated herself positively: She nodded her head, smiled, and occasionally indicated her agreement with such statements as "Yes, I think so too." Conversely, the interviewer would disapprove of the student's negative self-evaluations: She would shake her head, frown, or indicate her disagreement verbally. It became clear to the subject that the trainee took a very positive view of her.

As a consequence of this procedure, the women's self-evaluations became progressively more positive. This increase in self-esteem was significantly greater than the minimal change in self-esteem that occurred in the members of a control group, which consisted of young women who were also interviewed but did not receive the personal reinforcement of positive self-images.

But were the students misleading the interviewer? Were they merely conforming to the expectation that they reflect more positive self-images while secretly experiencing no increase in self-esteem? As a check on their private self-evaluations, the women were asked to produce honest self-ratings in an additional test that was not to be seen by the trainee interviewer. Gergen found significant increases in the self-esteem of students who had received the positive feedback; no such increases were found for students in the control group. One young woman later told Gergen: "You know, it's very strange; I spent the rest of the day whistling and singing. Something about that interview really made me happy." All this suggests that the women's elevated sense of self-esteem was genuine. The study, however, does not tell us how lasting was the effect produced by the positive feedback.

Another's Social and Personal Characteristics

In a later experiment, Gergen and an associate, Barbara Wishnov (1965), found that the characteristics of one person are sufficient by themselves to influence the self-esteem of another person. Young college women were asked to write descriptions of themselves. About a month later they participated in an experiment in which they were told that the self-description of each woman had been exchanged with that of another coed, whose identity was unknown to her, and that what was being returned to her was her "partner's" self-description. In fact, however, what they were being given was an evaluation that the experimenters had prepared in advance.

One group of students found themselves reading the words of a braggart: This coed enjoyed her work, loved school, had had a marvelous childhood, had a superb dating life, was beautiful and intelligent, and saw herself as having no faults. The other group received the words of a student who might have been a dropout from psychotherapy: She was a whiner, unhappy, ugly, and not particularly bright; she had had a miserable childhood, hated school, and was intensely fearful about the future.

The experimenter then asked each of the college women to respond to this supposed partner's description as honestly as possible, the form of the self-evaluations being of the same variety that had been made a month earlier. Self-ratings became much more positive among those reading the egotist's statement; these women discovered positive qualities in themselves that they had not discussed in the earlier self-descriptions, and they left out negative ones that they had mentioned earlier. It was as if the students were saying, "You think you're so great; well, I'm pretty terrific too!" In contrast, those receiving the humble self-evaluation portrayed themselves as much more fault-ridden. They seemed to be saying, "I know what you mean; I've got problems too." Our self-esteem, then, tends to be influenced by the comparisons we make of ourselves with others.

The Social Setting

In still another experiment, this time involving fifty naval-officer trainees, Gergen (1971) and an associate, Margaret G. Taylor, showed how the setting in which we encounter others influences our self-esteem. The researchers placed the ROTC students in two-man work teams and gave them the task of maneuvering, under stressful conditions, a mock submarine out of danger. The task was presented to half the teams in language that emphasized productivity: The two men were to work together with great precision in processing an array of complex information. In contrast, the task was described to the other half of the teams in language that stressed solidarity: The two men were to get along with each other as well as possible, paying special attention to each other's opinions and feelings. The men were then asked to evaluate themselves in terms of a variety of self-esteem items, a test they had also completed a month earlier.

A comparison of the results of the earlier and later self-evaluations revealed that the men in the productivity setting had become more positive about themselves. They especially viewed themselves as significantly more logical, well-organized, and efficient than they had considered themselves a month earlier. The opposite was true of the earlier and later self-evaluations of the men in the setting where compatibility was at stake; these men had come to emphasize negative aspects of self. In an apparent attempt to make themselves seem more "human" and less defensive, these students deemphasized their virtues and were more willing to admit faults.

Self-conceptions and Behavior

We have noted that our self-conceptions are forged, directed, and shaped in the course of our social interaction with others and the world about us. In turn, our self-conceptions have an impact on our subsequent behavior. For example, consider the case of so-called born losers—people whose lives are stalked by failure and misfortune. Often they appear to be on the verge of success only to have adversity mysteriously strike, snatching triumph from their grasp. Psychiatrists and clinical psychologists have termed such people *masochists*—individuals who are bent on making themselves miserable and who set up situations so that they ultimately fail. Various psychologists have advanced the view that masochists are people who have somehow acquired a conception of themselves as failures and who then seek to be "true to self" by failing. They bring about failure in order to maintain a consistent conception of themselves and the world (Aronson and Carlsmith, 1962; Brockner, 1980). Self-defeating behaviors may also occur under other circumstances, a matter examined in the boxed insert on "choking" and self-handicapping behaviors (pp. 170–171).

Using as subjects a group of college women, Jeanne Marecek and David R. Mettee (1972) studied the relationship between low self-esteem and success. Employing psychological tests, the researchers identified those women who had low self-esteem scores and those with high self-esteem scores. They further established which individuals in both groups were certain and convinced or uncertain and unconvinced of the validity of their self-esteem appraisals. The subjects were then given the task of matching geometric figures on a display board. At the halfway point (after ten of the twenty trials), all subjects were led to believe that their performance to that point was highly successful. But half were told that their success was totally a matter of luck, while the other half were told that performance depended on skill. The subjects were then instructed to complete the trials.

Marecek and Mettee found that (1) all high self-esteem subjects showed improvement in the remaining trials; (2) low self-esteem subjects who had been uncertain of their low self-appraisal improved as much as did the high self-esteem subjects in the remaining ten trials; (3) low self-esteem subjects who had been certain of their low self-appraisal and who had been informed that their first-half success was due to *luck* improved more than any other group; and (4) low self-esteem subjects who had been certain of their low self-appraisal and who had been informed that their first-half success was due to *their own skill* failed to show any improvement.

The study reveals that not all low self-esteem people attempt to minimize self-produced success. Rather, it is only those who have a chronic, consistent low self-esteem conception who do so. Even these individuals, however, are capable of enthusiastically embracing a successful outcome *provided* they interpret the success as *not* self-produced. When, in contrast, chronic low self-esteem subjects view success as the product of their own efforts, they experience pressure to behave in a self-consistent manner: They fail. Such individuals, then, are locked by their self-conceptions into patterns of self-imposed failure.

A study by Robert H. Coombs (1969) similarly points to the important part self-conceptions play in fashioning behavior. In the study, 220 male and 220 female college students were paired by computer for a student-sponsored dance. Before the dance the students completed a questionnaire that provided information about the extent of their previous dating experience and their self-conceptions regarding their desirability as dates. This was followed up by another questionnaire completed shortly after the dance and by still another six months later. Both follow-up questionnaires contained questions on how much the participants would enjoy additional dates with their partners. The study revealed the following:

1. The more dates an individual had averaged per month before the dance, the more likely it was that he or she would favorably impress his or her computer-selected date.
2. Those most favorably evaluated by their dates were the ones most likely to think of themselves as successful dating prospects.
3. Overall, those most assured of their dating success engaged most often in subsequent dates with their computer partner.

This study, then, suggests that previous dating experience increases the probability of being positively evaluated by a dating partner; positive evaluations foster a positive view of self; and a positive self-concept leads to more participation in dating. The findings can be generalized in a more encompassing statement as follows: Previous experience in a specific social situation (a_1) increases the likelihood that an individual will make a positive impression upon others in similar situations (b_1); making such an impression (b_1) enhances a positive view of self (c_1); and a positive self-concept (c_1) gives an individual incentive to participate further in situations of the same sort (a_2):

$$a_1 \rightarrow b_1 \rightarrow c_1 \rightarrow a_2$$

We thus observe the cyclical nature of self-conceptions and our social behavior; they are linked in a relationship where each molds, guides, and influences the other in a reciprocal fashion.

SUMMARY

1. We experience ourselves as entities separated from others and having continuity through time.
2. Considerable controversy within the social sciences surrounds the usefulness of the concept of the self.
3. One way in which an individual experiences the self as an object is as the "bodily me," the material self.
4. We achieve a sense of selfhood when we act toward ourselves in much the same manner that we act toward other people.
5. Selfhood entails a communicative process; only through communication can one, figuratively, get outside oneself, take the positions of others, and gain a view of oneself as an object from these other standpoints.
6. We employ much the same kind of evidence and logic in forming conclusions about ourselves as we do in perceiving others.
7. Our self-conceptions involve mental "scripts," "frames," or "schemata" by which we select and process information about ourselves. We bring to each new situation of social interaction the cognitive generalizations about the

"CHOKING" AND SELF-HANDICAPPING BEHAVIORS

We are often motivated to make a positive impression on other people (Schlenker and Leary, 1982). In so doing, we lay claim to certain desired identities, for instance, the identity of a "bright student," an "accomplished lover," or an "athletic superstar." Although we may possess the necessary attributes or abilities, we may not reach our goal because we engage in self-defeating behaviors. One of these is **choking**—under pressure we fail to perform up to our level of skills or capabilities (Baumeister, 1984). For instance, we frequently become self-conscious when we are asked to provide excellent performances. Thus in athletic contests, we may attempt to endure the correctness of our execution—the coordination and precision of our muscle movements—by monitoring the process of our performance. But such monitoring disrupts the automatic or overlearned nature of execution. Ironically, the reliability and success of many types of performance are impaired when we attempt to control them. For example, if you attempt to ensure the accuracy of your finger movements while typing by conscious monitoring (perhaps motivated by the thought that you are running out of correction fluid), the effort is likely to backfire and multiply your mistakes.

Choking is not uncommon in competitive events. As we will see in Chapter 12, the home team tends to enjoy an advantage in athletic contests. Likewise, in championship games, such as baseball's World Series, the home field seems to afford an advantage in the early games. For one thing, the home team is familiar with the ballpark and its idiosyncrasies. However, in the last and deciding game, the home park is a decided disadvantage (Baumeister and Steinhilber, 1984). When a team has a chance to win the final, de-

self that we have evolved from past experience. Once established, our self-conceptions function as selective mechanisms that influence the information we attend to, how we structure the information, how much importance we attach to it, and what we subsequently do with it.

8. Central to much theory and research within social psychology is this postulate: our self-conceptions arise from social interaction with other people, and in turn, our self-conceptions guide and influence our subsequent behavior. According to this school of thought, our self-appraisals are reflected appraisals. While the mirror metaphor captures something essential about the formation of our self-conceptions, it does not capture everything. For instance, people acquire cultural standards from others in the course of socialization. In turn, they apply these standards to themselves without necessarily receiving direct communications from others about their behavior.

cisive contest and is competing at home, it tends to choke. In early games, the home team fields the ball flawlessly nearly twice as often as does the visiting team. But it is otherwise in the seventh and deciding game. A home crowd typically claps, shouts, and moans in response to the breaks and exploits of the home team, whereas the visitors' exploits are met with either relative silence or expressions of frustration. Such behavior may be a source of inspiration under normal circumstances; but when a championship is imminent, failing to win it before a supportive audience compounds the pressures and intensifies the players' self-consciousness. Similar patterns emerge in National Basketball Association championships. Judged by free throw performance, the home team performs more poorly in the final game than in earlier games.

Self-handicapping—any action that helps exempt us from personal responsibility for failure—may also be a response to self-presentation difficulties (Berglas and Jones, 1978). We may construct an impediment to our performance when we are motivated to make a positive impression on others but doubt our ability to do so. Should failure occur, we can attribute it to the impediment and thus discount our lack of ability as a possible cause. Alcoholism, test anxiety, hypochondriacal symptoms, learned helplessness, shyness, and low achievement motivation are among the phenomena that have been identified as self-handicapping mechanisms (Kolditz and Arkin, 1982; Greenberg, Pyszczynski, and Paisley, 1985; Snyder et al., 1985). They serve to protect a person's self-esteem by (1) fending off negative self-attributions, (2) avoiding a threatening evaluative situation, or (3) maintaining environmental conditions that maximize positive self-relevant feedback (Snyder and Smith, 1982). In sum, whereas choking seems to be associated with situations in which self-awareness impedes the spontaneity of performance, self-handicapping is a "damage-control" strategy employed to insulate the self-image from failure.

9. Others' judgments of us, the characteristics of our associates, and the social setting in which we are immersed all come to bear in the forging of self-esteem.
10. Our self-conceptions and our social behavior are linked in a cyclical relationship: Each molds, guides, and influences the other in a reciprocal fashion.

GLOSSARY

Choking ☐   Under pressure, we fail to perform up to our level of skills or capabilities.

Egocentric bias ☐   We overperceive ourselves as the victims or targets of events that, in reality, are not directed toward us.

Generalized other ☐ A synthesized overview of the cultural workings of our community; the attitude imputed to the entire group or society.

Identity ☐ Our sense of placement within the world and the meaning we attach to ourselves within the broader context of human life.

Looking-glass self ☐ Our perception of ourselves as determined by the way we imagine we appear to others.

Material self ☐ An individual's experience of the stream of sensations that arise within the organism as the "bodily me."

Self ☐ The individual as known to the individual in a socially determined frame of reference.

Self-awareness ☐ Attention focused inward upon the self.

Self-conception ☐ The overriding view one has of oneself; a sense of self through time—"the real me" or "I myself as I really am."

Self-esteem ☐ The personal judgment we make of our own worth.

Self-handicapping ☐ Any action that helps exempt us from personal responsibility for failure by constructing an impediment to our performance.

Self-image ☐ A mental picture or concept of oneself that is relatively temporary, subject to change from one social situation to another.

Self-indication ☐ The process in which we internally note things, assess them, give them meaning, and entertain various actions on the basis of the meaning.

Self-perception ☐ The processes by which we come to know and think about ourselves—the characteristics, qualities, and inner states that we attribute to ourselves.

Self-schemata (singular, **self-schema**) ☐ Mental scripts or frames containing organized bodies of information in memory that we use in selecting and processing information about ourselves.

Significant other ☐ A particular person who has considerable influence on another individual's self-evaluation and acceptance of given social norms.

6 ATTITUDES AND ATTITUDE CHANGE

THE NATURE OF ATTITUDES
  The Components of Attitudes
  The Functions of Attitudes
  The Relationship Between
      Attitudes and Behavior
THE ORGANIZATION OF
      ATTITUDES
  Balance Theory

Congruity Theory
Cognitive Dissonance Theory
PERSUASION AND ATTITUDE
      CHANGE
  The Communicator
  The Message
  The Target

For the most part we do not view the world around us in neutral terms. People, events, and situations have consequences for us. Some of these consequences are positive while others are negative. It is hardly surprising, therefore, that we should evolve certain regularities in our feelings, thoughts, and inclinations to act toward various aspects of our environment. And indeed we do. We term such regularities attitudes.

THE NATURE OF ATTITUDES

So many men, so many opinions.

—Terence, *Phormio*, 160 B.C.

An **attitude** is a learned and relatively enduring tendency or predisposition to evaluate a person, event, or situation in a certain way and to act in accordance

173

with that evaluation. It constitutes, then, a social orientation—an underlying inclination to respond to something either favorably or unfavorably. As such, an attitude is a state of mind. Consequently, if we wish to influence other people's behavior, one way to go about it is to influence their state of mind. We may seek to win their support for programs of social change, to persuade them to favor the political candidates of our choice, to prefer our taste in television programs, to stop polluting the water, to quit smoking, or to donate money to our favorite cause. And others likewise attempt to persuade us to adopt their views. Given the importance of some of these matters, it is hardly surprising that the process by which people go about forming, maintaining, and changing attitudes has attracted considerable research interest. Social scientists have devised a number of sophisticated techniques for measuring attitudes (see boxed insert, pp. 176–177).

The Components of Attitudes

Social psychologists distinguish three components of an attitude—the cognitive, the affective, and the conative (Breckler, 1984). The **cognitive component** is the way we perceive an object, event, or situation—our thoughts, beliefs, and ideas about something. In its simplest form, the cognitive element is a category that we employ in thinking. Thus the category *car* includes station wagons, convertibles, Jaguars, Hondas, Cadillacs, and so on. Statements of the form "cars are this or that" and "cars have this or that" express ideas that are a part of this component (Triandis, 1971).

When a human being is the object of the attitude, the cognitive component is frequently a stereotype—the mental picture we have of a particular people. Walter Lippmann, to whom we owe the term "stereotype," observed that since the world is filled with "so much subtlety, so much variety, so many permutations and combinations . . . we have to construct it on a simpler model before we can manage with it" (Lippmann, 1922: 16). In brief, we find it virtually impossible to weigh every reaction of every person we encounter, minute by minute, in terms of its particular, individual meaning. Rather, we type individuals and groups in snap-judgment style: the "fighting Irish," the "inscrutable Orientals," the "stolid Swedes," the "grasping Jews," and the "emotional Italians." Although stereotypes are convenient, they lack the important virtue of accuracy. They are the unscientific and hence unreliable generalizations that we make about people either as individuals or as groups.

The **affective component** of an attitude consists of the feelings or emotions—the gut reactions—that the object, event, or situation, or its symbolic representation, evokes within an individual. Fear, sympathy, pity, hate, anger, envy, love, and contempt are among the emotions that may be excited by a given individual or group. The idea of using the same washroom as someone of another race, of drinking from glasses handled by, or of shaking hands with, a black, Jew, white, or Chinese produces disgust or discomfort in some individuals. The prospect of having blacks move into an all-white neighborhood may arouse fear and anxiety among some whites. The social standing of Jewish businessmen or doctors may elicit envy among some Gentiles. Although the emotional level is distinct from the cognitive, the two may appear together.

The **conative component** (also known as the **behavioral component**) of an attitude is the tendency or disposition to act in certain ways with reference to some object, event, or situation. The emphasis is on the *tendency* to act, not on the action itself. Some people may favor barring given groups from their social clubs, athletic associations, neighborhoods, and business and professional organizations—that is, they may be disposed toward discriminatory behavior. But as we shall shortly see, simply because people would like to act in certain ways does not necessarily mean that they do in fact act in these ways; they may fail to translate their inclinations into overt action. For example, some prejudiced individuals, recognizing the legal penalties attached to discrimination, may not in fact discriminate.

The Functions of Attitudes

All human beings harbor a wide variety of needs. Some needs are primarily biological (such as hunger, thirst, and the needs for sex and sleep); others are social (the needs for status, recognition, privilege, power).

Daniel Katz (1960) has advanced a **functionalist theory of attitudes** that is premised upon this fact. He takes the view that our attitudes are determined by the functions they serve for us. In brief, people hold given attitudes because these attitudes help them achieve their basic goals. Katz distinguishes four types of psychological functions that attitudes meet.

The Adjustment Function

Human beings typically seek to maximize rewards and minimize penalties. According to Katz, people develop attitudes that aid them in accomplishing this goal. We tend to favor a political party or candidate that will advance our economic lot—if we are in business, one that will hold the line on or lower corporate taxes; if we are unemployed, one that will increase unemployment and social welfare benefits. And we are likely to seek as a mate someone who provides us with a variety of rewards—a sense of self-worth, recognition, security, and so on—while avoiding someone who produces the opposite effect. Likewise, we are more likely to change our attitudes if doing so allows us to fulfill our goals or helps us avoid undesirable consequences (Smith, 1982).

The Ego-Defense Function

Some attitudes serve to protect us from acknowledging basic truths about ourselves or the harsh realities of life. They serve as defense mechanisms, shielding us from inner pain. *Projection* is such a device: We attribute to others traits that we find unacceptable in ourselves, and in so doing, we dissociate ourselves from the traits. To the alcoholic it may be the other fellow who overindulges; to the failing student it may be the teacher who is incompetent; to the hostile and aggressive child it may be the other child who started the fight.

MEASUREMENT OF ATTITUDES

Social scientists have developed a variety of devices for measuring attitudes. Here we shall briefly consider a number of these scaling measures. Our treatment is at best suggestive, since a thorough discussion is beyond the scope of this text.

THURSTONE SCALES

Louis Thurstone developed what is known as an *equal-appearing intervals* method. He would assemble a fairly large number of clearly formulated statements on an issue, such as attitude toward religion. Next he would have people judge the statements, not in terms of their own attitudes, but with respect to the extent to which the statements were favorable or unfavorable toward a given object—for instance, church. The statements were assigned numbers on a scale that usually ranged from 1 to 11, with 1 being extremely favorable and 11 being extremely unfavorable. Thurstone then selected for his *actual* questionnaire—the questionnaire to be employed in questioning subjects to determine their attitudes—the statements upon which the judges were in close agreement as to their degree of favorability or unfavorability.

The questionnaire would then be administered to a second group of people, the subjects of the study. Each subject would check the statements with which he or she agreed. For instance, the following might be included in an inventory of forty-five or so statements:

____ I believe that membership in a good church increases one's self-respect and usefulness.

____ I think the church is after money all the time, and I am tired of hearing about it.

____ I don't believe church-going will do anyone any harm.

In the above items, as rated by the initial group of judges on an 11-point scale, the first statement has a scale value of 2.7 (favorable); the second, 9.0 (unfavorable); the third, 5.3 (neutral). When the actual subjects of the study would later complete the questionnaire containing these statements, they would receive the scale value score for those questions with which they agreed (if they disagreed with the statement, they were instructed to leave it unmarked). The scale value scores of all the items checked by a subject could then be totaled, giving each subject a summated score.

LIKERT SCALES

Rensis Likert developed an attitude scale referred to as the *technique of summated ratings.* As with the Thurstone technique, a series of statements expressive of a wide range of attitudes, from extremely favorable to extremely unfavorable on a particular question, are compiled and carefully edited. For each statement, the subject checks or underlines one of five responses, such as *strongly approve, approve, undecided, disapprove, strongly disapprove.* For instance:

I believe that membership in a good church increases one's self-respect and usefulness.
definitely agree (5) agree (4) undecided (3) disagree (2) definitely disagree (1)

I think the church is after money all the time, and I am tired of hearing about it. definitely agree (1) agree (2) undecided (3) disagree (4) definitely disagree (5)

A total score for each subject is obtained by totaling the value of each item that is checked. The weights of 1, 2, 3, 4, 5, or 5, 4, 3, 2, 1 denote the degree to which the response is favorable or unfavorable. Note that on this scale the lowest value is assigned to an unfavorable response.

GUTTMAN SCALES

Louis Guttman developed a method of attitude measurement termed *scalogram analysis*. Knowing a person's score on a Guttman questionnaire enables us to tell, without having to consult the questionnaire itself, exactly which items he or she endorsed. In its simplest terms, the rationale of a Guttman scale is this: If an attitude (for instance, that toward the United Nations) falls along a continuum or gradient from favorable to unfavorable, then it should be possible to devise items for a questionnaire that tap the sentiment in a step-by-step fashion. As a consequence, the items on the scale have a cumulative relationship. An individual necessarily endorses *all* the items below the highest one he or she checks and *none* above it. Accordingly, if we know the *number* of items checked by the individual, we automatically know *which* items he or she checked.

By way of illustration, consider the following five items which are arranged in order from the least difficult to the most difficult to accept:

Issue: Women's Rights in Employment

1. Generally speaking, women should be able to secure any job for which they are qualified.
2. Employers should not discriminate against women in favor of men.
3. The state should actively support the idea of equal job rights for women.
4. There should be local review boards that pass on cases of extreme discrimination against women in employment.
5. The federal government should pass and enforce legislation guaranteeing equal job rights for women.

Thus if a person agrees with the third statement above, in most cases he or she would also agree with the first two statements.

SEMANTIC DIFFERENTIAL SCALES

Charles E. Osgood and his associates (1975) devised the *semantic differential* (see Chapter 3) to measure the connotative meaning of a concept (a person, a product, a group of people, a song, a political party, a candidate, or anything else). The subject is asked to rate the concept on a series of 7-point bipolar scales, as in the following format for a political candidate (in which the subject is asked to check the appropriate blank on the continuum):

Candidate Mary M. Doe

Weak	_ _ _ _ _ _ _	Strong
Cautious	_ _ _ _ _ _ _	Rash
Bad	_ _ _ _ _ _ _	Good
Kind	_ _ _ _ _ _ _	Cruel
Honest	_ _ _ _ _ _ _	Dishonest

The scale provides a method of measuring the similarities or differences among individuals in their concepts of a given object.

3

The Value-Expressive Function

While ego-defensive attitudes prevent us from revealing unpleasant realities to ourselves, other attitudes help give *positive* expression to our central values and to the type of person we imagine ourselves to be. Such attitudes reinforce a sense of self-realization and self-expression. We may have a self-image of ourselves as an "enlightened conservative" or a "militant radical" and therefore cultivate attitudes that we believe indicate such a core value; or we may see ourselves as a "swinger" or "someone really with it" and hence cultivate attitudes that reinforce this perspective.

4

The Knowledge Function

In life we seek some degree of order, clarity, and stability in our personal frame of reference; we search for meaning in and understanding of the events that impinge upon us. Attitudes help supply us with standards of evaluation. It was noted earlier in this chapter that stereotypes provide us with order and clarity with respect to the great and bewildering complexities of life that are due to human differences.

Katz's functionalist theory also helps to explain attitude change:

> The most general statement that can be made about the conditions conducive to attitude change is that the expression of the old attitude or its anticipated expression no longer gives satisfaction to its related need state. In other words, it no longer serves its function and the individual feels blocked or frustrated. Modifying an old attitude or replacing it with a new one is a process of learning, and learning always starts with a problem, or being thwarted in coping with a situation. (1960: 177)

A case in point is an adjustment need. A Honda owner who undergoes a change to a higher social status may also undergo a change of attitude toward his old car. He may decide that he now wants a Mercedes, because he believes a Mercedes to be more in keeping with his new social status. Thus attitude change is achieved not so much by changing a person's information about or perception of an object, but rather by changing the person's underlying motivational and personality needs.

The Relationship Between Attitudes and Behavior

Social psychologist Gordon W. Allport once observed that the concept of attitudes "is probably the most distinctive and indispensable concept in contemporary American social psychology" (1968: 59). The reason for this is not difficult to discern. Many investigators have assumed that attitudes occupy a crucial position in our mental make-up and as a result have consequences for the way we act (Cohen, 1964; Abelson, 1972; McGuire, 1976). Viewed from this perspective, attitudes serve as powerful energizers and directors of our behavior—they *ready* us for certain kinds of action. Hence, to understand our attitudes is to understand our behavior. Indeed, the assumption is frequently made that our attitudes serve as rather accurate predictors of our actions (Kahle and Berman, 1979).

*A*ttitudes and behavior

> *I have always been a strong advocate of a woman's legal right to have an abortion. In fact, in high school I had selected this topic for my "big" speech for my communications class. I never doubted for a moment that if necessary I would have recourse to abortion. Well, my period has been over two weeks late and I have been pretty scared. I went over to the health clinic this morning and had a pregnancy test done. They said I could not get the results until later today. So I went back to my room and called my boyfriend. He told me we should get married. But my roommates tell me I should get an abortion and finish school. Yet the fact of the matter is, I just can't "destroy" my own child. An abortion is just not for me. So I have decided to get married. This just goes to show the complexity of the relationship between attitudes and behavior. I never doubted for a minute what course of action I would take were I to become premaritally pregnant. I would opt for an abortion. But con-fronted with the actual situation, I find that I will have the baby. P.S. Written later. The crisis is past. The health service just called and told me the test came out negative.*

To a considerable extent, however, this basic assumption has not been borne out by observation. In fact, many studies have revealed a lack of correspondence or, at best, a low correspondence between verbally expressed attitudes and overt behavior (Wicker, 1969).

The findings of a classic study by Richard T. LaPiere (1934) are frequently cited as providing a striking example of such a discrepancy. LaPiere traveled throughout the United States—covering some 10,000 miles altogether—with a Chinese couple. He kept a list of hotels, auto camps, tourist homes, and restaurants where they were served and took notes on how they were treated. Only once were they denied service, and LaPiere judged that their treatment was above average in nearly half of the restaurants they visited. Several months later, he mailed questionnaires to the proprietors of these various establishments asking if members of the Chinese race would be accepted as guests. Approximately 92 percent indicated they would *not* accept Chinese, which was *clearly in contradiction to their actual behavior.*

Critics have faulted LaPiere's study because his presence with the Chinese couple undoubtedly had a biasing effect (Linn, 1965). Also, it is quite probable that, whereas the Chinese couple dealt with waitresses and desk clerks, the questionnaires were completed by proprietors. Since the time of LaPiere's study, however, a large number of additional studies have also failed to find a consistent relationship between people's attitudes and their behavior.

In one study undertaken in the period immediately prior to the civil rights movement, G. Saenger and E. Gilbert (1950) compared the attitudes of white customers buying from black clerks with the attitudes of white customers buying from white clerks in a large New York department store. Customers were followed out of the store, where they were then interviewed. In both groups 38 percent either disapproved of black clerks or wanted them excluded from some of the departments in the store (for example, from the food department). Despite this fact, a number of women who had insisted a short time previously that they would not buy from blacks later returned to the store and were observed buying from black clerks. Thus a considerable gap existed between what people said and what they did.

Various researchers (Rokeach, 1968, 1972; Wicker, 1971; Warner and de Fleur, 1969) have attempted to resolve these matters by suggesting that behavior is a function of at least two attitudes—an attitude toward the *object* and an attitude toward the *situation*. Indeed, multiple, diverse, and even contradictory attitudes may be activated in given situations.

Saenger and Gilbert, for instance, suggest a number of *situational* factors that might have accounted for the discrepancy between what white people in the study of department-store shoppers said about black clerks and the way they acted toward them. First, prejudiced individuals were caught in a conflict between two contradictory motivations: their prejudice, on the one hand, and their desire to shop where they found it most comfortable and convenient, on the other. They tended to resolve their dilemma by acting contrary to their prejudice and completing their shopping as quickly as possible. Second, prejudiced individuals were caught in still another conflict: whether to follow the dictates of prejudice or to act in accordance with America's democratic ideals. Third, people prefer to conform with prevailing public opinion; the fact that blacks were serving as clerks tended to suggest to many whites that the public approved of their presence (and that, by the same token, the public would disapprove of racist acts). Thus because of the intervention of situational factors, there is no simple way in which the behavior of one person toward another can be accurately predicted solely on the basis of knowledge of that person's attitude toward the other (see Figure 6.1).

Other factors besides the situational interfere with prediction of behavior on the basis of attitudes alone. For example, blacks differ from each other in such social properties as age, education, occupation, sex, and marital status; and attitudes toward these properties affect white behavioral interaction with blacks (Liska, 1974). And attitudes vary not only in their direction—that is, in being either positive or negative—but also in extremity (degree of favorableness and unfavorableness), intensity (strength of feeling), and the extent of the person's ego involvement with the attitudes (Petersen and Dutton, 1975). Further, attitudes that we form on the basis of our own direct experience predict our actions better than those attitudes we form indirectly through hearsay (Fazio and Zanna, 1978; Zanna, Olson, and Fazio, 1980).

As pointed out earlier in the chapter, attitudes typically consist of three components: the cognitive, the affective, and the conative. Each of these components has a somewhat different effect on behavior. Take contraception, or more particularly, the use of oral contraceptives, an IUD, a diaphragm, or a condom. Conation is a better predictor of contraceptive behaviors than is affect, which in turn is a better predictor than cognition (Davidson and Morrison, 1983).

Situational Factors

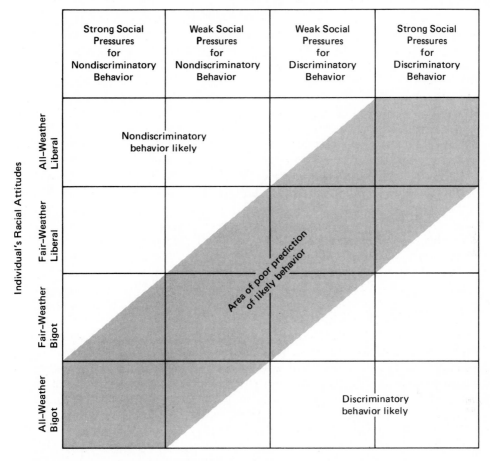

FIGURE 6.1 Racial Attitudes, Situational Factors, and Overt Action
Situational factors are assumed to account at least in part for divergence between
expressed racial attitudes and actual behavior.
(SOURCE: Adapted from L. G. Warner and M. L. de Fleur, "Attitude As an Interactional Concept," *American Sociological Review*, Vol. 34 [1969], p. 168.)

Icek Ajzen and Martin Fishbein (1973, 1977, 1980) have proposed a further
refinement for conceptualizing the relationship between attitudes and behavior.
They say that our attitude toward an object influences our *overall* pattern of
responses to the object. However, our attitude does not predict any *specific*
action toward that object. Ajzen and Fishbein concern themselves with the
behavioral *intentions* underlying our actions. They view our intentions as shaped
by three factors: (1) our attitude toward performing the act in question, (2) the
beliefs we hold about the likelihood that others expect us to perform the particular act, and (3) our motivation to comply with these beliefs.

Mark Snyder and Deborah Kendzierski (1982) direct our attention to still another matter. Before attitudes can be employed as guides to action, they must first be activated. More specifically, certain attitudes must be defined as relevant to the action choices that are being confronted. In other words, people need to link mentally the elements in the situation in which they find themselves with particular attitudes before they can bring these attitudes into play in guiding their actions. For instance, they may have positive attitudes toward affirmative-action programs for minorities. Yet it may not occur to them that the underrepresentation of minorities in their school or profession calls for the implementation of affirmative-action policies in these areas. They fail to see the relevance of the attitudes for the situation at hand. Consequently, believing does not guarantee doing.

Social psychologists, then, are coming to see the relationship between attitudes and behavior in increasingly complex terms—as involving multiple factors and mediating variables. They no longer ask *whether* people's attitudes can be used to predict their overt actions, but *when*. In any event, attitudes offer a convenient starting point for examining people's behavior as they enter situations and begin to construct their actions.

THE ORGANIZATION OF ATTITUDES

Underlying much social psychological theory and research is the notion of **attitude consistency**—the idea that people tend to organize their attitudes in a harmonious manner so that their attitudes are not in conflict. Thus civil rights activists do not ordinarily contribute to the Ku Klux Klan; Christian Scientists do not usually enroll in medical schools; and liberal and radical reformers seldom vote for conservative Republican candidates. The concept of attitude consistency presumes and underscores human *rationality*. It assumes that people experience inconsistency as a noxious state that they are impelled to eliminate or reduce (Zajonc, 1960).

The basic prediction to be derived from the principle of attitude consistency is that people typically seek to reconcile their conflicting attitudes—that the direction of attitude change will be from a state of inconsistency toward a state of consistency. Assume, by way of example, that you strongly support abortion laws, believing that a woman should have the right to terminate an unwanted pregnancy. Indeed, you feel so strongly about the matter that you have recently begun to campaign for pro-choice political candidates and to raise funds to support a local abortion clinic. Also suppose that your best friend vigorously opposes abortion, believing it to be an act of murder. How can you have deep and abiding ties with a person whose opinions about abortion are so different from your own? You may conclude that you really do not feel so strongly about abortion legislation after all; or you may decide that you do not like your friend all that much; or you may attempt to delude yourself into thinking that your friend is not really opposed to abortion. In any event, the chances are that you will change an attitude so as to bring about consistency.

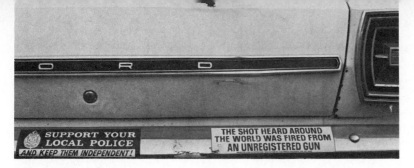

Attitude Congruity

Human beings tend to organize their attitudes in a harmonious manner. Politically conservative "law and order" advocates are commonly strong supporters of the local police *and* opponents of gun control legislation. The "shot heard around the world" was fired by a minuteman in Lexington, Massachusetts, in the first battle of the American Revolution. (Patrick Reddy)

There are several varieties of consistency theory, three of which we shall review here: balance theory, congruity theory, and cognitive dissonance theory.

Balance Theory Heider.

The initial formulation of the principle of attitude consistency came from Fritz Heider's **balance theory of attitudes** (1946, 1958). Heider was concerned with three elements in attitude change: (1) the person who is the focus of attention, labeled *P*; (2) some other person, labeled *O*; and (3) an impersonal entity—an object, idea, or event—labeled *X*. His primary interest was in discovering how relations among *P*, *O*, and *X* are organized by the person, *P*.

Heider's theory can be applied to the illustration involving abortion. In the illustration you would be *P*, your friend would be *O*, and support for abortion legislation would be *X*. The situation can be diagrammed according to Heider's version of balance as follows:

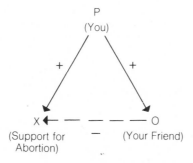

P
(You)

+   +

X ◄ — — — — — O
(Support for   —   (Your Friend)
Abortion)

Since you favor abortion, the link between you and abortion has a positive value, indicated by a plus sign. Further, since you and your friend have a close relation, the link between you and your friend has a positive value (+). Finally, since your friend opposes abortion, the link between your friend and abortion has a negative, or minus, value (−).

In mathematics, the multiplication of two positives and one negative produces a negative:

$$+ \times + \times - = -$$

Heider terms a minus state of affairs *imbalance*. This state is characterized by stress, discomfort, and unpleasantness. Hence you would be motivated to reduce the imbalance.

One way you might accomplish this would be to change *your* attitude toward abortion:

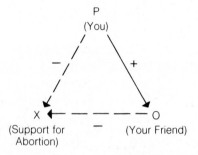

In this case you would multiply two negatives and one positive, which in mathematics gives you a plus sign:

$$+ \times - \times - = +$$

Since the sign is positive, balance has been restored.

Instead of changing your attitude toward abortion, you could reject your friend:

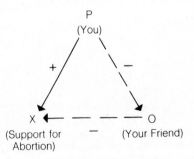

In this case you would also have restored balance:

$$- \times - \times + = +$$

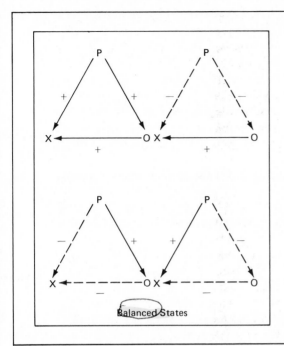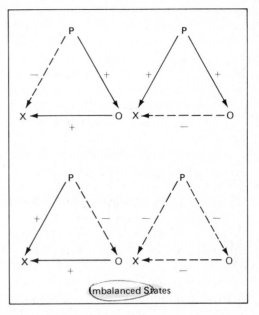

FIGURE 6.2 Heider's Balanced and Imbalanced State
A balanced state exists when there are no negatives or two negatives; an imbalanced state exists when there are one or three negatives. An imbalanced state is
one characterized by discomfort and unpleasantness. Accordingly, the individual is
under pressure to reduce imbalance, which means changing one's attitude toward
either the person or the impersonal entity (object, idea, or event). The arrows indicate the direction of the relationships.

Observe that a balanced state exists when there are either no negatives or two
negatives; an imbalanced state exists when there are one or three negatives (see
Figure 6.2).

Congruity Theory Osgood

The **congruity theory of attitudes,** which is an outgrowth of balance theory, was
advanced by Charles E. Osgood and his associates (Osgood and Tannenbaum,
1955). They recognize that we hold a great many attitudes, some of which are
consistent with one another, others inconsistent. Inconsistent attitudes generally
do not pose a problem for us *unless* they are somehow brought together within
the same context. Let us assume, for instance, that you hold a positive attitude
toward a given university professor and also toward the idea of pro-choice legislation. The two matters remain unrelated unless the professor expresses a

position on abortion legislation. Should the professor indicate support for pro-choice legislation, the two attitudes are congruent—that is, in harmony or agreement. If the professor opposes legislation permitting abortion, they are incongruent—out of harmony or agreement.

Thus far congruity theory remains undifferentiated from Heider's balance theory. Osgood and his associates proceed, however, to develop a scheme in which something is evaluated on a scale that runs from *good to bad,* or $+ 3$ to $- 3$. On the scale, $+ 3$ means that we have a maximum positive evaluation of something; $- 3$, a maximum negative evaluation of it; and 0, a neutral evaluation of it.

The recognition that we do not feel equally strong or intently about all matters has formed the basis for predictions by Osgood and his colleagues regarding the direction and degree of attitude change. They find that the stronger an attitude, the less likely it is to change when paired or linked with something of opposite strength.

Suppose we like a professor at the highest scale value of $+ 3$ and we learn that she or he opposes legislation permitting abortion, a position we dislike at the relatively moderate level of $- 1$. Osgood would predict that our attitude toward abortion would be more likely to "give" than our attitude toward the professor. Inasmuch as extreme attitudes are more resistant to change than neutral ones, there is a greater shift in the milder attitude.

Cognitive Dissonance Theory   *Festinger*

> *There are those who would misteach us that to stick in a rut is consistency—and a virtue, and that to climb out of the rut is inconsistency—and a vice.*
>
> —Mark Twain, *Consistency*

Few theories in social psychology have had the impact of Leon Festinger's theory of **cognitive dissonance.** Since its initial formulation in 1957, it has stimulated

Cognitive Dissonance Does this sign arouse cognitive dissonance for you? Explain your reaction to it. (Patrick Reddy)

Cognitive dissonance

Today I went to the auto show at the fair grounds arena. It cost $5 to get into the show. Once inside the show, the patrons could see all the cars with one exception. Curtained off from the other cars was John Lennon's limousine. You had to pay another 50 cents to see the car. Well, like the other suckers, I paid my 50 cents and saw the car. We were all raving about the car. Yet if I were to be honest, the car really was not all that special and a number of cars on the floor actually topped it. But we had paid 50 cents to see the car. To admit that we were fools for having paid an extra 50 cents would have been a difficult solution to our cognitive dissonance. So instead, having paid 50 cents to see the car, we brought our cognitions into balance by redefining the car as the greatest.

a vast amount of controversy, research, and theoretical development. And although severely challenged (Bem, 1967), the theory has overall shown considerable versatility, resilience, and predictive ability (Greenwald, 1975; Kiesler and Pallak, 1976; Fazio, Zanna, and Cooper, 1977, 1979; Croyle and Cooper, 1983). In his theory, Festinger replaces the concept of consistency or balance with that of *consonance,* and inconsistency or imbalance with that of *dissonance.* As viewed by Festinger, there is "pressure to produce consonant relations among cognitions and to avoid dissonance" (1957: 9). A *cognition* is any bit of knowledge ("it is below zero outside today"), belief ("below zero weather causes the flu"), or opinion ("I hate below zero weather") that people have about themselves, their behavior, or their environment.

Festinger developed his theory as a tool for interpreting some bizarre rumors that had appeared after an earthquake in India. Included among the rumors were the following: "There will be a severe cyclone in the next few days"; "There will be a severe earthquake on the lunar eclipse day"; "A flood is rushing toward the province." The rumors arose in an area where people had felt tremors but had not experienced personal injury or destruction of property. The prevalence of the rumors in this area seemed to contradict the prevalent psychological notion that people seek to avoid unpleasant things, such as anxiety and the prospect of pain. Interestingly enough, comparable data revealed that people in an actual disaster setting—an area of death and destruction—did not create rumors predicting further disaster.

The explanation arrived at by Festinger was that the rumors in the undamaged community had derived from cognitive dissonance. The people had a strong and persistent fear reaction to the tremors; yet in the absence of destruction, they could see nothing to fear. The *feeling* of fear in the absence of an adequate reason for fear was dissonant—nonfitting, or out of balance. The rumors of impending disaster provided explanations that were consonant with being afraid; the rumors functioned to justify fear and thus to reduce dissonance. The people, then,

WHEN PROPHECY FAILS

Some years ago the following story appeared in a midwestern newspaper.

Prophecy from Planet.
Clarion Call to City: Flee that Flood.
It'll Swamp Us on Dec. 21,
Outer Space Tells Suburbanite

Lake City will be destroyed by a flood from Great Lake just before dawn, December 21, according to a suburban housewife, Mrs. Marion Keech, of 847 West School Street. . . . It is the purport of many messages she has received by automatic writing, she says. . . . The messages, according to Mrs. Keech, are sent to her by superior beings from a planet called "Clarion." These beings have been visiting the earth, she says, in . . . flying saucers. . . . Mrs. Keech reports she was told the flood will spread to form an inland sea stretching from the Arctic Circle to the Gulf of Mexico. At the same time, she says, a cataclysm will submerge the West Coast from Seattle, Washington, to Chile in South America. (Festinger, Riecken, and Schachter, 1956: 30–31)

Mrs. Keech told her friends about the message and attracted a small following of believers. Leon Festinger, Henry W. Riecken, and Stanley Schachter (1956), three social psychologists, joined the movement for research purposes, concealing their identity as social scientists. Many of the members of the doomsday sect made considerable financial sacrifices in committing themselves to the group, resigning from jobs and giving away their belongings. Thus the way was prepared for a monumental instance of cognitive dissonance between prophecy and outcome.

Mrs. Keech set the hour (midnight, December 21) for the arrival of a visitor from outer space who would escort group members to safety by a flying saucer; at the appointed hour, however, nothing happened. When the visitor failed to arrive and the earth was not destroyed, the believers found themselves in intense confusion, apprehension, and despair. They checked and rechecked their watches in disbelief. Two facts were in dissonance—the members believed in their prophet and her prophecy had failed.

About five hours later, Mrs. Keech called the members together and announced that she had received a message: God had saved the world from destruction because of the faith spread throughout the world by the believers' actions. In so doing, Mrs. Keech offered a way by which cognitive dissonance could be reduced. Rather than reject their prophet, the members undertook to alter the other cognition—the doomsday belief. They reinterpreted the events and redirected their cause, finding a justification for their considerable commitment and investment. This illustrates how attitudes can be resistant to change even in the face of strong disconfirming evidence.

Dissonant Messages
The public is often exposed to clashing efforts to influence opinion and behavior. (Patrick Reddy)

undertook to reduce dissonance by *adding* new consonant elements—the fear-justifying rumors added new cognitions that were consistent with being afraid.

Still another method for reducing dissonance is to *change* certain cognitions. Here Festinger uses the example of people who believe that cigarette smoking causes cancer and who simultaneously know that they themselves smoke. Such people experience dissonance.

The most efficient way to reduce dissonance would be to stop smoking, but many people find this the most difficult solution. Instead, they undermine the other cognition—that cigarette smoking causes cancer. They may belittle the evidence that links smoking to cancer. Festinger (1957) cites a survey which found that 29 percent of nonsmokers, 20 percent of light smokers, but only 7 percent of heavy smokers believed that a relationship had been established between smoking and lung cancer. Or dissonance-experiencing smokers might switch to filter-tipped cigarettes, deluding themselves that the filter traps all the cancer-producing materials. Or they might convince themselves that cigarette smoking is worth the price—"I'd rather have a short but enjoyable life than a long, unenjoyable one." In taking any of these approaches, individuals seek to reduce dissonance by reducing the absurdity involved in making themselves cancer-prone (Aronson, 1969). The boxed insert provides another account of a change in a cognition when the world was not destroyed as the members of a doomsday cult believed it would be. Of interest, alcohol also reduces the unpleasant feelings associated with cognitive conflict, an effect that may reinforce alcohol consumption (Steele, Southwick, and Critchlow, 1981).

Cognitive dissonance explains in part why some patients realize benefits from psychotherapy. Social psychologists Danny Axsom and Joel Cooper (1985) find that the effort involved in therapy, plus the decision to undergo the effort, leads

REACTANCE

In the United States we place a premium on freedom. For many Americans, freedom is what their country is all about—"the land of the free and the home of the brave." Anything that jeopardizes freedom is seen as a menace to the American way of life—as "un-American." We like to believe that we control our own destinies. We experience anything that lessens our freedom to act as highly unpleasant. Indeed, compelling us to act against our wishes often boomerangs—we become "contrary" and attempt to reassert our freedom. If we feel *prevented* from doing something, commonly we will want to do it even more; if *forced* to do something, we will want to do it even less than we did before.

Jack W. Brehm (1966; Brehm and Brehm, 1981) undertakes to analyze these matters with his theory of **reactance.** Re-actance theory assumes that people view themselves as possessing a set of free behaviors (alternatives for action), any one of which they might engage in at any given time. When any of these behavioral freedoms is eliminated or threatened with elimination, psychological reactance is aroused. Reactance is a motivational state directed toward restoring or safeguarding the threatened freedom. The greater the importance of that freedom, the greater the magnitude of the aroused reactance. Many laboratory studies (Wicklund and Brehm, 1968; Sensenig and Brehm, 1968; Jones, 1970; Worchel and Brehm, 1970, 1971; Andreoli, Worchel, and Folger, 1974; Brehm and Brehm, 1981) have shown that when reactance is aroused, people display an increased appreciation of and desire for the threatened or eliminated freedom. Fur-

to positive outcomes through the reduction of cognitive dissonance. For instance, individuals in weight therapy programs apparently respond to the programs in part to justify the expenditure of effort. Not losing weight after undergoing highly effortful sessions would seem absurd. Losing weight justifies the effort.

Commitment and Volition

Research findings have led to various modifications of Festinger's original formulations. One of the most notable of these modifications has been proposed by Jack W. Brehm and A. R. Cohen (1962). They note that the theory holds only under certain conditions. Two key conditions are commitment and volition. Commitment is a state of being bound to or locked into a position or a course of action. It implies that people, by closing the door to alternative behaviors, have to "live with" their decisions. Accordingly, they need to reduce any dissonant elements deriving from their irreversible commitment.

Assume, by way of illustration, that a high school student praises Ivy League schools and ridicules the scholarly attributes of state universities. Later, he finds that no Ivy League school will accept him, and he then decides to enter a state

ther, reactance leads to an increased tendency to exercise the threatened freedom.

Michael B. Mazis (1975) has tested reactance theory in a marketplace situation where consumers' freedom of choice was restricted by government action. Mazis was able to study this kind of situation in Miami, Florida. As an antipollution measure, the county in which Miami is situated prohibited the sale, possession, or use of laundry detergents containing phosphates. Only a small number of popular brands were available in no-phosphate form. Thus shoppers found their choice of detergents drastically reduced.

Seven to nine weeks after the antiphosphate statute became effective, interviews were conducted among a sample of housewives in a middle-class Miami neighborhood and a similar neighborhood in Tampa, Florida (a city which had no such ordinance). As predicted by reactance theory, Miami housewives expressed more positive attitudes toward the eliminated alternative (phosphate detergents) than women did in Tampa. Further, the women who were forced to switch brands expressed less favorable attitudes about their no-phosphate detergents than the women who did not have to switch. (One leading manufacturer quickly began distributing no-phosphate versions of all its existing brands.) This finding is also in accordance with reactance theory, since the women who were compelled to switch brands should have experienced more psychological choice deprivation.

Thus reactance theory provides insight into violations of law and opposition to new laws restricting what people believe to be their freedom of action. A classic example is the dismal failure of Prohibition to prevent the manufacture, transportation, and sale of alcoholic beverages in the 1920s. Sometimes antipornography and antidrug laws have also had boomerang consequences.

university. By his actions, he has now *committed* himself to a state university. According to dissonance theory, it can be predicted that he will reduce dissonance by bringing his attitudes into line with his behavior: His attitude toward state universities will become more favorable, and possibly his attitude toward Ivy League schools will become more negative (Sherwood, Barron, and Fitch, 1969).

Volition refers to the degree of freedom individuals believe they possess in making a decision or choice. For individuals to experience dissonance, they must believe they acted *voluntarily* so that they feel responsible for the outcome of their decision (Goethals, Cooper, and Naficy, 1979). If, in contrast, they are *compelled* to act contrary to their beliefs, they can avoid dissonance by reasoning, "I was forced to do this; I really did not have any choice." If the student in the above illustration felt himself forced to attend the state university, he presumably would experience less dissonance—and thus less pressure to change his attitudes about state universities—than if he saw himself making a free choice (Sherwood, Barron, and Fitch, 1969). Closely associated with the processes of commitment and volition is that of reactance (see boxed insert).

Reward and Dissonance

Pursuing this matter further, dissonance theory makes a prediction that is surprising because it runs counter to common-sense thinking: The less the reward for engaging in behavior contrary to an attitude, the greater will be the resultant attitude change. And further, the less the coercion employed to force commitment, the greater the chance of attitude change. Presumably, people who by virtue of a large reward or coercion behave in a way that conflicts with their attitudes can deny responsibility for their behavior by saying, "How could I refuse such a large reward?" or "They made me do it!"

This is illustrated by a classic experiment of Festinger and J. Merrill Carlsmith (1959). They had subjects perform an exceedingly boring task for two hours. After the subjects had completed the task, most of them were instructed by the experimenter to tell the subjects who replaced them that the experiment had been fun and exciting; others, who served as a control group, were not asked to lie. Some of the subjects who lied were paid $1 for their compliance; others received $20. The subjects were next referred to the psychology department office, where they evaluated the experiment. The evaluations were actually part of the experiment, although the subjects were led to believe that the experiment was finished.

Among other questions, the students were asked the degree to which they had enjoyed the task they had performed. As can be seen in Figure 6.3, the subjects who were paid $1 rated the task more positively than those paid $20. These findings are in keeping with dissonance theory. The subjects who received only $1 found it necessary to rationalize their falsehood; for a trivial sum they had lied, and hence they undertook to resolve their dissonance by coming to believe that they really had liked the dull task. In contrast, the subjects who received the $20 experienced little dissonance and thus had little reason to alter their unfavorable attitudes toward the boring task.

Self-concept and Dissonance

Elliot Aronson (1968, 1969), among others (Bramel, 1968; Collins, 1969; Baumeister and Tice, 1984), has suggested a still further refinement in dissonance theory. He indicates that Festinger mislocated the source of dissonance. What is critical, he argues, and what Festinger overlooks, is the conflict between people's self-conceptions and their cognitions about a behavior that violates these self-conceptions. According to this view, dissonance does not arise between just any two cognitions; rather, it arises when one's behavior threatens to diminish the positive feelings one has about oneself.

Aronson argues that in the Festinger-Carlsmith experiment cited above, the dissonance did not occur, as Festinger and Carlsmith insisted, between the cognition "I believe the task is dull" and the cognition "I think the task is interesting." What instead was dissonant, according to Aronson, was the cognition "I am a good and decent human being" and the cognition "I have committed an indecent act; I have misled a person." Some research lends confirmation to this alternative view of dissonance (Nel, Helmreich, and Aronson, 1969; Steele and Liu, 1983).

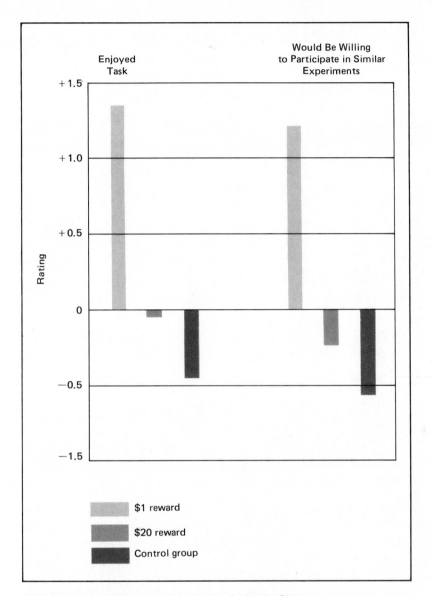

FIGURE 6.3 Amount of Reward and Attitude Change

The experiment by Festinger and Carlsmith bears out the theory that the less the reward for engaging in behavior contrary to an attitude, the greater will be the accompanying change in attitude; the greater the reward, the less the change in attitude.

(SOURCE: Adapted from L. Festinger and J. M. Carlsmith, "Cognitive Consequences of Forced Compliance," *Journal of Abnormal and Social Psychology*, Vol. 58 [1959], pp. 203–210.)

PERSUASION AND ATTITUDE CHANGE

Nothing is so unbelievable that oratory cannot make it acceptable.

—Cicero, 46 B.C.

Persuasion is a deliberate attempt on the part of one party to influence the attitudes or behavior of another party so as to achieve some predetermined end. As pointed out in Chapter 3, communication requires that a sender and a receiver become "tuned" together for a given message. Consequently, for persuasion to occur, three elements must be fitted together within some viable arrangement: the communicator, the message, and the target. The communicator sends a message to a target person hoping to evoke a particular response. Of course not all messages succeed in eliciting the desired outcome. Let us consider the communicator, the message, and the target in turn, examining the part each plays in persuasion and attitude change.

The Communicator

Persuasion is achieved by the speaker's personal character when the speech is so spoken as to make us think him credible. We believe good men more fully and more readily than others.

—Aristotle

Aristotle's observation is in keeping with common-sense notions: We are inclined to believe people and be influenced by people whom we judge to be honorable and trustworthy. But what about social psychological research? Do social psychologists find that we take the characteristics of the communicator into account in assessing his or her message to us? Additionally, what characteristics make a communicator more fully and more readily believable? (See the boxed insert on successful selling.) Much research has been directed to these matters.

Trustworthiness
Marketing agencies seem to share the belief that the character of the communicator has a considerable effect on the persuasiveness of their appeals. Advertisers select consumers whom they feel typify the target audience to present testimonials on their satisfaction with the advertiser's product. Manufacturers often attempt to win the seal of approval from independent product-testing agencies to substantiate their product claims. And politicians running for office commonly solicit the endorsement of prestigious individuals (Sternthal, Phillips, and Dholakia, 1978).

Common sense also suggests that untrustworthy communicators are not as effective as trustworthy ones. Presumably, if we think that communicators are attempting to advance their own self-interests, we view them as biased—as having

SUCCESSFUL SELLING

Psychologist Donald J. Moine (1982) has looked into those techniques that contribute to success in selling. He compared the approaches employed by successful and mediocre salespeople in real estate, automobiles, and stocks. Moine found that skilled persuaders use weapons from the arsenal of the clinical hypnotist. These techniques lead clients to a state of intensified attention and receptiveness.

Able salespeople first undertake to establish a climate of trust and rapport. They engage in "hypnotic pacing" through a mirrorlike matching of the customer's thoughts, tone of voice, speech tempo, and mood. This strategy is a way of communicating to the customer: "You and I are a lot alike. We're in sync." If the customer seems "up," the salesperson matches the upbeat mood; if the customer is "down," the persuader admits to feeling a "little down" recently. Thus the best sales agents attempt to share and reflect the customer's reality. In fact, superior insurance agents even agree with a customer that "insurance isn't the best investment nowadays" (although perhaps adding, "but it does have its uses").

Having achieved a bond of trust and rapport, effective salespeople move to the "soft sell." They often use blatantly obvious pacing statements to bridge the transition, saying, for instance, "Mr. Johnson, you are looking at this home and you can remember the joy of owning a first-rate place of your own." In the course of the soft sell, they embed direct commands to a customer in otherwise innocuous statements. For example, "If you can imagine yourself owning this lovely home and imagine how happy it will make you, you will want to, Mr. Johnson, buy this home." The statement carries the embedded command, "Mr. Johnson, buy this home." Top salespeople are also adept tellers of stories, parables, and anecdotes. They use these devices to handle customers' resistance and to "close" on them without threatening rapport and trust.

ulterior motives—and, therefore, we are less inclined to be influenced by them. Yet research on this matter has produced mixed results. While high-credibility sources often produce more *opinion change* than low-credibility sources, the high or low credibility of the source has not been found to affect *message learning*. Neutral sources produce an amount of opinion change halfway between that produced by high- and low-credibility sources, but neutral sources produce *more* learning of the message content (McGuire, 1969, 1985). When people know that the source is trustworthy, they can evaluate the conclusion without paying attention to the arguments; when people are unable to evaluate the source, they must evaluate the arguments themselves, and consequently are more likely to learn them (Bauer, 1965).

Further, when the communicator is seen as arguing against his or her own best interests, the person's influence may be increased. In one study, social psychologists found that when a criminal argued in favor of more individual freedom and against greater police powers, he produced little attitude change in his listeners. But when he argued in favor of a stronger police force, he produced considerable attitude change (Walster et al., 1966).

Additionally, rapid speech functions as a credibility cue and as such enhances persuasion. Fast speakers are perceived as more knowledgeable and more trustworthy. And a message is perceived as more complex but clearer and easier to understand when presented by a fast speaker (Miller et al., 1976).

We should not assume, however, that a high-credibility source is always superior to a low-credibility source (Romer, 1979). Under some circumstances, high credibility may be a liability. Some evidence suggests that a low-credibility source induces greater persuasion than a high-credibility source when the issue is one toward which we have a positive initial disposition. Presumably, when we encounter a highly credible source articulating a position we favor, we let the individual do all the work. We feel no need to retrieve supporting cognitive responses from our long-term memory. It is otherwise, however, when a low-credibility source expounds our position. Under these circumstances we feel mentally compelled to seek arguments that will support the position, in the process strengthening our initial opinion (Sternthal, Phillips, and Dholakia, 1978).

Expertness

Research reveals that experts are more persuasive than nonexperts (Maddux and Rogers, 1980). Elliot Aronson and his colleagues had students who had negatively evaluated nine stanzas of poetry read the evaluation of someone who praised the poetry (Aronson, Turner, and Carlsmith, 1963). The favorable evaluation read by one group of students was by the distinguished poet T. S. Eliot; the one read by the other group was by Agnes Stearns, "a student at Mississippi State Teachers College." The subjects then reevaluated the poetry. Perhaps it is not surprising that considerably more attitude change occurred among those who read the evaluation by T. S. Eliot, the expert, than among those who read the one by Agnes Stearns, the nonexpert. Overall, studies that have been made of credibility suggest that the expertness or perceived competence of the communicator increases persuasive impact more than trustworthiness does (McGuire, 1969, 1985).

Liking

Research reveals that the more we like the source of a persuasive message, the more likely we are to change our belief in accordance with that advocated by the source. This finding is in keeping with the predictions of Heider's balance theory and of Osgood's congruity theory. However, in some studies based on dissonance theory, the opposite relationship has been predicted and at times confirmed. As dissonance theorists explain this outcome, people who listen to a disliked person can find little justification for agreeing with the person. Accordingly, they are likely to have to justify their listening by saying that the message itself was worthy of attention and, hence, to be more influenced by it (McGuire, 1969). But other factors are also at work. For instance, a likable communicator is more persuasive in videotaped and audiotaped messages than in written messages. In contrast, disliked communicators are more persuasive when they employ written messages than when they use videotaped or audiotaped messages (Chaiken and Eagly, 1983).

Similarity

We tend to be influenced more by people who are similar to us than by people who are different. Presumably, if we perceive the communicator as being like ourselves we assume that he or she also shares with us common needs and goals. We conclude that what the source advocates is good for "our kind of people" and align our attitude accordingly. Further, similarity tends to produce liking for a source, and, as noted above, if we like a source, we are inclined to change our attitude to coincide with that advocated by the liked source. The impact is strengthened by an additional factor: Liking also enhances our perception that the person is similar to us (McGuire, 1969, 1985).

Multiple Sources

Common sense seemingly dictates that multiple sources are more persuasive than one source alone. At political conventions, several noteworthy supporters typically nominate a candidate. Television and magazine advertisers frequently expose their audiences to multiple testimonials for their product. And in courtrooms, attorneys commonly present multiple witnesses to verify or dispute a defendant's good character. Social psychologists Stephen G. Harkins and Richard E. Petty (1981) find merit in these approaches. Their experiments reveal that people have to "gear up" anew each time they encounter a new speaker. Consequently, increasing the number of sources compels listeners to think more intently about the message. Should each of the communicators present compelling arguments for a position, listeners typically generate more positive thoughts about the position than they do when the same high-quality arguments are provided by a single person. But multiple sources can also boomerang. Should each communicator present weak arguments, listeners find the messages more negative and less persuasive than they do if the same weak arguments are supplied by one source.

The Message

> *The receptive ability of the masses is very limited, their understanding small; on the other hand, they have a great power of forgetting. This being so, all effective propaganda must be confined to a very few points which must be brought out in the form of slogans until the very last man is enabled to comprehend what is meant by any slogan.*
>
> —Adolf Hitler, *Mein Kampf*, 1933

Central to the persuasive process is the message. A communicator wishes to achieve some goal—an attitude or behavior change. To be persuasive, the com-

THE EFFECTIVENESS OF ADVERTISING

Advertising is not necessarily as effective as we assume. Two studies reveal that in four out of ten cases, people see an ad but forget the message or miss the name of the sponsor (Abrams, 1983). Communicus, Inc., a Los Angeles research concern, found that only six of ten viewers of popular TV commercials could correctly recall the sponsor when the advertiser's name was omitted. Advertising techniques that seemed to work the best included celebrities or company executives as spokespersons (Lee Iacocca for Chrysler), continuing characters (Mr. Whipple for Charmin toilet paper), special graphic techniques (the Merrill Lynch bull), and musical themes (Miller High Life beer). Perception Research Services of Englewood Cliffs, New Jersey, studied magazine ads by using eye-tracking cameras that recorded what readers actually saw when they viewed 804 ads. In 43 percent of them, the subjects overlooked the sponsor's name.

When we are exposed to an advertisement or some persuasive communication, we commonly think that it has a greater effect on others than on ourselves. This is called the **third-person effect in communication** (Davison, 1983). We reason, "I will not be influenced, but they (a third party) may well be persuaded." When viewing the campaign materials of rival candidates or the advertisements of rival products, we typically believe that they are more effective than in fact they are. Indeed, people on both sides of an issue tend to see the media as biased against their particular point of view, and they assume that a disproportionate effect will be achieved by material supporting the "wrong" side of the issue. Likewise, when the *Roots* television series was first aired in January 1977, both professional researchers and the public assumed that the series would

municator must put some idea or feeling into a form in which it can be transmitted to the target (see boxed insert). Social psychologists have been interested in the factors that contribute to a communication's effectiveness.

Fear Appeals

One type of message for changing attitudes involves an appeal to fear. Fear appeals seek to influence or persuade people by telling them of impending danger or harm from following or failing to follow a given course of action. Communicators have successfully used fear appeals in attempts to influence a great many behaviors, including terminating cigarette smoking, securing vaccinations, and wearing auto seat belts (Rogers, 1983). Yet the arousal of fear alone may boomerang (Janis and Feshbach, 1953; Leventhal, 1970; McGuire, 1985). The anxiety

have a substantial impact on the attitudes of both blacks and whites. (The eight-part drama of Alex Haley's story about his forebears' painful progress through slavery attracted the largest television audience for any program up to that time.) Whites were expected to show greater tolerance and sympathy; blacks, to become more angry and bitter. However, when asked about their *own* reactions, substantial pluralities of both blacks and whites reported that a feeling of sadness was the chief effect that watching *Roots* had on them.

The third-person effect helps explain the phenomenon of censorship. Insofar as faith and morals are at issue, it is unusual to find a censor who admits to having been adversely affected by viewing the prohibited communication. The censor's associates are also thought to be immune to the "pollution." Rather, it is the general public—those with "impressionable minds"—who must be protected. Between 1916 and 1981, Maryland maintained a state board of censors to cut smut from motion pictures. The pornographic materials apparently left the censors themselves unscathed. One of the censors noted that over the course of twenty-one years she had "looked at more naked bodies than 50,000 doctors," but the experience had intruded more on her diet than on her morals. She observed, "I had to stop eating a lot of food because of what they do with it in these movies" (Davison, 1983).

The third-person effect can be seen as well in welfare. For instance, during World War II, the Japanese learned that there was a service unit consisting of black troops with white officers on Iwo Jima in the Pacific. Learning about the unit, the Japanese sent planes over it with propaganda leaflets. The leaflets stressed the theme that the war was a white man's war and urged the black soldiers to desert. There is no evidence that the leaflets had any effect on the black troops. However, it had a powerful effect on the white officers, who feared the black soldiers might be influenced by the leaflets. Accordingly, the white military command withdrew the black service units.

that fear appeals cause may lead people to think up counterarguments, suppress their thoughts about the danger, or rationalize why they need not have any worries. Accordingly, it seems that fear-arousing messages result in greater persuasiveness if they contain recommendations for reducing fear—for example, coping with the danger by stopping smoking, getting a tetanus injection, or wearing a seat belt.

The antismoking campaign has paid particularly large dividends (Warner, 1981). Per capita cigarette consumption in the United States has declined annually since 1973. In the absence of the antismoking campaign, cigarette consumption in 1978 would have exceeded the 1973 level by a third. The aim of fear appeals is usually to get people to think about the dangers they confront and to take protective action. In the process, they may gain a sense of effective coping or mastery. People may conclude, "Why should I take a chance?" and follow a strategy of precaution. Or they may think, "I have nothing to lose by

Persuasiveness
Which groups are likely to find this man "believable"? Which not? Why? What types of persuasion are contained within the message itself? How effective are they likely to be? (Patrick Reddy)

trying this approach and much to gain," and then pursue a strategy of defensiveness. In either case, the individual is made to feel safer (Maddux and Rogers, 1983).

Conclusion Drawing

Is it more effective, when presenting arguments, to state the conclusion explicitly or to leave it unstated? Social psychologists have debated this matter. If the conclusion is stated, the possibility that the audience may misinterpret the argument is avoided. On the other hand, by not stating the conclusion, the speaker may give the impression of having no ulterior motive and, therefore, may appear more credible. Further, if the audience members draw the conclusion for themselves, they may be more strongly persuaded than if the conclusion is drawn for them.

On the basis of his survey of the literature, William McGuire concludes: "In communication, it appears, it is not sufficient to lead the horse to water; one must also push his head underneath to get him to drink" (1969: 209). There does appear, however, to be an exception to this general principle. With relatively well-informed, sophisticated audiences or where the issue is a very simple one, it is usually more effective to let the audience draw the conclusion for itself (Thistlethwaite and Kamenetzky, 1955).

Multiple Messages

In the course of our daily lives, we are bombarded with a good many persuasive communications. For instance, we encounter ten to twenty-five messages per hour on commercial radio or television (Baumgardner et al., 1983). Accordingly, public opinion experts stress that a single advertisement or program may be relatively ineffective in reaching the public with a particular message. A campaign is necessary. Several related advertisements or programs often are capable of producing effects even greater than could be accounted for in terms of simple summation; multiple exposure tends to produce a pyramiding impact.

One-sided Versus Two-sided Communications

Is it more effective for a speaker to acknowledge the opposing arguments and refute them or simply to ignore the opposing view? If the message includes mention of arguments in support of the opposing view, the speaker has the advantage of appearing less biased, more knowledgeable, and less intent on trying to persuade. In brief, the speaker appears more credible, since the message comes across less like propaganda and more like a dispassionate talk. On the other hand, a one-sided communication is less complicated and easier for the hearer to grasp.

Research findings suggest that whether the one-sided or the two-sided communication is more effective depends partly on the audience. The one-sided communication appears more effective when the audience is poorly informed and poorly educated. To present such an audience with both sides of the issue serves merely to confuse the listeners and to provide them with counterarguments that they would not otherwise consider. One-sided communications appear to be more effective also when the audience already agrees with the message. Then such communications simplify matters and strengthen existing attitudes. But where audiences are well informed and well educated or are initially opposed to the message, a two-sided communication appears to be the more effective (McGinnies, 1966; McGuire, 1969, 1985).

Personal Involvement

Richard E. Petty and John T. Cacioppo (1981) distinguish between central and peripheral routes to persuasion. The central route aims to change people's attitudes by involving them in a diligent consideration of issues and arguments. This approach emphasizes comprehension, learning, and retention of the message argument. In contrast, the peripheral route does not necessarily entail issue-relevant thinking. Instead, attitude change is promoted through "cues" that link the persuader to the issue. These cues are associated with the nature of the communicator; for instance, the communicator is credible, attractive, or powerful. Petty and Cacioppo find that changes that are induced through the central route and that activate personal involvement are more enduring and predictive of subsequent behavior than changes induced through the peripheral route. Personal involvement can often be fostered by increasing the number of arguments in a message, thus giving people more information to think about (Petty and Cacioppo, 1984). Opening a message with a rhetorical question may also arouse people's interest and contribute to their personal engagement with the message (Burnkrant and Howard, 1984).

The Target

Our daily observations suggest that some people are gullible "pushovers" while others stubbornly "stick to their guns." Do people in fact differ in their susceptibility to persuasive communications? Evidence suggests that there is such a trait as general persuasibility—that there is some consistency in the degree to which a person can be persuaded by certain kinds of appeals and on certain kinds of issues (McGuire, 1969). Individuals also differ in their tendency to derive information from and elaborate on arguments provided by a message (Cacioppo, Petty, and Morris, 1983). But although people differ in their susceptibility to certain kinds of influence, a host of situational and other factors nonetheless intervenes to moderate the impact of any given appeal. Thus the relationship between personality and persuasibility cannot be determined without taking account of the source and nature of the appeal and the nature of the issue.

A sampling of research also reveals the following:

☐ The more a person's attitude is "anchored" through linkage and integration with logically related beliefs, the more resistant the individual is to a change in the belief (Holt, 1970). And the greater the individual's involvement with the issue and stake in the outcome, the greater the person's resistance to persuasion (Chaiken, 1980; Petty, Cacioppo, and Goldman, 1981; Jaccard, 1981). These tendencies are strengthened by the fact that we draw on our existing beliefs and prior experiences to evaluate the validity of message arguments (Schmidt and Sherman, 1984; McFarland, Ross, and Conway, 1984; Wood, Kallgren, and Preisler, 1985). Indeed, people selectively recall their past behaviors to make them consistent with their current attitudes (Ross et al., 1983).

☐ Making public one's position on an issue and then finding one's position attacked tends to make a person more resistant to counterpropaganda and more dedicated to the cause. In one study, women who favored the dissemination of birth control information and who had signed a petition in support of such a program were sent a leaflet attacking their stand. Follow-up investigation revealed that these women—when compared with a control group who had signed the petition but who did not receive the leaflet—increased their commitment to the cause and were subsequently more willing to do volunteer work on its behalf (Kiesler, 1971).

☐ Forewarning people of an upcoming communication that runs counter to their current position increases their resistance to persuasion. Warnings motivate people to consider more fully their own positions and to generate anticipatory counterarguments for the impending attack: Forewarned is forearmed (McGuire and Papageorgis, 1962; Petty and Cacioppo, 1977). However, over time some individuals either forget or dissociate the forewarning, thus permitting the full impact of the message to emerge (Watts and Holt, 1979). Social psychologists term this outcome **the sleeper effect**—a delay occurs before the impact of a communication is felt (Cook et al., 1979).

☐ Voluntary exposure to information tends to be highly selective. We seek out information that supports our beliefs and avoid information that challenges our position. This behavior allows us to minimize dissonance (Festinger, 1957). However, there are exceptions to this principle. For instance, our attention is also affected by the novelty and utility of the information. Additionally, norms of intellectual honesty and fairness can lead us to expose ourselves to information supporting the "other side" despite the dissonance aroused by such material (Olson and Zanna, 1979).

☐ People who hold strong opinions on social issues accept information confirming their own views at face value. Moreover, they remember it better than they do opposing information. Hence individuals respond to topics like compensatory education, water fluoridation, and energy conservation with biased mind sets. Indeed, a "rebound effect" often operates—people encountering opposing viewpoints and criticisms of their position not only stick with their original position but claim to be even more convinced than they were previously. Consequently, exposing contending factions in a dispute to an identical body of information may increase rather than decrease their polarization (Lord, Ross, and Lepper, 1979; McGuire, 1985).

Clearly, the effectiveness of communications that are designed to persuade depends on a good many situational and other factors. As a consequence, overriding generalizations regarding an individual's susceptibility to persuasion are difficult to make.

SUMMARY

1. An attitude is made up of three components: the cognitive, the affective, and the conative (or behavioral).
2. Attitudes serve a variety of psychological functions. Daniel Katz distinguishes between the adjustment function, the ego-defense function, the value-expressive function, and the knowledge function.
3. There is no simple way in which the behavior of one person toward another can be accurately predicted solely on the basis of knowledge of that person's

attitude toward the other. Situational and other factors interfere, so that people do not necessarily translate their behavioral inclinations into overt actions.

4. Underlying much social psychological theory is the notion of attitude consistency. It assumes that people experience inconsistency as a noxious state that they are impelled to eliminate or reduce.

5. There are several varieties of consistency theory, three of which are considered in the chapter: balance theory, congruity theory, and cognitive dissonance theory.

6. Research findings have led to various modifications of Leon Festinger's original formulations of dissonance theory. Commitment and volition play a vital part: For people to experience dissonance, they must believe they acted voluntarily and without the coercive impetus of a large reward so that they feel responsible for the outcome of their decision. Further, underlying much dissonance is a lack of balance between people's self-conceptions and their cognitions about a behavior that violates these self-conceptions.

7. Trustworthiness, expertness, likability, similarity, and a multiplicity of sources are factors that increase the effectiveness of a communicator in bringing about attitude change in the listener.

8. Factors that influence the effectiveness of a message include the employment of fear appeals, the explicit drawing of a conclusion, multiple presentations, and the presentation of only one side of an argument or of both sides.

9. Evidence suggests that there is such a trait as general persuasibility. But although there is an underlying general trait of susceptibility to influence, a host of situational and other factors affects a person's response to a given appeal.

GLOSSARY

Affective component □ The feelings or emotions that an object, event, or situation—or its symbolic representation—evokes within an individual.

Attitude □ A learned and relatively enduring tendency or predisposition to evaluate a person, event, or situation in a certain way.

Attitude consistency □ The tendency of people to organize their attitudes in a harmonious manner so that their attitudes are not in conflict.

Balance theory of attitudes □ Fritz Heider's theory of attitude change, which focused on three elements: (1) the person who is the focus on attention, *P;* (2) some other person, *O;* and (3) an impersonal entity, *X.* These elements interact so as to realize attitude consistency.

Behavioral component □ See **conative component.**

Cognitive component □ The way we perceive an object, event, or situation; our thoughts, beliefs, and ideas about something.

Cognitive dissonance □ The theory, formulated by Leon Festinger, that there is pressure to produce consistent relations among one's attitudes or behaviors and to avoid inconsistency.

Commitment □   A state of being bound to or locked into a position or a course of action.

Conative component □   The tendency or disposition to act in certain ways with reference to some object, event, or situation. The emphasis of the definition is on the tendency to act, not on the action itself.

Congruity theory of attitudes □   A theory of attitude change, formulated by Charles Osgood and his associates, which suggests that extreme attitudes are more resistant to change than more neutral ones.

Functionalist theory of attitudes □   The view that our attitudes are determined by the functions they serve for us; that people hold given attitudes because these attitudes help them achieve their basic goals.

Persuasion □   A deliberate attempt on the part of one party to influence the attitudes or behavior of another party so as to achieve some predetermined end.

Reactance □   A motivational state directed toward the restoration or safeguarding of an individual's freedom with respect to some matter.

Sleeper effect □   An effect that happens because a delay occurs before the impact of a communication is felt.

Third-person effect in communication □   The view that when we are exposed to a persuasive communication, it has a greater effect on others than on ourselves.

Volition □   The degree of freedom individuals believe they possess in making a decision or choice.

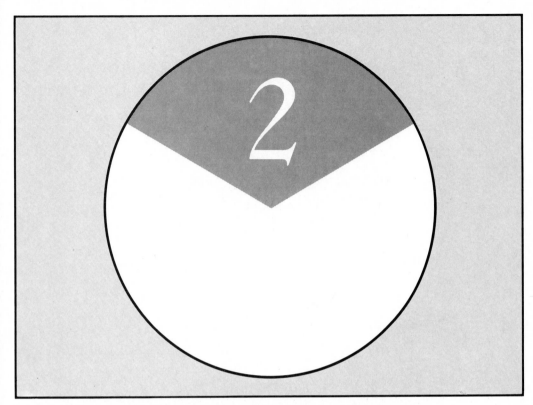

INTERPERSONAL
SOCIAL BEHAVIOR

NORMS: SOCIAL ORDER AND CONFORMITY

EFFECTING SOCIAL ORDER
Constructing Social Order
Norms
Accounts: Excuses and
  Justifications
Negotiated Order
CONFORMITY IN GROUP
  SETTINGS
Norm Formation
Conformity to False Group
  Judgments

Social Support as a Deterrent to
  Conformity
The Impact of a Minority
Obedience
COMPLIANCE IN THE ABSENCE
  OF EXTERNAL PRESSURE
The Foot-in-the-Door Technique
The Effects of Guilt on
  Compliance
The Obligation to Reciprocate
  Favors

We live our lives in a social world, one composed of people. This fact is obvious. What is not so obvious is how the social world is realized. Through the years this question has been variously phrased (Wrong, 1961): "What are the sources of social cohesion?"; "How is society possible?"; and "How do human beings become amenable to social discipline?"

However phrased, the question draws our attention to the fact that we must coordinate our actions if we are to achieve an integrated web of relationships and avoid destructive conflict. Whatever we want—food, clothing, shelter, sex, fame, material wealth, or football tickets—we can get it only by working with and through other people. We must fit our diverse actions together so that the work of the world gets done (Cohen, 1966).

Additionally, we must subordinate our needs and interests to those of the group as a whole. Our actions must be guided and constrained by the requirements of the larger human enterprise. All of this requires some understandings

209

Constructed reality

Toward the end of each year, most Americans prepare for a special, sentimental holiday—Christmas. For Christians, it is a day that commemorates the birth of Christ (although historians and biblical experts are uncertain as to the precise date of Christ's birth). Christmas Day and the days immediately preceding it are supposed to be filled with good cheer, the reassemblying of family members, the renewal of ties with old friends, gift giving, and entertaining. Schools, businesses, and government close on December 25. Special religious services take place in Christian churches. Radio and television programs carry traditional songs of yuletide cheer. And on Christmas Eve children await the arrival of a legendary elf, Santa Claus. The Christmas holiday affords a good illustration of a constructed reality. It exists because people "make" it exist by acting as if it exists. We assign meaning to given activities by placing the "Christmas" label on them. Once we define the situation in these terms, we establish social expectations for people's behavior. And in turn, people engage in "Christmas" behavior. The reality of "Christmas" does not exist independently of our social definitions. We manufacture "Christmas" by celebrating the "Christmas season."

about who is to do what and under what circumstances. And for the most part, we must be able to assume that the people about us will conform with these expectations. In the absence of predictable modes of conduct, chaos would reign.

EFFECTING SOCIAL ORDER

The art of progress is to preserve order amid change and to preserve change amid order.

—Alfred North Whitehead

Human life presents a picture of organization and regularity. Interaction seems patterned in flowing currents of activity. We feel ourselves caught up and bound within integrated wholes. We experience much of life as relatively stable and predictable.

Consider that we usually have little difficulty in attuning ourselves to new classmates and professors each semester—much of academic life is a replay of itself. Consider the recurrent and orderly flow of traffic into the city each morning and its outward flow to the suburbs in the evening. Consider the store clerks smoothly carrying out innumerable exchange transactions with streams of customers. Consider the layout of the city, with the central business district, ghetto

Social Regularity and Stability
Outdoors, unhampered by seats bolted to the floor, students still array themselves in the accustomed manner before the instructor. (Don McCarthy)

areas, "automobile row," manufacturing district, and middle-class suburbs. And consider the linkage of millions of people in the Medicare and Social Security system, with its monthly distribution of checks (Olsen, 1968). Accordingly, as we observe human behavior it seems in large measure to be organized and focused rather than haphazard and random. In other words, society gives the appearance of regularity and stability that social psychologists term **social order.**

Constructing Social Order

The fact that so much of social life is routine and repetitive permits us to treat certain activities and situations as things or objects. We give names to societies ("the United States of America"), organizations ("the University of Wisconsin"), communities ("Chicago"), families ("the Smiths"), courses ("Social Psychology 101"), athletic events ("the Superbowl"), holidays ("Thanksgiving"), reading our lecture notes ("studying"), getting married ("a wedding"), and so on. By singing the National Anthem, reciting the Pledge of Allegiance, celebrating the Fourth of July, honoring George Washington as "the father of our country," criticizing America's policy toward the Soviet Union, and extolling the virtues of the American way of life, we constitute and act toward the first kind of "object"—a nation-state (Hewitt, 1976).

Likewise, by attending classes and interacting with deans, faculty, and students we give existence to the University of Wisconsin. By acting toward one another

THE ETHNOMETHODOLOGICAL VIEW OF SOCIAL ORDER

A central concern of sociology has been how and why society is possible. Basic to this question is the assumption that there is a "real world"—that something exists out there, something independent of people's perception, and that this something is knowable through scientific study. Sociologists term the real world "society." They see society as made up of institutions, norms, values, roles, and so on. Viewed from this perspective, the task of social science is to uncover the regularities in people's behavior that together produce social order—the relatively stable, recurrent, and patterned aspects of human interaction.

Within the past twenty years or so, a new approach has emerged that challenges this traditional view. Rather than asking how social order is possible, it asks how a sense of order is possible. Termed *ethnomethodology* (see Chapter 1), this school has been prominently identified with Harold Garfinkel (1964, 1967), Harvey Sacks, Don H. Zimmerman (1976), Aaron W. Cicourel (1975), and Hugh Mehan and Houston Wood (1975, 1976). These ethnomethodologists raise a fundamental and disturbing question: How do people (including sociologists) create and sustain for each other the *presumption* that society has a real character? Thus ethnomethodologists ask, "Is there indeed anything more to 'society' than people's belief that it is 'out there'?"

From the ethnomethodological per-

in certain ways we "are" the University of Wisconsin. Additionally, since we are aware or conscious of these patterned relationships—we label them "the University of Wisconsin"—we can act toward these and related activities as an object ("I will graduate from the University of Wisconsin next June"; "the University of Wisconsin defeated the University of North Carolina in a basketball game"; "the University of Wisconsin closed for the Christmas holidays").

It matters little that a "Stone Age" Tasaday of the Philippines, if transported to North America, fails to comprehend "the United States of America," or, if visiting Madison, Wisconsin, does not grasp "the University of Wisconsin" (just as we fail to grasp various Tasaday social arrangements). In time, in the course of communicative and other interaction with "Americans" and "Badgers," the Tasaday may come to "construct" the same definitions of these activities as do "Americans" and "Badgers." Then the Tasaday will also have arrived at a similarly constructed reality or social order: "the United States of America" and "the University of Wisconsin." How this reality is arrived at is the concern of *ethnomethodology* (see boxed insert).

spective, the question of social order becomes one of studying *how* people come to agree upon an *impression* that there are such things as societies, norms, roles, and so on. What is real, say ethnomethodologists, is not society but the *methods* people employ in constructing, maintaining, and altering for each other a sense of order. Order, therefore, is not maintained by some society out there; instead order derives from people's capacity to convince one another that "out there" a society truly exists.

Ethnomethodologists, then, study how people create and maintain conceptions of a real world through their social interactions. These theorists do not question the existence of a real world; rather, they say that multiple perceived realities exist. They undertake to examine the many versions (including their own) of the way the world is assembled.

In sum, ethnomethodology is *not* a method but an approach that takes as its subject the study of the methods jointly used by members of society to organize the settings of their everyday activities. Ethnomethodologists focus on various "social structuring activities." Cicourel (1975), for instance, examines a doctor's practices in diagnosing the patient in a medical interview, transforming the data into summary statements on a medical chart, and utilizing medical summaries to treat other cases. Other ethnomethodologists have described the practices employed by police on the beat and judges and lawyers in the courtroom in assembling social structures. Ethnomethodology is a highly controversial school of thought (Coser, 1975). Although only in its infancy, it has attracted considerable interest, especially among the younger generation of sociologists.

Norms

Social order allows us to experience the world as stable and predictable. One way in which we achieve a sense of social order is through shared expectations. In much of human life, social behavior is prescribed for us in terms of do's and don'ts: Thou shalt be quiet and attentive while a professor is lecturing; thou shalt not cheat on examinations; thou shalt read the material a professor assigns; thou shalt not walk out of class simply because the class is boring. Conformity with these requirements generally has favorable consequences, while violation brings unpleasant results. Such social requirements are **norms**—standards for behavior that members of a social group share, that they are expected to follow, and that are enforced by positive and negative sanctions. Norms provide guidelines whose contours tell us what action is appropriate in particular situations.

Norms are vital to our lives. Day by day, we are able to act together with relative ease because we share common understandings about what each of us

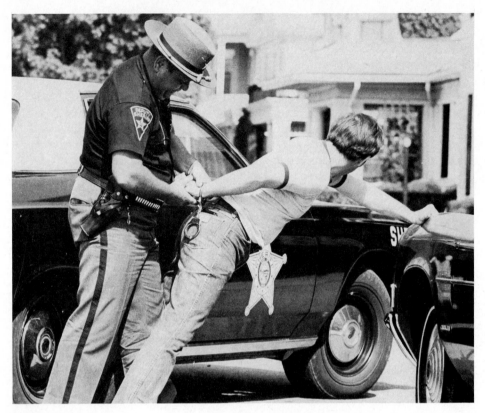

Law and Order
The law has teeth, and the teeth can bite. (Don McCarthy)

is supposed to do. We find that when we all take the same things for granted, cooperation is facilitated. We are prepared to wait in line at the supermarket, the bank, or the ticket office, on the assumption that we will be served when our turn comes (Dullea, 1982). We are willing to be paid for our work in pieces of paper that have no inherent value on the assumption that we can exchange the money later for the goods and services we want. Thousands of such shared assumptions characterize social life. Society is possible precisely because of the faith we place in our mutual willingness to act upon them (Shibutani, 1961).

For the most part, norms are not expressed in some official code. Rather, they are an abstract synthesis of the many separate times that the members of a society state their sentiments on a given issue. They are the accumulated understandings reached through time that come to serve as precedents for future understandings. Each time the group censures some acts as inappropriate—as deviant—it sharpens the contours of the rule. Indeed, one can argue that a certain amount of crime is necessary to the stability of a moral order, that without occasional violations there would be no occasion for society to reaffirm

---

N*orms*

Today I was in the men's restroom using a urinal. I was going about my business, and while standing there I noticed that I was looking straight ahead at the blank wall in front of me. When I realized this I looked to both sides and noticed several other guys also staring straight ahead. Everyone is afraid to look to the right or left for fear of being deemed a little "strange" or "queer." But it is interesting if you observe carefully, that upon lining up at the urinal, guys usually take a quick glance out of the corner of their eyes, checking out the people next to them. This is a good illustration of a folkway (a type of norm). You aren't supposed to size up other guys, or else people will think you are a homosexual. Yet most guys violate the norm when lining up at the uri-nal, but so quickly that they aren't caught.

---

the basic tenets of its moral code (Erikson, 1970). The deviant informs us what "evil" looks like and what shapes the "devil" can assume. The wrongdoer shows us the difference between the kinds of experience that belong within the group and the kinds of experience that belong outside it. Moreover, in the process of opposing the deviant, the group may strengthen itself. A common enemy arouses common sentiments and revives and maintains group solidarity (Coser, 1956; Lauderdale, 1976; Lauderdale et al., 1984).

Accounts: Excuses and Justifications

As noted above, norms provide expectations for behavior. Yet it is not always possible for us to live up to the expectations of others. At these times, we may attempt to explain our behavior, in hopes of minimizing damage to a relationship. We offer **accounts**—explanations we make for unanticipated or untoward behavior (Scott and Lyman, 1968; Riordan, Marlin, and Kellogg, 1983). We have no need of accounts when we engage in routine, common-sense behavior because its appropriateness is settled in advance by cultural definitions. But when our behavior is called into question, we may provide excuses or justifications for what we and others are likely to regard as inept, wrong, or unwelcome. **Excuses** are statements we provide that deny our responsibility for the negative conse-quences of our action and admit the behavior to be reprehensible. For instance, "I know I disrupted the party by punching him, but I was drunk and didn't know what I was doing." **Justifications** are statements we provide that admit respon-sibility for an action but reinterpret it in a more socially acceptable manner. For instance, "You would have hit him too if he had said that about your wife."

Excuses and justifications are so common because they are a social lubricant vital to the smooth operation of our daily lives (Snyder, Higgins, and Stucky,

1983). When we accept other people's accounts or they accept our accounts, interaction can proceed in a "normal" way. Asked why we have not completed our assignment, we may reply, "I have family troubles." The remark is likely to be taken as an account and honored because "everyone knows" that family problems are a cause for not doing an assignment. At times we are virtually obligated to make an excuse, and if we fail to make it, others may do so for us. Not making a proper excuse is too much of a threat to the ongoing social fabric for most people to let it pass. Accordingly, "white lies" are a standard of everyday interaction—"Sorry, I can't make your party. I have to study tonight."

Negotiated Order

According to one sociological view, social order appears to flow more or less spontaneously from the fact that we obey the norms of our group or society. Social cohesion and integration are seen as resulting from adequate socialization, for if we learn the relevant rules for behavior, our activities will mesh smoothly with those of other people. Additionally, social control is said to be achieved— we subordinate our own interests to those of the larger whole—since we internalize the norms of our society (for instance, the expected behaviors for men and the expected behaviors for women).

Most social psychologists recognize this view as much too simplistic. It portrays society as simply a community of organisms who blindly enact a programmed routine much in the fashion of robots. Such a perspective fails to recognize that social order is a process, not something that automatically happens. Social order must be worked at and fashioned as we repeat, reaffirm, and reconstruct social acts. We arrive at mutually shared agreements, tacit understandings, binding contracts, unhappy compromises, and coerced accommodations. And we do it all through processes of manipulation, persuasion, constraint, inducement, diplomacy, and bargaining. Order is **negotiated** out of a conflict of interests and sentiments in the process of social interaction. Hence life is never static; it is always in flux, ever-changing. While change seemingly undermines order, the process of change—social interaction—creates new working arrangements that we perceive as social order. In this manner there can be order under conditions of change, and change can be experienced by us as orderly.

Anselm Strauss (1964) and his associates provided insight into the process of change in their study of two psychiatric hospitals. To most of us, hospitals appear to be relatively fixed social organizations. Administrators, physicians, nurses, aides, and patients seem to interact in a fairly stereotyped, patterned manner as laid down by an array of rules. Yet Strauss and his associates found this to be a gross oversimplification of hospital life.

In the hospitals Strauss studied, no one knew all the existing rules, much less to whom they applied, in what situations, and with what penalties. This confusion came in part from the continual turnover in staff and patients. Rules, once made, would fall into disuse. Later a crisis might cause the new staff to reinvent them. Almost all "house rules" were more like general understandings than commands, and most rules could be stretched, negotiated, argued, ignored, or applied at

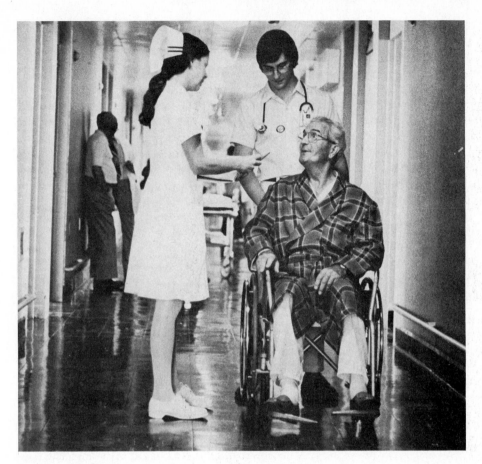

Negotiated Order
Each hospital case has unique qualities that require individuals to arrive at somewhat new working arrangements. (Patrick Reddy)

convenient moments. Thus an otherwise ignored rule might be invoked to serve someone's self-interest: "Sorry, we can't take Janet because we aren't allowed to take violent patients on this ward"; simultaneously, another violent patient who was already on the ward might be kept because of someone's special clinical interest: "Let's give it a try for a few more days, and see if this thing won't clear up with Ethel."

Further, each professional group in the hospital had received different kinds of training. Patients were viewed differently by the practicing private psychiatrists, psychiatric residents, nurses, nursing students, psychologists, occupational therapists, and social workers. Each group had a different rank in the hierarchy of the hospital, and the differences in training and rank resulted in clashing definitions of the hospital situation. The conflict was compounded among psychiatrists, since some of them had a psychoanalytic orientation, while others had a neurological background and tended to prescribe more drugs and far more electric shock therapy.

Within the context of clashing interests and sentiments, negotiation provided the means for piecing together workable arrangements in the hospital. A nurse might draw the physician into a ward management problem, persuading the physician to use the therapeutic sessions to calm a patient down. A private physician might persuade the resident psychiatrist to "work on" the nurses to keep an unruly patient on the ward and to take responsibility for blocking the patient's scheduled transfer to another ward. At times the nursing staff would grow restless when a patient was not "moving" (showing progress). If the physician disagreed with the staff's analysis, the nurses would negotiate among themselves to create a supplementary program.

The result of such negotiations among physicians, staff, and patients was that people struck bargains, made verbal agreements, and arrived at implicit understandings. But their "negotiated consensus" was limited in time. The hospital was a place where agreements were continually being terminated or forgotten even as others were being established, renewed, and revised. The operating agreements in effect at any given time were considerably different from those arrived at in the past and those likely to be fashioned in the future.

Strauss and his associates concluded:

> A skeptic, thinking in terms of relatively permanent or slowly changing structure, might remark that the hospital remains the same from week to week, that only the working arrangements change. . . . Practically, we maintain, no one knows what the hospital "is" on any given day unless he has a comprehensive grasp of the combination of rules, policies, agreements, understandings, pacts, contracts, and other working arrangements that currently obtain. In a pragmatic sense, that combination "is" the hospital at the moment, its social order. . . . It is necessary continually to reconstitute the bases of concerted action, of social order. (1964: 312)

In sum, social order is continually being negotiated in the course of social interaction.

CONFORMITY IN GROUP SETTINGS

When in Rome, do as the Romans do.

—Author unknown

To summarize, people experience a sense of social order—regularity and stability—within human affairs. In part this sense of order derives from norms. Norms provide us with guidelines that tell us what behavior is appropriate and applicable under given circumstances. In the course of social interaction, we arrive at various understandings (a working or negotiated consensus) regarding the norms—the mutual set of obligations and expectations—that will govern our behavior. Now let us consider the pressures that operate within group settings to bring about conformity. **Conformity** entails adherence to or behavioral change in accordance with social expectations.

Norm Formation

In a pioneering study, Muzafer Sherif (1936) investigated norm formation within a laboratory setting. His experiment utilized an optical illusion, the so-called **autokinetic effect.** If a small, fixed spot of light is briefly exposed in a darkened room, it appears to move—and it may seem to move erratically in all directions. People differ in their estimates of how far the spot "moves." Sherif found that when he tested subjects alone, each evolved a characteristic range for the reported movements. Although lacking an objective basis for gauging its extent, each person nonetheless developed a standard or norm. This standard or norm functioned as a reference point for the individual in comparing and judging each successive movement.

Sherif then organized groups made up of subjects who had established very *different* ranges and reference points in their solitary sessions. Within the group setting, each person was again exposed to the light and asked to report aloud on his or her appraisal of the light's "movement." The subjects soon converged toward a group standard of apparent movement. And later, when the individual sessions were resumed, the group-evolved norms persisted; individuals did not return to the norms they had evolved in the initial solitary sessions.

Sherif discovered still another fact:

> Every individual was not necessarily aware of the fact that he was being influenced by others, or that he and other individuals were converging toward a common norm. In fact, the majority of the subjects reported not only that their judgments were made before the others spoke but also *that they were not influenced by the others.* (Sherif and Sherif, 1969: 210)

Hence situational factors influence perception, although we are not necessarily aware of such influences. This finding has been experimentally confirmed by other researchers (Schofield, 1975; Moscovici and Personnaz, 1980; Sorrentino, King, and Leo, 1980).

Conformity to False Group Judgments

Success, recognition, and conformity are the bywords of the modern world where everyone seems to crave the anesthetizing security of being identified with the majority.

—Martin Luther King, Jr., *Strength to Love,* 1963

A very different kind of experimental manipulation of group factors was devised by Solomon Asch (1952). The Asch studies have attracted considerable attention,

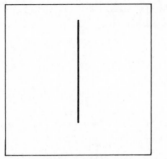
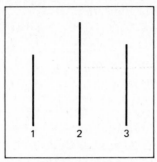

Standard Line   Comparison Lines

FIGURE 7.1 Cards in Asch-type Conformity Experiments
Two sets of cards like these are placed at the front of the
room, and subjects are asked to match the lines in length.
One card has a single black line (the standard). The other
card has three lines, one of which is the same length as
the standard while the other two are obviously either
longer or shorter. When answers are written anonymously,
control subjects match the lines with almost complete accuracy. But under experimental conditions where there is
pressure toward group conformity, many "naive" subjects,
who are asked to match the lines publicly after confederates in the experiment intentionally give incorrect answers, also give the incorrect answers.

and other social psychologists have developed variations on them. In his research, Asch would seat a group usually numbering seven to nine people side by
side. Unlike Sherif, he did not present his subjects with an ambiguous situation.
Rather, subjects were asked to match lines of the same length from two sets of
cards that were displayed at the front of the room. One card had a single line
(the standard). The other card had three lines, one of which was the same length
as the standard while the other two were clearly shorter or longer (see Figure
7.1).

Asch had the subjects give their answers aloud. Except for one person, the
"critical" subject, the group members were all confederates of Asch who unanimously provided incorrect answers on certain trials. Despite the fact that the
correct answer was obvious, nearly one-third of all the critical subjects' judgments contained errors identical with or in the direction of the rigged errors of
the majority. Further, 74 percent of the subjects conformed on at least one of
the trials.

Why did some of the subjects conform to the false group consensus even
though it contradicted the evidence of their own eyes? On 50 percent or more
of the trials, 30 percent of the subjects conformed. In follow-up interviews with

> ## Conformity to false group judgments
>
> *Today some of the guys at work decided to play a trick on Jim. The boss told Jim to go downstairs and bring up a big bucket of ice and a big jar of Coke for the pop machine. Jim first brought up the bucket of ice and then went downstairs for the jar of Coke. While he was gone we hid the bucket of ice. When Jim returned with the jar of Coke, he looked kind of puzzled. We all went about our business as usual and acted like we didn't know what was going on. He said, "Didn't I bring the bucket of ice here?" I answered, "Not that I know of! You were here once before, but all you brought up was this empty tray." Jim started insisting that he had set the bucket of ice on the table. One of the other guys said, "Jim, last time I saw you, you brought up this empty tray." And another guy said, "Ya, Jim." Jim was upset. He thought about it all for a moment and then said, "Now I remember. I brought up the tray. I better go down and get the bucket of ice." And off he went. The funny thing about this is that Jim is no hammerhead. He is in pre-med. This is a good example of how group pressure affects people's judgments and behavior. I can see how a group can brainwash its members.*

these subjects, Asch found that three different kinds of reactions had contributed to their conformity:

1. *Distortion of perception:* A number of subjects said that they were *not* aware that their estimates had been distorted by the majority. They came to perceive the rigged majority estimates as the correct estimates.
2. *Distortion of judgment:* Most of the subjects who yielded to the majority had concluded that their own perceptions were inaccurate. Lacking confidence in their own observations, they reported not what they saw but what they felt must be correct.
3. *Distortion of action:* A number of subjects frankly admitted that they had not reported what they in fact had seen. They said that they had yielded so as not to appear different or stupid in the eyes of other group members.

The type of conformity represented by *distortion of perception* points to **internalization**—the process whereby an individual incorporates within his or her personality the standards of behavior that are prevalent in the group (see Chapter 5). In contrast, conformity associated with *distortion of action* illustrates the distinction between private acceptance and compliance (Kiesler, 1969). **Private acceptance** refers to a behavior change accompanied by underlying attitude

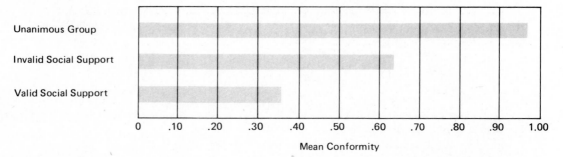

FIGURE 7.2 Conformity Scores in the Three Conditions of the Allen-Levine Study
When another member of the group breaks away from the majority opinion, even
to give a wrong answer (provide invalid social support), the subject is less likely to
conform.
(SOURCE: Adapted from V. L. Allen and J. Levine, "Social Support and Conformity: The Role of
Independent Assessment of Reality," *Journal of Experimental Social Psychology,* Vol. 7 [1971],
p. 55.)

change. **Compliance** refers to a behavior change without any underlying attitude
change (without private acceptance). Some individuals comply with the wishes
of others in order to be liked by them (Insko et al., 1983).

Social Support as a Deterrent to Conformity

In variations on the Asch type of group-pressure experiment, one of the confederates breaks with the majority on a critical trial. This results in a substantial
drop in a subject's conformity. (Asch himself found a decline of 32 percent
conformity to 6 percent under these conditions.) The "deviance" of one other
person emboldens the subject to stick to his or her judgment. Indeed, one study
reveals that the planted deviant need not give the correct answer (Allen and
Levine, 1971). Even where the deviant's answer is more incorrect than that of
the majority, the amount of conformity among subjects is greatly reduced.

In the study, the researchers employed three experimental conditions: (1) On
some trials all four confederates unanimously provided the incorrect answer; (2)
on some trials one of the confederates gave the correct answer but the other
three gave the wrong one; and (3) one of the confederates with a "severe visual
handicap" dissented from the group but did so correctly only 40 percent of the
time. (The confederate wore eyeglasses with extremely thick lenses and indicated
in response to a question by the experimenter before the experiment began that
he could not easily read a legible sign on the wall.) As revealed in Figure 7.2,
the fact of having social support made a considerable difference. And it made
the most difference when the subject had valid support (believed that the deviating confederate gave the right answer and was capable of seeing the card
sets).

The psychological mechanisms responsible for the effectiveness of social support are not yet completely understood, but social psychologists have identified some factors that seem to operate. The very fact that the consensus of the group is broken shows the subject that a variety of opinions and behavior is possible. Further, individuals find themselves less vulnerable to group pressure when they have "company in deviance." And finally, social support gives people an independent source of information against which they can assess reality.

The Impact of a Minority

The above discussion suggests that social influence is by no means limited to the impact that a majority has on a minority. A minority that firmly and resolutely pursues its ends can exert considerable influence on a majority, even when the minority has no obvious advantages such as wealth or recognized positions of power. Historical figures like Galileo, Abraham Lincoln, and Sigmund Freud steadfastly advanced a minority position and eventually induced the majority to adopt their beliefs. Serge Moscovici (1976) notes that a minority commonly finds itself in conflict with some majority standard for behavior. If the minority is to challenge the majority, it needs to provide a consistent and stable alternative norm (for instance, with respect to air pollution, women's rights, abortion, or the employment of immigrant workers). The consistency with which the minority promotes its program is critical because the majority interprets consistency as an expression of certainty and confidence (Maass and Clark, 1984).

However, should the majority perceive a minority as rigid, it finds it easy to discount the minority's opinions (Ricateau, 1971). Under these circumstances, the majority may simply define the minority as dogmatic and narrow-minded. Likewise, the majority can often dismiss the disagreement of a lone minority member as the product of the person's idiosyncracy (perhaps a lack of familiarity with the task, a visual problem, or pigheadedness). But the majority finds it more difficult to discount two or more minority members who support one another.

There has been a difference of opinion among social psychologists as to the point in time at which minority members might display their nonconformity. According to one view, the minority should initially conform to the majority position and show competence before taking a deviant position (Hollander, 1964). By attaining status in the group and demonstrating its dedication to group goals, the minority establishes its credibility. According to another view, the minority should consistently and resolutely show nonconformity from the outset (Moscovici and Faucheux, 1972). Research suggests that both approaches are effective, although much depends on the circumstances (Bray, Johnson, and Chilstrom, 1982). The first approach tends to be more effective than the latter if there is only one minority member. Should a lone individual dissent from the outset, the majority has little difficulty dismissing the person as a "crank" or as "obstinate." Much also depends on the ability of a minority to provide salient and convincing arguments for its position. At times it is less important *when* a minority steps forward than that it do so in ways that convince the majority of its competence.

---

*D*eviance

I am in AFROTC and attended a military social gathering this evening. Although it was a function involving military personnel, we were not supposed to wear our uniforms. Somehow the cadets from our detachment didn't know this, so we all showed up in uniform. Even though we knew everyone else present was military, we felt out of place. Deviance is not an absolute standard but is dependent on the situation. You can carry on the identical behaviors in different situations, and in the one be a conformist and in the other a deviant. In fact, it doesn't even have to be a different group with different standards. It can be the same group with different standards operating in a different situation.

Obedience

This free will business is a bit terrifying anyway. It's almost pleasanter to obey, and make the most of it.

—Ugo Betti, *Struggling Till Dawn*, 1949

Would you carry out orders that could result in the death of another human being if the orders were given by someone in authority? "Of course not," you reply. Any other answer awakens gruesome visions of Hitler's Germany, S.S. concentration camps, and Gestapo units. Certainly people of conscience do not behave that way, or at least, not democratic people like Americans.

Yet the enslavement of millions of blacks, the massacre of the American Indians, the internment of Japanese Americans during World War II, the use of napalm against civilians in Vietnam, the assassination plots against foreign leaders—all these harsh policies arose in a democratic nation. Additionally, the 914 deaths at the People's Temple settlement in Guyana led by Rev. Jim Jones provides stark testimony to the coercive qualities of obedience found in various cults (see Chapter 18). And startling—indeed, frightening—research by a social psychologist, Stanley Milgram (1974), reveals that there is a very good likelihood that you, or at least people like you, would carry out orders impairing another's life.

In his experiments, Milgram told the subjects, who were males aged twenty to fifty from a variety of occupations, that they were to take part in a study of memory and learning. Each subject was to press a switch administering an electric shock whenever the learner (in a reality a Milgram confederate) answered a test question incorrectly. The subject controlled a "generator" that supposedly provided graduated shocks from 15 to 450 volts. The switches had labels ranging from "slight shock" up through "danger: severe shock" and, for the last two switches—for 435 and 450 volts—simply "XXX."

According to plan, the learner provided wrong answers, so that before long the naive subject was instructed to give the strongest shock on the equipment.

The "Victim"
The victim in Milgram's experiment (who was in fact a confederate) was played by a forty-seven-year-old accountant. He appeared somewhat soft, avuncular, and innocuous. Most observers found him mild-mannered and likable. (SOURCE: Stanley Milgram, *Obedience to Authority* [New York: Harper & Row, 1974], Figure 2, p. 17. Copyright © 1974 by Stanley Milgram. Reprinted by permission of Harper & Row, Publishers, Inc.)

Each increase in shock level was met by increasing cries of agony, shrieks of discomfort, and vehement demands from the learner that the experiment be stopped. If the subject hesitated, the experimenter told him to continue with the procedure. (You can see why these studies have been criticized as unethical. Refer to Chapter 1 for the arguments against them and for Milgram's defense of his work.)

The result: 65 percent of the subjects gave the *highest* shock voltage—450 volts. No subject stopped before administering 300 volts, at which point the learner began kicking the wall. Here are excerpts from the responses of one fifty-year-old subject. Upon administering the 180-volt shock, the subject turned around in his chair and, shaking his head, addressed the experimenter in agitated tones (Milgram, 1974: 73–76):

Subject: I can't stand it. I'm not going to kill that man in there. You hear him hollering?
Experimenter: As I told you before, the shocks may be painful, but—
Subject: But he's hollering. He can't stand it. What's going to happen to him?
Experimenter (his voice is patient, matter-of-fact): The experiment requires that you continue, Teacher.
Subject: Aaah, but, unh, I'm not going to get that man sick in there . . . know what I mean?
Experimenter: Whether the learner likes it or not, we must go on, through all the word pairs.

At 195 volts the following exchange occurred:

Learner (screaming): Let me out of here, you have no right to keep me here. Let me out of here, let me out, my heart's bothering me, let me out! *(Subject shakes head, pats the table nervously.)*

> *Subject:* You see, he's hollering. Hear that? Gee, I don't know.
> *Experimenter:* The experiment requires . . .
> *Subject (interrupting):* I know it does, sir, but I mean—hunh! He don't know what he's getting in for. He's up to 195 volts!

After the subject had administered 450 volts, the highest voltage, the following dialogue occurred:

> *Subject:* That's that.
> *Experimenter:* Continue using the 450-volt switch for each wrong answer. Continue, please.
> *Subject:* But I don't get no anything!
> *Experimenter:* Please continue. The next word is "white."
> *Subject:* Don't you think you should look in on him, please?
> *Experimenter:* Not once we've started the experiment.
> *Subject:* But what if something has happened to the man?
> *Experimenter:* The experiment requires that you continue. Go on, please.
> *Subject:* Don't the man's health mean anything?
> *Experimenter:* Whether the learner likes it or not . . .
> *Subject:* What if he's dead in there? *(Gestures toward the room with the electric chair.)* I mean, he told me he can't stand the shock, sir. I don't mean to be rude, but I think you should look in on him. All you have to do is look in on him. All you have to do is look in the door. I don't get no answer, no noise. Something might have happened to the gentleman in there, sir.
> *Experimenter:* We must continue. Go on, please.
> *Subject:* You mean keep giving him what? Four-hundred fifty volts, what he's got now?
> *Experimenter:* That's correct. Continue. The next word is "white."
> *Subject (now at a furious pace):* "White—cloud, horse, rock, house." Answer, please. The answer is "horse." Four-hundred and fifty volts. *(Administers shock.)* Next word, "Bag—paint, music, clown, girl." The answer is "paint." Four-hundred and fifty volts. *(Administers shock.)* Next word is "Short—sentence, movie . . ."
> *Experimenter:* Excuse me, Teacher. We'll have to discontinue the experiment.

In other variations of the experiment, Milgram found that subjects were less obedient as they became "psychologically" closer (in auditory, visual, and physical terms) to the victim. Nonetheless, over 30 percent complied in giving the maximum shock, even when they had to touch the victim and place his hand on the shock plate (see Figure 7.3). This finding helps explain why bombardiers generally feel less guilt about unleashing a deadly cargo of bombs than foot soldiers do about killing people in hand-to-hand combat. In still other experiments, Milgram varied the experimenter's physical closeness and degree of surveillance over the subject. In one condition, the experimenter sat just a few feet away; in another, the experimenter left the laboratory and gave orders by telephone. Obedience dropped from 65 percent when the experimenter sat close by to 22 percent when the experimenter was simply a voice on the telephone. Thus the physical *presence* of an authority has an important influence on an individual's compliance or noncompliance.

From all of this Milgram concludes that obedience is not so much a product

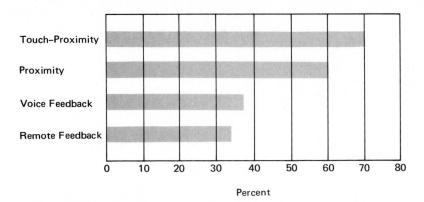

FIGURE 7.3 Percentage of Subjects Who *Defied* an Experimenter Under Varying Conditions
Subjects became less obedient as the experimental conditions put them into closer contact with the victim.
(SOURCE: Adapted from Stanley Milgram, "Some Conditions of Obedience and Disobedience to Authority," *Human Relations,* Vol. 18 [1965], p. 129.)

of a person's moral qualities or lack of them, but of the situation in which the person is placed. He interprets his study as revealing that the subjects were unwilling to appear rude, unwilling to embarrass either themselves or the experimenter. The subjects entered what Milgram calls an "agentic state," one in which they viewed themselves as agents of the experimenter (see boxed insert, pp. 228–229). The most difficult thing for the subjects was to break the ice. Once a subject refused to comply, his relationship with the experimenter altered. For these latter subjects, Milgram found that there was a perceptible moment when the strain is reduced and each subject surmounts a barrier of anxiety, refusing to go on.

COMPLIANCE IN THE ABSENCE OF EXTERNAL PRESSURE

The research described so far in the chapter has dealt with conformity under conditions of considerable pressure to conform. Milgram's experimenters ordered their subjects to follow instructions. And in the Asch type of experiment, subjects experience considerable group pressure to conform. But what about situations in which people are put under little or no pressure to comply? Many studies have been conducted to find out what happens then.

The Foot-in-the Door Technique

Compliance breeds compliance. If we can induce a person to comply with a small request at first, we stand a good chance of getting him or her to comply

OBEDIENCE TO ORDERS: ISSUES OF MORALITY IN COMBAT

The Milgram experiment has been referred to as "the Eichmann experiment." Adolf Eichmann, an infamous Nazi bureaucrat, contributed to the murder of millions of Jews in German gas chambers in the course of "carrying out his job." When captured in South America, where he had fled after World War II, and brought to trial in Israel, Eichmann portrayed himself not as an individual acting in a morally accountable way but as the agent of external authority: "So far as my participation is concerned, I must point out that I do not consider myself guilty from a legal point of view. I was only receiving and carrying out orders" (Faulkner, 1973: 135). Loyalty, duty, and discipline were his compelling values.

The Milgram experiments, conducted in the early 1960s, were often dismissed as simply the "German phenomenon." But the shocking atrocities committed by "ordinary" American soldiers in the course of the Vietnam War added a new dimension. It seemed that Americans were just as capable as Germans of committing crimes in the name of obedience. This was highlighted by the massacre at the Vietnamese village of My Lai. American soldiers under the command of Lieutenant William Calley landed near the village in helicopters. The troops moved into the village, rounding up men, women, children, and infants. One American soldier gave this account:

We made them squat down and Lieutenant Calley came over and said, "You know what to do with them, don't you?" And I said yes. So I took it for granted that he just wanted us to watch them. And he left, and came back about ten or fifteen minutes later and said, "How come you ain't killed them yet?" And I told him that I didn't think you wanted us to kill them, that you just wanted us to guard them. He said, "No. I want them dead." (*New York Times,* November 25, 1969, p. 16)

The Americans then backed away about 15 feet and fired their automatics into the group. The following exchange occurred between one American soldier and Mike Wallace of CBS News:

Q: How do you shoot babies?
A: I don't know. It's just one of those things.
Q: How many people would you imagine were killed that day?
A: I'd say about three hundred and seventy. (*New York Times,* November 25, 1969, p. 16)

Lieutenant Calley was later brought to trial and convicted for having ordered the death of the civilians. In his trial, Calley did not deny that he had personally ordered the slayings; rather, the defense insisted that Calley was acting in accordance with what he saw as his duty in carrying out orders from legitimate authorities. A major question in the Calley trial was not so much whether Calley was acting on the basis of an order from his superior, but whether a reasonable person should have followed such orders had they been issued. The court found that Calley, by virtue of his age, rank, experience, and training, should have known that such an order was illegal. In convicting Calley, the court reaffirmed the Nuremberg principle that soldiers must disobey an order that requires them to commit a war crime. In sum, it held that military personnel are not automatons but reasoning agents who must act on the basis of moral principles (Cockerham and Cohen, 1980).

Immediately after the trial, a Gallup telephone poll revealed that 79 percent of Americans *disapproved* (9 percent approved) of Calley's having been found guilty of premeditated murder. In another poll, conducted by the Roper Organization, 58 percent of Americans disapproved of Calley's having been brought to trial. At the beginning of the Roper interview, the interviewer described a hypothetical situation in which soldiers were ordered by their superior officers to shoot all inhabitants of a Vietnamese village who were suspected of aiding the enemy, including old men, women, and children. Of the sample interviewed, 67 percent thought most people would follow orders and shoot. Asked what they themselves would do, 51 percent said they would shoot and 33 percent said they would refuse to do so. The 51 percent who declared that they would follow orders were not admitting to moral weakness; for many of them, this response represented what they viewed to be their moral obligation (Kelman and Lawrence, 1972).

V. Lee Hamilton (1978) undertook to simulate in a laboratory setting a modified court-martial case resembling that of Lieutenant Calley. The "defendant" (a corporal) argued that he had followed the orders of a superior officer in killing unarmed prisoners and that he thought his orders were legal. "Jurors" attributed the burden of responsibility to the superior, although the superior was not the person on trial. This was even more likely when the superior was of considerably higher rank than the subordinate (a captain as opposed to a sergeant).

Although the "superior officer" did not testify at the simulated trial, the "jurors" (the subjects) viewed him as deserving to be tried for the crime and justified such a trial both in terms of his role responsibilities and his having given the specific orders. In contrast, the perceptions of the defendant varied with the verdict that was chosen. Subjects voting for acquittal stressed his role requirements, citing his orders and his duty to obey. Subjects voting for conviction on the charge of premeditated murder focused on the illegality of the actions, irrespective of the orders from a superior officer.

Other research suggests that enough ambiguity and disagreement prevail among current United States military personnel on the subject of immoral and illegal orders that it remains quite possible that incidents like My Lai can occur again (Cockerham and Cohen, 1980). However, individuals differ in their readiness or willingness to obey orders. Higher-ranking soldiers, individuals with favorable attitudes toward the military, and those who grew up in rural areas and small towns are more likely than other soldiers to *disagree* with the statement "A soldier should have the right to disobey any order he feels is immoral, even in combat."

with a larger demand later. During the Korean War, Chinese interrogators used this principle to their advantage. They would persuade American prisoners of war to sign noncontroversial documents as a first step in leading them eventually to sign damaging anti-American statements (Schein, Schneier, and Barker, 1961). People selling products from door to door likewise often try to get a customer to comply with a small request, such as allowing the sales representative to enter the customer's house, after which it is easier to get the customer to comply with a bigger request—purchasing the product. This is the so-called **foot-in-the-door technique.** If we can get someone to give an inch, we are more likely to be able to take a mile.

J. L. Freedman and S. C. Fraser (1966) demonstrated this effect in a safe-driving campaign. Experimenters visited homemakers and told them they were working for the Committee for Safe Driving. They asked the women to sign a petition that was to be sent to their state senator supporting safe-driving legislation. The vast majority complied. A few weeks later another experimenter visited the petition signers. This time the women were asked to place a large, unattractive sign—reading "Drive Carefully"—in their front yards. Of these women, 55 percent complied. In contrast, the experimenters obtained only 17 percent compliance from a control group composed of homemakers who had not previously been approached. Hence getting the women to comply with a small initial request more than tripled their compliance with a much larger request.

Freedman and Fraser explain their finding in these terms:

> What may occur is a change in the person's feelings about getting involved or about taking action. Once he has agreed to a request, his attitude may change. He may become in his own eyes, the kind of person who does this sort of thing, who agrees to requests made by strangers, and who takes action on things he believes in, who cooperates with good causes. (1966: 201)

This explanation parallels the self-perception and attribution theory of Daryl Bem (1972) described in Chapter 2. According to this view, people observe their own actions and draw inferences (make attributions) regarding their internal states. Thus a homemaker observes herself as taking action on a good cause without any external pressure. She then infers that she must be the sort of person—generous and compliant—who becomes involved with such causes. As a consequence of this change in self-perception, she becomes more disposed to later compliant acts of a similar sort.

A study by Mark Snyder and Michael R. Cunningham (1975) supports this interpretation. The experimenters telephoned subjects and asked some of them if they would be willing to answer eight questions (a small request) in a telephone survey to be conducted at a future time. Other subjects were asked if they would be willing to answer fifty questions (a large request) in the future survey. Two days later, each subject was called back by a different experimenter, who asked if the subject would be willing to answer thirty survey questions (a moderate request). In addition, a control group of subjects who had not previously been telephoned were asked if they would answer 30 questions. In the control group, 33 percent said yes. Of the subjects who had initially agreed to the small request,

64 percent agreed to the moderate-sized request. But of the subjects who had initially refused the large request (78 percent had refused the initial request), only 12.5 percent complied with the moderate request.

These findings are in keeping with the self-perception hypothesis (DeJong, 1979). The increase in compliance in the small-initial-request condition results from previous compliance with the small request. The decrease in compliance in the large-initial-request condition is associated with the previous noncompliance with the large request. In sum, a step-by-step program apparently brings about a change in people's self-perceptions that makes them either more or less susceptible to new requests. It needs to be pointed out, however, that for the foot-in-the-door technique to succeed, the first request must be of sufficient magnitude to commit the person to further compliance (Seligman, Bush, and Kirsch, 1976). Additionally, there is some question as to whether the foot-in-the-door procedure influences compliance with more substantial requests involving behaviors like donation of blood that are psychologically costly to perform (Foss and Dempsey, 1979).

A variation of the foot-in-the-door technique is what salespeople and researchers term "the low-ball technique." Consider, for instance, a panhandler who asks you for a quarter. You agree to the request and reach in your pocket or purse for the money. But as you do so, the panhandler asks, "Could you make it fifty cents?" You are more likely to give him the fifty cents than you would have had he asked you for the higher amount first. The automobile salesperson uses a similar approach in securing an agreement from a customer to purchase a car and then increasing the cost of the vehicle. Research suggests that the low-ball technique generates a sense of obligation to the individual who makes the request (Burger and Petty, 1981). The low-ball procedure seems to be even more effective than the foot-in-the-door technique in generating compliance.

The Effects of Guilt on Compliance

Common sense tells us that when we commit a wrong, we feel guilty. We seek to atone—balance the scales, so to speak—by complying with another person's wishes, especially if it entails performing a good act. Two social psychologists, J. Merrill Carlsmith and Alan E. Gross (1969), decided to test whether in fact this common-sense notion is true. Using a format similar to Milgram's obedience study, they told each subject that they were conducting a "learning" experiment.

Subjects were instructed to throw a switch whenever the "learner" (the experimenters' accomplice) made a mistake. Carlsmith and Gross told half of the subjects that when they closed the switch the learner received a painful shock. The other half were told nothing; they merely heard a buzzer sound when they threw the switch. After the experiment was completed, the learner (the confederate) asked the subject to participate in a telephone campaign to get signatures on a petition to save the redwood trees in northern California. Of those who had only heard the buzzer, 25 percent complied. In contrast, 75 percent, or three times as many, of those who thought they had administered shocks complied—presumably to lessen their feelings of guilt.

Social psychologists have found a similar effect operating in many different kinds of transgressions: ruining an experiment, breaking an experimenter's machine, causing someone to forfeit green stamps, scattering a graduate student's index cards, breaking a camera, and lying. Under such experimental conditions, people who felt guilty have agreed to sign a petition, donate blood, and volunteer to serve in future experiments for no pay.

But the principle of making restitution to the injured party does not appear to be the motivation behind compliance behavior. Experimenters (Freedman, Wallington, and Bless, 1967) have demonstrated similar compliance effects when the request is made by someone who lacks knowledge of the subject's transgression. Indeed, evidence suggests that a person who does harm may be even more inclined to help someone who is not the victim. Continued contact with the victim apparently results in uncomfortable feelings of obligation, or serves as an unpleasant reminder of the harm the subject inflicted (Carlsmith and Gross, 1969). Further, research by Dennis T. Regan, Margo Williams, and Sondra Sparling (1972) shows that guilt does not merely make people more compliant with requests; guilty people *seek out* ways to lessen their guilt by voluntarily engaging in a good deed.

Just why people who feel guilt should be more disposed to comply with a request or do a good deed is not entirely clear. One explanation, which has some experimental support, concerns our feelings of self-esteem. Doing harm apparently damages our self-esteem—our images of ourselves as decent people. By engaging in some activity that we believe has social merit, we can gain positive information about ourselves. In so doing we restore a positive self-image (McMillen, 1971; Apsler, 1975).

The Obligation to Reciprocate Favors

"You scratch my back and I'll scratch yours." "One good turn deserves another." We base many of our activities on the principle embodied in these sayings. Indeed, it is a familiar practice in the business world to wine and dine prospective clients and even give them gifts. The assumption is that the recipient will feel obligated to reciprocate the favor by complying with the other person's wishes.

D. T. Regan (1971) undertook to test this principle of reciprocation in a social psychological experiment. He had college students in pairs evaluate paintings for a study on "aesthetics." Unknown to each subject, the other person in the pair was the experimenter's confederate.

Regan provided periodic rest periods as the pair evaluated paintings. During the first five-minute break, the confederate left the room briefly and returned with two Cokes. The confederate would hand one of the Cokes to the subject and say: "I asked him [the experimenter] if I could go get myself a Coke, and he said it was okay, so I bought one for you, too." In another experimental condition, the confederate simply left the room and returned in a short while. And in still another condition, the experimenter provided Cokes for both the subject and the confederate.

During conversation in the second break, it would turn out that the confed-

Besides the factors considered in the body of the text, social psychologists have identified a number of other situational factors that influence conformity and compliance.

GROUP SIZE

Asch's research (1952, 1956) suggested that conformity increases as group size increases, up to about four members (a unanimous majority of three plus the subject), but then it levels out. However, Harold B. Gerard, Roland A. Wilhelmy, and Edward S. Conolley (1968) found a higher incidence of conformity when the majority numbered five or six. In any event, a majority need not be unusually large in order to exert maximal influence.

COHESIVENESS

The greater the cohesiveness of the group, the greater the conformity. In brief, the more attracted individuals are to the group, the more likely they are to conform to its dictates.

STATUS

George C. Homans (1974) takes the view that both high-status and low-status people conform less than those intermediate in status. He reasons that one deviation is unlikely to jeopardize the position of a high-status person, and that low-status people have little to lose in nonconformity. But for persons of intermediate status, the situation is different; they lack the credit standing of the high-status person; and unlike the low-status person, they have plenty of room for downward mobility. Not all research, however, confirms Homans' interpretation. Richard M. Emerson (1964), for instance, found in a group of Boy Scouts that it was the high- and low-status boys who, relative to moderate-status boys, were most conforming. Clearly, additional research is needed.

PUBLICITY AND SURVEILLANCE

The greater the publicity and surveillance associated with behavior, the greater the conformity. Where behavior is difficult to monitor—where transgressions may go unnoticed—the effectiveness of social sanctions is weakened (Milgram, 1974). In public settings, we are likely to experience pressures for compliance although private acceptance may be absent.

DIFFICULTY AND AMBIGUITY

The more difficult the task or the more ambiguous the stimulus, the greater the conformity. For instance, where the task is difficult, we are more likely to look to others as sources of information regarding appropriate courses of action.

FEAR AND ANXIETY

The greater the fear or anxiety, the greater the conformity (Schachter, 1959; Walters and Karol, 1960). Apparently misery loves company—particularly miserable company.

ALLOCATION OF RESOURCES

Compliance with rules is related to the allocation of resources within the group. Equitable sharing heightens people's tendency to comply and requires less surveillance to produce compliance. The reverse is true of inequitable sharing (Thibaut, Friedland, and Walker, 1974).

erate was selling raffle tickets for a good cause at 25 cents each. The story was that if the confederate sold the most tickets, he would win $50. As his measure of compliance, Regan used the number of tickets the subject agreed to buy.

There was no difference in compliance between subjects who did not receive a Coke and those who were treated to one by the experimenter. Thus simply receiving a soft drink did not lead to greater compliance. But receiving a Coke from the confederate more than doubled the proportion of the subjects buying more than a single ticket (58 percent when the confederate bought the Coke compared with 25 percent in the other two conditions).

These data strongly indicate that we are more likely to comply with a request by someone who has done us a favor than by someone who has not. Regan interprets such behavior as deriving from the *norm of reciprocity*—the expectation that people ought to return good for good (see Chapter 10).

Several other situational factors that influence compliance are discussed in the box on page 233.

SUMMARY

1. Human life presents a picture of organization and regularity. Interaction seems patterned in flowing currents of activity. We feel ourselves caught up and bound within integrated wholes. Accordingly, as we observe human behavior it seems in large measure to be organized and focused rather than haphazard and random. Social psychologists term this social order.

2. The fact that so much of social life is routine and repetitive permits us to treat certain activities and situations as things or objects. By acting toward one another in certain ways, we "are" social order. Additionally, since we are aware or conscious of these patterned relationships—we label them "the United States of America," "the University of Wisconsin," and so on—we act toward these activities as objects.

3. Social order allows us to experience the world as stable and predictable. One way in which we achieve a sense of social order is through shared expectations. In much of human life, social behavior is prescribed for us in terms of do's and don'ts. Such requirements are norms. When norms cannot be lived up to, we may offer excuses and justifications to maintain the social order.

4. Social order is not something that occurs automatically. It must be worked at and fashioned as we repeat, reaffirm, and reconstruct social acts. We negotiate social order in the process of social interaction.

5. Muzafer Sherif's work with the autokinetic effect shows how norms arise in social situations. Individuals are not necessarily aware of the fact that they are being influenced by others, or that they are converging toward a common norm. In fact, they often believe that they are not influenced by others. This work reveals the importance of situational influences.

6. Solomon Asch's work has added to our understanding of the conditions

under which individuals will conform to a false group consensus that they can plainly see is wrong.

7. When a confederate breaks with the majority in an experiment of the type Asch designed, there is a substantial drop in subject conformity. The "deviance" of one other individual emboldens the subject to stick to his or her judgment.

8. A minority that firmly and resolutely pursues its ends can exert considerable influence on a majority, even when the minority has no obvious advantage such as wealth or a recognized position of power. If the minority is to challenge the majority effectively, it needs to provide a consistent and stable alternative norm. The consistency with which the minority promotes its program is critical because the majority interprets consistency as an expression of certainty and confidence.

9. Stanley Milgram has added to our understanding of how human behavior can be dictated when an individual is in a situation in which he or she feels required to obey. Some 65 percent of his subjects would have gone "all the way," delivering what they thought were dangerous electric shocks to people who gave wrong answers in the test. From all of this, Milgram concludes that obedience is not so much a product of a person's moral qualities or lack of them but of the situation in which the person is placed. The subjects entered what Milgram calls an "agentic state," one in which they viewed themselves as agents of the experimenter. The most difficult thing for the subjects was to break the ice and disobey.

10. Compliance breeds compliance. If we can induce a person to comply with a small request at first, we stand a good chance of getting him or her to comply with a larger demand later. This is the basis of the foot-in-the-door technique. A prevalent social psychological explanation of this phenomenon is based on self-perception and attribution theory.

11. A powerful technique for obtaining compliance is to induce a person to do something that harms another. Guilt can lead to compliance, and this compliance does not necessarily involve the injured party at all.

12. Putting people under obligation by doing them favors tends to make them more inclined to comply with one's wishes. This derives from the norm of reciprocity.

GLOSSARY

Accounts □   Explanations we make for unanticipated or untoward behavior.

Autokinetic effect □   An optical illusion. If a small, fixed spot of light is briefly exposed in a darkened room, it will appear to move.

Compliance □   A behavior change without any underlying attitude change (without private acceptance).

Conformity □   Adherence to or behavioral change in accordance with social expectations.

Excuses ☐ Statements we provide that deny our responsibility for the negative consequences of our action and admit the behavior to be reprehensible.

Foot-in-the-door technique ☐ The idea that compliance breeds compliance. If we can induce a person to comply with an initial small request, we stand a good chance of getting him or her to comply with a larger demand later.

Internalization ☐ The process whereby an individual incorporates within his or her personality the standards of behavior that are prevalent in the group.

Justifications ☐ Statements we provide that deny responsibility for an action but reinterpret it in a more socially acceptable manner.

Negotiated order ☐ A system by which we arrive at mutually shared agreements, tacit understandings, binding contracts, unhappy compromises, and coerced accommodations through processes of manipulation, persuasion, constraint, inducement, diplomacy, and bargaining.

Norms ☐ Standards for behavior that members of a social group share, that they are expected follow, and that are enforced by positive and negative sanctions.

Private acceptance ☐ A behavior change accompanied by underlying attitude change.

Social order ☐ The configuration that makes human life usually appear to be organized and focused rather than haphazard and random.

8 ROLES

THE NATURE OF ROLES
  The Reciprocal Nature of Roles
  Role-taking
  Role-making
  Role Strain
  Role Distance and Role–Person
    Merger

SELF-PRESENTATION
  Impression Management
  Front
  Regions: Front-Stage, Backstage
  Altercasting
  Authentic Behavior
  The Self-monitoring of Behavior

All the world's a stage,/And all the men and women merely players./They have their exits and their entrances;/And one man in his time plays many parts.

—William Shakespeare, *As You Like It,* Act II, Scene 7

From Shakespeare down through the writings of contemporary social psychologists, the analogy between human behavior and the theater has often suggested itself. Much of social life resembles the acting on the stage of a theater, with its varied scenes, parts, masks, and airs. As actors perform their theatrical roles, they are governed by the script, what the other actors say and do, and the reactions of the audience.

Of course, the analogy of the stage has its shortcomings. Our parts are real, whereas the theater is a world of make-believe. Life presents us with actual scenes and players who are often not well rehearsed (Goffman, 1959, 1981). The scripts provided us by our culture are much too broad to cover many of the details and eventualities of social interaction. Indeed, few situations in everyday life supply us with a fixed script. Rather, as we experience much of life, we must

237

continually write our own lines as we devise our courses of action (Hewitt, 1976). Hence there is an element of tentativeness in our relations with other people.

THE NATURE OF ROLES

As we go about our everyday activities, we mentally attempt to place people in various social categories: neighbor, old man, child, pedestrian, aunt, shopper, student, Catholic, lawyer, minister, alcoholic, client, Republican, lover, and so on. We classify people—lump them together—in terms of their common attributes, their common behavior, or the common reactions others have toward them. In so doing, we undertake to define the situation. For instance, we must judge whether the person in the clothing department is a fellow customer or the salesclerk, whether the telephone caller is a poll taker or a salesperson, whether the answer seeker appearing at our university office door is a student or a faculty member, whether the friendly individual at the party is the bartender or a guest, whether the intruder on our property is a thief or a meter reader, and so on. We make such inferences in order to identify the set of expectations that will operate in the relationship—what we can expect of others and what they can expect of us. **Roles** allow us to do this. They specify the normative requirements that apply to the behavior of specific categories of people in particular situational contexts. Put in still other terms, roles specify *who does what, when, and where* (see boxed insert).

Roles permit us to formulate our behavior mentally so that we can fit our action to that of others. Through them we are able to collapse or telescope a range of behaviors into manageable bundles. We can collect particulars of an unfolding social scene under more general units or classes. And roles enable us to assume that in certain respects we can ignore personal differences; that people are interchangeable; and that as a practical matter we can deal with them in almost identical ways. We know what to expect of one another in certain situations because we "know" that particular "types" of people behave in typical ways under certain circumstances (Schutz, 1964). For instance, every American "knows" that a postal clerk is a "person who forwards the mail."

Roles involve a categorizing process. By means of roles we structure our social world in terms of classes or categories of potential coactors (individuals with whom we may interact). John Lofland observes:

> Roles are *claimed* labels, from behind which people present themselves to others and partially in terms of which they conceive, gauge, and judge their past, current and projected action. And roles are *imputed* labels toward which, and partially in terms of which, people likewise conceive, gauge and judge others' past, present and projected action. (1967: 9–10)

Of course the process of categorization involves a social loss. As Georg Simmel points out: "Man distorts the picture of another. He both detracts and supplements, since generalization is always both less and more than individuality is" (1971: 2).

FROM DEVIL TO SAINT

Our roles have an important bearing upon our identities. Our roles, by placing us in relation to others, establish *where* and *what* we are in social terms and thus *who* we are. It is not surprising, therefore, that a change in a role may be followed by a corresponding change in our expression of personality. In daily life we encounter many illustrations: the young woman turned mother who reveals new maturity, or the child who becomes a member of the school patrol and takes on new dignity. Here is a first-grade teacher's account of one such change:

This is my first year of teaching, and first grade is no picnic. One girl, Beth, has been giving me constant trouble. She is a very energetic child, a perpetual-motion machine. She's a regular little chatterbox—picks fights, takes other children's crayons, gets out of her seat continually, and fails to do her work.

I have tried everything I know to get her to behave. I have tried various combinations of "neighbors" in hopes of arriving at some workable arrangement. I have placed her at a table off by herself in a segregated part of the room. I have kept her in during recess and held her after school. I have tried to shame her in front of her classmates. I have sent her to the principal's office. I have had a meeting with her parents. But nothing worked.

You can imagine my concern when it was Beth's turn to be "leader" at her table last week. In fact, I entertained the thought of skipping over her, but she was observant and reminded me that she was to be leader. Not knowing what else to do, I let her. The leader's job is to make sure that the leader and the other children do their work properly, work quietly, behave themselves, and do something constructive during their free time.

To my surprise, Beth not only kept all the others in line but also took care of herself. She was quiet and conscientious, and she did the best work she has done all year. To tell the truth, if I had not known otherwise, I would have insisted that this was not the same Beth. It just shows the impact that role-taking can have in influencing the self-image and in turn guiding a person's actions. As I see it, Beth previously had a self-image as a "little devil" and was playing the part to the hilt. And she was being rewarded by getting all kinds of attention. When Beth had new expectations and obligations attached to her in the role of "leader," she found an avenue to win acceptance that was socially approved. She became the person of the role, "a responsible, conscientious leader."

Source: Adapted from the term paper of a teacher who was working on a master's degree. By permission.

The Reciprocal Nature of Roles

A role does not exist by itself (Athay and Darley, 1982; Stiles et al., 1984). Rather, it is a bundle of activities meshed into the activities of other people. Without students there are no professors; without clients, no lawyers; without

The Deviant Role
One role often taken by a child
is that of the "bad boy." (Patrick
Reddy)

husbands, no wives; without Jews, no Gentiles; without "offenders," no police; without "psychotics," no psychiatrists. And vice versa: Without professors there are no students; without lawyers, no clients; and so on through the list.

Roles impinge upon us as sets of norms that define our **obligations**—the actions others can legitimately insist that we perform—and **expectations**—the actions we can legitimately insist that others perform (Goffman, 1961*b*: 92). Every role is linked to at least one other role and is reciprocal to this linked role (or roles). Thus the obligations of the student role—to read assigned materials, take exams, attend classes—are the expectations of the professor role. The expectations of the student role—to receive authoritative material from lectures, to be given fair examinations, to be graded in terms of merit without regard to personal attributes, race, sex, or religion—are the obligations of the professor role.

As a consequence of the reciprocal character of roles, other social actors must recognize and respect our adoption of a given role. Hence, you *validate* your social psychology professor's role as a professor by acting as a student toward him or her. But should your social psychology professor claim to be a surgeon, you are unlikely to take his or her word for it and allow the professor to remove your gall bladder. You would refuse to accept the professor's claim to the surgeon's role; consequently, the professor could not "make like" a surgeon in actual life. Indeed, some roles, such as that of surgeon, require *legitimization* through professional licensing.

Roles are shorthand conceptions embracing expectations and obligations. We are locked by life into the same social arena through networks of reciprocal roles. In other words, *we are tied to one another through role relationships: The obligations of one end are the expectations of the other.* Human societies are characterized by peculiarly intricate complexes of interlocking roles, which we sustain in the course of interaction with one another. We experience these definable relationships as social order or social structure.

The reciprocal character of roles finds its reflection in selfhood (see Chapter 5). We take the stance of another person and imagine what he or she expects of us in a given role (say, as professor, lawyer, wife, Jew)—in brief we anticipate our obligations. In so doing, we have to take the role of the other person. In imagination, we place ourselves in other people's shoes—in their roles—and determine what is required to fit our actions to their actions (our obligations). But in taking the stance of the other, we also imagine his or her obligations toward us (say, as student, client, child, Gentile). It is as if we momentarily exchange roles to grasp the requirements for social interaction. We attempt to determine how others experience a given situation; we look for the intention or direction of their acts. We examine, evaluate, and interpret what they do; we seek to uncover the implications of their acts for our plans of action. In sum, we attempt to grasp people's point of view by mentally "penetrating" their consciousness.

We then form our own actions on the basis of our interpretations of theirs. We may abandon a given course, revise it, suspend it, intensify it, or replace it. We are seldom allowed to play our roles in exactly the manner we would like, and the same is true for others. Hence we have to build up interaction point by point as we take each other continuously into account. It is this process involving the self that enables us to *fit* our lines of action to the developing lines of actions of other people.

Role-taking

As we translate roles into action, even well-established and repetitive action, we find that in each instance we need to create the action anew. We continuously engage in a process of self-interpretation as we fit our behavior to that of others linked with us in a reciprocal network of roles. Since the roles of others can only be inferred rather than directly known, we constantly need to test our inferences about the behavior of others. In **role-taking**—the ongoing process of *devising* our performance—we start or stop, abandon or postpone, implement or transform our lines of action on the basis of the feedback we receive. As a consequence, interaction has a *tentative* quality to it (Blumer, 1969; Turner, 1962). Role-taking, then, involves us in a process in which we undertake to "get inside" the perspective of another in a particular situation and "observe" our own conduct from this other person's point of view (Hewitt, 1976).

In formulating our behavior, we act *as if* roles are real and objective entities; we treat them as things. We bring to social settings the familiar image of the people and roles that we have evolved in previous encounters. We hold as

*R*ole-taking

This past week we had a lot of midterms, so my roommates and I decided to go out and do a "little celebrating" since it was Friday night. "Celebrating" consists of hitting a local bar and getting drunk. Now the truth of the matter is that I don't drink and my roommates know that I don't drink. I can't stand the stuff. Even carbonated beverages seem to tear at my mouth and throat, ripping my internal organs apart. Nonetheless, I am very fond of my roommates and we're one big primary group. The bar waiter humorously added a drink-stirring stick to my water—water always being my "drink" of the evening. Well, the evening wore on, and we all started getting pretty "loaded." My girlfriends and I laughed and giggled, and made perfect fools of ourselves. I felt very lightheaded and I had difficulty keeping my balance on the dance floor. In fact, in my "state" I slipped and fell on at least two occasions. Somehow we all managed to make it home. But the real "clincher"—this morning I woke up with a bad "hangover." Now believe me, all I had was one glass of water all evening. But I had played my role so well, I so identified with the role, that I became the person of the role. By meeting the expectations of my roommates and having them "validate" my role for me, I had in fact gone so far as to cultivate and experience the symptoms of intoxication.

constant that stock of knowledge that concerns the other people—until we receive information to the contrary (Schutz, 1964: 39–42). Such information provides a framework in which we can again pick up interrupted social interaction; it gives us a sense of preestablished meanings by which we can formulate our actions and anticipate the actions of others. Such a priori knowledge minimizes the disruption and costs of exploratory behavior.

Role-making

We have stressed that role-playing—even in the case of a role that is well established and repetitive—entails the continuous creation of action. We constantly devise performances as we fit our behavior with that of others. Consequently, our action is always provisional and subject to revision in light of the perceived purpose and meaning we find in others' actions. Our ideal conceptions of our own and others' roles tend to be vague and incomplete. In some respects, each action is unique and each interaction involves an element of improvisation. For this reason, role-playing entails **role-making.**

As an example let us consider bureaucracies, since it is in them that we would least expect role-making to occur. Literature in the social sciences has traditionally emphasized that bureaucratic work rules are tightly prescribed and rigorously enforced. Yet William J. Haga, George Graen, and Fred Dansereau (1974) found that the fixed-role theory did not hold for managers entering new jobs in a state college housing and food-service division. Many of the managers brought with them a professional orientation to administrative work, which was reflected in subscriptions to professional journals and memberships in professional associations.

Haga and his associates found that over a nine-month period, the supervisors of these professionally oriented managers came to hold significantly *higher* expectations of them (in terms of counseling, planning, communication, and administering duties). The managers who were professionally oriented (as contrasted with their counterparts who were not) worked harder and longer on all tasks. Their professional orientation to administration provided an alternative source of guidance to that furnished by the bureaucratic organization. Through work—through their actions—the managers modified their supervisors' expectations of their role requirements (of what they *ought* to do); they *shaped* their own organizational roles. Rather than being brought into line with the organization's fixed-role prescriptions, they brought about *new* role definitions. Similarly, blacks and women have effected profound changes in their role definitions in recent years by *doing*—by acting as first-class citizens. Rigid arrangements of institutional racism and sexism bent and gave as new definitions were forged. And more recently, the relationship between physician and patient has been redefined by a consumerist perspective, in which the physician and patient "bargain" over the terms of the relationship (Haug and Lavin, 1981). Traditionally, the physician as practitioner was in charge, and the patient (the role of sick person) was obligated to cooperate unquestioningly with the physician's prescribed regimen.

Still other forces contribute to role-making. As Erving Goffman (1961: 82) observes, "We do not take on items of conduct one at a time but rather a whole harness load of them." In other words, we find ourselves bound in a network not only with one other reciprocal role but with many others. This web of multiple roles makes contradictory and conflicting demands upon us. We find it necessary to adjudicate, align, adjust, and balance their requirements—to *create* and *discover* "consistent" wholes. In brief, we need to engage in role-making.

Take the role of school superintendent. People in this role are not only managers of a financial enterprise but also personnel officers. They must deal with parents and parent-teacher associations, teachers and teacher organizations, school boards, taxpayers, politicians, patriotic organizations, and fundamentalist religious groups. They are immersed in a field of clashing expectations. Taxpayers oppose new revenue-raising tax levies pushed by educational groups. Professional principles of academic freedom conflict with demands for "loyalty" from patriotic organizations and with calls for strict biblical teachings from fundamentalist church groups. Politicians see school funds as lucrative sums to be diverted to cronies and special business interests. Teachers want higher salaries when money is scarce. In handling these contradictory pressures, superintendents juggle various requirements in an ongoing process—giving in to this group here, that group there—compromising, negotiating, holding the line, backtracking, advancing, maneuvering, in brief, hammering out, trimming, and

> ## *Role conflict*
>
> *For the past three years I have worked on the loading dock of a large retail appliance store. Well, five months ago I received a promotion and was made the supervisor. I used to load trucks with all the guys that now work under me, and at times I feel very uneasy when I have to get after the guys to work faster and harder. I understand how aggravating it is for a boss to constantly hound you for more work. All of these guys are my friends, but in my new role I am required to get them to do things that I always hated to do myself. I have to play the role of both supervisor and friend, and it isn't the best situation to be in, believe me! I am confronted with conflicting expectations because I am assuming two contradictory roles simultaneously—supervisor and friend. The boss expects me to get the most work I can out of the guys; the guys expect me to be understanding and take it easy on them.*

shaping the contours of their roles through action (Gross, Mason, and McEachern, 1958).

Role Strain

From the discussion thus far in the chapter, it should be clear that roles do not provide us with set, rigid scripts, carved once and for all time in granite. Rather, the fluidity and indeterminacy of human life continually compel us to modify our behavior and to define and redefine our roles. It is hardly surprising, therefore, that from time to time we should encounter difficulties in hammering out our courses of action and experience these difficulties as stress. **Role strain** is the term social psychologists apply to those problems we experience in meeting the requirements of a role (Goode, 1960).

One source of role strain is *role conflict*—individuals find themselves exposed to incompatible demands. The crux of the matter lies in the fact that social relationships involve at least two people, each of whom has a variety of expectations regarding the behavior of the other. Conflict often develops when the individuals disagree as to what each may legitimately expect of the other. As illustrations, consider the following three sources of role conflict:

1. Some roles are ascribed to us by virtue of our race, nationality, religion, gender, or family membership. Consequently, other people may expect us to act in ways that we find unacceptable or uncongenial. Chapters 15 and 16 detail some of the difficulties associated with being a member of a racial minority and with institutionalized sexist practices.
2. We find that some of our roles conflict with other roles. For instance, when a worker is promoted to supervisor, he or she often feels a conflict

Role Conflict
The police officer is ex-
pected to be a stern, formidable, tough representative
of authority yet simulta-
neously a kindly, sympa-
thetic, and helping friend.
(Don McCarthy)

between being a boss and being a friend to former co-workers. Likewise, workers at times experience conflict between working overtime (work role) and spending the time with their families (family role); this is particularly the case for women, who, more than men, also usually assume responsibility for household management and child care (Cooke and Rousseau, 1984). And college students sometimes report that they feel considerable stress when their parents pay them a campus visit. In some respects the life styles of their family and peers are at odds, making them feel they are "on stage" before audiences holding contradictory expectations.

3. Some roles contain incompatible elements in their repertoires. We have already noted that school superintendents find themselves pulled in

contradictory directions by parents, teachers, taxpayers, politicians, and others. They must somehow adjudicate the conflicting demands deriving from multiple interests. Likewise, physicians are supposed to be humanitarian, self-sacrificing saviors of the sick, yet simultaneously they are small-business retailers of knowledge. Although aggressive bill collecting may be consistent with the latter aspect of the role, it is inconsistent with the gentle healer dimension.

Mechanisms for dealing with role conflict run into the hundreds. One of the more common approaches is *compartmentalization*. We subdivide our lives so that in one context we act one way and in another context another way. Hence some college students act one way with their parents and another way with their peers, attempting to keep the two worlds separated. Another mechanism entails a *hierarchy of obligations*. We recognize that certain obligations take precedence over others. Many of our excuses take this form: "I would like to but I can't because . . . ," followed by the assertion of some higher priority.

Role ambiguity may be another source of role strain. Some roles are rather new and emergent, such as that of chiropractor. The expectations associated with the role lack clarity. For instance, should chiropractors be limited to spinal manipulations, or should they be permitted to perform surgery, deliver babies, and sign death certificates? Different states provide different answers to these questions. Similarly, rapid social change subjects some roles to ongoing redefinition—such as that associated with being a black or a woman in the United States in recent years. And still other ambiguities may be associated with the transition from one role to another. Take the transition from childhood to adulthood. At puberty, boys and girls are expected to stop being children but are not yet accorded the rights of adulthood. In many situations young people seem to be neither fish nor fowl, scarcely knowing whether they are supposed to act like children or like adults.

Role Distance and Role–Person Merger

Erving Goffman points out that some roles we **embrace**:

> To embrace a role is to be embraced by it. Particularly good illustrations of full embracement can be seen in persons in certain occupations: team managers during baseball games; traffic policemen at intersections during rush hours; landing signal officers who wave in planes on the decks of aircraft carriers; in fact, anyone occupying a directing role where the performer must guide others by means of gestural signs. (1961*b*: 106–107)

Goffman notes that not only can roles be *played;* they can also be *played at.* Indeed, when we must undertake roles that contradict our self-conceptions, we may take pains to display our detachment from the role (demonstrate our lack of personal involvement)—show **role distance**. The behavior of people riding the merry-go-round at an amusement park is revealing. Two-year-olds often find the prospect too much—the grimace upon their faces reveals terror and a determination simply to survive the ordeal. Three- and four-year-olds throw themselves into the role with abandon, playing it with a verve and vitality that reveal their thorough absorption. By age five, boys ride along flaunting a toughness and bravado—a "he-man" stance of control and mastery. By seven or eight, however, children have self-consciously dissociated themselves from the wooden horse; it is "kid stuff." Their daredevil antics or bored, nonchalant manner are designed to suggest the absence of genuine involvement. As for adults riding beside their two-year-olds, they often carefully assume an air of studied indifference. The merry-go-round provides a capsule glimpse of people's differential involvement in role-playing—the extent to which the behavior is stamped with serious intent.

Role distance may also be shown in "crucial" activity. The operating-room behavior of lesser medical personnel such as the intern and the junior resident is a case in point. The tasks given these juniors—holding retractors, cutting small tied-off veins, swabbing the operating area before the operation—are not large enough to support much of a surgical role. In this context, junior staff (especially those who will not specialize in surgery) undertake—through shows of sullenness, muttering, irony, joking, and sarcasm—to demonstrate that their real selves lie outside the constraints of the moment. Interns may take a rest by leaning on the patient or by placing a foot on an inverted bucket; their manner, however, is too contrived to convince anyone of their nonchalance. Similarly, interns often play the part of the jester.

> *Scrub Nurse:* Will there be more than three [sutures] more? We're running out of sutures.
> *Chief Surgeon:* I don't know.
> *Intern:* We can finish up with Scotch tape. (Goffman, 1961b: 117–118)

In this fashion, role distance is revealed.

Ralph H. Turner (1978) adds another dimension to our understanding of these matters. He points out that we put on and take off some roles like clothing, without lasting personal effect. In contrast, we find it difficult to put aside some of our roles even when the situation is changed; these roles continue to color the way in which we think about ourselves and act in varied circumstances. When the attitudes and behavior developed in the expression of one role carry over to many situations, Turner says that there is "a merger of role with person." When a role is deeply merged with the person, it has pervasive effects on the person's personality and self-conceptions.

Gender and race are roles that frequently assume the properties of a role–person merger. For this reason some social psychologists term such roles "core roles" or "master roles." In these cases, the roles are ascribed to us. But some core roles may be achieved roles. Take the case of the doctor, the judge, or the college professor who carries the bearing and air of authority of the professional role into family and community dealings; such individuals become the person of the role—"Doctor," "Judge," or "Professor." These individuals are not simply role incumbents; each *is* the role, having fully embraced it. Thus some professors have trouble distinguishing the classroom from social occasions, and at cocktail parties they may lecture others rather than engaging in casual conversation with them.

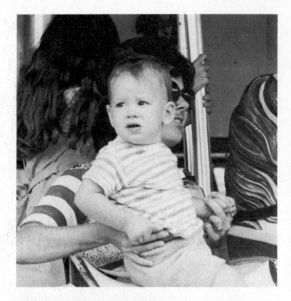

Role Distance
Children on merry-go-round horses reveal varying degrees of role embracement. The two-year-old displays role distance. The four-year-old fully embraces the role, completely absorbed in it. The nine-year-old, through his daredevil antics and bored act, dissociates himself from the role; his expression tells you that this is "kid stuff." (Patrick Reddy)

Other people also may see us and relate to us in terms of one particular role. This is especially true when they have little opportunity to encounter us in alternative or contradictory roles. Our astonishment over the timid but reliable bank teller who acts the hero during a bank robbery, or the one who is exposed as an embezzler, are cases in point. Such cases highlight how much we take for granted in our everyday lives that the role is the person when we encounter the individual in only one role. But when we encounter the individual regularly in alternative or contradictory roles, we are sensitized to the distinction between person and role; consequently, under these circumstances we do not make automatic assumptions about the person behind the role.

SELF-PRESENTATION

When we enter the presence of others, we typically seek to "size them up"—to gain information about them or to use information that we already possess. We look for **cues,** expressions given off or signals that will tell us crucial things about them, especially their roles. Such knowledge has very practical uses. It helps us to define the stituation (to determine in advance what they will expect of us and what we can expect of them). Only in this fashion will we know the best way to act in order to call forth the behavior we wish from them (Goffman, 1959, 1981). All this has implications for our self-presentations—the use of behavior to communicate some information about ourselves to others (Baumeister, 1982). Cues can also have very special uses; see the boxed insert on poker, pages 250–251.

Impression Management

If indeed social interaction is based on cues and the meanings they convey, then we possess the potential for manipulating various aspects of our performances in order to produce an outcome to our own advantage. We have ideas about who and what we are, ideas that we seek to present to others. We are concerned with the ideas that others develop of us. Only by influencing others' ideas can we hope to predict or control what happens to us. The process by which we tailor our presentations of self to different audiences is fundamental to social interaction. Erving Goffman (1959) terms it **impression management** when we seek to define the situation by generating cues that will lead others to act in accordance with our plans.

Although nearly all our behavior reveals information about us, not all behavior entails impression management. In self-presentational behavior, we have the goal of influencing how others perceive us. Nor does impression management necessarily involve conscious deception. In many cases, it involves merely bringing our actual attributes or accomplishments to the attention of others. For instance, we may perform deeds that normally win approval or provide information about ourselves that inspires confidence (Schlenker and Leary, 1982).

When we encounter someone for the first time and expect to have dealings with him or her, we start structuring definitions of the situation and lines of action. Consider how the skilled waitress accomplishes this:

> The waitress who bears up under pressure does not simply respond to her customers. She acts with some skill to control their behavior. The first question to ask when we look at the customer relationship is, "Does the waitress get the jump on the customer, or does the customer get the jump on the waitress?" The skilled waitress realizes the crucial nature of this question. . . .
>
> The skilled waitress tackles the customer with confidence and without hesitation.

POKER: TELLS AND LIES

Poker is the most popular card game in the United States. It is played in homes on kitchen tables, in legal casinos, and in illegal cardrooms. When occasional players go against professional players, they encounter formidable obstacles. Not only do they have an incomplete knowledge of the mathematical foundations of the game; occasional players also lack the impression management skills of the professionals. Poker involves a large element of deliberate deception in sending and receiving verbal and nonverbal signals. Some authorities estimate that professional players have at least a 20 percent edge over amateurs by virtue of their skills in fabricating impressions and correctly "reading" the cues of others. Avoiding bad calls while eliciting such calls from opponents can produce net differences of thousands of dollars a month for high-stakes players.

Anthropologist David Hayano (1979) has studied the uses made of impression management among professional poker players. He says that skilled poker players make extensive use of "tells," unintentional verbal or nonverbal messages that reveal the nature of a person's hand or intention to act. (*Tell* is derived from the word *"telegraph."*) When tells are intentional and faked they are called "lies."

Professional players find that inexperienced players "telegraph" information about their cards through such mechanisms as a cough, a straightening of the back, or an extra-loud voice when they have an unusually good hand. And players who grab a stack of chips or hold their cards tightly are usually signaling that

For example, she may find that a new customer has seated himself before she could clear off the dirty dishes and change the cloth. He is now leaning on the table studying the menu. She greets him, says, "May I change the cover, please?" and, without waiting for an answer, takes his menu away from him so that he moves back from the table, and she goes about her work. The relationship is handled politely but firmly, and there is never any question as to who is in charge. (Whyte, 1946: 132–133)

Social life entails the construction of meanings. If we are to elicit the responses we desire from others, we must take steps to fashion the meanings that these others employ within the situation. Some spheres, such as criminal law, seem to be more susceptible to impression management than others. Seymour Wishman (1981), a prominent and successful criminal lawyer, tells us that he has represented hundreds of people accused of crimes. He claims that most of his clients have not merely been guilty but have been guilty of atrocities: sons who hatcheted fathers, strangers who murdered strangers, and lovers who knifed lovers. Wishman (1981: 25) says, "I've struggled to win for clients who would go

when their turn comes they intend to call or raise the pot. On the other hand, excessive talking about a hand in a loud or strained voice is seen by professionals as a compensatory bluffing mechanism. Many professionals deliberately enact the tells displayed by amateurs as lies to befuddle other professionals.

Professional players tend to be of two types. The first is the continuously animated player. Through constant chatter and exaggerated gestures, they undertake to rattle their opponents. They find that by increasing the anxiety and nervousness of the amateur, they can throw the novice off guard, making the individual more likely to exhibit revealing tells.

The second type of professional poker player is the solid, stern individual who tries not to send any messages. Only infrequently do they talk, and they pattern their hand and body movements in a fixed, stereotyped presentation so that the movements are indistinguishable from one another. They, too, carefully scrutinize their opponents for tells. Indeed, many professionals have a memorized store of information—a working "book"—on the playing characteristics of several hundred players. Regarding his own perceptive capabilities, one professional recalls, "I had to use my eyes and ears, and neighbor, I can see a gnat's keister at a hundred yards and hear a mouse wet on cotton" (Hayano, 1979: 21).

Successful poker playing entails a wide variety of skills in acting and deception, while simultaneously gathering and interpreting cues that reveal tells and lies. Of course other professions also employ such devices. Actors, magicians, politicians, salespersons, and lawyers are likewise called upon to manage their own display of cues while sensitizing themselves to the displays of others.

out and commit new outrages." The heart of his courtroom effort rests on impression management. Consider the staging of anger. He observes, "I'm sure I'm not the first trial lawyer who knew exactly when he was going to 'lose' his temper, what he would do while his temper was 'lost,' and how long it would be before he recovered it."

But impression management is not limited to such obvious arenas as the courtroom. Teachers may pretend to be more knowledgeable than they actually are, judges more objective and neutral, and clergy more moral and altruistic (Buss and Briggs, 1984). Goffman (1981) also finds expressions of impression management in spheres that we often overlook. Take the public lecture sponsored by a college or civic organization. Goffman points out that the imparting of information is largely a pretext for an occasion in which the eminence of the speaker can be employed to confer prestige on the audience and the sponsoring organization. This fact helps explain the elaborate introductions, advertising, and publicity. Indeed, Goffman argues that an organization's advertising is not done in response to the anticipated presence of a prominent figure. Rather, a prominent figure is a device to present something that warrants wide advertising.

*I*mpression management

I went to see my doctor today as I had a sinus infection. While sitting in the waiting room, I noticed the magazines on the tables: Time, Harper's, New Yorker, Forbes, Newsweek, *and* The Atlantic. *After seeing the doctor, I went to get my hair cut. At the barbershop I also noticed the magazines:* Pro-Quarterback, Outdoors, Pro-Basketball, Playboy, Penthouse, *and* Argosy. *The doctor and the barber were both engaged in impression management. Each was seeking to project an image of himself. The doctor was portraying an intelligent individual with a well-rounded, educated background. It was as if he were saying to his patients, "I am a competent professional who can handle difficult matters." The barber was portraying a masculine individual with an interest in "manly" things. It was as if he were saying to his customers, "I am a real man, an outdoor type."*

Or take such common "response cries" as "Good God," "wow," "oops," and "whee." Goffman sees these responses as more than emotional ventings. A man reading the evening newspaper groans, "Good God!" in an implicit appeal to his wife to ask him to elaborate.

Barry R. Schlenker (1980) says that people are motivated to present themselves in ways that yield enhanced levels of self-esteem and social approval. As a consequence, they strive to associate themselves with desirable images and to dissociate themselves from undesirable images; he terms this the *association principle*. For this reason, individuals seek to bask in the reflected glory of the highly successful—an example is the often heard boast by people that they shook hands with a famous celebrity or sports figure. And college students wear more school-identifying apparel such as sweatshirts and school buttons on a Monday morning following a Saturday football victory than after a loss. Such behaviors constitute image-management tactics (Cialdini and Richardson, 1980). The techniques are characterized by indirect rather than direct tactics of self-presentation. They attempt to influence other people's images of oneself through the presentation of information about something with which one is associated (rather than through the direct presentation of information about oneself). All this suggests that impression management has many faces.

Front

Central to the process of impression management is **front**—the expressive equipment we intentionally or unwittingly use in presenting ourselves to others (Goffman, 1959; Ball, 1966). Front consists of setting, appearance, and manner.

Setting refers to the spatial and physical items of scenery (props) that we employ in staging our performance. Consider, for instance, the carefully laid out

*F*ront

I recently switched optometrists. The reason had nothing to do with the service I had been getting or the actual competence of my previous optometrist. However, I went with my friend to pick up her glasses at her optometrist's office, and I was quite favorably impressed by the setting. The waiting room was decorated attractively, and the office was located in a recently constructed building with modern landscaping. The whole arrangement seemed pleasant and professional. In contrast, my former optometrist had his office located in a wing of his home. The differing settings suggested to me that the two men must also differ in their competence. The contrasting appearances seemed to reflect a different underlying reality. Of course, the new optometrist also charges more for his services, but somehow I am "suckered" by the assumption that if a professional charges more than another professional, he must be better at his job.

office of the typical physician. Patients are herded together in a waiting room and impersonally distributed on couches and chairs along the walls. The arrangement immediately and forcefully conveys the difference in status and power that sets patient apart from doctor. A receptionist or nurse acts as a gatekeeper, regulating access to the physician's special chambers. The waiting room is often deeply carpeted, well furnished with couches, chairs, large lamps, and tables with "appropriate" magazines—all signaling luxury and the special station of the doctor. In due course the patient is ushered into an office or examining room to await an audience with the physician. The office exudes luxury; shelved medical books and framed diplomas convey a scientific mystique and competence; family portraits communicate trustworthiness by telegraphing that the occupant is a pillar of an established and "proper" community life. The examining room features medical paraphernalia—an aseptic table, stainless-steel pans and trays, bottles and vials enclosing colored liquids, gauze, hypodermic syringes, and other "equipment." These arrangements arouse awe and define the situation as one in which the patient should honor and defer to the physician.

Appearance refers to personal items that serve to identify an individual (Stone, 1970). Clothing, insignia, titles, and grooming are all elements of appearance. The doctor's white lab coat, stethoscope, and black bag provide cues to his or her identity; the title "Doctor" (linked with the last name or simply used by itself) establishes a social rank that elicits deference and social distance. Likewise, used-car sellers aim to present a favorable image, which in their case means avoiding the look of a con man (by avoiding villainous mustaches, loud clothes, and other stereotyped "con man" attributes). They must not dress too expensively, either; as one said, "If you're wearing a $150 sports coat and a $20 tie, you don't sell a car to a ditchdigger" (Davidson, 1975).

The Uniform: Certification of Legitimacy
By permitting use of its uniform, an organization—in this case a parking lot—indicates that an individual is its representative and assumes responsibility for his activities. The company would fire him and take away his uniform if he began to shirk his duties (Joseph and Alex, 1972). (Patrick Reddy)

Manner refers to those expressions that reveal the performer's style of behavior, mood, and disposition (Ball, 1966). The physician may display a brusque, coldly professional, businesslike manner: the conventional greeting, "How are you?" (the conventional answer, "Fine") as you step into the office, quickly followed by "What's the trouble?" as you seat yourself. Other physicians project a warm, kind, sympathetic manner (more chit-chat between the "How are you?" and the "What's the trouble?"). But whatever the manner, the physician sets the tone for the ensuing interaction. Used-car sellers, in contrast, notoriously "come on" as cheerful, smiling, friendly "good guys."

In sum, in presenting ourselves to others we employ front. We use a variety of expressive equipment to publicize the meanings that we wish to convey. This expressive equipment consists of setting, appearance, and manner.

Regions: Front-stage, Backstage

Part of impression management involves the manipulation of **regions**—places separating front-stage performances from backstage performances. Some of our behavior occurs **front-stage** before an audience, in a context that the previous section called "setting." Other behavior takes place **backstage.** Here, away from our audience, we engage in performances that contradict the impressions we are attempting to convey and that we seek to screen from the audience's view (Goffman, 1959).

We engage in front-stage behavior in our living rooms, where we entertain guests. Here we display our best behavior and present ourselves as respectable, upstanding, proper, good people. But backstage in our kitchens or bedrooms— areas commonly off-limits to guests—we may criticize or ridicule outsiders, wage

Backstage
Backstage activities are usually essential for front-stage performances. Very often, however, backstage operations contradict the impressions that the person is attempting to project front-stage. Hence backstage operations need to be screened from an audience's view, as these backstage restaurant activities are. (Patrick Reddy)

hard-fought family squabbles, "let down our hair," and generally live a somewhat cluttered and disorderly existence.

Although backstage performances would discredit our front-stage performance if the audience ever saw them, they may be essential for successful front-stage behavior. Restaurants seal off the dirty work of food preparation—the gristle, grease, and foul smells of spoiled food—from the appetizing and enticing front-stage atmosphere. Within the locker-room setting, football players can be the opposite of "good sports"; they may plot illicit actions that they can employ during the game to victimize their opponents. Furthermore, in the backstage region the tensions built up front-stage can be released. Teachers can laugh about the stupidity of their students, students can ridicule their teachers, doctors can make light of human suffering and death, and prostitutes can mock the "johns."

Altercasting

In impression management we attempt to present ourselves to others in such a way that they will act in accordance with our wishes. In so doing, we undertake to establish an identity or make a role for ourselves in a particular situation.

Altercasting involves the other side of the interaction equation (Weinstein and Deutschberger, 1963). In altercasting we attempt to shape the identity or define the role that will hold for the other person in a situation; we engage in behavior that casts another in an identity or role that will call forth from this other the responses we desire.

Perhaps a number of illustrations will help clarify altercasting. Take the case of a parent who says to a child, "Big boys don't act that way." By casting the child in the role of a "big boy," the parent hopes to elicit from the child those types of behavior that are in keeping with the role expectations of a "big boy." Or consider students who badger their professor with questions so as to keep the professor from introducing new material that could conceivably appear on a later test. A professor often becomes entrapped by this strategy, since the students manage to cast the professor in the teacher role with the obligation of responding to student questions. Finally, consider the practice of treating another person as a friend in order to win the favors that one can extract from a "friend": the extension of a financial loan, the use of a car, baby-sitting for one's child, and so on.

Throughout all these illustrations there runs a common denominator: By imputing roles to people, and then acting toward them in terms of these same roles, we place powerful constraints on their conduct. In sum, we put pressure on them to act in ways that are consistent with the normative requirements of the role in which we have cast them.

Authentic Behavior

The discussion so far may have suggested that social life consists of performances purposely contrived to create impressions that help us manipulate others. We have observed how people use the arts of both concealment and strategic revelation to impress their audiences. And it may appear that life is basically a fake, something painstakingly but artificially—even falsely—pasted together. Indeed, critics charge that Erving Goffman, the sociologist whose theory of role-playing has been described in this chapter, treats human life as a big con game. Of course, we do encounter situations in which people pretend to be someone other than who they really are. The clearest example is the con artist who convinces others that he or she is wealthy (and honest) and persuades them to entrust large sums to be invested "in partnership." In the Abscam operation, designed to trap members of Congress susceptible to bribes, FBI agents and others portrayed the role of rich Arab oil sheiks who were prepared to buy special legislative favors (Buss and Briggs, 1984). But what about honesty, sincerity, and genuineness—**authenticity**—in human life? Are people always concerned with controlling the image that others have of them?

The answer is no. There are many contexts in which we let down our guard. With friends, associates, and lovers, we experience relationships as ends in their own right—valued and appreciated—rather than simply as means to ends. And then there are times, such as during the subway rush hour, when the careful masks we often wear slip a bit—in a kind of temporary, uncaring exhaustion we reveal ourselves as we really are: "We no longer give a damn" (Fast, 1970: 65). Thus in some contexts we are not necessarily putting on a show for the benefit of others. Much of our behavior is authentic.

Nor should we assume that life is merely a drama acted out upon the world's stage. In everyday life, our actions are not distinct from social reality; they *are* reality (Perinbanayagam, 1974). At best the analogy of a theater is a somewhat contrived illusion. In ordinary life, real, vital, visceral things happen to us. We *experience*—we feel—these happenings. We are not dissociated from the experiences; we are the experiences. We do not take on roles only to cast them off when they are no longer convenient; we are the roles.

The Self-monitoring of Behavior

> *The image of myself which I try to create in my own mind in order that I may love myself is very different from the image which I try to create in the minds of others in order that they may love me.*

> —W. H. Auden

As most of us experience life, then, we are not engaged in a never-ending, studied "presentation" of ourselves to others. Not all of our behavior is "staged," though some of it is. When it is—when we do engage in impression management—are we all equally conscious of what we are doing? Are we all equally sensitive to various situational cues? In brief, do we all monitor our own and others' behavior to the same extent?

From his research, Mark Snyder (1974, 1980) concludes that individuals differ strikingly in the extent to which they observe and control their self-presentation. Some people are intensely concerned with the appropriateness of their behavior. These individuals, termed *high self-monitors* by Snyder, are actors on a social stage, more concerned with playing a role than with presenting a true picture of the self. They are especially sensitive to the ways they express and present themselves in social settings—at parties, job interviews, professional meetings, and chance encounters. In contrast, *low self-monitors* have little concern for the appropriateness of their presentation and expressive behavior. They pay less attention to the behavioral cues afforded by others, and they monitor and control their own presentations to a lesser extent.

Whereas high self-monitors vary with the situation, low self-monitors are more constant and less disposed to bend with changing social circumstances. The high self-monitor asks, "What behavior is called for here?" whereas the low self-monitor asks (should indeed the low self-monitor ask anything), "What behavior is most like me here?" When responding to the "Who am I?" test (see Chapter 1), high self-monitors depict themselves in terms of the roles they play. They provide answers like "I am a student," "I am an employee of General Electric," and "I am first violin in a chamber music group." Low self-monitors make greater use of adjectives than do high self-monitors in describing themselves: "I am friendly," "I am reliable," and "I am even-tempered" (Sobel, 1981).

THE QUALITY OF INTIMATE RELATIONSHIPS

High self-monitors are quite concerned with the appropriateness of their social behavior. According to Mark Snyder, "It is as if they [high self-monitors] chronically strive, in chameleonlike fashion, to appear to be the person called for by each situation that confronts them" (Snyder and Cantor, 1980: 223). Such individuals can swing with ease from bubbly sociability to reserved withdrawal, or even from conformity to noncomformity, as the situation dictates (Goleman, 1985*d*). By contrast, low self-monitors subscribe to the credo "To thine own self be true." Their behavior more closely approximates the attitudes, dispositions, and other traits that typify their personalities.

In keeping with their situationally guided orientation, high self-monitors seek to maximize the fit between their friends and the kinds of situations in which they interact with them. Low self-monitors, on the other hand, seek to maximize the fit between their friends and their own personal attributes. One way in which these differing social worlds are revealed is in the choice of friends that people make for leisure activities (Snyder, Gangestad, and Simpson, 1983). High-monitors prefer to have a wide range of friends and to have different friends for different activities. They play tennis with Fred and go sailing with Paul. Moreover, they pick friends who are highly skilled in a particular area. Thus

Low self-monitors have a firmer, more single-minded idea of what their "self" should be. They strive for congruence between "who they are" and "what they do." In contrast, high self-monitors present many "selves," fitting the "self" of the moment to the dictates of the situation. Self-monitoring individuals are more likely to laugh at a comedy when watching it with friends who are laughing at it than when watching it alone. But non-self-monitoring individuals show less difference in the two situations; their expression is internally controlled by their experience more than by their sensitivity to situational factors. These differences have implications for the intimate relationships of high and low self-monitors (see boxed insert). Snyder says that self-monitoring is neither good nor bad in itself and seemingly has no relationship to neurotic behavior (Sobel, 1981).

Perhaps not surprisingly, Snyder found that professional actors scored higher on a self-monitoring test than a sample of Stanford University undergraduates. Further, individuals with high self-monitoring scores were able to communicate emotion by voice and facial expression more successfully than those with low self-monitoring scores. And in a self-presentation task, individuals with high self-monitoring scores were more likely than others to seek out comparative information regarding their peers. Other researchers have also found that high self-monitors are more likely than low self-monitors to initiate conversations with

Fred is likely to be especially adept at tennis and Paul at sailing. In looking for friends, they tend to ask themselves, "How well suited is this person for this activity?" and "Does this person have what it takes to do this activity well?" In contrast, low-monitoring individuals pick as their friends people they like. They prefer to play tennis and sail with the same person. They tend to ask themselves, "How much do I like this person?" and "All other things being equal, how much do I like to spend time with this person?"

High self-monitors are also less willing to commit themselves to a romantic relationship, are more willing to end one romance in favor of an alternative one, and are slow to become emotional intimates of dating partners. Low self-monitors are more willing to commit themselves to a romantic relationship, are more faithful lovers, and are more willing to invest themselves emotionally with those they date (Snyder and Simpson, 1984). In so doing, both types of individuals seem anchored to their unique orientation. High self-monitors, in keeping with their situationally oriented focus, are likely to enter dating relationships on the basis of the specific competencies of their prospective dating partners. Low self-monitors, in contrast, look for partners on the basis of their relatively stable personality traits, leading to the greater longevity of and a stronger commitment to their dating relationships. It seems that for high self-monitors, the satisfaction of a relationship derives primarily from the pleasure of *doing* activities with their partners. For low self-monitors, the satisfaction derives primarily from the pleasure of simply *being* with their partners.

others (Ickes and Barnes, 1977). Of interest, high self-monitors are also more adept at detecting impression management in others. Snyder (1980) finds that they are more accurate than low self-monitors in identifying the "real Mr. X" when provided with the three contestants in "To Tell the Truth" programs.

SUMMARY

1. As we go about our everyday activities, we mentally attempt to place people in various social categories. In so doing, we undertake to define the situation. We make such inferences in order to identify the set of expectations that will operate in the relationship—what we can expect of others and what they can expect of us. Roles permit us to do this.

2. A role is a bundle of activities clearly meshed into the activities of other people. Every role is linked to at least one other role and is reciprocal to this linked role. Roles impinge on us as sets of reciprocal norms: expectations and obligations.

3. The reciprocal character of roles finds its reflection in selfhood. It is as if by imagining ourselves in the other person's place, we momentarily exchange roles to grasp the requirements for social interaction.

4. As we translate roles into action, we find that in each instance we need to create the action anew. Hence interaction has a tentative quality.

5. In some respects each action is unique, and each interaction involves an element of improvisation. For this reason, role-playing entails role-making.

6. In meeting role requirements, we sometimes experience role strain, as when we find ourselves exposed to incompatible demands (role conflict). We may deal with role strain by compartmentalizing our lives or establishing a hierarchy of obligations.

7. Some roles we embrace—we accept them and become absorbed in them. But not only can roles be played; they can also be played at. Under some circumstances we take pains to display our distance from roles that contradict our self-conceptions.

8. When we enter the presence of others, we typically seek to "size them up." We look for cues that will tell us what roles they hold. This enables us to define the situation—determine in advance what they will expect of us and what we can expect of them.

9. We often seek to define the situation by generating cues that will lead others to act in accordance with our plans. In brief, we undertake to manage the impressions we make on others.

10. Central to the process of impression management is front. Front consists of setting, appearance, and manner.

11. Part of impression management involves the manipulation of the backstage and front-stage regions of our lives. We may also try, by altercasting, to shape the identity or define the role of the other person in a situation.

12. Although at times we use the arts of both concealment and strategic revelation to impress our audiences, much of our behavior is authentic. We are not dissociated from our experiences; we are the experiences. We do not take on parts only to cast them off; we are the parts.

13. Individuals differ strikingly in the extent to which they observe and control their self-presentations. Some people are intensely concerned with the appropriateness of their behavior. These individuals, termed high self-monitors, are actors on a social stage, more concerned with playing a role than with presenting a true picture of the self. In contrast, low self-monitors have little concern for the appropriateness of their presentation and expressive behaviors. They pay less attention to the behavioral cues provided by others, and they monitor and control their own presentations to a lesser extent.

GLOSSARY

Altercasting □ The process by which we undertake to shape the identity or define the role that will hold for the other person in a situation; we engage in behavior that casts another in an identity or role that will call forth from this other the responses we desire.

Appearance □ Personal items that serve to identify an individual. Clothing, insignia, titles, and grooming are elements of appearance.

Authenticity □ Behavior that is honest, sincere, and genuine, as opposed to performances that are artificial and false.

Backstage □ A region in which our behavior contradicts the impressions we are attempting to convey front-stage. We seek to screen the backstage region from an audience's view, because our performances there would tend to discredit our front-stage performances.

Cues □ Signals, both verbal and nonverbal, that give us critical information about the nature and meaning of people's behavior.

Expectations □ The actions we can legitimately insist that others perform in relation to a role.

Front □ The expressive equipment we intentionally or unwittingly use in presenting ourselves to others. Front consists of setting, appearance, and manner.

Front-stage □ Behavior that takes place in this region is intended for an audience's viewing.

Impression management □ The process by which we manipulate the definition of a situation, generating cues that will lead others to act in accordance with our plans.

Manner □ Those expressions that reveal the performer's style of behavior, mood, and disposition.

Obligations □ The actions others can legitimately insist that we perform in relation to a role.

Regions □ Places separating front-stage performances from backstage performances; places bounded to some degree by barriers to perception.

Role □ The normative requirements that apply to the behavior of a specific category of people in a particular situational context. Roles specify who does what, when, and where.

Role distance □ A display of detachment from the set of norms applying to our behavior in a given situation.

Role embracement □ Commitment to given courses of action; absorption in and acceptance of the expectations and obligations defined by a set of normative rules.

Role-making □ The process of improvising new features of action as we devise our performance and fit our line of action to that of others. In role-making we use our acts to alter the traditional expectations and obligations associated with a role.

Role strain □ Problems that individuals experience in meeting the requirements of a role.

Role-taking □ The process by which we devise our performance and fit our line of action to that of others; the translating of roles into action.

Setting □ The spatial and physical items of scenery (props) that we employ in staging our performance.

9 RELATIONSHIPS AND INTERPERSONAL ATTRACTION

SOCIAL RELATIONSHIPS
  Types of Relationship Ties
  Networks
ATTRACTION IN THE DYAD
  Proximity
  Physical Attractiveness
  Love

Similarity
Complementary Needs
Social Exchange
RESPONSES TO
    DISSATISFACTION IN A
    RELATIONSHIP

Much of human life consists of **social interaction**—a process directed toward, stimulated by, or influenced by another person or persons. Human groups consist of acting people, and group life consists of their actions. The way we behave is in large measure determined by our relations with one another. In our daily lives we continually encounter others, cooperate with them, conform to their wishes, irritate them, ignore them, violate their standards, and compete with them.

SOCIAL RELATIONSHIPS

Who can enjoy alone?

—John Milton, *Paradise Lost, 1667*

Enduring Social Interaction
When people live together over an extended period of time, they typically develop a relatively stable set of expectations regarding one another's behavior. (Patrick Reddy)

A good many of our social interactions are casual, one-time encounters. In buying a pair of shoes, taking a seat on a bus, watching a movie, eating lunch at McDonald's, and checking a book out of the library, we deal primarily with strangers. Since such interactions generally lack continuity through time, we invest little of ourselves in them. Nonetheless, we still need to "plug" ourselves into the world of these others, if for no reason than to minimize our involvement with them. Thus at the very least we need to identify them, appraise them, attune ourselves to the meaning of their actions, and attempt to figure out what they intend to do.

Other casual interactions come to have a more enduring quality. An encounter on a bus or at McDonald's may lead to a date and grow into a "steady" relationship. A chance afternoon game of touch football in the corner lot may lead to a Saturday afternoon routine. A retail jeweler's order to a wholesaler may evolve into a standing business arrangement. A wartime alliance between nations may lead to mutual-aid and defense pacts. Some interaction, then, continues long enough so that people become linked together by a relatively stable set of expectations—a **social relationship.**

Social relationships lie at the very core of human existence (Berscheid and Peplau, 1983). Indeed, most of us recognize that our lives center on our relationships with others. When we are asked what it is that makes our life most meaningful, we typically answer in terms of friends, relatives, and lovers (Klinger, 1977). And we commonly mention the importance of "feeling loved and wanted." Public opinion surveys reveal that we believe our personal happiness is integrally bound to the state of our intimate relationships (Campbell, Converse, and Rogers, 1976). We consider it important to have "a happy marriage," "a good family life," and "good friends." Research corroborates that close relationships are vital to our well-being and are associated with our mental and physical health and longevity. It is not surprising, therefore, that a strong association exists between marital disruption and physical and emotional disorder (Bloom, Asher, and White, 1978; Greenblatt, Becerra, and Serafetinides, 1982). Divorced adults are at much greater risk than married adults for mental and physical illness, automobile accidents, alcoholism, and suicide.

Types of Relationship Ties

> There is no hope of joy except in human relations.
>
> —Saint-Exupéry, *Wind, Sand, and Stars,* 1939

The creation of social relationships involves **bonding,** a process whereby individuals or groups are linked together. Two common types of bonding are expressive ties and instrumental ties.

Expressive Ties

Many of our human needs can be realized only in association with other people, and meaningful people at that. Through these people we satisfy our needs for security, love, acceptance, companionship, and a sense of worth. We cannot be human all by ourselves. Accordingly, many gratifications require sustained social interaction in which we are deeply involved in bonded relationships with others. Only as we personally invest ourselves in others and commit ourselves to them— as we establish **expressive ties**—do we achieve this sort of reward.

Social interactions that rest upon expressive ties among people are called **primary relationships.** We view these relationships as ends in themselves, valuable in their own right. Within them we experience warmth, oneness, familiarity, and closeness. They provide us with a sense of meaning and richness; they fashion and sustain us as unique human beings. There are many types of primary relationships, including those with kin, friends, lovers, neighbors, and co-workers. Each type meets somewhat different needs. For example, we tend to socialize with friends who are the same age and to ask advice of associates who are of the same religion (Feld, 1984).

Instrumental Ties

Regardless of whether or not we care for one another, life confronts us with countless circumstances where we simply need each other to achieve certain goals. Only by cooperating, by pulling together—by establishing **instrumental ties**—can we reach our ends. At times this may mean working with our enemies, as in the old political saying, "Politics makes strange bedfellows." More often, it simply means that in contemporary societies we find large, complex networks of action involving an interlinkage of the diverse actions of diverse people—for instance, the division of labor extending from the farmers who grow wheat to the grocers who sell bread (Olsen, 1968; Blumer, 1969).

Social interactions that rest on instrumental ties among people are called **secondary relationships.** We view such relationships as means to ends, rather than as ends in their own right. We enter secondary relationships as *social elements;* we view ourselves as independent, autonomous units within these situations. We do not experience a broader commitment to or involvement with the other party, who may be a chance seatmate on a subway, the cashier at the store counter, the clerk in the registrar's office, or a gas station attendant. This is not the case in primary relationships, where we come to view ourselves as *social parts*—as integral, committed, and involved units (Olsen, 1968).

Expressive-Instrumental Continuum

Although some of our ties are predominantly either expressive or instrumental, others have a mixture of expressive and instrumental qualities. This is true, for instance, of friendly relations (Kurth, 1970). Friendly relations—acquaintance-ships—are not identical with friendships; they do not have the same intimacy and involvement of self. A friendly relation facilitates the interaction associated with fulfilling formal role requirements. Thus we establish friendly relations with fellow workers whose cooperation we rely on; we feel that if we keep on good terms with them, we will minimize many difficulties in the work setting. Further, they provide us with a pleasant basis of association. Thus for some purposes, it is useful to consider expressive ties and instrumental ties as poles on a continuum. Between these poles there is a variety of real-life ties:

Expressive	Instrumental
ties	ties

Networks

> *Relationship is life, and this relationship is a constant movement, a constant change.*
>
> —J. Krishnamurti, *You Are the World*

Beyond one-to-one relationships, human life encompasses multiple relationships organized into **networks.** These are webs of social relationships that center on a

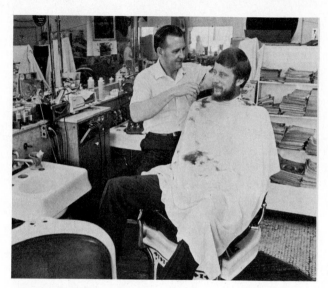

Conversations in Public Places
What thoughts pass through your mind as you sit down to have your hair cut by a barber or beautician? How do you go about establishing whether you will or will not carry on a conversation with the barber or beautician? What "taken-for-granted" aspects pervade your conversational interaction? (Patrick Reddy)

single individual and that tie him or her directly to other individuals and indirectly through these other individuals to still more people. Take an individual named Arlene Tracy. She may be linked in direct relationships with three people: Call them Ida Block, John Ford, and Isaac Kramer. In turn she may be indirectly linked to Bob Werner through Ida Block, and to Fran Walton through Bob Werner. Each of us is in touch with a number of other people, some of whom are directly in touch with each other and some of whom are not. (John Ford may also have a direct relationship with Isaac Kramer, but not necessarily with Ida Block.) Viewed as a social structure, a network can be depicted with persons as points and relations as connecting lines (see Figure 9.1). A method for studying networks is sociometry, discussed in the boxed insert on page 268.

One approach to networks has emphasized the paths or threads that prevail in a single network (White, Bourman, and Breiger, 1976). Social psychologists with this interest focus on the manner in which long chains of contact wind their way through large social systems. Stanley Milgram's "small world" studies, detailed in the boxed insert that appears on pages 270–271, are illustrative of this approach.

Another approach has stressed the "knittedness" of interconnections within a network (Fischer et al., 1977). This interest has led to the study of network *density*. Density is a measure of how nearly a network approaches a state in which each individual is directly linked to every other individual. More precisely, it is the ratio of observed to possible direct relations between people in a network (Friedkin, 1978). This approach has been employed in studying people's "sense of community." Research suggests that a crucial part of "belonging" is a dense network of social ties over a specified area, a place in which individuals con-

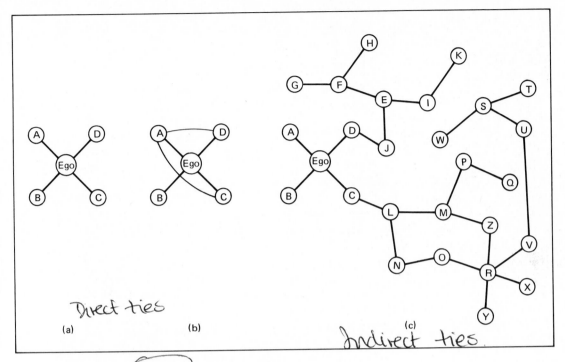

Direct ties

(a)   (b)   (c)

Indirect ties.

FIGURE 9.1 Networks of Varying Complexity
In network (a), ego is linked to individuals *A, B, C,* and *D.* Network (b) is identical
to (a) except that *A* and *D,* and *A* and *C,* are also bound within a social relationship. In network (c), ego is directly linked to only four individuals: *A, B, C,* and *D.* But
through individuals *C* and *D,* ego is indirectly linked to individuals *E* through *Z.*

stantly encounter familiar, friendly faces in the course of everyday life (Granovetter, 1976). To the extent that such multibonded relationships overlap and
crisscross among the members of society, they provide an encompassing web—
a meshed fabric—knitting and integrating people within a larger social whole.
The social bonds provided by dense networks act as support systems, not only
to maintain health but also to prevent physical or mental breakdown and maladjustment in times of stress (Greenblatt, Becerra, and Serafetinides, 1982).

Networks play an important part in our everyday lives. Consider, for instance,
our search for help in times of difficulty. When visited by misfortune—illness,
mental turmoil, grief, loneliness—we may seek assistance from those who professionally help people in trouble: doctors, psychologists, marriage counselors,
ministers, chiropractors, and others. Yet often we lack personal acquaintance
with specific professionals and tend to distrust those whom we do not personally
know. Under these circumstances we commonly turn to our own "lay referral
systems." For example, an acquaintance who got help for her "bad back" from a

Chiro-
referral

SOCIOMETRY

Sociometry is an objective method for assessing patterns of attraction, rejection, or indifference among members of a group. The technique has been widely employed in the study of influence and power, friendship, social adjustment, morale, group structure, race relations, political divergences within a community, and social status. Its usefulness has been demonstrated in studies of fraternities, graduate schools, high schools, college student bodies, summer camps, units of the armed forces, factories, and even entire communities.

The basic technique involves a sociometric questionnaire or interview in which people are asked to name the three (or five) individuals in the group whom they would most like to sit next to (or eat with, have as a close friend, live next to, go camping with, have on their team, and so on). Or the study can trace patterns of discrimination, rejection, or antagonism by asking people whom they would least like to interact with in a given context. Each person is assured that his or her choice will be kept confidential.

The data secured from sociometric questionnaires can be represented in a **sociogram,** which graphically shows the patterns of choice existing among members of a group at a given point in time (see Figure 9.2).

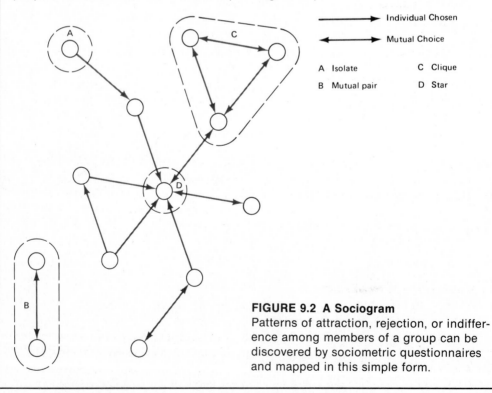

──────▶	Individual Chosen
◀──────▶	Mutual Choice

A Isolate	C Clique
B Mutual pair	D Star

FIGURE 9.2 A Sociogram
Patterns of attraction, rejection, or indifference among members of a group can be discovered by sociometric questionnaires and mapped in this simple form.

certain chiropractor will recommend that professional to us (Friedson, 1960; McKinlay, 1973; Rose, 1974).

Job seekers likewise commonly turn to informal acquaintance networks. Mark S. Granovetter (1973), in his study of professional, technical, and managerial job changers in Boston, found that in 39.1 percent of the cases the job information came directly from the prospective employer, whom the applicant already knew. In 45.3 percent of the cases there was one intermediary between the applicant and the employer, in 12.5 percent there were two intermediaries, and in 3.1 percent there were more than two. Similar patterns prevail within the academic community: The head of a department who must fill a teaching position generally prefers to canvass his or her acquaintances with, "Say, have you got any bright people coming out of grad school at your university?" Often, employers view people who list themselves in "situations wanted" columns or with employment agencies as being at the "bottom of the barrel." Similarly, job seekers often find that formal employment agencies list jobs that turn out to be "dogs." Both prospective employers and job seekers, then, prefer to rely on informal acquaintance networks (Rose, 1974). By reaching out to relatives, friends, and acquaintances, and advising them of our job skills and desires, we accomplish three tasks: (1) We learn about job openings that are not being advertised; (2) we have someone (our contact) who can speak for us and speak well of us prior to a job interview; and (3) we are able to bypass the personnel department and secure interviews directly with the people who have the power to hire us (Fader, 1984).

Networks also play a critical part in the growth and spread of social movements (Snow, Zurcher, and Ekland-Olson, 1980). They are a primary mechanism by which religious cults, student-activist groups, and political-protest organizations expand their ranks and mobilize support. The likelihood that a movement will recruit a person depends in large part on whether the person has prior personal ties with a movement member. And the intensity of a person's commitment is influenced by the movement's ability to encapsulate the individual within its network. In this manner, rivalrous counterforces and counterattractions are reduced. Likewise, social networks are the primary source for the diffusion of new medical procedures, technologies, and medications among physicians. Physicians tend to be skeptical of published sources of information and rely on the experiences of their colleagues when deciding on new methods of treatment (Anderson and Jay, 1985).

ATTRACTION IN THE DYAD

As interpersonal relationships progress from initial acquaintance to close friendship, the amount of interaction (breadth) and the intimacy level (depth) increase (Hays, 1985). Among university students, the period between the third and sixth weeks of a relationship appears to be particularly important as a building phase. This period serves as an exploratory time, in which potential friends get to know each other and sample the possibilities of a relationship before evolving more

"MY, IT'S A SMALL WORLD!"

When you are in some distant city or state, how often have you had the experience of meeting someone who has a mutual acquaintance with you back home? And then you both exclaim, "My, it's a small world!" Indeed, as part of the process of becoming acquainted, college students usually ask each other what their hometowns and academic majors are and then turn to the "small world game": "Do you know . . . ?"

Stanley Milgram and his associates (Milgram, 1967; Travers and Milgram, 1969; Korte and Milgram, 1970) experimentally studied social networks involving unexpected strands that link people who are widely separated in physical or social space. They selected an arbitrary "target person" (the wife of a divinity-school student who lived in Cambridge, Massachusetts, and a stockbroker who worked in Boston and lived in Sharon, Massachusetts) and a group of "starting persons" (individuals who lived in Wichita, Kansas, and Omaha, Nebraska). Each starter was given a booklet telling the target person's name, address, occupation, and a few other facts. The starter was instructed to begin moving the booklet on by mail toward the target. The booklet, however, could be sent only to a first-name acquaintance. Each person in turn was to advance the booklet in this manner until ideally the chain reached its target (see Figure 9.3).

Of course, in most cases the booklet failed to reach the target person. The proportion of chains completed ranged from 12 to 33 percent in the different studies. The fact that some were successful is testimony to the strength of the indirect linkages operating among people. The number of links in the completed chains ranged from two to ten, with averages between five and eight. Milgram describes one case involving two intermediate links:

> Our first target person was the wife of a student living in Cambridge. Four days after the folders were sent to a group of starting persons in Kansas, an instructor at the Episcopal Theological Seminary approached our target person on the street. "Alice," he said, thrusting a brown folder toward her, "this is for you." At first she thought he was simply returning a folder that had gone astray, but . . . we found to our pleased surprise that the document had started with a wheat farmer in Kansas. He had passed it on to an Episcopalian minister in his home town, who sent it to the minister who taught in Cambridge, who gave it to the target person. (1967: 64)

Most people are surprised to learn that only five to seven intermediaries will typically suffice to link any two randomly selected individuals, no matter where they happen to live in the United States. But although we deal with only a small number of intermediaries, behind each of them

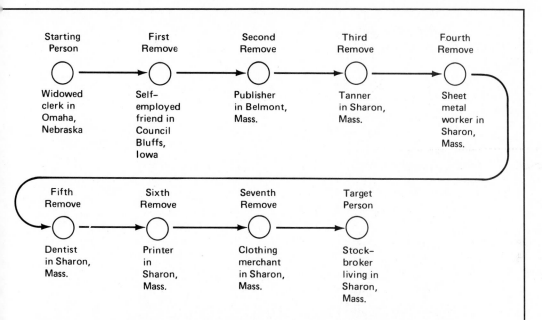

FIGURE 9.3 A Completed Chain in the Milgram Small-World Experiments
These studies show that social networks link people who are widely separated in physical or social space. Each link represents an individual's acquaintance pool of 500 to 2,500 people.
(SOURCE: Adapted from S. Milgram, "The Small-World Problem," *Psychology Today*, Vol. 1 [1967], pp. 61–67.)

stands a much larger group of 500 to 2,500 individuals. In other words, each sender has an acquaintance pool of 500 to 2,500 people from which he or she selects the person who is believed best able to advance the chain. Thus a screening procedure operates. Further, a process of geometric progression is implicit in the research procedure. (Analogously, if you earn a penny a day and the sum is doubled each day, you will have a sum of more than $10 million at the end of thirty working days.) Elements of geometric progression, with an increase rate far more powerful than mere doubling, underlie the small-world scheme; and thus, with just a few removes, the search extends to an enormous number of individuals (Killworth and Bernard, 1979).

stable patterns of interaction. They seek out one another for activities and share growing amounts of information with each other. One student observes: "We have become closer. We increasingly spend more time together. I also can tell her things that I may not have felt comfortable telling her three weeks ago" (Hays, 1985: 920). After an initial flurry, the rate of interaction drops off to some extent. It seems that as the school term progresses, students have less free time to devote to their friends. And they may also form other friendships that compete for the amount of time they have available.

In primary relationships—those characterized by expressive ties—**social attraction** is the principal cohesive tie. Social attraction refers to the property that draws two people together. At first sight it may seem that common-sense knowledge can adequately explain attraction with little need for social psychological study. But a little reflection reveals numerous examples in which common sense lacks reliability. Indeed common-sense knowledge is often contradictory: "Opposites attract," yet "Birds of a feather flock together." "Absence makes the heart grow fonder," yet "Out of sight, out of mind." "True love never dies," yet "Love is like linen, often changed." "There's no fool like an old fool," yet "Love, like wine, is best when aged." Clearly we cannot rely on common-sense knowledge for an understanding of attraction in the two-person group, or **dyad.** Research has shown that proximity, physical appearance, love, similarity, complementary needs, and social exchange are important determinants of the dyad.

Proximity

Proximity—nearness in physical space—has a considerable influence on our friendship choices. Other things being equal, we tend to like people who are geographically close to us. Various studies reveal that students typically develop closer friendships with those who share their classes, who sit near them, or who live near them in the dormitory (Segal, 1974).

The importance that physical proximity has for friendship choice is highlighted in a classic study by Leon Festinger, Stanley Schachter, and Kurt Back (1950). The researchers examined the development of friendships among married students in a new housing project. The complex consisted of seventeen two-story units, each containing ten apartments (see Figure 9.4). Residents were asked to name their three closest friends in the project. The results (see Table 9.1) revealed that they were most likely to be friends with their next-door neighbors (41.2 percent). Even living two doors away made a big difference—the percentage of close friends was 22.5 percent, only half that of next-door neighbors.

Friendships were also affected by (1) distance between houses and (2) the direction in which a house faced. As the distance between houses increased, the number of friendships decreased—and friendship rarely occurred between people separated by more than four or five other houses. Residents whose houses faced the street had less than half as many friends in the project as did those whose houses faced the court area. The simple architectural decision of turning certain houses toward the street made involuntary isolates out of their occupants. Other

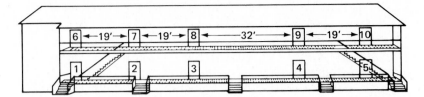

FIGURE 9.4 Layout of the Two-Story Buildings in a Housing Project That Was Studied for Friendship Patterns
The study revealed that proximity was the most important factor determining friendships in the project. Residents were most likely to be friends with their next-door neighbors.
(SOURCE: Adapted from L. Festinger, S. Schachter, and K. Back, *Social Pressures in Informal Groups* [New York: Harper and Row, 1950], p. 36.)

architectural features also played a part. For example, people who lived near the entrances and exits of stairways and near mailboxes generally had more friends than other residents.

Robert F. Priest and Jack Sawyer (1967) confirmed the importance of proximity in their study of friendships among college dormitory men. Although a room five doors away represented scarcely ten seconds' more travel time, five *closer* rooms had to be passed by. The actual physical distance was less important than the *perceived* distance. To borrow change for the Coke machine from someone five rooms away would raise the question, "Why didn't he ask someone closer?" Asking a next-door neighbor seemed less threatening and less awkward. And once initiated, contact was typically repeated.

These findings suggest that proximity plays a critical part in attraction by providing the *opportunity* for people to interact with one another—they are more available than those who are farther away. Proximity acts as a physical screen in determining the probability of initial contact (Priest and Sawyer, 1967;

TABLE 9.1
Sociometric Choice and Physical Distance

UNITS OF PHYSICAL DISTANCE*	NUMBER OF CHOICES GIVEN†	NUMBER OF POSSIBLE CHOICES‡	PERCENTAGE CHOOSING§
1	112	8 × 34	41.2
2	46	6 × 34	22.5
3	22	4 × 34	16.2
4	7	2 × 34	10.3

* All physical distances that can separate any two people living on the same floor.
† Total number of choices given to people living at each distance from the individuals who are doing the choosing.
‡ Correction factors for each distance of separation between apartments. (There are, for instance, many more possible 1-unit choices than 4-unit choices—see Figure 9.4.)
§ Choices given (column 2) divided by possible choices (column 3) times 100 (to secure percentage).
Source: Adapted from L. Festinger, S. Schachter, and K. Back, *Social Pressures in Informal Groups* (New York: Harper and Row, 1950), p. 38.

Proximity
Our close friends and marriage partners tend to be people we go to school with (people who are geographically close). (Patrick Reddy)

Nahemow and Lawton, 1975). Once people are in contact with one another, other factors come into play to determine the course of the relationship. For instance, an equal status ranking among the parties facilitates friendship; an unequal status ranking impedes friendship (Schutte and Light, 1978). Moreover, interaction in its own right has been found to induce interpersonal attraction (Insko and Wilson, 1977).

However, it is also true that familiarity may breed contempt. Police records reveal that aggravated assault and murder occur most frequently among family members, neighbors, and acquaintances. Although proximity may be a necessary condition for attraction, it also may function as a condition for hatred.

There is some evidence that the formation of negative relationships may be even more dependent on physical proximity than the formation of friendships (Ebbesen, Kjos, and Konečni, 1976). In theory as well as practice, we can always travel to find friends. But disliking is another matter. Take the case of "environment spoiling." We may dislike another because of the unpleasant things the other person does. For instance, in a suburban setting, a dog might be allowed to bark without control, music might be played too loudly at night, the other party might not mow his or her lawn or otherwise keep the yard well maintained, and so on. If events of this sort occur frequently enough, they can lead to disliking even in the absence of face-to-face contact. Since we cannot easily avoid such experiences in a neighborhood setting, proximity can play a direct part in the formation of negative relationships.

Physical Attractiveness

Beauty is a greater recommendation than any letter of introduction.
—Aristotle

Physical attractiveness

I am coming to believe that a person's physical attractiveness counts for much more than Americans are willing to admit. Take the dance I went to with my roommates Saturday night. There was a pudgy, stocky fellow who couldn't get a girl to dance with him. And the girls didn't seem particularly kind in turning him down. About an hour later, I heard everyone laughing and pointing to the dance floor. Out on the middle of the floor was this pudgy guy dancing all by himself. He would try to cut in on girls who were dancing together. But they would just shove him away. A little later in the evening, a number of us were riding one of our friends because he was putting the moves on a real ugly chick. Finally, he told us to bug off. He said he was no stud himself, and he had to take what he could get.

Within the United States, most of us share a fairly common standard of physical beauty. We generally like physically attractive people more than we do those who are unattractive. And as discussed in Chapter 2, we tend to think that attractive people are more likely to find good jobs, to marry well, and to lead happy and fulfilling lives—in brief, we think that "what is beautiful is good" (Dion, 1972; Dion, Berscheid, and Walster, 1972). In sum, we typically judge a book by its cover.

Social psychologists find that we prefer the companionship and friendship of attractive people to that of unattractive people (Reis, Nezlek, and Wheeler, 1980; Marks, Miller, and Maruyama, 1981). Likewise, even when appearance has no conceivable tie to the requirements of a job, people with good looks are more likely to be hired, even by experienced personnel officers. And when television technicians pan a football crowd, they stop and focus the camera on an attractive person. Apparently the advantages of being attractive start early. Newborn infants who are independently judged as attractive are held, cuddled, and kissed more than less attractive babies (Berscheid, 1982). Further, when Karen Dion and Ellen Berscheid (1974) asked nursery school children between four and six years of age to name the classmates they liked best, they found that the children preferred their good-looking peers; moreover, the youngsters thought that their homely classmates were unfriendly and aggressive. Contrary to democratic notions that all people are created equal, findings such as these suggest that an individual's physical appearance can have a profound impact on his or her life.

University of Minnesota social psychologists have shown the part that good looks plays in courtship behaviors (Brody, 1981). The researchers had young men talk on the telephone to strange women who were described to them as either physically attractive or physically unattractive. The social psychologists recorded the conversations and later asked outside observers to tell what kind of people the women were by listening to the taped calls. A woman who was

The dating and mating game

It is May Dance time at the junior high school that my two brothers attend. Last year Jimmy, my youngest brother, was in seventh grade. About ten days before the dance, some of the kids in his clique started bringing him the "word" that Jennie "liked" him and that he "ought" to ask Jennie to the dance. Well, he asked Jennie and everything worked out fine. Jimmy and Jennie were great friends, but six months ago Jennie moved away. A few days ago Jimmy asked Debbie to go with him to the May Dance but she refused. However, his friends have recently passed the "word" to him that Ginny "likes" him. But he doesn't like Ginny and swears he won't go to the dance this year.

Last year Ted, my other brother, was in eighth grade. He was friendly during the year with Kris. Both shared similar interests and he felt quite comfortable with her. So he asked Kris to the May Dance and Kris gave him an affirmative response. Well, Ted's friends quickly heard that he was taking Kris to the dance and really gave the poor kid a rough time. They said that Kris was a "real dog" and made all kinds of derogatory remarks about her. That same evening he came home from school and started sobbing uncontrollably. He told mom that he wasn't going to go to the dance, but mom insisted that since he had asked Kris, he had to follow through on it. Well, he took Kris to the dance, but he wouldn't even talk to her in the halls thereafter (this despite the fact that he and Kris had a lot going for them). Apparently, Ted's classmates had let him know that Kris was at a lower level in the peer group's erotic-popularity hierarchy than he was.

Well, another dance has now rolled around. Ted has had a "crush" on one girl since both were in seventh grade. She is a petite number, a real "All-American girl." She ranks at the very top of the erotic-popularity hierarchy. For the past four weeks Ted has been putting the "moves" on her and the other day asked her to go to the May Dance with him. She outright refused. I had guessed as much before he asked her, as Ted is somewhat lower in the ranking system.

talking to a man who believed her to be attractive was judged, on the basis of her verbal behavior alone, to be more poised, more sociable, and more vivacious than was a woman who was talking with a man who believed her to be unattractive. In self-fulfilling prophecy fashion, the men—through their differential behavior—brought out of the women the very behavior they had expected the women to demonstrate. Not surprisingly, the outside observers also judged the men who believed they were talking to attractive women to be more sociable, sexually warm, interesting, outgoing, humorous, and socially adept.

The power of physical attractiveness is also revealed by research dealing with couples on blind dates. In one study, social psychologists arranged a "computer

In any event, a few days ago Ted was in his Spanish class and got the whispered question that had been passed down the row among his classmates, "Are you taking Dot to the May Dance?" Ted responded, "No." The message was then relayed back among the students as the teacher was writing on the blackboard. Yesterday various of his class-mates were telling him, "You ought to ask Dot to the May Dance." But Ted told me last evening that he didn't care that much for Dot. Today Ted learned that the kids in study hall had "polled" one another and decided that he ought to ask Dot to the dance. And another girl informed Ted that she had talked with Dot and that Dot had said that if Ted asked her, she "probably" would go with him. So Ted now has asked Dot and they're going to the dance together.

All of this seems to me to be very interesting. Certain patterns seem to be at work in the dating game at the junior high school. For one thing, the students have pretty well arrived at some sort of erotic hierarchy—the relative physical attractiveness and popularity of their peers. In turn they engage in "matchmaking" based on this informal hierarchy. If you violate the ranking system, the girl is likely to refuse to go out with you if she is of a higher rank; if she is of a lower rank, your peer group bugs you to death. It seems to me that this arrangement gives a new twist to the matching hypothesis of mate selection. The theory says that we tend to choose partners who have a similar degree of physical attractiveness to our own. But such selection is not merely a function of one's own behavior—translating one's own options into reality. It is also a product of one's group bringing pressure upon individuals to date and mate with others of like ranking. We also see from the experience of my broth-ers how one's clique or network operates to "arrange" certain pairings. In this way it smooths the way for the "coupling" of a boy and a girl and saves each from the embarrassment of rejection. Mate selection is clearly a social or group happening.

dance" in which the students were paired on a random basis except that the man was always taller than the woman (Walster et al., 1966). Before the individuals actually met, the researchers obtained data on each subject's personal characteristics, including a rating for attractiveness. Later, after having attended the dance together, the subjects were interviewed and asked how much they liked their partners and whether they wanted to see them again. To their surprise, the researchers found that only ratings of a man's or woman's attractiveness were useful predictors of liking—personality, intelligence, and social skills did not seem to matter.

In *hypothetical* situations, research shows that we think in terms of idealized

The Matching Hypothesis of Mate Selection
We tend to choose partners with about the same degree of physical attractiveness as we have ourselves. (Patrick Reddy)

visions and prefer a date or mate of considerable physical attractiveness. Very simply, physical beauty seems to be rewarding for both sexes, both as an individual experience and for the reflected status it brings. But the supply of unusually beautiful or handsome partners is limited. Real-life situations generally confirm the **matching hypothesis of mate selection**—namely, that we tend to choose partners who have a similar degree of physical attractiveness to our own (Walster and Walster, 1970; Berscheid et al., 1971; Murstein, 1972; White, 1980). Hence, although we strongly prefer physically attractive individuals as dates (and also like them more), those of us who are unattractive tend to choose similarly unattractive others as our dates (Shanteau and Nagy, 1979).

Support for the matching hypothesis is provided by Bernard Murstein's (1972) study involving ninety-nine couples who were either engaged or "going steady." The individuals rated both themselves and their partners on a 5-point scale ranging from "extremely good-looking" to "considerably below average in looks." Using the same scale, judges who did not know the subjects rated both them and a control group of randomly matched couples. The study revealed that (1) actual couples were less discrepant (more similar) in physical attractiveness than the randomly matched couples, (2) individuals' self-ratings were similar to the judges' ratings of them, and (3) individuals typically rated their partners as slightly above themselves in physical attractiveness.

It appears that whereas we would ideally like to associate with beautiful or handsome people (hypothetical situations), in practice we reduce our aspirations.

Apparently in real-life situations, we fear rejection in the "mating and dating game" and select partners who are most likely to reciprocate our advances. In other words, we generally experience the greatest payoff and the least cost when we direct our efforts toward someone of approximately equal physical attractiveness (White, 1980).

Love

Love is one of the most intense of human emotions. In the United States, we expect that all of us will eventually experience it. Pulp literature, women's magazines, "brides only" and traditional "male" publications, movies, television, and popular music reverberate with themes of romantic ecstasy. In sharp contrast to the American emphasis on love, consider these words of the elders of an African tribe. They were complaining to the 1883 British Commission on Native and Custom about the problems of "runaway" marriages and illegitmacy: "It is all this thing called love. We do not understand it at all. This thing called love has been introduced" (Gluckman, 1955: 76). The elders saw romantic love as a disruptive force. In their culture, marriage did not necessarily involve a feeling of attraction for the spouse-to-be; marriage was not the free choice of the couple marrying; and considerations other than love played the most important part in mate selection.

The Nature of Love

All of us are familiar with the notion of love, yet social psychologists have found it exceedingly difficult to define. If letters to "Dear Abby" and "Ann Landers" are any indication, it seems that a good many Americans—particularly teenagers— are also uncertain about what love is supposed to feel like and how they can recognize the experience within themselves. Common questions include "How can I be sure that I'm in love?" "How can I tell if my partner loves me?" "What can I do to get my partner to be more committed to our relationship?"

Social scientists and laypeople alike recognize that the intense emotion of love entails more than mild feelings of liking (Berscheid, 1983). Indeed, in our everyday lives we readily distinguish between friends and lovers and value each differently (Davis, 1985). However, social psychologists have had difficulty specifying how these two essential relationships differ. Even so, one aspect seems clear. Love, or more particularly romantic or passionate love, commonly has both positive and negative emotions and cognitions associated with it:

> A preoccupation with another person. A deeply felt desire to be with the loved one. A feeling of incompleteness without him or her. Thinking of the loved one often, whether together or apart. Separation frequently provokes feelings of genuine despair or else tantalizing anticipation of reuniting. Reunion is seen as bringing feelings of euphoric ecstasy or peace and fulfillment. (Pope, 1980: 4)

Although the emotional intensity may be absent from friendships, the two types of relationships tend to be similar in such characteristics as enjoyment, accept-

Love
A number of social psychologists say that passionate
love involves physiological arousal—increased heart
rate, accelerated breathing, and the like—and then the
assignment of the label "love" to the arousal. (Patrick
Reddy)

ance, trust, respect, understanding, spontaneity, and confiding (Davis, 1985).
(See the boxed insert on successful marriages, pp. 282–283.)

Love may take different forms (Kelley, 1983). One type of love has been
variously termed *romantic love, passionate love,* and *limerence* (Tennov, 1979;
Berscheid, 1983). It entails intense absorption in, acute longing for and dependency on, and strong bodily sensations in response to a loved one. Romantic
love is quite fragile and dwindles after long interaction. Thus marriage partners
find that the abrasions of ordinary living dull the idealization of the partner, and
regular sexual gratification and growing predictability of the partner undermine
high levels of arousal. Another type of love is *pragmatic love*. It occurs among
mature adults and is found in lengthy relationships, such as marriage. Trust and
tolerance of the other's idiosyncracies highlight pragmatic love relationships.
Each party is likely to view the relationship as equitable, getting out of it rewards

commensurate with what they put into it. Still another type of love is *altruistic love*. The caring component assumes an important part in altruistic love, usually thought to be epitomized by "mother love." The caring behavior is intrinsically motivated rather than performed to elicit similar behavior from the partner. However, in many enduring relationships it is difficult to distinguish altruistic behaviors from helpful behavior motivated by expectations of eventual reciprocity (see Chapter 10). In actual close relationships, love is frequently a blend of these three forms. And whatever is different among the types of love, there is a core cluster of traits that they share in common, including needing, caring, trust, and tolerance of the other's faults (Kelley, 1983; Sternberg and Grajek, 1984).

Love as Labeling

Writing *The Art of Love* in first-century Rome, Ovid noted that an excellent time for a man to arouse romantic passion in a woman was while watching gladiators disembowel one another in the arena. Presumably the emotions of fear and repulsion excited by the grisly scene were somehow converted into romantic interest (Rubin, 1977). Recent studies of "falling in love" suggest that there may be some truth to Ovid's observation. Social psychologists like Zick Rubin (1977), Ellen Berscheid, and Elaine Hatfield (Berscheid and Walster, 1974*a*) say that passionate love, like other emotional states, requires arousal and then the assignment of a label to that arousal. They suggest that intense attraction is most likely to occur when people find themselves in situations in which they experience physiological arousal such as during an exciting football game, the bombardment of a city, or a frightening storm.

An experiment undertaken by Donald G. Dutton and Arthur R. Aron (1974) helps our understanding of this matter. These researchers undertook a study near two footbridges that cross the Capilano River in North Vancouver, Canada. The first bridge was suspended 230 feet above the rushing rapids below, had a tendency to tilt, sway, and wobble, and had low handrails of wire cable—in brief, a bridge having many arousal-inducing features. The second bridge was a solid wood bridge further upriver that was only 10 feet above a small, shallow stream.

An attractive female experimenter approached men who had crossed either of the bridges and explained that she was doing a project for her psychology class on "the effects of exposure to scenic attractions on creative expression." The men merely had to complete a questionnaire with a number of brief "filler items" and write a short dramatic story based on a picture she showed them. When the subjects had completed their questionnaires, the woman gave each man her name and telephone number in the event he desired more information about the study.

As revealed by the content of their stories, the researchers found that the men on the frightening suspension bridge were more sexually aroused than the men on the solid bridge. Additionally, half of the men on the high-fear bridge called the young women, ostensibly to find out more about her study. (In contrast, only 13 percent of those on the low-fear bridge called the experimenter.) Presumably, the men on the rickety bridge had relabeled their inner stirrings of fear as the product of sexual arousal and romantic attraction. This sort of labeling

SUCCESSFUL MARRIAGES

More than a million couples each year end their marriages by divorce. Even so, there are a good many Americans whose marriages endure. In recent years, a number of social scientists have turned their attention to the study of happy marriages to identify the ingredients that make for marital success. Jeanette Lauer and Robert Lauer (1985) surveyed 300 happily married couples, asking them why their marriages survived. The most frequently named reason was having a positive attitude toward one's spouse. The partners commonly said that "my spouse is my best friend" and "I like my spouse as a person." One woman observed: "I would want to have him as a friend even if I weren't married to him" (Lauer and Lauer, 1985: 24). A second key to a lasting marriage was a belief that marriage is a long-term commitment and a sacred institution. In one way or another, many individuals indicated that sometimes marriage demands that you grit your teeth and remain on track despite the difficulties. A man married for more than twenty years said:

> Commitment means a willingness to be unhappy for a while. I wouldn't go on for years and years being wretched in my marriage. But you can't avoid troubled times. You're not going to be happy with each other all the time. That's when commitment is really important. (Lauer and Lauer, 1985: 25)

A common theme among couples in the Lauers' study was that they were grateful to have married a person whom they found basically appealing and likable. More particularly, they often mentioned such qualities as caring, giving, integrity, and a sense of humor as important to them. Yet they were hardly blind to each other's faults. They recognized flaws in their mates and acknowledged that they had had their share of rough times. But when all was said and done, they felt that their

is encouraged by the popular stereotype that portrays falling in love as entailing such symptoms as a pounding heart, shortness of breath, and trembling hands (also the physical symptoms of fear). In sum, according to this view, love does not exist unless we define our inner feelings of arousal as love. Consequently, it is easy for people to follow the romantic clues that abound in their environment and decide that they are "in love."

Further confirmation for this interpretation of love is afforded by Gregory L. White and his associates (1981). They first stirred up a number of male subjects by having the men jog or listen to either a funny tape by comedian Steve Martin or a grisly tape describing a missionary's death at the hands of a mob. Next they showed the men a videotape of an attractive woman who told about her family and school experiences. The men then completed a questionnaire concerning the woman. Another group of men also saw the same videotape and completed

mates' likable qualities outweighed the deficiencies and the difficulties. Perhaps surprisingly, sex was far down on the list of reasons couples cited for a happy marriage. Less than 10 percent of the spouses believed that good sexual relations kept their marriage together. Although some couples were contented with their marriages despite a less-than-ideal sex life, most couples were satisfied with their sex lives.

Some marriage counselors stress the importance of spouses freely venting their anger, letting out all the stops short of physical violence. But the Lauers found that happily married couples felt otherwise. The vast majority emphasized the importance of restraint and the need not to say things that one will be sorry about later. Other researchers confirm this finding (Goleman, 1984b). Happy couples have the ability to deescalate conflict. It seems that when tensions are high, it is typically the husband who attempts to deflect in a gentle way his partner's negative feelings. Happily married men seem to find marital arguments particularly punishing and try

to head off arguments more often than do their wives. But when things flare up, it is usually the wives who take the crucial role in managing things, since men tend to respond to anger with anger.

Research by Robert J. Sternberg and Susan Grajek (1984) suggests that the best predictor of how satisfied and happy a couple are is not how much or how little the spouses love each other, but rather how equal their love is. The least happy situation is where one partner perceives the other partner as not reciprocating his or her love to a like degree. This finding is supported by a longitudinal study of dating couples (Hill, Rubin, and Peplau, 1976). Those couples who initially reported unequal levels of involvement in the relationship were more likely than other couples to break up later. Nonmutual relationships may break up in a kind of implicit bargaining, with the more dependent person leaving after finding his or her position too insecure and exploitable or the less dependent person leaving for a better alternative.

the same questionnaire, but they had not been physiologically stirred up. The men in the aroused condition rated the woman's personality as more sympathetic, humorous, sexy, and exciting than did the men who had not been physiologically aroused. Further, they gave higher ratings to how much they would like to know the woman, work with her, date her, and kiss her. But when the study was repeated with an unattractive woman, the effect worked in reverse. The physiologically aroused men found her less desirable and less attractive than did the nonaroused men.

Love as Brain Chemistry

Not all researchers accept the notion that love is physiologically indistinguishable from other arousal states, such as fear. Michael R. Liebowitz (1983), a clinical psychiatrist, believes that love has a unique chemical basis, associated with phenylethylamine (a compound related to the amphetamines). Amphetamine is thought to affect the human nervous system indirectly by inducing the brain to release vast amounts of the neurotransmitters norephinephrine and dopamine (chemicals released by nerve and brain cells that influence the action of other nerve and brain cells). Liebowitz contends that neurochemical pathways in humans, somewhat analogous to electrical circuits wired into machines, activate the response we call romantic attraction. The action of the chemicals norepinephrine and dopamine seems to affect the threshold, or activation level, of the brain's pleasure center. Love brings on a giddy response, much like an amphetamine high. The crash that follows a breakup resembles an amphetamine withdrawal. Endorphins may also be involved. When first discovered in brain and certain other body tissues, endorphins were called "the body's own morphine," because they are neurotransmitters that have the capacity to dull pain and produce euphoric feelings.

Studying patients with a history of roller-coaster love affairs, Liebowitz finds that the individuals often have a craving for chocolate after a breakup. Chocolate has a high supply of the mood-altering chemical phenylethylamine. Perhaps, reasons Liebowitz, the brain pours out its own chemical correlate to amphetamine—phenylethylamine—when the person is in love, and halts production of the substance in a breakup, leaving the person to suffer from its absence. Chocolate binges may simply be an attempt at self-medication.

Psychologist John Money of Johns Hopkins University also claims that love has a distinctive physiological basis. He finds that individuals who undergo surgery before or during their teens for the removal of pituitary tumors confront lifelong difficulty falling in love. Although such individuals are capable of experiencing a wide range of emotions, they do not seem able to have full-blown love affairs. Consequently, Money believes that the place to look for answers to love is not on high bridges in Vancouver but "inside people's heads" (quoted in Ansen, 1980; Sobel, 1980).

Similarity

A good deal of research reveals that we tend to like others who are similar to us. In experiment after experiment, subjects say that they like people whom the experimenter suggests are close to them in beliefs and attitudes. Indeed, the greater the proportion of similar attitudes held by two people, the greater their attraction to each other tends to be (Gonzales et al., 1983). Conversely, we are less favorable toward people who disagree with us. Studies of marriages also point to the impact of **homogamy**—the tendency of "like to marry like." More than a hundred studies have been conducted on homogamy. They have dealt with such diverse characteristics as age, race, religion, nationality, social class, social attitudes, education, previous marital status, intelligence, neuroticism, emotional stability, deafness, health, and physical height. With few exceptions, people who are similar marry more often than would be expected by chance. (Homogamy appears most influential in the realm of social variables. The evidence is less clear with regard to various psychological and personality components.) Why should this be so; why should similarity lead to liking? A number of explanations have been advanced by social psychologists.

Cognitive Consistency

Following Fritz Heider (see Chapter 6), Theodore Newcomb (1956, 1961, 1963) suggests that people strive for cognitive consistency among their attitudes and behavior. He predicts that people who agree on important matters will become attracted to each other because they satisfy one another's need for consistency. To test this hypothesis, Newcomb studied the development of friendships among a group of university men who lived in a campus house over a sixteen-week period.

At first, roommates were most attracted to each other, irrespective of similarity in attitudes and values. With the passage of time, however, similarity in attitudes and values increasingly became a factor in attraction. Shared attitudes toward other group members, and similarity between the attitudes an individual held toward himself and the attitudes held toward him by another, assumed critical importance. Knowing the degree of similarity that existed among the men *before* they moved into the house enabled Newcomb to predict who would be attracted to whom by the end of the period. Evidently it took the men a certain amount of time to learn who held values similar and dissimilar to their own. And people who experience a like world are able to communicate more effectively with one another (Padgett and Wolosin, 1980).

Anticipation of Being Liked

We may also be attracted to others who are similar to us because we assume they will like us. And being liked can in turn produce liking for the would-be friend. Researchers find, for instance, that if people believe a stranger will like them, they like the stranger (McWhirter and Jecker, 1967).

To go a step further, would we choose to associate with people dissimilar to us if we could feel sure that they would like us? To answer this question, Elaine Hatfield and G. William Walster gave college students the choice of joining a discussion (on why people dream) made up of similar people (fellow students) or dissimilar people (factory workers, psychologists, and so on). When the students were told that the members of *both* groups would be disposed to like them, they vastly preferred the *dissimilar* group. But when they were told that the members of both groups would be disposed to dislike them, they chose similar people. Apparently, when we are concerned about whether or not others will like us, we feel anxious and tend to "play it safe" by associating with others similar to us (Walster and Walster, 1963).

Reinforcement

Donn Byrne, in an extensive research program with various associates, has provided evidence of a positive linear relationship between attraction to a stranger and the proportion of attitudes held in common with that stranger

(Byrne, 1971, Clore and Byrne, 1974; Lott and Lott, 1974). According to Byrne, attraction toward another person is determined by the proportion of reinforcements and punishments associated with that person. He says that the perception of similarity is rewarding: the perception of dissimilarity, nonrewarding—even punishing. Similarity, Byrne believes, leads to liking because it provides people with independent evidence of the correctness of their interpretation of social reality. People find this rewarding. They feel that their point of view is validated and that they can confidently and effectively cope with their environment. Similarity, then, reinforces people's "need for competence" and as such feeds attraction. In contrast, dissimilar attitudes are presumed to threaten the person's view of the world.

Similarity provides a second kind of potential reinforcement. When we perceive others as similar to us, it encourages us to expect more positive outcomes from interaction with them (Schlenker, Brown, and Tedeschi, 1975; Lott and Lott, 1974).

Social Comparison Processes

Leon Festinger (1954) suggests a social comparison theory to account for the strong relationship between attitude similarity and interpersonal attraction. He says that we possess a basic "drive" to evaluate our opinions, attitudes, personality characteristics, and abilities—to know the truth about ourselves. Indeed, we find that to be incorrect or to do poorly in front of others is painful. For example, we may raise our hand in class to answer a question only to learn when called on that we have provided the wrong answer. Or we may continually miss the hoop in basketball practice before our physical education classmates. If we are to avoid or cope with these unpleasant experiences, it is necessary that we have some basis for appraising ourselves and our performance.

We usually prefer *physical reality* as a source of relevant information, since we can check our beliefs or capabilities against certain objective standards. Thus if we wish to know if we can throw a baseball sixty feet, we can throw the ball as far as we can and then measure the distance between where we were standing and where the ball landed. But physical reality is not always available to us, and hence we must rely on *social reality*. This requires that we appraise ourselves by comparing our abilities or opinions with those of appropriate other people.

We especially desire to compare ourselves with others who are relatively similar to us in opinion, ability, or ideals (Wetzel and Insko, 1982; Miller, 1982). Only in this manner will the resulting comparison be stable and subjectively precise. For instance, if we are a graduating senior in business administration trying to decide about a job opportunity, we do not seek out the opinions of music majors, registered nurses, or electrical engineers. Rather, we attempt to compare our thinking with that of others like ourselves such as other business administration majors or our roommates—individuals of similar age, training, and academic level.

In sum, when we are in a state of uncertainty about impending events or what we should do, we can determine the "correctness" of our projected course of action by comparing our attitudes or beliefs with others who are similar to us.

Complementary needs

I recently ran into an old girlfriend of mine and discovered something about my preferences in women. Although Ann and I went together for nearly a year and seemed to care a good deal for one another, something was wrong with the relationship. I'm a very outgoing, extroverted, talkative, and aggressive person. In many ways, Ann shared these characteristics, although to a somewhat lesser extent. And I think this was part of the difficulty. I'm now going with Marie, and we plan to get married in June. Marie is a quiet, retiring person—even shy. We seem to complement one another in this respect, whereas Ann and I always seemed to be engaged in an underlying tussle to see who would be out front and who would be in command of the relationship. We just didn't seem to find a good fit. In contrast, Marie is no rival for me. She welcomes my taking the lead in the world and prefers a more dependent role. Of interest, Ann is now going with a guy who strikes me as being on the passive side.

Presumably, the more uncertain or unverifiable an opinion is, the greater the need for social evaluation and support.

Complementary Needs

People with some personality traits "rub us the wrong way," whereas we feel comfortable with individuals who have certain other traits. Robert F. Winch (1958) has formulated a theory of attraction based on this everyday observation. Rather than stressing the similarities between people, Winch stresses differences. He focuses on the part that **complementary needs** play in producing attraction. This term refers to two different personality traits that are the counterparts of each other and that provide a sense of completeness when they are joined. They mutually supply each other's lack. Although the theory includes attraction between friends of the same or opposite sex, it is seen most clearly in the area of mate selection. According to Winch, we typically seek within the field of eligible mates a person who gives the greatest promise of providing us with the maximum gratification of our needs.

Winch notes that many of our needs are met in a complementary manner. People who possess a strong desire for recognition may love and be loved by deferential people who prefer to bask in the achievements of others. Within such relationships, each person finds his or her needs satisfied. People with a nurturance need—a need to sympathize with or help others in difficulty—find fulfillment with people having a succorance need—a need to be helped and taken care of. Dominant people find a complementary relationship with submissive people. Talkative people find themselves attracted to taciturn people.

The wife in the following illustration tells how she depends on her husband to guide her and how he in turn receives a sense of accomplishment from her dependence:

> I need someone to check my impulsiveness. I can never say no or refuse a favor. Besides, I overestimate my physical capacities. Consequently, I am always trying to do too many things at one time, and I end up running around in circles, not knowing which way to turn. Bob is always able to straighten me out and help me find the right direction. I depend on his ability to extricate me from my own maneuverings. I wouldn't be surprised if he gets a kick out of straightening me out too. (Blood, 1969: 38–39)

Bernard Murstein (1967, 1972, 1976) suggests a somewhat different version of the theory. He stresses the part that role compatibility plays in interpersonal attraction—how well each partner fulfills the role expectations of the other and how mutually gratifying their role "fit" is. For instance, a bedroom athlete is likely to be attracted to a lusty, passionate partner rather than a cool, cerebral one with little "animal" sensuousness. Thus, according to Murstein, the essential determinant of marital adjustment is the degree to which each spouse fulfills the other's expectations of the ideal husband or wife.

Richard V. Wagner (1975) has undertaken to integrate Winch's theory of complementary needs and Murstein's notion of role compatibility. His research, involving working relationships among counselors in three summer camps, supported such a formulation. Interpersonal attraction was dependent on the extent to which individuals *both* gratified one another's social needs *and* fulfilled the obligations of the role context in which the relationship existed.

Although the theory of complementary needs appears to find confirmation in everyday life (the domineering male and the mousy wife, or vice versa), actual studies have produced mixed findings. While a number support the theory (Kerckhoff and Davis, 1962; Becker, 1964; Rychlak, 1965), others fail to confirm it (Bowerman and Day, 1956; Shellenberg and Bee, 1960; Levinger, Sen, and Jorgensen, 1970; Meyer and Pepper, 1977; Antill, 1983). One problem is that some of our personality needs are complemented by similarity rather than by contrast (Rosow, 1957; Levinger, 1964). For instance, a quiet, thoughtful, introverted person usually prefers a similar companion rather than a loud, active extrovert. Overall, the usefulness of the theory remains to be determined; further refinements are clearly needed.

Social Exchange

A number of social scientists have stressed the view that we like those who reward us and dislike those who punish us. They have undertaken to apply various economic concepts to the realm of social behavior, suggesting that attraction occurs when rewards outweigh costs (Thibaut and Kelley, 1959; Homans, 1961, 1974; Blau, 1964). According to this view, the general determinants of attraction have to do with reciprocal rewards and punishments that are realized

Exploring New Relationships
These nursery school children are taking turns whispering in each other's ear, a form of social exchange. (Patrick Reddy)

SELF-DISCLOSURE AND TRUST WITHIN THE DYAD

Self-disclosure is the act of revealing one's "real" self to another. Typically it involves telling another about oneself. Self-disclosure implies that in some situations we can choose how much or how little we divulge to another. In brief, we can voluntarily alter the degree of openness we maintain in the course of a social relationship (Altman, 1975; Derlega and Chaikin, 1977).

Social scientists find that communication plays a critical part in marriage, underlying and supporting most other processes and outcomes. Self-disclosure is one type of marital communication. Through self-disclosure one partner expresses feelings, perceptions, fears, and inner doubts to the other partner. Not surprisingly, self-disclosure is significantly associated with marital satisfaction (Jorgensen and Gaudy, 1980; Hendrick, 1981). It can also promote **trust**—a belief by one person in the integrity of another person (Larzelere and Huston, 1980). By the same token, trust fosters self-disclosure. Trust implies that individuals believe that other people are genuinely interested in their welfare and that these others are honest when telling about their future intentions.

Social psychologists have repeatedly found that increased self-disclosure on the part of one party increases self-disclosure by the other party—what some have called the *dyadic effect* (Cozby, 1973; Chaikin and Derlega, 1974; Goodstein and Reinecker, 1974; Lynn, 1978; Berg and Archer, 1982). Although the effect is firmly documented, social psychologists have provided three somewhat different explanations for it.

Social exchange theorists point out that self-disclosure has been found to be positively related to liking (Worthy, Gary, and Kahn, 1969; Certner, 1973). Mutual disclosure spirals upward as a relationship develops, with people disclosing more and more about themselves at each encounter. Presumably, by disclosing personal information to others, we reveal to them that we value and trust them. Additionally, self-disclosure is often rewarding to the one who makes the disclosure. This may result from the ego-satisfying nature of the disclosure or from the catharsis realized through disclosure. The net result is that mutual self-disclosure is experienced by many individuals as a rewarding outcome—a mutual exchanging of rewards having reinforcement properties.

A second approach, *equitable exchange theory* (Walster, Berscheid, and Walster, 1973; Davidson, Balswick, and Halverson, 1983), says that the "norm of reciprocity" obligates us to exchange

in *social exchange*. In brief, a great many of our acts are based on our confidence that from these acts will flow a reward—perhaps some desired expression of love, gratitude, recognition, sense of security, or material benefit. Unless our expectations remain unfulfilled, the rewards we give one another in the course of social interaction maintain mutual attraction and continuing association (Blau, 1964;

Self-disclosure
Social psychologists find that increased self-disclosure by one party increases self-disclosure by the other party. (Patrick Reddy)

comparable behaviors and maintain equity in a relationship. When we exchange disclosures, we help achieve equity in that the ratio of our inputs and outputs is equal to that of the other party. Inequity is said to be aversive, a quality that contributes to tension and strain. To reduce this condition, we are motivated to make disclosures about ourselves to others when they make disclosures about themselves to us. Such disclosure is postulated to occur independent of our liking for another.

A third approach takes its cue from Sherif's experiments with the autokinetic phenomenon and Asch's work with distortions of judgments in group settings (see Chapter 7). The exchange of disclosures is seen as resulting because the partner who first provides a disclosure defines for the other party what constitutes appropriate behavior in an otherwise ambiguous situation (Rubin, 1975). An emergent norm is fashioned that sets forth situational demands affecting disclosure response. Thus we may provide self-disclosures not because of a feeling of attraction for our partner or because of a felt obligation to reciprocate, but because we perceive the situation as calling for this type of behavior (Lynn, 1978).

Lott and Lott, 1974; Burgess and Huston, 1979). In sum, the mutual exchange of rewards results in mutual reinforcement.

In exchange theory, the rewards-costs relationship assumes critical importance. *Profit* is total reward minus cost. Exchange theorists say that in the course of our social interaction we keep track of our profits; a relationship tends to persist only so long as both parties receive profit. *Costs* include not only punishment but physical or mental effort (fatigue, anxiety, emotional aggravation, embarrassment). Accordingly, people are viewed as engaged in mental bookkeeping—they keep a mental ledger on their rewards and costs.

Cost is value forgone, and hence the individual employs some evaluative standard—a *comparison level*. He or she weighs the attractiveness of a relationship in terms of some minimum level of expectation. The person asks internally, "Is the payoff what I deserve in terms of the costs?" Further, "What is the lowest level of reward I will accept to continue the relationship?" Or put in other terms, "What rewards do I forgo if I continue to engage in this interaction as opposed to alternative activities?" In sum, exchange theory proposes that a dyad engaged in a mutually satisfying relationship will exchange behaviors that have low cost and high reward to both members. However, some research suggests that rewards may play a more important part in many relationships than do costs. A study of heterosexual dating relationships found that increases over time in rewards led to corresponding increases in satisfaction and commitment, whereas variations in costs did not significantly affect either (Rusbult, 1983). And a study of long-term friendships among college students showed that benefits scores, and not costs or benefits-minus-costs scores, are the best predictor of the current and long-term status of relationships (Hays, 1985).

On the basis of exchange principles, Peter M. Blau (1964) says that we usually end up with the friends, lovers, and marriage partners that we "deserve." If we want to reap the benefits of associating with others, we must offer them enough to entice them to enter into and maintain a relationship with us. The more individuals have to offer, the greater will be the demand for their company. Consequently, we will have to provide such people with more benefits if we hope to win their friendship. The principle of supply and demand ensures that we will get partners only as desirable as we are ourselves.

Blau points out that a similar principle influences a couple's involvement in a love relationship. He says that love, like water, seeks its own level. If one lover is more involved than the other, this greater commitment invites exploitation and provokes feelings of entrapment, both of which undermine love. Only when two lovers' affection expands at roughly the same pace do they mutually reinforce their love.

Of course not all relationships are characterized by a balance between a person's rewards and another's behavior. The more a person's outcomes are dependent on the behavior of another, the less that person's relative power in an exchange arrangement. Consequently, the person with the more attractive alternative options enjoys a power advantage in the relationship.

Richard M. Emerson (1969) suggests that where both parties are equally dependent on each other, the relationship is in a stable state that discourages the use of power by either partner. But where the balance is unequal, the less dependent person is likely to employ his or her power advantage. Yet, Emerson says, the use of one's power serves to erode that very power, for it increases the power wielder's dependence on the exchange relationship—the rewards he or she is extracting from it. Accordingly, unbalanced relations tend to move toward balance with time: "To have a power advantage is to lose it" (1969: 391).

*T*he reacquaintance process

My boyfriend attends another college so we only get to see each other on weekends. Whenever he comes down to see me, I notice that we seem to go through a subtle reorientation process. It is rather like having to get acquainted again. In the past this bothered me somewhat. I felt that since we care so much about each other, we should be able to pick up our relationship right where we left off the previous time. We feel so close at the end of a visit—I just wish we did not have this continual readjustment. Having taken social psychology, I now realize that life is an ongoing process, one that is continuously changing. During the period we are apart, each of us changes ever so slightly, enough so that our actions cannot remain fixed and static. We individually experience new things that the other person does not experience. We do not have day-to-day continuity in our interaction. Consequently, we are unable to synchronize our actions on a regular basis and a gap becomes apparent when we later do get together. Further, our working definitions of the situation which we evolved during the previous visit seem to fade in the course of the week. Such definitions no longer have the vivid force that they maintain over shorter periods of time, especially when they are strengthened on a daily basis. Consequently, my boyfriend and I must refit our actions together and arrive at somewhat new definitions of the situation at the beginning of each visit.

A major advantage of exchange theory is that it enables us to identify unifying principles that underlie the other factors of attraction. Take the matter of physical beauty, discussed earlier in the chapter. Suppose that a man who is physically unattractive desires a woman who has the asset of beauty (Murstein, 1972). Other things being equal, she would gain less profit from the relationship than he would; thus he reasons that his suit is likely to be rejected. Moreover, rejection would constitute a cost to him, since he would lose in self-esteem. If he should try to date a woman less attractive than he is, on the other hand, he feels confident of success; the cost is low, because he would risk little chance of rejection. But the reward (profit) in such a conquest is also low. He can obtain the greatest reward at the least cost when he directs his efforts toward a woman approximately equal to him in physical attractiveness—thus the proposition that people tend to select partners of physical attractiveness comparable to their own.

Exchange theory is also helpful in explaining other factors in attraction. People who are geographically close (proximity) are more likely to interact because of the low cost of initiating the interaction. People whose attitudes and values are similar can give each other the reward of attitudinal validation and social support at very low cost. And the participants in complementary relationships also offer each other high rewards at low cost to themselves.

RESPONSES TO DISSATISFACTION IN A RELATIONSHIP

How do people respond when they become dissatisfied with a relationship? There seem to be four basic approaches that they may take (Rusbult, Zembrodt, and Gunn, 1982; Rusbult and Zembrodt, 1983). The first, *exit,* entails formally separating from the other person, such as moving out of a joint residence, deciding to be "just friends," or getting a divorce. The second, *voice,* involves active verbal attempts to resolve difficulties—for example, asking a partner what is troubling him or her, compromising, or seeking help from a therapist or member of the clergy. The third, *loyalty*, implies remaining passively loyal to the relationship or waiting for conditions to improve. And the fourth, *neglect,* entails passively allowing the relationship to atrophy, including ignoring the partner, refusing to discuss problems, treating the partner badly, or just letting things fall apart.

The responses differ from one another along two dimensions. The first is a constructive-destructive dimension. Whereas voice and loyalty are intended as constructive responses that tend to maintain a relationship, exit and neglect tend to be relatively destructive. The second is an activity-passivity dimension. Exit and voice are active behaviors—the person attempts to do something about the relationship. In contrast, loyalty and neglect are more passive responses.

Three conditions influence whether an individual will take one response rather than another: (1) the degree of satisfaction with the relationship prior to the emergence of problems, (2) the magnitude of a person's investment of resources in the relationship, and (3) the quality of the best available alternative to the relationship. In cases in which prior satisfaction is high, voice and loyalty tend to be the responses. Similarly, increases in a person's investment in the relationship encourage voice and loyalty. More attractive alternatives promote exit and hamper loyalty behaviors.

SUMMARY

1. Much of human life consists of social interaction. Human groups consist of acting people, and group life consists of their actions.
2. Some of our social interactions are casual, one-time encounters. Others continue long enough so that people come to be linked by a relatively stable set of expectations—social relationships.
3. We can distinguish between two types of ties that bond people together: expressive ties and instrumental ties. Expressive ties characterize primary relationships; instrumental ties, secondary relationships.
4. Beyond one-to-one relationships, human life encompasses multiple relationships organized into networks. Viewed as a social structure, a network can be depicted with persons as points and relations as connecting lines. One approach to networks has emphasized the paths or threads that prevail in a single network. Another approach has stressed the "knittedness" of interconnections within a network.

5. Other things being equal, we tend to like people who are geographically close to us.

6. Physical attractiveness plays a critical part in people's perception of the desirability of a relationship. We tend to choose partners who have a similar degree of attractiveness to our own.

7. Romantic love, which involves strong negative and positive emotions and cognitions, is an important factor in mate selection in our culture, though not in others. Mature love relationships often involve pragmatic and altruistic love as well.

8. A number of social psychologists say that passionate love, like other emotional states, requires arousal and then the assignment of a label to that arousal. According to this view, love does not exist unless we define our inner feelings of arousal as love. Consequently, it is easy for people to follow the romantic clues that abound in their environment and decide that they are "in love."

9. We tend to like others who are similar to us, apparently because of cognitive consistency, anticipation of being liked, reinforcement, and social comparison processes.

10. Within the field of eligible mates, we typically seek a person who gives the greatest promise of providing us with the maximum gratification of our needs. Many of these needs are met in a complementary fashion.

11. A great many of our acts are premised on confidence that they will bring a reward. We weigh the attractiveness of a relationship in terms of some minimal level of expectation. In interaction, people keep track of their "profits"; the relationship tends to persist only so long as both parties receive profit. This is the social exchange view of attraction.

12. There seem to be four basic approaches that people employ when they become dissatisfied with a relationship: exit, formally separating from the other person; voice, actively pursuing verbal discussions to resolve difficulties; loyalty, remaining passively loyal to the relationship or waiting for conditions to improve; and neglect, passively allowing the relationship to atrophy.

GLOSSARY

Bonding □   A process whereby individuals or groups are linked together.

Complementary needs □   Two different personality traits that are the counterparts of each other and that provide a sense of completeness when they are joined.

Dyad □   A two-person group.

Expressive tie □   A social linkage formed when one invests oneself in and commits oneself to another person.

Homogamy □   The tendency of "like to marry like." People who are similar marry more often than would be expected by chance.

Instrumental tie □   A social linkage formed when one cooperates with another person to achieve a certain limited goal.

Matching hypothesis of mate selection □   The tendency to choose partners who have a similar degree of physical attractiveness to our own.

Network □   A web of social relationships that center on a single individual and tie him or her directly to other individuals and indirectly through these other individuals to still more people.

Primary relationship □   A social interaction that rests on expressive ties between people. In primary relationships people experience warmth and closeness; they participate as integral, committed units.

Proximity □   Nearness in physical space.

Secondary relationship □   A social interaction that rests on instrumental ties between people. In secondary relationships, people view themselves as independent, autonomous units, not as totally committed participants.

Self-disclosure □   The act of revealing one's "real" self to another.

Social attraction □   The property by which two people are drawn together.

Social interaction □   A process directed toward, stimulated by, or influenced by another person or persons.

Social relationship □   An association that develops when social interaction continues long enough for two people to become linked together by a relatively stable set of expectations.

Sociogram □   A graph or chart that shows the patterns of choice among members of a group at a given point in time.

Sociometry □   An objective method for assessing patterns of attraction, rejection, or indifference among members of a group.

Trust □   A belief by one person in the integrity of another person.

ALTRUISM AND HELPING BEHAVIOR

POSITIVE FORMS OF SOCIAL
   BEHAVIOR
Prosocial Behavior and Altruistic
   Motives
The Effects of Personality
   Characteristics
The Effects of Mood States
Prosocial Behavior in Ambiguous
   Situations

Prosocial Behavior in
   Unambiguous Situations
NOTIONS OF A JUST WORLD,
   EQUITY, AND EQUALITY
The Just-World Hypothesis
Equity Theory
The Norm of Reciprocity
Self-interest, Equality, and Need

In the early hours of a spring morning in 1964, Kitty Genovese was returning home from a night job when a male assailant attacked and stabbed her. In response to her screams, at least thirty-eight residents in a respectable New York City neighborhood looked out their windows and witnessed the attack. A number shouted, "Leave the girl alone." The attacker ran away, came back, and stabbed the young woman again. Once more there was commotion and the assailant fled, only to come back a third time and complete the murder. No one went to the woman's assistance or called the police until after she was dead. Then one person called the police, but only after he first checked with a friend by telephone about the advisability of doing so. The case attracted national attention. News and other media commentators branded the incident "a national disgrace" and spoke of "the dehumanization of society," "a case of moral callousness," "the cold society," "apathy," "indifference," and "a loss of human decency and compassion."

Happenings such as the Genovese case are not unique to New York City. Newspapers throughout the nation periodically report similar incidents. In Columbus, Ohio, a man punched a woman several times in the face and made off with her wallet. The attack took place in a downtown bank parking lot in clear view of at least a half-dozen witnesses. The onlookers did nothing. Indeed, they quickly left the scene lest they be asked to identify the assailant (*Columbus* [Ohio] *Dispatch,* July 25, 1981). In the same city some 300 spectators, many of whom brought their children and binoculars, gathered outside Mt. Carmel West Hospital and repeatedly urged a man perched atop the building to jump. In the carnival-like atmosphere, a vendor sold ice cream from his refrigerated truck. After some ninety minutes, a priest persuaded the man to leave the roof. Many of the spectators were disappointed when the drama ended. One man said, "What a waste of time. Nothing happened." Another noted, "I wanted to see some blood" (Berens, 1984). And in New Bedford, Massachusetts, a young mother of two entered a bar to buy cigarettes. A man grabbed her, stripped off her clothes, and raped her on the barroom floor. Other men then lifted her onto a pool table and raped her again and again, to the cheers and applause of other bar patrons. Although the woman was assaulted and raped repeatedly for more than an hour before the eyes of at least fifteen other male customers, no one came to her aid or called the police (*Newsweek*, March 21, 1983, p. 25).

Probably no one incident has led social psychologists to pay as much attention to a single aspect of social behavior as Kitty Genovese's murder. In the intervening twenty years more than 1,000 articles and books trying to explain the behavior of bystanders in crises have been written (Dowd, 1984). Social psychologist Stanley Milgram observes:

> I've often wondered why the bystander event is so important, why we respond to it. And I think it's because it really touches on a fundamental issue, one that all of us think about, our primordial nightmare. If we need help, if we are in distress, are people going to help us? If we are attacked by someone on the street, will those around us stand around and let us be destroyed or will they come to our aid? Is there meaning to community and our relationship to others? . . . Are other creatures out there to help us sustain our life and values or are we individual flecks of dust just floating around in a vacuum? (Quoted by Cunningham, 1984a: 30)

Helpful behavior by bystanders is an aspect of **prosocial behavior**—behavior involving acts that benefit other people; ways of responding to other people that are sympathetic, cooperative, helpful, rescuing, comforting, and giving. To many social psychologists, interpretations of the Genovese murder that pointed to human "callousness," "indifference," "apathy," and "dehumanization" were too simplistic. Any number of observers of the human condition subsequently assembled impressive lists of incidents that revealed human helpfulness.

POSITIVE FORMS OF SOCIAL BEHAVIOR

A certain man went down from Jerusalem to Jericho, and fell among thieves, which stripped him of his raiment, and wounded him, and departed, leaving him half dead. And by chance there came down a certain priest that way: and when he saw him, he passed by on the other side. And likewise a Levite, when he was at the place, came and looked on him, and passed by on the other side. But a certain Samaritan, as he journeyed, came where he was: and when he saw him, he had compassion on him. And went to him, and bound up his wounds, pouring in oil and wine, and set him on his own beast, and brought him to an inn, and

Prosocial Behavior
Prosocial behavior is required both for the functioning of society and for the welfare of its individual members. (Patrick Reddy)

took care of him. And on the morrow when he departed, he took out two pence, and gave them to the host, and said unto him, Take care of him; and whatsoever thou spendest more, when I come again, I will repay thee.

—Luke 10:30–35

Prosocial behavior is crucial both for the functioning of the social group and for the welfare of its individual members (Staub, 1978). At its most fundamental level, human society is based on the willingness of people to work with one another and share the benefits of their mutual labor. It is questionable whether a society could long endure unless people were willing to assume responsibility for one another's welfare and to behave in positive, helpful ways.

Prosocial Behavior and Altruistic Motives

A large part of altruism, even when it is perfectly honest, is grounded upon the fact that it is uncomfortable to have unhappy people about one.

—H. L. Mencken, *Prejudices: Fourth Series, 1924*

Prosocial behavior can take a good many forms (Wispé, 1972). Consider sympathy, cooperation, donating, helping, and altruism. *Sympathy* commonly makes reference to a concern with, or a sharing of, the pain or sadness of another. *Cooperation* implies that individuals are able and willing to work with others, usually but not always for a common benefit. *Helping* involves rendering assistance to another party so that this other party can attain some object or end. *Aid* has to do with providing another party with what is needed to achieve some object or end. *Donating* refers to the act of making a gift or giving a contribution, usually to a charity. And **altruism** concerns behavior carried out to benefit another person without expectation of an external reward (Macaulay and Berkowitz, 1970).

Social psychologists have been especially intrigued by altruistic behavior. They have asked, "Why should an individual engage in behavior that benefits another when this behavior demands great self-sacrifice and provides no tangible self-benefit?" This question has to do with motivation. **Motivation** entails those inner states and processes that prompt, direct, and sustain activity. Of course we never directly observe motivation. Rather, we observe people's behavior and the environment in which it occurs. On the basis of these observations, we make inferences with respect to people's inner states.

Most of us assume that behavior is functional, that people do and say certain things because the consequences somehow meet their needs (Levine, 1975). Thus altruistic behavior poses a puzzle. According to one philosophical perspective, the solution lies in the "hedonistic paradox" that says that even the most unselfish act may produce a psychological reward for the actor (Cohen, 1972). André Gide, in his novel *Lafcadio's Adventures,* suggests that a truly gratuitous act is impossible; either good or bad, rewarding or punishing effects will always flow from it. Likewise, many psychologists (especially those who follow in the behaviorist tradition) reject the premise that altruistic behavior requires no reinforcement. They insist that all behavior is influenced by its consequences, both real and anticipated. If behavior that demands great sacrifice is not reinforced, then it will simply extinguish over time. Thus altruism is seen as self-gratifying and, consequently, as a form of hedonism (Baumann, Cialdini, and Kenrick, 1981).

Some sociobiologists, such as Edward O. Wilson, say that there is no need to postulate a hedonistic motivation for altruism (see boxed insert, pp. 302–304.) They claim that altruism springs from genetic preprogramming. In support of their position, sociobiologists point to a recent study on altruism undertaken by psychologists in Canada and Great Britain that involved pairs of identical and fraternal twins (Zuckerman, 1985). The psychologists estimated that about half of the altruism scores were due to genetic influences and the other half to environmental factors. But many social psychologists find genetic arguments untenable, or at least in need of modification (Campbell, 1975; Batson, 1983). On the whole, they have preferred to look to social and psychological factors as motivational sources of altruism.

One social psychological motive for engaging in prosocial behavior is the expectation that we will realize some gain or avoid some loss. We may behave prosocially to gain material benefits, social approval, and honor, or to escape group sanctions, social disapproval, and ostracism. But self-gain need not only

Altruism
Passers-by are more likely to do-nate money to a "good cause" if they have observed a model making a donation (Macaulay, 1970). Researchers have also found that motorists are more likely to stop and help a woman fix a flat tire if they have previ-ously driven past a model help-ing a person (a confederate) fix a flat tire (Bryan and Test, 1967). (Patrick Reddy)

derive from this-worldly motivations. The belief that God will reward or punish us can have powerful motivating properties. Even revenge may motivate altruism. Anthropologist Ronald Cohen reports: "I have witnessed a Hare Indian near the arctic circle of Canada in a near frenzy of decision-making because he had killed a moose and was plotting how to give it away for both prestige purposes *and* revenge against those who had up to now slighted him" (1972: 44). Of course, it can be questioned whether acts motivated by such intentions are truly altruis-tic. But since, as noted earlier, the attribution of intent is always inferential, we can never be certain of the accuracy of our assumptions regarding others' mo-tives.

A second motive identified by some social psychologists as underlying altruis-tic behavior has to do with our personal values and norms (Staub, 1978; Schwartz and Fleishman, 1978; Batson and Gray, 1981). Through socialization and moral development we build up internalized standards for behavior, which we experi-ence as obligations to act in certain ways (Alper, 1985). (See Chapter 4.) We feel good about ourselves when we act in accordance with these principles and bad when we act contrary to them. In sum, our self-reactions have motivating prop-erties. We experience positive self-evaluation, various forms of self-reward, and the generation of positive emotions when we act in accordance with internalized norms; we experience negative self-evaluation, various forms of self-punishment,

ALTRUISM AND SOCIOBIOLOGY

The chicken is only an egg's way of making another egg.
                    —Samuel Butler

Considerable scientific controversy has been generated by Edward O. Wilson's *Sociobiology: The New Synthesis* (1975) and *On Human Nature* (1978a). Wilson, a Harvard zoologist specializing in the study of social insects, has in recent years expanded his interest to encompass the entire animal kingdom. **Sociobiology** is a new discipline that focuses on the biological basis for social behavior in species ranging from amoeba colonies to human societies. It seeks to integrate Darwinian theory regarding natural selection with the evolution of social behavior as reflected in groups, colonies, or societies. Its central thesis is that social behavior evolves as a mechanism to maximize the fitness of a species for survival. Consequently, a hereditary foundation is said to underlie social behavior.

Sociobiologists claim that a wide variety of behavior is built into human genes, including territoriality, aggression, the incest taboo, sex-role differences, sibling rivalry, nepotism, fear of strangers, and homosexuality. Wilson says that although the variation among the world's cultures appears enormous, in fact their summed content comprises only a tiny range of the realized social arrangements displayed by the thousands of social species on earth:

Many social scientists see no value in sociobiology because they are persuaded that variation among cultures has no genetic basis. Their premise is right, their conclusion wrong. We can do well to remember Rousseau's dictum that those who wish to study men should stand close, while those who wish to study man should look afar. The social scientist is interested in the often microscopic but important variations in behavior that are due to culture and the environment. The sociobiologist is interested in the more general features of human nature and the limitations that exist in the environmentally induced variation. (Wilson, 1978b: 12)

Perhaps the most startling assertion of sociobiology has to do with altruism— once regarded as a uniquely human type of behavior. Altruism is defined by sociobiologists as behavior that is potentially harmful to the acting organism but beneficial to genetically related members of its group. Wilson finds altruistic suicide among many forms of life. A honeybee, for instance, will attack an intruder in the hive with its fishhook-shaped sting. The sting remains embedded in the skin of the enemy, pulling out the bee's entire venom gland and much of the viscera with it. The bee soon dies, but the venom gland continues to leak poison into the wound. From the point of view of the colony as a whole, the suicide of the individual supports the survival of the hive. For similar purposes, some birds will sound an alarm that draws a predator toward them and away from their nests. And to allow others in the troop to escape, baboons will charge a prowling leopard, thus facing certain death. Perhaps of even greater interest, human beings are known during wartime to throw themselves on top of grenades to shield comrades.

Classical Darwinian theory has had difficulty providing an answer to the question, "How is it that natural selection can favor patterns of behavior that apparently do not favor the survival of the individual?" Wilson provides a new twist to evolutionary theory by advancing an explanation for altruism that is in keeping with natural selection. Consider the social insects. When a honeybee or a soldier ant sacrifices its own life for other members of the colony, it improves the chances of kin survival—the chances that genes like many of its own will survive. Evolution favors such genes (kin selection) because, although some individuals are sacrificed, the society as a whole survives (and has the capacity to reproduce the lost member's genes many times over). Thus Wilson observes:

> In a Darwinist sense the organism does not live for itself. Its primary function is not even to reproduce other organisms; it reproduces genes and serves as their temporary carrier. (1975: 3)

A central concept to sociobiologists is that of inclusive fitness. "Fitness" is a measure of how successfully a creature passes its genes on to future generations, that is, how many offspring it produces and how well they are equipped to survive. "Inclusive fitness" extends the principle to a group of individuals who share some of the same genes. Sociobiologists employ inclusive fitness to predict the extent of altruism: Each organism is viewed as having a 100 percent genetic interest in itself, a 50 percent interest in its parents, offspring, and full siblings, a 25 percent in-terest in half-siblings, grandparents, grandchildren, uncles, aunts, nephews, and nieces, a 12½ percent interest in first cousins, half-nephews,. great-grandchildren, and so on.

Inclusive fitness is also used to explain "double altruism" or reciprocity. Reciprocity can take place between any two individuals, whether they are genetically related or not. It is based on the conscious expectation that beneficent behavior will be returned. For instance, people who have risked their lives to help a stranger commonly say they did so because they would expect the other person to do the same for them under similar circumstances. Sociobiologists claim that reciprocity is the foundation for complex levels of social organization such as those found in human societies.

In sum, Wilson says that the emotions of altruism and reciprocity that we experience ultimately stem from hereditary factors. What evolves through genes is the underlying emotion, not the specific form that altruism takes in a given society. Altruism finds differing expressions in different cultures. Genes, then, do not necessarily prescribe a particular behavior; they provide the capacity to develop certain behaviors—even more, the tendency to develop them in specific environments.

Sociobiology has become the focus of a longstanding battle between those who believe human beings are perfectible and others who claim that biology is destiny. In the past, the debate swirled around such issues as race and IQ, and the biological foundations of aggression. A good deal of the fury once reserved for individuals like William Shockley and Arthur R. Jensen,

Box continues on next page

who have argued that the poorer performance of blacks on IQ tests has a genetic basis, is now being directed against Wilson (Pines, 1978). Critics claim that sociobiology provides a genetic justification of the status quo and of the privileges that certain groups hold according to class, race, or sex. Hence the basic issue is that old bugaboo of the behavioral sciences: the nature-nurture controversy. By giving an entirely new kind of respectability to the notion that there is an important genetic component in human behavior, Wilson's approach was bound to prove explosive.

Critics of sociobiology point to the slowness of genetic evolution in comparison with the evolution afforded by culture. Behavior patterns wired in organisms by genes do not permit quick adaptation to changing conditions. In contrast, cultural evolution is rapid and easily diffused. In the view of some social scientists, cultural evolution has swamped biological evolution as the chief source of behavioral change for human beings. The human

brain, the argument goes, is no longer rigidly tied to the calculus of the selfish gene. At most, genes have prescribed the construction of a liberated brain, one permitting a flexible repertoire of behavioral responses. The more culture human beings had, the more biological capacity for culture then evolved, leading to more culture, and so on (Barkow, 1978).

Sociobiology has afforded science both a major hope and a challenge. The new field permits scientists to move beyond the nature-nurture controversy. By now science has pretty well established that both nature and nurture play critical parts in development. Human behavior does not flow in some magical manner from genes, nor does environment imprint a human personality on a blank and infinitely plastic brain. Science can now tackle the task of finding answers to the questions of how and why nature and nurture interact in the ways they do. In truth, human behavior is an amalgam of biological potential and environmental experience.

---

and negative emotions (including guilt) when we deviate from these standards. Thus to one degree or another, many of us have internalized a humanistic value system that leads to a concern for others' welfare and a sense of obligation toward people in need.

 Some social psychologists single out empathic emotion as a third motivating factor producing altruistic behavior (Batson et al., 1981; Underwood and Moore, 1982; Toi and Batson, 1982; Batson et al., 1983). According to one formulation, empathy leads us to take another person's perspective and to see the world as he or she sees it. By taking the perspective of a person in need, we increase the likelihood that we will recognize the need and then act to reduce it. Hence empathy is said to have a *cognitive* impact, providing a potential helper with the information that he or she uses to define the situation as one requiring help. According to an alternative view, empathy results in our identifying with another person and feeling vicarious physiological arousal. (We feel emotional distress through imagined participation in the other person's experience.) By acting to assist another person, thereby reducing the person's plight, we simultaneously reduce our *own* emotional discomfort. Thus, empathy is said to have an *affective*

> ## *N*orm of social responsibility
>
> *Today I went over to a private blood center where you receive $10 for giving a pint of plasma. I needed the money badly. Although the experience was not painful, I've decided that my visit today was my first and last. The reason is that I felt terribly guilty afterwards. I had received money for blood needed by sick people. And I benefited from their misfortune. I feel I should have donated the blood to the Red Cross. As it is, I violated the norm of social responsibility, and I'm quite distressed about it.*

impact, providing the potential helper with "vicarious arousal" that leads to self-centered, egoistic behavior designed to reduce the distress. And still another formulation says that the cognitive and affective processes come together in motivating helping behavior.

The Effects of Personality Characteristics

> *True kindness presupposes the faculty of imagining as one's own the suffering and joys of others.*
>
> —André Gide, *Pretexts,* 1903

Many psychologists have been interested in identifying relatively enduring ways in which individuals differ, termed **traits.** Traits refer to descriptive characteristics: An individual may be more or less passive, more or less cooperative, more or less adventurous, and so on. We infer people's traits—as we do their motives—from their behavior in various environmental settings. (We attribute consistency and similarity to their behavior over time and across situations.)

A variety of personality characteristics can influence prosocial behavior, especially in combination with certain situational factors (Schwartz and David, 1976; Wilson, 1976; Staub, 1978). Social psychologists have approached the study of prosocial personality traits in various ways. Perry London (1970) interviewed persons who rescued Jews in Nazi Germany and helped them escape. By some estimates, some 200,000 Jews were saved from the Nazis by non-Jewish rescuers. London found that these men and women shared an adventurous spirit, a sense of being on the margin of society, and a close identification with a morally committed and frequently moralistic parent. One rescuer explained:

> My mother said to me when we were small, and even when we were bigger, she said to me . . . "Regardless of what you do with your life, be honest. When it comes to

the day you have to make a decision, make the right one. It could be a hard one. But even the hard ones should be the right ones." (1970: 247)

Yet other researchers find that espousing such values was not by itself enough (Goleman, 1985a). Rescuers were also distinguished by a sense of competence. They viewed themselves as in control of their lives and were inclined to take calculated risks. Moreover, the rescuers had to have at their disposal the where-withal to put their values and sense of competence into action. They may have been expert skiers who could escort Jews across the Alps to Switzerland, or they may have had a large home or estate where they could hide Jews.

Often the rescuers of Jews made only a small commitment at the beginning—to hide a person for a day or so. However, once they took the first step, they began to define themselves differently, as persons who help others. For instance, Raoul Wallenberg, the Swedish diplomat who used his position to save hundreds of Hungarian Jews, started by rescuing a Hungarian-Jewish business partner. Soon Wallenberg was manufacturing passes that made Jews eligible for Swedish citizenship, and hence exempt from German capture. As Wallenberg's involve-ment grew, he exposed himself to considerable risk by providing passes to Jews waiting in line for deportation trains (Goleman, 1985a).

We should not conclude that the good Samaritan is necessarily a saint. Ted L. Huston, Gilbert Geis, and Richard Wright (1976) have wondered how the rather flawless image we have of the good Samaritan matches the flesh-and-blood Samaritan in the street. In 1965, California passed a "good Samaritan" law that compensates private citizens for injuries suffered trying to prevent a crime, catch a criminal, or help out in an emergency situation. Through interviews and psychological testing (for humanitarianism, religious feelings, attitudes toward criminal justice, and so on), Huston and his associates have built up a composite portrait of the good Samaritan from a sample of Californians who benefited from that state's law.

The researchers have found that most of the California good Samaritans were risk takers, men (with few exceptions all were men) who were familiar with violence and on rather amiable terms with it. Some 81 percent of one sample owned guns, and some carried them in their cars. These men defined themselves as preeminently qualified to provide assistance. The good Samaritans were taller, heavier, and better trained to cope with crimes and emergencies than were noninterveners (many with lifesaving, medical, and police training). They were also more likely to describe themselves as physically strong, aggressive, emo-tional, and principled (Huston et al., 1981). Indeed, the good Samaritans seemed jealous of others who also wished to render help or invade the limelight. They expressed considerable anger toward criminals. Surprisingly, the good Samaritans seemed unsympathetic toward the victims, often saying that they brought the trouble on themselves through their own stupidity. The men saw their interven-tion primarily as a contest between themselves and the criminal, with the victim almost a side issue. For example, they were likely to take off after the wrongdoer, leaving the victim unattended and unassisted (in some cases, even dying).

The California good Samaritan research deals with the behavior of individuals who intervene in situations with a high degree of violence. It is conceivable that many other individuals, intimidated and frightened by crime and violence (especially when the attacker is still present and the possibility exists that a potential helper may be the next victim), would nonetheless render help in less threatening emergencies. A review of responsive-bystander research suggests that this is indeed the case. The research reveals: (1) There are some people who are more disposed than others to help people in distress, even at cost to themselves; (2) altruistic behavior appears rooted in early socialization experiences; (3) prosocial behavior tends to be correlated with sympathetic attitudes toward the welfare of others; (4) good Samaritans tend to be characterized by a spirit of adventurousness and unconventionality; and (5) prosocial assisters have a tendency to reduce their own distress by social actions designed to reduce the distress of another (Huston and Korte, 1976). However, the data are inconsistent as to whether individuals living in small communities are more likely to intervene in emergency situations than those living in large communities (Weiner, 1976; Holahan, 1977; Takooshian, Haber, and Lucido, 1977; House and Wolf, 1978; Amato, 1983).

Not all psychologists accept the notion that human behavior is sufficiently consistent and stable to warrant conceiving of it in terms of prosocial or other

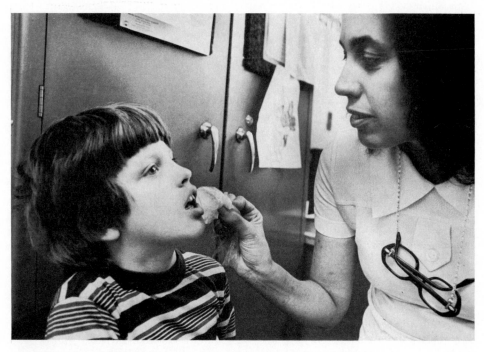

Altruism Among Children
Helping responses among children are influenced more by what adults do than by what they say. (Patrick Reddy)

traits. On the basis of his review of the psychological literature, Walter Mischel (1968, 1969, 1973, 1977) concludes that the consistency we experience in people's behavior is merely in the eye of the beholder, more illusory than real. He says that we are motivated to believe that our world is predictable and orderly. Consequently, we perceive our own and other people's behavior as patterned and recurrent. Mischel does not deny that there is a high degree of consistency in our cognitive functioning; he admits that our performances on various tasks measured by intelligence tests are reasonably correlated with one another. But he finds that consistency in interpersonal behavior is low; correlations between scores on personality tests and behavior are high only when the situations in which the behavior is tested are *highly* similar.

Mischel's reasoning suggests that a person who engages in altruistic behavior on one occasion need not do so on another occasion (Staub, 1978; Hampson, 1984). Thus it has come as no surprise to some psychologists that a variety of experiments have found no relationship between certain personality characteristics (including Machiavellianism, authoritarianism, social desirability, alienation, and social responsibility) and helping (Latané and Darley, 1968, 1970; Korte, 1971; Yakimovich and Saltz, 1971; Darley and Batson, 1973). These findings are reminiscent of those of Hugh Hartshorne and Mark A. May (1928; Hartshorne, May, and Maller, 1929; Hartshone, May, and Shuttleworth, 1930). In their monumental and classic study carried out over a half century ago, Hartshorne and May were unable to locate a stable personality trait such as honesty. It was not possible for the researchers to predict whether a person who cheated on an arithmetic test would also cheat on a spelling test. Honesty, self-control, service, good temper, truthfulness, justice, and bravery were not a "bag of virtues" that individuals either did or did not have. Rather, behavior was a function of the specific situations in which people found themselves.

More recently, John M. Darley and C. Daniel Batson (1973) have reached somewhat similar conclusions based on a study in which they tested the influence of religiosity on helping. The subjects were students at Princeton Theological Seminary. None of the religious variables predicted whether a seminarian would help the victim or not (a confederate of the experimenters who sat slumped motionless in an alleyway, coughing and groaning with his head down and eyes closed). Nor did it matter that some of the young men were on their way to deliver a lecture on the biblical parable of the good Samaritan. Indeed, on several occasions Darley and Batson report that a seminarian would literally step over the victim as the student hurried to give his lecture.

It should be noted, however, that Darley and Batson measured only one personality characteristic (religiosity). This is also true of the other studies reporting no relationship between a personality trait and helping. A more comprehensive approach would look at several characteristics and determine their relationship, singly and in combination, in producing prosocial behavior (Huston and Korte, 1976). Further, it is important that researchers examine how personality factors interact with a situation in determining helping responses (Wilson, 1976). Although there is admittedly limited experimental evidence documenting the influence of personality on helping others in physical distress, some social psychologists nonetheless believe there is enough to generate hope of finding more evidence (Huston and Korte, 1976; Staub, 1978; Shotland, 1985).

The Effects of Mood States

Another factor influencing whether or not we assist others in need of help is how we feel at the time. Research shows that "good moods" induce helpful behaviors (Weyant, 1978; Staub, 1978; Rosenhan, Salovey, and Hargis, 1981). When subjects in experiments are led to believe that they have done well on tasks requiring motor-coordinating, creative, or problem-solving abilities, they are more likely to volunteer, work, or sacrifice for the benefit of others. Other studies reveal that generosity is fostered by positive mood imagery, induced by thinking "happy" thoughts, reading "elation" statements, or listening to radio broadcasts containing "good news." Still other studies demonstrate that being fortunate enough to find a dime in a phone booth or being given a packet of stationery enhances the likelihood that shoppers or individuals at home will help others. Perhaps not surprisingly, sunny days encourage helping behavior; cloudy days and bad weather discourage it (Cunningham, 1979).

But unlike the favorable effect of positive mood states on prosocial behavior, the influence of negative mood states varies with the circumstances (Rogers et al., 1982; Manucia, Baumann, and Cialdini, 1984). "Bad moods" sometimes increase helping, sometimes decrease it, and sometimes have no significant effect. As pointed out in Chapter 7, guilt induced by doing harm increases helping behaviors. Under these conditions, prosocial behavior seems to serve a self-therapy or image-repair function. But in many settings in which guilt is absent, a negative mood curtails helping tendencies.

Ervin Staub (1978) says that the experience of being competent or incompetent and successful or unsuccessful affects our psychological states. People who fail on a task may become preoccupied with how others evaluate them, engage in self-criticism, and become susceptible to negative thoughts. Consequently, their attention turns inward, away from happenings in the outer world. They do not feel "free" to attend to others, nor do they experience the ease or comfort necessary to move outward in the direction of other people. For instance, students who have done poorly on an exam or have been rejected in an interpersonal relationship report that they often watch television or engage in other "time-out" and withdrawing activities; it is as if some inner, self-correcting system operates, with time, to effect recuperation.

Some social psychologists, like D. L. Rosenhan, Bert Underwood, and Bill Moore (1974), say that positive experiences create a generalized mood of benevolence that embraces both oneself and others, whereas negative experiences have the opposite effect. And in a related vein, Alice M. Isen and her associates (1978) claim that a good mood involves thinking about positive material. They find that people in good moods are more likely than others to retrieve positive than negative information from memory. In turn, helpful acts are more likely to follow from these circumstances (especially when helping is compatible with pleasant thoughts). In sum, good mood, pleasant material from memory, and prosocial activities mutually reinforce one another.

Prosocial Behavior in Ambiguous Situations

As noted earlier in the chapter, the Kitty Genovese murder provided a major impetus to the social psychological study of prosocial behavior. Like many others, social psychologists wondered why people may fail to assist an individual in an emergency (Latané and Nida, 1981). Is the reason simply that apathy and alienation are so rampant in contemporary society that people are insensitive, indifferent, and unconcerned with the misfortunes of others? Questions of this sort led Bibb Latané and John M. Darley (1970) to launch a research program exploring the *situational* factors that influence prosocial behavior.

Latané, Darley, and their colleagues undertook experiments in a number of different contexts. In one experiment, heavy smoke filtered into the room where the subjects were working (Latané and Darley, 1968). In another, subjects overheard a person who was stricken by an epileptic seizure in an adjoining room (Darley and Latané, 1968). And in still another, subjects overheard a woman experimenter fall and cry out for help (Latané and Rodin, 1969). The researchers varied the conditions under which subjects learned of the emergency: In one condition the subject was alone, in a second condition the subject was with other naive subjects, and in a third condition the subject was with passive, nonreacting people (confederates of the researchers). All these experiments pointed to the critical importance of group size. The probability that an individual will help in an emergency decreases as the number of strangers who witness the emergency increases (Howard and Crano, 1974).

Many emergencies begin as *ambiguous* events. A man staggering about may be having a heart attack, experiencing the onset of a diabetic episode, or simply suffering from drunkenness. What appears to be smoke pouring from a building may be caused by fire or may be merely steam escaping.

Before bystanders can decide to intervene in an emergency, they must take a number of preliminary steps. First, they must *notice* the event. Second, they must *interpret* it as an emergency. And third, they must *decide* that it is their personal *responsibility* to act. At any of these preliminary steps, individuals can remove themselves from the decision process and refrain from helping. They can fail to notice the event, they can fail to interpret it as an emergency, or they can fail to assume responsibility for taking action. The fourth and fifth steps in the sequence involve more practical questions: *what* to do and *how* to do it. Intervention may be *direct*—swimming out to someone who is drowning—or *indirect*—notifying a lifeguard (Latané and Darley, 1970). (See Figure 10.1.)

When confronted with an *ambiguous* event, individual bystanders observe the reactions of others and are powerfully influenced by them (step 2—*interpreting* the event). If others take the event calmly, without apparent concern or anxiety, a bystander is led to interpret the emergency as not serious and thus as not requiring personal action. For example, in the Latané and Darley (1968) experiment where smoke filtered into the workroom, 75 percent of the subjects

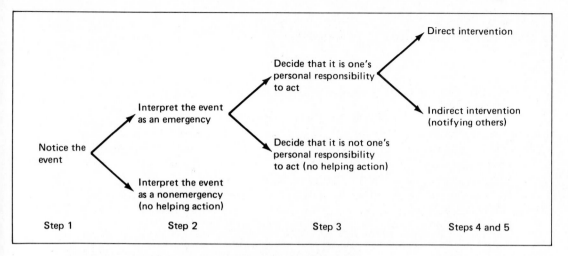

FIGURE 10.1 Steps Involved in Prosocial Assistance
Before bystanders can decide to intervene, they must (1) notice what is happening, (2) interpret it as an emergency, (3) decide that action is up to them, and (4) and (5) figure out what to do and how to do it.

who were alone reported the smoke, compared with 38 percent of the pairs in the naive condition, and only 10 percent of the pairs in the passive-confederate condition. Thus individuals take cues from the behavior of others in the social situation; if no one else is helping, they have doubts about whether the victim is in fact in need of help. In everyday life, they may assume that someone else has already called the police or the hospital.

This interpretation rests on social comparison theory (see Chapter 9). Since social reality is often ambiguous, we rely to some extent on other people's reactions to define the meaning for us. On the basis of our observations of what other people say and do—whether they are responsive or unresponsive to a stimulus—we conclude that the situation is either one that merits or does not merit our intervention. Our concern with how others will evaluate us may either enhance or inhibit helping (Schwartz and Gottlieb, 1980). Typically, we assume that other witnesses will view our intervention as appropriate and consequently we conclude that they will evaluate our helping in a positive fashion. But when cues in the situation imply that other witnesses consider intervention to be inappropriate, we fear that our helping actions will appear foolish or that our assistance will be judged incompetent (Staub, 1978; Latané and Nida, 1981).

In some circumstances, norms favoring intervention may undergo weakening in the third step of the decision-making process—*deciding* that the event is one's personal *responsibility* (Mynatt and Sherman, 1975; Latané and Nida, 1981). Where others are present, **diffusion of responsibility** may occur. Both the obligation to assist and the potential blame for not acting are spread around. Something of this sort apparently occurred in the Kitty Genovese murder: Each

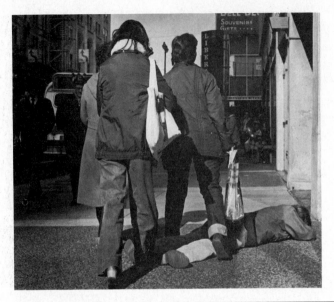

Diffusion of Responsibility
Where many people are present, bystanders are less likely to aid a stricken person. The obligation to assist and the potential blame for not acting are spread among the crowd. (Patrick Reddy)

observer, seeing lights and figures in other apartment-house windows, knew that others were also watching. But when only one bystander is present in an emergency, help must come from the bystander if it is to come at all, so the pressures to intervene are focused on an individual.

Diffusion of responsibility seemingly accounts for the outcome in the Darley and Latané (1968) experiment where subjects overheard a person having an epileptic seizure. Whereas 85 percent of the subjects who were alone reported the seizure, only 31 percent of those who thought four other people were present did so. In sum, Latané and Darley conclude that safety does not necessarily lie in numbers (1970). A "surplus" of helpers reduces responsibility, a finding known as the *bystander effect*.

Most research conducted on the bystander effect has involved individuals who were strangers at the time of the emergency. In such settings, group cohesiveness is usually low. However, when bystanders are cohesive—where they know one another and have ties with one another—they are *more* likely to intervene when they are part of a larger group than a smaller one (Rutkowski, Gruder, and Romer, 1983). It seems that cohesiveness increases responsiveness to social norms. One norm that is prevalent in American culture is the *norm of social responsibility*. People are expected to help others who are in need and who are dependent on them. Hence social cohesiveness tends to cancel the negative effect of diffusion of responsibility in a group of bystanders by increasing the bystanders' adherence to the social responsibility norm.

Diffusion of responsibility can also be reduced by having people commit themselves in advance to assist another person under given circumstances. For instance, Thomas Moriarty (1975) found that bystanders at a public beach would more readily intervene to stop the theft of a portable radio from an unattended beach blanket if they had previously agreed to watch the victim's belongings. The same held true for people in two Automat cafeterias in midtown Manhattan. Individuals who were asked to watch another person's suitcase intervened substantially more often to stop the theft of the suitcase than those who were not asked. Presumably, the prior commitment to help served to minimize the need for a decision and freed the individual from conflict, thereby producing greater responsiveness when an emergency arose. Similarly, if bystanders expect to have future face-to-face interaction with a person in distress, they are more likely to provide help than if they do not expect future interaction (Gottlieb and Carver, 1980). Indeed, even informal social contact seems to activate a latent sense of obligation. "Familiar strangers"—for instance, the person one may see at the bus stop every day without ever exchanging a word—have been known to display extraordinary acts of kindness in a crisis (Cunningham, 1984*a*).

Leonard Bickman and Dennis P. Rosenbaum (1977) have investigated the impact that verbal communication between bystanders has on people's reporting of crime and on their sense of responsibility for making such a report. According to the decision-making model for prosocial intervention, bystanders will report a crime only after noticing the event, interpreting the event as a crime, taking personal responsibility to act, and deciding how to report the crime. In real-life situations, which are often ambiguous, this sequence of decisions must often be made quickly.

Bickman and Rosenbaum find that one bystander can influence another bystander's decision making by making a few verbal comments. In an experiment undertaken in a field setting, weekday shoppers in a supermarket checkout line witnessed a "shoplifter" steal a number of items. A confederate-bystander was found to discourage a bystander from reporting the thief by observing, "Say, look at her. She's shoplifting. She put that into her purse. But it's the store's problem. They have security people here." In contrast, reporting was encouraged when the confederate-bystander said: "Say, look at her. She's shoplifting. She put that into her purse. We saw it. We should report it. It's our responsibility." Such verbal comments help a bystander define whether or not a particular incident is a crime. Additionally, by indicating a course of action, a few verbal comments can suggest the appropriate course of action and consequently have a strong impact on one's tendency to report a crime to the proper authorities.

Prosocial Behavior in Unambiguous Situations

Man is not so wedded to his own interest but that he can make the common good the mark of his aim.

—John Wise, *A Vindication of the Government of New England Churches,* 1717

The previous section dealt with prosocial behavior in ambiguous situations— situations whose meanings are doubtful or uncertain. Within such settings, people may have considerable difficulty in interpreting an event. By way of illustra-

LEGISLATING GOOD SAMARITANISM

Many states have "good Samaritan" laws that relieve individuals of liability when they render aid in an emergency. Laws have also been passed that hold public officials, employers, and landlords responsible for the safety of others. But laws in four states—Vermont, Rhode Island, Massachusetts, and Minnesota—go a step further by mandating bystander help in crises. (For instance, the Minnesota law provides up to a $100 fine for people who fail to aid in an emergency.) However, duty-to-rescue laws have resulted in few, if any, arrests. One problem is that overburdened criminal justice systems find them exceedingly difficult to enforce.

Social psychologists are also doubtful whether mandatory good Samaritan laws are capable of motivating bystanders to render help (Shotland, 1985). For instance, it is questionable whether bystanders in the Kitty Genovese case would have been affected by the legislation. The bystanders had an easy out: They could claim to be sound sleepers or to have observed and heard nothing. Likewise, the witness who finally did call the police might have been subject to prosecution because he called when it was too late. (Would duty-to-rescue law have discouraged him from calling the police at all?) Bystanders have to act promptly if they are to aid in apprehending a criminal. Research undertaken in Kansas City suggests that if bystanders report a crime while it is in progress, an arrest occurs about 35 percent of the time. Should bystanders delay reporting the crime until immediately after the event ends, the chance of capture drops to 18 percent. Waiting a full minute lowers the capture rate to 10 percent, and delaying by one to five minutes brings it down to 7 percent.

Proponents of duty-to-rescue laws admit the difficulty associated with enforcing them. But they point out that such laws may tip the balance toward intervention if bystanders find the situation ambiguous: People can feel it safe to assist, since doing so also guards them against a penalty. Moreover, proponents contend that mandatory good Samaritan legislation has symbolic value in pointing out to citizens what society expects of them. Such laws, it is argued, set a moral tone and tell people what constitutes proper behavior. In short, social behavior can be influenced by community sentiment that defines what is good (Cunningham, 1984a).

tion, consider the following account by Robert A. Baron and Donn Byrne of an incident a number of years ago at the University of Texas in which a sniper in a library tower shot down dozens of people:

Some of the people who were shot had actually heard the shooting when it began and a few saw the bodies of the earliest victims as they lay dead or injured on the sidewalks and lawns surrounding the tower. Rather than take cover, however, a surprising number of people simply continued on their way to wherever they were going and thus became victims themselves. Some who were only wounded described their reactions in terms of feeling confused about what was going on—some thought the rifle shots were sounds made by construction-workers, the dead and wounded were perceived as actors in a fraternity stunt, and the puffs of gunpowder visible at the top of the tower were interpreted as evidence of a small fire. One wounded graduate student said afterward that he decided it would be silly to interrupt his lunch plans when he wasn't sure what was going on. If he postponed lunch and hid behind a wall just because of some noise from a construction site or because some undergraduates were putting on a skit, he would have felt totally ridiculous. Instead, he was shot and badly wounded. (1977: 375–376)

In light of these considerations, it is perhaps not surprising that experimental evidence should show that prosocial behavior is much more likely to occur in *unambiguous* situations, especially emergencies (Shotland and Huston, 1979). Russell D. Clark and Larry E. Word (1972, 1974) set up an "emergency" that was designed to be less ambiguous than those provided by Latané and his associates. In a room adjoining the subjects' workroom, a maintenance worker (a confederate) climbed a metal ladder, fell off it, and pulled the ladder over on top of him. He grunted heavily and exclaimed, "Oh, my back; I can't move!" He continued groaning with each breath; then he gave a cry for help. In *all* conditions—whether they were alone, with other naive subjects, or with confederates of the researchers—100 percent of the subjects went to the aid of the victim. In a second experiment, Clark and Word staged the same fall in an ambiguous manner without any verbal cues of injury. Under these circumstances only 30 percent of the subjects helped. Further, subjects in two- and five-person groups were less likely to help and intervened more slowly than would have been expected on the basis of the responses by subjects who were alone.

Irving M. Piliavin, Judith Rodin, and Jane Allyn Piliavin (1969) found that help was forthcoming in sixty-two out of sixty-five trials (95 percent) involving a faked emergency on a New York subway train. Shortly after entering the train, a young man with a cane staggered forward and collapsed. As in the Clark and Word experiments, this emergency was unambiguous; indeed, it was not only heard but seen.

Piliavin, Rodin, and Piliavin (1969, 1975) offer a **cost-reward analysis of altruism.** They suggest that whether or not a person intervenes in an emergency depends on his or her assessment of costs relative to rewards: (1) costs associated with helping (effort, embarrassment, possible distasteful experiences, and potential bodily harm), (2) costs associated with not helping (self-blame and potential censure from others), (3) rewards associated with helping (praise from oneself, the victim, and others), and (4) rewards associated with not helping (benefits derived from continuing other activities). In real-life situations in which bystanders may expect negative outcomes—possible retaliation from the criminal or days spent in court testifying—the cost plays a major part in discouraging helping behaviors.

Piliavin, Rodin, and Piliavin (1969) found support for their model in a variation of the subway experiment. When a drunk (a young man smelling of liquor and carrying a liquor bottle) was substituted for the sober victim with a cane, help was given in only 50 percent of the trials. Presumably a drunk is helped less

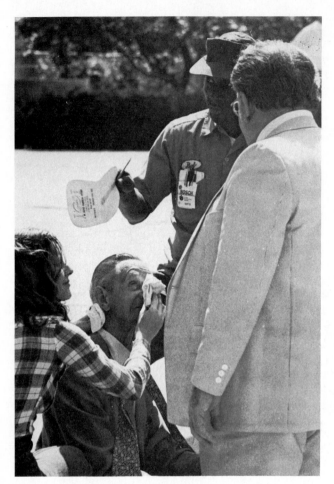

Helping Behavior
Piliavin, Rodin, and Piliavin suggest that whether or not a person aids another depends on an assessment of costs relative to rewards. The person is more likely to help if the victim is well-dressed and seems non-threatening. (Patrick Reddy)

Costs: neg.
Attribution
(control)

because costs associated with helping are higher (since disgust is greater) and costs associated with not helping are lower (less self-blame, since the individual is seen as partially responsible for his difficulty). In still another test of the model, Piliavin and Piliavin (1972) employed a victim with a cane who collapsed in a moving subway car and either "bled" from the mouth or did not. As they predicted, help was significantly slower and less frequent with the bloody victim. (Greater cost was presumably associated with the blood because of the fear or revulsion that many people experience at the sight of it.) The same was true in a similar test using a man who had a large birthmark on his face (Piliavin, Rodin, and Piliavin, 1975).

Bernard Weiner (1980) proposes a further interpretation of the outcomes in the illness and drunkenness studies. He points out that bystanders typically make inferences (attributions) regarding the causes of a person's difficulties. In the case of illness, people are usually viewed as having little personal control over their misfortune. In contrast, drunkenness is perceived as personally controllable. Consequently, illness is more likely than drunkenness to elicit sympathy in bystanders and to result in their rendering assistance. But drunkenness typically triggers feelings of disgust. Emotion, then, is seen as the primary motivational flywheel in helping behavior.

NOTIONS OF A JUST WORLD, EQUITY, AND EQUALITY

We will not be satisfied until justice rolls down like waters and righteousness like a mighty stream.

—Martin Luther King, Jr., Washington, D.C., June 15, 1963

Although others' misfortunes at times elicit our sympathy and compassion, this is not always the case. Our society tolerates the suffering of a good many disadvantaged people. We permit sick children to go untreated and patients at state mental hospitals to suffer because of grossly inadequate budgets. Many comfortably situated Americans condemn the unemployed, the lower classes, and ghetto blacks as "idlers" and "welfare chiselers." Indeed, at times human beings can be extremely cruel, selfish, and destructive in their treatment of their fellow human beings. Contemporary Beirut provides us with daily reminders of humankind's potential for brutality. And many Germans living under the Nazi regime either denied the fact of the mass murders of Jews or else concluded that those who were sent to the death camps were members of an inferior race who deserved their fate.

The Just-World Hypothesis

Behold, God will not cast away an innocent man, neither will he uphold evildoers.

—Job 8:20

The question of why people do so little to alleviate the suffering of their fellow human beings has provoked considerable interest among social psychologists. One explanation, the **just-world hypothesis,** is advanced by Melvin J. Lerner (1970, 1974, 1975, 1980). Lerner suggests that we have a need to believe we live in a just world—one where people get what they deserve and deserve what they get. In such a world, deserving people are rewarded and the undeserving are punished. Moreover, Lerner says that any evidence that others are not getting what they deserve distresses us, for it leads us to question whether we can trust others and the world around us. Only by believing that there is a just world can we confront our physical and social environment as though they are stable and orderly. Without such a belief, we would find it difficult to commit ourselves to the pursuit of long-range goals or even to the socially regulated behavior of everyday life.

The just-world belief leads us to be concerned that others get what they deserve. If others can suffer unjustly, then we must admit to the unsettling prospect that we too could suffer without cause. Consequently, we will be psychologically motivated to reestablish justice. Only in this way can we resolve our cognitive dissonance (see Chapter 6). However, the just-world concern will not always be translated into helping behavior. Another way of accomplishing this is to persuade ourselves that the victim deserves to suffer (Wyer, Bodenhausen, and Gorman, 1985). We derogate a seemingly innocent victim in order to convince ourselves that there is no injustice in the victim's suffering, that the victim got exactly what was deserved. We assume that responsibility lies in some bad quality within the victim. Consequently, we lower our opinion of the victim. To arrive at this position, however, two additional conditions are necessary: We must believe that the suffering will continue, and we must feel that we are powerless to help the victim (Lerner and Simmons, 1966; Lincoln and Levinger, 1972).

In an early demonstration of the just-world hypothesis, Lerner (1965) showed that even when we *know* that the outcomes are *random* (that the people involved cannot affect the outcomes), those outcomes still influence our opinions of the people. Lerner asked subjects to observe two people working at a task. In the experiment only one of the workers could receive payment—the person who happened to draw the even number from a hat. After watching the workers, observers rated their performance and personal characteristics. Consistent with the just-world hypothesis, the observers judged the performance of the paid worker as superior to that of the unpaid worker. Presumably the subjects persuaded themselves that having been rewarded (paid), the paid worker in fact deserved the reward.

In still another test of the hypothesis, Lerner showed subjects a televised session in which a supposed victim (actually a confederate) received painful electric shocks for incorrect responses in a "learning" experiment (Lerner and Simmons, 1966). In one condition, subjects saw the victim willingly enter the room where the experiment was to be held. In another, the "martyr condition," the victim at first refused to enter the room. She reluctantly agreed only after she was told that as a result of her refusal, the subjects would not receive course credit for participating in the experiment. And in a third condition, the confederate received no shocks; all her responses were correct and she was rewarded for them. Later, subjects were asked to rate the confederates on their general attractiveness.

The confederate in the martyr condition was judged *least* attractive. In order to justify her misfortune (the shocks), especially when she appeared to be so noble, the subjects devalued her; in effect, she was made to deserve her suffering. In contrast, the confederate who had been rewarded was judged most attractive; in effect, she was defined in positive terms to justify her good fortune. A number of other studies have been interpreted as providing support for the just-world hypothesis (Simons and Piliavin, 1972; Apsler and Friedman, 1975). These studies suggest that dominant-group members of our society, seeing the disadvantaged circumstances of minority-group members, may find it easy to conclude, "They only get what they deserve." In sum, they blame minority-group victims for the misfortunes that befall them. As Lerner states, "Once the rejection is accomplished, the observer can again rest easy—his world is just, and he need not feel impelled to act to reestablish justice" (1974: 344).

There may be occasions, however, in which we find it difficult to dismiss the misfortune of others as the product of their own misdoings. When we perceive the victim as being similar to us—perhaps in age, race, or other attributes—we find it disconcerting to fault the person. To do so would be much like devaluing or blaming ourselves. Accordingly, we assign less responsibility for their own victimization to people who are similar to us than people who are dissimilar. Moreover, we attribute the misfortune of dissimilar victims more to their character than to situational factors. With similar victims, we reverse the pattern of blame; we rely to a greater extent on situational explanations than on explanations based on people's character (Thornton, 1984).

Equity Theory

> *Awards should be "according to merit"; for all men agree that what is just in distribution must be according to merit in some sense.*
>
> —Aristotle

The Declaration of Independence proclaims as a self-evident truth that "all men are created equal." Yet this pronouncement by the founding fathers is contradicted by widespread social inequality. How do Americans reconcile the dream and the reality? How can the disadvantaged classes be expected to feel loyalty for a system that gives them less than their share of America's good things? Part of the answer lies in American conceptions of equity.

In the American dream, any poor child can make good, just as a rail splitter, Abe Lincoln, could become President. But the American promise has been equality of *opportunity,* not equality of *results.* It has been a vision in which individuals—freed from discrimination based on race, family, religion, sex, or community—find their places on the basis of fair competition. Rewards go to those who merit them through talent, ambition, and hard work. The American dream, then, is not of a classless society where all people enjoy equal status, privilege, and power; rather, it is of a class society in which all have equal access to the top positions. It means *equality* of opportunity but *inequality* of outcomes.

George C. Homans (1974) and J. Stacy Adams (1965) have advanced a theory of equity (sometimes also termed *distributive justice*) to explain these matters. **Equity theory** holds that group members will be satisfied with a distribution of rewards (outcomes) that is proportional to each member's contribution to the group (inputs). People define it as "fair" or "just" when each person receives as much as someone who has provided the same input. They feel that a person who invests more deserves more, while a person who invests less deserves less.

Experimental evidence offers some support for the proposition that people participating in inequitable relationships experience distress, no matter whether they are the victims or the beneficiaries of the inequity. Those who receive less

Social Inequality
Considerable inequality prevails
in the United States in the distribution of income. (Patrick Reddy)

than they deserve often feel anger; those who receive more, guilt. Further, equity
theory suggests that people in an inequitable relationship seek to eliminate their
distress by restoring equity (Walster, Berscheid, and Walster, 1973; Austin and
Walster, 1974; Berkowitz and Walster, 1976; Reis and Burns, 1982).

Equity may be restored in one of two ways. One approach entails restoring
actual equity, which can be achieved in one of four ways: We can seek to alter
(1) our own outcomes, (2) our own inputs, (3) the outcomes of others, or (4)
the inputs of others. For instance, workers who feel that they are underpaid may
respond by slacking off (lowering their inputs), by demanding a raise or stealing
from the firm (raising their outcomes), by forcing their employer to work harder
(raising their employer's inputs), or by sabotaging company equipment (lowering
their employer's outcomes). A second approach entails restoring *psychological
equity*—individuals distort their perception of their own or the other's outcomes
and inputs. For instance, an exploitative employer may restore psychological
equity by exaggerating his own inputs ("Without my drive and brains this company would fall apart"), by minimizing his workers' input ("They're just stupid"),
or by exaggerating his workers' outcomes ("Work gives them a chance to see
their friends and keeps them from getting bored").

It is important to stress, however, that equity ultimately lies in the eye of the
beholder. As Aesop observed, "The injuries we do and those we suffer are seldom

weighed on the same scales." Thus people are more distressed by inequity when they are victims than when they are the harm doers. Those who materially benefit from inequity are more tolerant of inequity than those who materially suffer from it (Blumstein and Weinstein, 1969; Walster, Berscheid, and Walster, 1973). And those who materially suffer from inequity are quicker to demand a fair distribution of resources than those who do not suffer (Leventhal and Lane, 1970).

Individuals also typically take more credit for an activity or event than a partner is willing to grant them (Ross and Sicoly, 1979; Thompson and Kelley, 1981). Egocentric biases occur among marriages partners, baseball teammates, and collaborators in laboratory experiments. It seems that people have better access to information concerning their own contribution than to information concerning that of a partner. Consequently, they conclude that their contribution is greater than that with which a partner credits them. All this influences their feelings of satisfaction with the partner.

Adherence to equity standards is influenced by people's concerns about what others will think of them (Greenberg, 1980, 1983; Ancok and Chertkoff, 1983). Thus Ellen Berscheid and Elaine Hatfield have found that harm doers seek to make restitution to a degree equal to the harm they imagine they cause others (Berscheid and Walster, 1967). In an experiment with women's church groups, parishioners were led to cheat others out of trading stamps in the expectation that they could then win additional stamps for themselves. Subsequently, the women were provided an opportunity to make restitution to the victim. Women who could compensate exactly by giving a partner the same number of books they had taken were considerably more likely to do so than women who were limited to insufficient compensation (a few stamps) or who would have had to make excessive compensation (a great many stamp books). This research has interesting implications for real-life restitutions. Exploited individuals frequently attempt to win restitution by stressing how much they have suffered. The Berscheid-Hatfield study suggests, however, that in some instances it might be a more effective strategy to minimize one's suffering than to exaggerate it.

restitution

The Norm of Reciprocity

There is no duty more indispensable than that of returning kindness.

—Cicero

One good deed deserves another.

—Popular proverb

Equity implies that people believe they should receive returns equal to what they put forth—that the resources they expend on behalf of others should be equal to the resources others expend on their behalf. Underlying equity is the

The norm of reciprocity

A few weeks ago it was my birthday. Well, Ken—the guy who lives across the hall—gave me two six-packs of beer. It didn't take us long to finish it off with the help of a couple of our friends. Well, yesterday it was Ken's birthday. A bunch of us went to Papa Joe's (a local bar) and we all got drunk. I paid for all the beer. In so doing, I was conforming to the norm of reciprocity: One good deed deserves another.

norm of reciprocity, a social rule that sociologist Alvin Gouldner (1960) says is a prerequisite for organized society. The norm of reciprocity stipulates that (1) people should help those who have helped them, and (2) people should not injure those who have helped them. More broadly, social psychologists have viewed the norm of reciprocity as embodying the expectation that people return good for good and evil for evil. Thus in addition to its positive form, the norm of reciprocity has a negative component guiding retaliation. Although people differ in their feelings regarding retaliation, negative reciprocity is embodied in the ancient code "A tooth for a tooth and an eye for an eye." Social psychological formulations regarding the norm of reciprocity have been strongly influenced by social exchange theory (see Chapters 1 and 9).

The norm of reciprocity underlies some forms of helping behavior. Social psychologist Elliot Aronson (1972) provides an interesting exception to the principle of diffusion of responsibility, which we discussed earlier in the chapter. While spending the night in a Yosemite National Park campground, Aronson was awakened by a scream. He grabbed his flashlight and rushed to the rescue. But as he did so, dozens of other campers with flashlights and lanterns also converged on the scene. Reflecting on the incident, Aronson speculates that responsibility may not have diffused because the campers were bound by a feeling of mutuality that arose from a sense of shared threat. A more cynical possibility suggested by C. Daniel Batson and his associates (1979) is that people offer more help to those with whom they share a common threat because they are aware that they too may soon need help. Consequently, they extend help to others because they want to ensure that the other person will reciprocally assist them should they need help in the future. For instance, a mother with two young children says she is involved in her church's activities to transport and hide illegal immigrants from Guatemala and El Salvador because "I'm a mother and I would want another mother to shelter my children from a war" (King, 1985: 6).

The norm of reciprocity has implications that extend even to the international level, where policies such as foreign aid are directly concerned with reciprocity. In interviews with some fifty officials from more than a dozen nations, Kenneth Gergen and Mary Gergen (1971) found considerable animosity among foreign-aid recipients toward their benefactors (see Figure 10.2). International gifts accompanied by clearly stated obligations were preferred both to gifts that were not accompanied by obligations and to gifts that had many strings attached.

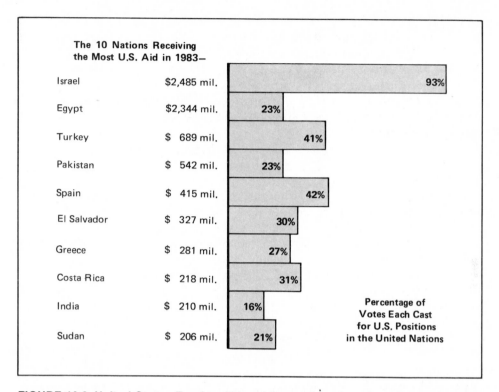

The 10 Nations Receiving the Most U.S. Aid in 1983—

Israel	$2,485 mil.	93%
Egypt	$2,344 mil.	23%
Turkey	$ 689 mil.	41%
Pakistan	$ 542 mil.	23%
Spain	$ 415 mil.	42%
El Salvador	$ 327 mil.	30%
Greece	$ 281 mil.	27%
Costa Rica	$ 218 mil.	31%
India	$ 210 mil.	16%
Sudan	$ 206 mil.	21%

Percentage of Votes Each Cast for U.S. Positions in the United Nations

FIGURE 10.2 United States Foreign Aid and Support for American Stands at the United Nations
The United States mission to the United Nations studied voting trends at the 1983 General Assembly. On ten key issues, the ten major recipients of American military and economic aid supported the United States less than half the time. Despite receiving more than $1 billion, African states backed the Americans in only one of every five votes. The most consistent support came from Western European nations, which get little aid.
(SOURCE: Agency for International Development, U.S. Department of State.)

Seemingly, gifts that can be exactly reciprocated by the fulfillment of definite obligations are preferred to gifts that cannot be reciprocated or that require excessive reciprocation—especially if the attached "strings" restrict people's freedom of action (Brehm and Cole, 1966).

Laboratory research by Kenneth Gergen and his associates (1975) has supported the conclusion that people like a benefactor more when they are expected to reciprocate the help. In a series of experiments, subjects were provided with poker chips (which could be exchanged for money) and then required to wager them in a game of chance. At a critical point in the game, when a subject was about to be forced out because of his consistent losses, another "player" gave him more chips. In one experimental condition, the subject was informed that he need not repay the chips (low-obligation condition); in a second, that he could pay the chips back later (equal-obligation condition); and in a third, that he should do something for the donor later on (high-obligation condition). In subsequent evaluations of the donor, recipients in the equal-obligation condition evaluated him more positively than did the recipients in the other two conditions. The results of the Gergen studies tend to confirm an observation made by the Roman historian Tacitus in the first century: "Benefits are only acceptable so far as they seem capable of being requited: Beyond that point, they excite hatred instead of gratitude."

All of this suggests that people do not like to be in the debt of others (Shumaker and Jackson, 1979). While reciprocal exchange breeds cooperation and good feelings, gifts that cannot be reciprocated breed discomfort, distress, and ultimately dislike. It seems to be important to people that they maintain equity (a proper ratio between their own inputs and their own outcomes), both in their own eyes and in the eyes of others. In general, people who receive greater amounts of help return greater amounts of help, and those who receive more valuable help tend to give more valuable help in return (DePaulo, Brittingham, and Kaiser, 1983). It is not surprising, therefore, that not being able to reciprocate a favor, or accepting assistance that is not part of an ongoing relationship characterized by mutual cooperation and help, tends to reduce both our overall social esteem and our self-esteem (Staub, 1978).

Self-interest, Equality, and Need

The nature of things continually tends to the destruction of equality.

—Jean Jacques Rousseau, *The Social Contract,* 1761

In deciding how to distribute a group reward, allocators are faced with at least four potential strategies: *equity,* in which rewards are distributed proportionally among members relative to their inputs; *self-interest,* in which an allocator maximizes his or her own rewards, independent of inputs; *equality,* in which each member receives the identical quantity of rewards as every other member regardless of inputs; and *need,* in which rewards are allocated in terms of each individual's wants or requirements. Societies differ in the emphasis that they and their members place on one strategy or another (Leung and Bond, 1984; Murphy-Berman et al., 1984).

Equity appears to be employed when the allocator is primarily interested in maximizing the performances of group members (Leventhal, 1976). Additionally, when the stakes are high and co-workers have equal retaliatory power, an allocator is likely to follow equity principles (Greenberg, 1978). Presumably an equity arrangement allows a person to make a response that is both socially justifiable and more profitable (assuming the allocator has also contributed more). Simultaneously, an allocator may attempt to obligate his or her co-workers to reciprocate by adhering to equity standards and not exploiting their power when their turn comes to allocate rewards.

Under circumstances of self-interest (sometimes termed "greed"), the allocator keeps a substantially greater portion of the rewards than would normally be judged appropriate in terms of his or her inputs. This is most likely to occur in situations where the rewards are lucrative and the allocator need not be concerned with the retaliatory power of co-workers. In contrast, the expectation of future dealings and the opportunity for retaliation deter an allocator from maximizing personal gain at the expense of others (Greenberg, 1978).

Equality is based on the credo of "All for one and one for all—share and share alike." Distribution based on equality occurs most often within families and closely bonded we-groups. It tends to be used by an allocator who is desirous of preventing intragroup conflict and of maintaining a high level of harmony and satisfaction among group members (Leventhal, 1976; Morgan and Sawyer, 1979; Stake, 1983). Further, individuals are more likely to endorse a division of labor that benefits the least-advantaged person at the expense of the most-advantaged person when they do not know their own positions in the division of labor than when they do (Bickman and Rosenbaum, 1977). Equal distribution has the added advantage of being relatively easy to implement because it requires neither complicated formulas nor worries about ascertaining the respective contributions of group members (Elliot and Meeker, 1984).

Finally, distribution may rest upon notions of justice in which need assumes central importance. It is expressed in the Marxist slogan "From each according to ability, to each according to need." In one study, for instance, Gerald S. Leventhal and Thomas Weiss (1971) found that when subjects were given the opportunity to divide joint earnings with a co-worker, they gave the partner more money when his monthly income was relatively low than when it was high. The subjects' decisions were based on their perceptions of comparative need. Norms of social responsibility are likely to be activated when an allocator has lucrative rewards and feels concern for the fate of co-workers (Greenberg, 1978; Lamm and Schwinger, 1980).

It seems that men and woman differ in the ways that they allocate rewards between themselves and others (Major and Deaux, 1982; Major and Adams, 1983). When asked to split rewards between themselves and a partner with performance inferior to their own, women tend to allocate the rewards equally, whereas men tend to allocate the rewards equitably. When the partner's performance is superior to their own, both women and men tend to divide the rewards equitably, but women generally take less for themselves than men do. Even when their performances are equal to those of a partner, women take less reward for themselves than do men. This pattern holds regardless of the sex of the partner. Various explanations have been suggested for these differences. One explanation is that women, by virtue of their socialization, show greater concern than men for maintaining good relations with a partner, and they place their emphasis on people rather than on end results (Kahn et al., 1980; Gilligan, 1982a). Another explanation is that women have a tendency to be more tolerant in their judgment of individual differences (Stake and Katz, 1982). Still another explanation is that women attribute different motivations than do men to slow workers; for instance, women are more likely to view slower workers as more conscientious or as working under internal constraints such as poor training or lower ability (Stake, 1985).

SUMMARY

1. Social psychologists have asked, "Why should an individual engage in behavior that benefits another when this behavior demands great self-sacrifice and provides no tangible benefit?" One motive advanced for engaging in prosocial behavior is the expectation that we will realize some gain or avoid some loss. A second motive involves conformity to our personal values and norms. A third motivating factor derives from empathic emotion.

2. Research reveals that there are some people who are more disposed than others to help people in distress, even at cost to themselves. However, not all psychologists accept the notion that human behavior is sufficiently consistent and stable to warrant conceiving of it in terms of prosocial or other personality traits.

3. Research shows that "good moods" induce helpful behaviors. But unlike the favorable effect of positive mood states on prosocial behavior, the influence of negative mood states varies with the circumstances. Guilt induced by doing harm seems to increase helping behaviors. But in many settings in which guilt is absent, a negative mood curtails helping tendencies.

4. Many emergencies begin as ambiguous events. Before bystanders can decide to intervene in an emergency, they must take a number of preliminary steps. First, they must notice the event. Second, they must interpret it as an emergency. Third, they must decide that it is their personal responsibility to act. In the fourth and fifth steps in the sequence, they must determine what to do and how to do it.

5. Altruistic behavior is considerably more likely to take place in unambiguous situations where help is plainly needed than in ambiguous situations. Irving M. Piliavin, Judith Rodin, and Jane Allyn Piliavin say that whether or not an individual intervenes in an emergency depends on his or her assessment of costs relative to rewards.

6. Although others' misfortunes at times elicit our sympathy and compassion, this is not always the case. Our society tolerates the suffering of a good many disadvantaged people. One explanation of why people do so little to alleviate the suffering of their fellow human beings is the just-world hypothesis. The just-world belief leads us to be concerned that others get what they deserve. One way we accomplish this is to persuade ourselves that victims deserve to suffer.

7. The equity model of justice is built on the criterion of investment or "input." Equity theory holds that group members will be satisfied with a distribution of rewards that is proportional to each member's contribution to the group. People participating in inequitable relationships experience distress, no matter whether they are the victims or the beneficiaries of the inequity. Those

who receive less than they deserve often feel anger; those who receive more, guilt.

8. The norm of reciprocity embodies the expectation that people return good for good and evil for evil. Thus in addition to its positive form, the norm of reciprocity has a negative component guiding retaliation. Research reveals that gifts that can be exactly reciprocated by fulfilling clearly stipulated obligations are preferred both to gifts that cannot be reciprocated and to gifts that have too many strings attached.

9. Other potential strategies for allocating group rewards in addition to equity are self-interest, equality, and need. In self-interest, an allocator maximizes his or her own rewards. In equality, each member receives the same quantity of rewards as every other member regardless of inputs. In need, rewards are allocated in terms of each individual's wants or requirements.

GLOSSARY

Altruism □   Behavior carried out to benefit another person without expectation of an external reward.

Cost-reward analysis of altruism □   The theory that whether or not a person intervenes in an emergency depends on his or her assessment of costs relative to rewards: (1) costs associated with helping, (2) costs associated with not helping, (3) rewards associated with helping, and (4) rewards associated with not helping.

Diffusion of responsibility □   A process in which the obligation to help in an emergency and the potential blame for not helping are spread among observers.

Equity theory □   The hypothesis that group members will be satisfied with a distribution of rewards (outcomes) that is proportional to each member's contribution to the group (inputs).

Just-world hypothesis □   The theory that people need to believe they live in a world where the deserving are rewarded and the undeserving are punished. According to the just-world hypothesis, the victim deserves to suffer.

Motivation □   Those inner states and processes that prompt, direct, and sustain activity.

Norm of reciprocity □   A social rule which stipulates that (1) people should help those who have helped them, and (2) people should not injure those who have helped them.

Prosocial behavior □   Acts that benefit other people; ways of responding to other people that are sympathetic, cooperative, helpful, rescuing, comforting, and giving.

Sociobiology □   A discipline that focuses on the biological basis for social behavior in species ranging from amoeba colonies to human societies.

Traits □   Relatively enduring ways in which individuals differ; descriptive characteristics of people.

11 AGGRESSION AND CONFLICT

AGGRESSION
  Preprogrammed Aggression: The
    Human as Beast
  Frustration-Aggression
  Social Factors Influencing
    Aggressive Behavior
  Deindividuation
  Institutional Aggression
Erotic Materials and Aggression
Rape
CONFLICT
  Clashing Interests
  Clashing Values
  Conflict Models
  Intensity of Conflict
  Coalitions

Men! This stuff we hear about Americans wanting to stay out of war—not wanting to fight—is a lot of bullshit. Americans love to fight, traditionally. All real Americans love the sting or clash of battle.

—General George Patton

Terror, violence, and aggression seem everywhere about us. War, internal strife, violent repression, terrorism, and rampant crime haunt people on all continents. The United States is no exception. The black leader H. Rap Brown once observed, "Violence is as American as cherry pie." The 1969 National Commission on the Causes and Prevention of Violence came to similar conclusions:

Americans have always been a violent people. . . . But Americans have been given to a kind of historical amnesia that masks much of their turbulent past. Probably all nations share this tendency to sweeten memories of their past through collective repression, but Americans have probably magnified this process of selective recollection, owing to our historic vision of ourselves as a latter-day chosen people, a new Jerusalem. (1969: 792)

Indeed, Abraham Lincoln claimed in 1838 that domestic violence was this nation's worst domestic problem. And today many Americans believe that violence remains our number one problem. Each year more than 50,000 Americans are murdered or commit suicide. The average American's chances of having his or her life end in homicide is 1 in 150. Much of the homicide takes place within the family (see boxed insert, pp. 330–332).

The commission asserted that in recent decades violence in the United States has risen to "alarmingly high levels," is "disfiguring our society," is "making fortresses of portions of our cities," and is "poisoning the spirit of trust and cooperation" essential for democratic functioning. Six hundred years before the birth of Christ, the prophet Ezekiel had similar concerns: "The land is full of bloody crimes and the city is full of violence" (Ezekiel 7:23). And Henry Fielding, the London Bow Street magistrate, wrote in 1751:

> The innocent are put in terror, affronted and alarmed with threats and execrations, endangered with loaded pistols, beat with bludgeons and hacked with cutlasses, of which loss of health, of limbs, and often of life, is the consequence, and all this without any respect to age or dignity or sex. (Quoted by Hughes, 1979: 3)

Indeed, it appears that aggression and conflict are as old as humankind itself.

AGGRESSION

All of us are familiar with the word **aggression,** and doubtless we all feel that we know what we mean by it. Yet when we set out to define it, we encounter difficulties. Albert Bandura observes:

> Aggression is typically defined as behavior that has injurious consequences, accompanied by ten to twenty qualifiers. The same destructive behavior can be labeled aggressive or otherwise depending on subjective judgments of whether it was intentional or accidental. If the dispenser of aggression is a sanctioned authority, his injurious behavior is minimized as vigorous pursuit of duty; but if a free-lancing individual does it, he is judged to be acting violently. The same act is regarded differently, depending upon, among other factors, the sex, age, and socioeconomic level of the performers. (1973*b*: 203–204)

Some social psychologists (Berkowitz, 1965*a;* Feshbach, 1971) have attempted to deal with the problem by distinguishing between two types of aggression: hostile and instrumental. *Hostile aggression* aims to harm or otherwise injure another party. In *instrumental aggression,* harming another party is carried out only to gain some other objective. For most purposes, social psychologists simply view aggression as behavior that is socially defined as injurious or destructive.

FAMILY VIOLENCE

The problem of family violence has long been neglected by both society and the academic community. Indeed, the view that the family is and ought to be a warm setting has contributed to a perceptual blackout on family violence. Yet the family is the single most frequent location for violence of all types, including homicide. Only during the past decade have steps been taken to correct this situation (Gelles, 1980, 1983; Goodstein and Page, 1981; Bowker, 1983).

WIFE ABUSE

The expression "coming out of the closet" is quite apt when applied to battered wives. Abused women have been as reluctant to reveal their plight as have gay persons to reveal their sexual preferences. Indeed, evidence suggests that the battered wife may spend more energy attempting to keep her secret than in finding a way to escape from her trap. Until relatively recently, most women sought to keep the indignities that they experienced at the hands of their husbands locked inside the family home (Martin, 1976; Straus, Gelles, and Steinmetz, 1980). However, domestic violence is not limited to married couples. There is a higher level of violence in ongoing cohabiting relationships than in ongoing marriages (Yllo and Straus, 1981). A study of 369 engaged couples found that 37 percent of the women and 34 percent of the men had physically assaulted their fiances at least once (Findlay, 1984). And in a survey among Arizona State University juniors and seniors, 60 percent of the students said that they had experienced some

form of violence during dating and courtship (Joseph, 1981).

Estimates of wife battering vary widely. The National Crime Survey, based on interviews every six months with some 132,000 Americans over age twelve, finds that an average of 456,000 cases of domestic violence take place each year in the United States. However, Justice Department officials and experts on domestic violence believe this number seriously understates the problem (*New York Times,* April 24, 1984, p. 5). *Time* magazine estimates that nearly 6 million wives are abused by their husbands each year and reports that the nation's police officers spend one-third of their time responding to domestic violence calls (O'Reilly, 1983). Both men and women engage in violence. However, since men are usually stronger than women, they can typically do more damage than their female partners can. Likewise, men often find it easier to control the weaker members of the family by force. It is usually easier to control than to negotiate because negotiation requires skills. At times sexual abuse accompanies the battering of women. Although alcohol is found in some cases of wife abuse, many psychologists say that alcohol is not so much a causative factor as another expression of the tensions underlying a relationship (Goodstein and Page, 1981).

Why does a woman who is beaten by her husband remain with him? To answer this question, sociologist Richard J. Gelles (1980) undertook in-depth interviews with members of forty-one families in which women had been beaten by their husbands. Three major factors emerged from this research. First, on the whole, the less severe and less frequent the violence, the more likely a wife is to remain with her husband. Of the women in the sample, 42 percent of those who had been struck at least once during their marriage had sought some type of outside assistance. This contrasts with 100 percent of those who had been hit at least once a month, and 83 percent of those assaulted at least once a week. Gelles suggests that women who are abused at least once a week may be less likely than those abused once a month to seek outside intervention because they are more terrorized by their violent husbands and fear provoking even more lethal reactions from them.

Second, the more a wife was struck as a child by her parents and witnessed violence in her childhood home, the more likely she is to remain with her abusive husband. Presumably, experience with violence as a victim and observer teaches a person to tolerate and even approve of the use of violence. In sum, exposure to violence provides a role model for violence (Kalmuss, 1984). Many of the women's lives seem structured around their husbands' violent episodes, just as their parental family was preoccupied with the father's violence (Hilberman, 1980).

Third, the fewer the resources a wife has and the less power she enjoys in the marriage, the more likely she is to stay with her violent husband (Kalmuss and Straus, 1982). The more resources a woman has in the way of education or job skills—the better able she is to support herself and her children—the less is her willingness to acquiesce in violence and the more likely she is to reach out for assistance. Indeed, in the opinion of battered wives, the most important factor in their husbands' willingness to end the battering is fear of divorce (Bowker, 1983).

It should be stressed, however, that just because a woman calls the police or seeks the intervention of a social agency does not guarantee that she will receive meaningful assistance (Ford, 1983; Sherman and Bouza, 1984). Most legal organizations and agencies are unprepared to provide beaten women with help. Unless a victim dies, the chances that the court system will deal in a serious manner with the offender are slight. Much official acceptance exists regarding family violence, encompassed in the belief that such matters are a "private affair." Additionally, many women fear exposing their circumstances to public attention lest the myth of a peaceful family life be exploded. And many women point to the futility of entering official complaints with the law. The husbands are seldom detained by the police. Consequently, the men are free to return and inflict even greater suffering on the women. Even so, arrest and brief incarceration have a deterrent effect on wife-beating husbands (Sherman and Berk, 1984).

A variety of other factors have also been cited by a number of researchers (Truninger, 1971; Hilberman, 1980; Strube and Barbour, 1983, 1984). For one thing, many of the women have negative self-concepts, which inhibits them from seeking outside assistance. Then too, many abused women believe that their husbands will reform. And in practical terms, it is often difficult for unskilled women with children to get work.

Box continues on next page

All of this points to the need for an overhaul of the legal system, from police policy and practice to court proceedings and actions. Social service agencies should be restructured so that the battered wife can find meaningful help. Remedial laws need to be enacted. And more refuges should be established to shelter abused women and their children during crises. Perhaps of even more importance, a cultural revolution of attitudes and values is required to eradicate wife abuse (Martin, 1976; Hilberman, 1980).

CHILD ABUSE

Beating of women in the home is often accompanied by physical and even sexual abuse of children. Officials of the United States Department of Health and Human Services estimate that more than 1 million children within the United States suffer abuse or neglect each year. Research sponsored by the National Institute of Mental Health suggests that these figures may even be on the low side. From interviews with 2,143 married couples representing a demographic cross section of American families, sociologists estimate that parents kick, punch, or bite as many as 1.7 million children a year, beat 460,000 to 750,000 more, and attack 46,000 others with knives or guns (Straus, Gelles, and Steinmetz, 1980). Researchers find both immediate and long-lasting deficits in physical, intellectual, and emotional development among neglected and abused youngsters (Brenner, 1985; Wolfe, 1985).

Child abuse is a catchall term referring to nonaccidental physical attack on or injury to children (including emotional and social injury) by individuals caring for them. Child abuse is found among families from all social, religious, economic, educational, and racial backgrounds. Although it is difficult to generalize about parents who abuse children, a number of facts nonetheless stand out. Abusing parents are generally low in self-esteem, are emotionally immature and self-centered, and feel incompetent as parents. On the whole they demand a great deal from their children, far more than the children can understand or respond to:

> Henry J., in speaking of his sixteen-month-old son, Johnny, said, "He knows what I mean and understands it when I say 'come here.' If he doesn't come immediately, I go and give him a gentle tug on the ear to remind him of what he's supposed to do." In the hospital it was found that Johnny's ear was lacerated and partially torn away from his head. (Steele and Pollock, 1968: 110)

Frequently, abusive parents feel insecure and unsure of being loved, and look to the child as a source of reassurance, comfort, and affection:

> Kathy made this poignant statement: "I have never felt really loved all my life. When the baby was born, I thought he would love me; but when he cried all the time, it meant he didn't love me, so I hit him." Kenny, age three weeks, was hospitalized with bilateral subdural hematomas [multiple bruises]. (Steele and Pollock, 1968: 110)

Child abusers frequently were raised in the same authoritarian style that they later recreate with their own children. They possess an intense fear of spoiling their children, of showing them gentleness, tenderness, and kindness. All of this suggests that the pattern of abuse is unwittingly transmitted from parent to child, generation after generation (Steele and Pollock, 1968; Spinetta and Rigler, 1975).

Preprogrammed Aggression: The Human as Beast

Man is a gaming animal. He must be always trying to get the better in something or other.

—Charles Lamb, *Essays of Elia,* 1823

Some two decades ago, Konrad Lorenz (1966), Robert Ardrey (1966), and Desmond Morris (1968) published immensely popular books that viewed the human being as the most brutal and uninhibitedly aggressive of all animals. According to these writers, war and other murderous, destructive impulses are encoded in the human race by genes, so that aggression is *instinctive.* They believe that the human nervous system contains a biochemically preprogrammed blueprint that impels aggression.

Lorenz, a Nobel Prize–winning ethologist, begins *On Aggression* (1966) with vivid accounts of brilliantly colored coral-reef fishes in tanks and in the sea. He describes cases in which one of these fishes, excited by another's invasion of its territory, attacks and drives off the trespasser. Lorenz says that aggression within the same species serves a function in spacing out individuals over the available habitat to ensure that adequate food is available. Still another benefit of aggression, according to Lorenz, is sexual selection—the selection of the best and strongest members of the species for reproduction. Thus Lorenz views aggression as an adaptive mechanism evolved to promote the survival of a species: "Aggression, far from being the diabolical, destructive principle that classical psychoanalysis makes it out to be, is really an essential part of the life-preserving organization of instincts" (1966: 48).

Lorenz suggests that predatory animals other than humans can put a brake on the aggressive drive so that aggression stops short of murder. *Ritualization* is supposedly one such mechanism:

> The wolf turns his head away from his opponent, offering him the vulnerable, arched side of his neck; the jackdaw holds under the beak of the aggressor the unprotected base of the skull, the very place which these birds attack when they intend to kill. . . .
>
> When the loser of a fight [between two dogs] suddenly adopted the submissive attitude, and presented his unprotected neck, the winner performed the movement of shaking to death, in the air, close to the neck of the morally vanquished dog, but with closed mouth, that is, without biting. (Lorenz, 1966: 132–133)

But whereas in lower animals instinctive aggression works to the advantage of the species, Lorenz says that it has gotten out of hand in human beings. He contends that people lack inborn inhibitions against severely injuring and killing their fellows. He suggests that natural selection is responsible for this tragic state of affairs. Dangerously armed carnivores evolved strong aggression-inhibiting mechanisms to prevent self-extermination of the species. In contrast, the human race evolved as puny, harmless, omnivorous, but intelligent creatures. Paradoxically, it is intelligence that has almost done us in. People have used their

The Human: Nature's Most Aggressive Animal?
Controversy surrounds the question as to whether human beings are more violent than other animals. (Patrick Reddy)

intelligence to develop lethal weaponry for which they lack inborn biological inhibitors.

This view has been popularized by Robert Ardrey (1966), a former playwright, who argues that human beings have an innate and ineradicable compulsion to gain and defend exclusive territory and property, and that far from hating war, people really find it "outrageously satisfying." Such theories have profound political and social implications. If people are inherently greedy, aggressive, and warlike, it is absurd to be hopeful about world peace or to think that we can do much to lessen poverty and crime.

As might be anticipated, the human-as-beast perspective has aroused considerable controversy. Critics (Montagu, 1973; Freedman, 1975; Kagan, 1985) have challenged the view that an "instinct" for aggression explains the behavior of even the lower animals. They regard the notion that genes incorporate fixed action patterns as overly simplistic. They argue that even in low-level creatures a continuous give-and-take interaction occurs between heredity and environment.

As a case in point, critics cite the behavior of cats: The so-called instinct to kill mice is the complex end product of a series of learning experiences based on biological tendencies. A kitten automatically watches a moving object. This leads to playful chasing, which leads to seizing and biting, which leads, in turn, to tasting blood. Each experience affords new gratifications and builds toward the mouse-killing pattern. But if the kitten misses the crucial steps at the critical period of its development, it may never become a mouser and may remain forever indifferent to mice (Hunt, 1973).

Some students of animal aggression question the view that human beings are more violent than other animals (Marler, 1976). They suggest that wounding and killing occur more often among animals than has been supposed. Naturalist Jane Goodall became famous for her studies of the chimpanzees in Tanzania's Gombe National Park. She said:

> I had once thought that chimpanzees resembled humans only in their gentler traits, like holding hands, embracing, and kissing. The horrifying thing is they bear a strong similarity to humans in other ways. We saw one community of chimps systematically attack and kill another. (Quoted by Horn, 1978: 18)

Additionally, hosts of animals are pushed into unsuitable habitats through the aggression of their companions, thereby dooming them to higher mortality and poorer prospects of reproduction.

Critics also call it naive to assume that evidence and arguments advanced for lower animals necessarily hold for human beings. They say that even if insects and lower animals are largely guided by instincts, people are virtually instinctless. The higher an animal on the evolutionary scale, the more likely that its behavioral tendencies arise out of interactions with the environment and that the behavior is learned. A cricket will chirp under the right conditions without ever having heard another cricket chirp. But as Chapter 3 explained, people need to learn every word of the language they speak even though they may have an innate tendency to use language (Hunt, 1973).

What is striking about human beings is the remarkable diversity of behaviors found among quite different societies. If we say that the murderous raids of Brazilian Indians are caused by an inborn aggressive instinct, how are we to account for the peacefulness of the Eskimos? If we explain the very warlike habits of the Vikings in genetic terms, how are we to interpret the peace-loving habits of their contemporary progeny, who are among the most pacific people in the world (Cordes, 1984)? And critics of Lorenz, Ardrey, and Morris ask, would it not make more sense to conclude that by nature, people are neither aggressive nor peaceful, but a product of complex interactions between their biology and their environment (Eisenberg, 1972)?

Anthropologist Richard Leakey (1982) is deeply troubled by the popularity of the notion of humankind as "killer apes." Many Americans have grown up with stereotypes drawn from comics of the cave man as a hairy brute with a club who dispatches his rivals and drags women off by their hair to his den. Such beliefs, Leakey says, create a psychological acceptance of violence and aggression as rooted in our primitive past. Yet he claims that violence and its acceptance are "purely cultural." Cooperation, not aggression, is the hallmark of humankind. Leakey asserts that even warfare requires cooperation and that the most extreme form of cooperation is the fielding of a modern army. Likewise, a number of sociologists have challenged the theory that human beings are biologically fated to be aggressive. They point to recent paleoanthropological evidence suggesting that many of the oldest human tools thought to have been hunting weapons were actually tools used in scavenging. Such evidence suggests that human ancestors were scavengers, sneaking the kill of other carnivores, rather than chest-pounding killer apes themselves (Cordes, 1984).

Frustration-Aggression

If the Tiber rose to the walls of the city, if the inundation of the Nile failed to give the fields enough water, if the heavens did not send rain, if an earthquake occurred, if famine threatened, if pestilence raged, the cry resounded: "Throw the Chistians to the lions."

—Tertullian, early Christian leader

Literature and religion inform us that suffering is ennobling. Unpleasant conditions and tragic circumstances are supposed to make better people of us. Novels and television series extol the virtues of affliction, deprivation, and even torment in compelling us to "grow" and search for spiritual peace and personal nobility. However widespread this theme might be, a long tradition in psychology suggests that harsh experiences are much more apt to bring out the worst in us than to improve our social conduct (Berkowitz, 1983). For over forty years, the **frustration-aggression hypothesis** has been a popular explanation for aggressive behavior (Dollard et al., 1939). According to the original version of the theory, frustration produces aggression; aggression *never* occurs without prior frustration. **Frustration** refers to the interference with or blocking of the attainment of some goal. For instance, frustration might arise from interference with the satisfaction of some biological need (say, for food, water, sex, or sleep) or social need (for recognition, love, or security). But critics quickly pointed out that frustration need not result in aggression. Some individuals respond to frustration with new or added efforts to realize the goal; some substitute a different goal; and some abandon the goal, become apathetic, or doubt their self-worth (Mark, 1985). The theory was soon amended (Miller, 1941) to say that frustration may produce other kinds of behavior besides aggression.

A classic study testing the frustration-aggression hypothesis was carried out by Kurt Lewin and his associates (Barker, Dembo, and Lewin, 1941). The experimenters allowed one group of children to play with a number of attractive toys. Another group was allowed to look at the toys but not play with them—a frustrating situation. Later when the children in the second group were permitted to play with the toys, they smashed them on the floor, threw them against the wall, and displayed considerable destructive activity. In contrast, the first group of children, who had not been frustrated, played quietly and constructively.

Critics of the frustration-aggression theory have pointed out that whether or not an individual displays aggression depends in large measure on the extent to which his or her culture *permits* aggression. In some societies, like the Kwakiutl Indians of the Pacific Northwest, aggressive behavior is viewed as the mark of a "real man" and hence is encouraged and rewarded. And among some groups within the United States—sailors, marines, lumberjacks, longshoremen, and oil field workers—a macho-male subculture actively fosters violent interpersonal aggression; the man who exclaims, "I don't believe in fighting," wins no popularity contest. But in other societies, like the Zuñi Indians of the American Southwest, aggression is viewed as an evil force that disrupts group harmony. And some groups in the United States define overt aggression and fighting as sinful, or at least ungentlemanly and uncivilized (Westie, 1964).

Moreover, research by Arnold Buss (1961, 1963, 1966) suggests that frustration is at best only a weak antecedent of aggression. In his experiments, he manipulated the degree of frustration people experienced by varying the rewards the subjects could obtain for successful task performance. In some cases they could experience the simple satisfaction of completing a task, in others they could actually win some money, and in others they could earn a favorable report that would be sent to their psychology instructor. In all cases, subjects were blocked from achieving the goal by a frustrater (a confederate of the experimenter). But variations in the magnitude of frustration produced only minimal effects on the level of the subjects' aggression.

In another experiment, Russell L. Geen (1968) found support for Buss's conclusion, although he discovered that subjects display considerably more aggression if they have previously been provided with aggressive modeling influences. (Geen's subjects watched a prize-fight sequence from the movie *Champion* in which Kirk Douglas is viciously beaten.) Further, in laboratory settings, verbal abuse and insults lead to more aggression (willingness to deliver electric shocks to another subject) than does interference with an ongoing task (Geen, 1968; Gentry, 1970). In sum, other determinants may be more important sources of aggression than frustration.

Social psychologist Leonard Berkowitz (1983) takes these arguments a step further and contends that unpleasant events instigate escape *and* attack behaviors. In certain social conditions, we strike out at an available target, inflicting injury because we ourselves are experiencing physical pain or psychological distress. Intense discomfort activates meanness, if not outright hostility. Berkowitz says that it is not frustration itself that produces aggression. Rather, it is the aversiveness of many frustrating experiences—the sense of physical or psychological pain—that is the source of aggressive behavior.

Displacement

According to frustration-aggression theorists, frustration activates an aggressive drive. Presumably frustration remains a motivating force until it is discharged in aggressive behavior. As a consequence, the aggressive impulse may become "free-floating"—detached from the frustrating source and discharged on another person, group, or object. Frustration-aggression theorists term this process **displacement**. Displacement (also called "scapegoating") has been a popular explanation for racism, anti-Semitism, and other kinds of prejudice. Hitler and Goebbels allegedly gave the German people—frustrated by their defeat in World War I, plagued by poverty and wild inflation, and exasperated by the problems of life in general—Jews, Reds, and international bankers as targets on which to vent their rage. And in ancient Rome, the Christian minority was allegedly "thrown to the lions" at public circuses to divert popular attention from the problems, failures, and corruption of the Roman state.

Although a number of studies have tended to confirm the displacement hypothesis (Feshbach and Singer, 1957; Cowen, Landes, and Schaet, 1959; Weath-

Frustration-aggression

This evening after football practice my girl came by and walked with me back to my apartment. I was really upset and raging inside. I got hurt in practice today, and after talking to the trainer, the coach said I won't be making the trip to the coast this weekend. We'll be on television and the pros should be scouting the game. So here I go and blow it and get hurt. As we were going down the alley to my apartment, a black speeds by in his classy-looking car. I started cursing blacks and calling them every dirty name under the sun. This shows that people often get angry but cannot direct their anger at the source, so consequently their anger becomes detached from its source and displaced upon a scape-goat, in this case blacks.

erley, 1961; Stricker, 1963; Konečni and Doob, 1972; Berkowitz, 1978; Berko-witz, Cochran, and Embree, 1981), others have contradicted it (Zawadzki, 1948; Lindzey, 1950; Morse and Allport, 1953; Stagner and Congdon, 1955). The predictive value of the hypothesis has been limited by its emphasis on the motivational state of the individual—the simple state of being frustrated. Other factors, however, intervene to influence how frustration is handled. For instance, it may depend on the individual's personality (Berkowitz, 1962), the kind of frustration involved (Feshbach and Singer, 1957), the qualities of the potential target (Berkowitz, 1962), and the likelihood of counteraggression (Donnerstein et al., 1972). These qualifying factors do not deny the existence of aggressive displacement. Rather, they suggest that we need to be careful in specifying the conditions under which displacement does and does not occur.

Catharsis

Still another process closely associated with the frustration-aggression hypothesis is **catharsis**—a purging and lessening of aggressive energy through discharging it in aggressive behavior. According to this view, anger is depicted as blocked energy in a hydraulic system: To feel better, the enraged person should vent anger fully and forthrightly. The notion of catharsis has wide popularity. Many of us have experienced a sense of relief after engaging in some aggressive behavior (perhaps an emotional outburst): "I just had to get that out of my system," or "Gee, I'm glad I let off steam." Since the frustration-aggression theory postulates that all forms of aggression are functionally equivalent, one type of aggressive response can be substituted for another. Presumably we can drain off our aggressive energies by fantasizing physical assaults or by watching someone behaving vio-lently (as when we watch a boxing match or a football game).

Once again, however, experimental evidence contradicts the popular notion. Although some researchers have found that aggressive behavior lowers subse-quent aggression (Thibaut, 1950; Thibaut and Coules, 1952; Feshbach, 1955;

Manning and Taylor, 1975), in other cases it has produced a rise in aggression (Kenny, 1952; De Charms and Wilkins, 1963; Nelson, 1969; Geen, Stonner, and Shope, 1975). Moreover, watching someone behave aggressively appears to *increase* the likelihood of aggressive behavior (see Chapter 4). Watching aggression provides an opportunity to learn new ways of behaving in an aggressive manner (Bandura, Ross, and Ross, 1961, 1963). In addition, certain stimuli become associated or linked with aggressive behavior and later serve as cues that trigger similar actions in the viewer (Berkowitz, 1965*b*; Geen and Berkowitz, 1967).

A number of treatment therapies, including primal-scream techniques, are based on the notion that people must unearth and release their deep-seated anger if they are to rid themselves of joy-robbing emotional ghosts. However, research suggests that ventilative ("get it out") therapies, aimed at reducing aggressive drives, may inadvertently reinforce them (Berkowitz, 1970*a*; Bandura, 1973*b*). Letting rage out is rarely cathartic and usually produces more anger, not less, by serving as a rehearsal for future outbursts (Tavris, 1983). As individuals recite their grievances, their emotional arousal builds up again. It makes them feel as angry as they did when the infuriating event first happened, all the while more deeply entrenching the angry attitudes. For instance, a study of laid-off aerospace engineers in San Diego found that men who were invited to ventilate their anger became more hostile toward the company or their supervisors than did men who were asked to evaluate their own performance. And third-grade children who were instructed to express anger toward a child who had frustrated them ended up liking that child less than did children who were not encouraged to express anger. Significantly, as noted in Chapter 9, happily married couples typically contain angry outbursts and defuse tension-generating confrontations. And scientists are taking a new look at the claim that there is a direct link between suppressed anger and illness.

According to social psychologist Carol Tavris (1983), anger is not a fixed amount of energy that bounces through the system but a process, a transaction, and a way of communicating. In brief, angry episodes are social events. They acquire their meaning only in terms of the social interaction that takes place among the participants. Let us now examine a number of social factors that influence aggressive behavior.

Social Factors Influencing Aggressive Behavior

Leonard Berkowitz and his associates at the University of Wisconsin have shown the part that social factors play in the selection of *targets for aggression*. In some of these experiments, subjects watched a seven-minute violent film clip from *Champion* (Geen and Berkowitz, 1967). Then they were told that they could give electric shocks to an individual (a confederate of the experimenter) who had previously insulted and angered them within the experimental setting. Berkowitz varied the nature of the target person by varying his name: One-third of the subjects were told that the person who had angered them and to whom they could apply shocks was Bob Kelly, one-third that it was Bob Dunne, and the other third that it was Bob Riley. In the movie *Champion,* a boxer named Midge Kelly is given a bloody beating by another boxer named Dunne.

Competition Reward Structures
Some social psychologists believe there is a link between competition and aggression. Competition pervades a great many aspects of contemporary schooling. It is little wonder that most students within the United States see school as competitive, become increasingly competitive the longer they remain in school, and are more competitive than children in most other cultures. (Patrick Reddy)

Berkowitz expected that after witnessing the boxing film, subjects would administer more shocks to Bob Kelly than to the other confederates. This proved to be true. When the confederate's name was the same as that of the victim in the film, subjects gave him an average of 5.40 shocks. When the confederate was called Riley, a name not mentioned in the film, they gave him 4.40 shocks. Thus subjects made the strongest attack on a target with the *same* name as the target in the movie. In another of Berkowitz's studies, subjects who were shown the fight film gave more shocks to their tormentor in the next room when they were told that he was a boxer—like the victim in the movie—than when they were told he had some other occupation (Berkowitz, 1965b). In brief, the frustrater's name or occupational category evidently associated him with the fight victim. As a consequence of the association, the target had the stimulus characteristics that elicited the strongest aggressive reactions.

On the basis of this and other research (Berkowitz and Knurek, 1969; Berkowitz, 1973), Berkowitz concludes that persons having characteristics that the angry individual has previously learned to dislike are especially apt to be victimized. Thus as children grow up, the significant people in their environment may repeatedly make negative responses toward members of given groups. When the significant people encounter a Jew or a black, or when they see or hear the label "Jew" or "black," they may make unpleasant remarks or otherwise display distaste:

> Whatever the specific manner in which this is done, the child comes to associate these minority groups with unpleasantness, so that eventually his own meetings with members of these groups are unpleasant to him. Even a person only labeled as belonging to these groups can produce this negative reaction in him. (Berkowitz and Knurek, 1969: 205)

Thus if Jews or blacks are culturally defined in negative terms, it becomes easier to attack them.

Berkowitz (1981) finds that the mere presence of guns can also have an aggressive influence on behavior, what he terms the *weapons effect*. He disputes the claim of the National Rifle Association that "Guns don't kill people; people kill people." His research and that of his associates suggest that a gun is not simply a convenient way for settling an argument. The weapon itself acts as a stimulant to violence.

In one experiment, Berkowitz had frustrated and angry subjects deliver shocks to their partners if the latter provided unimaginative ideas for an advertising campaign. One group of subjects worked individually at a table with nothing on it but the telegraph key that sent the shocks. A second group worked at the same table, but for this condition the experimenters also placed badminton rackets and shuttlecocks on the table. Finally, a third group was tested under similar circumstances except that the badminton equipment was replaced by a 12-gauge shotgun and a snub-nosed .38 revolver. The presence of the weapons had a decided effect. Those subjects in the weapons group administered more shocks to their partners and held the key down longer for each shock than did the subjects in the other two groups. Berkowitz concludes that "the finger pulls the trigger; but the trigger may also be pulling the finger" (1981: 11).

Social psychologists have also demonstrated that social factors influence the way we define aggression and come to perceive it (Epstein and Taylor, 1967; Shortell, Epstein, and Taylor, 1970). Research reveals that the physical discomfort experienced by a person (as in the case of electric shocks) is subordinate to the symbolic elements of the attack. Thus subjects respond *more* aggressively when the physical discomfort is *mild* and the symbolic attack is *strong* than when the physical discomfort is strong and the symbolic attack is relatively mild. Specifically, subjects respond more aggressively when they perceive the attacker's behavior as being intentional rather than accidental, and hostile rather than helpful. Indeed, the perception of the opponent's intent is more important in arousing aggression than is the physical attack itself (Maselli and Altrocchi, 1969; Greenwell and Dengerink, 1973; Kulik and Brown, 1979).

Deindividuation

Some of the guys in my fraternity decided it would be a good prank to streak in front of the house of our university president. The idea appealed to me because it was daring and adventuresome to make a run of this sort in the nude. But I also found it frightening. I did not want to be recognized and then later picked up by the police. So I was defensive and hesitant when a few of the guys stopped by my room and asked me to join them. When they told me that a whole bunch of guys were going to streak and that we would wear stockings over our heads, I immediately changed my mind and agreed to participate. And tonight we showed our wares in the front yard of the president's home. I had initially been unwilling to streak because I was afraid that I would be identified. However, when I learned I would be in a large group and my head would be covered, I felt I would be anonymous and thus safe. This deindividuation allowed me to do what I otherwise would have been unwilling to do. And I did not feel particularly self-conscious streaking.

Deindividuation

The matter of crowd violence has intrigued laypeople and social psychologists alike (Le Bon, 1895; Mann, Newton, and Innes, 1982). Crowds gathered at the site of a suicide threat have often taunted and urged the victim to jump (Mann, 1981). And any number of observers have documented the savage cruelty of the lynch mob (Cantril, 1941). Or take the episode that occurred after midnight on June 27, 1981, in New York City's Times Square. A twenty-six-year-old man was mugged and then mugged again, stripped of his clothes, and chased nude through the square by a jeering mob. They threw bottles at him and laughed at him. Attempting to elude his attackers, the man fled for safety into a subway station where he jumped on the tracks and died of electrocution. His death was just another bit of "fun" and excitement for the shadowy figures, drug peddlers, con artists, vagrants, flower peddlers, prostitutes, tourists, and others who haunt Times Square in the early morning hours (Barbanel, 1981).

One factor that makes individuals susceptible to aggressive and violent behavior in crowd settings is **deindividuation.** Deindividuation is a psychological state of diminished identity and self-awareness. *Anonymity* contributes to deindividuation. In a laboratory study, Philip G. Zimbardo (1969) produced anonymity in half of the subjects by dressing them in hoods, never using their names, and conducting the experiment in the dark. The other half of the subjects, in the *identifiability* condition, were greeted individually, given large name tags, and encouraged to use one another's names. The procedure entailed administering shocks to a target person. The total duration of electric shocks delivered by the subjects who felt anonymous was twice as high as the duration of shocks delivered by subjects whose individuality was emphasized. Presumably anonymity produces an overall disinhibiting effect for behavior that is otherwise socially disapproved. Individuals need not fear the application of negative sanctions. Accordingly, they feel less accountable for their behavior. It seems that a similar process operates in riots and lynchings when people commit acts that they ordinarily would not (see Chapter 17).

Other studies show that reduced self-consciousness and lowered concern for social evaluation also contribute to the deindividuation process (Diener, 1979; Prentice-Dunn and Rogers, 1980, 1982; Mann, Newton, and Innes, 1982). Feelings of distinctiveness and self-consciousness diminish as individuals increasingly make the group their focus. They become less aware of their usual thoughts, moods, bodily states, and other internal processes. And as noted in Chapter 10, a large number of people contributes to diffused responsibility.

However, antisocial behavior does not inevitably result from deindividuation. Kenneth J. Gergen and his associates (1973) found in one study that darkness and anonymity led to increases in touching, caressing, and affectionate behaviors. In this case, darkness seemed to suggest intimacy to the subjects rather than aggression. Apparently much depends on the cues that lead people to define the situation in one way or the other. Whether prosocial or antisocial behavior is enhanced by deindividuation depends on which situational cues are salient (Johnson and Downing, 1979).

Institutional Aggression

A good deal of aggression occurs within institutional contexts. People—ordinary people—commit aggressive and even violent acts as part of "doing their job." This is **institutional aggression.** It can be seen most clearly in the case of the military, the police, and certain sports. A freshman linebacker for the Ohio State football team says, "When I hit somebody and I see him hurting, just grimacing, it sends something through me that's hard to explain. A bolt. A charge. You play to hurt somebody. You've got to be clean, but you play to put them out of the game" (Harden, 1984: B-1). Chapter 7 detailed Stanley Milgram's experiments in which he found that most individuals will commit aggressive and violent acts in the name of obedience to authority. Within institutional settings, people come to see themselves as being absolved of personal responsibility for their acts. They view themselves as "pawns" rather than as "originators of behavior." If they place any blame at all, they pin it on the institution, excusing themselves by the rationalization, "If I don't do it, someone else will" (De Charms, 1968; Kipnis, 1974).

Perhaps even more shocking than the results of the Milgram study are those revealed in an experiment by Philip G. Zimbardo and his associates (Zimbardo, Haney, and Banks, 1973; Haney, Banks, and Zimbardo, 1973). To investigate the consequences of being a prisoner or a prison guard, the researchers converted the basement of the Stanford University psychology building into a mock prison. Some seventy-five male student volunteers were given intensive clinical interviews and personality tests, and twenty-one were selected for their maturity and stability. About half of these were assigned at random to serve as "guards," half

Sport: Institutional Aggression
Boxing, wrestling, football, and hockey are sports in which people commit aggressive and violent acts as part of their expected role-playing behavior. (Patrick Reddy)

to serve as "inmates." To enhance the realism of the experiment, the prisoners were unexpectedly picked up at their homes by city police in a squad car. Each subject was charged with a felony, told of his constitutional rights, spread-eagled against the car, searched, and handcuffed; then he was delivered to the station for fingerprinting and preparation of an information file.

At the mock prison the men were stripped naked, skin-searched, sprayed for lice, issued a uniform, bedding, soap, and a towel, and placed in a 6- by 9-foot barred cell with two other "convicts." The prisoners were required to obtain permission from the guards to perform routine activities such as writing letters, smoking a cigarette, or using the toilet.

"Guards" worked on three eight-hour shifts and went home when they were not on duty. They were instructed not to use physical violence, although they were given considerable latitude to improvise and develop strategies for maintaining "law and order" in the prison. They wore khaki uniforms and carried billy clubs, whistles, and handcuffs as symbols of power.

Over a six-day period, a "perverted" symbiotic relationship developed. As the guards became more aggressive, the prisoners became more passive. The guards' assertion led to the prisoners' dependency, the guards' self-aggrandizement to the prisoners' self-deprecation, and the guards' authority to the prisoners' helplessness. The guards' sense of mastery and control was inversely related to hopelessness and depression among the prisoners.

As the guards fell into their roles, they became increasingly authoritarian. They made the prisoners obey petty, meaningless, and even inconsistent rules. They forced the prisoners to undertake tedious and useless work (moving cartons back and forth and picking thorns out of their blankets after the guards had dragged the blankets through thorn bushes). They made the prisoners sing songs, laugh, or refrain from smiling on command. They regularly called prisoners out of their cells and counted them, and they encouraged the prisoners to curse and vilify one another publicly during some of the counts. One guard said later:

> I was surprised at myself. . . . I made them call each other names and clean the toilets out with their bare hands. I practically considered the prisoners cattle, and I kept thinking: I have to watch out for them in case they try something. (Zimbardo, Haney, and Banks, 1973: 42)

As mentioned in Chapter 1 in the section on ethics in research, this treatment had a devastating impact on the prisoners. They became resigned to their fate and behaved in ways that helped justify their dehumanizing treatment. Tape-recorded private conversations among them revealed that 85 percent of the evaluative statements prisoners made about one another were uncomplimentary. Although the experiment had been organized to run for two weeks, it had to be discontinued after only six days in order to prevent permanent psychic damage to the subjects. Four of the ten prisoners had to be released within the first five days as a result of fits of rage, crying, acute anxiety, and symptoms of severe depression. A fifth had to be released when he developed a psychosomatic rash all over his body. Although the prisoners were pleased when the experiment was terminated, the guards were reluctant to give up their positions of power.

The study revealed that normal, healthy, educated college men can be radically transformed under the institutional pressures of a prison environment. Had psychiatrists diagnosed the guards after observing their behavior, the men would undoubtedly have been labeled "psychopathic," while the prisoners would have been diagnosed as suffering from character defects and personality maladjustment. Yet the bizarre social and personal reactions of the subjects cannot be attributed to preexisting personality differences or pathologies, since such factors were eliminated by the careful selection processes and the random assignment. Rather, the guards' aggressive behavior and the prisoners' submissiveness arose *Conc !* out of situational factors in an institutional environment. What would otherwise have been termed "pathological" behavior became "appropriate" behavior in the prison.

Erotic Materials and Aggression

Until relatively recently, the prevailing view among social scientists was that exposure to pornography does not contribute to sexual crimes. This conclusion was also the principal finding of the Presidential Commission on Obscenity and Pornography (1971). However, more recent research has shown that erotic material can influence aggressive behavior in a variety of ways. Since human sexuality and aggression are both quite complex forms of behavior, it is hardly surprising that social psychologists are finding extraordinarily complex ways in which the two interact.

Social psychologists typically study the relationship between sexual arousal and aggression by exposing some subjects to a sexually arousing stimulus like an erotic film or written passage. Another group of subjects watch a neutral film or read a neutral passage. All the subjects are then provided with an opportunity to act aggressively against someone else, generally a confederate who makes a preset number of errors in a guessing game. For each error, the subject administers an electric shock to the other party, the intensity of which is determined by the subject. (Unknown to the subject, the wires do not carry an actual electric shock but simply lead to a recording device.) The average intensity level of the shock that the subject administers over several trials is taken as an index of the subject's level of aggression (Feshbach and Malamuth, 1978).

Research shows that men typically become more aggressive toward women after viewing sexual violence (Donnerstein, 1980; Donnerstein and Berkowitz, 1981). Men who watch films depicting sexual violence administer more electric shocks to their female partners than men who watch nonviolent sexual films. And when they have been previously angered, the men are even more willing to administer shocks to women.

But even relatively nonviolent pornography may increase aggressive behavior. It seems that as erotic stimuli become more arousing (especially as precoital and coital activity are depicted), aggressive behavior increases (Meyer, 1972; Zillmann, Hoyt, and Day, 1974; Donnerstein and Hallam, 1978). In contrast, at a low level of arousal (for instance, photographs of nudes), erotic stimuli act to lower the intensity of aggressive reactions (Donnerstein, Donnerstein, and Evans, 1975; Baron, 1977; Baron and Bell, 1977; Ramirez, Bryant, and Zillmann, 1982). Apparently, mild erotic materials are experienced by most people as hedonic and pleasing (Zillmann and Sapolsky, 1977).

One interpretation of these findings is that the increase in aggression following exposure to highly erotic material is the result of a person's overall arousal. Any number of social psychologists have demonstrated that people become similarly aggressive if aroused by vigorous exercise or environmental stressors such as loud noise, overcrowding, and high temperature (Griffitt and Veitch, 1971; Zillmann, Katcher, and Milavsky, 1972; Baron and Bell, 1976; Donnerstein and Wilson, 1976; Mann, 1981). Viewed from this perspective, heightened arousal of any sort serves to exaggerate *any* behavior that is already prevalent at the time. Accordingly, sex and aggression become linked because the arousal elicited by sexual stimuli can add to the arousal elicited by aggressive and violent stimuli (Zillmann, 1984). Some social psychologists express concern that when erotic scenes are followed by violence, viewers "misattribute" their arousal from the sex to the violence, and the two merge cognitively. Some people, especially children and adolescents, may then be led to combine sex and aggression in their own lives.

Seymour Feshbach and Neil Malamuth (1978) consider the interpretation that overall arousal accounts for increased aggression following exposure to erotic material to be excessively simplistic. They argue that the tie between erotic arousal and aggression derives from the cultural linkage Western societies make between the two behaviors. Common taboos affect sex and aggression and hence generalize from one to the other. They find confirmation for this interpretation in a number of studies they have conducted (Malamuth, Heim, and Feshbach, 1980).

Perhaps of greatest interest is the Feshbach-Malamuth research dealing with rape and sadomasochistic literature. In sadism and masochism, the source of sexual gratification is pain. In one study, the researchers had college students read one of two versions of a story taken from *Penthouse*. One group read the original story, in which a woman experienced sexual pleasure at being mistreated, while another group read a nonviolent version. After completing the story, the students completed a questionnaire assessing their level of sexual arousal and other emotions. (The students had volunteered for a study called "Evaluation of Erotica.") Next the students read a story about a rape. In the story, the terrified woman, compelled to yield at knife-point, exhibited moderate pain cues although she was not portrayed as sexually excited. The students then completed a second questionnaire evaluating their responses to the story.

Whether previously exposed to the sadomasochistic or nonviolent condition, the female students reacted negatively to the rape story. However, men who read the sadomasochistic story tended to be much more sexually aroused by the account of the rape than men who had read the nonviolent version. Presumably the men in the first group interpreted the victim's pain in the rape scene as a sign of her sexual excitement and were in turn sexually aroused. In contrast, those men who had read the nonviolent account were more likely to perceive the rape victim's responses as pain and were in turn more likely to be sexually inhibited. This research suggests that the inhibitions most men experience to pain cues are altered by exposure to sadomasochistic material.

Other research also suggests that pornographic films that depict women as enjoying sexual assault serve to justify aggression, reduce men's sensitivity to rape, and lower men's inhibitions against sexual aggression. And the men find it easier to make the women responsible for the assault, shifting the responsibility for rape to the victim (Donnerstein and Berkowitz, 1981). For instance, research by Edward Donnerstein suggests that as men watch "slasher" movies that feature graphic scenes of bloody violence inflicted on young women over a number of days, they become emotionally desensitized to violence against women (Donnerstein and Linz, 1984). When he and his associates showed sexually violent films to young men and then asked the men to judge a simulated rape trial, the men were less likely to vote for conviction than were men who had not seen the films. Likewise, after viewing sexually violent films in which a rape victim appears to enjoy the attack, the young men were more likely to believe that a woman who was raped wanted to be and that hitchhikers or provocatively dressed women *deserve* to be raped. In short, the men had become more calloused toward women. Given such evidence, social scientists are increasingly coming to conclude that any kind of publicity about violent acts can stimulate aggressive behavior, even in normal people. For those individuals who already have aggressive tendencies or who are emotionally disturbed, violent pornography can implant violent notions and spur violent behavior (Bishop, 1981).

Rape

Concern with pornography's role in violent behavior has gained impetus from reports of an increasing number of physical assaults on women. The FBI's *Uniform Crime Reports* shows a doubling of reported rapes since 1970. In part, this rise may reflect a greater willingness to report assaults. Even so, a Justice Department report concludes that only about half the rape victims in the United States ever report the crime to the police (*New York Times*, March 25, 1985, p. 13). Victims fail to come forward for a variety of reasons (Williams, 1984). Some women fear retaliation from the rapist. Others wish to avoid the notoriety and stigma that society attaches to the rape victim. Still others say they feel embarrassed and ashamed, or wish to protect their family members from the publicity that often attends rape cases. Practical concerns may also be involved. Many women lack confidence in the ability of the criminal justice system to apprehend or punish rapists. (Government figures reveal that rapists serve less then one-third of the average prison sentence of nine to ten years.)

Although rape has had a long and disturbing history, societal attention to the problem is a relatively recent phenomenon. It seems that a crime receives attention only when the victims have enough power to demand attention. Consequently, the current focus on rape has paralleled the emergence of the women's rights movement (Cann et al., 1981). Yet the extent to which rape is rooted in the social system should not be underestimated (see Chapter 16). For instance, a 1981 study of 432 teens by social scientists at UCLA found that 54 percent of the boys and 42 percent of the girls believed forced sexual intercourse was permissible under some circumstances (Seligmann, 1984). Likewise, accumulating evidence suggests that marital rape is a common form of family violence and brutality (Russell, 1982). Yet as of 1985, only twenty-three states had laws allowing prosecution of husbands for raping their wives.

Rape myths abound among the American population. Martha R. Burt (1980) found that over half of her representative sample of 598 Minnesota residents agreed with such statements as "In the majority of rapes, the victim was promiscuous or had a bad reputation," and "A woman who goes to the home or apartment of a man on a first date implies she is willing to have sex." And over half of her sample thought that 50 percent or more of rapes are reported as rapes because "the woman was trying to get back at the man she was angry with or was trying to cover up an illegitimate pregnancy." These rape myths form a part of a larger and interrelated attitude structure that includes acceptance of traditional sex-role stereotyping, interpersonal violence (especially when directed against women), and the view that sexual relationships are adversary relationships.

Women who press rape charges are as much on trial as their alleged rapists. Researchers who observed thirty-seven Indianapolis sexual assault trials and interviewed 360 jurors found that jurors admit to being influenced by a victim's character, appearance, reputation, and life style (Brozan, 1985). They treat more seriously the rape of a woman who seems chaste or is conventional in her life style. They are more likely to exonerate men charged with raping women who reputedly are sexually active outside of marriage or women who knew the assailant. A woman becomes suspect if mention is made that she uses birth control pills, has an illegitimate child, has a child with a different last name than her own, or has the same address as a boyfriend. And jurors judge harshly such behaviors as going to a bar alone, accepting a ride with a strange man, drinking, keeping late hours, or using marijuana. Accused men are usually placed in one of two categories. If the men come across as losers, are scruffy, lack a job, or are unmarried, jurors tend to be biased against them. If the men are attractive, have a girlfriend, or are married, a juror finds it difficult to believe that they would commit rape. But in fact these characteristics provide no pointers to who is or is not a likely rapist (see boxed insert, pp. 350–351). Although women made up 53 percent of those surveyed, they did not differ markedly in their attitudes from male jurors.

In a series of studies, Neil M. Malamuth (1981) asked college males to indicate the likelihood that they personally would rape if they could be assured of not being caught and punished. Across the varied studies (involving students in the Los Angeles and Stanford areas in California and the Winnipeg area in Canada), an average of about 35 percent of the men indicated some likelihood of raping. Other research suggests that the figure may approach 44 percent (Check and Malamuth, 1983). A 1982 survey of 190 male undergraduates at Auburn University found that the men had engaged in a wide range of sexually coercive practices (Rapaport and Burkhart, 1984). Fifty-three percent of the men had kissed a woman against her will; 61 percent had placed a hand on an unwilling woman's knee or breast; 42 percent had removed or disarranged a woman's clothing against her will; and 15 percent acknowledged that they had had intercourse with a woman against her will (that is, they had raped her). When the researchers analyzed the personality characteristics of the male college students, they found that the more sexually coercive men were more likely to be immature, be irresponsible, lack a social conscience, and hold values that legitimized aggression against women.

Studies of convicted rapists reveal two types of responses that typically distinguish rapists from men in the general population: greater acceptance of rape myths and relatively high sexual arousal to rape depictions (Malamuth, 1981, 1983; Check and Malamuth, 1983). These responses are also more typical of college males who admit to rapist inclinations. Men who rape women typically believe that their actions do not in fact constitute rape (Scully and Marolla, 1984). They employ rape stereotypes to make their victims appear culpable. The single most used cry of a rapist to his victim is, "You know you want it. You *all* want it"; and afterward, "There now, you really enjoyed it, didn't you?" Justifications of rape are buttressed by the cultural view of women as sexual commodities. Of interest, the incidence of rape varies across cultures, with some societies, such as the Gusii of southwestern Kenya, being "rape prone" and other societies, such as the Tuareg of the Sahara, being relatively "rape free" (Sanday, 1981).

AVERTING RAPE

Advising women on strategies to avert rape is admittedly perilous, since no single formula exists. Take the case of Caroline Isenberg, a New York City drama student. She had returned home from the theater on December 2, 1984, and was confronted in the elevator by an attacker, who forced her to the rooftop. She resisted and was stabbed nine times. On her death bed she said that she wished she had not resisted. This declaration has reinforced the conviction of some women that if attacked they should submit to save their lives. But others, including Susan Brownmiller, author of the best-selling *Against Our Will: Men, Women, and Rape* (1975), are worried by this attitude. Says Brownmiller: "It took decades to get society to look at rape as a crime of violence that women did not provoke and now all this talk about 'if you just submit, everything will be O.K.' is taking us backwards" (quoted by Franks, 1984: 13).

As in many other matters, the best defense against rape is to take reasonable precautions. In appearance and demeanor rapists are as typical as men in general. Yet research suggests that there may be some telltale signs of men who are more likely to be dangerous and that should make women wary (Dubrow, 1984):

—— The man displays a good deal of anger against women.

—— The man interprets many nonsexual things a woman does as inviting sex. (For instance, asking a man in for coffee is seen as her wanting sex.)

—— The man comments that there is no such thing as rape.

—— The man treats a woman as if she is his property and shows rage should another man pay attention to her.

—— The man puts women on a pedestal, so that he is bound to be disappointed and enraged by real-life women.

In practice, however, it is not always possible to steer clear of potential rapists. All women encounter men in their everyday lives who are capable of rape. Indeed, although precise statistics are difficult to come by, it is likely that most women are raped by someone they already know and not by a stranger. Most experts agree, however, that resistance early in an attack has the best chance of success (Franks, 1984). Rapists often look for a woman who they think will not put up a fight or make a scene. For instance, victims are often women who are afraid to establish eye contact or hold a glare when threatened. Some experts, like Pauline Bart, a sociologist at Chicago's Medical School, suggest that fighting back is effective in stopping a rape, particularly date rape, because it shows the man that a woman is serious and means no. Such a strategy becomes even more effective when combined with trying to flee and yelling. (Screaming or shrieking alone, in contrast, reinforces the hysterical woman concept.) However, acting "crazy," telling a man one has venereal disease, getting a man to see one as a human being, and other related verbal techniques typically are useless and often are counterproductive.

A study undertaken by clinical psychologists at the Massachusetts Treatment Center in Bridgewater, the state's facility for treating "sexually dangerous criminals," identifies four major types of rapists and suggests different strategies for dealing with each type (Goleman, 1985e). About half of rapists are in the category termed "exploitative"—men for whom rape is a spur-of-the-moment event and who view a victim purely as an object for sexual gratification. They interpret a woman's resistance as a sexual maneuver, heightening their arousal. Another quarter of rapists are "compensatory"—men who feel acutely inadequate as men and who are obsessed by sexual fantasies. Still another 20 percent of rapists are men for whom sex is a way of humiliating women and displacing anger toward their mother, lover, or wife. Finally, about 5 percent of rapists are sadistic. This latter category of men is the most dangerous. Their assaults are frequently premeditated and involve enacting a compulsive, ritualized fantasy.

The Massachusetts psychologists offer guidelines that rape victims might use. The first is to flee if possible. If this fails, the psychologists recommend that a woman talk to the rapist, keeping the conversation "real" and "in the here-and-now" (for instance, conveying to the man that she is a stranger). If the rapist listens, he is most likely a compensatory rapist and can be stopped by active resistance, such as yelling for help. If the rapist pays no attention to what the victim says but does not seem to be employing gratuitous violence, he is very likely an "exploitative" rapist. It is suggested that the woman divert the man by asking him questions about himself, thus breaking the initial tension of confrontation and "derailing" the rape. If the rapist responds to talk by increasing his aggression and seems to want to humiliate and demean his victim, the best strategy seems to be an empathic response, one that demonstrates some sense of concern or caring. Finally, if the rapist makes bizarre sexual demands, he is likely to be a sadist. In this case, the psychologists suggest that the woman feign participation and at a critical moment make maximum use of surprise, attacking the genital or facial areas as viciously as possible and fleeing.

But again, there are no pat answers. There are simply too many variables in a rape situation, and it usually happens so quickly that it is impossible for a woman to judge the psychological profile of her assailant. And the rapist may also have a weapon. Whatever the case may be, most experts on rape suggest that a woman remain calm and constantly monitor her options. Moreover, resistance at the beginning of an attack, when people are in earshot, can often be successful. A woman's options drastically decrease thereafter. And experts warn that if a woman reaches to poke out an assailant's eye or crush his testicles, she had better have the courage and capacity to do it. Force and violence are on the side of the rapist, and most assailants are used to being "bad guys."

REACTIONS TO VICTIMIZATION

We become victims in a good many ways. We can have a serious accident, contract a serious disease, be assaulted, raped, robbed, or abducted, experience a tornado, earthquake, or fire, or bear the impact of a technological disaster. When we become victims, we must deal not only with any physical injury that may ensue but also with the psychological toll produced by the event. Much of the psychological toll derives from the shattering of a number of basic assumptions that we hold about ourselves and the world (Janoff-Bulman and Frieze, 1983). Prior to victimization, most of us go about our daily activities imbued with an "illusion of invulnerability"—the notion that "it can't happen to me." But after victimization, we become preoccupied with a fear that misfortune will recur—for instance, that we will again be raped or robbed or that we will suffer a recurrence of disease. In brief, once victimized, we find it easy to see ourselves in the role of victim again. Our assumption of invulnerability rests in part on the view that events in the world are comprehensible and orderly. Clearly, victimization does not fit with such notions, and so we experience the world as "senseless." Moveover, victimization challenges our conceptions of ourselves as worthy, decent people. It activates negative self-images and leads us to see ourselves as weak, helpless, needy, frightened, and out of control.

The shattering of such basic assumptions results in intense stress and anxiety. The coping process involves reestablishing conceptions that will allow us to function effectively once more. To do so, we must fashion assumptions that incorporate our experiences as a victim. One successful way of coping is to redefine the event so as to minimize the threat it poses to our assumptions about life (Taylor, Wood, and Lichtman, 1983). We may compare ourselves with a less fortunate person (for instance, a woman with breast cancer may view herself as doing better than other women coping with the same crisis). We may create a hypothetical world that envisions an even worse scenario (as when

The threat of rape affects women whether or not they are actually victimized (Riger and Gordon, 1981; Warr, 1985). It limits their freedom, keeps them off the streets at night, and often serves to imprison them at home. Many women are kept in a state of anxiety by the threat of rape, and they consequently restrict their behavior in a quest for safety. Women who carry the highest burden of fear are those with the fewest resources to cope with victimization—the elderly, ethnic minorities, and those with low incomes. Women living in high-crime neighborhoods typically seek to avoid rape by staying away from particularly dangerous areas and through "street savvy" (for instance, wearing shoes that permit them to run and keeping an eye out for suspicious-looking men). None-a rape victim notes that she could have been murdered). Or we may construe some benefit from the experience ("I am a better person for having experienced adversity and I now pay less attention to mundane concerns").

Anothe way of reacting to victimization is self-blame (Miller and Porter, 1983). Contrary to conventional wisdom, people who blame themselves, at least in part, for their misfortune have less difficulty coping with their misfortune. For example, if individuals can attribute their difficulty to having been careless (not locking a door or walking in a dangerous neighborhood late at night), they can again see the world as orderly and controllable. Accordingly, rape victims need not blame themselves for their assailant's actions but instead can blame themselves for having become victims. All they have to do is modify their behavior, and they need not be victimized in the future. Even victims of a technological disaster, such as the radiation accident at Three Mile Island, seem to suffer less stress if they attribute some of the blame to themselves ("I should not have lived so near a nuclear plant"). But it is otherwise if individuals attribute their misfortune to an enduring personality trait ("I am a sinful person and deserve misfortune"). This latter type of interpretation feeds feelings of depression and helplessness.

Still another way to responding to victimization is to undertake new behaviors that are consistent with the changes wrought by new definitions. For victims of rape and muggings, formal training in self-defense and assertiveness are often effective vehicles for minimizing feelings of vulnerability. Victims may also turn to others for emotional and other forms of help. Where one has supportive family and friends, this approach can be helpful. But not all people are compassionate toward victims; many see victims as responsible for their fate (see the discussion of the just-world hypothesis in Chapter 10). Self-help groups may prove helpful by giving victims a feeling that they are not abnormal. But they can have negative outcomes when individuals, seeing the distress of others in a support group, conclude that their problems are more serious than they thought and may even get worse (Coates and Winston, 1983).

theless, victims frequently are assaulted in their homes and know their attacker (Bart, 1981).

Rape victims usually suffer injury and emotional trauma as a result of the assault (see the boxed insert on reactions to victimization). Women vary in their immediate reactions following the rape incident. Some become very tearful and agitated; others attempt to maintain their control and display little open emotion. A particularly prevalent reaction is fear. (It is not unusual for rape victims to fear being alone.) Other feelings include guilt, shame, and loss—in part, products of society's rape myths and the woman's loss of control over her body. Such disturbances as loss of appetite, insomnia, nightmares, sexual dysfunction, and social withdrawal are quite frequent. Many women also change their life style: They obsessively check doors to see if they are locked, change telephone numbers, move to a new residence, and change jobs. Seventy-four percent of rape victims report that it took them several months to several years to recover. Another 26 percent report that even after four to six years they still do not feel recovered from the rape trauma (King and Webb, 1981; Kilpatrick, Resick, and Veronen, 1981; Nadelson et al., 1982).

Women may also rape men (Timnick, 1983). The suggestion that men can be "raped" by women typically elicits either skepticism or lewd comments like "Lucky guy!" Male victims describe varying levels of fright, panic, and confusion at the time of the assault. Even so, many of them have erections, and in some cases they ejaculate. However, the aftereffects are similar to those experienced by women who have been raped. They include impotence, a lack of sexual desire, sexual aversion even to the point of nausea and vomiting, depression, and feelings of inadequacy and abnormality.

CONFLICT

Conflict is a form of interaction in which people (individually or in groups) perceive themselves as being involved in a struggle over scarce resources or social values. People in conflict find themselves at odds; they feel separated by incompatible objectives. They see one another as competitors or threats, and thus their interaction is antagonistic. Rather than fitting their lines of action together to realize common ends, people contend against one another; their actions and counteractions are opposed. Each side aims to eliminate, or in any event neutralize, the other (Kriesberg, 1973; Scherer, Abeles, and Fischer, 1975).

We commonly think of harmony as good and conflict as bad. In our dreams of a "good life"—whether it be of an other-worldly heaven or a this-worldly utopia—we see an existence free of human friction, family quarrels, discrimination, ill-will, turmoil, and wars. We want a world where peace, brotherhood, and comradeship reign. Yet unhappily, it is not quite so simple (Wheaton, 1974). Philosophers like Georg Wilhelm Hegel and Karl Marx tell us that conflict is a necessary instrument of change and progress. And sociologists like Georg Simmel (1955) and Lewis Coser (1956) see conflict as a vehicle for the formation of groups—as a social glue knitting people together within social units.

Clashing Interests

Under some conditions of human life, individuals and groups find that they simultaneously desire the same scarce resources. Some of these desires are needs that derive from our existence as biological organisms. When conditions depart from some physical optimum, our bodies experience tension and discomfort, even pain, as in the case of hunger, thirst, sensitivity to temperature, and fatigue. Food, water, clothing, and shelter give us the means for minimizing distress, and when they are available in ample supply, enable us to enjoy creature comforts.

Conflict

> *During the past summer two privately owned ice cream establishments in my hometown were carrying on a price war with each other. The locality can support only one shop; there is not enough business for two. Each tried to best the other. And depending on the special of the day, one might pick up a few customers here or there at the expense of the other. They even tried to supplement their ice cream business with an occasional pizza extravaganza or some other sort of promotion. But it became clear that they could not continue their intense competition much longer or both would flounder. When I was home last weekend, I noticed that one of the shops has now switched over to sandwiches and carryout lunches. Both shops could not occupy the same ecological niche and survive. Now that one of the shops has changed its product line, perhaps both can draw on a roughly similar clientele by meeting a somewhat different set of needs.*

Normally the goods and services essential for health and survival are in limited supply, a recurring problem throughout human history. In stationary societies, the more there is for some people, the less there is for others. One individual or group can gain only at the expense of others; in brief, one can rise only by pushing another down. This is the so-called "Duchess law" (Boulding, 1962), based on one of the morals of the Duchess in *Alice in Wonderland*—the more there is of yours, the less there is of mine.

We are not, however, simply biological organisms. We also experience various social and psychological needs, including the need for **status**—for an expansive feeling of being somebody special and valuable, so that our self-images are positively illuminated. To be thought well of by ourselves and our fellows appears to be an overriding human concern. We tend to associate self-esteem, prestige, and worthiness with a sense of well-being. Concern with status influences almost every kind of decision that a person makes, from the choice of a college to the choice of a spouse or lover. The matter of status—of honor and worth in the eyes of God, our friends, and our family—is one of the few motives that make people willing to lay down their lives on the field of battle. The late Robert Lowie, a leading anthropologist, wrote that "primitive man" was not a miser, sage, or beast of prey, but rather a peacock (quoted in Lenski, 1966: 37–38). And the same might be said of us today.

One peculiarity that we have as human beings, in contrast to plants and to other animals, is our *insatiable appetite for goods and services*. No matter how much we produce and consume, we seem to desire more. This craving derives from the fact that goods and services have not only utilitarian value but *status value*. Homes, clothing, and food not only meet organic needs but also function as status symbols. Since our status is usually not an absolute matter but one

Clashing Interests: Labor Versus Business
Conflict may derive from the fact that wealth, power, and status are scarce and divisible, so the more there is for some, the less there is for others. Strikes are one means employed by workers to improve their chance of obtaining the things they define as desirable. (Patrick Reddy)

that is relative to the status of others, the very nature of status striving makes it inevitable that the demand will exceed the supply (Lenski, 1966).

A once-and-for-all solution does not exist to the problem of distributing scarce resources among the members of a society. At any given moment some arrangement operates for apportioning the good things desired and sought by most, including privilege, power, and status, among the society's individuals and groups. Some people are advantaged; others are disadvantaged. Those who are better off have a stake—a vested interest—in conserving, consolidating, and even expanding their share. Those who are less privileged seek to improve their outcome with respect to what they define as good and desirable. Indeed, our definition of the situation varies with our place in the social system. The very social arrangements that create misery and suffering for some contribute to the freedom and security of others. Privileged groups do not voluntarily relinquish their advantaged position. The result of the clash of these opposing interests is conflict (Oberschall, 1973).

Clashing Values

A **value** is an ethical principle to which people feel a strong emotional commitment and which they employ in judging behavior. In group life we evolve shared

Clashing Values: The Abortion Controversy
Few issues in contemporary America excite the passions that sur-
round abortion. The proponents argue that a woman has the right to
exercise control over her own body and to determine whether or not
she wishes to become a parent. The opponents insist that abortion is
murder. (Patrick Reddy)

sentiments regarding what is good or bad, commendable or deplorable, important
or unimportant. Values impart meaning to life. Through what we value, we
experience the world—people, objects, happenings—not in cold, aseptic terms
but in human terms: We "feel" about them. Indeed, social values are "what life
is all about"—the touchstone of human existence.

Values provide us with our conceptions of good and evil. They tell us what is
noble, holy, and vital—for instance, God, country, and motherhood. And they
tell us what is vile, dishonorable, and shameful. Often we see our social values
as sacred, immortal truths given us by our gods or our wise ancestors (our
Washingtons, Jeffersons, and Lincolns). Small wonder that social values fuse like-
minded people together (Rabbie and Horowitz, 1969), especially when these
people confront others whom they see as the embodiment of evil: the antichrist
Jew, the infidel Moor, the treacherous Jap, the barbarous Hun, the despicable
Communist, or the Wall Street imperialist. Our common enemies infect us with
a feeling of kinship. We cease being simply Dick, Ilse, Ivan, Miriam, or Anwar
and become an American, a German, a Russian, a Jew, or an Arab (Hoffer, 1951).

Social values at times arise from a clash of interests, as in class or racial
conflict. Thus elitist and racist notions of superiority function as rationalizations
and justifications for class and racial oppression. Social values may also evolve
independently of such conditions, as in religious antagonism. (Here too, however,

there is often a linkage between interests and social values: Pope Urban II, preaching the First Crusade in Clermont in 1095, did not omit to mention that there was a good deal of excellent real estate in the Holy Land simply awaiting occupation by the Christians, and the Spaniards combined their concern for extending the power of the holy Catholic Church with a compelling interest in increasing their store of gold and silver.) Whatever the source of the clash in social values, it is common for individuals or groups to disagree about whose standards should operate in controlling and regulating social interaction. Where each undertakes to ensure that its own social values predominate, conflict results.

Conflict Models

Three different and somewhat contrasting models have found expression in social psychological approaches to the conflict process (Pruitt and Gahagan, 1974): the aggressor-defender model, the conflict-spiral model, and the structural-change model.

Aggressor-Defender Model

The aggressor-defender view of conflict dominates the thinking of many leaders in public life. Whether the conflict involves warfare among nations, strife between racial groups, disagreement among politicians, controversies among scientists, or whatever, one party typically views the other as the "aggressor." Depending on the observer's bias, one side in the dispute (the "bad-guy villain") is seen as motivated by ignoble, evil, and illegitimate aims; the other ("the good-guy hero") by noble, morally correct, and legitimate aims. The Vietnam War and this nation's longstanding difficulties with the Soviet Union have commonly been defined in these terms. When the aggressor-defender model is accepted, it follows logically that the "good guys" must increase their deterrent power to ensure that the "bad guys" are held in check—that "law and order" prevails.

The major problem with this approach is its highly moralistic focus. It commonly leads to a one-sided analysis of causation that places the blame on the "aggressor's" behavior. Further, scholars who allocate blame inevitably end by distorting various facts.

Conflict-Spiral Model

According to the conflict-spiral view, conflict breeds conflict. Each party in turn extends and intensifies the conflict by reacting in a punitive or defensive manner to the other party's behavior. As a consequence, a continuing spiral of escalation unfolds that traps both parties. Viewed from this perspective, the initial source of friction may have been inconsequential—neither intended nor defined as aggression. But rather than focusing on a "first cause" (as in the case of the aggressor-defender model), the conflict-spiral model describes the dynamic, interactive process by which individuals or groups find themselves caught in an upward spiral of hostilities. Deescalation may also occur in spiral fashion. The Strategic Arms Limitation Talks (SALT) and summit talks between the United States and the Soviet Union have had as their aim a step-by-step retreat from nuclear confrontation. Presumably each step increases trust and leads to ever more limited armament—perhaps ultimately even to disarmament.

The model provides a useful tool for examining the student power and antiwar clashes that occurred on college campuses across the nation in 1970. Not uncommonly, a few students would stage a sit-in or a demonstration. School or local authorities would respond by bringing in police units. Arrests, name-calling, scuffling, and other incidents would follow. College or state administrators might then bring in more police or National Guard units, serving to inflame student anger and activating previously uninvolved and uncommitted students. In short, aggression bred counteraggression in a spiral of intensified confrontation.

The conflict-spiral model falls short, however, in that it neglects the part played by strategic planning in conflict and does not take account of the fact that one party may be better organized than the other. Also, action does not inevitably result in reaction. The cumulation of effects may be checked by some turn of events or by the intervention of a third party.

Structural-Change Model

Like the conflict-spiral model, the structural-change model is concerned with the dynamic interaction between the parties in the course of conflict. But unlike the conflict-spiral model, it holds that certain *enduring* changes take place that perpetuate the conflict. The changes can occur in various areas: in the social structure of the parties; in people's images, attitudes, and motives; in the salience of issues; and in people's depth of commitment. For instance, military elites often gain considerable power during a war. They may come to have a stake in perpetuating hostilities so that they will not lose their power and privileges to civilian authorities. The same holds true for war industries and for the workers who become dependent on a war economy.

Of course, not all conflicts last long enough to bring about major institutional changes. Further, societies often possess considerable resilience, rebounding after the conflict to what are essentially preconflict conditions. Nor are the conflict-spiral and structural-change models necessarily contradictory. Spiraling conflict and structural change may operate simultaneously, as in the case of America's involvement in the Vietnam War.

Intensity of Conflict

As the discussion in this chapter has implied, a variety of forces come into play in influencing the **intensity of conflict**—the degree to which the parties are committed to expending resources and energy in the effort to defeat or neutralize their opponents. (For example, are they committed to engage in physical conflict, or will they limit themselves to verbal debate?) A variety of factors determine the intensity of conflict.

Common Allegiances and Memberships

Where the parties to conflict share common loyalties and identities, bonds exist between them that lessen the magnitude of their discord. Within the United

States, for instance, the clash between Republicans and Democrats is mitigated by overriding national considerations, especially in the realm of foreign policy.

Crosscutting Identifications

Contemporary nation-states commonly contain a variety of antagonistic groups—classes, races, nationality groups, religious denominations, and political parties. Where individuals have crosscutting identifications—where they are antagonists in one conflict (for example, class) and allies in another (say, race or religion)—the conflict tends to be less intense. But where identities are superimposed—where, regardless of the arena, some individuals are consistently the top dogs and others consistently the underdogs—conflict is likely to be more intense. For instance, class and race tend to be overlapping identities within the United States and thus serve to intensify black-white polarization (Dahrendorf, 1959).

Third Parties as Referees

A powerful third party—often the government—may intervene in conflict in order to limit or encapsulate it. Third parties, however, are seldom entirely neutral, or disinterested. Governments generally take a dim view of unregulated internal strife, since it tends to undermine national unity and thus diminish a nation's strength in the international arena. Further, as E. E. Schattschneider observes, private conflicts may be taken into the public arena precisely because someone wants to make certain that the power ratio among the private interests most immediately involved will not prevail. For instance, a vulnerable corporation confronted by a well-organized, powerful labor union may have a strong interest in securing governmental intervention (Schattschneider, 1960: 23).

Cooperative Bonds

Individuals or groups may impose self-contained limits on conflict lest it imperil other rewarding aspects of the relationship. Thus many husbands and wives "pull their punches" in a marital disagreement because they recognize that they wish to continue living together. They do not want to jeopardize the broader companionship or the sexual, security, and affectional aspects of the marriage. Similarly, nation-states may "take it easy" in disputes with allies in order to preserve the overriding interests of the alliance.

Salience of Costs

Individuals or groups often minimize or contain conflict because they feel that the expenditure of greater resources or energy "just isn't worth it." In other words, as they appraise the situation, the costs of conflict outweigh the gains to be derived from it (Brockner, Shaw, and Rubin, 1979).

Coalitions

Joint undertakings stand a better chance when they benefit both sides.

—Euripides, *Iphigenia in Tauris,* 414 B.C.

Conflicts are not always restricted to two parties. At times three or more parties have an interest in a competitive outcome. By forming an alliance with one or more others, people can combine their resources in order to advance their own individual interests. However, as sociologists have long recognized, situations involving three or more persons are quite different from those involving two people (Simmel, 1902). The difference is a qualitative one that is not as simple as the difference between two and three (Luce and Raiffa, 1957). This fact derives from the possibility of alternative coalition arrangements. A **coalition** consists of two or more parties who coordinate their efforts in order to achieve their ends against the opposition of one or more competing parties. By joining their efforts, a number of parties can determine the allocation of rewards within a group or force their will upon other group members. Coalition formation occurs at all levels of social interaction—among family members, politicians, special interest groups, ethnic groups, cartel participants, nations, and blocks of nations (Komorita and Tumonis, 1980).

Interest in coalitions stems from their importance in family relationships, business transactions, domestic politics, and international relations. The resources that parties may pool include status, expertise, special abilities, votes, money, natural resources, weapons, and troops. Social psychologists are concerned with three central issues: (1) which coalitions will form, (2) how the parties will apportion the resources or payoffs of the coalition among themselves, and (3) how bargaining proceeds from the initiation of negotiations to their conclusion (Rapoport and Kahan, 1976).

Social psychologists commonly study coalition behavior by confronting two or more individuals with a game situation in which the players must try to maximize their share of the rewards. A number of studies have employed Parcheesi, a popular board game found at most toy stores. In such games, no single player enjoys dictatorial or veto power and no single alternative will maximize the payoff to all participants. Researchers focus on the processes by which potential coalition partners offer various divisions of the winnings to form a successful coalition.

In some coalition studies, the players are assigned unequal resource units at the beginning of the game. For instance, 16 resource units may be distributed among four players as follows: A has 7 units, B has 5 units, C has 3 units, and D has 1 unit. The quota needed to win the game is 9 units. The general form for symbolizing this type of arrangement is Q:A-B-C-D. Q refers to the quota necessary to win; A, B, C, and D designate the resources held by the four members, with A being the strongest, B being the second strongest, and so on. Substituting resource units for the symbols, we arrive at 9:7-5-3-1. Thus individuals A and C (7 and 3 units respectively) can form a coalition to win the game; so can individuals B, C, and D (5, 3, and 1 units respectively).

Researchers find that the resolution of the social psychological issues involved in coalition behavior depends on the number of players, their personalities and resources, their previous experience in bargaining, the rules governing communication among the players, and the information initially made available to the players (Miller, 1980*a,b,c*; Kravitz, 1981; Komorita, Hamilton, and Kravitz, 1984). It is not surprising, therefore, that coalition research can become quite

THE PRISONER'S DILEMMA GAME

One way social psychologists study competition and cooperation within a laboratory setting is by employing the *Prisoner's Dilemma Game*. In this game, subjects confront the following type of predicament:

Two suspects are taken into custody and separated. The District Attorney is certain that they are guilty of a specified crime, but he does not have adequate evidence to convict them at a trial. He points out to each prisoner that he has two alternatives: to confess to the crime the police are sure they have done, or not to confess. If they both do not confess, then the D.A. states he will book them on some very minor trumped-up charge such as petty larceny and illegal possession of a weapon, and they would both receive minor punishments; if they both confess, they will be prosecuted, but he will recommend less than the most severe sentence; but if one confesses and the other does not, then the former will receive lenient treatment for turning state's evidence, whereas the latter will get "the book" slapped at him. (Luce and Raiffa, 1957: 95)

The Prisoner's Dilemma Game provides a mixed-motive situation in which subjects must choose between cooperation and competition. Consider the situation in which the dilemma places you, using Figure 11.1 as your point of reference. If you both remain quiet—"stonewall" it—you and your co-conspirator will receive two years in prison. If only you confess, you will receive a four-month prison term and your partner will receive a ten-year sentence. If your partner confesses and you hold out, you will receive the ten-year term. If both of you confess, each of you will receive a seven-year sentence.

From the standpoint of the game, the "don't confess" choice is the cooperative one (viewed from the perspective of the co-conspirators and not that of the prosecutor). In taking this route, you demonstrate that you trust your partner not to take advantage of the situation by turning state's evidence. But you also run the risk that your partner will confess and you will pay dearly. The "confess" choice is the competitive one, since you are attempting to improve your circumstances by betraying your partner. But again, you must run the risk that your partner will also confess, ensuring that you both will receive stiff sentences. In sum, what is the best choice for each person considered individually results in a particularly punishing outcome if chosen by both.

Experimenters can adapt the game to various situations by replacing the numbers representing months and years in prison with other numbers. Additionally, the game can be modified so that subjects play for money or points rather than prison sentences. Subjects may play one game or several hundred games (trials) under varied reward structures. In most cases, unknown to the subjects, the game is played not against another subject but against a nonexistent person whose responses are supplied by the experimenter.

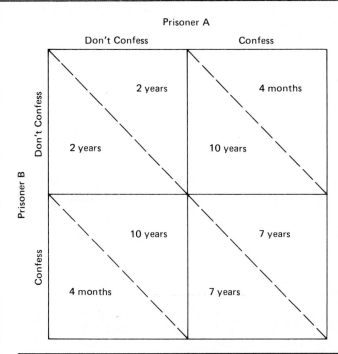

Prisoner A

Don't Confess   Confess

Prisoner B

Don't Confess

2 years

4 months

2 years

10 years

Confess

10 years

7 years

4 months

7 years

FIGURE 11.1 The Prisoner's Dilemma Game
Each of the numbers in the matrix represents the number of months or years each person would spend in prison.

Personality characteristics influence individuals' typical responses to the game. Some people are inclined to compete, others to cooperate, and still others vacillate between approaches (Bennett and Carbonari, 1976). Additionally, subjects who describe their intentions as competitive at the outset of a gaming study commonly believe that others are competitively inclined as well. Those who attribute cooperative tendencies to themselves similarly expect others to be in their "motivational neighborhood" (Kuhlman and Wimberley, 1976).

Cooperation is facilitated where the players can communicate with each other, thereby establishing mutual trust and coordinating their strategies (Wichman,

1972). The strategy pursued by one's opponent also influences one's own strategy. Where an opponent is consistently (and even foolishly) cooperative, subjects respond in a competitive and exploitative manner. Should the opponent reciprocate a cooperative move while remaining ready to compete if cooperation is in turn not reciprocated, subjects respond with a high degree of cooperation. And as might perhaps be expected, competition breeds competition.

Real life provides a large number of dilemmas like those posed in the prisoner's game. For instance, it is in each individual's self-interest to exploit the environ-

Box continues on next page

ment, pollute, and in some countries over-populate, whereas the net outcome is worse for everyone than if each person exercised restraint (Dawes, McTavish, and Shaklee, 1977). Roger Brown (1965) has also noted that the game resembles escape panics and crazes. And some have used it as a model for labor-management bargaining (Nemeth, 1972).

Political scientist Robert Axelrod (1984) finds that the simplest and most effective strategy for playing the Prisoner's Dilemma Game is one he terms *tit for tat.* The strategy consists of starting with cooperation as the first move, and then doing whatever one's partner does on the previous move. Tit for tat appears to be successful because it combines four crucial properties of a winning strategy: It is nice, retaliatory, forgiving, and clear. It is nice because it avoids unnecessary conflict so long as the other side reciprocates. It is retaliatory because it responds to provocation. Should the other player make an unjustified competitive move, immediate retaliation is called for. Delay runs the risk of sending the wrong signal that competition can pay. The strategy is forgiving in allowing the other party to back off following retaliation. Thus if the other party resumes cooperation after having retaliated, forgiveness and a return to cooperation become the order of the day. Finally, tit for tat is clear and predictable. Clarity is critical to enable the other party to adapt its pattern of action, thereby fostering long-term cooperation. Axelrod believes the tit for tat strategy has applications extending from marital relationships to American-Soviet relationships.

However, in some respects real-life situations often differ from the Prisoner's Dilemma Game. Commonly, the parties communicate with each other (although they may attempt to bluff and deceive each other). Further, the parties seldom enjoy equal power, and hence one party can bring more resources to bear to gain a favorable outcome. Moreover, the actual risks are seldom limited to those contained within the game setting but reach out to encompass other phases of one's life (Brickman, Becker, and Castle, 1979). And finally, group norms and expectations serve to facilitate or inhibit particular types of responses (Bonacich, 1976).

---

complex and that the findings should vary greatly depending on experimental conditions. A consideration of these matters would lead us far afield. Consequently, the discussion that follows is limited to a brief consideration of four theories of coalition formation.

The *minimal resource theory* says that people try to maximize their gains. In so doing, they import into the coalition situation the norm of equity, which prescribes that individuals should divide rewards in proportion to the resources they have contributed (see Chapter 10). The theory predicts that the most likely coalition is the one that minimizes each person's contribution (is the cheapest available) (Gamson, 1961, 1964).

The *pivotal power theory,* like the minimal resource theory, assumes that people seek to get the largest possible share of the reward. The theory says, however, that people expect the payoff to be divided in proportion to their pivotal power, not in proportion to their resources. Pivotal power is determined by examining those potential winning coalitions of which a person is a member and deciding which of these arrangements would no longer win were this person to withdraw from membership. An individual's bargaining position derives from the number of potential winning alliances he or she can cause to fail by withdrawing from a coalition. The theory predicts that the coalition that will form will be the one that minimizes the coalition's total pivotal power (Shapley and Shubik, 1954).

The *bargaining theory of coalition formation* places heavy emphasis on the negotiation process. Like the other two theories, it assumes that people try to maximize their payoffs. Each potential coalition member is said to have a maximum expected outcome, a minimum expected outcome, and a most probable expected outcome. For a person with below-average resources, the maximum outcome is equality (rewards divided equally), the minimum outcome is equity (rewards divided in proportion to resources), and the most probable outcome is halfway between equality and equity. For a person with above-average resources, the maximum outcome is equity, the minimum outcome is equality, and the most probable outcome is halfway between equity and equality. At the outset of coalition bargaining, a person with below-average resources is likely to advocate equality, while a member with above-average resources is likely to advocate equity. The typical negotiated agreement is assumed to be midway between equity and equality. The theory predicts that the most likely coalition is one that minimizes each person's temptation to defect from the coalition (Komorita and Chertkoff, 1973; Komorita and Moore, 1976; Michener, Fleishman, and Vaske, 1976; Chertkoff and Esser, 1977; Komorita and Kravitz, 1981; Urruti and Miller, 1984).

Weighted probability theory also assumes that people are expected to maximize reward (Kravitz and Iwaniszek, 1984). The theory goes on to say that the problem of communicating offers and counteroffers among individuals becomes more difficult in larger coalitions. Consequently, as the size of a potential coalition increases, the problem of achieving unanimous agreement among the coalition members increases, and the number of potential defectors from the coalition also increases. This means that a large coalition is not only more difficult to form but is also more difficult to maintain. The theory predicts that the most likely coalition is the one that is the smallest (Komorita, 1974; Komorita and Meek, 1978).

SUMMARY

1. Konrad Lorenz views aggression as an instinctive mechanism evolved to promote the survival of a species. Critics call this theory excessively simplistic and argue that it overlooks the continuous give-and-take interaction between heredity and environment.

2. The original version of the frustration-aggression hypothesis postulated that frustration produces aggression, and aggression never occurs without prior frustration. The hypothesis was soon amended to say that frustration may produce other kinds of behavior besides aggression.

3. According to frustration-aggression theorists, aggression remains a motivating force until it is discharged in aggressive behavior. Aggression may find expression in displacement or catharsis.

4. The work of Leonard Berkowitz suggests that people having characteristics that the angry individual has previously learned to dislike are especially apt to be objects of an angry person's aggression.

5. The perception of the opponent's intent is more important in arousing aggression than a physical attack itself.

6. One factor that makes individuals susceptible to aggressive and violent behavior in crowd settings is deindividuation. Anonymity contributes to deindividuation by producing an overall disinhibiting effect for behavior that is otherwise socially disapproved. Reduced self-consciousness and lowered concern for social evaluation also contribute to the deindividuation process.

7. Aggressive behavior often arises out of situational factors in an institutional environment. People commit aggressive and even violent acts as part of doing their jobs; this is called institutional aggression.

8. Until relatively recently, the prevailing view among social scientists was that exposure to pornography does not contribute to sexual crime. However, more recent research has shown that erotic material can influence aggressive behavior in a variety of ways. For instance, research reveals that men typically become more aggressive toward women after viewing sexual violence. Indeed, even relatively nonviolent pornography may increase aggressive behavior.

9. Rape myths abound among the American population, and they form a part of a larger and interrelated attitude structure that includes acceptance of traditional sex-role stereotyping, interpersonal violence, and the view that sexual relationships are adversary relationships. The threat of rape affects women whether or not they are actually victimized. It limits their freedom, keeps them off the streets at night, and often serves to imprison them at home. Rape victims usually suffer injury and emotional trauma as a result of the assault.

10. In conflict, people find themselves at odds; they feel separated by incompatible objectives. They may perceive themselves as involved in a struggle over scarce resources or social values.

11. Three different models of the conflict process are the aggressor-defender model, the conflict-spiral model, and the structural-change model.

12. The intensity of conflict is influenced by common allegiances and memberships, crosscutting identifications, third parties who function as referees, cooperative bonds, and the salience of costs.

13. Conflicts are not always restricted to two parties. At times, three or more individuals have an interest in a competitive outcome. By forming an alliance with one or more others, people can combine their resources in order to advance their own individual interests. However, as sociologists have long recognized, situations involving three or more persons are quite different from those involving two people. The difference is a qualitative one that derives from the possibility of alternative coalition arrangements.

GLOSSARY

Aggression □ Behavior that is socially defined as injurious or destructive. Instrumental aggression, which has as its aim the realization of goals other than the victim's suffering, is distinguished from hostile aggression, which has as its aim the deliberate infliction of suffering or injury on another.

Catharsis □ A purging of aggressive energy through discharging it in aggressive behavior.

Coalition □ Two or more parties who coordinate their efforts in order to achieve their ends against the opposition of one or more competing parties.

Conflict □ A form of interaction in which people (individually or in groups) perceive themselves as being involved in a struggle over scarce resources or social values.

Deindividuation □ A psychological state of diminished identity and self-awareness.

Displacement □ The detachment of an aggressive impulse from the frustrating source and the discharge of that aggression on another person, group, or object.

Frustration □ Interference with or blocking of the attainment of some goal.

Frustration-aggression hypothesis □ The theory that frustration produces aggression.

Institutional aggression □ Aggression within institutional contexts, when people commit aggressive and violent acts as part of "doing their job."

Intensity of conflict □ The degree to which the parties in a conflict are committed to expending resources and energy in the effort to defeat or neutralize their opponents.

Status □ An expansive feeling of being somebody special and valuable, so that a person's self-image is positively illuminated.

Value □ An ethical principle to which people feel a strong emotional commitment and which they employ in judging behavior.

THE PHYSICAL ENVIRONMENT AND INTERPERSONAL BEHAVIOR

TERRITORIALITY
  The Social Roots of Territoriality
  Expressions of Territoriality
  Crowding
HOW PEOPLE HANDLE SPACE
  The Interpersonal Dynamics of
    Space

Territorial Violation
Reactions to Invasion
Territorial Defense
The Language of Space

As human beings, we behave in physical settings. The point is an obvious one. What is not so obvious are the ways in which the nature, organization, and meaning of various physical settings influence our behavior and experience. Consider the behavioral consequences produced by such natural conditions as terrain, climate, and vegetation, and such human-built aspects as streets, study halls, hospital wards, schoolrooms, bedrooms, elevators, subway trains, apartment houses, and shopping centers. "Spaces and places" affect our sense of self-esteem, infant-care practices, the lovemaking of newlyweds, the mutual hostility of ethnic groups, the anxiety or tranquillity of the shut-in, the productivity of workers, the consumption of alcoholic beverages, illness, accident rates, life expectancies, and the study of behavior (Proshansky, 1976; Altman, 1978).

368

TERRITORIALITY

The dog is a lion in his own house.

—Persian proverb

The human being is a territorial animal:

- □ By the second or third class period, most college students come to occupy the same seat in a lecture hall. They feel irritated when someone else takes "their seat."
- □ Dad is distressed and uncomfortable if a visitor sits in "his" chair.
- □ Mom gets annoyed when a visitor comes to stay and takes over "her" kitchen. Dad is teed off when someone "messes" with "his" tool table.
- □ We have our favorite seat on the bus, our favorite bench on campus, our favorite spot on the beach, our favorite chair in the lounge, our favorite fishing place on the pier, and our favorite table in the park.
- □ In monasteries and convents, monks and nuns come to feel possessive about their individual cells.
- □ In communes stressing ideals of equality and sharing, individuals commonly have a sense of ownership about a room, bed, chair, or table—one that is "theirs" by virtue of consistent use.
- □ The family has its home, the juvenile gang its "turf," the ethnic group its neighborhood, the state its national territory. Indeed, virtually every piece of the earth's surface is divided up among people so that, at least in theory, there are no blank land spaces on the map.

Territoriality involves behavior in which individuals or groups maintain, mark, and defend areas against intrusion by members of *their own* species. It has long been recognized that birds and many animals have a strong sense of territory. But the matter of territory among human beings, like the topic of sex, has only recently been subjected to scientific scrutiny (Hall, 1966). Indeed, a good many resemblances exist between hedges, fences, and flower beds in human communities and territorial boundaries in the animal kingdom (Hediger, 1950).

One facet of territoriality is, in Robert Ardrey's (1961) words, that the "home team always wins." On its own territory an animal will fight with greater vigor—indeed, a male on its home territory is almost invincible against other males of the species (Tinbergen, 1939; Lorenz, 1966). Among captive animals—fish, lizards, mice, chickens, and monkeys—a *home-cage effect* operates: The "owner" of the cage, even if it has been there only a short period, is usually victorious over a newcomer (Braddock, 1949; Leary and Moroney, 1962; Sommer, 1966). In general, the winner of a fight is likely to be the animal that is on its home territory rather than the animal that is bigger and stronger.

Evidence also suggests that a home-cage effect operates among human beings. Count Leo Tolstoy (1869/1957) portrayed territorial dominance as contributing to the outcome of epic human battles, including the retreat from Moscow of the French forces under Napoleon. Coaches are well aware of the "home" court, park, and field advantage in professional and college sports: In professional baseball, the home team wins about 53 percent of the time, compared with 58 percent in professional football, 60 percent in college football, 64 percent in professional hockey, and 67 percent in professional basketball (Schwartz and Barsky, 1977). A ten-year survey of the performance of basketball teams in the Atlantic Coast Conference found that on the average the teams won 65.8 percent of their games at home while winning only 34.2 percent of their games on the road. Crowd hostility to visiting teams causes them to perform below their normal level of play, while crowd support gives a lift to the home team (Varca, 1980; Greer, 1983). (However, as we saw in Chapter 5, when a title is on the line, exuberant home crowds can lead home-team players to "choke.") Likewise, children often display the home-cage effect in play and at school. Police interrogation is based on the same principle: Never question suspects on their home ground but on the detective's home ground—the police station (Inbau and Reid, 1962). And research by Julian J. Edney (1975) reveals that residents of dormitory rooms allow themselves to be controlled by others less than visitors to these same rooms do. Moreover, visitors see residents as more relaxed, secure, impulsive, warm, and uninhibited than residents see visitors. In fact, a resident exerts influence over visitors even if they outnumber the resident and even if the resident is not a particularly dominant person (Taylor and Lanni, 1981). There may be profound truth in the saying that one's home is one's castle, since on home territory we enjoy a special sovereignty that we may not possess elsewhere.

The Social Roots of Territoriality

As discussed in the previous chapter, clashing interests and social values underlie much human conflict. But aggression, given full rein and allowed to run its full course in a constant war of all against all, would jeopardize the survival of the species. Therefore aggression must be regulated. This can be accomplished in many ways, two of which entail territoriality and hierarchy. In territoriality, people establish monopoly rights over resources in an area and impose a given set of social values within the area. In the development of a hierarchy, people create an order of precedence in the distribution of good things (and thus an order of social inequality), and high-ranking people in the social order impose their own value standards.

Territoriality serves to limit aggression to the extent that individuals or groups refrain from going where they are likely to be involved in disputes (see the boxed insert on the ordering of slum life, pp. 372–373). A hierarchy serves to limit aggression because, on the basis of their knowledge of who is above and below them in rank, individuals or groups engage in ritualized dominance-subordination behavior rather than actual combat (Sommer, 1969). We find many illustrations of territory and hierarchy in the animal kingdom. Male house mice, for instance, typically remain territorially isolated and chase away other mice that happen into their area. But as population density increases among mice, the number of areas defended decreases, until eventually none can be defended successfully. Rather than defending any individual areas, the mice group together and develop a social hierarchy (Davis, 1958). Hence crowded confinement among mice tends to eradicate territorial boundaries and to produce social rank behavior.

These observations led David E. Davis (1958, 1959) to advance the hypothesis that territoriality and hierarchy are two poles of a continuum of behavior that is dependent on population density. Thus situations range from those that are exclusively territorial at one extreme to those that are exclusively hierarchical at the other. Mockingbirds, for instance, are territorial for practically the entire year and apparently never form a social rank. In contrast, sage grouse are always ranked and never defend a territory. Other species such as cardinals, gulls, and starlings fall at various points on this continuum (Davis, 1959). Among primate species as well, there tends to be an inverse relationship between territoriality and hierarchy. (Gibbons, for example, are primarily territorial; baboons are principally hierarchical.) But just how closely we can draw parallels between animal and human territoriality is still an open question (Edney, 1975). Certainly we cannot assume that territoriality among human beings necessarily has an instinctual basis (Fischer, 1975; Mazur, 1973, 1975; van den Berghe, 1975; Dyson-Hudson and Smith, 1978).

What is unique about human beings is that they are *both* highly territorial and hierarchical. So long as boundaries and hierarchies go unchallenged, aggression is inhibited. But a once-and-for-all solution does not exist to the problem of distributing scarce resources among the members of a society, nor is there an ultimate answer to the problem of determining whose social values shall prevail. Social order, although it is a negotiated process, is in the last analysis a function of power. Power determines which individual or group will translate its preferences into the reality of human life.

Since power is a matter of social interaction, a given social order is not fixed for all time; ongoing negotiation and renegotiation are required. The boundaries and hierarchy imposed by the advantaged are not suffered gladly by the disadvantaged. Hence the disadvantaged subject the inequitable order imposed by an elite to continual challenges—sometimes frontal, sometimes subtle—through passive resistance. As a result, territory and hierarchy not only help to control aggression but also breed counteraggression:

> The fundamental contradiction in territoriality and hierarchy is that, while they appear to regulate aggression, and, therefore, to provide a solution to it, they also contain within them a dialectic of conflict: territorial rights and hierarchical privileges are both aggressively defended and challenged. (van den Berghe, 1974: 787)

Territory is one means by which elites appropriate privilege: Not only are their homes and offices located in the most desirable places, but their command of territory—mines, factories, and plantations—makes them gatekeepers in the distribution of good things. In American society, for example, blacks, women, institutional inmates, and young people are especially deprived. Additionally, territory is an instrument for achieving control over a subject people. The disadvantaged can be relegated to "reservations"—blacks to ghettos; women to kitchens; "deviants" to prisons and mental institutions; and young people to campuses, where a growing army of young adults is diverted, managed, and kept

TERRITORIALITY IN THE ORDERING OF SLUM LIFE

Middle-class Americans commonly view city slums as grim islands of pathology. From the suburban perspective, morality in the slums seems to have been stood on its head. Slum people appear to be drowning in a swamp of "urban ills" largely of their own making: high delinquency and crime rates, unwed mothers, high unemployment, urban blight, and juvenile gangs. But viewed from the inside, life in slum neighborhoods is often rich, orderly, disciplined, and composed mostly of conventional people.

Territorial groups are an important element of social organization in slum neighborhoods. The Addams area on Chicago's "Near West Side" provides a good illustration. The area is less than half a square mile in size, but it contains some 20,000 residents and four ethnic neighborhoods: Italian, black, Puerto Rican, and Mexican. The Italians form the largest group, although they are slowly being displaced by the other groups. In its heyday, the area was the stronghold of Al Capone and

Frank Nitti, and it served as the kindergarten for several figures still active in the underworld.

Addams-area residents make four basic distinctions among themselves: age, sex, ethnicity, and territoriality. Each street-corner group, for example, contains about twelve to fifteen *men—young* men. It is limited largely to members of one *ethnic* group. And it has a highly *localized* membership (a fact reflected in group names, which usually include a reference to the street where they "hang"). These groups function to ease the problem of urban anonymity for their members.

Residents know the boundaries of each ethnic section of the Addams area. They all share a kind of mental map that specifies the associations that are and are not to be pursued in each neighborhood:

The boundaries of the neighborhood itself form the outermost perimeter for restricting social relations. Almost all the residents caution their wives,

off the streets without threatening the jobs of the working population (Bird, 1975). Hence subject peoples, besides forfeiting the full fruits of territory, are controlled by means of territory.

It would be incorrect, however, to assume that aggression and its management are the only roots of territoriality. It is also true that people are deeply attached to their homelands. Russians from the Great Steppes who were quartered in Swiss mountain resorts during World War II pined for flat country. Pygmy peoples from the primeval forests feel exposed and helpless in clearings. European settlers feel trapped and depressed in the gloom of the tropical rain forest. Saskatchewan prairie dwellers begin feeling uncomfortable as they enter the Canadian brush country. The exact mechanism for such preferences—whether they are a product of learning or imprinting, or both—is still unknown (Sommer, 1966).

daughters, children, and siblings against crossing Roosevelt, Halsted, Congress, and Ashland. Within each neighborhood, each ethnic section is an additional boundary which sharply restricts movement. Adults cross ethnic boundaries to shop or go to work, while children do so in running errands or attending school. Free time and recreation, however, should be spent within one's own ethnic section. (Suttles, 1968: 225–226)

In addition, each ethnic group is subdivided internally within relatively segregated age, sex, and residential groupings. On warm summer nights hardly a stoop, corner, alley, or doorway is not staked out by some regular group. It is a pattern, partitioned by age and sex, that fans out from the household. Nearest the house stoops are the women and the old people, followed in order by infants, young girls, young boys, and adult males. It is the young males who range most widely beyond this perimeter.

Age, sex, and ethnic groups, as they find territorial reflection, constitute the basic units of conflict and opposition. Trouble usually starts when peer groups of the same sex confront one another and gradually draw in other groups. However, conflict may occur at any level: between street-corner bands of the same ethnic group, between territorial units of the same ethnic group (such as Italians in the Addams area against Italians "over on Western"), between ethnic groups, and between Addams-area residents and non-Addams residents (such as the "people from Eighteenth Street").

In turn, various groups combine (street-corner group with street-corner group, ethnic group with ethnic group) at the threat of trouble. At times, disputes reach a high pitch: Street groups coalesce, adult men sit on their front steps with guns, and women retire inside. Usually, however, the friction fails to go beyond the "preparation stage." In sum, life in the Addams area—both cooperative and competitive—is fashioned largely in terms of territorial groupings.

Source: Adapted from Gerald D. Suttles, *The Social Order of the Slum* (Chicago: University of Chicago Press, 1968).

Territoriality has still other social roots. By exerting control over a particular segment of space, we experience a sense of freedom of choice within our environment (Proshanksy, Ittleson, and Rivlin, 1970). We feel that somehow we are the masters of our fate, at least within the bounds of our own little world. And we achieve a sense of identity, a feeling of being separate and distinct from others. Undoubtedly, social psychological study in the years ahead will come to identify additional sources of territoriality.

Expressions of Territoriality

In the United States, territoriality has a number of expressions. First there is **personal space**—the area we actively maintain around ourselves into which

Maintaining Personal Space
These individuals maintain their personal "spatial bubble" by alternating a vacant stool between them. Notice in each case how the men apportion the vacant stool among themselves—each laying claim to a part of the territorial space—through the positions of their knees and feet. (Patrick Reddy)

others cannot intrude without arousing our discomfort (Sommer, 1969; Hayduk, 1978). Personal space differs from other forms of territorial behavior in four ways: (1) Personal space is portable, going wherever we go; (2) the boundaries of territory are usually marked, whereas those of personal space are invisible; (3) personal space has our body at its center whereas territory does not; and (4) intrusion into personal space most usually leads to withdrawal, whereas territorial intrusion frequently leads to threats or fights (Hayduk, 1978).

Personal space has been likened to the shell of a snail and to an aura, halo, or "invisible bubble" that surrounds a person. It is not spherical, however. The distance that individuals seek to maintain between themselves and their fellows tends to be an irregularly shaped "balloon." People demand more space directly in front of their faces than at their backs, and less at their ankles than at their waists and heads (Goffman, 1971; Hayduk, 1978). Significantly, blind people require spaces virtually identical in size, shape, and permeability to those required by sighted persons (Hayduk and Mainprize, 1980).

Our sense of personal space becomes activated in a crowded setting, such as a packed elevator. But if crowding continues, we eventually give up the effort to maintain a defensive niche and experience intense discomfort, as indiscriminate packing violates our spatial bubble. Indeed, pickpockets strategically violate a victim's personal space—"pratt in a mark"—to get the victim to position his body in a way that makes his wallet accessible (Goffman, 1971). The size of this buffer zone tends to vary as a function of such factors as culture (Hall, 1966; Baxter, 1970), personality (Leipold, 1963; Williams, 1963), and age (Willis,

1966). Gender also plays a part (Baxter, 1970; Liebman, 1970; Hartnett, Bailey, and Gibson, 1970; Fisher and Byrne, 1975; Giesen and McClaren, 1976). Women have been found to have smaller zones of personal space and can seemingly tolerate closer interpersonal contacts than males. (Presumably, it is more culturally acceptable for women to display physical warmth, whereas same-sex contact has homosexual overtones for many men.)

Another form of territoriality finds expression in **situational territory**—a temporary tenancy of space while in use. Here the territory is in the public domain, but it "belongs" to one person and then another for short periods. Jurisdictional control arises from temporary use of the space for a specific purpose—as in libraries, cafeterias, parks, beaches, telephone booths, and public transportation (Becker, 1973).

In **fixed territory,** space is viewed as belonging to some individual or group even when it is not being used (Goffman, 1971; Becker, 1973). Invasion or violation of the space arouses active defense, either by the occupant or by a third party. Newcomers in old people's homes quickly discover that chairs are staked out by specific people; title to the chairs is supported by the behavior of both patients and staff (Lipman, 1968). In the case of formal property—yards, fields, houses, and buildings—the state commonly backs up the formal rights of ownership.

Public territory is an area where an individual has freedom of access but not necessarily freedom of action. While public territory is officially open to all, certain images and behaviors are expected; violations lead to the removal of "lawbreakers" by police, as in cases of public nudity, drunkenness, and rowdyism. It is important to note, however, that some categories of people may be granted only limited access to certain public territories: Children are not allowed in playgrounds after midnight, and blacks may be stopped by police if they are found strolling leisurely in white neighborhoods (Lyman and Scott, 1967).

Crowding

Popular belief has it that crowding is bad for people. It is said to breed violence, crime, family breakdown, mental illness, alcoholism, and suicide. The belief that high density produces pathology comes in part from studies of animal populations. These findings reveal that after population buildups, interaction intensifies, leading to progressively greater levels of stress (Evans, 1978). J. J. Christian (1963), in a classic study of the Sika deer population on James Island in Chesapeake Bay, advanced the thesis that as overcrowding increased, so did stress. Prolonged stress produced severe metabolic disturbance (an overactivity and enlargement of the adrenal glands). Metabolic disturbance when combined with shock (a winter cold spell) resulted in a sudden and massive die-off. John Calhoun (1962), in studies of the Norway rat, found that overcrowding led to the disintegration of family life, high infant mortality rates, small litters, inadequate nest building, abandonment of the young, cannibalism, and sadism—a situation Calhoun termed a "behavioral sink." Some question exists, however, as to whether these responses are primarily a function of the amount of space available per individual or a product of the size of the group (Freedman, 1979).

TABLE 12.1

The Twenty-five Most Densely Congested Cities in the United States*			The Twenty-five Least Congested Cities in the United States*		
	AREA (SQ. MI.)	PEOPLE PER SQUARE MILE		AREA (SQ. MI.)	PEOPLE PER SQUARE MILE
1. New York	302	23,453	1. Anchorage	1,732	100
2. Jersey City	13	16,934	2. Chesapeake, Va.	340	336
3. Paterson, N.J.	8	16,623	3. Oklahoma City	604	668
4. San Francisco	46	14,633	4. Jacksonville, Fla.	760	712
5. Newark	24	13,662	5. Lexington-Fayette, Ky.	285	717
6. Chicago	228	13,174	6. Columbus, Ga.	217	779
7. Philadelphia	136	12,413	7. Nashville-Davidson	479	950
8. Boston	47	11,928	8. Virginia Beach	256	1,026
9. Yonkers, N.Y.	18	10,675	9. Huntsville, Ala.	114	1,256
10. Washington, D.C.	63	10,170	10. Waco, Tex.	74	1,367
11. Miami	34	10,115	11. Chattanooga	124	1,370
12. Baltimore	80	9,798	12. Independence, Mo.	81	1,387
13. Berkeley, Calif.	11	9,480	13. Montgomery, Ala.	128	1,389
14. Elizabeth, N.J.	12	9,077	14. Kansas City, Mo.	316	1,417
15. Detroit	136	8,874	15. Bakersfield, Calif.	74	1,435
16. Bridgeport, Conn.	16	8,745	16. Kansas City, Kans.	107	1,500
17. Buffalo	42	8,561	17. Fort Worth	240	1,604
18. Providence	19	8,297	18. Beaumont, Tex.	73	1,618
19. Hartford	18	7,662	19. Mobile	123	1,630
20. Pittsburgh	55	7,652	20. Irving, Tex.	67	1,634
21. Hialeah, Fla.	19	7,487	21. Fremont, Calif.	78	1,683
22. Santa Ana, Calif.	27	7,435	22. Davenport, Iowa	59	1,736
23. St. Louis	61	7,379	23. El Paso	239	1,778
24. Cleveland	79	7,264	24. Amarillo	80	1,863
25. Long Beach, Calif.	50	7,256	25. Jackson, Miss.	106	1,910

* Among cities with 1980 population of 100,000 or more. Source: U.S. Department of Commerce.

But while population buildup has bad effects on deer, rats, and a variety of other creatures, it does not necessarily have a similar impact on human beings. Take the matter of crime. Although it may sound implausible, over the past few decades American urban population density *and* household crowding have sharply *declined,* while crime rates have soared. Since people are for the most part less crowded than they used to be, high density cannot be responsible for the nation's crime increase. Furthermore, crowded cities as diverse as Tokyo, London, Buffalo, and Providence have low crime rates in comparison with relatively uncrowded cities such as Los Angeles, Houston, and New Orleans (see Table 12.1). And in New York City, no relationship has been proved to exist between neighborhood crowding and the crime rate: When economic level is equated, population density is not associated with crime rate or any other kind of social, mental, or physical pathology. And although a number of investigators have recently attempted to link crowding to aggression, studies generally show that there is *no* significant independent association (Loo, 1972; Mitchell, 1971; Fischer, Baldassare, and Ofshe, 1974; Freedman, 1975; Sundstrom, 1978). Obviously, the source of social pathology must be sought elsewhere.

But these findings do not suggest that crowding has no impact on human behavior; it does. In studying its influence, social psychologists make a distinction between density and crowding (Stokols, 1972). **Density** is a physical con-

Crowding and Density
We often find ourselves in settings with a high density of people. Yet we define the situation as in keeping with our expectations and hence as tolerable. (Patrick Reddy)

dition of population that involves spatial limitations. **Crowding** is the perception people have of themselves as receiving excessive stimulation from social sources (Desor, 1972). This distinction draws attention to the social factors that influence people's *definitions of situations* and lead them to differing judgments of being crowded or uncrowded (Cohen, Sladen, and Bennett, 1975; Baron and Needel, 1980). (A related concept, privacy, is discussed in the boxed insert, pp, 378–379.)

J. A. Desor (1972) found that architectural design (of doors, windows, partitions, and dividers) that reduces interpersonal perception within a space—that provides more privacy—leads people to feel themselves "less crowded," even though the actual density remains constant. Likewise, researchers find that they can lessen the sense of crowding and stress experienced by residents living in long-corridor dormitories by modifying the hallways so as to cluster students in small groups of less than twenty members (Baum and Davis, 1980).

The finding that stress does not always accompany high density has led social psychologists in a quest for those factors that induce people to define their settings as crowded (Sundstrom, 1978; Worchel and Brown, 1984). Duration of exposure is one factor: Individuals often find it easier to tolerate a brief exposure to conditions of high density, such as a ride on a crowded elevator, than a prolonged exposure, such as a ride on a crowded cross-country bus. Another

PRIVACY

Central to the American political system is the doctrine of the separation of the public sphere (the state) from the private sphere (the citizen, the church, and so on). In recent years, the rapid expansion of information technology has eroded this traditional separation. The growth in information technology has been encouraged by the decreasing unit costs of computer data banks and the increasing demands of governments and businesses for information that will aid their decision making. The United States is rapidly becoming an information-based society, with personal information an important component of the data base. Today, the average person's name and aspects of his or her life appear in an estimated thirty-nine federal, state, and local government data banks plus an additional forty public- and private-sector files (tax agencies, state motor vehicle agencies, employers, schools, selective service, customer records, credit bureaus, and so on). On a typical day, every name passes from one computer to another five times (Galloway, 1984). A good many Americans are distrustful of these developments. They fear that public and private agencies will misuse the personal information in people's files and undermine individual autonomy and dignity (Margulis, 1977a; Garfield, 1985).

Privacy involves the claim of individuals or groups to determine for themselves when, how, and to what extent information about themselves is communicated to others (Westin, 1967: 7). When Maxine Wolfe and Robert S. Laufer (1974) asked a sample of children and adolescents what privacy meant to them, four predominant themes emerged: "controlling access to information," "being alone," "no one bothering me," and "controlling access to space." These same meanings have also been found among middle-management executives in an office setting (Margulis, 1977b). In sum, privacy represents people's attempt to control their transactions with others so as to enhance their autonomy and minimize their vulnerability.

Irwin Altman (1977) distinguishes privacy from social isolation and crowding. Privacy refers to selective control over access to the self. It is a boundary-control process whereby people at certain times make themselves open and accessible to others and at other times close themselves off from others. Social isolation describes a deviation from a desired level of interaction in the "too little" direction. Crowding is a deviation in the "too much" direction. Privacy is also to be distinguished from secrecy (Warren and Laslett, 1977). Privacy entails a socially recognized and legitimated right to carry on certain behaviors in private settings. The heterosexual family provides a good illustration of this. In contrast, secrecy does not involve any such socially recognized and legitimated right. Stigmatized or disadvantaged social groups who have little or no access to privacy employ secrecy to conceal their behavior. The behaviors that secrecy protects are commonly viewed by members of the larger society as illegitimate and as involving the interests of the excluded. The homosexual world provides a good example of this.

Altman (1975) points out that privacy performs three functions: (1) the management of social interaction, (2) the establishment of plans and strategies for interacting with others, and (3) the development and maintenance of self-identity. The first two functions are self-explanatory. But of the identity function, Altman observes:

> Privacy mechanisms define the limits and boundaries of the self. When the permeability of these boundaries is under the control of a person, a sense of individuality develops. But it is not the inclusion or exclusion of others that is vital to self-definition; it is the ability to regulate contact when desired. If I can control what is me and what is not me, if I can define what is me and not me, and if I can observe the limits and scope of my control, then I have taken major steps toward understanding and defining what I am. Thus, privacy mechanisms serve to help me define me. (Altman, 1975: 50)

First-year students in college dormitories typically evolve mechanisms to regulate their "openness" and "closedness" to others in their new and strange environment (Vinsel et al., 1980). Contact-seeking mechanisms include opening the door to one's room, phoning someone, visiting others' rooms, inviting people to one's room, and going to the dorm lounge. Avoidance mechanisms include shutting the door to one's room, finding a quiet place, and going for a walk alone. Students who remain at the university for more than a year are more adept at using privacy-regulating mechanisms than are dropouts. Since dormitory settings provide many opportunities for social contact, it may be necessary for students to develop effective avoidance techniques if they are to survive in such a setting.

Societies of the world differ in the extent to which they attempt to minimize or maximize privacy (Altman, 1977). For instance, certain groups in the Javanese culture have little physical privacy. Families live in unfenced bamboo homes, outsiders freely wander in and out, and people go from room to room without announcement. Nonetheless, the Javanese seek to regulate their social interaction with others and have evolved various mechanisms to achieve this end: Social contacts are restrained, people hide their emotional feelings, etiquette is elaborate, and people speak softly. In contrast with the Javanese, the Tuareg (a Moslem nomadic-pastoral people who live in Northern Africa) take great care to protect their physical privacy. The Tuareg wear a sleeveless under-robe and a flowing outer garment that reaches from the shoulder to the ankle. Men dress in a turban that covers the forehead and a veil that covers the face below the bridge of the nose. Men wear the veil even when eating and sleeping. They adjust and readjust the veil, however slightly, to reflect openness or closedness to others. Altman says that societies evolve mechanisms that permit various balances between openness and closedness, with different mechanisms and different levels of accessibility shifting over time and with circumstances.

factor is predictability: People find aversive conditions more stressful when they are unpredictable than when they are predictable. Still another factor has to do with people's current desire for social stimulation: There are times during which individuals welcome solitude and times during which they prefer intensive social interaction. And finally, people's reactions are influenced by whether the crowding occurs in a *primary* environment (personal settings such as one's home or apartment) or in a *secondary* environment (impersonal settings such as a shopping center, an airline terminal, and so on). Overloading or thwarting generally poses a greater threat to "psychological security" in the former than in the latter settings (Stokols, 1978).

Some but not all types of task performance are negatively affected by high densities (Paulus et al., 1976; Heller, Groff, and Solomon, 1977; Sundstrom, 1978). Density is most likely to produce stress when it involves conditions that disturb an individual's sense of control over interpersonal interactions (Edney, 1975; Sundstrom, 1975). Within situations of high room density, people at first experience discomfort; excessive eye contact and touching constitute inappropriate signs of intimacy. And people may be subjected to unwanted social interactions with others (Baum and Valins, 1977). But as people remain in the high-density setting, they resort to various coping behaviors that partly neutralize the effects of other people's intrusion. As a consequence, individuals usually come to feel increasingly comfortable in the setting. Where people find that their goals are blocked in high-density situations, however, their initial stress continues or even increases (Sundstrom, 1975; McCallum et al., 1979; Cox, Paulus, and McCain, 1984).

Further, studies conducted at Columbia University suggest that crowding intensifies the perceived characteristics of a situation (Freedman, 1975; Freedman and Perlick, 1979). If people are fearful and antagonistic, crowding increases their fear and antagonism; the same is true of excitement, stimulation, and friendliness. Crowding usually makes a doctor's waiting room and a subway car all the more unpleasant. In contrast, a football game and a party benefit from high density. And while a crowded New York subway car is a complete turn-off, a crowded San Francisco cable car, crammed with people hanging over the sides, is a "tourist attraction."

Although crowding has been shown to have only minor pathological effects when examined on the neighborhood level, some researchers find that overcrowding in the home is strongly associated with poor mental health, poor social relationships, and poor child care, and less strongly associated with poor physical health (Gove, Hughes, and Galle, 1979; Gove and Hughes, 1983). In contrast, others find that household congestion has little or no effect on family relations (Booth and Edwards, 1976; Baldassare, 1978; Edwards, Booth, and Edwards, 1982; Loftin and Ward, 1983). The evidence regarding the relationship between household density and physical illness is somewhat uncertain (Booth and Cowell, 1976). However, it has been reported that sailors on more crowded ships have more illnesses and that the same relationship holds between illness complaints and crowding in prisons (Dean, Pugh, and Gunderson, 1975; McCain, Cox, and Paulus, 1976). And increases in prison populations where facilities are not increased proportionately are associated with increased rates of death, suicide, disciplinary infraction, and psychiatric commitment (Cox, Paulus, and McCain, 1984).

One social psychological explanation for some of the adverse consequences of crowding is based on the notion of "overload" or "too much stimulation." We find that complicated or disorderly settings tax our attentional capacity and our ability to assimilate information. More thermal and olfactory cues are picked up when we are forced closer together physically, and our visual cues are accentuated. Such settings apparently produce greater stress than simple, orderly ones (Cohen, 1978; Evans, 1978; Schaeffer and Patterson, 1980). This renders the primary tasks of everyday living even more problematic. Simultaneously, excessive interpersonal proximity makes us feel that our personal space is being invaded (Karlin, Epstein, and Aiello, 1978). To complicate matters further, high density is generally associated with spatial constraint, so that it seems to us that our behavioral options and freedom for physical movement are reduced (Saegert, 1978; Schmidt and Keating, 1979). More broadly, density restricts our sense of personal control. This finds expression in the colloquialism "Don't crowd me" (Pennebaker et al., 1977; Rodin, Solomon, and Metcalf, 1978; Darley and Gilbert, 1985). Even so, people differ greatly in their experience of crowding. For instance, individuals who effectively screen sensory inputs—who construct a priority-based pattern of attention to information and disregard low-priority inputs—cope more successfully with a crowded environment than do nonscreeners (Baum et al., 1982).

HOW PEOPLE HANDLE SPACE

Space is not neutral. It has social meaning. Theodore H. White provides a good example in *The Making of the President, 1960,* when John F. Kennedy's nomination became a certainty. As Kennedy entered his "hideaway cottage" in which a number of Democratic party leaders had assembled, he moved to the corner where his brother Bobby and his brother-in-law Sargent Shriver were chatting.

> The others in the room surged forward on impulse to join him. Then they halted. A distance of perhaps 30 feet separated them from him, but it was impassable. [After a few minutes, Shriver crossed the separating space and invited the leaders over.] First Averell Harriman; then Dick Daley; then Mike DiSalle; then, one by one, Kennedy let them all congratulate him. Yet no one could pass the little open distance between him and them uninvited, because there was this thin separation about him, and the knowledge they were there not as his patrons but as his clients. They could come by invitation only, for this might be a President of the United States. (White, 1961: 171)

The Interpersonal Dynamics of Space

Many of the terms we use to refer to status are based on spatial analogies: "central figure," "dominant position," "head chair," "upper echelon," and "high

THE SOCIAL SIGNIFICANCE OF SPACE

Edward T. Hall (1966), an anthropologist, has contributed to our knowledge of how people formulate definitions of the situation in terms of spatial distance. On the basis of observations and interviews with middle-class Americans, Hall identifies four distances (each with its close and far phase):

INTIMATE DISTANCE

Close phase—actual contact. This is the distance for making love and showing warmth in friendships. Children clinging to a parent are using this phase.

Far phase—6 to 18 inches. Although heads, thighs, and pelvises are not easily brought into contact, people can readily clasp hands. They can also detect the heat and odor of another person's breath. Americans tend to experience considerable discomfort at this distance in the presence of strangers—as on a public conveyance—lest accidental bodily contact occur. Speaking tends to be very low or even in a whisper.

PERSONAL DISTANCE

Close phase—1½ to 2½ feet. At this distance, individuals can still hold or grasp hands. Wives and husbands often find it threatening if another woman or man moves into this zone with their partner, since it may signal that the person has designs on their spouse. Nonetheless, this is the comfortable distance at cocktail parties. Conversations are carried on in soft voices indoors and at moderate volume outside.

Far phase—2½ to 4 feet. Since we cannot comfortably touch one another at this distance, it lends a measure of privacy to an encounter; it keeps others at "arm's length." When we encounter people on the street we usually chat at this range. Voice level is moderate.

SOCIAL DISTANCE

Close phase—4 to 7 feet. At this distance Americans tend to shift their gaze back and forth from eye-to-eye or from eyes-to-mouth. We use it to transact our impersonal business—for example, between customers and clerks in stores, or householders and delivery personnel. A boss employs this distance to dominate a seated subordinate, such as a secretary or a receptionist. Speaking is at full voice.

Far phase—7 to 12 feet. We use this distance when we say to another, "Stand away so I can look at you." It is the range at which office desks hold visitors; it enables a boss to remain seated and look up at a subordinate without losing status. It requires continual eye contact, or else the other person is shut out and the conversation is terminated. Voices are notably louder and can usually be heard in an adjoining room if the door remains open.

PUBLIC DISTANCE

Close phase—12 to 25 feet. At this distance our words and sentences become more formal and carefully chosen. It is suited to a variety of gatherings, including small classroom settings involving a lecturer and students. Or in situations of possible danger, at this distance an alert person can take evasive or defensive action. Voices are loud but not necessarily at full volume.

Far phase—25 feet or more. This is the distance given to important public figures such as the President of the United States. Voices tend to be at full volume.

The Limits of Comfortable Conversation
Strangers align themselves at about five-foot intervals, the distance at which conversation is no longer comfortable. When possible, people observe this distance in seating themselves on a wall or bench and in spacing themselves while awaiting a bus. (Top: Don McCarthy; bottom: Patrick Reddy)

Spatial distance and status

I got off the bus today and saw an unusual sight. Walking down the sidewalk was COACH—the man who brought glory days to the university in football. It was the closest I had ever been to him and I was awed at the sight. There was a crowd from the bus on the sidewalk but as COACH came by we all moved aside to give him room on the sidewalk. I noticed that the distance we gave him was at least three times that which we give any other person. Here was one of the great ones: the image of football and the "god" of victory. We show recognition of a person's special status through what Erving Goffman calls "avoidance rituals." Since close association would violate the aura of respect, awe, and dignity associated with high status, we of lesser rank are required to maintain distance from the "great one." He would become "soiled" through too close contact with us.

status" (Sommer, 1967; Schwartz, Tesser, and Powell, 1982). This is not surprising; territory and privilege usually go hand in hand. The "big boss" can walk into a subordinate's office unannounced, but the subordinate must wait outside the boss's office for an invitation. If the boss is on the phone, the subordinate may unobtrusively peek into the room, see that the boss is busy, and tiptoe off. But if a subordinate is on the phone, the boss enters and asserts his or her status by standing *above* the subordinate until the subordinate murmurs, "Let me call you back later." In office buildings, firms frequently reserve the highest floor for their top-ranking personnel. On any given floor, the highest-ranking employees receive the corner offices, the next in rank have offices with windows, the lesser-ranked occupy partitioned cubicles with no windows, and the lowest in rank sit at desks in an open room (Fast, 1970).

The relationship between status and territory is reflected in other interpersonal contexts. In barracks-style prison dormitories, dominant inmates possess the most desirable bunks and locations: single rather than double-decked bunks, bunks in the least congested areas, and bunks with the best view of the television set (Austin and Bates, 1974). Eric Sundstrom and Irwin Altman (1974) found similar patterns among youths in a juvenile detention center. Studies of small groups reveal that leaders gravitate to the head position at a rectangular table, while other people arrange themselves so that they can see the leader (Sommer, 1961). Studies of juries show that the person seated at the head of the table in the jury room is very likely to be elected foreman, that jurors from managerial and professional classes select the head chair more often than do lower-status individuals, and that individuals seated at the head position participate more in the deliberations (Strodtbeck and Hook, 1961). And studies of college classrooms reveal that dominant ethnic- and racial-group members occupy the seating area near the front and center of the room more often than minority-group members, who more often occupy the spatial peripheries of the room (Haber, 1982).

Dynamics of Space
Notice the distribution of the students in the library reading room, in particular the mechanisms by which each student lays claim to a given territory. (Patrick Reddy)

Territorial arrangements reflect still other aspects of a relationship. Robert Sommer (1969) found that college students, in seating themselves at tables, overwhelmingly choose a corner-to-corner or face-to-face arrangement for casual conversation (see Figure 12.1). The students give as their reasons both the convenience of physical proximity and the advantage of seeing one another clearly. They select a side-by-side arrangement for cooperative activity, explaining that it is easier to share things in this manner. Competing pairs, however, generally prefer face-to-face seating, although some employ a distant seating pattern. Various distant or catty-cornered arrangements are selected by students who are working separately at the same table (co-acting pairs). As Figure 12.2 shows, somewhat similar arrangements are selected at a round table. A nonfacing L-shaped arrangement decreases involvement and increases discomfort in small-group discussions (Patterson et al., 1979). In standing relationships, people who like each other stand closer together than those who do not—a linkage between a psychological state and spatial behavior (Mehrabian and Diamond, 1971; Aiello and Cooper, 1972; Storms and Thomas, 1977).

Territorial Violation

We generally view territory as the possession of a given individual or group. As such, it is subject to violation by both invasion and contamination. **Invasion** involves entry into a party's territory against that party's wishes. The invader may simply cross the territory with no intent to occupy it, or may make temporary use of the territory, as children do who play football across one's front

Percentage of Subjects Choosing This Arrangement

Seating Arrangement	Condition 1 (Conversing)	Condition 2 (Cooperating)	Condition 3 (Co–acting) *separate*	Condition 4 (Competing)
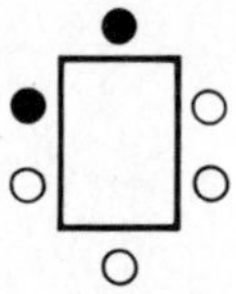	42	19	3	7
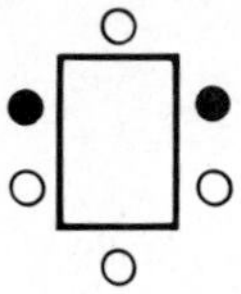	46	25	32	41
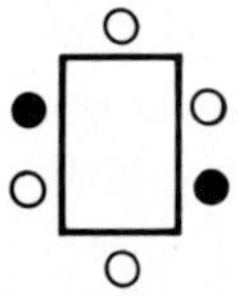	1	5	43	20
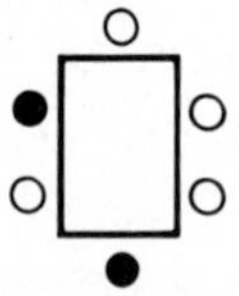	0	0	3	5
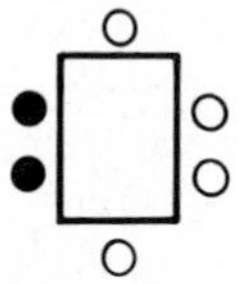	11	51	7	8
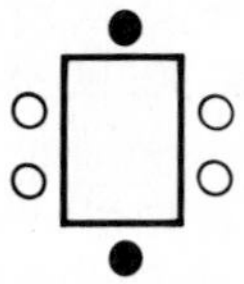	0	0	13	18
Total	100	100	100	99

FIGURE 12.1 Seating Preferences at Rectangular Tables
People tend to choose a corner-to-corner or face-to-face arrangement for conversation, a side-by-side arrangement for cooperating on a task, distant or catty-cornered patterns for co-acting (working separately), and either a face-to-face or a distant arrangement when they are competing.
(SOURCE: From the book *Personal Space: The Behavioral Basis of Design,* by Robert Sommer.
© 1969 by Prentice-Hall, Inc. Published by Prentice-Hall, Inc., Englewood Cliffs, NJ 07632.)

Seating Arrangement	Percentage of Subjects Choosing This Arrangement			
	Condition 1 (Conversing)	Condition 2 (Cooperating)	Condition 3 (Co-acting)	Condition 4 (Competing)
⬭	63	83	13	12
⬭	17	7	36	25
⬭	20	10	51	63
Total	100	100	100	100

FIGURE 12.2 Seating Preferences at Round Tables
People's seating patterns at round tables are similar to those at rectangular tables. Most subjects sit side by side for conversing or cooperating and face to face for co-acting or competing.
(SOURCE: From the book *Personal Space: The Behavioral Basis of Design,* by Robert Sommer. © 1969 by Prentice-Hall, Inc. Published by Prentice-Hall, Inc., Englewood Cliffs, NJ 07632.)

yard. But at times an invader undertakes to make continual use of the territory, as squatters do who settle on land without title or payment. Some territories are invaded simply by the fact of unwarranted entry; this is true of sacred sanctuaries, nunneries, locker rooms, and bathrooms that are for the use of a particular category of people (Goffman, 1971; Lyman and Scott, 1967).

Contamination entails the defilement of one party's territory or property by another. The pollution may be viewed as having primarily a physical origin:

☐ *Bodily excreta*—spittle, mucus, perspiration, blood, semen, vomit, urine, fecal matter, or pus.
☐ *Odor*—flatus, tainted breath, or body smells.

ARCHITECTURE AND PUBLIC SPACES

Architects and planners are drawing on the findings of the social sciences to make the urban landscape a more pleasant place for people (C. Levine, 1984). They are directing increasing attention to the linkage between design and human needs. Central to the problem of designing public spaces is the matter of what people find desirable, useful, and comfortable. A large number of factors—biological, social, cultural, and emotional—influence how we respond to a place. Structures that stimulate all our senses are more likely to evoke a sense of well-being than those that depend on only one sense. For instance, medieval cathedrals, with the color of stained glass, the scent of burning incense, and the tactile warmth of wooden pews, provide a fuller emotional experience than do modern skyscrapers that depend primarily on their visual impact.

Although it is not practical to remake whole cities, it is possible to revamp parts of cities, such as residential neighborhoods, shopping areas, buildings, and plazas. At times very simple remedies are effective. For example, researchers wondered why some public spaces in New York City are frequented by people while others are avoided. They found that the availability of sitting places makes a big difference. Too often architects had overlooked the fact that people tend to congregate where they can sit. Additionally, the places should be comfortable: benches with backrests and chairs with well-contoured seats.

In trying to explain why some public areas attract people and others repel them, social scientists have found that the elegance and purity of the design seem to matter very little. The shape of the space likewise appears to be unimportant. And the amount of space is not particularly critical, since in some instances the more space that is available, the less people use it. Although people claim that they wish to avoid crowds, their actions indicate otherwise. They seek out crowded places, and they typically choose to sit and stand in the mainstream of pedestrian traffic. Many people say that what they like about a particular park or plaza is that it is calm and restful. Yet observers often note that such places are actually quite noisy. In some cases, the noise of park activities ("white noise") masks annoying street noises. The presence of food vendors, trees, water fountains, and a clear line of sight to and from the street also make public places "friendlier." All this suggests that a truly public architecture is one that promotes and symbolizes the condition of civil life and possesses the virtue of civility (Scruton, 1984).

□ *Body-heat defilement*—the thermal warmth found on a chair, bedding, or clothing recently used by another.
□ *Auditory assault*—excessive and loud noise, idiomatic slang, obscenity, or personal narratives inflicted by strangers.

Pollution may also have religious origins, as in the case of upper-caste Hindu Brahmans, who consider themselves defiled by contact with Untouchables. The notion of defilement similarly finds expression in Orthodox Judaism, where dinnerware must be destroyed when a milk product is accidentally put on meat dishes (Lyman and Scott, 1967; Goffman, 1971).

Reactions to Invasion

Robert Sommer and his associates (1969) have studied people's responses to intrusions into situational territory—territory controlled temporarily by the person using it, as in the case of library and cafeteria tables. Sommer or a colleague would invade situational territory by sitting next to someone on a park bench even though other benches were readily available, or occupying a chair next to someone in the library and then moving progressively closer to the victim. In these settings they found that the victim rarely voiced disapproval. Rather, people responded through *body language*. They would move their heads toward the intruder and give him an aggressive look, frown, or raise and lower their hands. Or on a less aggressive level, the victim would engage in rocking movements, leg swinging, or tapping that said, "You're too close. You're making me uneasy." These signs of tension might then be replaced by closed eyes, withdrawing the chin into the chest, hunching, and crouching that said, "Go away. You're intruding on my territory." If defensive gestures, shifts in posture, and unobtrusive attempts to slide over did not work—if all body signals were ignored—the victim would commonly take off and move to another location: *flight*.

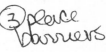

Another approach to territorial invasion was to treat the intruder as a *nonperson*. The victim reacted as if the intruder were an object or a part of the background. The implication was that a nonperson can no more invade one's space than a tree or a chair can. Such psychological withdrawal from others makes crowding on buses and subway trains bearable. Still another defense involved placing *barriers*—books or a coat—between oneself and the intruder.

In everyday life, most of us respect others' territorial claims and seat ourselves at vacant tables or benches. When library or cafeteria crowding does not permit this approach, a variety of **recognition ceremonies**—deferential gestures—ease the way for our intrusion. Sometimes we apologize and ask, "Is this seat taken?" or "May I sit here?" Or body language may serve a similar purpose: We lower our eyes as we sit down and then keep our eyes off our seat mate. By doing so, we attempt to minimize the threat of our territorial invasion.

Territorial Defense

In human societies as well as in the animal kingdom, an area that cannot be defended against intruders is generally not considered to be private territory. The three-mile coastal limit for countries was originally based on the maximum range of coastal artillery batteries, the idea being that a nation could not claim any more space than it could defend. Thus the question arises: How do we

CAPTIVITY: HOSTAGES AND LOSS OF PRIVACY

In response to the rise in terrorist kidnappings over the past decade, nations and major cities have organized SWAT (special weapons and tactics) teams and antiterrorist units. Established procedures in hostage situations call for authorities to position sharpshooters, establish communication with the terrorists, sustain continuous dialogue with the terrorists where possible, trade food for hostages, buy time, compromise, and wait. Of greatest concern is the fate of the hostages, not only during their immediate ordeal but also following release.

Studies of war prisoners, of the victims of the 1977 takeover of the B'nai B'rith office in Washington by a group of Hanafi Moslems, and of the fifty-two American hostages held by the Iranians reveal the traumatizing nature of being held captive. Captivity results in a loss of autonomy and control over one's body and destiny. Privacy is lost. Where hostages become utterly dependent on their captors for food, loosened shackles, and even permission to go to the bathroom, a Stockholm Syndrome can develop. The phenomenon (although recognized among American captives during the Korean War) takes its name from a 1973 Swedish incident in which four hostages used their own bodies to shield their two captors from a fusillade of police bullets. The hostages had temporarily come to identify with and support their captors. Patricia Hearst, who joined the Symbionese Liberation Army after her 1974 kidnapping, is considered a classic illustration of the Stockholm Syndrome. The Stockholm Syndrome seems to arise as a response to the tremendous fear that captives experience, and it embodies a desire to see their captors as less dangerous than they are. If the captors can be seen as less threatening, then the captives in turn can feel less frightened. Moreover, since the captors hold the power of life

---

undertake to defend situational territories in everyday life? Again Sommer (1969) provides us with some answers. He observes that we employ two positioning styles in gaining privacy in library and cafeteria settings. One method involves avoidance—sitting as far away from other people as we can. The other entails offensive displays—aggressively asserting ownership of an entire area.

If we enter a library or cafeteria that we anticipate will become crowded, we often gravitate to end chairs and corners of tables—an avoidance stance. In body language we say: "Share the table if you must, but leave me alone here in my corner." Or if we take an offensive posture, we sit in the middle of a long table, spread out our possessions "as if we own the place," and hope that timid invaders will slink away rather than risk our displeasure. We say to potential intruders: "This is my table, so get lost." Sommer also finds that when we prefer retreat,

and death, when they allow their captives to live, the victims feel they owe their captors something. Arthur W. Toga, a captive held for seventeen days in Beirut after Shiite gunmen seized TWA Flight 847 in 1985, observed: "You don't ever bite the hand that feeds you. When a man brings you food every day, you learn to like him" (Butterfield, 1985: 5).

Captivity is humiliating, debasing, and destructive. On release, victims often undergo a heightened sense of vulnerability, anxiety, depression, sexual problems, self-deprecation, and psychosomatic illnesses (such as headaches, heart palpitations, and numbness); on occasion, they even attempt suicide. For some, like rape victims (see Chapter 11), unpleasant memories and vague fears persist for years. And those who collaborated with their captors often experience a lingering sense of embarrassment and guilt.

Additional difficulties may ensue from the celebrity status hostages enjoy following their release. They become media events. However, as public interest wanes, the former hostages once again feel victimized. They believe themselves betrayed when the "entitlements" they feel they deserve are no longer forthcoming.

When the captives have been separated from their families for an extended period, new adjustments await them. Their families have usually undergone their own ordeal, including feelings of despair, grief, and loss. Because of the open-endedness of the hostage event, the families cannot find resolution or closure. Further, growing children become accustomed to the absence of a parent. And spouses often become more independent and assertive. When the families are reunited these changes may result in increased conflict and in some cases divorce.

The hostage experience may also change the former captive's outlook on life. Some hostages undergo a profound religious experience or a deepening of religious faith. Captivity may move them to clarify their values and goals, particularly those relating to loved ones. A number of the B'nai B'rith hostages returned home and quickly followed up on a decision to marry or have children. Many reported an increased awareness of the "fragileness of life."

we tend to face away from the door. When we wish to hog a table, we tend to face toward the door.

Markers—signs that communicate the fact of ownership or legitimate occupancy—also play a part in territorial defense (F. D. Becker, 1973). Bears mark their territories by clawing the bark from tree trunks, deer secrete a smelly substance from a gland near their nostrils, and wolves urinate around the periphery of their territory (Thiessen and Rice, 1976). Human beings employ a "silent language" for marking—symbols such as name plates, fences, hedges, and personal belongings. We place books, handbags, and coats on a table or empty chair to reserve our place in the library, sunglasses and lotion on a towel to lay claim to a spot on the beach, and a drink on a bar to assert "ownership" of a bar stool (F. D. Becker, 1973; Shaffer and Sadowski, 1975). A major problem

Territorial Defense
Territory may be defended against intrusion by placing a barrier—in this case a purse—between oneself and others. (Patrick Reddy)

with employing a personal possession as a marker, however, is that it may be stolen; to hold our places, we may have to expose something to theft (Goffman, 1971).

In public territories where the ability to use physical markers is restricted, such as at game arcades, individuals use bodily behaviors to establish and maintain territorial control (Werner, Brown, and Damron, 1981). For instance, individuals are more likely to touch a machine and prolong their touch of it even though they are not currently playing the game when a stranger approaches them than when a friend approaches them. Others also get "the message," for they are less likely to attempt to use a machine if a person stands near it and touches it than if a person stands off and does not touch it. Hence, touching frequently serves as a symbolic territorial marker.

The Language of Space

Individuals of different societies are culturally "programmed" somewhat differently. Through social interaction, we are alerted to the importance of the things our culture views as important; other things are played down or ignored by our culture. Without even being aware of the process, we learn to screen out one kind of information and pay close attention to another. The work of the anthropologist Edward T. Hall (1966) has shown the part that the language of space plays in social interaction.

Hall observes that Americans commonly find Arabs pushy and rude. Paradoxically, Arabs also consider Americans pushy. This is the product of two different

The Language of Space
Among Arabs, interaction has a highly physical quality; the participants often touch one another. Since Arabs do not have our sense of
a private spatial bubble, touching is not the threatening experience
that it is among Americans. (Patrick Reddy)

languages of space. Americans find exceedingly offensive the Arab tendency to
shove one another in public and to feel and pinch women on public conveyances.
This behavior, Hall explains, derives from the fact that the typical Arab lacks a
sense of a private spatial bubble that envelops the body. Rather than viewing a
person as extending in space beyond the body, the Arab sees the person as
existing somewhere down *inside* the body. Thus Arabs violate the American ego
by invading Americans' private space.

For their part, Arabs are infuriated by Americans who think nothing of cutting
ahead of others on the highway. To do so is to violate the Arab sense of "use
space." Arabs feel that the territory into which they are moving belongs to them—
that they acquire rights to the space in front of them as they move.

Americans and Arabs have other difficulties arising from their different languages of space. The visual interaction of Arabs is intense; they are directly and
totally involved. Arabs stare—Americans do not. American men feel that their
masculinity is being challenged by the way an Arab looks at them, although in
reality the Arab means no offense. Further, Arabs bathe the other person in their
breath. To smell another is not only desirable, it is mandatory; to deny another
one's breath is to act ashamed. Whereas Arabs stay inside the olfactory bubble

of others, Americans stay outside of it. Hence Americans communicate shame to the Arab when in fact the American is trying to be polite. A "polite" American diplomat is an "ashamed" diplomat; diplomacy among Arabs is not only "eyeball to eyeball" but breath to breath.

Distancing in conversations is also affected by the language a bilingual person is using (Sussman and Rosenfeld, 1982). For instance, Venezuelans represent a high-contact culture and Japanese a low-contact culture. But Venezuelans typically sit closer together when speaking Spanish than English, and they sit farther apart than do North Americans when speaking English. In contrast, Japanese conversing in English sit more closely together than when they speak in Japanese. All this suggests that communicative competence in a foreign culture is a total multichannel behavior package.

People of different societies also handle "privacy" differently. Americans gain privacy by going to their rooms and closing the doors. Arabs, in contrast, have no sense of *physical* privacy; they even lack a word for privacy. Since privacy is "internal," Arabs who want to be alone simply stop talking. The English do likewise. Arabs and English who shut themselves off in this way are not indicating that anything is wrong, but merely that they want to be alone with their thoughts. Americans who show displeasure toward Arabs and English by giving them "the silent treatment" will obviously fail in their purpose; this behavior will not be interpreted as anything out of the ordinary.

For their part, Arabs and English are puzzled by the American "need" for an individual room or office. Even members of the British Parliament have no offices and often conduct their business on the terrace overlooking the Thames. Despite our preoccupation with physical privacy, Americans find the German approach to space difficult to grasp. To Germans, an entire room of their home can be a bubble of privacy. Germans conceive of space as an extension of the ego. Thus German prisoners during World War II, rather than pooling available materials to build a warm, shared shelter, constructed tiny individual units no larger than foxholes. To do otherwise would have constituted an extraordinary invasion of the German ego. Not surprisingly, Germans also build sand-castle walls around their chosen spot on a public beach (Smith, 1981).

SUMMARY

1. One facet of territoriality is the home-cage effect. Animals will fight with greater vigor on their home territory, and the same effect operates with human beings: The "home team" has the advantage.

2. Aggression, given full rein and allowed to run its full course, would jeopardize the survival of the species. Two common approaches for regulating aggression are territoriality and hierarchy.

3. Within the United States, territoriality finds expression in personal space, situational territory, fixed territory, and public territory.

4. While crowding has bad effects on deer, rats, and a variety of other creatures, it does not seem to have a similar impact upon human beings. Although a

number of studies have attempted to link crowding to various social pathologies and aggression, generally they have not found a significant association.

5. Social factors influence people's definitions of situations and lead them to different judgments of being crowded or uncrowded.

6. Territorial arrangements reflect various social aspects of a relationship. For example, college students choose different seating patterns at a table, depending on whether they anticipate cooperative or competitive relationships. Territory and privilege tend to go hand in hand. For example, the boss has a larger office than subordinates.

7. We generally view territory as the possession of an individual or group. As such, it is subject to violation: invasion and contamination.

8. Sommer's studies suggest that we respond to intrusions into situational territory in any number of ways: through body language, flight, treating the intruder as a nonperson, and placing barriers between ourselves and the intruder.

9. We commonly employ two positioning styles for defending situational territories: avoidance, in which we place ourselves as far away from other people as we can, and offensive displays, in which we aggressively assert ownership of an entire area. Markers also play a part in territorial defense.

10. Individuals of different societies are culturally "programmed" somewhat differently. This finds reflection in what Edward T. Hall terms the language of space.

GLOSSARY

Contamination □   The defilement of one party's territory by another.

Crowding □   The perception that people have of themselves as receiving excessive stimulation from social sources.

Density □   A physical condition of populations that involves spatial limitations.

Fixed territory □   Space that is viewed as belonging to some individual or group even when it is not being used.

Invasion □   Entry into a party's territory against that party's wishes.

Language of space □   The different perceptions that people of different societies have regarding territorial privacy.

Markers □   Signs that communicate to people the fact of ownership or legitimate occupancy of territory.

Personal space □   The area we actively maintain around ourselves into which others cannot intrude without arousing our discomfort.

Positioning □   A strategy of locating oneself or one's personal effects in space so as to lay claim to a given territory.

Privacy □   The claim of individuals or groups to determine for themselves when, how, and to what extent information about themselves is communicated to others.

Public territory □   An area, such as a street or playground, where an individual has freedom of access but not necessarily freedom of action. (For example, people can be arrested in public territory for nudity or drunkenness.)

Recognition ceremonies □   Deferential gestures employed to ease the way for intrusion into another's territory.

Situational territory □   A temporary tenancy of space while in use. Although the territory is in the public domain, it "belongs" to one individual and then to another for short periods—as when a person uses a telephone booth.

Territoriality □   Behavior in which individuals or groups maintain, mark, and defend areas against intrusion by members of their own species.

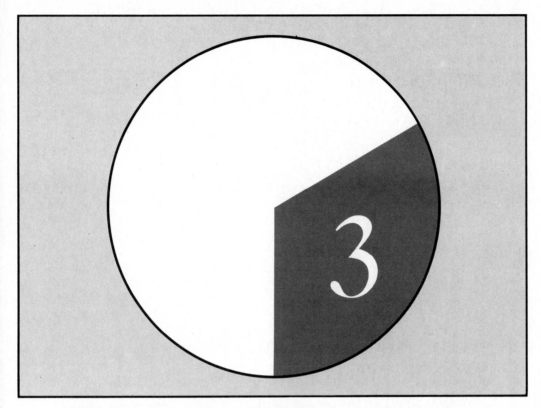

SOCIAL BEHAVIOR
IN GROUPS

13 GROUPS AND GROUP BEHAVIOR

CHARACTERISTICS OF HUMAN
   GROUPS
  Boundaries
  Products of Social Definitions
  Consciousness of Oneness
  Rituals
PRIMARY GROUPS AND
   SECONDARY GROUPS
  The Importance of Primary
   Groups

Primary Groups Within
   Secondary Groups
REFERENCE GROUPS AND
   MEMBERSHIP GROUPS
  Group Polarization Effects
  Groupthink
  Social Loafing
  Mock Jury Research

As human beings we are a great many things, but above all we are *social* animals. Our behavior is affected by others—indeed, our humanness derives from our social being. We cannot be human all by ourselves. Chapter 4 discussed the cases of Anna, Isabelle, and Genie, children who spent their early years under conditions of extreme isolation. By the time they were "discovered," they were little more than biological vegetables. The cases highlight the fact that the group is the foundation—*the* critical element—in human life. We are wretched and incomplete if we are not part of a group existence. Studies show that social support contributes to our psychological well-being and reduces the adverse consequences of a wide variety of stressful events (House, 1981; Williams, Ware, and McDonald, 1981; Mitchell, Billings, and Moos, 1983). (See boxed insert, pp. 400–401.)

SUPPORT NETWORKS AND HEALTH

The quality of our lives depends in large measure on our interpersonal relationships. As social beings, we meet our needs in interaction with other people. Our patterns of health and illness provide striking evidence of our need for such interaction (Shumaker and Brownell, 1984). One strength of the human condition is our propensity for giving and receiving support from one another. **Social support** consists of the exchange of resources among individuals based on their interpersonal ties. Group and community supports affect our physical and mental health through their health-sustaining and stress-buffering functions.

People with social ties live longer and have better physical and mental health than do those without such ties (Berkman and Breslow, 1983). Research dealing with a vast range of illnesses, from depression to arthritis to heart disease, shows that the presence of interpersonal support helps people fend off illness, while the absence of such support makes poor health more likely (Cohen and McKay, 1984; Ruberman et al., 1984; Reis et al., 1985). Likewise, death from all causes is greater among people with relatively low levels of social support (Blazer, 1982; House, Robbins, and Metzner, 1982). And studies reveal that college students immersed in social environments that are low in cohesion, participation, and social activities have a higher incidence of health problems than do those from social environments high in these qualities (Moos and Van Dort, 1976). In brief, support systems have a beneficial effect on people irrespective of whether or not they are under stress.

When we are integrated in social networks and groups, we have regular access to positive experiences and a set of stable, socially rewarded roles in the community. Such support fosters our physical and mental well-being because we are more

CHARACTERISTICS OF HUMAN GROUPS

The group forms the human being. Our first and most immediate experiences are small-group experiences. From infancy onward we are immersed in groups—families, childhood gangs, organizations, and teams. And as adults, even though we may work in large firms, factories, or government departments, our immediate work experiences take place in small-group settings with a few people (Homans, 1950: 1–2). A **group** can be defined as two or more people who share a feeling of unity and are bound together in relatively stable patterns of social interaction.

Three characteristics of human groups stand out in considerable relief. First, groups have boundaries. Second, groups are products of social definitions. Third, people are commonly aware of their own membership in groups—that is, they have a consciousness of oneness. Thus the boundaries of the group are the same

likely to have a positive frame of mind, feel that our social world is predictable and stable, and achieve a sense that we are worthwhile individuals. Additionally, a support network may encourage us to exercise and maintain good self-care.

Support systems also buffer or protect us from the potentially harmful influence of stressful events. Those of us with a strong support system appear better able to cope with major life changes and daily hassles. Social support cushions stress in a number of ways (Cohen and Wills, 1985; Seeman, Seeman, and Sayles, 1985). First, friends, relatives, and co-workers may let us know that they value us. Our self-esteem is strengthened when we feel accepted by others despite our faults and difficulties. Second, other people often provide us with informational support. They help us to define and understand our problems and find solutions to them. Third, we typically find social companionship supportive. Engaging in leisure-time and recreational activities with others helps us to meet our social needs while simultaneously distracting us from our worries and troubles. Finally, other people may give us instrumental support—financial aid, material resources, and needed services—that reduces stress by helping us resolve and cope with our problems.

There are, however, circumstances when our support systems may have negative effects (Shinn, Lehmann, and Wong, 1984; Rook and Dooley, 1985). For instance, bereaved people frequently receive well-intended but inappropriate remarks from friends and relatives that prematurely seek to stem their expression of grief ("It's probably for the best," "Don't take it so hard," or "He's better off now"). Moreover, well-meaning people may also put obstacles in our paths, violate our privacy, or provide us with "help" that does not fit our circumstances. At times lay support also interferes with our seeking professional assistance from physicians or mental health workers. And support for some medical patients inadvertently undermines their independent coping while reinforcing sick-role behaviors.

for the "insider" as for the "outsider." Let us consider each of these characteristics in turn and then see how they may be established.

Characteristics of Groups

Boundaries

Groups have **boundaries;** people either belong or do not belong to them. Thus groups are discrete entities—bounded units; they begin and come to an end somewhere (Nadel, 1957; Phillips and Conviser, 1972). To one degree or another, groups serve to "encapsulate" people, so that the flow of their action is internally contained (Mayer, 1961; Knowles, 1973; Knowles et al., 1976). Group boundaries act not as physical barriers but as discontinuities in the flow of interactions. An important aspect of social boundaries is that they face in two directions. Not

Families as Social Groups
Members of this family have a consciousness of oneness. Notice the body language—the mutual touching; the "encapsulating" quality of the interaction; the subtle drawing together of each individual into the larger whole. (Patrick Reddy)

only do they prevent us and those like us from moving out of our social spheres to interaction possibilities beyond these spheres, but they prevent others unlike us from entering our spheres (McCall and Simmons, 1966).

People define a group's boundaries in many ways:

- *Geographical location,* such as a neighborhood (South End), community (Milwaukee), nation-state (United States)
- *A set of time-honored traditions,* as in ethnic groups (Chicanos, Irish, Chinese, Italians)
- *Particular religious or political viewpoints*—for example, Christianity, communism, conservatism
- *Occupational specialty,* as with medical doctors, teamsters, machinists
- *Common language,* such as English, French, Russian
- *Formal membership rosters*—for example, the Kiwanis Club, the Church of Christ, the parent-teacher association
- *Social ranking,* such as classes, castes
- *Kinship,* in families, clans

Whatever the boundary criteria, people are aware of the contours of a group; they know what kinds of experiences "belong" within its precincts and what kinds do not (Erikson, 1970).

Groups differ in the extent to which their boundaries are penetrable or perme-

Boundary Permeability
Youths in their early and middle teens tend to coalesce in groups of
the same sex. And they explore relationships with the opposite sex in
groups rather than in one-to-one interactions. Thus a same-sex
group, although in essence a "closed group," is the vehicle for
"opening the door" to new avenues of social interaction. (Patrick
Reddy)

able (Milgram and Toch, 1969). More often than not, the barrier to "outsiders"
is like a screen rather than a solid wall—an interaction membrane filtering out
some people but permitting the entry of others. Groups, then, differ in the extent
to which they are **closed** or **open.** Racial, ethnic, and nationality groups are
commonly closed groups (for example, groups that are white, Chicano, or Irish);
entry tends to be a function of *birth* rather than choice, and hence membership
is termed *ascribed* status. Occupational, religious, and political groups tend to
be open groups (at least, within the United States); membership is commonly a
function of merit (possessing certain qualifications) or allegiance, and hence is
termed *achieved* status. Still other groups fall somewhere between the open and
closed categories, as in the case of many cliques, neighborhoods, and community
groups. Social psychologists find it useful, therefore, to think of permeability in
terms of a continuum:

Open group |————————————| Closed group
(permeable boundaries)   (impermeable boundaries

Products of Social Definitions

First and foremost, groups are states of mind—mental models or images at
varying levels of awareness. They are not tangible things that have actual sub-

stance in the real world. Rather, we fabricate groups in the course of social interaction by clustering people together in social units: families, races, teams, cliques, parties, organizations, unions, fraternities, and the like. Groups, then, are products of social definitions—sets of shared ideas; they are human-constructed "realities." In short, we conceptualize groups; we attribute real substance to them and treat them *as if* they were real and exact things.

As observed in Chapter 2, if we define situations as real, they are real in their consequences. This is true of groups. We make them real by treating them as real. By grouping certain of our fellows together into social units, we fashion and create an existence *beyond* the individuals who are involved. Thus groups have an existence as social entities *apart from* the particular relationships that individual people have with one another. For example, the parent-teacher association at a given school has continuity through time as a distinct, recognizable, and enduring entity, even though its membership continually changes. The same holds for ethnic groups, religious orders, political parties, labor unions, business corporations, colleges, and nation-states, all of which have an existence extending beyond the life spans of specific people.

What has been said about groups adds up to this: The whole is greater than the sum of its parts. Groups have a distinctive character in their own right, a character that lies in the linking of people apart from the particular individuals who are linked. Groups are more like chemical compounds than mixtures: For instance, although hydrogen and oxygen are both gases at room temperature, they come together in the chemical compound water, a liquid with properties that are qualitatively different from hydrogen or oxygen. Thus the *joining* (bonding) of people or molecules produces a synthesis, a qualitatively new entity with a distinctive character. We can therefore speak of such groups as corporations, families, and communities without having to break them down into the separate interactions that compose them (Blumer, 1969).

Consciousness of Oneness

In human life we commonly find that by joining together and marshaling our efforts and resources within groups, we are able to reach goals that would be beyond each individual's reach. The effectiveness of groups is associated with their internal cohesiveness. To a considerable extent, cohesiveness depends on the degree to which the members are aware of their common identity—the degree to which they share a **consciousness of oneness** (sometimes termed a consciousness of kind). Consciousness of oneness entails a sympathetic identification with others in the same group.

Ingroups and Outgroups

Social psychologists commonly distinguish between ingroups and outgroups. An **ingroup** is a social unit that we either belong to or identify with. An **outgroup** is a social unit that we either do not belong to or do not identify with. Sometimes ingroups are termed *we-groups* and outgroups *they-groups*.

Feelings of loyalty, solidarity, attraction, and cooperation tend to prevade ingroups. Social psychologists commonly term this sense of "we-ness" **cohesive-**

Developing a consciousness of oneness

One of the guys in my dorm suite is joining a fraternity. The rest of us think he must be crazy to put up with what he does. He has been beaten, humiliated, deprived of sleep, and made to run ridiculous errands at ridiculous hours, and his school work is messed up because he does not have enough time to study. And believe it or not, he hasn't gone through "Hell Week" yet. When we ask him what he is getting out of it all, he only laughs and says his efforts will be worth it in the end. The fraternity is compelling my suitemate to undergo various group rituals. In doing so, they are promoting a "consciousness of oneness"—an identity as a fraternity member. Such rituals emphasize the gulf between the ingroup and the outgroup. Also, by making my suitemate pay such a high human price for admission, they are telling him the high value placed on fraternity membership. In the course of the socializing process, he too is coming to acquire an even higher regard for fraternity life.

ness. Cohesiveness refers to the forces that act to keep individuals within a group and prevent them from leaving it (Collins and Raven, 1969a, b). Research reveals that members of highly cohesive groups, in comparison with members of groups low in cohesiveness, are more satisfied with one another, interact more frequently and freely, receive a greater sense of security from each other, have greater influence on one another, and communicate more often and in a more cooperative manner (Cartwright, 1968; Shaw, 1971; Ryen and Kahn, 1975; Terborg, Castore, and DeNinno, 1976; Shiflett, 1979; Scott and Scott, 1981). The presence of an outgroup increases our consciousness of ingroup ties and promotes conformity to ingroup norms (Lauderdale et al., 1984; Wilder and Shapiro, 1984). And strong ingroup identities—especially those associated with allegiance to a racial or ethnic group—provide powerful props to individual feelings of self-worth and self-esteem (Vander Zanden, 1983; Meindl and Lerner, 1984).

As a result of ingroup identifications, we come to assume that our inner experiences and emotional reactions are closer to those of ingroup members than they are to those of outgroup members (Shibutani and Kwan, 1965; Allen and Wilder, 1975). Moreover, since we expect differences between ourselves and members of an outgroup, we behave so as to create such differences (Sherif et al., 1961; Markides and Cohn, 1982). (See boxed insert, pp. 406–407) Our appraisals of outgroup members are more extreme than appraisals of ingroup members (Linville and Jones, 1980). We strip outgroup members of their individuality and become more likely to act toward them in an unfriendly and negative fashion (Wilder, 1978a). Thus guards in Nazi concentration camps treated Jews more leniently when the guards knew their names than when they were anonymous members of the Jewish outgroup (Zimbardo, 1970).

"WE" VERSUS "THEY"

Muzafer Sherif and his associates undertook a series of ingenious field studies dealing with intergroup conflict (Sherif et al., 1961). The subjects were boys eleven and twelve years old who did not know one another at the beginning of the experiment. They were healthy, socially well adjusted, and somewhat above average in intelligence. They came from stable middle-class white Protestant families. Thus the experimenters ruled out any group behavior caused by differences in family, religious, ethnic, or socioeconomic backgrounds.

The boys were taken in separate buses to a summer camp run by the researchers. They were settled in cabins at a considerable distance from each other. Contact between the groups did not occur until stage 2 of the experiment.

In stage 1, the boys in each group camped out together, cooked meals, worked on improvements for their swimming place, canoed, and played various organized and informal games. Gradually they evolved into two cohesive groups characterized by recognized status hierarchies, individual role assignments, norms (regarding cursing, toughness, and rowdy behavior), names (one group called itself the "Rattlers," the other the "Eagles"), their own jargon, special jokes, secrets, and preferred places.

In stage 2, the Rattlers and the Eagles "discovered" each other's existence and challenged each other to competitive sports. The experimenters arranged a tournament in which cumulative scores were recorded for each group. The events included baseball, touch football, a tug-of-war, skits, and a treasure hunt. In the course of the week, good sportsmanship gradually gave way to accusations, friction, name calling, scuffling, and fighting. Eagles and Rattlers raided each other's cabins, causing some destruction. Interviews and observations at the end of the second stage revealed that hostile attitudes and negative stereotypes had developed toward the outgroup, while ingroup cohesiveness had increased. Shared threats served as a social glue increasing each group's cohesiveness.

In stage 3, the experimenters undertook to unite the warring groups. Following the common-sense notion that "contact breeds friendliness," Sherif and his associates mixed Eagles and Rattlers together for pleasant social contacts: movies, meals, shooting fireworks on the Fourth of July, and the like. But far from reducing conflict, these situations served as new occasions for the rival groups to call names and attack each other. In the dining-hall line they shoved and scuffled, and at meals they started "garbage wars," throwing paper and food.

The method that turned out to be effective in bringing the groups together was suggested by a corollary to the experimenter's hypothesis of intergroup conflict. Sherif's hypothesis was that conflict develops from mutually incompatible goals, and the corollary said that common goals should promote cooperation. Accordingly, *superordinate* goals were introduced into the intergroup situation. They consisted of a number of urgent and "naturally" occur-

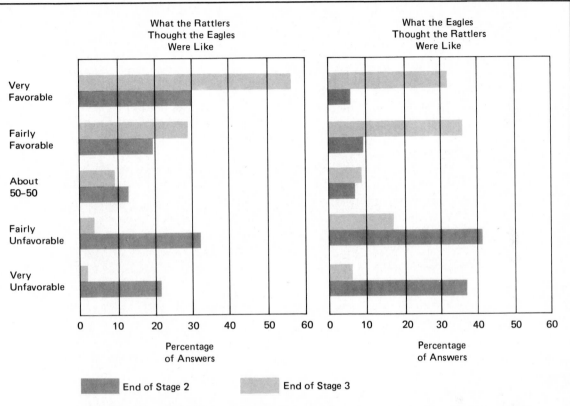

FIGURE 13.1 Attitudes of the Rattlers and the Eagles Toward Each Other at Two Stages of Their Group Relations
Hostility developed between the two groups of boys when their goals were mutually incompatible (stage 2). The hostility gave way to more favorable attitudes when the boys had to work together toward common goals (stage 3).
(SOURCE: M. Sherif et al., *Intergroup Conflict and Cooperation: The Robbers Cave Experiment* [Norman: Institute of Group Relations, University of Oklahoma, 1961], Table 4, p. 191.)

ring situations that made it necessary for the boys of both groups to come together and jointly tackle the problem. For example, it was arranged for the camp truck to break down when it was taking both groups on a camping trip. All the boys were needed to push the truck up the hill and get it started again. Gradually a series of activities requiring interdependent action reduced conflict and hostility between the groups. Interviews with the boys at the end of stage 3 confirmed a change in attitudes. From choosing their best friends almost exclusively in their own group, many shifted to listing some boys in the other group. Further, group stereotypes became more positive (see Figure 13.1).

Territorial Insiders and Outsiders
People locate themselves in space—divide up territory—on the basis of insider-outsider divisions. In the use of public facilities, we tend to draw social boundaries between "my racial group" and "that other racial group." (Patrick Reddy)

Social Distance

Because of a consciousness of oneness, we are not merely *in* the group; we are *of* the group. As pointed out in Chapter 2, we categorize or structure stimuli as a means of simplifying the abundance of information available to us. Likewise, we often "chunk" or categorize people within groups (Wilder, 1978*b*). But the mere conceptualization of our world into "us" and "them" is enough to arouse ingroup sympathies and bias (Dion, 1973; Gerard and Hoyt, 1974; Tajfel and Billig, 1974; Brewer, 1979; Locksley, Ortiz, and Hepburn, 1980; Moreland, 1985). Perhaps the most intriguing aspect of this biasing tendency is the relative ease with which it is produced. Social categorization produces ingroup-outgroup biases even when the basis for categorizing people into groups is arbitrary. It induces us to discriminate against outgroup members and to favor ingroup members in the allocation of rewards, heightens ingroup attractiveness, and fosters the assumption that ingroup members are similar to one another (Rabbie and Horowitz, 1969; Tajfel and Billig, 1974; Holtz and Miller, 1985). Consequently, we become set apart from others who are not, as we are, in and of the group. We experience **social distance** from them. Social distance does not so much refer to spatial separation as to a subjective sense of being set apart from (as opposed to being near to) certain people:

> When social distance is low, people can enter imaginatively into one another's minds and share their experiences; they are able to sympathize with one another's

pains, joys, sorrows, hopes, and fears. Those who feel close to each other are more relaxed and tend to be less defensive, for each feels that he can understand those around him. He feels "at home," that he "belongs" in this company. . . . When social distance is high, the other individual is seen as a representative of a different category. We feel apprehensive before a creature unlike ourselves, for we are not sure of what he will do. Even after long acquaintance there remains a residue of uncertainty—a vague apprehension, especially if the stranger maintains his reserve. In speaking of social distance, then, we are referring to the psychological barriers that facilitate or deter easy, spontaneous interaction. (Shibutani and Kwan, 1965: 42–43)

We commonly experience high social distance from people who engage in quite different practices and customs. Under such circumstances, it is not difficult for us to perceive outsiders as objects of loathing. The outsider is

a symbol of strangeness, evil, and danger to the community as a whole. His existence disturbs the order of life in the sense in which order is understood and experienced by the in-group. His customs are scandalous, his rites sacrilegious. His laws are incomprehensible, so that he appears to be lawless. His gods are false gods. (Speier, 1941: 445)

Thus we often see outsiders as deviants because their behavior differs from ours. **Ethnocentrism** is the tendency to view our own group as the center of everything and to rate all other people with reference to it (Sumner, 1906).

Many of our "social problems" derive from a conceptual scheme in which we create social entities that include some people and exclude others: capitalists-workers, whites-blacks, Gentiles-Jews, honest citizens–criminals, sane-insane, young-old, rich-poor, and so on. We draw social boundaries between "us" and "them." We cut up the world, organize it into categories, and assign meanings to it; we impose lines of demarcation on the great range of human behaviors. But in doing so, we create the sort of "social problems" that derive from insider-outsider divisions.

We see this principle highlighted in the nationalist and ethnic-group frictions that have underlain many wars. Consider Europe, for example. Almost every European territory has at one time or another combined with almost every one of its neighbors. It is impossible to align each European ethnic nationality with a distinct territory. Ethnic groups are found in segmented local pockets or scattered by residence and place of occupation throughout the territory of the dominant group. Most European nation-states contain multiple nationality groups: Great Britain (English, Welsh, Scotch), Switzerland (French, Italians, Germans), Czechoslovakia (Czechs and Slovaks), Belgium (Flemish and Walloons), Yugoslavia (Serbs, Croatians, Slovenes, Macedonians, and Montenegrins). Therefore, political self-determination for one people is incompatible with political self-determination for others.

National minority status is not inherent in human affairs. Rather, it is *created* by "social entity" awareness (consciousness of oneness), which causes us to include some people in, and exclude others from, certain flows of interaction. It derives from an image—a social definition—of what a "society" or "nation-state" is (a conception of "my kind of people"). Hence we create minority–dominant

Ritual
Fourth of July celebrations are staged public occasions by which our inner consciousness of group identity is made a collective consciousness. We fuse ourselves in a fellowship of sentiment—a communion of patriotic fervor—as we reenact our "sacred past" through the symbolic device of rituals. (Don McCarthy)

group "problems," which are not inherent in the mere existence of human differences.

Rituals

The foregoing discussion of groups has stressed a number of points. First, groups have boundaries—people either belong to them or not. Second, groups are products of social definitions; we mentally fashion social entities by grouping some people together and by treating such groups as if they are real things. Third, the cohesiveness of groups is fostered by a consciousness of oneness: We are not merely in the group; we are of the group. Each of these elements may be established, heightened, and rejuvenated by means of **rituals**—social acts of symbolic significance that are performed on certain occasions by prescribed tradition. The social sciences owe much to Emile Durkheim (1954)—a pioneer French sociologist (1858–1917)—for an understanding of the part rituals play in human life. He pointed out that religious rituals, performed with all their pomp and ceremony for the gods, serve to renew and reaffirm the social order.

Robert K. Merton (1968), another distinguished sociologist, points out that our conscious motivation in carrying out ceremonies may have little to do with the objective consequences of our behavior. Take the rain ceremonials of the Hopi Indians. Meteorologists tell us that the ceremonials do not perform the

Rituals

Example

Regularly scheduled college athletic events have the properties of rituals. They are social events rife with symbolic significance and are performed on certain occasions by prescribed tradition. Basketball games are a good illustration of this. The events and activities associated with a game between two schools takes place in a patterned way that gives them structure. There are crowd members, the opposing teams, referees, coaches, concession-stand workers, ushers, security personnel, media people, and maintenance workers, all with unique roles for the event. Players wear uniforms that bear the school colors, and the home court and the home fans are decked out in these same colors. Fans sing the school's "alma mater" and related "fight" songs. Cheerleaders orchestrate "cheers," the "wave," chants, and other expressions of school loyalty. A mascot—a Badger, Wolverine, Lion, Cardinal, Trojan, Hawkeye— symbolizes the intangible university and gives it a tangible existence. The net result of these activities is that the boundaries between "our" school and "their" school are highlighted. Students, faculty, staff, and alumni mentally come to think of themselves as a social unit and act toward this social unit as if it were real (making it a social reality). And a consciousness of oneness is awakened and solidified. Consequently, people who have very little else in common find themselves bonded together in a larger social enterprise—that group or social structure we term the "university."

function that the Hopi attribute to them: obtaining abundant rainfall. But Merton says that the ceremonials serve other functions that are not recognized by the Hopi. First, the ceremonials provide occasions during which the scattered members of the society assemble and renew their social bonds. Second, they allow the Hopi to "manage" the emotional tension associated with a drought and to feel that they can control the otherwise uncontrollable forces of nature. And third, the ceremonials permit the Hopi a periodic escape from reality through the collective ecstasy and exuberance provided by the ritual activities themselves.

Rituals take forms other than simply the religious: flag salutes, the singing of the national anthem before sporting events, Fourth of July parades, Thanksgiving and Christmas festivities, graduation exercises, marriage and funeral ceremonies, birthday parties, sports events like the Kentucky Derby and the Superbowl, and in some countries, public executions. Social psychologists say that all such activities have a common function: They serve to recharge our sense of collective solidarity. Rituals symbolize the reality of the group and our relation to it.

Consider flag salutes, the singing of the national anthem, and Fourth of July parades. We carry out these stereotyped actions in a collective setting and manner. We perform them with an appropriate sense of sacredness, awe, and reverence, all of which serve to evoke a single definition of reality and a mutually held emotion. The rituals identify group boundaries—our incorporation within a nation-state, the United States of America; they identify the group, the United States, as a distinctive social entity having a superindividual existence; and they provide a consciousness of oneness, a heightened sense of involvement and commitment to the nation.

Colleges employ athletic events, especially basketball and football games, as rituals to achieve a collective consciousness among students, faculty, and alumni. Traditional games, such as a homecoming game or a game against a longtime rival, cement group ties. Hugh Hindman, Ohio State University's athletic director observes:

> Football is the rallying point for all those people out there. It is their tie to the university after they're gone. . . . Football Saturdays are when you have the reunions of grads from different colleges. The colleges [within the university] use the games to get people in here. Then they work on them for development fund contributions while they're here. (Baptist, 1984: C-1)

The college mascot—for instance, the buckeye, the badger, the lion, the warrior, the cougar, the horned frog, the bulldog—serves as a symbolic embodiment of a university and the focus for heightening a consciousness of oneness.

Durkheim observes that if we are left to ourselves, our individual consciousnesses—our internal states—are closed to one another. Our separate minds cannot come in contact and communicate with one another except by "coming out of themselves." We accomplish this by making that which is internal external. Our inner consciousness is transformed into a *collective* consciousness through the symbolic device of rituals. By uttering the same cry, pronouncing the same word, or performing the same gesture, we inform one another that we are in harmony and that we are aware of this unity. In addition, through the collective representations of rituals, we fuse ourselves in real communion; we experience a fellowship of sentiment (a common emotional bond) as we create in unison through ritualistic symbols a shared state of mind. In sum, rituals operate in two directions: First, they serve as instruments or vehicles for *revealing* our individual mental states; second, they serve to *create* common, shared mental states.

PRIMARY GROUPS AND SECONDARY GROUPS

One of the broadest and most fundamental distinctions made by social psychologists is that between primary groups and secondary groups. **Primary groups** involve two or more people who relate to one another in direct, intimate, personal ways. The family, work groups, friendship groups, old-fashioned neighborhoods, and children's play groups are examples of primary groups (see Table 13.1).

The formation of primary groups is encouraged by (1) physical proximity that involves face-to-face contact, (2) a small number of people, and (3) intense and frequent interaction (Davis, 1949; McGrath, 1984). Physical proximity permits intimate communication; when people can see and talk with one another, they can carry on the subtle exchange of moods, feelings, and opinions. Size is important for the simple reason that large numbers of people cannot relate to

TABLE 13.1
Primary and Secondary Groups

PRIMARY-GROUP CHARACTERISTICS	SECONDARY-GROUP CHARACTERISTICS
Small number of people	Large number of people
Involves the whole person	Involves behavioral segments
Personal	Impersonal
Continuous interaction	Sporadic interaction
Long duration	Short duration
Informal expectations	Formal prescriptions
Informally imposed constraints	Formally imposed constraints
Expressive ties	Instrumental ties
EXAMPLES OF PRIMARY GROUPS	EXAMPLES OF SECONDARY GROUPS
Family	Labor union
Clique	College
Work group	Corporation
Old-fashioned neighborhood	City
Friendship group	Military unit

one another directly and personally. And finally, the duration and intensity of the interaction are critical. Other things being equal, the more often we are together, the more numerous and more profound the ties between us. As we associate with one another, we evolve interlocking habits that bind us together.

The opposite of primary groups are **secondary groups** (two or more people who relate to one another in indirect, nonintimate, impersonal ways). They involve us in everyday transitory relationships in which we have little or no knowledge of others. Colleges, the air force, urban communities, government bureaus, the AFL-CIO, factories, General Electric, and the Roman Catholic church are examples of secondary groups. Within such settings we are more careful and calculating, more inclined to "watch ourselves." Typically we invest only a segment of our lives and personalities in secondary groups—not our total selves, as in primary groups. Secondary groups are often special-interest groups that perform particular functions—educating youth (schools), making money (corporations), protecting the country (the military), and worshipping (churches). In sum, relationships in secondary groups are impersonal; communication is rational and purposeful; role expectations are specifically defined; and interaction is goal-oriented, not person-centered.

The Importance of Primary Groups

Primary groups are basic—"primary"—in a number of respects. First, they are agents or vehicles by which we are introduced to society. Kingsley Davis observed:

The primary group, in the form of the family, initiates us into the secrets of society. It is the group through which, as playmates and comrades, we first give creative

Primary Groups
Primary groups supply us with companionship, a feeling of ego worth, affection, acceptance, and a general sense of well-being. (Patrick Reddy)

expression to our social impulses. It is the breeding ground of our mores [rules and customs], the nurse of our loyalties. (1949: 290)

Thus primary groups function as agents of socialization. They fit us for participation in society—a point highlighted for anthropologists during field work, when they must become "outsiders" in another society. As described by the anthropologist Edmund Carpenter, who lived for a period among the Aivilik, an Eskimo people:

> For months after I first arrived among the Aivilik, I felt empty, clumsy. I never knew what to do, even where to sit or stand. I was awkward in a busy world, as helpless as a child, yet a grown man. I felt like a mental defective. (1965: 55)

Only as Carpenter was inducted into Aivilik primary groups did he learn the appropriate cultural patterns and become comfortable in the society.

A second reason why primary groups are basic is that they are the source by which we realize various social satisfactions. Within them we find companionship, a feeling of ego worth, affection, acceptance, and a general sense of well-being. We come to appreciate this quality of primary groups when we leave home to attend college, get married, or take a job. We feel "homesick"—nostalgic for a primary group from which our immediate ties have suddenly been severed. Charles Horton Cooley, who originated the concept of primary groups, observed:

> The result of intimate association, psychologically, is a certain fusion of individualities in a common whole, so that one's very self, for many purposes at least, is

*S*mall groups and culture creation

*During high school, Ginny was my best friend. Both of us are now col-
lege sophomores. I went away to school, but Ginny is living at home
and attending a local college. When I was home over Easter break,
Ginny invited me to a party that she gave for her clique at college.*

*I was the only person at the party who was not a member of this
group of friends. I didn't know anyone except Ginny. The people were
very nice and friendly to me. However, I felt uncomfortable and out of
place. Much of what they talked and laughed about was Greek to me.
They giggled and carried on about the "golden grouse" and their "Wood-
side women." From time to time the guys would sing out "ding-dong,"
which seemed to tickle and amuse everyone but me. They gossiped
about people they knew, kidded about happenings in various classes,
and made references to prior parties. All these things were beyond me.*

*My experiences brought to mind the observations of Gary Alan Fine
(1979), a sociologist. He pointed out that small groups evolve their own
cultures—what he calls "idioculture." These cultures are various shared
elements that are (1) known to the members of a group, (2) usable in
facilitating group interaction, (3) functional in supporting group goals
and fulfilling individual needs, (4) appropriate in supporting the status
hierarchy of the group, and (5) triggered by events that arise in group
situations. As a consequence of their idioculture, the members of this
small, intimate group were immersed in their own little world of which
I was not a part. No wonder I felt awkward and clumsy.*

the common life and purpose of the group. Perhaps the simplest way of describing
this wholeness is by saying that it is a "we"; it involves the sort of sympathy and
mutual identification for which "we" is the natural expression. One lives in the
feeling of the whole and finds the chief aims of his will in that feeling. (1909: 23–
24)

The primary group, then, satisfies a variety of social needs and gives us a sense
of social affiliation.

A third way in which primary groups are basic is that they function as agents
of social control. The members of primary groups enjoy unparalleled opportunities to make their attitudes known, to check, modify, or correct one another's
views, and to bring dissenters into line:

Their power is further augmented by their extraordinary capacity for rewarding
conformity and punishing deviation, and, what is equally important, for doing so

immediately, directly, and tangibly. Other associations, in contrast, must rely upon "reinforcements" that are often more distant in time, more dimly perceived, more ambiguous, and likely, therefore (as numerous experiments in the psychology of learning make plain), to be far less effective. . . . Should the use of rewards fail, a primary group may, and often does, win obedience by rejecting or threatening to ostracize the deviants—measures with a potency that increases in proportion as the latter esteem the group or find no alternative groups to turn to. (McClosky and Dahlgren, 1959: 759)

Thus primary groups serve not only as "carriers" of norms but as "enforcers" of them.

Primary Groups Within Secondary Groups

Except for people in small societies that have only one or two hundred members, we live our lives within large, complex societies and formal organizations characterized by impersonal, secondary relationships. Within this context, primary groups provide an essential bridge between the individual and the "great society." We have observed how primary groups function to transmit, interpret, and in the end, sustain society's norms. Indeed, primary groups are the principal "carriers" and repositories of a people's cultural ways. In this sense, primary groups serve a mediating function binding individuals to the larger society. The capacity of a large organization to mobilize and control members is increased if the members belong to it through intermediary primary groups. The stronger the mediating group—such as the family—the firmer the bond between the organization and the individual (Broom and Selznick, 1973).

It is hardly surprising that primary groups often play a critical part in mobilizing people to work for the goals of larger organizations. An army is a case in point. Why should people endure situations where they can be killed and where they have to kill others? In brief, why should soldiers enter combat—behavior that is extremely hazardous to life and limb? Part of the answer is to be found in the functioning of small face-to-face groups and the sense of solidarity they provide (Moskos, 1984). Indeed, much research suggests that the stronger the primary-group ties of the troops fighting together, the better their combat record. In a study of the German army during World War II, Edward A. Shils and Morris Janowitz (1948) found that the Wehrmacht's fighting effectiveness stemmed from its ability to reproduce in the infantry unit the intimacy and ties previously furnished by the soldiers' civilian primary groups. Except among a minority of hard-core Nazis, political and ideological convictions had little impact on determination to fight. As one captured German said, "Nazism begins ten miles behind the front line." Unlike the Americans, German soliders who trained together went into battle together. And whereas American fighting units were kept up to strength through individual replacements, German units were "fought down" and then pulled back to be formed anew (Van Creveld, 1982). The result was that the German units often fought better than their American counterparts.

The German soldiers showed considerable ignorance and apathy regarding the course of the fighting. Shils and Janowitz report:

> For the ordinary German soldier the decisive fact was that he was a member of a squad or section which maintained its structural integrity and which coincided roughly with the *social* unit which satisfied some of his major primary needs. He was likely to go on fighting, provided he had the necessary weapons, as long as the group possessed leadership with which he could identify himself, and as long as he gave affection to and received affection from the other members of his squad and platoon. In other words, as long as he felt himself to be a member of his primary group and therefore bound by the expectations and demands of its other members, his soldierly achievement was likely to be good. (1948: 284)

Studies of American soldiers after World War II reveal similar motivations (Shils, 1950; Moskos, 1969). Influenced by social psychological research, the United States Army has moved decisively toward keeping soldiers together throughout their military careers. It has concluded that "a soldier's loyalty is to the primary group with which he identifies and interacts." The army anticipates that stabilization in a regiment will "overcome the transitory nature of soldiers in units and will provide a solid basis for cohesion and bonding" (Middleton, 1983: 10).

We have observed that primary groups may function as *intermediaries* binding individuals to a larger organization. But they can also operate to undermine the official goals and commands of the larger group. This double-edged potential is often seen in **informal groups**—social organizations that evolve within a formal organization although they are not defined or prescribed by the formal organization.

Informal groups that arise in work settings develop norms that enable workers to increase their control over the work environment and to lessen their dependence on management. Peter M. Blau and W. Richard Scott have summarized some of these group norms and the measures employed to support them:

> In the course of interaction a set of common rules of conduct emerged, which included the following prohibitions: Don't be a rate-buster by working too fast. Don't be a chiseler by working too slow. If you are a straw boss, act like a regular guy; don't try to get bossy. Don't be a squealer. Conformity to norms was rewarded by approval that bestowed a relatively high position in the informal status structure. Norm violations were punished by group members in a variety of ways. Minor violations might be met with "binging"—striking the offender on the upper arm— or with ridicule. Continued violation of important norms resulted in a loss of popularity, a reduction in social interaction, and ultimately in complete ostracism. One worker was isolated because he violated the most serious group norm: he "squealed" on his fellows to the foreman. (1962: 92)

In prisons, military units, the postal service, hospitals, schools, and factories, studies have revealed elaborate patterns of "kidding," gambling, illicit drug trafficking, unauthorized work breaks, and "goldbricking," all derived from informal-group relationships.

REFERENCE GROUPS AND MEMBERSHIP GROUPS

> *If a man does not keep pace with his companions, perhaps it is because he hears a different drummer.*

> —Henry Thoreau, *Walden,* 1854

More than a century ago, Henry Thoreau pointed out that the apparent nonconformist—the person out of step with the procession—may merely be marching to the tune of a different drummer. Implicit in Thoreau's observation is the concept of the **reference group.** The term refers to the social unit with which people identify. People use the standards of their reference group to define their behavior and evaluate themselves. A reference group may or may not be a **membership group**—a social unit to which an individual actually belongs.

Reference-group affiliation derives from *psychological* identification. It helps account for seemingly contradictory behavior: the upper-class revolutionary, the renegade Catholic, the reactionary worker, the shabby gentleman, the quisling who collaborates with the enemy, the assimilated immigrant, and the social-climbing chambermaid. Such individuals have taken as their reference group people other than those in their own membership group (Hyman and Singer, 1968). A good many college students aspiring to membership in various professions also fit this description. Indeed, their schooling is a form of *anticipatory socialization*—they are cultivating the behaviors (professional skills, manner, ethics, and outlook) associated with full-fledged nurses, doctors, engineers, lawyers, accountants, scientists, and so on. They hope that their reference group will ultimately become their membership group.

Reference groups perform two functions (Kelley, 1952). First, they provide us with norms and attitudes—a frame of reference for guiding our behavior. Social psychologists term this the *normative function* of reference groups. We view ourselves as being members in good standing within a certain group, or as wishing to be members in good standing. Hence we take on the group's political views, its clothing and hair styles, its religious beliefs, its sexual practices, or its drug-using behaviors. The group's views and norms become our views and norms. In this sense our behavior is group-anchored.

Second, reference groups provide a *comparison function*—they serve as a standard or comparison point against which we judge or evaluate ourselves. We continually make self-assessments regarding our physical attractiveness, intelligence, health, social ranking, and standard of living relative to others. When our reference group is not our membership group, we may experience a sense of *relative deprivation*—dissatisfaction derived from the gap between what we have (the conditions or circumstances of our membership group) and what we believe we should have (the conditions or circumstances of our reference group). These sentiments may contribute to alienation and foster social discontent and revolution (see Chapter 17). In contrast, a sense of *relative gratification* may render us satisfied with the "system" (Singer, 1981).

Not all reference groups are positive. We also employ *negative reference groups,* groups with which we compare ourselves in order to emphasize the

*R*eference groups

I spent Memorial Day with my best friend. Tony has been a truck driver for the past year, hauling livestock. I noticed a tremendous change in his behavior during this time. Previously, he was a dignified, middle-range executive with the regional IBM office. When he was with IBM, he played golf, loved bridge, attended middle-class social gatherings, drank bourbon, and dressed in a suit with a white shirt and a tie. Now that he has become a truck driver, his behavior has drastically changed. He sold his golf clubs, plays little bridge, no longer attends middle-class social gatherings (preferring the company of truckers and blue-collar workers), and drinks primarily beer. I never see him in "business" suits anymore. Now he wears only Levis, a Western shirt, cowboy boots, and to top it all off, a $40 cowboy hat. Even his accent now has a drawl like the Texas cattlemen he is in contact with, and his speech reflects the "toughness" of truck drivers. Tony conforms to the patterned behavior characteristic of his trucking associates. He is "in" with the truckers and "out" with the local businessmen.

We can understand the shift in Tony's behavior in terms of reference groups. When he worked for IBM he had the business community as his reference group. When he became a truck driver, he attached himself to a new reference group. This explains the very marked change in his behavior.

differences between ourselves and others. For Cuban-Americans in southern Florida, the Castro regime serves as a negative reference group (Carver and Humphries, 1981). Most of them fled their homeland after the 1959 revolution, which brought Fidel Castro to power. Opposition to Castro's Cuba helps the Cuban-Americans to decide what they really believe in and to determine who they really are. But even more than this, the negative reference group provides a mechanism of social solidarity, a vehicle by which the exile community knits itself together. It facilitates their acceptance within the community and ensures them the benefits of social interaction with like believers.

Group Polarization Effects

It long has been thought that a group tends to be more conservative than its individual members—that groups have a dampening impact on boldness, creativity, innovation, and daring. William H. Whyte (1956), in his best-selling book *The Organization Man,* which became a bible of the business world, suggests that the administrator who wants conservative advice should ask a committee rather than an individual for recommendations. Yet as is often true of common-sense knowledge, this prediction is contradicted by an impressive and growing body of social psychological evidence.

Anticipatory Socialization
Although he is a truck driver, this young man has aspirations to "move up" in the business world. In reading the *Wall Street Journal* he is cultivating the skills and attributes that will facilitate upward mobility. (Patrick Reddy)

Research on the matter originated in James Stoner's (1961) unpublished master's thesis at the Massachusetts Institute of Technology. His study revealed that people tend to make more daring decisions when they are in groups than when they are alone—a phenomenon termed the risky shift. Experiments studying the risky shift generally begin by having subjects individually read about a hypothetical case of a person who must choose between two alternatives—one that is safe but unattractive and one that is attractive but exposes the person to a much higher possibility of failure.

Subjects are presented, for instance, with the case of an electrical engineer who has a secure job with a modest but adequate income. He is offered another position at a considerably larger salary with a small, newly founded company that has an uncertain future. Subjects are asked the lowest probability of success in the new venture that they would consider acceptable before recommending that the engineer take the new job: 1 chance in 10, 3 in 10, 5 in 10, 7 in 10, or 9 in 10. After the pretest, subjects are requested to discuss the issue as a group and arrive at a decision. Results vary somewhat owing to the type of risk item employed or the social setting, but there is an overwhelming tendency (over the diverse conditions of more than a hundred experiments) for riskier choices to be made in the group than in the solitary condition (Pruitt, 1971*a,b;* Cartwright, 1971, 1973).

A good many explanations have been advanced to account for the risky-shift effect. Although no hypothesis has achieved universal confirmation, one that has gathered considerable support is the **value hypothesis,** advanced by Roger Brown

Value Hyp: ①

*T*he risky-shift phenomenon

Last night three of my sorority sisters and myself snuck over to the fraternity house where we are "little sisters." Using a "stolen" key, we got inside and worked our mischief in the front room. This all was taking place about 3:30 A.M. I knew our behavior was against the rules and I was scared of getting caught. But I realized that I was not half as scared as I would be if I were engaged in prankstering alone. As a matter of fact, I would not even have thought of or considered the idea had I been by myself. This is a good example of the risky-shift phenomenon. Through discussions with my sorority sisters, we arrived at a course of action that was more risky than any of us would have considered in isolation.

in 1965 and since modified and expanded in several versions (Morgan and Aram, 1975; Muehleman, Bruker, and Ingram, 1976; Hong, 1978). According to this view, daring and risk taking are highly valued behaviors in Western culture. People want to be at least as daring as their peers. But in group discussions, some people find that they are not really so adventurous as they would like to believe, and they consequently shift to riskier options.

On some tasks, however, people shift not in risky but in *cautious* directions. For instance, when experimental tasks involve the alternative of divorce (a culturally disfavored option) as a solution to marital discord, a cautious shift occurs. Thus we find not only risky-shift effects but also cautious-shift effects in group behavior. Social psychologists call both phenomena **choice shifts.** According to the value hypothesis, people shift in social situations toward the dominant value of a given reference group (risky or cautious, depending on whether the behavior is viewed as being socially desirable or undesirable). Consequently, group discussion polarizes individual judgment. It enhances the tendency of group members to shift toward the already preferred pole, *the group polarization phenomenon* (Myers and Lamm, 1976). Norris R. Johnson (1974; Johnson, Stemler, and Hunter, 1977) says that crowd behavior provides a good illustration of group polarization; the average response of group members becomes even more extreme, although in the same direction, than had been the case in the precrowd context. It seems that group members perceive a norm, and group consensus regarding it, as more extreme than is in fact the case. By virtue of their identification with the group, individuals accept what they believe to be the group's norm (Mackie and Cooper, 1984).

Dean G. Pruitt (1971a,b) has advanced another explanation of the choice shift—release theory—that has also gained experimental support. He suggests that we find ourselves in conflict when we are asked to make decisions. On the one hand, risk taking is attractive because it implies that we are confident of our ability to cope with the environment. On the other hand, we find a cautious approach compelling because of widely held values attached to moderation and being reasonable. Release theory portrays people as acting like Walter Mitty in

James Thurber's short story of a man who lived a cautious, mundane life with a domineering wife. Although Mitty's actual behavior was cautious, his inner life was characterized by daring, adventurous daydreams. According to **release theory,** the risky shift occurs in group discussions because the discovery of another person who endorses high risk taking *releases* the more cautious group members from their social constraints—it gives them the "courage of their convictions." However, considerable controversy still surrounds the risky-shift phenomenon and current explanations of it.

Groupthink

In 1961, some of the most respected and competent leaders in America's history unanimously undertook a diastrous policy: the ill-fated Bay of Pigs invasion of Cuba. President John F. Kennedy's policy-making group included Robert Kennedy, Arthur Schlesinger, Jr., Dean Rusk, McGeorge Bundy, Douglas Dillon, and Robert McNamara. These men decided to send some 1,400 CIA-trained Cuban exiles to Cuba with the intent of overthrowing the Castro regime. Although the invaders were assisted by the CIA and the United States Navy and Air Force, nothing went right. Castro's forces crushed the attack, capturing 1,200 of the exiles and killing most of the others. The Bay of Pigs invasion proved to be a colossal blunder: Not only did it deeply embarrass the United States, but it solidified the Cuban-Russian alliance and led to a Russian attempt to put nuclear missiles in Cuba.

The President later asked, "How could we have been so stupid?" Yet John F. Kennedy was hardly stupid; nor was his brother Bobby, or Arthur Schlesinger, Jr. (a distinguished professor of history from Harvard), or Robert McNamara (previously a Ford Motor Company official, an administrator credited with a computerlike mind), or the other presidential advisers. Yet the basic assumptions on which the Bay of Pigs operation depended were absurd when examined in the light of evidence available at the time. Even such elementary facts as the size and strength of the Castro forces had been overlooked. Indeed, in some cases the President and his advisers had failed to seek relevant information.

How could such seemingly competent individuals go so wrong? Irving Janis (1971, 1972), a Yale social psychologist, says that the answer lies in groupthink. **Groupthink** refers to a decision-making process occurring within highly cohesive groups in which the members are so preoccupied with maintaining group consensus that their critical abilities become ineffective. Under circumstances of external threat, a hidden agenda emerges, stipulating that group members must maintain friendly relations with one another at all costs. Individuals come to place a premium on unanimity and concurrence, all of which interfere with their capacity for critical thinking. As a consequence, group members are willing to sanction policies that entail excessive risk taking. Janis identified eight symptoms or characteristics of groupthink:

1. *An illusion of invulnerability:* The Kennedy group took office on a wave of confidence in their wisdom and abilities—they viewed themselves as immune to failure. Arthur Schlesinger, one of the inner circle, notes:

*G*roupthink

I share an apartment with three other guys from my hometown. We've known one another since we played in the same midget football league. We knocked one another around and tested one another out. As the years rolled by we played football together in junior and senior high school. We hung out together and now we're in college together. Well, the other guys have been talking for sometime about getting a rather costly stereo. Now they want to go ahead with it. I'm not hip to the idea. Frankly, I don't care for music—for some reason I find it just a lot of noise and it bothers me. Not only that, but it is expensive and will take my bucks as well. I would like to express my true feelings and tell them to count me out. But I have shut up and am going along with the idea. I do not want to violate our group's illusion of unanimity and impair our sense of solidarity. And I know that if I were to voice opposition, the other guys would jump all over me and I'd feel real low. So I'm exercising self-censorship. P.S.: Now they got the damn thing and I'm living with it: the insidious qualities of groupthink.

Everything had broken right for him [Kennedy] since 1956. He had won the nomination and the election against all the odds in the book. Everyone around him thought he had the Midas touch and could not lose. (1965: 259)

2. *Shared stereotypes:* The Kennedy advisers conceived of Castro and the Cubans in oversimplified and ideologically stereotyped terms. They assumed that the communists were so stupid, incompetent, and weak that their air force and army would be ineffective against the highly trained CIA exiles.

3. *A sense of morality:* Groupthink victims look upon themselves as highly moral agents of good in a battle against evil—in this case, communism.

4. *Rationalization:* President Kennedy and his advisers justified the invasion by arguing that it was the will of the Cuban people, whom the American strategists expected to rise up in support of the invaders. Yet U.S. government surveys were available showing that Castro had considerable popular support.

5. *An illusion of unanimity:* Although some advisers had doubts about the operation, not one expressed them. Schlesinger notes:

   Our meetings were taking place in a curious atmosphere of assumed consensus. Had one senior adviser opposed the adventure, I believe that Kennedy would have canceled it. Not one spoke against it. (1965: 259)

6. *Conformity-group pressures:* Closely associated with the illusion of unanimity are strong groupthink pressures for conformity. Individuals who have misgivings are reluctant to express them lest they incur the disapproval of other group members.

7. *Self-censorship:* Under the influence of groupthink, the cohesiveness of the group becomes such an overriding consideration that individuals censor their own divergent opinions. Again Schlesinger observes:

> In the months after the Bay of Pigs I bitterly reproached myself for having kept so silent during those crucial discussions in the cabinet room. . . . I can only explain my failure to do more than raise a few timid questions by reporting that one's impulse to blow the whistle on this nonsense was simply undone by the circumstances of the discussion. (1965: 255)

8. *Mindguards:* Within highly cohesive groups, one or more individuals generally emerge who undertake psychologically to protect the warm glow of group unanimity by stifling dissent. In effect they become self-appointed "mindguards." Robert Kennedy assumed this role in the Bay of Pigs deliberations.

It is chilling to think that both the risky-shift group effect and groupthink can operate in decision-making processes concerning war and peace in an atomic age.

Other researchers also find that a leader's characteristics make a difference in group decision making. Some leaders foster groupthink by their tendency to show low "integrative complexity"—a manner of processing information that is relatively simple and uncomplicated (Tetlock, 1979). Similarly, power-oriented leaders promote and sustain a closed style of group functioning that discourages creative and imaginative thinking and instead encourages groupthink (Fodor and Smith, 1982). Hence, factors other than a need for group solidarity foster groupthink processes.

Social Loafing

An old saying has it that "Many hands make light the work." The proverb suggests that we can achieve our goals more easily through collective than through individual action. Yet research by Bibb Latané and his associates reveals that when people work in groups, they work less hard than they do when working individually (Latané, Williams, and Harkins, 1979a,b; Williams, Larkins, and Latané, 1981). Latané terms this process **social loafing** (see also the box on social dilemmas, pp. 426–427.)

Initial evidence for social loafing came from the work of a number of German psychologists during the 1920s. They tested individuals singly and collectively in a rope-pulling task. When working in groups, a division of labor did not typically result and performance depended on the sum of individual efforts. We might expect that three individuals could pull three times as much as one person and that eight could pull eight times as much. Yet, whereas persons individually averaged 130 pounds of pressure when tugging on a rope, in groups of three they averaged 352 pounds (only two-and-a-half times the solo rate) and in groups of eight only 546 pounds (less than four times the solo rate). Some psychologists have speculated that faulty coordination is the source of this group inefficiency. But when Alan G. Ingham and his associates (1974) replicated the work of the

German researchers with blindfolded subjects who *believed* they were pulling with others, the subjects also pulled less in the group setting than when alone. (They pulled only 90 percent of their individual rate when pulling with "another person" and at only 85 percent when they believed two to six others were pulling with them.)

Latané and his associates have likewise encountered social loafing when they have asked undergraduate men to make as much noise as possible by shouting or clapping in concert with others. Their results show that the men produce only twice as much noise in groups of four and 2.4 times as much in groups of six as when alone. And when the men wear headphones that control their auditory feedback, they shout more loudly when they believe they are alone than when they think they are in a group.

It seems that people slack off in groups because they feel they are not realizing their fair share of the credit for the outcome or because they think that in the crowd they can get away with doing less work. In comparable situations, Soviet peasants are much more productive when they individually cultivate a small plot of land for their own use than when they work on collective farms (although the private plots occupy less than 1 percent of Soviet agricultural lands, they produce 27 percent of the total value of the nation's farm output).

Latané cautions that his findings should not lead us to do away with work groups. He stresses that groups are an essential element in all societies and that they can accomplish things individuals cannot. And social psychologists point out that such groups as Alcoholics Anonymous, Parents Without Partners, and Weight Watchers may have desirable influences and outcomes.

Instead, Latané calls for the exploration of ways to combat social loafing. He notes, for instance, that successful football teams like those at Ohio State University undertake to highlight and make visible the contribution of each player to the outcome of a play. The coaching staff screens and grades each play and computes the average performance of each individual. Teammates know one another's scores, and the scores influence which players start the next game. At weekly press luncheons, coaches announce "lineman of the week" honors and award "buckeye" decals to adorn players' helmets, signifying superior performance to the player, his teammates, and Ohio State enthusiasts. The success of Ohio State football teams suggests that identifiability and individual reward may serve as effective deterrents to social loafing. Likewise, when individuals conclude that they can make a unique contribution to a group effort, social loafing is reduced (Harkins and Petty, 1982).

Mock Jury Research

The trial of all crimes, except in cases of impeachment, shall be by jury.

—Constitution of the United States, Art. III, 1789

The right of trial by a jury of one's peers is one of the oldest and most cherished rights of Americans. Because of the critical role juries play in the American system of justice, they have come under increasing public and scientific scrutiny.

SOCIAL DILEMMAS

Task-performing groups rarely achieve their productive potential. The difference between a group's potential productivity and its actual productivity arises from at least two sources. First, *coordination losses* derive from a group's failure to coordinate or combine optimally the contributions of its individual members. Second, *motivation losses* occur when individuals do not exert their maximal effort in a group setting. The social loafing phenomenon is a good illustration of a motivation loss. There are also situations, termed **social dilemmas,** in which members of a group are faced with a conflict between maximizing their personal interests and maximizing the collective welfare (Komorita and Barth, 1985). Garrett J. Hardin (1968) provides the example of the "tragedy of the commons," in which the long-run consequences of self-interested individual choice result in social disaster. In a situation where a number of herders share a common pasture, each individual may reason that he or she will realize a benefit by placing an additional cow to graze in the pasture. But should each person follow this course, the commons will soon be overgrazed and each will be a loser. Hardin had in mind the problem of population growth. But the notion can also be applied to pollution problems, where harmful matter is placed in the environment.

In social dilemma situations, one member of the group often can and will provide for the public good, making one's own contribution unnecessary (Kerr, 1983). This "let George do it" approach is termed the **free-rider effect**. Take the choice confronting a soldier in a foxhole at the outset of a battle. The safest course for each soldier is to remain in the foxhole and not assault the enemy position. But if every soldier makes this choice, the battle will be lost and everyone in the unit will be

In particular, recent publicity has focused on "scientific jury selection." Of course prosecuting and defense attorneys, aware of the importance of a jury's attitudes, have always tried to size up potential panel members. The liberal lawyer Clarence Darrow (famous for his defense of John Scopes, a teacher who in the mid-1920s had taught evolutionary theory in violation of a Tennessee state law) evolved a formula for choosing a jury likely to be sympathetic to an "underdog" client: Prohibitionists, Presbyterians, Baptists, Scandinavians, and the wealthy were apt to convict and thus were to be avoided. Far more forgiving, he believed, were Jews, agnostics, Irish, and especially people who laugh a lot.

More recently, a number of social scientists have assisted defense attorneys in selecting jurors in a number of highly publicized trials of activists, war protesters, and minority-group members (including the Harrisburg Seven, the defendants in the Attica prison trial, the Camden 28, Angela Davis, the Indian defendants in the Wounded Knee case, and Katherine Boudin in the Brinks

killed or taken prisoner. The free-rider effect inclines individuals to resist appeals to unite with others for the public good (Olson, 1965). This was seen, for instance, in the Three Mile Island area, following the serious nuclear accident in 1979, in which radiation was leaked from the Unit 2 reactor. Although some area residents became active politically, the vast majority, while agreeing with the goals of the citizen protest groups, never contributed any time or money to the movement. Instead, they became free riders on the efforts of others (Walsh and Warland, 1983).

There is also a second basis for social dilemmas. In many group settings, there is not only the possibility that you can free ride on another person's contributions. There is also the danger that other people may free ride on your contributions. Such circumstances lead to the **sucker effect.** We are usually reluctant to "play the sucker," and instead we may reduce our own contributions to the group. The soldier in the foxhole may reason that if he alone were to assault the enemy position he would surely be killed, and thus he may choose not to fight.

Given the existence of social dilemma problems, what mechanisms are available to the members of a group to encourage one another to act cooperatively rather than selfishly? Hardin sought an answer in social controls that restrict individual actions deemed detrimental to the common good. Government frequently serves this function by regulating access to critical resources. Group norms may operate toward a similar end through the operation of informal sanctions. But there are other measures as well. Among these mechanisms are those that highlight group boundaries and foster a superordinate group identity (see the box " 'We' Versus 'They' " earlier in the chapter). Likewise, where individuals are made to feel that they are being rewarded for cooperative behavior (for example, by sharing in the benefits or profits equally), they are less disposed to engage in self-centered, individualistic behavior (Komorita and Barth, 1985).

robbery-murder case). The social scientists undertake to draw up a "jury profile" favorable to acquittal. Then defense lawyers exercise their twenty peremptory challenges to eliminate potential jurors lacking the desired characteristics. The practice has since spread to other types of cases, including those in which attorneys seek to determine the characteristics of jurors who are most likely to hold a defendant liable for large monetary damages (Andrews, 1982; Hunt, 1982). The implications of such behavioral research are significant: Jurors are seen not as free moral agents, able to assess impartially where the truth lies, but as beings whose mental and emotional processes are determined by such predictable variables as social status, education, age, gender, ethnic origin, religion, and personality traits.

Social scientists have studied juries in a number of ways. One approach is to interview various population samples in order to discern those characteristics— race, age, marital status, religion, political orientation, income, and education—

that serve to identify individuals with particular kinds of sympathies. Social scientists have also attempted to surmount the substantial difficulties that arise in attempts to study actual trial juries by using simulations, or "mock juries." Most usually the experimental subjects are college students. However, a group of University of Chicago sociologists has assembled, within real courtrooms, groups of twelve jurors selected from actual jury pools in Chicago, St. Louis, and Minneapolis (Strodtbeck, James, and Hawkins, 1957; Strodtbeck and Mann, 1956; James, 1959).

Private marketing firms have also employed simulated or mock juries to determine the best tactics for winning a favorable verdict (Andrews, 1982). On the basis of this research, the firms provide feedback to lawyers on how to try a case and how to speak and dress so as to enhance their popularity with the jurors. In 1980, the law firm representing MCI Communications in an antitrust suit against AT&T hired research consultants to develop a profile of potentially favorable jurors. The firm then arranged mock juries made up of such individuals, before whom the MCI attorneys practiced their arguments. Witnesses who were to give testimony favorable to MCI were videotaped and then advised as to how to present their testimony more effectively before the real court. Of interest, the MCI attorneys won their case before the real jurors, and MCI was awarded $1.8 billion, the largest antitrust verdict in history up until then. "When you get right down to it," said one of the MCI attorneys, "the process we used was the standard procedure for marketing a new toothpaste."

Jury research reveals that status, measured by either occupational or educational level, is related to the amount and kind of comments a juror makes during the process of deliberation (Gerbasi, Zuckerman, and Reis, 1977). On the whole, higher-status jurors have higher participation rates and make more procedural comments than do low-status jurors. Persons of high status are also more likely to be selected as "foremen." Men tend to participate more in the deliberations than do women. However, men and women do not appear to differ in their sympathy for a defendant or in their susceptibility to persuasion (Nemeth, Endicott, and Wachtler, 1976). Rita James Simon (James, 1959) finds that approximately 50 percent of the jurors' time is devoted to discussing opinions and personal experiences (either directly or indirectly related to the trial), 25 percent of the time to discussing procedural matters, 15 percent of the time to considering testimony, and 8 percent of the time to discussing the judge's instructions.

Some evidence suggests that whether a defendant is of high or low status has little effect on the verdict reached by a jury (Bray et al., 1978). But a juror is more likely to hand out harsher punishment to high-status defendants if they misuse the skills and talents associated with their high status (for instance, physicians who have committed murder). Likewise, when a crime is related to the attractiveness of the person, as in the case of a con game or swindle, an attractive defendant is punished more severely than an unattractive defendant. But when the crime is unrelated to the person's attractiveness, as in the case of burglary, the unattractive defendant is punished more severely (Sigall and Ostrove, 1975).

In recent years the twelve-person unanimous jury has been replaced in some states for certain crimes and civil litigations by juries as small as six and by decision rules that permit a verdict when two-thirds of the jurors agree. The U.S. Supreme Court has upheld these changes in a series of divided, but landmark, decisions (*Williams* v. *Florida,* 1970; *Johnson* v. *Louisiana,* 1972; *Apodaca et al.* v. *Oregon,* 1972; *Colgrove* v. *Battin,* 1973). In the case of *Williams* v. *Florida,* the nation's highest court said that six-person juries could achieve the functions of a jury no less successfully than could twelve-person juries:

> The performance of this role is not a function of the particular number of the body that makes up the jury. To be sure, the number should probably be large enough to promote group deliberation, free from outside attempts at intimidation, and to provide a fair possibility for obtaining a representative cross-section of the community. But we find little reason to think that these goals are in any meaningful sense less likely to be achieved when the jury numbers six, than when it numbers twelve. . . . And, certainly the reliability of the jury as a factfinder hardly seems likely to be a function of its size.

The Supreme Court upheld these changes in the structure and functioning of juries, not on the basis of legal or historical analysis, but on the grounds that social scientists have found that size and decision rules have no effect on the verdict produced by a jury (Saks, 1977). However, social scientists have accused the Supreme Court of misreading and misinterpreting their research findings (Gerbasi, Zuckerman, and Reis, 1977; Wrightsman, 1978). Moreover, recent studies have intensified the questioning process (Hastie, Penrod, and Pennington, 1983; Kerr and MacCoun, 1985). For instance, with respect to jury size, Michael J. Saks has found:

> Large juries, compared to small juries, spend more time deliberating, engage in more communication per unit time, manifest better recall of testimony, induce less disparity between minority and majority factions in their ratings of perceived jury performance and in sociometric ratings, . . . facilitate markedly better community representation, and, though not achieving statistical significance, tend to produce more consistent verdicts. [In contrast] small juries allow jurors to initiate more communication per member (although the total group communication was less than in twelve-person juries), share more equally in the communication, better recall arguments as a percentage of total arguments, obtain higher sociometric ratings of reasonableness and contributions to the jury's task. (1977: 105)

The change from unanimity to a two-thirds majority rule also makes a difference. Unanimous juries tend to deliberate longer, are more likely to air divergent views fairly, and make decisions in a more considered fashion (Hastie, Penrod, and Pennington, 1983). Further, only in unanimous juries can the minority effectively alter the course set by the majority (Saks, 1977; Tanford and Penrod, 1983). A good illustration of this is provided by the conspiracy trial for John Mitchell and Maurice Stans in 1974, in which former Attorney General Mitchell and Richard Nixon's campaign finance director Stans were charged with conspiracy to impede a U.S. Securities and Exchange Commission investigation of Robert L. Vesco in return for an alleged $200,000 contribution to the President's reelection campaign. The first vote was eight for conviction and four for acquittal.

Ordinarily, with such a split, the chances are 86 out of 100 against a jury eventually reaching a unanimous verdict of acquittal. But in this case, one of the four jurors who was for acquittal was able to persuade the others to vote his way (Wrightsman, 1978). Additionally, when incriminating evidence is strong, it is to the defendant's advantage to have a twelve-person jury (Gerbasi, Zuckerman, and Reis, 1977).

Robert D. Foss (1981) finds that juries that are required to reach unanimity rather than a specified quorum (for instance, concurrence among ten of twelve jurors) take longer to decide a case and are more likely to hang (be incapable of reaching a verdict). At first, the extent of disagreement in both types of juries is basically the same. But within fifteen minutes, disagreements in quorum juries drop to virtually half the level found in unanimous juries. Seemingly, jurors are less contentious in quorum juries and more opinionated in unanimous juries. Foss speculates that in quorum juries the members know that one or two of their number cannot block a verdict. Consequently, the members work toward consensus, even should one or two jurors remain steadfast in a contrary view. In contrast, differences among jurors in unanimous juries are more likely to build into sharp opposition, so that polarization ensues. Further, Foss conjectures that jurors in quorum juries may be less insistent in their views because they lack the power to block a verdict.

Other evidence from experimental juries suggests that lawyers should maintain eye contact with witnesses or jurors and change their vocal pitch and body movements at significant moments to stimulate juror attention. Strong evidence should go first and last, and weak material in the middle (Hunt, 1982b). The order in which a jury takes up decision tasks is also important. Conviction on charges considered first significantly increases the relative frequency of conviction on later charges (Davis et al., 1984).

SUMMARY

1. Groups show three major characteristics. First, they have boundaries. Second, they are products of social definition; they exist as social entities apart from the particular relationships people have with one another. Third, they are characterized by a consciousness of oneness. All three characteristics are highlighted and reinforced by rituals.

2. One of the broadest and most fundamental distinctions made by social psychologists in classifying groups is that between primary groups and secondary groups.

3. Primary groups are basic because (a) they function as agents of socialization, (b) they are the source by which we realize various social satisfactions, and (c) they are vehicles of social control.

4. Primary groups may function as intermediaries binding individuals to a larger organization. But they may also operate to undermine the official goals and commands of the larger organization.

5. Social psychologists distinguish between reference groups and membership

groups. Reference groups serve two functions: a normative function and a comparison function.

6. People tend to make more daring decisions when they are in groups than when they are alone—the risky-shift phenomenon.

7. Two explanations have received considerable support in accounting for the risky-shift phenomenon: the value hypothesis and release theory.

8. Groupthink is characterized by an illusion of invulnerability, shared stereotypes, a sense of morality, rationalization, an illusion of unanimity, conformity to group pressures, self-censorship, and mindguards.

9. When people work in groups, they work less hard than they do when working individually. Apparently people slack off in groups because they feel they are not realizing their fair share of the credit for the outcome or because they think that in the crowd they can get away with doing less work. However, identifiability and individual reward may serve as effective deterrents to social loafing.

10. Because of the critical role juries play in the American system of justice, they have come under increasing public and scientific scrutiny. Jury research reveals that status, measured by either occupational or educational level, is related to the amount and kind of comments that a juror makes during the process of deliberation. Evidence suggests, however, that whether a defendant is of high or low status has little effect on the verdict reached by a jury. In recent years the twelve-person unanimous jury has been replaced in some states for certain crimes and civil litigations by juries as small as six and by decision rules that permit a verdict when two-thirds of the jurors agree. Such changes make a difference in jury functioning.

GLOSSARY

Boundaries □ Demarcation lines between discrete social units; points or zones where social interaction begins or ends.

Choice shift □ A shift—whether toward risk or toward caution—that occurs when people make decisions in groups rather than individually.

Closed group □ A social unit with impermeable boundaries and therefore high or maximal barriers to entry by outsiders.

Cohesiveness □ Forces that act to keep individuals within a group and prevent them from leaving it; a feeling of "we-ness."

Consciousness of oneness □ A sympathetic identification with others in the same group; a sense of "we-ness," so that individuals are not merely in the group but of the group.

Ethnocentrism □ The tendency to view one's own group as the center of everything and to rate all other people with reference to it.

Free-rider effect □ One member of the group often can and will provide for the public good, making one's own contribution unnecessary.

Group □ Two or more people who share a feeling of unity and are bound together in relatively stable patterns of social interaction.

Groupthink □   A decision-making process occurring within highly cohesive groups in which the members are so preoccupied with maintaining group consensus that their critical abilities become ineffective.

Informal group □   A social organization that evolves within a formal organization, although it is not defined or prescribed by the formal organization.

Ingroup □   A social unit that a person either belongs to or identifies with.

Membership group □   A social unit to which an individual belongs.

Open group □   A social unit with permeable boundaries and therefore low or minimal barriers to entry by outsiders.

Outgroup □   A social unit that a person either does not belong to or does not identify with.

Primary group □   Two or more people who relate to one another in direct, intimate, personal ways.

Reference group □   The social unit with which people identify. They use the standards of their reference group to define their behavior and evaluate themselves.

Release theory of the risky-shift phenomenon □   The theory that the risky shift occurs in group discussions because the discovery of another person who endorses high risk taking releases more cautious group members from their social constraints.

Risky-shift phenomenon □   People's tendency to make more daring decisions when they are in groups than when they are alone.

Ritual □   A social act of symbolic significance that is performed on certain occasions by prescribed tradition.

Secondary group □   Two or more people who relate to one another in indirect, nonintimate, impersonal ways; the opposite of a primary group.

Social dilemmas □   Situations in which members of a group are faced with a conflict between maximizing their personal interests and maximizing the collective welfare.

Social distance □   A subjective sense of being set apart from (as opposed to being near to) certain people.

Social loafing □   When people work in groups, they work less hard than they do when working individually.

Social support □   The exchange of resources among individuals based on their interpersonal ties.

Sucker effect □   A situation in which other people free ride on our contributions and lead us to reduce our own contributions to the group.

Value hypothesis of the risky-shift phenomenon □   The theory that in social situations, people shift toward the dominant value of a given reference group.

14 POWER AND INFLUENCE

THE NATURE OF POWER
  Power: A Two-Way Street
  Attributions of Interpersonal
    Power
  A Clash of Wills
POWER AS PROCESS
  Shaping Definitions of the
    Situation

Assessment and Reassessment
Bases of Power
Power Preference
FROM MIGHT TO RIGHT
Elites
Control, Influence, and Authority
From Force to Authority
From Force to Influence

To discuss power—black power, imperialist power, gay power, communist power, Jewish power, labor power, Catholic power, military-industrial power, Jesus power—is to excite human passion. And no wonder, for power is like the formless inkblot of the Rorschach test—everyone is capable of "seeing" an extraordinary number of things in it. Power is the magic engine that propels us to the promised land; in the hands of the blessed, it can end tyranny and usher in an age of justice and freedom. Power is also the soulless machine that subjects us to misery and suffering; in the hands of the unworthy, it breeds oppression and exploitation. Indeed, the recurrent rallying cry crossing the ages of time has been "Power to the people." It has found expression in the question: "Shall power be the servant of the people (translated: 'me and my group') or the slave of selfish interests (translated: 'them and their group')?" In truth, of course, power usually serves someone's interest and advances some goal (Gamson, 1968).

THE NATURE OF POWER

Power implies that in human affairs one party (either an individual or group) is able to realize its will over the will of another party. Change is brought about in one party—in attitude, behavior, intention, motivation, or direction—that would not have occurred in the absence of power (Pruitt and Gahagan, 1974; Gamson, 1974). Indeed, if by social interaction we mean people mutually influencing and affecting one another, then every instance of social interaction involves power. Take such a simple matter as eye contact. Low-power individuals typically look less at a person's face when they are speaking to a high-power associate than when they are listening. In contrast, high-power individuals exhibit nearly equivalent rates of looking while speaking and while listening (Ellyson et al., 1980; Dovidio and Ellyson, 1982). And high-power individuals dominate a conversation by using a disproportionate amount of the available time and by interrupting low-power individuals (Kollock, Blumstein, and Schwartz, 1985). Clearly, as Amos H. Hawley observes: "Every social act is an exercise of power, every social relationship is a power equation, and every social group or system is an organization of power" (1963). Although we commonly equate power with big organizations—big government, big business, big unions, and so on—in reality it pervades all human interaction. Thus it finds expression in one-to-one, family, and couple relationships, a fact that has been raised to recent consciousness by the women's movement. Some social psychologists do not require that one party receive its preferred outcome in order for them to say that power has been exercised. If one party has increased the *probability* of a favorable outcome, that party is said to have exercised power (Gamson, 1968; Kaplowitz, 1978).

Power: A Two-Way Street

One cannot be powerful all by oneself. By ourselves we are neither powerful nor weak. To say someone has power is meaningless unless we indicate in relation to whom. Being powerful is an aspect of social interaction. It is a question of outcomes, or more precisely, the degree to which one party is able to translate its preferences—its will—into the reality of human life. Power, then, is often power over others. It frequently implies clashing interests and clashing social values—indeed, resistance and opposition.

Power is exerted even when both parties are equal in strength. One party's power may exactly balance and so cancel out the other party's power, or the two sides may have to arrive at some compromise that neither finds entirely satisfactory. Other arrangements may also prevail. For example, married couples often evolve spheres or domains where one or the other partner has strong interests in controlling decisions (Huston, 1983). In most cases, however, the dimensions of power are unbalanced; the interchange is uneven and unequal. Even so, power is hardly ever a one-way street. The reciprocity of influence persists as the parties piece together a working arrangement, whether it is between a child and his or her parents, a new nation and a superpower, or the poor and city hall (Olsen, 1970). Each still finds it necessary to take the other into account. Individuals exercise mutual control over each other's outcomes (Molm, 1981*a,b*). Thus as Machiavelli said over four centuries ago, even a victory is not absolute (Goode, 1972).

The powerful are dependent on the weak to grant or deny—facilitate or

Display of Power
One of the most extreme expressions of power in the United States
occurs in parental control and domination of children. An ever-pres-
ent, taken-for-granted aspect of the relationship is the power differential. Notice in this photo how the father and mother physically establish control of their sons by "locking them in" with their bodies.
(Patrick Reddy)

hinder—their gratification (Emerson, 1962). Power is not simply an instrument
to stop certain acts; it is a vehicle whereby people are activated to behave in
certain desired ways. Thus the strength of the poor and downtrodden is **passive
resistance:** Noncooperation, meaning the withholding of participation from an
ongoing enterprise, can exert considerable pressure on the dominant party.

Under slavery, blacks employed passive resistance by feigning illness in the
fields and on the auction block (Franklin, 1952; Genovese, 1974). Mohandas
Gandhi used this weapon against the British in gaining independence for India.
And blacks under the leadership of the late Reverend Martin Luther King, Jr.,
successfully launched a massive boycott in 1955 to force an end to segregation
on buses in Montgomery, Alabama, a tactic of nonviolent resistance that came
to be the hallmark of the civil rights movement of the early 1960s. Where a
minority lacks access to major power resources and finds the coercive remedies
of the state arrayed against it, acts of "omission" (for instance, failure to ride
the buses or patronize racist establishments) render the resisters less subject to
direct retaliation than acts of "commission," or more directly aggressive tactics
(Vander Zanden, 1965).

Since power involves at least two parties, Karen S. Cook and Richard M. Emerson (1978) seek to extend social exchange theory to encompass power. They view power as the ability of one party to exploit another party. Exchange enters the picture through notions of equity, which place normative restraints on exploitation. (People define it as "fair" or "just" when the members of a group receive rewards proportional to each individual's contribution.) David A. Baldwin (1978) takes exchange theory even further. He converts a threat like "Your money or your life" into exchange terminology as follows: "You give me your money and I will give you your life." Some social scientists object to calling such a transaction an exchange (Blau, 1964; Boulding, 1963, 1965). But Baldwin responds: "The phrase is rarely attributed to the physician who has just informed the patient that he will die within a year unless he can afford the expensive operation required to save his life. In such a situation, depicting 'your money or your life' as a proposed exchange may not seem quite so objectionable" (1978: 1230).

Attributions of Interpersonal Power

The human mind seemingly does not rest easy until it identifies the cause of a perceived effect—the attribution of a cause-and-effect relationship to a succession of two paired events (see Chapter 2). We are all interested in figuring out how much of a change in one person's behavior is caused by that of another person. For example, a mother may enter the family room where her daughter is watching television. The mother exclaims, "Now that's enough of that! Go practice your piano lesson." The daughter proceeds to shut off the television and begins playing the piano. From this course of events we infer that the mother influenced her daughter's behavior. We make the attribution of causality on the following basis: Given the daughter's state at time 1 (watching television), the mother has influence over the daughter if the mother gives direction to the daughter, who then does something at time 2 (playing the piano) that does *not* follow from the daughter's state at time 1 (Schopler and Layton, 1974).

John Schopler and Bruce Layton (1972) undertook to investigate the attribution of power under experimental conditions. Each male subject was assigned as an adviser to a partner who had previously done well or poorly on a social judgment task. This performance provided the basis for the adviser's expectations regarding his partner's performance on the next task. The subject did not know whether the partner accepted or rejected the advice, although presumably he accepted it. Later the subject was told the overall results of his partner's performance, which in some conditions was reported as having remained the same (low-low or high-high) and in other conditions as having changed (low-high or high-low). The subject then filled out a questionnaire in which he evaluated his influence over his partner.

As would be expected, the subject-advisers claimed more influence when their partners' performances changed than when the performances remained the same. But the interesting result was that subjects rated themselves as most influential when their partners succeeded, not when they failed. In sum, when the change

Disadvantage: A Function of Limited Power
Power answers the distributive question: Who shall get what, when, and how? (Patrick Reddy)

was in a *positively* valued direction, the subject's attribution of power was greatest. When the change was in a negative direction (the partner failed), the subject claimed considerably less influence.

A Clash of Wills

> *Power never takes a back step—only in the face of more power.*
>
> —Malcolm X, *Malcolm X Speaks*, 1965

We have observed that power generally implies opposition—clashing interests and social values. Within this context, power determines whose will shall prevail. More particularly, it provides an answer to the **distributive question** of *who shall get what, when, and how* (Lasswell, 1936). Or put in other terms, power largely decides who will be advantaged and who disadvantaged—who will be the haves and who the have-nots.

Power enables some individuals or groups to impose limits on the ability of others to compete and negotiate; one party can screen others off from access to knowledge, skills, and resources. In brief, some individuals or groups can fashion the flow of good things to themselves by continuously imposing their definitions of the situation in the arena of social interaction. They define what is possible, what is rational, what is real, and what is right.

And some individuals or groups can structure the working arrangements of life so as to make advantage self-perpetuating. Thus advantage becomes hereditary in fact, if not by law. Even when positions are theoretically open to all on the basis of merit (when academic degrees, scientific training, and special aptitudes as measured by standardized tests are the qualifications for offices), some people have a head start in the race for the good things. The disadvantaged seldom possess the resources for meeting the expense of long preparation or the connections and kinship that set them promptly on the right road. Thus many blacks have come to realize that equality of opportunity does not produce equality of results, a point President Johnson recognized when he asserted, in a Howard University commencement address in 1965:

> You do not take a person who for years has been hobbled by chains and liberate him, bring him up to the starting line of a race and . . . say, you're free to compete with all the others, and still justly believe that you have been completely fair.

The foundation of privilege is the production of social surplus—of goods and services over and above what is necessary for human survival. In the Neolithic period, human beings increasingly came to master nature through the cultivation of crops and the domestication of animals (agriculture). From that time, people were less dependent on the whims of nature than their hunting and gathering ancestors had been.

As social surpluses were created, some humans were released from the obligation of spending all their time in subsistence activities. They could apply their abilities to new occupations, such as pottery, masonry, and weaving. Not everyone needed to farm, and some could live off the surplus produced by others. Thus some could enjoy **privilege**—the possession or control of a portion of the surplus produced by a people (Lenski, 1966). Kenneth Prewitt and Alan Stone note:

> If craftsmen produce artifacts and ornaments, these status symbols become the possessions of the ruling class. If warriors venture forth to conquer and return with slaves and women, the slaves will serve in the fields and kitchens of the ruler and the women will be placed in their harems. If the productive labor of society is used to build palaces, temples, and monuments, these edifices will be inhabited by or dedicated to the members of the ruling class. It has been a constant fact of history that much more than an equal share of the social surplus is retained by the rulers for private pleasures. (1973: 12–13)

Power not only provides an answer to the distributive question of who shall get what, when, and how. If also answers the question of whose social values shall govern human affairs. That is to say, power determines which individual or group will make its behavioral preferences the operating normative rules for others. Power decides which party will be able to translate its social values into the accepted standards for defining situations, and which can make these standards stick through the manipulation of rewards and the imposition of penalties.

The women's movement has sensitized us to the political nature of morality. Women are punished for a variety of behaviors—sexual and otherwise—that are considered permissible to men. Nonconformity to prevailing male chauvinist standards confronts women with many personal problems. But rather than attacking the social arrangements producing these problems, the male-dominated order traditionally shunted women to control agents—clinical psychologists and

*S*tatus

> *Each evening for the past two weeks my friend and I have been playing frisbee out on the Oval. I can honestly say that we are the best throwers and catchers on campus. We are good, darn good! Actually I never thought that I would become so hooked on such a stupid thing. After all, how far can you get in the world with a frisbee? We do it for the status it provides—an expansive, even a euphoric feeling of being special and important. A lot of people stop and watch us. We enjoy their comments on how good we are and their encouragement to do more.*

psychiatrists—who defined the women as deviant, maladjusted, hung up with "unresolved oedipal complexes," and perhaps even "crazy." Women "got well" to the extent they made their peace with—buckled under to—prevailing male standards. Much the same point could be made as to whose "morality" shall prevail in the realm of sexual behavior (who will be judged "perverted," as in the case of homosexual behavior) and in the abortion debate.

POWER AS PROCESS

In life, we usually try to maximize the experiences that we perceive as being satisfying, desirable, and good. Since we are social beings, with few exceptions we realize the things we value—goods, services, status, information, sex, security, or love—through the facilitating actions of others. Life confronts us with the reality of our mutual dependency. Thus to achieve our goals, it is essential that we be able to control or influence other people's conduct. To some degree each of us is in a position to grant or deny, facilitate or hinder, one another's gratification (Emerson, 1962). Many of our needs can be satisfied only by creating appropriate behaviors in others (Kipnis, 1974).

Shaping Definitions of the Situation

> *The most important quality in a leader is that of being acknowledged as such. All leaders whose fitness is questioned are clearly lacking in force.*

> —André Maurois, *The Art of Living*

To get others to act in accordance with our wishes, we need to shape their definition of the situation in such a way that they will fit their acts to our acts in the desired manner. By manipulating various aspects of our performance, we seek to fashion others' perception of reality. In brief, through *impression management* (see Chapter 8), we try to create an image that will lead others to act as we wish them to act (Goffman, 1959; Stone, 1970; Blumstein, 1975).

Still another technique involves *altercasting* (see Chapter 8)—behavior that seeks to cast another person in a role that will bring forth the desired response (Weinstein and Deutschberger, 1963). For instance, another person may undertake to cast us in the role of a friend, hoping to activate the norms associated with the obligations of friendship: "Hey Jim, ole buddy, how about helping out your ole pal and. . . ." Similarly, altercasting processes operate upon leaders, who experience pressures to exemplify their followers' values and meet their followers' expectations with respect to leadership style (Beckhouse et al., 1975).

Whether we are engaged in impression management or altercasting, we need to make an assessment of two factors: (1) what resistance others are likely to pose to our desires, and (2) what resources we would need to expend in order to overcome their resistance. We are required, therefore, to engage in a process of self-indication. Through taking the role of the other (the process associated with the self—see Chapter 5), we make calculations of what it would take to get them to act or stop acting in certain ways. Simultaneously, the others are engaged in the same process regarding us.

It is important to stress that the application of power, even physical force, does *not* result in others' conforming to our wishes, or vice versa. Rather, conforming follows from the perception—the definition of the situation—that the cost of resistance is too high, whether the toll is expressed in physical suffering (pain) or psychological discomfort (loss of status, affection, property, and so on). It is for this reason that force need not be applied to be effective. Actually, even most cases of overt force are instances of force threats, promises of more to come:

> In few robberies is the victim physically subdued. Instead, he is threatened. If a bullying policeman shoves a citizen, the latter correctly perceives the action less as force than as a threat of more force, a possible escalation to death. (Goode, 1972: 512)

Usually force can remain, so to speak, unapplied in the wings. An American businessman does not ship arms to an unfriendly country, because he knows federal authorities would confiscate them. A divorced husband does not remove his children from his wife's custody, because he knows that she would haul him into court. Indeed, the use of physical force reveals a failure of the force-control processes (Goode, 1972).

Assessment and Reassessment

The reputation of power is power.

—Thomas Hobbes

As people fashion their actions in relation to the actions of others, all the parties make ongoing assessments of their resources and their willingness to commit varying amounts of these resources to the situation. It is a continual process of assessment and reassessment, as people weigh the relative costs and results of their past, present, and anticipated acts. They are literally engaged in an ongoing guessing game—one in which each party continually makes estimates of probable outcomes and then guides behavior accordingly. Hence the actual outcomes of interaction are problematic.

In considering power, we are again confronted with the axiom that if people define situations as real, they are real in their consequences. It is not so much actual resources that count in human affairs as people's beliefs about these resources—particularly their beliefs regarding the availability of resources and the willingness of various parties to commit them to the encounter (Wrong, 1968). Consequently, the appearance of power can be as useful as the real thing (Kaplowitz, 1978). General Erwin Rommel understood the tactical significance of this fact. When he arrived in North Africa in 1941 to assume command of the German panzer forces, he found that he had very few tanks in his Afrika Korps. The wily general—aptly nicknamed the "Desert Fox"—quickly ordered his workshops to fabricate dummy tank frames and mount them on Volkswagen chassis. These vehicles, equipped with devices to churn up clouds of dust, created the impression of enormous armored might when seen by his British adversaries across the desert terrain (Lewin, 1968). At the present time, notions of deterrence have assumed a prominent position in international diplomacy and domestic politics. The MX missile, whatever its military usefulness may be, is frequently seen as a weapon whose importance is largely symbolic, more a tool for manipulating perceptions than an instrument for fulfilling a real military need (Goleman, 1985b).

H. Andrew Michener, Edward J. Lawler, and Samuel B. Bacharach (1973) undertook a laboratory appraisal of the part that the perception of power plays in conflict situations. They distinguished four critical perceptual processes: (1) the *magnitude of damage* that an attacker can potentially inflict on a target, (2) the *probability* of actually exercising control over the target, (3) the target's ability to *block* the attacker's efforts, and (4) the target's ability to *retaliate* after the aggressor has struck an initial blow.

In order to examine the part played by these factors, student subjects were given a number of situations to evaluate. One depicted a confrontation between a salesman and his regional manager. (1) The manager could *damage* the salesman's commission-based income by either 10 or 90 percent (depending on two sets of conditions specified by the experimenter). (2) There was either a 10 or a 90 percent *probability* that the manager would actually do so. (3) The salesman had either a 10 or a 90 percent chance of *blocking* the manager's onslaught by appealing to a higher official in the organization. (4) The salesman could *retaliate* by moving to another company and taking either 10 or 90 percent of his customers with him (thus hurting the manager's sales record). The subjects were asked to make judgments regarding the respective power of the adversary and the target.

All four factors affected the subjects' judgments of the adversary's power: They saw it as greater under conditions of (1) high damage, (2) high probability, (3) low blockage, and (4) low retaliation. In short, the subjects ascribed greater power to an adversary when the adversary can and will wreak severe damage

MACHIAVELLIANISM

Since the publication of *The Prince* in 1532, the name of its author, Niccolò Machiavelli, has come to be associated with the use of ingratiation, hypocrisy, deceit, guile, and opportunism in human affairs. The Italian philosopher proposed various strategies for succeeding in politics. Central to his thinking was a view of human nature in which people are characterized by their underlying baseness, impersonal opportunism, and absence of ethical standards.

Two social psychologists, Richard Christie and Florence L. Geis (1970), undertook a series of experiments exploring **Machiavellianism,** an approach in which a person manipulates others for his or her own purposes. They scanned Machiavelli's writings for statements that could be translated into scale items—for instance, "The best way to handle people is to tell them what they want to hear," and "Anyone who completely trusts anyone else is asking for trouble." They also formulated various un-Machiavellian statements, for instance, "Honesty is the best policy in all cases," and "Barnum was very wrong when he said there's a sucker born every minute." In their experiments, Christie and Geis have found that subjects who endorse high-Mach (Machiavellian) statements are more likely than those who endorse low-Mach statements to employ manipulative and exploitative practices in their dealings with others.

In one such experiment, the "Ten Dollar Game," ten $1 bills are placed on a table in front of three subjects. The subjects are told they can make some money if they are good at bargaining: The money will go to any *two* of them who can agree with each other on how to divide the $10. (The subjects are not permitted to divide the money three ways.) The game ends when any two players make an agreement that a third party cannot break. In the experiments, the low-Machs lost while the high-Machs won

and when the target cannot intercept the assault or retaliate. The researchers suggest that the threatened use of a coercive power base—rather than mere possession of the power resource—exerts a great influence on attributed power:

> Even persons who are outgunned or trapped in low-power positions can manipulate the power attributed to them by vigorously activating (or pretending to activate) their limited resources. The consequences for impression management seem obvious, given that one can frequently fake the probability of initiating action with relative ease. (Michener, Lawler, and Bacharach, 1973: 158)

In sum, as pointed out earlier, it is not so much actual resources that count in human affairs as people's beliefs about these resources—their perceptions and definitions of situations.

overwhelmingly; no high-Mach failed to be a member of the winning coalition. In sum, high-Machs manipulated more, were persuaded less, and persuaded others more than did their associates.

High-Machs differ from low-Machs primarily in their cool detachment. Low-Machs, in contrast, are characterized by their openness to emotional involvement. High-Machs are thick-skinned enough to withstand the enticements and dangers of interpersonal involvements that might interfere with task achievement. Consequently, the high-Machs show a general lack of susceptibility to social pressures urging compliance, cooperation, or attitude change. The more personal, open orientation of the low-Machs makes them less effective as strategists, but they are more sensitive to others as individual persons. On the whole, high-Machs have little defensive investment in their own self-image and their own beliefs, being strongly task-oriented. Not surprisingly, it seems that high-Mach lawyers are more successful than low-Mach lawyers in extracting from a witness the testimony they desire (Sheppard and Vidmar, 1980). And individuals who hold a Machiavellian view of life are more convincing liars than non-Machiavellians (Geis and Moon, 1981).

Christie and Geis admit that at first their image of the high-Machs was a negative one, associated with shadowy and unsavory manipulations:

> However, after watching subjects in laboratory experiments, we found ourselves having a perverse admiration for the high Machs' ability to outdo others. . . . Their greater willingness to admit socially undesirable traits compared to low Machs hinted at a possibly greater insight into and honesty about themselves. . . . This does not mean that our admiration was unqualified; it might better be described as selective. (Christie and Geis, 1970: 339)

In short, the researchers ended up with different emotional reactions to the term "Machiavellianism" than they had when they began the experiments.

Randall Collins (1975) observes how this principle operates in maintaining a dictatorship. The dictator exerts control not because he can personally coerce every single person, but because his police or army can. Further, he controls the police and army not by his personal might, but because he enjoys a position where he can bring power to bear against dissidents and rebels. Even if everyone in the organization should feel antagonistic toward him, the organization makes it risky for any person to rebel:

> The dictator reigns by organizing matters so that his followers watch each other and are afraid to take the lead in acting against him. . . . In effect, power creates a self-fulfilling prophecy—men who are powerful are so because others believe they are powerful. It is this belief, in turn, which makes subordinates maintain the sanctions that keep their rulers powerful. (Collins, 1975: 367)

Bases of Power

> *Power over a man's subsistence amounts to a power over his will.*

> —Alexander Hamilton, *The Federalist,* 1788

Underlying much of our discussion is the notion of **bases of power.** These are the resources that individuals or groups can muster in the attempt to impose their will in human affairs. The bases of power include *what* is used and the means to decide *how* it is used. Resources tend to fall into three categories (Gamson, 1968; Rogers, 1974):

1. *Constraints* are resources that enable one party to add *new disadvantages* to the situation. They are generally viewed by participants as punishment. Constraints involve doing harm to the body, the psyche, or the possessions of another. Examples are sit-ins, imprisonment, and the use of weapons.
2. *Inducements* are resources that enable one party to add *new advantages* to the situation. They are generally viewed by participants as rewards. Inducements usually entail a transfer of socially defined good things— such as material items, services, or positions of status—in exchange for compliance with the wishes of the power wielder.
3. *Persuasion* includes all resources that enable one party to change the minds of others *without* adding either advantages or disadvantages to the situation. Through persuasion, individuals or groups are led to prefer the same outcomes that the power wielder prefers. Persuasion may be a function of one party's reputation for wisdom, personal attraction, or control of communication media and skills.

To gain mastery of critical resources is to gain mastery of people. To control key resources is to interpose ourselves or our group between others and the means whereby these others meet their biological and social needs. It is to render people vulnerable and susceptible to our wishes by giving us leverage over their definitions of the situation. Elites achieve this leverage through their command of rewards, punishments, and persuasive communications. To the extent that elites control critical resources, they are able to dictate the terms by which the game of life is played. At times, to play the game "by the rules" means that it is no game at all, because "the deck is stacked"—the outcome is a foregone conclusion.

A somewhat different approach for describing the sources of social power was first advanced by John R. P. French and Bertram Raven in 1959 and later modified by Raven (Collins and Raven, 1969*a, b*; Raven, 1974). This approach, which has had a considerable impact on the social psychological study of power (Podsakoff and Schriesheim, 1985), distinguishes among the following bases of power:

☐ *Reward and coercive power* derive from the ability of one party to mediate rewards or punishments for another party. The rewards and punishments may be impersonal (for instance, financial benefits or fines; promotions or dismissals) or personal (for instance, love or hate; acceptance or rejection).

☐ *Expert power* derives from the knowledge, experience, skills, or special competence that one party possesses or is believed to possess (Tedeschi, Schlenker, and Bonoma, 1973; Horai, Naccari, and Fatoullah, 1974; Huston, 1983). Accepting an attorney's advice in legal matters provides a good illustration. Expert power may be lost if individuals transmit their special knowledge or skills to others, as teachers do.

☐ *Informational power* depends less on the social relationship than on the specific content of the communication or new cognition that is transmitted. An example would be a housewife who is persuaded by a vacuum cleaner salesman that his machine is far superior to her present model.

☐ *Referent power* operates when one party uses another party as a "frame of reference" for self-evaluation. If one party (a person or group) is highly attracted to another, it undertakes to think and act like the admired party. People adopt the suggestions and ideas of people with whom they identify (Huston, 1983). Referent power may be either positive or negative. When it is negative, as it is among countercultural youth, one party seeks to think and act in a fashion opposite to the standards of the other party.

☐ *Legitimate power* derives from some code or standard by which one party is recognized as having a right to assert power over another party. For instance, a superior in a university, business, church, or other organization is commonly recognized as having legitimate power (Michener and Burt, 1975).

Although social psychologists may differ in the scheme they prefer for conceptualizing power, we should not assume that they are talking about wholly different things. As you probably noted, the two schemes described in this section display considerable overlap. Neither is right or wrong; both are tools that are more or less useful for some specific scientific or scholarly purpose. And they draw attention to the idea that power finds expression in a good many different ways.

Power Preference

If people have several bases of power available to them, how do they decide which to use? When French and Raven (1959) first compiled their list of the sources of power, they assumed that people were basically rational, and that power holders would therefore use the form of power requiring the least surveillance and producing the longest-lasting results. Logically this meant that power holders would choose informational power wherever they could. Coercion would be their last choice, since it requires considerable surveillance and tends to arouse the anger of the subordinate.

Raven (1974) has since concluded that these expectations were oversimplified and naive. He now says that a large number of factors influence power prefer-ences and many of these are not "rational." Likewise, David Kipnis (1976) points out that power holders do not always have a free hand in selecting their means of influence (Relatively low rank in the organizational hierarchy may preclude their employing some possibilities) and in other instances they may not recognize that a particular tactic can be legitimately used by them.

In some situations, people prefer to use coercive power for the personal satisfaction it provides, as when one feels a good deal of hostility toward the person being influenced (Raven and Kruglanski, 1970; Raven, 1974; Zimbardo, Haney, and Banks, 1973). People's need for self-esteem may also influence their choice of power. (They may select expert power in order to appear "knowledge-able" or coercive power to demonstrate how "tough" and "manly" they are.) And at times, holders of power may need to experience the feeling that they them-selves are the source of the social influence (Fodor and Farrow, 1979). This is essentially the advice that Frantz Fanon (1966), a black psychoanalyst from Martinique who served with the Algerian rebels, gave to the "wretched of the earth." Because the systematic violence of colonialism deadened and degraded the natives, Fanon said, they can achieve psychic wholeness only by committing acts of violence against the white rulers and masters whom they wish to supplant: "At the level of individuals, violence is a cleansing force. It frees the native from his inferiority complex and from his despair and inaction; it makes him fearless and restores his self-respect (1966: 73). The subjugated, then, gain self-respect by seeing that *they,* not their former oppressor, are the source of change (Raven, 1974).

An accumulating body of social psychological research in business and indus-try suggests that the following ten factors influence power holders in selecting a given source of power:

1. A supervisor does not necessarily use rewards to influence workers who tend to do their job well, who are similar to the supervisor, and whom the supervisor likes. Power holders usually feel that they can count on the continued compliance of workers whom they like and who tend to do the job well, so that reward is not necessary to gain compliance (Kipnis, 1976).

2. The presence of noncompliant workers—workers who deliberately re-fuse to obey orders—increases the number of rewards given to com-pliant workers. Fewer rewards are given to compliant workers when all workers are compliant (Goodstadt and Kipnis, 1970).

3. Power holders are most likely to use rewards when the power holders wish to secure the goodwill of their subordinates or when the power holders have some doubts that the subordinates will continue their compliance (Kipnis, 1976).

4. Informational and persuasive sources of power are most likely to be directed at subordinates whose unsatisfactory performance is attributed by superiors to a lack of motivation. The supervisor's concern is to find out the causes of a subordinate's poor attitudes and, if possible, to persuade the subordinate to change (Kipnis and Consentino, 1969; Kipnis, 1974).

Power and Control
Those who control other people's sources of livelihood can dictate the terms on which the game of life is played. They possess the leverage to translate their wishes into reality through specifying working hours, production quotas, the assembly-line layout, length of the lunch break, and the like. Unions provide a source of counterpower. Here, auto workers gleefully race to their cars when the afternoon whistle sounds at 4:30. (Patrick Reddy)

5. Where a supervisor attributes a subordinate's poor performance to ineptness, persuasion is rarely attempted. Rather, a supervisor invokes his or her expert powers and devotes time to training the subordinate (Kipnis and Consentino, 1969; Kipnis, 1974).

6. Coercion is employed against subordinates who reveal "poor attitudes" and deny the legitimacy of the superior and the goals of the organization. In brief, a leader's choice of coercive measures often stems from the perception that the subordinate's resistance is willful and voluntary (Kipnis and Consentino, 1969; Goodstadt and Kipnis, 1970; Goodstadt and Hjelle, 1973; Kipnis, 1984).

7. Coercion is employed most frequently by superiors who lack self-confidence, who are oppressed by feelings of powerlessness, or who have so many subordinates that they cannot devote personal attention to them (Kipnis and Lane, 1962; Kipnis and Consentino, 1969; Kipnis, 1974; Goodstadt and Hjelle, 1973).

8. Once a supervisor has employed coercion, it becomes more difficult for the supervisor to shift to a more subtle approach (like persuasion) in later influence situations (Kipnis, 1976; Kipnis and Schmidt, 1985).

9. When power holders use stronger means of influence (especially coercion), they are more likely to devalue the subordinate and therefore to

THE USE OF POWER

Power tends to corrupt and absolute power corrupts absolutely.
—Lord Acton, letter to Mandell Creighton, April 5, 1887

The absence of power renders individuals vulnerable to the wishes and dictates of others. But the possession of power may also present problems. Research by social psychologist David Kipnis (1984) shows that the control of power produces significant psychological changes in people. Power holders become less reluctant to exploit those they control; they overestimate their own importance; and their moral values become increasingly self-serving. These changes occur whether the power holders are men or women who dominate their spouses, executives who manage businesses, or political leaders who govern nations.

In order to study the effects of power on people, Kipnis distinguished among three types of tactics: *soft tactics*—ingratiating, flattering, and pleading behaviors; *rational tactics*—explaining, discussing, and compromising behaviors; and *strong tactics*—ordering, threatening, and angry behaviors. He found that the use of strong tactics typically sets in motion a train of events. First, when the tactics result in success, the power holder concludes that he or she controls the other person. When the same tactics succeed time after time, the notion is reinforced and strengthened. Second, the power holder begins to devalue the individuals he or she controls.

By making other people do what we want, we attribute their behavior, no matter how well they do their tasks, to our orders rather than to their own drive and abilities. Consequently, we do not give them credit for what they accomplish. And third, the power holder finds it increasingly easy to exploit the less powerful.

In research involving 195 couples, Kipnis found that partners who used strong tactics saw themselves as having the final say in making decisions. Yet significantly, those who unilaterally controlled decision making had less satisfactory relationships than did those who employed rational tactics and undertook to share power. Indeed, dominance and power were negatively related to feelings of affection. Even couples' sexual relations were evaluated as less satisfactory when one partner was seen as the final decision maker. Power had its price not only in domestic relations. In business situations, authoritarian leaders routinely complained that their employees lacked motivation to work hard. And the authoritarians evaluated their employees' work as less satisfactory than did democratic leaders. Since the authoritarian leaders told their employees exactly what to do and how to do it, they downplayed their workers' skills and abilities and rated them as less suitable for promotion. Over time, these attributions of control led to a steady denigration of the work force and a disruption of harmonious management-employee relationships.

believe that they themselves are more powerful (Kipnis, 1976; Kipnis and Schmidt, 1985).

10. When power holders lose faith in their own effectiveness, they are more likely to be attracted to coercive remedies (Kipnis, 1976). Coercion tends to be the means of last resort when other measures have failed (Raven and Kruglanski, 1970; Kipnis, 1974; Kipnis and Schmidt, 1985).

On the whole, it appears that power holders anticipate the possible effectiveness of each of their bases of power and avoid using those that they believe are ineffective (Raven and Kruglanski, 1970; Kipnis, 1976). Overall, expert and referent power tend to be positively associated with the job performance of subordinates, their satisfaction with their supervisors, and their satisfaction with their work; coercive and legitimate power more often are negatively associated with these components (Podsakoff and Schriesheim, 1985). Even so, the best power tactic depends on the situation and the people involved. It seems that any of the types of power can work if it is used at the right time by the right person (Kipnis and Schmidt, 1985). (See boxed insert.)

Psychologists have focused primarily on power holders as individuals. In contrast, sociological interest has centered on various structural characteristics of power in organizational settings. For instance, Robert Michels (1911/1966) claims that large-scale organization inevitably leads to the concentration of power in the hands of a few. In turn, the few use their positions to advance their own fortunes and selfish interests. He terms this the **iron law of oligarchy.** Michels says that factors inherent to organizational life feed this tendency: Power holders become adept at organizational manipulation; they establish machinery that makes it difficult for opponents to challenge their leadership; they dominate the organization's communication networks and disciplinary agencies; they control the organization's finances; they buy off or absorb (coopt) potential rivals; and they benefit from the indifference and apathy of the rank-and-file members.

Michels says that the developmental course of European labor unions and socialist parties demonstrates that power holders seldom reflect the democratic aspirations that theoretically are espoused by their organizations. Some sociological research has found that the iron law of oligarchy does tend to hold for many labor unions, professional associations, private clubs, and legislative bodies (Selznick, 1952; Lipset, Trow, and Coleman, 1956; Tannenbaum, 1965; Schlesinger, 1965). Nonetheless, most sociologists insist that tendencies toward oligarchy hardly constitute an "iron law" (Gouldner, 1955; Olsen, 1968; Collins, 1975).

FROM MIGHT TO RIGHT

> *The state calls its own violence law, but that of the individual crime.*
>
> —Max Stirner

Force is an act performed by an individual or group aimed at compelling another individual or group to follow a given course of action. Force implies coercion; an

*P*roperty redefinition

I borrowed a television set from a guy on my floor. A gang of about seven of us were watching a baseball game when the owner came in and wanted to repossess the television. There was one problem. The group wanted to watch the game and told the owner to go to hell. Under the circumstances, the guy was helpless to enforce his claim to the television. For the duration of the game we had in effect redefined whose "property" the television was. As pointed out in the lecture, property does not consist of physical items, but a set of rights indicating what one party can do and what another party cannot do. Property consists of an enforceable claim with respect to some scarce object. We were able to enforce our claim to the television, and the "owner" was not.

individual or group is induced to follow directions because the power holder can take their life or inflict physical and psychological suffering on them. In effect, force is the final court of appeals in human affairs; there is no appeal from force except the action of superior force (Lenski, 1966; Walster and Walster, 1975).

Force is the foundation of the **state,** an arrangement consisting of people who exercise an effective monopoly in the use of physical coercion within a given territory. The state may be many things, but above all, it is the military and the police. One popular belief is that the state is merely a kind of grade-school assembly in which people get together to operate for their common good. Under some circumstances this may indeed be the case. But when vital interests are at stake—when "the chips are down" or "push comes to shove"—the issue becomes who will threaten and fight whom, and who will win. It is in this context that we speak of the state; it is the dominant apparatus of violence (Collins, 1975).

Elites

The great question which, in all ages, has disturbed mankind, and brought on them the greatest part of those mischiefs which have ruined cities, depopulated countries, and disordered the peace of the world, has been, not whether there be power in the world, nor whence it came, but who should have it.

—John Locke, *Two Treatises on Civil Government,* 1690

The word **elite** grates on the ears of many Americans. It comes close to denying that all people are created equal, and this is to deny (or so it seems to some) the Declaration of Independence. But the term finds a useful place in the social sciences. It draws our attention to the fact that some individuals or groups enjoy more power than other individuals or groups in the making of the crucial decisions that affect people's daily lives. By their exercise of control over particular

Property: An Enforceable Claim
Property does not consist of physical objects but of socially recognized rights.
Elites can draw upon the state to enforce their "no trespassing" claims. (Patrick
Reddy)

spheres of social activity, elites are the gatekeepers of privilege. They open or
close the gates that regulate the flow of good things to various individuals and
groups.

Although many contemporary observers of society accept the existence of
elites, they do not all draw the same conclusions. Some see the privileges of the
elite and conclude that the rulers exploit and manipulate the rules for their own
benefit. The elite live—and live well—from the efforts of others. Other observers
argue that rulers perform essential and beneficial tasks. They say that if rulers
monopolize power, it is only to give uniform direction to society and to muster
the necessary force to withstand the attacks of internal and external foes. These
observers agree that the elite live well, but they claim that it is the just reward
for the elite's special skills and devotion to duty. Thus one view stresses the
rulers' privileges and their exploitation of the ruled, while the other focuses on
the rulers' responsibilities and public service (Prewitt and Stone, 1973; Della-
Fave, 1980).

Control, Influence, and Authority

In considering matters relating to the state and elites, it is helpful to distinguish
among various types of power. One useful distinction is based on people's motives
in complying with superior power. **Control** suggests that people *submit* to the
power of others; resistance is overcome not because people come to prefer a

given course of action, but because resistance has been made prohibitively expensive or impossible. **Influence,** in contrast, suggests that in the course of interaction, people undergo an authentic change in their preferences in accordance with the preferences of power wielders. Given the same situation, they would not choose the same course of action that they favored before power was exercised.

It is also useful to distinguish between people's perception of power as legitimate or illegitimate. **Authority is legitimate** power—power used in accordance with the social values of those who are ruled and under conditions that the ruled view as proper. ("Legitimate," however, does not necessarily imply that the ruled *prefer* the course of action they take in obedience to authority. Army officers have the authority to lead their men into battle, but this does not mean that the men prefer combat as a course of action.) Illegitimate power, in contrast, is seen by those who are ruled as operating both against their preferences and against their sense of right and wrong (Etzioni, 1968; Della-Fave, 1980).

Max Weber (1864–1920), a distinguished German sociologist, pointed out that power can be legitimated in three ways. In *legal-rational* authority, power holders claim obedience on the grounds that their dictates and orders fall within the province of their office. Obedience is not owed to the person but to a set of impersonal principles contained within the law. People subscribe to the law and consequently follow the policies and instructions of those who rule in accordance with the law. Legal-rational authority is "a government of laws, not of people." The governments of Western democracies are built upon this bedrock concept.

In *traditional authority,* power holders look to the sanctity of custom to legitimate their exercise of power. Often the ruler's right to be obeyed derives from an "eternal," inviolable, and sacred tradition. This was the case with medieval kings who ruled in the name of "a divine right" ordained by God. And many Roman Catholics believe that the Pope enjoys divine guidance when acting on spiritual matters, making his decisions in these areas infallible.

Charismatic authority rests on the extraordinary, superhuman, or supernatural qualities that followers attribute to their leader. Religious prophets and political and military heroes often provide this type of leadership. People associate miracles, revelations, heroic feats, and baffling successes with charismatic persons. Christ, Muhammad, Napoleon, Joan of Arc, Hitler, Mao, and Lenin possessed charismatic authority with their followers.

From Force to Authority

> *Might is right, and justice is the interest of the stronger.*
>
> —Plato, *The Republic,* 370 B.C.

> *The more might, the more right.*
>
> —Plautus, *Truculentus,* 190 B.C.

Edmund Burke (1729–1797), English statesman and orator, observed that "the use of force alone is but temporary. It may subdue for a moment; but it does not remove the necessity of subduing again: and a nation is not governed, which is perpetually to be conquered." Authority (*legitimate* power), then, becomes the grand prize.

Though force (control) may be an effective means for seizing power, and though it remains the ultimate foundation of any system of privilege, it is not the most effective means for maintaining and exploiting a position of advantage. For one thing, it is both inefficient and costly. Much of the profit is consumed by the costs of coercion. (A large portion of the time, energy, and wealth of the elite is drained in supervising a garrison state.) Further, honor, which normally is a prized value, is denied those who rule by force alone. And finally, if the elite was motivated by revolutionary visions for building a new social order, the dreams and ideals remain unfulfilled until the masses come to embrace the new order as their own. Thus those who seize power by force find it to their advantage to legitimize their rule, to transform force into *authority* (Lenski, 1966). What might otherwise seem immoral must be given the appearance of morality. The strength of an elite lies not in its ability to rule through coercion and violence but in its ability to induce the masses to accept its vision of the world.

This task may not be as difficult as it seems at first. To begin with, the elite is in a good position to rewrite the law as it sees fit. Since legal statutes are stated in general, impersonal terms, law gives the appearance of supporting abstract principles of justice rather than special interests. And since a law exists before the events that it is applied to, it gives the appearance of objective impartiality. Yet laws are not neutral; they favor some individuals or groups. Anatole France, the French novelist and satirist, wrote: "The law in its majestic equality forbids the rich as well as the poor to sleep under bridges, to beg in the street, and to steal bread." And an impoverished bank robber receives a sentence in the state penitentiary, while a bank officer who embezzles money is placed on probation and ordered to receive psychiatric counseling.

In many cases, a new elite does not need to change the laws to advance its ends. Normally the old laws were written to serve the interests of the previous elite. Once the positions of the old elite have been seized, the new elite can simply use them as vehicles for furthering their own interests (Lenski, 1966).

From Force to Influence

Those in power want only to perpetuate it.

—Justice William O. Douglas

Elites find it to their advantage not only to transform force into authority, but to transform force into *influence*—to secure approval and support from the masses for elite decision making. Whereas authority refers to the masses' acceptance of their rulers as legitimate, influence refers to the masses' approval of their rulers' policies. Engineering such approval entails **political impression management**. Power is achieved by controlling, fashioning, and sustaining the elite's definition of the situation. By inducing people to share its view of reality, the elite can persuade them to act in the manner it prescribes. To define situations

The Non-neutral Law

Laws are neither neutral nor neutrally enforced. Ghetto residents are more likely to be accosted by the police than middle-class individuals. Indeed, police efforts are focused on maintaining "law and order" within the ghetto. Here a policeman stops two ghetto residents who are carrying stereo equipment. The policeman detains the two until he can "check out" the equipment. He proceeds to call their names and the stereo serial numbers in to his superiors. As it turned out, the equipment had not been stolen, nor were the two men "wanted." (Patrick Reddy)

for people is to control the situations and thus the people. Political impression management can be analyzed in terms of (1) controlling the flow of information and (2) symbolic mobilization of support (Hall, 1972).

Flow of Information

Basic to political impression management is the need to gain control over the flow of information. The rulers limit the *outflow* to the public, releasing only information that reflects positively on elite rule, and they maximize the *inflow* of accurate information concerning the political pulse of the public and the plans of the opposition. This activity primarily occurs *backstage*. It involves insulation, concealment, and secrecy. As revealed by the tapes from the Nixon White House, considerable planning, structuring, and rehearsing of performances take place backstage. Hidden from public view are the manipulative, selfish, cynical, uncertain, informal, and immoderate activities of the elite that, if they were known, would discredit its leadership before the public. There are countless examples of cases in which illegal acts occurred, the public was deceived, and Congress was deliberately misled through backstage elitist arrangements. These practices were not limited to the Nixon White House; the Pentagon papers reveal similar differences in the Johnson administration between backstage and front-stage behavior. Similarly, the Reagan administration, like its predecessors, has engaged in political impression management. For instance, Murray L. Weidenbaum, then chairman of the President's Council of Economic Advisers, admitted to a 1982 congressional hearing that the Reagan administration was aware of the severe 1981 economic recession for eight months before the White House acknowledged the downturn (*Columbus Dispatch,* June 10, 1982, p. A5).

Symbolic Mobilization of Support

Also basic to political impression management are *front-stage* performances, where elites employ verbal and nonverbal symbols to strengthen and maintain their position. In our time, mass anxiety and uncertainty have intensified as more and more of everyday life is caught up in the swirling and threatening currents of international happenings—wars and confrontations moving to the brink of war, the politics of oil and oil embargoes, hijackings, kidnappings, bombings, riots, and terrorism. Indeed, political scientist Murray Edelman argues that the masses, unorganized and overwhelmed with a sense of their essential powerlessness, look for the alleviation of their anxiety through the symbolic reassurances provided by the elite. The bulk of political talk serves to reassure the masses that they are in good hands and that all goes as well as can be expected (Edelman, 1967, 1975).

Elites mobilize support for their policies in a variety of ways. For one thing, they enjoy a considerable advantage over others in their ability to define issues. Their prominence (or the prominence of their representatives) enables them to upstage others through news conferences, press briefings, public speeches, and television interviews, as well as indirectly through news leaks, trial balloons, and off-the-record confidences. Further, elites undertake to shape the ideas people hold—their ideologies—so that listeners are turned into believers and believers into actors. For instance, support for American foreign policy in the post–World War II period has been mobilized through instilling in the populace a sense of mission against the menace of international communism.

Front-stage performances similarly entail the fashioning of a "personality cult" around an elite leader. Efforts are made to project the leader as a magnetic, wise, able, deliberate person capable of heroic feats, baffling successes, and even miracles. Whereas the elite leader is cast in heroic terms, the leaders of discontented groups are portrayed as villains, hypocrites, and scoundrels (as in the FBI attempts to smear Reverend Martin Luther King, Jr.). The elite's ability to label dissenters as deviants means that the issue represented by the dissenters is destroyed or deflected. Public opinion polls after the 1968 Chicago police riot and the 1970 Kent State University massacre clearly showed that the public blamed the demonstrators, not the police or the National Guard (Hall, 1972).

The mass media play an important part in these processes. In her study of newsrooms, Marilyn Lester (1980) shows that everyday life is not broken down and packaged into neat and distinct public events that news workers simply mirror. Newsworthiness is not inherent to certain occurrences. Journalists must select the happenings that they will portray and then translate them into public events for a mass constituency. Consequently, occurrences are successively filtered through a set of news gates. Values, norms, and rules function as screens that journalists employ in measuring the newsworthy character of various events.

The creation of "news" by individuals who have practical reasons for producing one sort of news instead of another is reflected in press coverage of the oil spill from Union Oil's Platform A off the Santa Barbara, California, coast in January 1969. Conservationists and local officials opposed the offshore oil-drilling program. They sought to promote news stories that oil drilling in the Santa Barbara Channel was unsafe, that the oil leak was never brought under complete control, and that considerable ecological damage was occurring. In contrast, the oil companies and the federal government were promoting statements and reports minimizing the oil damage and encouraging the offshore drilling program.

Nationwide press coverage of activities favorable to the oil companies was much more extensive than that given to conservationists (93.2 percent versus 6.8 percent), especially in comparison with the alternative coverage provided by the *Santa Barbara News Press* (54.5 percent versus 45.5 percent). It was not so much that the oil companies did inherently more newsworthy things. In fact, the oil companies could do rather routine things and get coverage, whereas the conservationists could do nonroutine and occasionally bizarre things (for instance, engage in sit-ins, sail-ins, and fish-ins) and get less coverage.

Clearly, news is a product of reality-constructing activities and not simply of reality-describing ones. Groups have differing and competing uses for occurrences and hence differing and competing conceptions of what is and is not newsworthy. One dimension of power is the ability to make one's own preferred account the perceived reality of others. In sum, a crucial dimension of power is the ability to "create" events and fashion their portrayal in ways that conform with one's needs and interests.

SUMMARY

1. Power entails a social relationship. One cannot be powerful all by oneself. Power is often power over others.
2. We are most likely to attribute influence to ourselves when another person, in response to our behavior, changes for the better.
3. Power provides answers to the distribution question of who shall get what, when, and how, and to the question of whose values shall govern human affairs.
4. Many of our needs can be satisfied only by inducing appropriate behaviors in others. Through impression management or altercasting, we seek to induce others to fit their acts to our acts in the desired manner. In brief, we seek to influence others' definitions of the situation.
5. It is not so much actual resources that count in human affairs as people's beliefs about these resources—particularly their beliefs regarding the availability of resources and the willingness of various parties to commit them to an encounter.
6. The bases of power can be classified in several ways. One approach distinguishes among constraints, inducements, and persuasion; the other distinguishes among reward and coercive power, expert power, informational power, referent power, and legitimate power. Neither approach is right or wrong; both are simply tools for analysis.
7. On the whole, power holders anticipate the possible effectiveness of each of their bases of power and avoid using those that they believe are ineffective.
8. In effect, force constitutes the final court of appeals in human affairs; there is no appeal from force except the action of superior force.
9. The state is the dominant apparatus of violence. To gain legitimate power is the grand prize.
10. Elites find it to their advantage not only to transform force into authority, but to transform force into influence. This entails political impression management, which involves controlling the flow of information and symbolic mobilization of support.

GLOSSARY

Authority □ Legitimate power; power used in accordance with the social values of those who are ruled, and under conditions that the ruled view as proper.

Bases of power □ The resources that individuals or groups can muster in the attempt to impose their will in human affairs. The bases of power include what is used and the means to decide how it is used.

Control □ Submission to the power of others; resistance is overcome not because people come to prefer a given course of action, but because resistance has been made prohibitively expensive or impossible.

Distributive question □ Who shall get what, when, and how?

Elite □ Those who rule, as opposed to those who are ruled.

Force ☐ An act performed by an individual or group aimed at compelling another individual or group to follow a given course of action.

Influence ☐ An authentic change in the preferences of an individual or group in accordance with the preferences of power wielders; given the same situation, an individual or group would not choose the same course of action that they favored before power was exercised.

Iron law of oligarchy ☐ The formulation by Robert Michels that large-scale organization inevitably leads to the concentration of power in the hands of a few; in turn, Michels says, the few use their positions to advance their own fortunes and selfish interests.

Machiavellianism ☐ An approach in which a person manipulates others for his or her own purposes.

Passive resistance ☐ Noncooperation; the withholding of participation from an ongoing enterprise.

Political impression management ☐ The achievement of power by controlling, influencing, and sustaining one party's definition of the situation; the elite induces people to share its view of reality, and therefore to act in the manner it prescribes.

Power ☐ The realization in human affairs of the will of one party (either an individual or group) over the will of another party.

Privilege ☐ The possession or control of a portion of the surplus produced by the members of a society.

State ☐ An arrangement consisting of people who exercise an effective monopoly in the use of physical coercion within a given territory.

15 PREJUDICE AND RACISM

INTERGROUP RELATIONS
  Minority Groups
  Prejudice
  Institutional Racism
  Gatekeeping

SOURCES OF RACIAL AND
    ETHNIC ANTAGONISM
  Competition
  Unequal Power
  Reference Groups
  Self-fulfilling Prophecies
  Personality Variables

As most of us see the contemporary world, the critical question that divides humanity is where people stand relative to Marxist ideology: whether they support capitalism or socialism—the "free world" or the "communist bloc." Yet as sociologist Andrew M. Greeley observes:

> The conflicts that have occupied most men over the past two or three decades, those that have led to the most appalling outpourings of blood, have had precious little to do with this ideological division. Most of us are unwilling to battle to the death over ideology, but practically all of us, it seems, are ready to kill each other over noticeable differences of color, language, religious faith, height, food habits, and facial configuration. (1974: 10)

Indeed, much of the world is consumed with tribal frictions and intergroup hatred: Turks and Greeks on Cyprus; Arabs and Jews in the Middle East; Protestants and Catholics in Northern Ireland; blacks and whites in the United States and South Africa; Jews, Ukrainians, and Great Russians in the Soviet Union; English and French in Quebec; the Hausa, Yoruba, and Ibo in Nigeria; Flemish and Walloons in Belgium; and Shiites, Druses, Palestinians, and Christians in Lebanon. Although many social scientists once believed that modernization and

459

industrialization would bring about a decrease in the importance of ethnic distinctions, this has hardly been the case. Indeed, ethnicity remains a powerful basis for mobilizing people—even more powerful than social class (Nielsen, 1985).

INTERGROUP RELATIONS

People in modern societies are evaluated and rated in terms of a great many attributes, including race, ethnic membership, gender, occupation, income, education, accumulated wealth, age, physical attractiveness, and social skills. Conceived in this fashion, individuals and groups are ranked from high to low and from better to worse, which results in differences in power, privilege, and status. What significantly distinguishes racial and ethnic hierarchies from other hierarchies is the fact that minority groups have the *potential* to carve their own autonomous nation from the existing state (Geertz, 1963). For instance, class conflicts, no matter how severe, do not intentionally threaten the existence of the nation-state. They threaten governments and forms of government with revolution; but they do not menace the nation itself, because they do not involve alternative definitions of the nation or its territory. In contrast, discontent and conflict based on race, language, or culture threaten partition or merger—a redrawing of the very limits of the state, a new definition of its domain. This difficulty confronts the Israelis and Palestinians on the West Bank and in the Gaza Strip, Christians and Moslems in Lebanon, Catholics and Protestants in Northern Ireland, and the French and English in Quebec. The issue, then, is not one of replacing one party or elite by another, or even of working a revolutionary change in the political system. Rather, the issue is whether the minority will be willing to participate in the existing nation-state arrangement (Lieberson, 1970).

Minority Groups

> *You can't hold a man down without staying down with him.*
>
> —Booker T. Washington

What is distinctive about the groups we term "minorities"? What characteristics do they have in common? Students of dominant-group–minority-group relations agree in general on a number of distinguishing features of a minority (Wagley and Harris, 1964), although a number of them have suggested that the term be replaced by "oppressed group" (Meyers, 1984).

Oppression and Various Disabilities

A minority is a group whose members suffer oppression and various disabilities at the hands of another group. As a consequence of their power disadvantage (see the treatment of power in Chapter 14), some groups—minorities—find

An Ethnic Minority: Appalachian Whites in Urban Centers
Although they are Protestant, native white descendants of early Anglo-Saxon Americans, migrants from the south Appalachian and Ozark regions constitute an ethnic
minority within a number of this nation's large cities. In many respects their way of
life conflicts with that of other urban dwellers. Their rural background has not
prepared them for the highly formal, circumscribed behavior required by American
industrial and urban life. The discrimination experienced by these whites is all the
more distinctive since the group has no "strikes" against it in terms of race, religion, or national origin. (Patrick Reddy)

themselves likewise disadvantaged in terms of privilege and status relative to the
dominant group. But it is not simply a matter of disadvantage. The minority is
the *source* of the dominant group's advantages. The oppression of one people
confers privilege on another.

A minority is not merely exploited; it is commonly victimized by prejudice,
discrimination, and racism. Its members are physically and psychologically degraded, abused, and humiliated. The functioning of the dominant group's social
order continually confronts them with a social definition of their worthlessness,
ignorance, despicableness, and bestiality. At times its members may be hounded,
persecuted, lynched, murdered, imprisoned, segregated, tortured, and raped with
relative impunity.

It is important to stress that the concept "minority" lacks any numerical
connotation. Despite the literal meaning of the word, a minority is not a statistical
unit. In many cases a minority is larger in population than the dominant group.
For example, blacks form a majority of the population in the Republic of South
Africa and in some American cities and southern counties. And until recently,
small numbers of Europeans dominated "minority peoples" throughout Africa,
Asia, and the Pacific islands. "Minority," then, is a social, not a numerical,
concept.

Racial Awareness
The vast majority of children in our society can accurately identify a person's racial membership by the time they reach five years of age. (Patrick Reddy)

High Social Visibility

A minority group is symbolically identified by certain traits having high social visibility. As is true of groups in general, a minority is a human-constructed reality. It is *not* a naturally self-constituted or self-contained entity; rather, it is a mental model fabricated through the process of social interaction. For whatever historical reason, people come to be lumped together on the basis of some shared physical attribute—perhaps their skin color, hair texture, head shape, stature, or facial features—or on the basis of their way of life—say, their language, dress, diet, religious belief, or social customs (Williams, 1964). Groups that are distinguished on the basis of hereditary physical traits are called **racial groups** (for instance, blacks and whites in the United States). Groups that are distinguished on the basis of socially acquired lifeways are called **ethnic groups** (for instance, Italians, Irish, and Jews within the United States).

Races present the clearest example of the social nature of minorities. Although we commonly conceive of races as separate, sharply delimited biological categories, in point of fact populations throughout the world grade into one another. It is next to impossible to say where one population ends and another begins. If, for example, we were to go on foot from the Congo northward through the Arab countries, then across Turkey through Bulgaria on into Central Europe, then across the Baltic Sea to Sweden, finally swinging eastward into Russia and heading toward Mongolia, we would not find any difference of physical type between the peoples of neighboring points on the route.

"Black" and "white" are not naturally occurring biological or genetic categories but human-constructed pigeonholes for placing people (Montagu, 1963, 1964; Livingstone, 1962). Thus in Barranquilla, Colombia, the term "Negro" is applied only to slum dwellers of the city. In the new housing developments, where no one is seen who would not qualify as a "black" in the United States, we are told, "Only white people live here." In northern Colombia, distinctions are made according to a person's hair and eyes, and to a certain extent according to stature. Skin color and the shape of the lips or nose are hardly taken into account. A person whose features are predominantly "Negroid" but whose hair is long and wavy is considered a "Spaniard." A person with predominantly Caucasoid features and a light skin, but with straight hair, slightly oblique eyes, and small stature, is an "Indian." An individual who would be classified as a "black" in the United States might, by traveling to Mexico, become "moreno" or "prieto," then "canela" or "trigueño" in Panama, and end up in Colombia with the label "white" (Pitt-Rivers, 1967).

Self-conscious Social Units

Minorities are self-conscious social units; they have a consciousness of oneness. Members of a minority experience an intense social and psychological affinity with others like themselves. They possess a primal sense of kinship, a solidarity springing from the roots of a real or mythical common ancestry in ages past. Frequently, they are so strongly bound together by a common identity that all other differences and conflicts become submerged in a spiritual loyalty and allegiance to the "people"—"my people": the Jews, Turks, blacks, Armenians, or Greeks.

Such feelings of spiritual allegiance are often solidified by common suffering, a sense of isolation, and a common sense of burden. Indeed, it is said with considerable truth that Jews have survived as a people *because* of their persecution, not in spite of it. Persecution highlights a group's boundaries, setting "us" off from "them." It solidifies the membrane that filters out "foreign" and "alien" ways, and plugs the pores by which assimilation might otherwise occur. Thus as anti-Semitism has declined in the United States, Jewish group existence has become endangered. Nahum Goldmann of the World Zionist Organization insists that assimilation, "if not halted and reversed, threatens Jewish survival more than persecution, inquisition, pogroms and mass murder of Jews did in the past" (Vander Zanden, 1983).

Ascribed Membership

For the most part, a person does not voluntarily become a member of a minority; he or she is born into it. Minority-group members commonly think of themselves as being alike because of common ancestry. Often if only one parent is a member of a minority, the children of that family also belong. In certain instances, a single grandparent or great-grandparent is enough to confer membership. In Nazi Germany, for example, it did not matter if a "Jew" looked like thousands of German non-Jews, had been converted to Christianity, and had taken a Christian

INTERGROUP MARRIAGE

Intergroup marriage represents an important means through which cultural and social assimilation and racial amalgamation take place. In the United States, intermarriage between peoples of differing ethnic groups is a frequent occurrence, religious intermarriage is somewhat less common, and racial intermarriage is infrequent. If we accept intergroup marriage as a particularly sensitive barometer of ethnic and racial prejudice, the most sharply drawn line in American society now divides the Americans of European origin in general from blacks, Hispanics, and American Indians (Glazer, 1984; Collins, 1985). Even so, Americans of European origin are still aware of their ethnic backgrounds. In response to the ancestry question in the 1980 census, only 6 percent of Americans said they were Americans or that they were from the United States; 83 percent of Americans reported some ethnic identification.

Data from the 1980 census revealed that among whites of non-Hispanic origin, only 27 percent were married to someone whose parentage was entirely the same. The net result has been that growing numbers of Americans are of mixed ancestry. Among younger native-born Americans, those born after 1960, some 60 percent had mixed ancestry, compared to only 31 percent of Americans born before 1920. The difference was particularly pronounced for some ethnic groups. For instance, of Americans of Italian descent born prior to 1920, 8 percent had some non-Italian ancestry; but of those born after 1970, 70 percent were the children of intermarriage. Among Americans of Polish descent under the age of thirty, more than 80 percent had married someone with no Polish ancestry, and among Americans of French descent of the same age group, 75 percent of men and 66 percent of women had married outside their own group.

The 1980 census revealed that there were 613,000 interracial couples, about 1.3 percent of all married couples. The number was about double that reported in the 1970 census. More than 72 percent of Americans of Asian origin and 71 percent of Americans with Hispanic ancestry were married to a member of their own group. However, 54 percent of American Indians were married to someone outside their group, mostly to a white. Such evidence suggests that within the United States the melting pot has melted only so far. Prejudices and intergroup barriers still persist, particularly in the realm of interracial marriage.

---

spouse; by Nazi definition, the person was a "Jew." Similar rules operate in many communities of the United States, where a person with all "white" ancestry except for a "black" grandparent is grouped with "blacks."

Ingroup Marriage

By choice or necessity, members of a minority usually marry within their own group. Ingroup marriage may be enforced by the dominant group or by the minority group; often it is urged by both. Accordingly, intergroup marriage is a particularly sensitive barometer of ethnic patterns. If intermarriage is high, it suggests that ethnic identities and allegiances are weakening. Some social scientists see the increase in Jewish-Gentile couples in this light. Today, 40 percent of Jews marry non-Jews, up from 15 percent in the early 1960s (Stewart, 1985). It would seem that within the United States traditional barriers between Christians and Jews have waned in recent years (see boxed insert).

In sum, a **minority** is any racially or ethnically self-conscious social aggregate, with hereditary membership and a high degree of ingroup marriage, which suffers oppression at the hands of a dominant segment of a nation-state (Williams, 1964).

Prejudice

> *Sometimes, it's [racial prejudice] like a hair across your cheek. You can't find it with your fingers, but you keep brushing at it because the feel of it is irritating.*
>
> —Marian Anderson, September 1960

Prejudice refers to an attitude of aversion and hostility toward the members of a group simply because they belong to it and are therefore presumed to have the objectionable qualities ascribed to the group (Allport, 1954). As Herbert Blumer (1961) observes, four basic types of feelings commonly characterize prejudice in the dominant group: (1) a feeling of superiority, (2) a feeling that the minority is inherently different and alien, (3) a feeling of proprietary claim to power, privilege, and status, and (4) a fear and suspicion that the minority harbors designs on the power, privilege, and status of the dominant group.

In many respects, racial and ethnic groups are special-interest groups (Blumer, 1961; Bobo, 1983; Jackson and Muha, 1984). Thus at root, prejudice is frequently a matter of a relationship between groups—a sense of group position. The dominant group comes to view itself as being entitled to advantages. These advantages may include the ownership of choice property; the right to certain jobs, occupations, and professions; the claim to positions of power; the exclusive right to use given schools, churches, and recreation facilities; the claim to positions of status and to the display of the symbols associated with such positions; and the claim to certain areas of intimacy and privacy.

Components of Prejudice

Prejudice is an attitude—a state of mind. And like any attitude, it has a *cognitive* component, meaning the mental image or picture we have of a people; an *affective* component, meaning the feelings or emotions aroused by a people; and a *behavioral* component, meaning our tendency or predisposition to act in certain ways toward a given people (Kramer, 1949; Mann, 1959). These components were described in detail in Chapter 6.

Stereotyping is an aspect of the cognitive component (see Chapter 2). It seems

*S*tereotypes

The stereotypes we learn about races are amazing when considered from an objective point of view. In physical education today I observed the reactions of the guys to a large, stocky, well-built Oriental student. We learn early in life that Orientals are excellent in gymnastics, self-defense, and Karate. So this Oriental student caused quite a "ruckus" in touch football. Although he really wasn't bigger than most of the guys, he was viewed as being awesome because of the stereotype. Most of the guys were afraid to try and block him. They would try to block someone on the other side of the line, even if he was just as big or bigger than the Oriental student. However, as the game went on we saw that the Oriental was "only human" and he was then dealt with as such. In life, we employ stereotypes in dealing with various categories of people. Although they are convenient, they are not necessarily accurate, as revealed in this illustration.

that stereotypes result from our need for coherence, simplicity, and predictability in the face of an inherently complex social environment (Tajfel, 1981; Bodenhausen and Wyer, 1985). The world is filled with so much variety and subtlety, so many permutations and combinations, that we feel impelled to fashion a simpler model in order to manage it. In brief, it is almost impossible for us to weigh every behavior of every person, minute by minute, in terms of its individual meanings. Instead, we type individuals and groups in snap-judgment style. Without stereotypes we would find it necessary to interpret each new social situation as if we had never met anything of the kind before. Stereotypes are convenient and have the virtue of efficiency, although not always of accuracy. We may come to think of Jews as "intelligent," Orientals as "inscrutable," Swedes as "stolid," Italians as "emotional," and so on. In sum, one way our minds organize information about people is by grouping certain individuals together in terms of what are believed to be their common traits.

The components of prejudice are interrelated, although they are not necessarily fully congruent (Abelson et al., 1982). Should negative feelings—the affective component—become attached to a stereotype, the attribute can assume a different meaning (Hamilton, Dugan, and Trolier, 1985). Thus "intelligent" can be taken to mean "cunning." Sociologist Robert K. Merton observes how a behavior may undergo a complete change of evaluation in its transition from the ingroup to the outgroup:

Did Lincoln work far into the night? This testifies that he was industrious, resolute, perseverant, and eager to realize his capacities to the full. Do the out-group Jews or Japanese keep these same hours? This only bears witness to their sweatshop mentality, their ruthless undercutting of American standards, their unfair competitive practices. Is the in-group hero frugal, thrifty, and sparing? Then the out-group villain is stingy, miserly and penny-pinching. All honor is due to the in-group Abe

Racism

Last night the guys on my dorm floor threw a "beer blast." We invited all the girls from the third floor of another dorm as a kind of mixer. There were a lot of good-looking girls and lots of beer, so everyone had a pretty good time. I met a girl, Lois, who was beautiful, charming, and bright. We had a great time talking, drinking, and dancing. She was a great conversationalist and a fantastic dancer. Near midnight Lois told me she had to be going since she had a midterm the next morning, and she had to do well on it because she's pre-med and has to keep her "accum" up. As I got up to walk her to her dorm, I got a few strange looks, quite a few stares (mostly hostile), and a couple of "knowing" winks. Lois is black and I am white.

This is a good illustration of racism. For one thing, Lois was discriminated against by the white guys. Only one other white guy even talked with her; the rest ignored her. When I left to walk Lois back to her dorm, the guys clued me in to the fact that a white guy shouldn't get involved with a black. And the "knowing" winks implied that if a white guy gets involved with a black, it is only for purposes of sexual exploitation. In this latter case, the behavior would be acceptable.

for his having been smart, shrewd, and intelligent and, by the same token, all contempt is owing the out-group Abes for their being sharp, cunning, crafty, and too clever by far. (1968: 428)

Given negative stereotypes and feelings toward a group of people, we are inclined to act toward them in negative ways. Prejudiced individuals easily retain evidence that confirms their negative attitude while ignoring or discounting evidence to the contrary. The hallmark of prejudice is that the negative belief persists despite contrary evidence. Indeed, we do not even know that our judgments are prejudiced (Hepburn and Locksley, 1983).

Discrimination

Prejudice, then, is merely a predisposition to act—a preference for a certain kind of behavior. It does not entail the actual response itself. A white grocer may feel considerable prejudice toward blacks; nonetheless, he may display friendship toward his black customers in order to secure their patronage. Thus his negative attitudes are not translated into overt action. On the other hand, a white barber who is *not* prejudiced may discourage black patrons because he believes their presence would offend his substantial white clientele. Under such circumstances, he fails to translate his nonprejudiced feelings into overt action. We need, therefore, to distinguish between prejudice and discrimination. **Discrimination** entails the arbitrary denial of power, privilege, and status to members of a minority group whose qualifications are equal to those of the dominant group. Prejudice

COMBATING RACISM

Until justice is blind to color, until education is unaware of race, until opportunity is unconcerned with the color of men's skins, emancipation will be a proclamation but not a fact.
—Lyndon B. Johnson

With the growing recognition that the findings of social science can be used to change behavior, social scientists are being increasingly called upon to help bring racial practices in the United States into line with the country's democratic creed. Three frequently suggested remedies for combating racism are education, intergroup contact, and legal intervention. How effective are these remedies? Contemporary research has some answers (Pate, 1981; Vander Zanden, 1983; Miller and Brewer, 1984).

EDUCATION
"Give people the facts, and prejudice will disappear." This assumption underlies many efforts to combat racism. It assumes that prejudice comes from "warped social perceptions" and that "correct facts" will alter hostile feelings. During the late 1920s and 1930s a variety of studies were undertaken to test this premise. On the whole, the results were discouraging. By 1948 Robert M. MacIver, a prominent sociologist in the field of race relations, observed, "All we can claim for instruction of a purely factual kind is that it tends to mitigate some of the more extreme expressions of prejudice" (1948: 222). This continues to be the verdict of most specialists in race relations.

Antiprejudice education is one thing. But what about education in general? Does its emphasis on rational processes contribute to lower levels of prejudice among better-educated people? Findings such as those by Gertrude J. Selznick and Stephen Steinberg (1969), based on a national sample, lend some support to this view (see Figure 15.1). Nonetheless, the evidence is contradictory. Selznick and Steinberg also found that college graduates are the most likely of all educational groups to defend exclusiveness (meaning discrimination) in their social clubs. Further, education is unrelated to attitudes toward intergroup marriage. Perhaps the question is not so much which group—educated or uneducated—is the most prejudiced. The issue might be phrased more appropriately in terms of where the two groups converge and where they differ in prejudice and behavior.

INTERGROUP CONTACT
"Bring ethnic and racial groups into contact with one another, and their prejudices will wither away." This folk wisdom is widely accepted in the United States—indeed, Americans have an almost mystical faith in "getting to know one another" as a solution to racial difficulties. Yet Muzafer Sherif's study of the arousal and resolution of conflict in a boys' camp (described in Chapter 13) showed that contact may merely provide an arena in which groups translate their hatreds into overt hostilities.

Research suggests, however, that contact may undermine racism where contributing conditions are favorable (Cook,

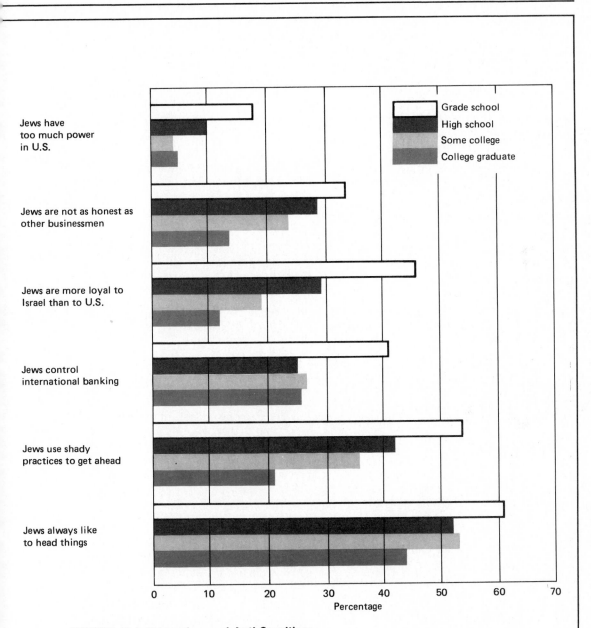

FIGURE 15.1 Education and Anti-Semitism
Some evidence suggests that the percentage of people agreeing with the six anti-Jewish statements falls as educational level rises.
(SOURCE: Adapted from G. J. Selznick and S. Steinberg, *The Tenacity of Prejudice* [New York: Harper & Row, 1969], p. 71.)

Box continues on next page

1972; Foley, 1976; Amir, 1969, 1976; Vander Zanden, 1983). The situation is favorable when:

1. The contact occurs between status equals (Cook, 1972; Amir, 1976; Riordan and Ruggiero, 1980; Patchen, 1982).
2. The behavior of the objects of prejudice contradicts the beliefs of the prejudiced individuals (Deutsch and Collins, 1951; Cook, 1972).
3. The contact is of sufficient duration and intimacy to challenge the beliefs of prejudiced individuals (Amir, 1976; Wilder and Thompson, 1980; Wilder, 1984).
4. Prevailing social norms dictate that prejudice and discrimination are inappropriate (Cook, 1972; Foley, 1976).
5. The members of the different groups have a common interest, task, or goal that is the focus of their interaction (Amir, 1976; Norvell and Worchel, 1981; Schofield, 1982).
6. Positive support for cooperative interaction comes from salient reference groups (Amir, 1976; Schofield, 1982).

Where such conditions are met, as in some interracial housing projects, contact may contribute to more positive intergroup relations (Deutsch and Collins, 1951).

LEGAL INTERVENTION

It has long been a popular view that "You can't legislate against prejudice." Yet over the past thirty years, legal remedies have been effective in undermining traditional segregationist institutions through legislative, executive, and judicial action. As Lewis M. Killian's studies of southern white migrants in Chicago reveal, what people do in intergroup situations appears to be almost independent of how they feel or what they think. (Refer back to the section on reference groups in Chapter 13.) The *social setting* seems to be the critical factor. As Gordon W. Allport notes, "Segregationists act like integrationists where social prescription requires; integrationists behave like segregationists when it is socially appropriate to do so" (1962: 123). And laws may make an important contribution in defining the social setting for people.

Many people believe that the fight against discrimination is more important than the fight against prejudiced attitudes. Discrimination affects the right of a minority to realize equality and freedom of opportunity. Attitudes, on the other hand, are often considered to be a private matter—a position summarized by Robert M. MacIver:

No law should require men to change their attitudes. . . . In a democracy we do not punish a man because he is opposed to income taxes, or to free school education, or to vaccination, or to minimum wages, but the laws of a democracy insist that he obey the laws that make provisions for these things. (1954: viii)

By the same token, laws against murder and theft do not attempt to root out the desire to kill or steal; rather, their aim is to prevent these desires from becoming translated into overt behavior. Much the same case can be made for laws against discrimination.

may or may not be associated with discrimination—a one-to-one relationship does not necessarily hold between our attitudes and our overt actions (see Chapter 6).

Symbolic Racism

A number of social scientists detect the emergence in recent years of a new form of prejudice toward blacks among relatively affluent, suburban segments of the American white population, what has come to be termed **symbolic racism** (McConahay and Hough, 1976; McConahay, Hardee, and Batts, 1981; Brewer and Kramer, 1985). It is not, they say, the racism of the Old South with its doctrines of racial inferiority and legally instituted segregation. Rather, three elements coalesce to make up symbolic racism. First, there is the feeling that blacks have become too demanding, too pushy, and too angry, and that blacks are getting more than they deserve. Second, there is the belief that blacks are not playing by "the rules of the game" (in accordance with traditional American values of hard work, individualism, sexual repression, and the delay of gratification). And third, there is a gathering of these elements within an imagery of black welfare, urban riots, black mayors, crime in the streets, affirmative-action programs, and quota systems. In sum, symbolic racism derives from the view that blacks are violating cherished values and are making illegitimate demands on whites for social change. Many whites resent the economic improvement made by blacks in the 1960s and 1970s (Ross et al., 1976; Farley et al., 1978). In its behavioral component, this new prejudice finds expression in voting against blacks and candidates favorable to black programs (Kinder and Sears, 1981; Sears and Kinder, 1985). "Racism" is seen as "somebody else's" problem, while white suburbanites concentrate on their own private lives.

The shift that has taken place among American whites from blatant forms of discrimination to more subtle forms of racism has occurred since World War II (Crosby, Bromley, and Saxe, 1980). Over the past fifty years, the National Opinion Research Center (NORC) has monitored racial attitudes within the United States (Smith and Sheatsley, 1984). In this interval, white Americans have displayed a steady but gradual shift toward greater liberalism on racial issues. In 1942, only 30 percent of whites thought that blacks and whites should attend the same schools. By 1984, a pro-integration consensus of 90 percent had emerged. The greatest change occurred between 1970 and 1972. Much of the long-term change can be credited to the changing composition of the population in age. Racial tolerance is highest among whites who are younger and who have been raised in liberal cultures, with above-average education and social standing. Overall, advanced education, greater occupational standing, and higher income are all associated with racial tolerance.

Yet despite these changes, the United States has hardly turned into a color-blind society (Ickes, 1984). Experiments employing college subjects reveal high levels of white prejudice toward blacks (Crosby, Bromley, and Saxe, 1980). Whites are most likely to discriminate against blacks in situations where the possibility of negative consequences is minimal. Moreover, they are more likely to assist blacks whom they perceive to occupy a subordinate or nonassertive role than blacks who do not conform to traditional stereotypes. And when the conditions are "safe" (no retaliation is possible), whites experimentally deliver more intense shocks to blacks than to whites. Additionally, although whites are opposed to educational and occupational discrimination, they draw the line at compensating blacks for past discrimination and disadvantaged backgrounds by applying racial quotas or other preferential treatment. In 1984, 35 percent of whites placed themselves at the extreme "no special treatment" position, on a 5-point scale, while only 7 percent were favorable. However, it is not the notion of helping blacks that whites seem to reject but the antiegalitarian principle of special treatment—the idea of reverse discrimination. Over 32 percent of whites favor more government spending to improve the condition of blacks, as opposed to 19 percent who want less spending (Smith and Sheatsley, 1984). In sum, many whites are willing to take steps to further racial tolerance and equality without endorsing affirmative-action programs.

Institutional Racism

The problem of the Twentieth Century is the problem of the color-line.

—W. E. B. Du Bois, *The Souls of Black Folk,* 1903

In his introduction to the Kerner Commission's report on civil disorders, Tom Wicker of the *New York Times* wrote: "What white Americans have never fully understood—but what the Negro can never forget—is that white society is deeply implicated in the ghetto. White institutions have created it, white institutions

Institutional Racism
Whites have traditionally made the critical decisions affecting the black community. (Patrick Reddy)

maintain it, and white society condones it" (1968). The Kerner Commission (1968) warned: "Our nation is moving toward two societies, one black, one white—separate and unequal." A decade later the *New York Times,* surveying racial progress in the nation, concluded: "The division between white and black Americans still exists, and the prospects of healing the rift may be more dismal today than they were 10 years ago" (Herbers, 1978). In 1985, a series of articles in the *New York Times* reiterated this conclusion (Reed, 1985; Shipp, 1985; Schmidt, 1985).

Institutional racism involves those social arrangements and enduring patterns by which people of one racial group oppress and exploit the members of another racial group. It is an inclusive concept. It entails prejudice as well as discrimination. But it involves *more than* simply prejudice and discrimination. It means, as Samuel Friedman notes, that "decisions are made, agendas structured, issues defined, beliefs, values, and attitudes promulgated and enshrined, commitments entered into, and/or resources allocated, in such a way that non-whites are systematically deprived or exploited" (1969: 19). In brief, institutional racism entails inequality in who gives and who receives.

The emphasis of institutional racism, then, is on the *consequences* of racial practices rather than the intentions of the people involved. Some of these consequences are shown in Figures 15.2 and 15.3. According to the U.S. Bureau of Labor Statistics, average weekly earnings of black and Hispanic families were $370 in 1983, compared to $502 for white families (Mitchell, 1984). Indeed, privilege in racial and colonial orders cannot be avoided by dominant-group members, even by those who consciously reject the society and its privileges. The "iron law" of white privilege means that children of the middle class who have "dropped out" to live in poverty conditions still hold their racial rights in reserve when and if they decide to reenter the mainstream (Blauner, 1972). Further, racism involves a kind of social imperialism in which the dominant group seeks to impose its values, morality, and lifeways on the minority. We find this in white middle-class definitions of black ghetto life as "pathological," "deficient," and "deviant."

Gatekeeping

In recent decades minority-group militancy has come to challenge and undermine the more traditional, blatant, and overt expressions of white Anglo-Saxon Protestant (WASP) dominance. As a consequence, covert and subtle mechanisms now occupy an even more important place in the establishment and maintenance of WASP advantage. In the forefront of these mechanisms is gatekeeping, one of the processes of institutional racism.

The Nature of Gatekeeping

Within the United States, a great many offices and positions are, *at least in theory,* open to individuals on the basis of merit. The doctrine of equality of opportunity has always enjoyed a prominent place in the American democratic creed. It insists that individuals must not be judged on the basis of race, ethnicity,

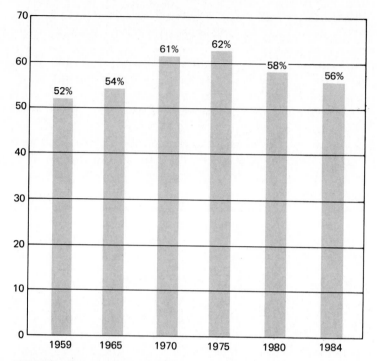

FIGURE 15.2 Median Income of Black Families as a Percentage of White Family Income
Just after the 1964 Civil Rights Act, which forbids discrimination on the basis of race or color, the median income of black families came to about 54 percent of that of white families. The percentage climbed for a period but then started down again.
(SOURCE: U.S. Departments of Commerce and Labor.)

class, family, community, or other group attributes. Rather, each individual should be evaluated on the basis of objective qualifications relating to talent and skill.

In the last analysis, however, talent and skill are relative matters. Which group's values will be used in determining who is "bright," "industrious," "resourceful," and "proficient"? Will the standards of excellence be those of the WASP community? the Irish community? the Italian community? the Chicano community? the black community? Equally important, who will be the *judges* of which individuals meet the standards of excellence? Who will control the gates that regulate the flow of people into those positions that provide access to the society's good things? Will the judges be WASPs, Irish, Italians, Chicanos, or blacks? **Gatekeeping** refers to the decision-making process by which individuals are admitted to scarce positions and offices of power, privilege, and status within a society.

Percent of Cohort*

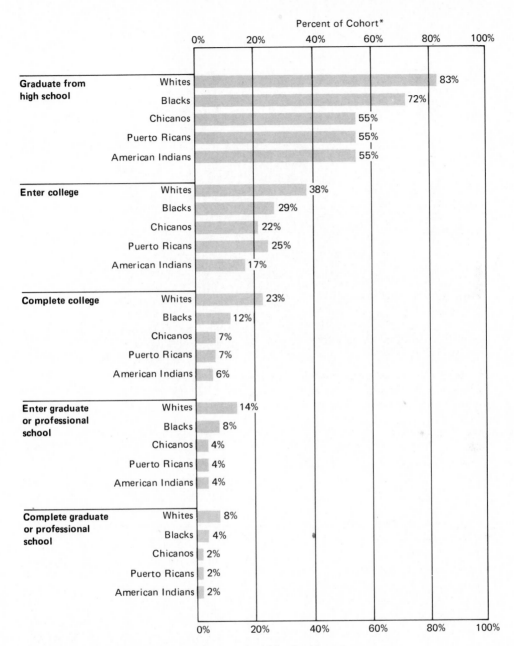

*Percentages are of the number of students entering high school in each group.

FIGURE 15.3 The Education Pipeline for Minority Students
Minority youth are disadvantaged in the race for professional careers.
(SOURCE: The Ford Foundation, 1982.)

Gatekeeping
The ethnic and racial membership of gatekeepers in schools and colleges, in employment agencies, and in the hiring offices of government and business makes a difference in the allocation of desirable positions. (Don McCarthy)

Most gatekeepers are white. They are usually professionals with experience and credentials in the fields they monitor. They are found in schools and colleges, in real estate offices, in employment agencies, and in the hiring offices of business and government. Even when white gatekeepers are well intentioned—dedicated to objective, nonprejudiced hiring, and sympathetic to the American democratic creed—non-WASP ethnics, Chicanos, and blacks frequently find themselves victimized in their encounters with "the Man" (WASPs who have power and influence). What actually occurs in such interactions to produce this effect? School counseling interviews provide many insights into the gatekeeping process (Erickson, 1975).

Gatekeeping and Ethnicity
One task of counselors is to regulate the flow of students to courses and school programs of higher rank, encouraging some students to pass through the gates

and preventing others from entering. Since American society places high value on credentials, the decisions of school gatekeepers have vast consequences for the subsequent placement of individuals. Counselors also function as advisers who describe mobility channels and offer encouragement or discouragement to students. And they may assist students by writing letters, making telephone calls, and bending or overlooking organizational rules.

People project many facets of their social identity in social interaction. One of these is ethnic membership. The two examples that follow show how a counselor's assessment of a student's ethnic background influences the help she or he gives the student. The first interchange took place when an Italian-American counselor at a junior college questioned an Italian-American student about the previous semester's grades:

Counselor: Data Processing 101. Whadja get for a grade?
Student: A "B."
Counselor: Data Processing 111?
Student: An "F."
Counselor: (Stops smiling momentarily, looks straight across at the student and then resumes smile) That's your major, data processing, right?
Student: (Smiling) Yeah, well I was . . . I just talked with him and he said it was 'cause of excessive absences.
Counselor: (Smiling, speaking with a slightly sarcastic tone) Good for you, good for you . . . Math 101?
Student: A "B." (Erickson, 1975: 48)

According to formal standards, the student had failed a course in his major and should have been in trouble. But the counselor, who shared the same ethnic background, did not reprimand him; the interview continued in a friendly tone.

Now consider the same counselor talking with a Polish-American student who spoke with a slight accent. Again the topic is grades:

Counselor: (Unsmiling and formal) What did you get in your Biology 101 last semester?
Student: Whad' I get?
Counselor: What did you get for a grade?
Student: "B."
Counselor: "B"?
Student: Yeah.
Counselor: How about Speech 101?
Student: Speech, ah . . . ah, I th . . . , I think, I didn't get that one.
Counselor: (Looks straight at the student without smiling) What do you mean you "didn't get it"?
Student: I got some incomplete.
Counselor: Ah, . . . how come?
Student: Th . . . then I, ah, ma . . . I did complete them. You know, then I make up the test . . . and then they give me tha . . .
Counselor: Did you make up the tests?
Student: The grades . . . yes, I did.

Counselor: (Looks down at the student's transcript) You don't know all the grades you got, though.
Student: I didn't (unintelligible) and "C."
Counselor: (Looks up at student without smiling) You didn't fail anything did you?
Student: No. No fail. (Erickson, 1975: 48–49)

Note the counselor's unfriendly and at times intimidating tone. When the Polish-American student showed confusion at the beginning of the exchange by responding to a question with a question, the counselor seemed direct, formal, and cold. And throughout the session the counselor continually challenged the student's answers, even when they were not ambiguous. Further, because the student had difficulty communicating, the counselor inferred incorrectly that the student was having academic difficulties.

These exchanges show how individuals forge rules and meanings in the course of social interaction. Rules of relevance (decisions as to which traits of an individual will be important to the interaction) and rules of irrelevance (aspects that are to be ignored) become part of the participants' definition of the situation. Hence counselors do not interact with and advise students in accordance with a single, stable set of rules pertaining to a generalized student; instead, they speak to an *Italian-American* student and a *Polish-American* student. In the course of interaction, social identities other than that of "student" (for instance, ethnic memberships) are activated that change the complexion of the encounter.

Gatekeeping and Race

In interaction, students and counselors rely heavily on a variety of implicit cues. The participants communicate not only verbally but nonverbally through gestures, tone of voice, figurative meanings, and what is left unsaid. Seldom do white counselors directly tell black students not to continue their education. Even so, the message may be communicated:

White counselor: As far as next semester . . . why don't we give some thought to what you'd like to take there . . . (Leans forward) Do you plan on continuing along this P.E. major?
Black student: Yeah, I guess so. I might as well keep it up . . . my P.E., and (Shifts in chair) I wanna go into counseling too, see . . . you know, to have two-way . . . like equal balance.
White counselor: I see, Ah . . . What do you know about counseling?
Black student: Nothing. (Smiles and averts eyes, then looks up)
White counselor: Okay . . .
Black student: (Shifts in chair, smiles and averts eyes) I know you have to take psychology courses of some sort . . . and counseling.
White counselor: (Leans back) Well . . . (Student stops smiling, looks directly at counselor and sits almost immobile while counselor talks and shifts in chair repeatedly) it's this is a . . . It'll vary from different places to different places . . . But essentially what you need . . . First of all you're gonna need state certification . . . state teacher certification . . . in other words you're gonna have to be certified to teach in some area . . . English or history, or whatever happens

to be your bag . . . P.E. Secondly, you're gonna have to have a Master's Degree . . . in counseling . . . which as you know is an advanced degree. (Short laugh) That's what you have to do to get a counseling . . . to be a counselor. (Erickson, 1975: 54)

On first sight, this exchange may appear fairly straightforward. Yet the white counselor and the black student had different reactions when they viewed a tape of the interview separately. The counselor's impression was relatively positive:

Right now we both seem to be concentrating on giving information. . . . He on the other hand is concentrating . . . on accepting the information and putting it together . . . he's got aspirations for the future. P.E. and uh . . . uh counseling . . . he's a little bit ahead of himself as far as the counseling . . . as the year progressed, I guess I got the question so often that it became one of my favorite topics an' I was ready to uh numerate . . . essentially what he did was he started me off on my information. (Erickson, 1975: 54–55)

The black student interpreted the interchange negatively. When asked whether the counselor's information was satisfactory, he responded, "Not especially." When asked to explain, he said:

Well . . . well I couldn't really say, but I wasn't satisfied with what he wanted to push. . . . I guess he didn't think I was qualified, you know. That's the way he sounded to me. . . . This guy here seems like he was trying to knock me down, in a way, you know. Trying to say no. . . . I don't think you can handle anything besides P.E. You know he just said it in general terms, he just didn't go up and POW like they would in the old days, you know. This way they just try to use a little more psychology . . . they sugar-coat it this way. (Erickson, 1975: 55)

Although the counselor did not literally tell the black student not to go into counseling, his hesitant and roundabout talk about certification and requirements served the same end. Whether they do it intentionally or unintentionally, white counselors often serve to "cool out" minority students.

A related process frequently operates within the housing market. Despite the apparent liberalization of white racial attitudes over the past decade or so (Taylor, Sheatsley, and Greeley, 1978), segregated housing patterns remain basically unchanged (Simkus, 1978). Although more whites are exposed to token integration than in the past, the predominant residential experience of most Americans remains that of a relatively homogeneous racial neighborhood. Real estate agents, acting as community gatekeepers, play an important part in perpetuating these patterns. Any number of studies have been undertaken to investigate these matters. Typically, two couples who are basically alike except for race separately approach a realtor as prospective clients. This research reveals that agents commonly differentiate among people by race, both as to whether homes are shown and as to where the homes are located (Pearce, 1979). Such racial steering is an expression of institutional racism.

Competition and racism

I have a good friend who works in a factory. He has a wife and son, having been forced to quit college and marry his pregnant girlfriend. His job is menial and he would like to move ahead and get a higher salary. There are a number of men in the same job category, so there are only a limited number of opportunities for advancement and the competition is fairly keen. When a job opportunity as assistant supervisor of the unit opened up, Hank thought his chances for promotion were pretty good. He had the most time and experience on the job. However, the company under government pressure recently instituted a system to promote blacks. So Hank was passed over for promotion and a black with little experience was hired. To complicate matters, Hank went to high school with the black and felt his record was superior in terms of academic achievement and aptitude testing. Before this, Hank was a pretty liberal guy on race matters. He felt blacks were screwed in American life. But now he has become a real bigot. I think this is the product of the competition he feels with blacks to get ahead in his relatively unskilled job.

SOURCES OF RACIAL AND ETHNIC ANTAGONISM

Racial and ethnic antagonism issues from many springs, all of which are interconnected and reinforce one another. It is not simple to identify or disentangle them. This section suggests a few such sources: competition, unequal power, reference groups, self-fulfilling prophecies, and personality variables.

Competition

In Chapter 11 it was shown how clashing interests find expression in social conflict. Edna Bonacich (1972, 1973, 1975, 1976) takes the matter a step further. She stresses the part that economic competition plays in the development of ethnic antagonism, especially within the context of a **split labor market.** This is an economic area where there is a large differential in the price of labor for the same occupation. In a split labor market, conflict develops among three groups: business, higher-paid labor, and cheaper labor.

The business class aims at securing as cheap and docile a labor force as possible in order to compete effectively with other businesses and maximize profits. To do so, it frequently imports cheap labor—African slaves in the pre–Civil War South, Oriental labor on the West Coast in the last half of the nineteenth century, workers from Eastern and Southern Europe for the coal mines and steel mills in the early twentieth century, blacks from the rural South for northern industry during and after World War I, and Mexicans for agriculture and industry in the Southwest.

Cheap labor, however, would displace higher-paid labor. Thus higher-paid labor finds its interests threatened. Where cheap labor is of a different racial or ethnic membership, class antagonism commonly takes the form of racial or ethnic conflict. What is basically class conflict becomes translated into the rhetoric of racism. The success with which higher-paid white labor has managed to defeat competition from blacks is revealed by a long-term unemployment rate for blacks that is twice that of whites.

Higher-priced labor seeks to block its own displacement (hold its position) through exclusion or caste systems (Cheng and Bonacich, 1984). *Exclusion movements* attempt to bar the immigration of cheaper labor through restrictive immigration acts. The anti-Chinese movement on the Pacific Coast in the 1870s is a good illustration. When the Republican and Democratic parties failed to heed the demands of native labor, the Workingman's party arose, sweeping elections with the campaign cry of "The Chinese must go!" As a result, various Oriental-exclusion laws were passed beginning in 1882.

In *caste systems,* higher-paid labor undertakes to create an aristocracy of labor based on exclusiveness rather than exclusion. The higher-paid workers attempt to deal with the potential of cheaper labor by denying it certain jobs—restricting the education and training of the cheaper labor and denying it the franchise and other rights of full citizenship. An example is the segregationist arrangement that evolved to block competition from blacks in the South following the Civil War—a trend that reached its peak during the 1890s. Both exclusion and caste systems represent a victory for higher-priced labor.

Unequal Power

> *When asked by an anthropologist what the Indian called America before the white man came, an Indian said simply, "Ours."*
>
> —Vine Deloria, Jr.

Most situations of intergroup contact involve an established population and a group migrating into the area. Where the incoming group enjoys superior power resources, it is able to dominate through conquest and the imposition of its control apparatus. This is **classic colonialism.** Usually such dominance derives from superiority in technology (especially weapons) and a more tightly organized state apparatus. Warfare often occurs early in the contacts between the two groups, as the newcomers undertake to seize the land and exterminate the native population or impose some form of slavery or serfdom on it (Lieberson, 1961; van den Berghe, 1967).

In large measure, classic colonialism has been the story of contact between

Anglo-Americans on the one hand and Native Americans (Indians) and Chicanos (people of Mexican ancestry) on the other:

> The most fundamental difference [between America's other minorities and Native Americans and Chicanos] is that Native Americans and Chicanos are this nation's only territorial minorities. Both were here first. Both had well-developed, viable institutions and societies before the Anglo arrived, and both have roots that go deeper than any planted by the Anglo. The Chicano and Native American did not immigrate to this nation; on the contrary, they fought to protect their lands from Anglo invaders. They were defeated, but they did not abandon their claims to the land nor did they forsake their cultural heritage. In effect, Anglo Americans imposed colonial rule upon the Native American and Chicano peoples. (De la Garza, 1973: 5)

Not all dominant-minority situations, however, fall into the category of classic colonialism. Blacks are a case in point. Africans did not come to America as traditional immigrants; certainly the element of free will was absent. Further, rather than being conquered and controlled in their native land, Africans were captured and transported to America and worked as slaves on southern plantations. In this respect, the black experience in America has been different from that of many Third World peoples under classic colonialism. But since black oppression and the circumstances of blacks in America closely parallel those of Third World peoples, the term **domestic colonialism** is often applied to the American situation. It is reflected, for instance, in the fact that black families are trying to live on $56 for every $100 received by white families (see Figure 15.2).

Reference Groups

In Chapter 13, the part reference groups play in human behavior was described. A reference group is the social unit with which people identify and whose standards they use for defining their behavior and evaluating themselves. Studies reveal that many of our racial attitudes and behaviors are rooted in our reference groups. Indeed, reference groups largely account for the fact that prejudice often develops before we even have contact with a minority people. Social psychologists find that ethnic slurs and noxious labels for outgroupers among ingroup members are powerful sources in the development of prejudice (Greenberg and Pyszczynski, 1985). Similarly, attitude change is associated with a shift in reference groups. Leonard I. Pearlin (1954) found in a study of college women that the process of changing to more favorable attitudes toward blacks is twofold: It involves both *disattachment* from previous reference groups unfavorable to blacks and *attachment* to new reference groups favorable to them. And James M. Fendrich (1967) found that readiness to participate in interracial activity is more closely associated with a subject's perception of the attitudes of friends, parents, roommates, and respected older people than with the subject's own attitudes.

Our sensitivity to various reference groups is also reflected in our overt behavior. Lewis M. Killian's (1952, 1953) studies of southern white migrants in Chicago revealed behavioral contradictions that can only be explained by the disparities between their reference groups. As patrons of a "hillbilly" bar, these whites would rather have beaten up a black man than permit him to be served. But within the context of a different reference group—the nonsegregated restaurant next door—the same southern whites regularly ate lunch on a nonsegregated basis. Further, many of the men not only worked in plants with blacks, but shared rest rooms and dressing rooms with them. Although the South generally continued to function as these southerners' reference group for racial attitudes, Chicago was the reference group for most of their actions.

Self-fulfilling Prophecies

> *If men [people] define situations as real, they are real in their consequences.*
>
> —W. I. Thomas, *The Relation of Research to the Social Process,* 1931

In life we respond not only to the objective features of a situation, but also to the *meaning* the situation has for us. Even though our original definition of the situation is *false*, we often create conditions that make it come true. Thus the definition is a **self-fulfilling prophecy** (also termed *interpersonal expectancy effect*) (Merton, 1968; Darley and Fazio, 1980; Harris and Rosenthal, 1985). Suppose a rumor—a false definition—spreads that a bank is insolvent. A run starts on the bank as people try to withdraw their funds. Then, since no bank can immediately honor all claims upon it, the bank is forced to close. No conspiracy existed to make the false definition come true. Rather, the fulfillment occurred unintentionally when people acted *as if* it were true.

In race relations, the self-fulfilling prophecy operates to bring about minority disadvantage (Blanchard, Weigel, and Cook, 1975). Many whites define blacks as inferior and regard this definition as gospel truth. In doing so, they do not necessarily intend to harm blacks, but a series of consequences flows from the definition. By virtue of their gatekeeping roles, whites—believing blacks to be "inferior" or at the very least different—allocate fewer privileges and opportunities to them. Whites thereby create the very "inferiority" they assume to be true: Blacks end up poorly educated, poorly housed, working at menial jobs, and with various health problems. Even when the evidence does not confirm some "stereotype" information, individuals selectively perceive and process information in a way that leads them to believe their stereotype is confirmed (Darley and Gross, 1983).

A series of experiments by Robert Rosenthal (1966) points to the part played in learning and education by self-fulfilling social expectations. He found that rats performed better in carefully controlled tests if their handlers were told, falsely, that the animals had been especially bred for intelligence. Likewise, rats consistently turned in poor performances when the handlers had been falsely told that

THE EFFECTS OF SCHOOL DESEGREGATION

In its 1954 school desegregation decision, the Supreme Court ruled that mandatory school segregation was unconstitutional. Relying in part on testimony given by social scientists, the nation's highest court said:

> Does segregation of children in public schools solely on the basis of race, even though the physical facilities and other "tangible" factors may be equal, deprive the children of the minority group of equal educational opportunities? We believe that it does. . . . To separate them from others of similar age and qualifications solely because of their race generates a feeling of inferiority as to their status in the community that may affect their hearts and minds in a way unlikely ever to be undone. (*Brown v. Board of Education of Topeka, Kansas,* 1954)

During the 1950s a rather naive optimism pervaded the scientific community that school desegregation would almost automatically improve intergroup relationships. However, the intervening three decades have not borne out this optimism. Numerous studies have shown that while the changes produced by desegregation are sometimes positive, they are also at times negative, and often there are no changes or the effects are mixed (Gerard, 1983; Cook, 1984, 1985).

ACADEMIC ACHIEVEMENT

In 1966 the voluminous Coleman Report appeared, apparently affording support for the Supreme Court's conclusion. The study, funded by Congress, involved tests and surveys of 645,000 pupils and 60,000 teachers in 4,000 schools. The data from the work of sociologist James S. Coleman and his associates seemed to show that the academic performance of blacks increased as the proportion of white students in a school increased. Social scientists assumed that this was due to the higher levels of educational motivation and background present in predominantly white student bodies—the "lateral transmission of values" hypothesis. According to this notion, black students acquire the achievement-related values held by whites when immersed within predominantly white schools (Bradley and Bradley, 1977). However, critics say that insistence on racial balance in the schools perpetuates the demeaning assumption that blacks must have a majority white presence in order to learn effectively. And some black leaders have insisted that it is not the presence of white children per se that leads to a higher achievement for black children; it is the quality of the education that is provided *because* white children are there that makes the difference (Bell, 1980). Martin Patchen (1982), who studied the academic performance of black students in twelve Indianapolis high schools, came to the same conclusion. He found that it was not necessarily the contact between black and white students that helped to improve the blacks' academic performance, but rather the higher standards to which teachers and administrators hold predominantly white classes.

Although a goodly number of studies

have investigated the relationship between the racial composition of a school and the academic achievement of its students, the evidence is inadequate, inconclusive, and even contradictory. On the basis of her survey of more than 120 studies. Nancy St. John (1975) could determine only that desegregation rarely lowers academic achievement for either black or white pupils. Many other social scientists agree that academic achievement, as measured by conventional standardized tests, is usually not negatively affected (Hawley, 1979). Overall, the effects of desegregation on black children's achievement are not uniform (Patchen, 1982; Schofield, 1982). This is because other factors like socioeconomic status, family background, degree of racial tension, and interracial acceptance in the schools also play a part. Moreover, it seems that when desegregation begins at kindergarten age, the effects are positive; in contrast, students desegregated in secondary school are far less likely to experience positive outcomes (Crain and Mahard, 1983). In sum, there is much more to effective integration than simply mixing together children from different racial backgrounds.

One further point, schools do more than teach academic skills; they also socialize youngsters for membership in the larger society. Desegregation brings children of different races together so that they can learn to coexist. Studies show that desegregation of schools contributes to desegregation in later life—in college, in social situations, and on the job (Braddock, Crain, and McPartland, 1984). One of the long-term results of racial segregation is its tendency to become self-perpetuating. School segregation gives birth to and nurtures avoidance learning that serves to maintain the separation of blacks and whites in later life. Consequently, minority members who have been educated in segregated schools generally move into segregated niches in adult society.

SELF-ESTEEM

Prior to the late 1960s, two decades of research seemed to show that black students in segregated settings suffer poor self-esteem (McCarthy and Yancey, 1971; Zirkel, 1971; Adam, 1978). As pointed out earlier, the Supreme Court assigned major importance to the argument that psychological damage results from segregation in reaching its 1954 school desegregation decision. This notion grew out of the work of Kenneth and Mamie Clark (1939, 1947, 1950). They found that black preschool children preferred white dolls to black dolls and concluded that the white-doll choice reflected black self-hatred. A proliferation of child studies followed that appeared to confirm the existence of low self-esteem in black children (Goff, 1949; Morland, 1962; Porter, 1971).

Over the past decade, this early research has come under careful scrutiny. Critics have noted that the doll studies employed faulty procedures for testing children's racial self-attitudes (Katz and Zalk, 1974; Banks, 1976). More recent research has shown that black children's preference for whites or blacks is a function of a great many factors, including the social situation (Banks and Rompf, 1973), the tester's race (Katz and Zalk, 1974), and the cleanliness of the dolls (Epstein, Krupat, and Obudho, 1976).

Perhaps of even greater interest, recent investigators have found that the levels of

Box continues on next page

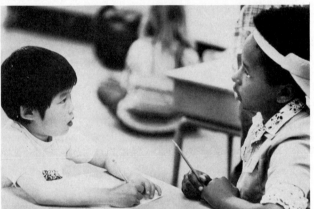

Benefits of School Desegregation
The benefits of school desegregation are greatest when
it begins in kindergarten and the early grades. But
schools teach more than academic skills. They prepare
children for interracial membership in the larger society.
(Patrick Reddy)

self-esteem among black children and adolescents are either higher than or no different from the levels among white youth
(Yancey, Rigsby, and McCarthy, 1972; Rosenberg and Simmons, 1972; Paton, Walberg, and Yeh, 1973; Cummings, 1975;
Simmons et al., 1978; Wylie, 1979; Phillips
and Zigler, 1980; Hoelter, 1983). Indeed,
some research suggests that the children
who show the highest self-esteem in American schools are black children in all-black
schools, especially in the South (St. John,

1975; Sage, 1978; Simmons et al., 1978; Drury, 1980). But here again there is room for controversy, for many individual factors (age, sex, and social class) and situational factors (teachers' attitudes and racial climate) play an important part (Gerard and Miller, 1975; Stephan and Rosenfield, 1978; Krause, 1983).

Social scientists now recognize that a variety of factors may intervene to blunt the impact of the negative racist feedback that minority groups receive (McCarthy and Yancey, 1971; Heiss and Owens, 1972; Hoelter, 1982). First, blacks do not necessarily judge themselves by the standards prevailing in the white society, the assessments of blacks being much more relevant. Second, racist institutions allow blacks to blame the system rather than themselves should they be unable to realize American goals of success. And third, an increase in black militancy has contributed to enhanced feelings of black dignity, pride, and unity.

"WHITE FLIGHT"

James S. Coleman has more recently said that the results his work promised in 1966 have not been realized. On the basis of more current research, he concludes that school desegregation has contributed to "white flight" from big cities and is fostering resegregation of urban districts (Coleman, 1975, 1976; Coleman, Kelley, and Moore, 1975). He claims that the policies pursued by the nation's courts are actually defeating the purpose of increasing overall contact among races in the schools.

Coleman's recent study has provoked bitter attacks from proponents of activist desegregation policies (Ravitch, 1978). Scholars committed to desegregation lost no time in taking issue with his findings. They have leveled three criticisms at Coleman's work (Pettigrew and Green, 1976;

Rossell, 1976; Frey, 1979, 1980; Farley, Wurdock, and Richards, 1980; Willie, 1984): His conclusions are invalid because his sample of school districts was not sufficiently large; white outmigration from central cities is a long-term trend that has predated school desegregation; and desegregation does not cause white outmigration, since the same level of movement can be observed in big cities whether or not they have implemented desegregation plans.

Looking at the "white flight" controversy as objectively as one can, it is clear that studies have provided conflicting evidence on the relationship between school desegregation and white enrollment stability (Giles, 1978; Farley, Wurdock, and Richards, 1980). Consequently, the appropriate query is not whether school desegregation leads to white outmigration. Instead, attention needs to be directed to the conditions under which white school enrollments decrease as a result of desegregation. A survey of the literature suggests the following tentative conclusions:

1. School desegregation accelerates the long-term decline in white public school enrollment in the year of implementation if a school district is above 30 to 35 percent black or if it involves the reassignment of whites to formerly black schools (Rossell, 1976; Levine and Meyer, 1977; Giles, 1978; Hawley, 1979).
2. Metropolitan plans (involving a central city and its suburbs) result in less "white flight" from desegregation than city-only plans (Hawley, 1979).
3. Voluntary school desegregation plans (including plans employing magnet schools) typically result in little or no protest or "white flight" because they

Box continues on next page

produce little desegregation (Hawley, 1979).

4. White reassignments to formerly predominantly black schools result in more than twice the "white flight" than do black reassignments to predominantly white schools. White reassignments to Hispanic or Asian schools appear to result in less "white flight" than reassignment to black schools (Hawley, 1979).

CONCLUSION

An intriguing current seems to run below the surface in virtually all school desegregation research. There are always indications that desegregation can work if we really want it to work, and there are disturbing signs of ulterior motives for not really wanting it to work (Sage, 1978). Further, we should abandon the simplistic question "Does desegregation work?" and move to develop and test theory concerning conditions for effective desegregation and for maximizing its benefit to students (St. John, 1975). Finally, we should recognize that desegregation failures may occur because they mirror the status order of the larger society. We cannot expect the schools to eliminate behaviors the larger society recreates in its day-to-day functioning.

---

the animals were dull. And when teachers were falsely told that certain children's IQ tests showed that they were about to "spurt ahead" academically, those children often surpassed their classmates on IQ tests given a year later (Rosenthal and Jacobson, 1968).

A study by Pamela C. Rubovits and Martin L. Maehr (1973) found that white teachers expect less of black children than they do of white children. The teachers, white college undergraduates, each met with four students—two white and two black. The experimenters had randomly assigned a high IQ (between 130 and 135) to one white and one black student, each of whom was labeled "gifted." The other white student and the other black student were assigned lower IQs (between 98 and 102) and labeled "nongifted." The study revealed that the teachers gave the "gifted" white more attention than the "gifted" black; as Table 15.1, p. 490, shows, the "gifted" white was called on more, praised more, and criticized less. Another interesting result, in view of the fact that the children had been randomly labeled "gifted" or "nongifted," was that in informal interviews the teachers chose the "gifted" white child most frequently as being the best-liked student, the brightest student, and the student who was certain to become leader of the class.

The study also provided evidence of white racism that was especially disturbing because it occurred among young, idealistic teachers, most of whom expressed liberal beliefs. As documented in Table 15.1, both black students were given less attention, ignored more, and criticized more than were the white students. Most startling was the fact that the "gifted" black was given the least attention, was praised least, and was criticized most, even compared with the "nongifted" black. Generalizations from these data should be made cautiously, but they do suggest answers to the questions of why teachers are frequently unable to equalize the performance levels of blacks and whites.

Educational Self-fulfilling Prophecies
Minority-group children often have difficulty with school because those responsible for teaching them do not expect them to be able to learn much. (Patrick Reddy)

Personality Variables

The frustration-aggression theory—detailed in Chapter 11—provides a popular explanation for prejudice and discrimination. Another explanation that likewise has roots in the writings of Sigmund Freud and the psychoanalytic school is that of projection. **Projection** is people's tendency to attribute to others traits that they find unacceptable in themselves. Supporters of the projection theory call attention to two facts (Dollard, 1937; MacCrone, 1937; Hernton, 1965; Fanon, 1967): First, whites in the United States and South Africa attribute to minorities, especially blacks, unbounded sexual energies and capabilities. Second, these whites are also immersed in a strong Puritanical, "uptight" cultural tradition that depicts sexual desire as "dirty," "filthy," "nasty," and "sinful." Projection theorists believe that the two facts are significantly linked.

The explanation runs along these lines. Whites find themselves in a dilemma: They experience sexual tensions but define sexual desire as wrong. So they resolve the problem by unconsciously projecting their unacceptable sexuality onto blacks. As a consequence, whites, having invested blacks with supersex-

TABLE 15.1
Mean Number of Teacher Responses
to "Gifted" and "Nongifted" White and Black Students*

TYPE OF INTERACTION	BLACK	WHITE
Total attention		
Gifted	29.6	36.1
Nongifted	30.3	32.3
Encouragement		
Gifted	5.5	6.2
Nongifted	5.3	6.3
Ignoring		
Gifted	6.9	5.1
Nongifted	6.9	4.6
Praise		
Gifted	.6	2.0
Nongifted	1.6	1.3
Criticism		
Gifted	1.9	.8
Nongifted	.9	.7

*The labels "gifted" and "nongifted" were assigned at random by the experimenters.
SOURCE: Adapted from P. C. Rubovits and M. L. Maehr, "Pygmalion Black and White," *Journal of Personality and Social Psychology,* Vol. 25 (1973), p. 212.

uality (superstar status in the bedroom), find blacks sexually tempting and attractive. But attraction to blacks would be too painful to acknowledge. In projection, the attraction becomes attributed to the black male. It is the black male that whites see as the aggressor, as being ever the potential rapist (Schulman, 1974; Stember, 1976). In this fashion the white man protects his pride. (He can discount the possibility that white women may find black men sexually attractive.) The white man's sense of masculinity has been preserved at the cost of all blacks who have ever been lynched under the faintest suspicion of intercourse with a white woman.

Plausible as the projection theory appears, it is highly speculative. It lacks the rigid experimental testing that is essential to science. Indeed, one theory could be—and frequently is—substituted for another, and there can be any number of theories to explain the same phenomenon. Thus it is advisable to use caution in applying projection theory.

Still another theory, also with roots in the Freudian tradition, claims that prejudice is closely and inseparably linked to an *entire* personality structure. Prejudice is seen not as an isolated trait that can appear in any kind of personality, but as an ingredient of the **authoritarian personality.** This is a set of traits characterized by rigid, conventional thinking, an obsession with power, submission to authority, highly judgmental values, and a cynical outlook. According to T. W. Adorno and his associates (1950), people with authoritarian personalities have essentially "fascist" mind-sets. Although the approach has been subjected to rigorous criticism (Christie and Jahoda, 1954), research has generally supported the idea of a linkage between prejudice and authoritarianism.

SUMMARY

1. People in modern societies are evaluated and rated in terms of a great many attributes, including race, ethnic membership, gender, occupation, income, education, accumulated wealth, age, physical attractiveness, and social skills. Conceived in this fashion, individuals and groups are ranked from high to low and from better to worse, which results in differences in power, privilege, and status. What significantly distinguishes racial and ethnic hierarchies from other hierarchies is the fact that minority groups have the potential to carve their own autonomous nation from the existing state.

2. A minority group is characterized by oppression at the hands of another group, high social visibility, a consciousness of oneness, ascribed membership, and ingroup marriage.

3. Prejudice is a state of mind. At root, prejudice is a matter of relationship between groups—a sense of group position.

4. Institutional racism is an inclusive concept. It entails both prejudice and discrimination. But even more, it points to the fact that a society's institutions operate systematically to the advantage of one group and the disadvantage of another. It is based on racial practices rather than the intentions of the people involved.

5. In theory, offices and positions in the United States are allocated to individuals on the basis of merit, not of their group attributes. But WASPs (white Anglo-Saxon Protestants) determine the standards of excellence to be used in judging qualifications. And WASPs are the judges who decide which individuals meet the standards. As a consequence, WASPs tend to have the advantage in the race for good things in American life.

6. Where workers offering cheap labor are of a different racial or ethnic group than those working for higher pay, class antagonism takes the form of racial or ethnic conflict. What is basically class conflict comes to be translated into the rhetoric of racism. Higher-priced labor seeks to block its own displacement through exclusion or caste systems.

7. Most situations of intergroup contact involve an established population and an incoming group. When the incoming group has superior power resources, it is able to dominate. This is the foundation of classic colonialism. In contrast, where the established population is dominant and brings in subject peoples, domestic colonialism is the result.

8. A good many of our racial attitudes and behaviors are rooted in our reference groups.

9. We respond not only to the objective features of a situation, but to the meaning the situation has for us. Under circumstances where we start out with a false definition of the situation, we may unintentionally act to fulfill the definition. This is called a self-fulfilling prophecy. It is the means through which dominant groups create the very inferiority that they claim exists in minority groups.

10. A number of approaches with roots in the psychoanalytic tradition seek to explain prejudice: the frustration-aggression theory, the projection theory, and the authoritarian personality theory.

GLOSSARY

Authoritarian personality □ A set of traits characterized by rigid conventional thinking, an obsession with power, submission to authority, highly judgmental values, and a cynical outlook; a "fascist" mind-set.

Classic colonialism □ Domination of an established, indigenous population by an incoming group through conquest and the imposition of a control apparatus.

Discrimination □ The arbitrary denial of power, privilege, and status to members of a minority group whose qualifications are equal to those of the dominant group.

Domestic colonialism □ The victimization, oppression, and subjugation by an established, indigenous population of another people, who are brought into the society against their wishes and will.

Ethnic group □ A group distinguished on the basis of socially acquired lifeways.

Gatekeeping □ The decision-making process by which individuals are admitted to scarce positions and offices of power, privilege, and status within a society.

Institutional racism □ Those social arrangements and enduring patterns by which people of one racial group oppress and exploit the members of another racial group.

Minority □ Any racially or ethnically self-conscious social aggregate, with hereditary membership and a high degree of ingroup marriage, which suffers oppression at the hands of a dominant segment of a nation-state.

Prejudice □ An attitude of aversion and hostility toward the members of a group simply because they belong to it and are therefore presumed to have the objectionable qualities ascribed to the group.

Projection □ The tendency of people to attribute to others traits that they find unacceptable in themselves.

Racial group □ A group distinguished on the basis of hereditary physical traits.

Self-fulfilling prophecy □ A false definition of a situation which creates conditions that make it come true.

Split labor market □ An economic arena in which there is a large differential in the price of labor for the same occupation; in a split labor market, conflict develops among three groups: business, higher-paid labor, and cheaper labor.

Symbolic racism □ A set of beliefs in which the underlying racial content is disguised but nonetheless finds expression in white notions that blacks are violating cherished values and making illegitimate demands on whites for social change.

16 GENDER ROLES, IDENTITIES, AND SEXUALITY

GENDER ROLES AND
    IDENTITIES
Gender Roles
Gender Identities
Gender Identities: Anatomy and
    Gender Identity
Gender Identity: Transsexuals,
    Transvestites, and
    Homosexuals

Acquiring Gender Identities
Sexual Symbols and Meanings
Androgyny
SEXISM
Sexism in the Home
Sexism in the Wage Economy

All societies contain two sexes, men and women. This fact has far-reaching implications for our personal behavior and for the structuring of social life. Being male or female affects how we view ourselves and others. And it shapes our fortunes, particularly our lot in life. Throughout human history, men and women have enjoyed different rights and opportunities. In practice this fact has been translated into social inequality, what has come to be termed **sexism.** Sexism involves those social arrangements and enduring patterns by which members of one gender group realize more benefits and fewer burdens than members of the other gender group. Most commonly, sexism has operated to the advantage of men and to the disadvantage of women. The term **male chauvinism** is often used to refer to patterns of behavior involving male sexism toward women. Gender differences are also related to sexuality, a significant component of our personalities. The images we have of ourselves are strongly influenced by our feelings about our sexuality. And aspects of our sexual beings express themselves in our interactions with others, even in situations that we do not usually define as being sexual. In sum, overtones and undertones of gender and sexuality permeate the human experience.

GENDER ROLES AND IDENTITIES

Within social psychology, the women's movement has given impetus to the study of gender roles and identities. Needless to say, there is no denying the obvious anatomical distinctions between males and females. These differences derive from hormones that begin working shortly after conception. But anatomical distinctions and hormonal differences are one thing; what human beings make of them is still another. And it is what people make of things that is a key interest of social psychologists.

Gender Roles

Apparently all societies have seized upon the anatomical differences between men and women as the basis for assigning **gender roles.** Gender roles are sets of expectations that define the ways in which the members of each sex should behave. Anthropologists suggest that gender roles may well represent the earliest division of labor among humans.

Anthropologist George P. Murdock (1935) analyzed the division of labor by sex in some 224 societies and found considerable differences in the types of activities assigned to each sex (see Table 16.1). It is noteworthy that the allocations of duties do not necessarily correspond to our own. Within many sections of the United States, for example, local laws restrict the weights that a working woman may lift. Yet among the Arapesh of New Guinea, women regularly carry heavier loads than men "because their heads are so much harder and stronger" (Mead, 1935, 1949). In some societies women do most of the manual labor. In others, such as the tribes of the Marquesas Islands, cooking, housekeeping, and baby tending are male occupations. (The Marquesas people explain that women are not nurturant.) And although in most societies it is believed that men should take the initiative in sexual matters, women are expected to do so among the Maoris and the Trobriand Islanders (Ford and Beach, 1951).

The wide variety found in the behavior patterns of men and women from one society to another points to a social foundation for a great many such differences. What is defined as normal masculine behavior in one society may be viewed as normal feminine behavior in another (see Chapter 7). And the changes that occur in sex-linked behavior patterns within the same society from time to time point to a similar conclusion. Not far back in Western history, the dashing cavalier wore long curls and perfume; he had a rapier and a stallion, but he also went in for powder and lace and soft leather boots that revealed a well-turned calf. Closer to our own time, men who wore long hair in the 1950s were defined as "sissies" and "queers." By the early 1970s long hair came to be viewed as masculine, and today more intermediate hair styles have come into vogue. Clearly these matters are a function of social definitions and socially constructed meanings.

Questions about gender roles frequently elicit from men and women statements that embody prevailing stereotypes. Indeed, given only a gender label, people will infer a variety of gender-related characteristics (Deaux and Lewis, 1984). Within the United States, men are typically stereotyped as dominant,

TABLE 16.1
Division of Labor by Sex in 224 Societies

Activity	NUMBER OF SOCIETIES AND SEX OF PERSON BY WHOM ACTIVITY IS PERFORMED				
	Men Always	Men Usually	Either Sex	Women Usually	Women Always
Hunting	166	13	0	0	0
Trapping small animals	128	13	4	1	2
Herding	38	8	4	0	5
Fishing	98	34	19	3	4
Clearing agricultural land	73	22	17	5	13
Dairy operations	17	4	3	1	13
Preparing and planting soil	31	23	33	20	37
Erecting and dismantling shelter	14	2	5	6	22
Tending and harvesting crops	10	15	35	39	44
Bearing burdens	12	6	35	20	57
Cooking	5	1	9	28	158
Metalworking	78	0	0	0	0
Boat building	91	4	4	0	1
Working in stone	68	3	2	0	2
Basket making	25	3	10	6	82
Weaving	19	2	2	6	67
Manufacturing and repairing of clothing	12	3	8	9	95

SOURCE: Adapted from G. P. Murdock, "Comparative Data on the Division of Labor by Sex," *Social Forces,* Vol. 15, (1935), pp. 551–553.

independent, competitive, self-confident, aggressive, and logical; women as submissive, dependent, emotional, conforming, affectionate, and nurturant. These stereotypes have proven amazingly consistent across the past several decades (Skrypnek and Snyder, 1982). This fact should not surprise us since stereotypes reflect the social structure and division of labor in a society. They mirror social patterns in which child care and household responsibilities are borne primarily by women, and men garner the more prestigious, higher-paying, and responsible positions in business and government (Eagly and Steffen, 1984). Complicating matters, people selectively perceive and remember gender-conforming behaviors. They more readily notice and learn evidence that confirms their stereotypes. Consequently, people overestimate the extent to which the actions of men and women actually verify gender stereotypes (see the boxed insert on facial prominence in pictures of men and women, pp. 498–499).

Berna J. Skrypnek and Mark Snyder (1982) advance and experimentally confirm an additional explanation for the persistence of gender stereotypes. When men and women use their stereotyped beliefs as guides for interacting with one another, they restrict one another's behavioral options in ways that generate traditional gender behaviors. In ongoing relationships, one person's stereotyped convictions often initiate a chain of events that cause another person to act in ways that accord with these stereotyped beliefs. Not surprisingly, social psy-

*F*emale-labeled professions

I am a student in the school of nursing. We have one or two men in the school but the rest are all women. The university attempts to recruit men for nursing but it has little success. The problem seems to be that nursing is labeled a "female profession" and men steer clear of it. The profession has evolved as an adjunct to the nurturing and caretaking duties traditionally assigned women in Western society. In fact, during the Civil War many of the women who functioned as nurses were the wives and sweethearts of men, who followed their men when they were inducted into the army. Many were perceived to be prostitutes—hence the name "hookers" after General Hooker and his unit. Nurturing and caretaking roles are typically defined as "unmanly," and men feel their masculinity would be put in jeopardy were they to become nurses. In fact, the men who are nurses are often thought to be gay or at the very least effeminate. Although nurses have technical skills that often surpass those of physicians (particularly interns and residents), they nonetheless are placed in subordinate roles and all too often are seen as merely "doctors' helpers." By virtue of these social definitions, nursing is a low-paying profession.

chologists have found that coeds portray themselves to a desirable male partner as quite traditional when they imagine his outlook to be conventional and as nontraditional when they imagine his outlook to be nonconventional (Zanna and Pack, 1975). And female job applicants dress more traditionally when they expect to be interviewed by a male holding traditional views of women than they do when they believe the interviewer to hold untraditional views of women (von Baeyer, Sherk, and Zanna, 1981).

Gender Identities

How do people conceive of themselves? How important to them are their **gender identities**—their self-conceptions of being either male or female? One way to answer this question is to ask the people themselves. The question "Who am I?" is placed at the top of a piece of paper that has lines for twenty answers—the Twenty Statements Test (TST). Social psychologists have employed this measure of social identities in a variety of studies.

For the most part, people give the response "I am a female" or "I am a male" to the "Who am I?" question with only moderate frequency, although men give it much more often than women. Instead, people usually employ a gender-specific marital or family role identification. They describe themselves as "mother" or "father" rather than "parent," and as "wife" or "husband" rather than "spouse." Overall, "Who am I?" studies reveal that gender-related identities tend to pre-

Touching
Men typically are the ones who initiate touching in male-female interaction. Should women take the initiative, men often construe the touching as a sexual invitation. (Patrick Reddy)

dominate over other self-characterizations (Mulford and Salisbury, 1964; Wellman, 1971).

Chapter 5 stressed the view that our identities arise from social interaction and in turn influence our subsequent interactions. Little wonder, then, that the women's movement should focus attention on sexist social definitions. How others define us in the course of social interaction has a profound effect on how we come to define ourselves (see Chapter 5). Even when we reject others' definitions of us, their social messages still have an impact, if only because we experience a sense of rejection, frustration, and rage. And how much more devastating it is when others command the power resources—jobs, social acceptance, and love—that compel us to play the game of life on their terms, in accordance with their needs and definitions!

The women's movement has highlighted the sexist nature of much of contemporary life and its consequences for the identities of women. In many social contexts, a woman gains a reflection of herself not as a person with individual worth, talents, and dignity, but as a commodity (Landy and Sigall, 1974). In American culture, people rely heavily on a person's physical appearance and attractiveness to make inferences about other aspects of the person (Webster and Driskell, 1983; Deaux and Lewis, 1984). But even more for women than for men, the ultimate test of their value has traditionally been their beauty. Indeed, a woman historically has been compelled to barter her looks in exchange for a man, not only for the food and shelter he provides, but for love. Repeatedly, women get the message, "If you are unlovely, you are unloved" (Stannard, 1972; Dion, Berscheid, and Walster, 1972; Berscheid and Walster, 1974b). In turn, a man is judged by the beauty of "his woman"—her looks are viewed as a tangible

FACIAL PROMINENCE IN PICTURES OF MEN AND WOMEN

American women spend millions of dollars each year on facial care and make-up. Yet according to Dane Archer and his colleagues (1983), men are more often represented in the mass media by their heads and faces whereas women are featured showing more of their bodies. These researchers conclude that the essence of a man is sought in his face whereas that of a woman is sought in her body. In investigating these matters, they gathered and coded 1,750 published photographs drawn from *Time, Newsweek, Ms.,* the *San Francisco Chronicle,* and the *Santa Cruz Sentinel.* They excluded photographs that featured the body as a whole, such as those of a performing athlete, a person modeling clothes or cosmetics, or an individual in a before-and-after weight-loss ad. Those photographs that met their criteria received a "face-ism" score computed by measuring the proportion of the total picture devoted to a person's face. A picture cropped at the shoulders would have a relatively high score, whereas one that showed the entire body would have a low score. On average, approximately two-thirds of a photograph was devoted to a man's face. In contrast, less than half of the average picture was devoted to a woman's face. These results showed up in all of the publications, even *Ms.* magazine—a publication identified with women's rights.

The sex differences were not limited to the United States. Archer and his colleagues examined face-ism in thirteen publications from eleven other nations and

measure of his manhood and erotic ranking (Zetterberg, 1966). It is not surprising that Grace Kelly, movie star and princess of Monaco, said when she turned forty that although forty is a marvelous age for a man, it is torture for a woman because it means "the end." And Brigitte Bardot, defined as a "sex siren" in the 1960s, attempted suicide on her forty-ninth birthday, observing, "It's really tough to age. . . . It's half a century. Welcome to the senior citizens' club" (*Columbus Dispatch,* September 20, 1984, p. 3). In a very real sense, every day in a woman's life has connotations of a Miss America contest.

It is often noted how men benefit from institutional sexism. Yet men also pay a price for their dominance. They become entrapped within the same system as women (Spence and Helmreich, 1978). Although the male prison may be much bigger and more luxurious, it is still a prison (Gitlin, 1971; Komarovsky, 1976). Men are expected to live up to male stereotypes. Within the United States, three expectations predominate (Cicone and Ruble, 1978). First, there are those stereotypes having to do with the way men handle their lives—they "should be"

found similar patterns. The researchers then studied portraits across six centuries, including the works of Leonardo da Vinci, Raphael, Rembrandt, Velázquez, Renoir, Cézanne, Modigliani, and Matisse. With the exception of the very earliest work, significant sex differences in facial prominence occurred across the time periods. Next, Archer and his colleagues had eighty undergraduate students draw separately a woman and a man, with instructions "to capture the character of a real person." The amateur artists—both men and women—not only made men's faces more prominent, but they also gave more detail to men's facial features (eyes, nose, and mouth). In sum, there is consistent asymmetry in images of the sexes in published photographs across a number of different cultures and in artwork across several centuries.

Archer and his colleagues also found that when they manipulated the degree to which they displayed the face and body to subjects, the attributions made about a person's qualities changed. Subjects perceived the person more favorably when the face was prominent than when it was not. Both men and women judged individuals who were depicted high in facial prominence as more intelligent, more ambitious, and more attractive. All this has implications for the conceptions that we have about the relative importance for women and men of hearts and minds. The defining, identifying, and pivotal qualities associated with men seemingly center on their intellect, personality, character, wit, and other dimensions of mental life. In contrast, the qualities uniquely associated with women appear to be more corporal than cerebral. The fact that women are portrayed in the media in ways that downgrade their facial prominence slights their intellectual qualities. Thus face-ism not only mirrors sexist stereotypes but helps perpetuate them.

active and achievement-oriented, displaying adventurous, ambitious, independent, courageous, competitive, dynamic, and active qualities. Second, there are those stereotypes depicting how men handle others—they "should be" dominant, exhibiting such qualities as aggressiveness, powerfulness, and assertiveness. Third, there are those stereotypes dealing with how men handle their emotions— they "should be" level-headed, demonstrating a "cool," realistic self-control. These expectations have weakened over the past decade, and many men, especially younger ones, no longer subscribe to them.

Marc F. Fasteau (1974) points out that traditional stereotypes had consequences for almost every aspect of men's lives. The need to project a tough, impersonal front and to maintain a competitive stance often made friendships between men shallow and superficial. Tenderness, warmth, and sensitivity were defined as weakness, even in relating to women and one's own children. And by making women sex objects, men became sex machines, which, when pushed to extremes, could lead to impotence.

---

*G*ender and drinks

Tonight I was out at a night club. It is interesting to observe what drinks people order. Females tend to drink such things as "Pink Squirrel," "Grasshopper," and "Singapore Sling," drinks with rather modest and neutral-sounding names. Guys tend to drink such things as "Black Russian," "Harvey Wall Banger," and "Hairy Buffalo," drinks with rather mean, nasty, and tough-sounding names. Night club owners cater to the normative requirement that women appear feminine and guys masculine in their drinking behavior.

Gender Identities: Anatomy and Gender Identity

The possession of a vagina, labia, and clitoris, or a penis and scrotum is neither a necessary nor sufficient condition for developing a female or male gender identity, respectively.

—Suzanne J. Kessler and Wendy McKenna, *Gender,* 1978

A six-foot two-inch, twenty-year-old human being with X and Y chromosomes, penis, scrotum, and facial hair is by *gender role* definition a male. By *self-gender identification* "he" may or may not be male. Freud's old formula notwithstanding, anatomy is not destiny. John Money, a psychologist at Johns Hopkins Medical Center, and his associates have done much to uncover the pathways by which we become male or female (Money and Ehrhardt, 1972; Money and Tucker, 1975; Ehrhardt and Meyer-Bahlburg, 1981). Until recently, it was assumed that there are two quite separate roads, one leading from XY chromosomes at conception to manhood, the other from XX chromosomes at conception to womanhood. However, Money's work and that of other medical researchers suggest that there are not two roads but one road with a number of forks where each of us turns in either the male or the female direction. In brief, we become male or female by stages within the mother's uterus (Wilson, George, and Griffin, 1981).

Critical biological forks occur at a number of points. For six weeks after conception, XX and XY embryos proceed along the same sexually neutral road. At this point, the Y chromosome sends a message to the two gonads to become testicles. As soon as the gonad fork is passed, the neutral and female roads converge. At this and every subsequent fork of the road, without a push in the male direction, the fetus will take a female turn. Nature's first choice is to make an Eve, not an Adam. At each critical stage, development as a male requires effective propulsion. Unless the required "something more" occurs in the correct proportions at the proper times, the fetus will follow the female pattern of development. Other critical points in shaping a male or a female occur when sex hormones are secreted and when sex organs take shape.

We erroneously assume that all babies are born either male or female, that the distinction is categorical and absolute. But **hermaphrodites** are individuals who have the reproductive organs of both sexes. By virtue of prenatal detours at critical junctures, individuals may develop both male and female internal reproductive organs, or external reproductive organs that are so ambiguous that the persons appear to be one sex at birth only to find at puberty that they are the other.

Money's research with hermaphrodites reveals the part that social definitions play in influencing a child's gender identity. At birth the infant is classed as a boy or a girl. This labeling—which is repeated countless times each day—launches a stylized treatment of the child. Thus how the child is reared provides the final and perhaps the most significant fork in the road to maleness or femaleness:

> The label "boy" or "girl" . . . has tremendous force as a self-fulfilling prophecy, for it throws the full weight of society to one side or the other as the newborn heads for the gender identity fork, and the most decisive sex turning point of all. (Money and Tucker, 1975: 86–87)

Money's case studies are highlighted by the case of the identical-twin boy whose penis was inadvertently cauterized during circumcision. His parents opted for surgical reconstruction to make him a female, and the child is progressing well, having developed a female gender identification (Money and Tucker, 1975). By the time the children reached four years of age, there was no mistaking which twin was the girl and which the boy. At five the girl preferred dresses to pants, enjoyed wearing hair ribbons, bracelets, and frilly blouses, headed her Christmas list with dolls and a doll carriage, and unlike her brother, was neat and dainty.

In still another case, a genetic female labeled a "male" at birth learned at puberty, when breasts began to develop, that he harbored female sex organs. He demanded and received medical assistance that enabled him to marry and, save for reproduction, live an impeccably male life. Cases of this sort have led Money to conclude that once a person's gender identity has been established, it cannot be easily reversed. During the preschool years this identification typically becomes firmly rooted.

Money does not deny that biological endowment plays a part in determining gender behavior. He and his associates have studied girls whose mothers had received hormonal supplements to prevent miscarriage, resulting in high levels of "male" hormones in their bodies before birth. These girls tend to be less interested in playing with dolls than most girls. Although interested in marriage and children, they are less so than most other girls their age. But they are not as aggressive and competitive as many boys. Moreover, their gender identity does not seem to be affected, nor do they show indications of lesbianism in their erotic interests.

Money has concluded that the human embryo has a bisexual potential. Certain very broad behaviors become programmed in the fetus by the relative proportions of the sex hormones received at critical developmental junctures. It seems to Money as if some inner behavioral dial is set at "male" or "female." Certain of the embryo's neural circuits become "imprinted" and subsequently affect the threshold for the elicitation of "male" or "female" behaviors. Consequently, by virtue of this prenatal dial setting, individuals are more or less sensitive to certain kinds of environmental experiences (Money, 1977).

In sum, Money says that anatomy per se does not provide us with our gender identification. We attain our gender identities in much the same way we attain speech (Money and Tucker, 1975). Although we are born "wired" for language, we are not programmed for any particular language. Analogously, we are wired but not programmed for gender identity.

Money's formulations are controversial. Some critics say that he assigns insufficient weight to social factors in the fashioning of gender identities and behaviors (Quadagno, Briscoe, and Quadagno, 1977). Others take the opposite tack and accord greater significance than does Money to biological factors. One group of researchers finds that women's gender-role identities are related to their level of *testosterone* (a male hormone secreted by the testes in males and by the ovaries and adrenal glands in females) (Baucom, Besch, and Callahan, 1985). Women with high levels of "masculine" attributes exhibit a higher level of testosterone than do women with high levels of "feminine" attributes. Likewise, medical researcher Julianne Imperato-McGinley and her colleagues (1979) at the Cornell University Medical Center have described shifts from female to male gender identities among adolescents in two rural communities in the Dominican Republic. They infer that exposure to the male hormone testosterone during the fetal period and again at puberty is the most important factor in the shaping of a male gender identity.

As of 1979, there were thirty-eight individuals from twenty-three interrelated Dominican families who displayed "male pseudohermaphroditism." At birth their external genitalia appeared to be female. Consequently, they were raised as girls in a very traditional and conservative culture where differences between the sexes are emphasized and where definitions based on male and female gender roles are firm and explicit. A strict gender division of labor prevails. Girls are physically and socially restricted at home; boys are free to roam and play. At twelve years of age, males start going to bars and cockfights; at age fourteen, they begin visiting prostitutes. Although the individuals in question appear to be females at birth and are reared as girls, the vast majority shift their gender identities during adolescence when the hormonal events of puberty give them a masculine appearance. (The child's voice deepens, muscles enlarge, a normal-looking penis and scrotum develop, and breasts do not emerge.) Apparently they first experience morning erections and nocturnal emissions, and they initiate masturbation and sexual intercourse at ages that do not appreciably differ from males reared as boys.

Some medical researchers have questioned the emphasis that the Cornell group has assigned to biological factors in the shaping of the gender identities of the Dominican pseudohermaphrodites (Bleier, 1979; Keen, 1979; Rubin, Reinisch, and Haskett, 1981). They note that the early appearance of the genitalia, while distinctly not masculine, is not normally female either. Further, sometime between the ages of seven and twelve the individuals begin realizing that they are different from girls and start questioning their true gender. Finally, the culture rewards the male gender role and deprecates the female role, encouraging the selection of the male role. Of interest, a number of individuals in the United States with a condition resembling that of the Dominican pseudohermaphrodites do not shift their identities, retaining female gender identities and roles.

What are we to conclude from these controversies? Probably the safest conclusion we can draw is that gender identity is a function of neither nature nor nurture alone. Hormonal and environmental factors interact to influence behavioral developments in human beings (Rubin, Reinisch, and Haskett, 1981). Hormones may serve to "flavor" a person for one kind of gender behavior or another. Even though hormones may predispose an individual to learn a particular gender role, they do not insist that the role be learned. Hormones simply make it easier for the individual to learn a particular behavior. And the behavior can be greatly modified by environmental conditions.

Gender Identity: Transsexuals, Transvestites, and Homosexuals

Homosexuality is assuredly no advantage but it is nothing to be ashamed of, no vice, degradation, it cannot be classified as an illness. . . . Many highly respectable individuals of ancient and modern times have been homosexuals, several of the greatest men among them (Plato, Michelangelo, Leonardo da Vinci, etc.). It is a great injustice to persecute homosexuality as a crime and cruelty too.

—Sigmund Freud in a letter to an American mother requesting treatment for her son, April 9, 1935

A good many people lump transsexuals, transvestites, and homosexuals together—as people whose sexual preference or behavior differs from that of the "straight" heterosexual culture. Few if any people are more scorned, feared, or stigmatized within contemporary American life. As recently as 1973, a third of the adults in a national poll felt that homosexuals should be jailed or put on probation, and the majority endorsed job discrimination against them (Money and Tucker, 1975). Moreover, until 1974, the American Psychiatric Association considered homosexuality a "sickness," listing it as a mental disorder. In the past several years, however, American opinion has relaxed its attitudes on what constitutes "permissible"—or perhaps more accurately, "tolerable"—sexual behavior, especially if performed by consenting adults in private. A 1983 national poll revealed that just under half of those questioned would not let a candidate's homosexuality influence their vote, and 52 percent supported antidiscrimination laws for homosexuals. Even so, 52 percent said they opposed homosexuals' way of living, and by a margin of two to one said they were "unsympathetic" to the homosexual community (Schneider and Lewis, 1984). Strong opposition to homosexuality is found among fundamentalist Protestant denominations, Eastern Orthodox churches, Orthodox Judaism, and the Roman Catholic church (Goodman, 1984).

Although the public commonly lumps the behaviors together, social psychologists distinguish among transsexism, transvestism, and homosexuality. **Transsexuals** are individuals with normal sexual organs who psychologically feel like

AN ETHNOMETHODOLOGICAL VIEW OF GENDER

There is no such biological entity as sex. What exists in nature is a dimorphism [division] within species into male and female individuals, which differ with respect to contrasting characters. . . . Sex . . . is merely a name for our total impression of the differences.
—F. R. Lillie, *Biological Introduction,* 1932

As we go about our daily activities, we assume that every human being is either a male or a female. We treat the existence of two sexes as an irreducible fact of life. When we encounter a person for the first time, we class this person as a male or a female. For the most part, the process is deceptively easy. Until relatively recently, scientists have done much the same thing. Even in the case of hermaphrodites, biologists have traditionally tried to sort individuals into one or the other gender category rather than creating a third category.

Occasionally, we see people whose gender identity is not obvious, as in the case of teenagers wearing "unisex" clothes. At such times we consciously scrutinize the individuals for gender cues as to what each person "really" is. But what do these cues consist of? If we ask people how they tell men from women, they usually provide an answer having to do with "genitals." Yet in most of our day-to-day dealings with people, we rarely, if ever, see the genitals of persons we "know" to be male or female.

Harold Garfinkel (1967: 122–128) points out that in the United States people accept the followng "facts" about gender:

1. There are two, and only two, genders [female or male].
2. One's gender is invariant. [If you *are* female/male, you always *were* female/male and you always *will be* female/male.]
3. Genitals are the essential sign of gender. [A female is a person with a vagina; a male is a person with a penis.]
4. Any exceptions to two genders are not

members of the opposite sex (Stoller, 1975; Feinbloom, 1977). They should not be confused with hermaphrodites—people in whom development of the sex organs took an incompatible turn at one of the forks in the road prior to birth, giving them mixed male and female organs. The sexual identities of transsexuals have swung in total opposition to their anatomy—it is "as if their mind is in the wrong body." James/Jan Morris (1974) put it in these terms: "I was born with the wrong body, being feminine by gender but male by sex, and I could achieve completeness only when the one was adjusted to the other."

Male transsexuals reject their penises; women transsexuals loathe their breasts. In some cases, as with Jan Morris, Christine Jorgensen, or Roberta Cowell, medical science has found a way, through surgery and hormones, to reduce the incompatibility by modifying the person's anatomy in conformity

to be taken seriously. [They must be jokes, pathology, etc.]
5. There are no transfers from one gender to another except ceremonial ones [masquerades].
6. Everyone must be classified as a member of one gender or another. [There are no cases where gender is not attributed.]
7. The male/female dichotomy is a "natural" one. [Males and females exist independently of scientists' (or anyone else's) criteria for being male or female.]
8. Membership in one gender or another is "natural." [Being female or male is not dependent on anyone's deciding what you are.]

Of course these "facts" about gender do not necessarily hold (Kessler and McKenna, 1978). For instance, hermaphrodites and transsexuals afford disconfirming illustrations. Yet by disconfirming the "facts," they provide us with insights as to how we go about constructing a world of gender in our everyday interactions. Take the case of transsexuals. Although transsexuals take their own gender for granted, they cannot assume that other people will do likewise. Consequently, they must "manage" themselves as "males" or "females" so that others will attribute the "correct" gender to them.

Transsexuals make obvious what non-transsexuals do "naturally." They have to learn gender-specific speech skills (for instance, talking like a "man" or a "woman" and using a "masculine" or "feminine" vocabulary). They need to present their bodies in gender terms that go beyond merely dressing as a male or female (for example, wearing padding, a scarf, and gloves to camouflage broad shoulders, an Adam's apple, and large hands). Additionally, preoperative transsexuals must manage their bodies so that others do not see them undressed. (Postoperative transsexuals generally do not experience this problem since genital surgery can be so successful that most people are unlikely to question the authenticity of transsexuals' genitals.) Finally, transsexuals must create the impression that they have always had the gender to which they lay claim. In sum, research with transsexuals highlights for us our use of various "gender markers" in making day-to-day gender attributions to people.

with gender identity. In changing a male to a female, surgeons remove the penis and testicles and construct an artificial vagina. They administer female sex hormones and may enlarge the breasts surgically. In changing a female to a male, surgeons remove breast tissue and seek to construct a scrotum and a penis (from skin flaps). Male sex hormones are also administered. An estimated 3,000 to 10,000 self-labeled transsexuals have received sex-reassignment surgery.

During the 1960s, the medical community had accepted the belief that traditional psychiatric intervention is useless with transsexuals and that sex-reassignment surgery is the treatment of choice. But during the 1970s, this thinking shifted. Researchers at the Johns Hopkins Gender Identity Clinic—the prestigious hospital that had pioneered sex-change operations—completed a follow-up study of one hundred patients who had applied for sex-reassignment surgery at their facility. They concluded that surgery confers no advantages over psycho-therapy in terms of social rehabilitation (Meyer and Reter, 1979). The release of these findings was used as evidence to close the clinic and to cease sex-change operations.

Currently, the medical community is taking a cautious approach toward sex-reassignment therapy, employing it primarily as the last resort for a highly select group of patients (Lothstein, 1982). While acknowledging that some individuals do benefit from the surgery, physicians find that a great many of their patients suffer from other psychological disorders. In many instances, individuals pre-senting themselves for the operation are persons who are encountering difficulty in social adjustment or experiencing a life crisis. They seek a gender change as a way out of their difficulties. However, surgery merely complicates their situa-tion. Further, while sex-reassignment surgery provides an individual with artifi-cial genitals, it does not supply the developmental history of a man or woman essential for being a male or female. For instance, it does not provide a man turned woman with the unique identifications with the mother, the experiences of participation in a girls' social group, the initial psychological encounter with menses, or the continued reactions to female physiological development.

Transvestism involves an overpowering urge to impersonate and dress in the clothes of the opposite sex. King James I of England frequently wore women's garb. So did Edward Hyde, Lord Cornbury, who was governor of New York and New Jersey during Queen Anne's reign. He would astonish the colonists by appearing in public toying with a fan and wearing a hoopskirt and feminine headdress (Money and Tucker, 1975). There is reason to believe that Joan of Arc was also a transvestite (Bullough, 1974, 1976).

Transvestites have ambiguous gender identities. Unlike transsexuals, however, they do not wish to give up their penises or breasts. When dressed in the garb of their own sex, their behavior appears quite normal. Nor are transvestites in clinical terms homosexual; their preference is commonly for the opposite sex.

Homosexuality entails erotic response to persons having the same sexual anatomy as oneself. It is important to distinguish between a person's gender identity and choice of a sexual object (Storms, 1980). Contrary to popular belief, homosexuals are not necessarily deficient in their sense of masculinity or femi-ninity—their gender identity conforms with their anatomy. They differ from heterosexuals in that homosexuals prefer sexual partners of the same gender. The homosexual's desire for objects of the same gender may be exclusive or partial. Some people are exclusively homosexual, whereas others are *bisexual* (finding both men and women acceptable sex objects). Situational homosexuality may arise in prison settings during periods of deprivation from the opposite sex. Individuals who engage in homosexual activity under such circumstances revert to heterosexuality, however, when the opportunity exists (Weinberg, 1974). American society has stigmatized homosexuality. However, in 64 percent of the societies for which such information can be identified, homosexual activities of one sort or another are considered normal and socially acceptable for all or at least certain members of the community (Ford and Beach, 1951).

Researchers at the Institute for Sex Research (founded by Alfred C. Kinsey) completed a study of about 1,500 homosexual men and women living in the San Francisco Bay area (Bell and Weinberg, 1978). The sample was derived from public advertising, personal contacts, mailing lists, and visits to gay bars and steam baths. About three quarters of the white homosexual men and a somewhat smaller percentage of the black homosexual men considered themselves exclusively homosexual in their current sexual behavior. This contrasted with two-thirds of the white lesbians and about three-fifths of the black lesbians.

Although homosexuals are stereotyped as sexually hyperactive, the study found them neither more nor less sexually active than their heterosexual counterparts. Overall, males tended to be more interested in impersonal sexual encounters, whereas the lesbians were more likely to seek a continuing, durable relationship that placed a premium on mutual fidelity. Almost half the white homosexual males and one-third of the black homosexual males reported that they had had at least 500 different sexual partners during the course of their homosexual careers. The majority of lesbians, whether black or white, had had fewer then ten female sexual partners. The researchers believe that the relative instability of male homosexual liaisons is partially due to the strong social opposition to such relationships. However, the number of male homosexuals living as couples has increased dramatically in recent years (Dullea, 1984). This trend is partly a reflection of a general movement toward conservatism in sexual behavior and partly a response to the fear of such diseases as acquired immune deficiency syndrome (AIDS) and genital herpes, which tends to discourage casual sex and encourage monogamy. A recent survey of homosexual men in San Francisco found that 42 percent of them were in monogamous relationships (*New York Times*, November 23, 1984, p. 13). Researchers find many parallels in the relationships of heterosexual couples and homosexual couples (Blumstein and Schwartz, 1983; Harry, 1984).

Researchers at the Kinsey Institute have investigated the development of sexual preferences in men and women (Bell, Weinberg, and Hammersmith, 1981). Under the influence of Freudian psychoanalytic thought, many psychiatrists have traditionally believed that family background is the critical factor in the shaping of sexual preferences. They have assumed that boys who grow up with weak fathers and dominant mothers have a tendency to become homosexuals. In contrast, girls who have rejecting mothers and unsatisfactory relationships with their fathers have a tendency to become lesbians. But the researchers found that distant fathers and overbearing mothers—or any other cluster of parenting qualities—had little or nothing to do with either homosexual or heterosexual development. Nor did they find evidence that homosexuality results from a lack of heterosexual opportunities, traumatic heterosexual experiences, or homosexual seduction. Because the researchers were unable to identify a pattern of feelings and reactions within the child that could be traced back to a single social or psychological source, they reached the controversial conclusion that a child's sexual preference may arise from "a biological precursor that parents cannot control."

For homosexual men, the researchers found that "gender nonconformity" was the single most important factor in predicting their eventual sexual preference.

For boys, this often meant little interest in sports and an enjoyment of solitary activities like drawing, reading, and music. But by the same token, one-fourth of the heterosexual men in the study said that they also were nonconforming as youngsters (and half of the homosexual males had typical masculine interests and activities in their childhood). For homosexual women, "gender nonconformity" was the second most important predictive factor, surpassed by homosexual involvement in adolescence. But of interest, only a third of heterosexual women described themselves as "highly feminine" in childhood. Since "gender nonconformity" occurred early in childhood, the researchers concluded that it was a reflection of an already-established homosexual orientation and not a cause of it. Other researchers confirm that significantly more homosexual than heterosexual men recall as children being called "sissy," being social loners, wanting to be girls, playing with girls, and cross-dressing (Harry, 1982; Green, 1985).

In summary, social psychologists distinguish among transsexuality, transvestism, and homosexuality on the basis of gender identity and sex-object preference. The gender identity of transsexuals is opposite to that of their anatomy—for instance, the male transsexual wants to live, work, think, and make love as a woman (Money and Primrose, 1969). Transvestites have an ambiguous gender identity but generally prefer sexual relations with members of the opposite sex. Homosexuals have a gender identity conforming with their anatomy but prefer individuals of their own sex as sexual objects (Storms, 1980). These categories, however, are not necessarily exclusive. Overlap may occur, as in the case of transvestite homosexuals (Person and Ovesey, 1974).

Acquiring Gender Identities

How do boys come to take on the behavior of boys, and girls the behavior of girls? Freudian psychoanalytic theory indicates that a normal child identifies with the same-sex parent and learns the details of a gender role through *imitation*. Along somewhat similar lines, social learning theory emphasizes *conditioning*—a product of selective reinforcement (see Chapter 4). Children are usually rewarded for modeling the behavior of individuals of the same sex. Boys and girls are actively rewarded and praised by adults and their peers for what are generally seen as sex-appropriate behaviors, and they are ridiculed and punished for behaviors deemed inappropriate to their sex. In sum, members of a society structure activities in ways that teach the gender roles favored by their culture (Bussey and Bandura, 1984; Perry, White, and Perry, 1984).

Albert Bandura (1971, 1973a) gives social learning theory a slightly different twist. He points out that children do not simply do what they see other people doing. They also learn by observing the behavior of others, although they themselves may not immediately act in the identical fashion. Bandura says that children mentally *encode* the behavior they watch and in this manner build up a large repertoire of potential behaviors. However, they *perform* the behaviors only if they anticipate a positive outcome for doing so. Bandura (1965) has experimentally shown that boys and girls learn aggressive acts about equally well from watching a movie (see Chapter 4). Nonetheless, boys are more likely to translate this knowledge into overt action in their own play behaviors. Consequently, Bandura concludes that boys and girls learn essentially the same information but, by virtue of their different socializing experiences, differ in the extent to which they activate particular types of behavior. In brief, by observing that men and women differ in certain behaviors, children come to encode some responses as male-appropriate and other responses as female-appropriate (Perry and Bussey, 1979). In turn, they find themselves rewarded for responses that they have encoded as same-sex–appropriate and punished for those that they have encoded as appropriate for the opposite sex.

Still another approach, the cognitive-developmental, is identified with Lawrence Kohlberg (1966; Kohlberg and Ullian, 1974) and focuses on *self-socialization* (see Chapter 4). In this view, the child first learns his or her gender identity and then attempts to acquire and master the behaviors that fit the gender concept. According to Kohlberg, children form an image based on what they have observed and have been told about what it means to be a boy or a girl. A limited set of features that are highly visible and describable from the child's viewpoint make up the concept. They include traits relating to hair style, dress, and stature. A child's gender-role conceptions are cartoonlike—oversimplified, exaggerated, and stereotyped. Once children acquire a clear conception of themselves as a "boy" or "girl," they strive to assume the behaviors appropriate for their sex. Sex-typed behavior is said to be motivated by children's desire to behave in a way consistent with their gender label.

Kohlberg (1966: 89) succinctly notes the differences between his cognitive-developmental approach and social learning theory. According to the social learning model, the following sequence occurs: "I want rewards. I am rewarded for doing boy things; therefore I want to be a boy." In contrast, Kohlberg suggests a different sequence: "I am a boy; therefore I want to do boy things; therefore the opportunity to do boy things (and to gain approval for doing them) is rewarding." Whereas both psychoanalytic and social learning theories see the child as essentially *passive* (the stress falling on the overpowering influence of parental actions), Kohlberg's cognitive-developmental approach emphasizes the child's *active* part in the socialization process.

Research suggests that by age six a child's gender identity is already fixed and provides an organizing focus for his or her social interaction (Vander Zanden, 1985). The critical years in gender-identity formation are from two to six. By age three a child will label himself or herself correctly and will name the gender of others with partial accuracy. By four, the child will label gender correctly and will show some awareness that gender cannot change. Allan Katcher (1955) found, for instance, that when four- or five-year-olds are asked to assemble dolls so that the genitals match other parts of a doll's body and clothes, most children are confused or ignorant about the genital basis of sex differences. Nonetheless, they know that the categories "boy" and "girl" exist, and they identify with their own gender category.

Rather than counterposing gender-acquisition theories so that the issue is

THE PSYCHOLOGY OF SEX DIFFERENCES

For centuries ignorance, superstition, and prejudice have surrounded both the popular and the scientific views of male-female differences. To find out which generalizations are justified and which are not, Eleanor E. Maccoby and Carol N. Jacklin (1975) spent three years compiling, reviewing, and interpreting over 2,000 books and articles on sex differences in motivation, social behavior, and intellectual ability. On the basis of sifting and weighing the psychological literature, they conclude that the following notions are *myths:*

□ Girls are more sociable, empathic, and socially oriented than boys.

□ Girls are more suggestible and susceptible to outside influences than boys.

□ Girls have less self-esteem and less self-confidence than boys.

□ Girls are better than boys at rote learning and simple repetitive tasks; boys are better at tasks requiring creative thinking.

□ Boys are better than girls in tasks requiring analysis.

□ Boys are more affected by environment, girls by heredity.

□ Girls lack the achievement motivation, or drive, of boys.

On the other hand, Maccoby and Jacklin find four fairly well-established sex differences between boys and girls:

□ Beginning at about age eleven, girls show greater verbal ability than boys.

□ Boys perform better than girls on visual-spatial tasks in adolescence and adulthood, although not in childhood.

□ At about age twelve or thirteen, boys move ahead of girls in mathematical ability.

□ Males are more aggressive than females.

Not surprisingly, these summary findings have been the source of considerable controversy. Other psychologists have undertaken their own surveys of the literature and have come up with differing conclusions and computations. Take, for instance, the three cognitive-gender differences that Maccoby and Jacklin find to be "well-established" (verbal ability, visual-spatial ability, and mathematical ability). Julia Sherman (1978) and Janet Shibley Hyde (1981) have independently reviewed the evidence and have concluded that the magnitude of the differences is quite small. And in the case of the spatial-visualization dimension (including picturing how objects will look after they are rotated or folded), Sherman (1980) finds no sex-related differences, a position confirmed by other researchers (Caplan, MacPherson, and Tobin, 1985).

The controversy surrounding sex differences in mathematical ability has heated up in recent years. Two psychologists at Johns Hopkins University, Camella P. Benbow and Julian C. Stanley (1980), have compared the 1972 through 1979 Scholastic Aptitude Test (SAT) scores of 9,927 intellectually gifted junior high school students. Although the boys and girls performed equally well on the verbal sections, more than twice as many boys as girls had math scores greater than 500 (1,817 versus 675). The largest differences were between the top-scoring boys and girls. On the basis of this evidence Benbow and Stanley hypothesize that sex differences in mathematics achievement derive from "superior male mathematical ability." Benbow told the *New York Times* "the reasons for male superiority in math are not understood, but may result from a combination of inborn factors such as hormonal or brain differences and environmental factors such as the way children are raised and the toys they play with" (December 7, 1980, p. 102). Subsequent analyses of SAT data suggest that male-female differences occur primarily on algebraic items and are not evident on arithmetical or geometric problems (Becker, 1983).

Any number of psychologists have challenged Benbow and Stanley's interpretation (Schafer and Gray, 1981; Tobias, 1982). They point out that until and unless girls experience the same world as that experienced by boys, one cannot assume that gender differences in math have a genetic basis. Current stereotypes lead many women to believe that mathematics is a "male domain." Such notions influence their career and educational aspirations and their attitudes toward mathematics. In brief, expectations may be instigated in which people play out social stereotypes. Further, women are more likely than men to be discouraged by parents, peers, teachers, and school counselors from pursuing mathematics-related careers. It is hardly surprising, therefore, that many behavioral differences between men and women result from conscious self-presentational strategies (Deaux, 1977).

The matter of biological differences between men and women in innate levels of aggressiveness remains an unsettled issue. Researchers find that males of many species are hormonally primed for aggression. Moreover, hormones seem to "masculinize" or "feminize" the brain prenatally. For instance, female rhesus monkeys who are prenatally injected with male hormones exhibit after-birth behaviors typical of male monkeys. They engage in much of the rough-and-tumble play, the threatening gesturing, and the sexual mountings characteristic of males. And on occasion a masculinized female works her way up to the dominant position in her troop by sheer aggressiveness (Phoenix, Goy, and Resko, 1969).

Psychologist Judith M. Reinisch (1981) has found some evidence to buttress the hormonal argument for human beings as well. She studied seventeen girls and eight boys whose mothers had been treated in pregnancy with synthetic progestins to prevent miscarriage. The progestins biochemically mimic the action of male sex hormones. Reinisch administered to the children and their siblings a standard test measuring aggressive responses. The progestin-exposed males scored twice as high on aggression as did their brothers. Twelve of the seventeen females scored higher on aggression than did their sisters. These findings led Reinisch to suggest that the differentiation of hormone-organized behaviors observed in laboratory animals may also apply to human behavior.

Box continues on next page

However, the evidence in support of gender differences in aggression is by no means firmly established. Janet Shibley Hyde (1984) has reviewed the Maccoby-Jacklin studies and more recent research. She found that the magnitude of such differences is small and that gender differences in aggression are smaller in recent than in earlier studies. Maccoby and Jacklin have since undertaken their own research on behavioral differences between boys and girls in the first six years of life. Some 275 children were monitored at ten periods between birth and age six. These researchers could find no significant differences between the boys and girls in aggression, timidity, or activity level (Elias, 1984).

It should be stressed that even when researchers find gender differences between males and females, the average differences between the sexes allow considerable room for individual variation. Men and women fall along the whole continuum of behavior. It should also be clear from our discussion that the psychology of sex differences is controversial. This condition will very likely persist in the future because the findings of the social sciences can be used to buttress or challenge various social arrangements and institutions.

defined in either-or terms, some social psychologists see psychoanalytic, social learning, and cognitive-developmental theories as complementing one another. Janet Shibley Hyde and B. G. Rosenberg write:

> No theory is completely wrong. Each contributes something to our understanding. Freudian theory was important historically in emphasizing the notion that individual sex identity and behavior have their roots in previous experiences. . . . Social learning theory is important in its emphasis on the social and cultural components of sex-role development—the importance of society in shaping sex-typed behaviors. . . . Social learning investigators have . . . contributed some very impressive laboratory demonstrations of the power of reinforcements in shaping children's behavior, in particular sex-typed behaviors. Social learning theory also highlights the importance of imitation in the acquisition of sex roles. . . . Finally, cognitive-developmental theory emphasizes that sex role learning is a part of the rational learning process of childhood. . . . Children actively seek to acquire sex roles. (1976: 48–50)

In sum, each theory has relevance, its usefulness depends on which variables are being considered and which parent-child relationships are involved (Rosenberg and Sutton-Smith, 1972).

Sexual Symbols and Meanings

We commonly think of sexual arousal and orgasm as a purely physiological experience. Although it undeniably has a biological aspect, sex—like any other activity—is approached by human beings in terms of symbols and meanings. The part that meanings play in turning a biological into a relevant psychological experience is also encountered in research on drug effects. Different reports on

Rough Play
What is a "real" boy?
(Patrick Reddy)

Gentle Play
What is a "real" girl?
(Patrick Reddy)

the internal experiences produced by LSD ("good trips," paranoid trips, multi-sensational hallucinations, meetings with God) and even marijuana seem more attributable to the individual's definitions of the drug, mood, situation, and previous history of usage than to the drug itself (Blum and Funkhouser-Balbaky, 1967; Goode, 1969; Barber, 1970). The same holds for sexual experiences. Young people in puberty often report feelings of anxiety, nausea, and even fear for what they finally categorize (or disregard, even though the feelings still occur) as sexual arousal. Indeed, a vast number of physiological events are filtered through social definitions so as to be either ignored or highlighted as "experience"; how we interpret an internal state has a profound impact on our experience of it (Gagnon and Simon, 1973). This fact is highlighted by people's sexual daydreaming and fantasizing, since the content of sexual fantasies is quite varied (Arndt, Foehl, and Good, 1985). Indeed, people's sexual fantasies can be at odds with their sexual orientation (Schwartz and Masters, 1984).

As Kenneth Plummer (1975) observes, much sexual behavior may have "nonsexual" sources. The health faddist may take sex at prescribed regular intervals in the same way as health foods and for the same purpose. A married couple may engage in sexual relations because each believes the other expects it, even though neither may want it. A prostitute or stripper employs sex as a means of earning a livelihood. A man may seek a regular flow of sexual partners in the belief that this will sustain his public image of masculinity and virility. And a student may masturbate as a mechanism of tension reduction.

Symbols and meanings pervade a vast range of behavior that we commonly label sexual. Take kissing. Most preadolescent boys regard kissing as "sissy stuff"; girls consider it asexual. But as adolescents begin "hanging out" together, they come to define the same physical act in sexual terms. Accordingly, they experience the result as erotically exciting. No change has occurred in the act, only in the meaning attached to it (Gagnon, 1975).

Many of the same physical acts that occur in male-female sexual sequences also occur in other situations—the palpation of the breast for cancer, the gynecological examination, the insertion of tampons, and mouth-to-mouth resuscitation. For an activity to be sexual, a variety of words and gestures must commonly be introduced into the situation to give it "sexual" meaning—saying the "right things," wearing "seductive" clothing, establishing "sexy" eye contact, "deftly" removing clothing, and petting in the "proper" ritualistic sequence. Further, we need to define another person as an "appropriate" sexual partner in terms of age, gender, physical attractiveness, and social status. Hence social interaction is critical to sexual functioning. Genitals, copulation, and orgasms do not have "sexual meaning" in their own right; meaning must be bestowed on them through social encounters (Gagnon and Simon, 1973; Plummer, 1975).

Androgyny

In the United States, "feminine" traditionally was assumed to mean all that is soft, tender, and helpless; "masculine," everything hard, tough, and independent. For years psychologists took these polar opposites as evidence of psychological health. More recently, some mental health experts have challenged this view. They insist that a new standard of psychological health is required, one that allows individuals to express the full range of human emotions and role possibilities without regard to gender stereotypes. They term the expanded range of human possibilities **androgyny,** from "andro," male, and "gyne," female. According to this view, androgynous individuals should be more flexible in meeting new situations and less restricted in the way they express themselves. This notion has generated a good deal of research and has contributed to much debate. Although some researchers have found support for the "androgyny equals mental health" position, others have not. And several investigators have presented strong evidence for a competing claim—namely, that a greater number of masculine traits enhance the mental health of both men and women, irrespective of the presence or absence of feminine traits (Lubinski, Tellegen, and Butcher, 1981; Taylor and Hall, 1982; Frank, McLaughlin, and Crusco, 1984; Heilbrun, 1984).

The controversy began in the 1970s when Sandra Lipsitz Bem (1975*a,b,* 1979) and her colleagues investigated gender roles among more than 1,500 Stanford University students. Semester after semester, they found that roughly 50 percent of the students adhered to "appropriate" (sex-typed) roles, about 15 percent were cross-sex–typed, and some 35 percent were androgynous. Bem and her associates then undertook five experiments to determine whether sex-typed people are more restricted and androgynous people more adaptable in carrying out a variety of actions that commonly confront adults.

In one such experiment, students were called on the telephone and given an unreasonable request: When would they be willing to spend over two hours, without pay, to fill out a questionnaire about their reactions to various student insurance policies? The students were not asked *whether* they would participate; participation was simply assumed. To refuse would require that the student assert his or her preferences over those of the caller. "Feminine" women found it harder to be assertive than any other group. When asked later how difficult it was to turn down the caller, 67 percent of the "feminine" women said they found it very difficult, compared with 28 percent of the "masculine" men and androgynous students.

Other experiments required students to relate to a baby and a person with troubles. Bem and her colleagues found that "masculine" men did "masculine" things very well, but "feminine" things badly. They could be independent and assertive, but they were relatively unresponsive to a baby or a person in need; they lacked the ability to express warmth, playfulness, and concern. "Feminine" women were responsive to the baby and to people in difficulty, but they lacked independence and assertiveness. In contrast, androgynous men and women could be independent and assertive when these traits were called for, and on other occasions they could be appropriately warm and responsive. Bem (1981, 1982, 1984) also claims that sex-typed individuals—"masculine" males and "feminine" females—are more likely to encode and process information in terms of cultural definitions of gender than are androgynous individuals. But other researchers have had difficulty confirming her position (Crane and Markus, 1982; Mills and Tyrrell, 1983).

Bem's work has been interpreted as confirming arguments that sexism locks

Androgyny
More American fathers
are coming to partici-
pate in the care and
rearing of their children.
(Patrick Reddy)

both men and women into roles that rob them of a broad range of human
emotions and possibilities. Traditional masculinity and femininity are seen as
penalizing men and women by restricting their behaviors. Androgynous men and
women, on the other hand, are depicted as more resourceful in diverse social
situations. A number of studies have supported Bem's notion of androgynous
flexibility and suggest that androgynous individuals enjoy a larger repertoire of
behaviors than do sex-typed individuals (Flaherty and Dusek, 1980); La France
and Carmen, 1980). Further, androgynous individuals tend to be evaluated as
more likable and better adjusted by other people than do sex-typed persons
(Major, Carnevale, and Deaux, 1981). And they seem to be more capable of
expressing love and tolerating a loved one's faults (Coleman and Ganong, 1985).

Initially, Bem portrayed androgyny as a balance between masculinity and
femininity (a scale ranging from high masculinity at one end to high femininity
at the other end, with androgyny defined as the middle range). But after considerable debate, she and other investigators (including Spence and Helmreich,
1978) have come to view as androgynous individuals who score high in masculinity *and* in femininity. Consequently, a person can be simultaneously high in
masculine and feminine attributes, high in one but low in the other, or low in
both. They class an individual with high scores on both masculine and feminine
attributes as "androgynous," an individual high on masculine but low on feminine
attributes as "masculine," a person scoring high on feminine but low on masculine
attributes as "feminine," and persons with low scores on both masculine and

*A*ndrogyny

One of my male friends, Gary, is an unusual individual, probably the closest of any person I know to a self-actualized individual. He is now touring with a ballet company and is rapidly gaining recognition as a first-rate professional. We went to high school together, where he excelled in gymnastics. Gary was also first-string wide receiver on the football team in his senior year. To top it all off, he has a marvelous singing voice. In short, he is truly a gifted individual. Moreover, Gary is quite sensitive, perceptive, and introspective. He is capable of displaying the full range of emotions. I have seen him break down and cry on occasion, as when one of our classmates was killed in an auto accident. Yet I have witnessed his aggressiveness on the football field where he won all-conference second-string honors. Nevertheless, I have found him to be the most compassionate and tender person I've ever known. Thus, it makes me extremely angry when people who hardly know him dismiss him as a "fag." Yet he is hardly a "fag" in the bedroom. I ought to know, as we were lovers for over a year. Gary is an androgynous individual. He seems to enjoy activities that our society labels as "girl" just as much as he enjoys various "boy" activities. Gary seems to find a comfortable integration of roles and is not restricted by societal gender stereotypes.

feminine attributes as "undifferentiated." Hence, as viewed by Janet T. Spence and Robert Helmreich, androgynous persons are characterized by the presence of both masculine and feminine attributes rather than the absence of both. How one defines androgyny and how one measures it have profound impact on the findings afforded by research (Myers and Gonda, 1982; Whitley, 1983; Deaux, 1985).

Spence and Helmreich find that androgynous individuals tend to be superior parents, to possess high self-esteem, and to enjoy high achievement motivation. However, not all studies have confirmed the superiority of androgynous patterns over those of one or the other sex types, suggesting that the advantages or disadvantages of particular patterns may have much to do with the situational context in which individuals find themselves (Heilbrun, 1981, 1984; Lubinski, Tellegen, and Butcher, 1981; Lippa and Beauvais, 1983; Zeldow, Clark, and Daugherty, 1985). At the present time there is much confusion regarding androgynous research, with some social psychologists finding that neither the Bem nor the Spence-Helmreich formulations have much predictive power (Taylor and Hall, 1982; Lubinski, Tellegen, and Butcher, 1983). Although the notion of androgyny has stimulated much interest, its scientific status is questionable, and it has not lived up to the promise its proponents anticipated a decade ago (Deaux, 1985).

SEXISM

Chapter 15 considered the part that race and ethnic hierarchies play in human affairs. Individuals are also ranked in hierarchies based on their gender. Indeed, the sexual hierarchy—the subjugation of women—may well be the oldest human ranking arrangement.

With respect to power, privilege, and status, men have enjoyed advantages relative to women. Women possess less power over their communities and over human affairs than men, earn less money than men, and have more difficulty becoming eminent than men. The distributive question of who shall get what, when, and how has for the most part been answered in favor of males: It is males who enjoy top political office, who get the best jobs, who usually escape from menial household labor, who schedule sexual intercourse, and who traditionally got most of the orgasms.

Sexism in the Home

> *Men of sense in all ages abhor those customs which treat us only as the vassals of your sex.*
>
> —Abigail Adams, Letter to John Adams, March 31, 1776

In the past, women provided unpaid child-rearing and domestic services. Although most men in American society have always belonged to the wage sector of the economy, most women were until recently left out of the wage economy altogether. Since household labor and child care typically take place outside of trade and the marketplace, they were not considered "real work"—reflecting a sexist value system. In a society where money defines worth, women's domestic labor was long belittled because it did not yield a monetary return.

Traditionally, the American family system has operated to bind women to their reproductive function. Until relatively recently, motherhood has been central to our society's definition of the adult female—the notion that a woman must have children and rear them well (Hardin, 1974; Russo, 1976). American family patterns have implied that sex is inevitably connected with reproduction (the availability of contraception and abortion notwithstanding). Additionally, the motherhood mandate has ordained that the woman who bears a child must be the major person responsible for his or her rearing. Each woman raises one man's children in an individual household viewed as private property and private space (Gordon, 1970). This has led to the slow development of institutions providing child-care services outside the home. Moreover, studies show that husbands of women working in the wage economy do not engage in more work around the house than do husbands whose wives stay at home (Riche, 1980). One recent survey found that only 14 percent of husbands in two-earner families perform as much as half the housework, and 60 percent do less than a quarter (Townsend, 1985). (See the boxed insert on excuses.) Hence, working wives typically must do two jobs while their husbands do but one. Even if a husband

EXCUSES OF A MALE CHAUVINIST HUSBAND

I am willing to share the housework. I'm just not good at it. Why don't we each do what we're best at?

Meaning: You stay home, grocery-shop, cook, do dishes, clean the house, and do the laundry, I'll bring in the money and maybe help out by changing light bulbs and moving furniture.

I'm willing to help out, but first you'll have to show me how to do it.

Meaning: Every time I do it, you'll have to show me over again. And don't plan to read or watch television, because I'll annoy the hell out of you until you find it easier to do it yourself.

I just hate this work. You don't mind it as much as I do.

Meaning: This is crap work. It degrades someone of my intelligence, but it's okay for women of your intelligence.

Gee, we used to be so happy! (When it is the husband's turn to do a task.)

Meaning: I used to be so happy before you got on this women's liberation kick.

I'm willing to help share the housework. But you can't make me do it on your schedule. That wouldn't be fair.

Meaning: I'll never get around to doing it, so just make up your mind that if you want it done, you had better do it yourself.

Among the wolves and other animals, the top animal is the male because of his brute strength, cunning, and intelligence.

Meaning: Baby, biology ordained you to play second fiddle. It justifies my keeping you down.

Source: Adapted in part from Pat Mainardi, "The Politics of Housework," in Leslie B. Tanner (ed.), *Voices from Women's Liberation* (New York: New American Library, 1970), pp. 336–342.

is unemployed, he does much less housework than a wife who puts in a forty-hour week (Blumstein and Schwartz, 1983). And young, educated professional men—yuppies—who claim to be for sexual equality, are no more likely to do the dishes or change diapers than their blue-collar counterparts (Lee, 1984). Not surprisingly, nearly half of working women report difficulty in keeping up with housework, and more than a third feel guilty about work left undone. Half say they have too little time for themselves (Townsend, 1985).

Within the Western world, male dominance has involved the notion of sexual property, namely, the tenet that men "own" female sexuality. All too frequently, men appropriated women for their beds and likewise pressed them into service in their fields and kitchens. Within this context, women exchanged sexual and

Role Specialization and Segregation by Gender
The American nuclear family has bound women to their reproductive function.
Even in public gatherings they are shunted off from the main activities to take care
of the children. (Patrick Reddy)

domestic services for male financial support. A sexual double standard, however, traditionally permitted men considerable sexual freedom and adventure, a right withheld from women. Indeed, until the past few years, marital "swinging" was referred to as "wife swapping" (as opposed to "husband-and-wife swapping"), clearly suggesting the view that a man owned his wife's sexuality. And feminists point out that a woman's virginity has long been defined as the property of her father and her sexuality as the property of her husband. By virtue of this definition, rape has been seen less as a crime perpetrated by a man against a woman than a crime perpetrated by one man against another man (LeGrand, 1973). Additionally, sexual assault within marriage is not legally rape in many states. (Some states have recently either modified or are in the process of modifying this provision; see Chapter 11.)

Until the twentieth century, English and American common law viewed women as entering "civil death" upon marriage. The woman lost her legal identity—indeed, her social identity, for she had to forsake her own name for that of her husband. In the eyes of the law, women became "incorporated and consolidated" with their husbands. The common-law doctrine of *femme couverte* held that a married woman was covered or veiled by her husband's name and authority. A wife could not own property in her own right or sign a contract; she could not sue or testify against her husband. The husband had claim to all her property, inherited or earned. And in the view of the court, a husband was legally liable

Sexual property

Tonight my boyfriend Fred, myself, and another couple went to a campus bar to drink and dance. When we left, about midnight, Jan (my girlfriend) and I walked out ahead of the two guys. As we passed the bar, another guy reached out and pinched me. I slapped his hand and quickened my pace. Fred came up to the guy and said, "Hey, that's my girl. What do you think you're doing pinching her?" A big argument developed between Fred and the guy on the bar stool. The guy said that he didn't mean any harm but that I had a "damn cute butt." Well, Fred is a big guy, six feet eight inches tall. The other guy, eventually intimidated, backed down and apologized to Fred for pinching me. None of the guys ever thought that maybe he should be apologizing to me. After all, I was the one who was molested. Rather, the apology went to Fred. It was Fred who was "wronged," not me. By pinching me, the other guy had "violated" Fred's property—me. Within our society, women are considered to be sexual property.

for criminal acts committed by his wife in his presence. He could require his wife to submit to sexual intercourse against her will and to live wherever he chose.

Sexism in the Wage Economy

Equality is not when a female Einstein gets promoted to assistant professor; equality is when a female schlemiel moves ahead as fast as a male schlemiel.

—Ewald B. Nyquist, 1975

As of 1984, more than two-thirds of American women twenty-five to fifty-four years old were in the labor force. Three of five women with children worked, including 46 percent of those with children younger than three and 52 percent of those with children younger than six. Overall, 53 percent of American women were in the labor force, up from 33.9 percent in 1950, 37.7 percent in 1960, and 43.3 percent in 1970 (Serrin, 1984). The acceptance of women in the labor force—even mothers with young children—has grown with considerable speed over the past two decades. By the late 1960s, it was generally considered acceptable for women to work out of economic necessity. More recently, the notion that married women might work by choice, assuming their husbands approve, has also achieved almost universal acceptance. Although in 1968 one-third of women aged twenty to twenty-four still disapproved of this idea, by 1978 only 6 percent found the idea unacceptable (Mott, 1982).

   The entry of women into the wage sector of the economy has constituted one of the most significant social and demographic developments of recent decades.

Sexual Property
What do you think this
couple is trying to com-
municate? (Patrick Reddy)

A number of factors have contributed to the expansion of the female work force. Economists point to the shift from a manufacturing to a service economy, which has been accompanied by an increased demand for white-collar workers. Demographers cite the increasing availability of new contraceptive methods and legal abortions, and the trend toward later marriage and smaller families—all of which increase the number of years women can spend in the labor force. And sociologists note such factors as the increased educational attainment of women (educated women are more likely to enter the wage economy), changing attitudes toward careers for women outside the home, and legislation that has broken down discriminatory barriers.

Despite these changes, many of the current figures on the employment of women in the American economy bear a striking resemblance to those of previous decades. Although the proportion of women in the labor force has greatly increased, there has been little substantial change in the sex labeling or sex segregation of occupations since 1900 (Gross, 1968; Scott, 1982). Much of the increase in the employment of women has been achieved through the displacement of men by women in some low-paying jobs and through the rapid expansion of the "pink-collar" occupations (primarily, clerks, secretaries, receptionists, and typists). In the United States, women fill more than 90 percent of all secretarial, bookkeeping, and receptionist positions (see Table 16.2). Furthermore, many jobs in the service industries entail an extension of the work that women do as homemakers—preparing food, teaching children, and nursing the sick. Additionally, men are overrepresented in higher-level positions within the "female" professions (Grimm and Stern, 1974). For instance, although women constitute 71

TABLE 16.2
Sexism in the Labor Force, 1982

OCCUPATION	% WOMEN	% MEN	MEDIAN INCOME
Secretaries	99.2		$12,636
Receptionists	97.5		10,764
Typists	96.6		11,804
Registered nurses	95.6		18,980
Sewers, stitchers	95.5		8,632
Keypunch operators	94.5		12,480
Bank tellers	92.0		10,348
Telephone operators	91.9		13,988
RR switch operators		100.0	22,828
Firefighters		99.5	20,438
Plumbers, pipefitters		99.2	21,944
Auto mechanics		99.1	15,964
Carpet installers		98.8	15,392
Surveyors		98.5	17,472
Truck drivers		97.9	17,160
Garbage collectors		97.3	12,116

SOURCE: Bureau of Labor Statistics, 1984.

percent of the nation's classroom teachers, only 20 percent of elementary-school principals and less than 2 percent of secondary-school principals are women (and less than 1 percent of school superintendents are women). Further, women have steadily lost ground in educational administration over the past eighty years. (In 1928, some 55 percent of elementary-school principals were women.) Overall, the positions that still elude American women are those at the top. Only 5 percent of top executives are women. In Congress, fewer than 5 percent of the 534 members are female.

In large measure, women who work in the wage economy are relegated to low-paying or part-time jobs. In clerical jobs, the average wage received by women is only slightly better than 60 percent of that earned by men; and in managerial and administrative categories, the percentage is only 50 percent (Linden, 1984). In terms of median earnings of full-time, year-round workers, the "pay gap" has remained relatively constant over the past three decades: 64 percent in 1955, 61 percent in 1960, 60 percent in 1965, 59 percent in 1970, 57 percent in 1975, 60 percent in 1980, and 64 percent in 1984. By the year 2000, Rand Corporation economists predict women will still earn only 74 cents to every dollar a man will make (Stewart, 1984). Sociologists David L. Featherman and Robert M. Hauser (1976) calculate that discrimination accounted for 85 percent of the earnings gap in 1962, and 84 percent in 1973. Sexism seems to penalize women even more than racism has penalized blacks. Black men currently earn 72 percent as much as white men (up 16 percentage points since the 1950s), and black women earn 92 percent as much as white women (Thurow, 1981). Sexism has contributed to what has come to be termed the "feminization of poverty." For every 100

> # "Sex bait"
>
> *I'm in dental hygiene. A few years ago there were some guys in the program, but now all the dental hygiene students are women. My boyfriend made an interesting observation about us today. He said, "You know, Jinny, all the dental hygienists are cute. Not one of them is a fat, ugly broad." And he's right. The other day a dentist in the clinic was talking with a number of us during a break, and he said something that angered me at the time. He said that dentists want attractive dental hygienists because they bring the guys in and the guys are also more likely to come back again. I guess what made me mad is that dental hygienists perform a necessary and useful health function. However, we are used for sexist purposes, almost as if we were "sex bait."*

men who earned less than $10,000 per year in 1983, there were 140 women who did so, and for every 100 men who made more than $50,000, there were only nine women who did so (Francese, 1984).

The Western definition of marriage as an institution in which the husband provides for his "dependents" has contributed to sexist patterns. Wage labor for women was seen as a premarital pastime or as a marital supplement. However, even though women's earnings are low, their financial contribution is becoming an increasingly important component of total household income. (Additionally, many women are the sole support of their families.) Thus it is often the wife's income that makes the difference between middle-income and low-income status—or that catapults the family into affluence (Townsend, 1985). One out of three working wives contributes between 30 and 50 percent, and one in eight earns at least half of the family's total income. In households with annual incomes of $30,000 to $35,000, more than two-thirds of the wives work; in households with incomes of $40,000 to $50,000, more than 70 percent work (Linden, 1984).

The wage gap between men and women is narrowing in some areas more than others. In 1982 and 1983, there was little or no difference between the beginning salaries offered male and female bachelor's degree candidates in a number of scientific, engineering, and social science professions. In 1983, women under twenty-five years old earned 90 percent as much as men. Female elementary-school teachers earned 87 percent as much as male teachers, female lawyers 88 percent as much as male lawyers, and female computer programmers 81 percent as much as male programmers. However, in sales, where women comprise a larger percentage of workers, they earned less than 50 percent as much as male salesclerks (Serrin, 1984). Women are also closing the educational gap with men. More than half of all college and university students now are women, up from about 40 percent in 1970. Women are currently securing over 30 percent of all law degrees, up from only 5 percent in 1970, and more than 23 percent of all medical degrees, up from less than 9 percent a decade ago (Linden, 1984).

Working Mothers
Children whose mothers
work outside the home
find that the workplace
clock is not calibrated
with that of the school.
(Patrick Reddy)

SUMMARY

1. Apparently, all societies have seized upon the anatomical differences between men and women as the basis for assigning gender roles. But there are considerable cross-cultural differences in types of activities assigned to members of each sex. Thus a great many of the differences found in the behavior patterns of men and women have a social foundation.
2. Our gender identities arise from social interaction, and, in turn, guide our subsequent actions.
3. Gender-role definitions and gender identities do not necessarily parallel one another. This is most clearly reflected in cases of hermaphrodites, transsexuals, transvestites, and homosexuals.
4. The work of medical researchers leads us to conclude that gender identity is a function of neither nature nor nurture alone. Hormonal and environmental factors interact to influence behavioral developments in human

beings. Hormones may serve to "flavor" a person for one kind of gender behavior or another. Even though they may predispose an individual to learn a particular gender role, they do not insist that the role be learned. Hormones simply make it easier for the individual to learn a particular behavior. And the behavior can be greatly modified by environmental conditions.

5. The gender identity of transsexuals is opposite to that of their anatomy. Transvestites have an ambiguous gender identity but generally prefer sexual relations with members of the opposite sex. Homosexuals have a gender identity conforming with their anatomy but prefer individuals of their own sex as sexual objects.

6. Various theories try to explain how gender identities are acquired. According to Freudian psychoanalytic theory, a normal child identifies with the parent of the same sex and learns the details of a gender role through imitation. Social learning theory emphasizes conditioning, a product of selective reinforcement. The theory assumes that parents reward and punish children's behaviors in accordance with parental perceptions of appropriateness of the behaviors for boys or girls. Cognitive-developmental theory focuses on self-socialization. In this view, the child first learns its gender identity and then attempts to acquire and master the behaviors that fit the gender concept.

7. Genitals, copulation, and organisms do not have "sexual meaning" in their own right; meaning must be bestowed upon them through social encounters.

8. Research by Sandra Lipsitz Bem suggests that androgynous individuals are more flexible in meeting new situations and less restricted in the way they express themselves than traditional "feminine" or "masculine" individuals.

9. Individuals are ranked in sexual hierarchies. With respect to power, privilege, and status, men have generally enjoyed the advantage relative to women.

10. Traditionally, the American family system has operated to bind women to their reproductive function. Until relatively recently, motherhood has been central to our society's definition of the adult female—the notion that a woman must have children and rear them well. Within the Western world, male dominance has involved the notion of sexual property, namely, the tenet that men "own" female sexuality.

11. Women who work in the wage economy are nearly all relegated to low-paying or part-time jobs. Sexism appears to penalize women even more than racism penalizes blacks. Discrimination has played an important part in producing these inequalities.

GLOSSARY

Androgyny □   A standard that allows individuals to express the full range of human emotions and role possibilities without regard to gender stereotypes.

Gender identity □   A person's self-conception of being either male or female.

Gender roles □   Sets of expectations that define the ways in which the members of each sex should behave.

Hermaphrodite □   An individual who has the reproductive organs of both sexes.

Homosexuality □ Erotic response to persons having the same sexual anatomy as oneself.

Male chauvinism □ Male sexism toward women.

Sexism □ Those social arrangements and enduring patterns by which members of one gender group realize more benefits and fewer burdens than members of the other gender group.

Transsexual □ An individual with normal sexual organs who psychologically feels like a member of the opposite sex.

Transvestism □ An overpowering urge to impersonate the opposite sex and dress in the clothes of the opposite sex.

17 COLLECTIVE BEHAVIOR AND SOCIAL MOVEMENTS

ELEMENTS OF COLLECTIVE
   BEHAVIOR AND SOCIAL
   MOVEMENTS
Structural Conduciveness
Structural Strain
The Growth and Spread of a
   Generalized Belief
Precipitating Factors
The Mobilization of Participants
   for Action
The Operation of Social Control

CROWD BEHAVIOR
   Contagion Theory
   Convergence Theory
   Emergent-Norm Theory
SOCIAL PROBLEMS
   The Nature of Social Problems
   Clashing Interests and Values
   Legitimizing Social Problems
   Official Public Policy
   Second-Order Consequences

On a spring evening a local television station in a southeastern state carried the following report:

> Officials of Montana Mills* shut down their Strongsville plant this afternoon because of a mysterious sickness.
>
> According to a report just in from Strongsville General Hospital, at least ten women and one man were admitted for treatment. Reports describe symptoms as severe nausea and a breaking out over the body.
>
> Indications are that some kind of insect was in a shipment of cloth that arrived from England at the plant today. And at the moment the bug is blamed for the outbreak of sickness. (Kerckhoff and Back, 1968: 3)

---

* The names used by the researchers in the report are fictitious, although in no case does the failure to disclose the identity of persons or places involve a distortion of essential information.

528

In due course, some 40 of 200 employees in the dressmaking section of the plant were afflicted by the illness. Although no one symptom was common to all cases, the most frequently mentioned complaints included nausea, fainting, weakness, nervousness, dizziness, and headache. The workers attributed the illness to insect bites. In all, the "epidemic" came and went in about a week's time.

Public health doctors and officials (including experts from the U.S. Public Health Service Communicable Disease Center) undertook a careful investigation. However, they could find no evidence of the presence of any insects that could account for the illness. Nor could they find any evidence for a viral infection (since no fever was involved) or food poisoning. They concluded that the ailment could be traced to a "bug," but one that was mental. Seemingly, the source of the illness was *hysterical contagion*—the dissemination of a set of behaviors that are heavily laden with fear of some mysterious force.

The Montana Mills case is not an isolated happening. Similar outbreaks have been reported on assembly lines, where each worker performs the same repetitious task over and over. (Occupational psychologists have termed such disorders "assembly-line hysteria" and "mass psychogenic illness.") Recent examples have included plants packing frozen fish, punching computer cards, assembling electrical switches, sewing shoes, and manufacturing aluminum lawn furniture (Stahl and Lebedun, 1974; Colligan and Stockton, 1978; Peterson, 1979; Colligan, Pennebaker, and Murphy, 1982). In most cases, the workers, usually women, complain of headaches, nausea, dizziness, weakness, and breathing difficulty. But physicians, industrial hygienists, and toxicologists can find no toxic agents, no bacteria, or no virus that might have caused the symptoms.

This conclusion should not be taken to mean that the illness is simply in the workers' "heads." Afflicted workers do suffer in a physical sense. Typically, something causes them to breathe rapidly (hyperventilate). This condition is a medically recognized disorder in which the faster the person breathes, the more carbon dioxide is blown off, and the higher becomes the pH level (acid-alkaline content) of the blood. The human body does not function well at high pH levels, and the result is neurological problems like headache, nausea, numbness in the feet and hands, and weakness.

ELEMENTS OF COLLECTIVE BEHAVIOR AND SOCIAL MOVEMENTS

Such unusual events as those recorded among the industrial workers are hardly new. Since the "dance mania" of 1374 in Europe, numerous episodes labeled "psychic epidemics," "collective seizures," "group outbursts," "mass delusions," "crazes," and "group pathology" have been recorded. In societies throughout the world, people have thrown themselves into these and other types of mass behavior: social unrest, riots, manias, fads, panics, mass flights, lynchings, crowd excitement, rebellion, and religious revivals. Social psychologists term such phenomena **collective behavior**—relatively spontaneous and unstructured ways of thinking, feeling, and acting that develop within a group or population as a consequence of interstimulation among the participants. It is behavior that is not governed by traditional, established norms and hence is not institutionalized.

Like collective behavior, social movements typically occur outside the institutional framework that forms everyday life and break through the familiar web of ordered expectations. Furthermore, both collective behavior and social movements frequently appear in times of rapid social change, while simultaneously providing an impetus to social change. Although collective behavior and social movements resemble each other, and arise from many of the same sources, they differ in one important respect (Traugott, 1978; Jenkins, 1983). Whereas collective behavior is characterized by spontaneity and a lack of internal structure, social movements are characterized by purposeful direction and a good deal of internal order. It is this organizational component that enables social movements to challenge established institutions. We may view a **social movement**, then, as a more or less persistent and organized effort on the part of a relatively large number of people to bring about or resist social change.

Ordinarily, individuals make their way about life assuming that "nothing unusual is happening" (Emerson, 1970). But from time to time, for whatever reasons, they label an emergent situation as outside the "normal" province of everyday life. Consequently, they no longer take the happenings for granted. Instead they begin defining a set of circumstances as unordinary, extraordinary, and even as unreal—in brief, as problematic. This suspension of people's ordinary frame for perceiving reality frequently marks the beginning of collective behavior or a social movement, especially when undertaken by sizable segments of the population. Episodes of robbery, mugging, financial loss, illness, and death also involve suspending the customary definitions associated with everyday life. But the private and individual character of these episodes leads people to label them as deviance, crime, or personal tragedy rather than collective action (Lofland, 1981).

Any number of social psychologists and sociologists have undertaken to provide a framework for examining collective behavior and social movements. One approach, that of Neil Smelser (1963), has attracted considerable interest. Smelser identifies six determinants. In order of occurrence, they are (1) structural conduciveness, (2) structural strain, (3) the growth and spread of a generalized belief, (4) precipitating factors, (5) the mobilization of participants for action, and (6) the operation of social control. Each determinant is shaped by those that precede it and shapes the ones that follow it.

Smelser's formulation is borrowed from the economists' notion of "value added." Take as an example the stages by which iron ore is converted into finished automobiles. As raw ore, the iron can be made into an auto fender, a kitchen range, a steel girder, or the muzzle of a cannon. Once it is converted into thin sheets of steel, however, its possible uses are narrowed. Although it can still be fashioned into an auto fender or a kitchen range, it can no longer be used for a steel girder or the muzzle of a cannon. After the steel sheet is cut and molded in the shape of a fender, its use is further limited; it cannot then be used for making a kitchen range. Each step in the process adds a specific "value" to the iron ore; simultaneously, each stage subtracts from its previous possibilities.

According to Smelser, episodes of collective action are like automobiles in

Panic behavior

In our dorm we had a fire drill at 2:30 this morning. Being awakened in the middle of the night is bad enough, but to a fire alarm is really scary. My roommates started screaming and running to the window to look outside and see if anything was happening. Someone down the hall started yelling "Fire!" and ran for the stairs. Naturally everyone dropped the idea of it being only a false alarm (which it really was) and thought the dorm really was on fire. We all jammed up at the stairway door and could not get through. We were pushing and shoving. It was just horrible. It seemed forever before we managed to get outside.

This illustrates panic behavior and shows the part Smelser's determinants of collective action played in it. Structural conduciveness existed in that a lot of us were clustered in the same wing of the dorm and hence could be affected by each other's reactions. In this case, preexisting structural strain was not in evidence, but the fire alarm (which signaled "fire" to us) produced intense anxiety; our anxiety was compounded by our being disoriented after having been jolted from sleep. A generalized belief came into existence regarding imminent danger posed by fire. The precipitating event was really not one thing but two events: first, the sounding of the fire alarm; second, the cry, "Fire!" We were mobilized for action, in this case flight, when one girl bolted for the stairway door. This set off a chain of fleeing girls.

that they are produced by a sequence of determinants. In both value-added sequences, as each successive determinant is added, the range of possible final outcomes is progressively narrowed. After each stage, the outcome becomes more certain and more specific. However, in some cases of collective action, all six stages do not occur or they do not take place in the sequence that Smelser specifies (Milgram, 1977). Although critics have found fault with aspects of Smelser's theory (Marx and Wood, 1975), it provides us with a convenient and useful framework for exploring collective behavior and social movements.

Structural Conduciveness

Structural conduciveness refers to the broad social conditions that are necessary for an episode of collective behavior to occur. Thus a necessary condition for a financial panic—such as that associated with the stock market crash of 1929—is a money market in which assets can be freely and quickly exchanged. A financial panic cannot arise in a society where property can be transferred to the eldest son only on his father's death. Under such conditions, holders of property lack maneuverability in disposing of assets on short notice.

The episode of hysterical contagion among the textile workers cited earlier in the chapter could not have taken place in the absence of social ties among the women. Two Duke University social scientists, Alan Kerckhoff and Kurt Back (1968), undertook a study of the "bug bite" epidemic. Their work revealed that the hysteria was transmitted through social networks, primarily friendship groups (women in the same car pool and women who ate lunch together). On the whole, the more ties a woman had with "affecteds" (individuals who had symptoms and saw a doctor), the more likely she was to become affected herself. In contrast, only 7 percent of the 232 women who had no ties with affecteds became affected. At most, however, conduciveness is permissive of a given type of collective behavior. Social networks set the stage, so to speak, for a wide variety of collective behaviors. Only later, as other elements are assimilated on a continuous, step-by-step basis, does the range of outcomes progressively narrow and find expression in a specific form or episode of collective behavior.

Structural Strain

Structural strain exists where various aspects of a system are in some way "out of joint" with one another. War, economic crises, geographical and social mobility, catastrophes, and technological change disrupt people's traditional or anticipated ways of life. People experience these developments as sources of frustration, conflict, deprivation, ambiguity, and tension. Over time, the cumulation of stress makes people susceptible to courses of action not defined by existing social arrangements—by traditional norms and roles. They experience *social malaise*— a feeling of pervasive dissatisfaction and disgruntlement. Indeed, Smelser suggests, the more severe the strain, the more likely it is that people will be disposed to episodes of collective behavior.

In their study of the "bug epidemic," Kerckhoff and Back isolated physical and psychological strain as a major underlying ingredient. Affected women were more likely than nonaffected women to supply half or more of the family income. They were also more likely to have preschool children *and* to have worked a great deal of overtime. Presumably, the affected women faced greater strain than nonaffected women due to the conflicting demands of their maternal and work roles. As such, these women were more susceptible than other women to an episode of hysterical contagion.

Other research also suggests that victims of assembly-line hysteria are under pressure to increase production. At times, this pressure involves large amounts of overtime to meet a production schedule. Frequently, the workers do not have the option of refusing overtime or they may need the additional income. Not uncommonly, a poor management-labor relationship characterizes the affected plants. The causes of the friction between management and labor may range from discontent over dress codes to the absence of adequate communication between workers and their supervisors (Colligan and Stockton, 1978; Colligan, Pennebaker, and Murphy, 1982). Additionally, the jobs of affected workers usually afford little opportunity for advancement, and the noise level is almost always high. What the workers seem to be saying when they get ill is, "This place makes me sick" (Peterson, 1979).

Social scientists have also noted the part that psychological and social strains play in the emergence of social movements (Champagne, 1983). The Ghost Dance that spread among the Plains tribes in the 1890s is a case in point. This nativistic or revitalization movement grew out of conditions in which white culture and encroachment had devastated Native American (Indian) societies and lifeways. One of the beliefs of the movement was that a cultural hero or messiah would one day appear and lead Native Americans to a terrestrial paradise.

A central ingredient in the movement was a dance in which participants would shake with emotion and fall into hypnotic trances. During the trances, individuals would experience visions of departed relatives in the spirit world who were engaged in dancing, playing games, gathering for war dances, and preparing for traditional ceremonials. Upon the arrival of the messiah and the inauguration of the golden age, the dead ancestors would return from the spirit world, and all would be reunited on a regenerated earth.

The movement arose at a time when the Native American population had been decimated through disease, starvation, relocation, and genocide. This timing suggests that the movement was, at least in part, an attempt to recover population losses (Thornton, 1981). And it represented an effort to revive and perpetuate aspects of Native American life and culture (Mooney, 1973).

Given that structural strain is one of the determinants of collective action, investigators have differed as to the nature of the conditions that serve as a precipitating cause for action. Some see relative deprivation as the spur to action; others, resource mobilization; and yet others, a synthesis of the two.

Relative Deprivation

Over the past several decades, social psychologists and sociologists have concerned themselves with the types of strain underlying episodes of collective action. One strain in particular, relative deprivation, has gained considerable attention. **Relative deprivation** refers to a state of mind in which a gap exists between what people seek and what seems attainable (Gurr, 1970; Folger, Rosenfield, and Robinson, 1983).

A good illustration of relative deprivation occurred during World War II. Within the American air force, promotions were rapid and widespread; within the military police, they were slow and piecemeal. Most of us would assume that the men in the air force were more satisfied with their chances for promotion than the men in the military police. After all, in absolute terms air force personnel were moving ahead faster in their careers. Yet research (Merton and Kitt, 1950) has revealed that the men in the air force felt considerably more frustrated over promotions than those in the military police. Among air force men, it was not the *absolute* level of attainment that made for poor morale but a sense of *relative* deprivation—the dissatisfaction aroused by the gap between what the men anticipated and what they had attained. In contrast, the military police did not expect rapid promotions; they learned to live with relatively few advances in rank.

TERRORISM

Terrorism is commonly seen as the use of force or violence against persons or property to intimidate or coerce a government, a formal organization, or a civilian population in furtherance of political, religious, or social objectives. In practice, however, terrorism is a function of our social definitions. Hence it is extremely difficult to differentiate "your terrorist" from "our freedom fighter," or to distinguish between "aid to terrorists" and "covert support of friendly forces" like the Nicaraguan contras, or counterrevolutionary fighters. (In 1984, an 89-page booklet was prepared under the auspices of the Central Intelligence Agency that advocated blackmailing, kidnapping, and assassinating Nicaraguan government officials.) Similarly, the Federal Bureau of Investigation labeled a "terrorist" the antinuclear activist who in 1982 drove up to the Washington Monument in a truck that he pretended was loaded with explosives, whereas the agency has failed to apply a similar label to those responsible for firebombing abortion clinics in various American cities.

According to Risks International, Inc., of Alexandria, Virginia, a decade ago the world experienced an average of ten incidents of terrorist violence (bombings, assassinations, air hijackings, kidnappings, and maimings) per week. By early 1985, there were nearly ten incidents each day. Between 1970 and 1985, terrorists struck 22,171 times, killing an estimated 40,394 persons and wounding 24,588 *(U.S. News & World Report,* 1985: 27). Terrorism functions as an avenue of political expression for individuals and groups motivated by ideology, ethnicity, or religion. At times it has been linked to insurgency (Halloran, 1982). During the first phase, insurgents

Relative deprivation may occur under a variety of conditions. The case of the air force men involved *rising expectations.* As a group experiences improvements in its conditions of life, it may also experience a rise in its expectations. But the expectations may rise more rapidly than the actual improvements, leading to dissatisfaction.

It was rising expectations—rather than despair—that bred the black protest and ghetto riots of the 1960s (Geschwender, 1964; Abeles, 1976). Blacks were led to believe that they were going to be much better off in the very near future. The early gains of the civil rights movement made it seem probable that blacks would rapidly gain a fair share of America's good things. But as it turned out, many blacks found themselves in the position of the underprivileged urchin who has his nose pressed against the bakery window, longing for the goodies inside. Previously, segregation had barred blacks from entering the store at all. Now they could walk in like any other customers, but they had no money with which to buy the goodies. Thus the new expectations went unfulfilled, or were perceived as being fulfilled too slowly.

often seek publicity—for instance, by blowing up power stations, assassinating politicians, or hijacking planes. In the second phase, they may rob banks for money, raid army outposts for weapons, and organize guerrilla operations. Next, the insurgents commonly challenge the government for control of the streets or parts of the nation, with ambushes, raids, sabotage, and bombings. In the fourth phase, insurgents seek to paralyze the economy by mobilizing the masses with general strikes. Finally, the guerrillas go over to direct assaults, as they did in the 1968 Tet offensive and the 1975 final offensive in Vietnam.

Increasingly, terrorism has also become an instrument of state policy among some governments. They are adopting terrorist tactics and employing terrorist groups or exploiting terrorist incidents as substitutes for warfare. The 1983 attack on the U.S. Marine barracks in Beirut that resulted in the death of 240 Americans is a good illustration of this. Complicating matters, violence often pays, encouraging additional violence. Thus anti-American terrorism in Lebanon has drastically reduced the U.S. presence there.

Another feature of contemporary terrorism has been the extent to which it has become a media event. Often, terrorism is aimed at a media audience and not at the actual victims. Measured in terms of the attention it garners, and not in terms of the suffering it causes, terrorism is an exceedingly effective method for gaining media coverage at relatively low cost to the perpetrators. Additionally, media preoccupation with hostage situations frequently enhances the importance of "the problem" that the terrorists are attempting to call world attention to. Newspaper readers and television viewers come to view "the problem" as of substantially increased importance and as justifying resolution by national or international measures (Cunningham, 1984b).

Further, the millennium that President John F. Kennedy had so eloquently promised blacks, if only a civil rights program were enacted, did not come to pass. President Lyndon Johnson successfully steered the program through Congress in 1964. In the same year he declared "unconditional war on poverty in America" and called for the building of a "Great Society," a dream that was largely forgotten as America became increasingly preoccupied with still another war, that in Vietnam. Blacks were led to believe that they would quickly find their circumstances bettered, but little dramatic improvement occurred. The heritage of black disadvantage lived on. Perhaps the closest a society can come to social dynamite is to raise people's expectations for a new day and then deliver crumbs. It served to intensify feelings of relative deprivation among blacks, and ghetto riots and the black power movement followed. Such feelings may be individual (when an individual compares his or her situation with that of others), fraternal (when an individual compares the situation of his or her group as a whole to that of an outgroup), or both (Guimond and Dubé-Simard, 1983).

James Davies (1962, 1969, 1974) notes that relative deprivation may be fostered under still another condition—that characterized by his "rise-and-drop," or "J-curve," hypothesis. He shows that rebellions and revolutions are likely to occur when a prolonged period of objective economic and social improvement is followed by a short period of reversal. People fear that the ground they gained with great effort will be lost, and their mood becomes revolutionary. Davies illustrates the rise-and-drop hypothesis by events as varied as Dorr's Rebellion in Rhode Island in 1842, the Pullman Strike of 1894, the Russian Revolution of 1917, and the Egyptian Revolution of 1953.

The relative deprivation thesis has proved popular among social psychologists, especially because it has strong links to so many other theories. It intersects with frustration-aggression theory, since individuals frustrated in pursuit of their goals are thought to be susceptible to aggressive behaviors (see Chapter 11). Its focus on people's definitions of what is their rightful due brings it within the same arena as equity theory, distributive justice, and just-world formulations (see Chapter 10). Its emphasis on the discrepancy between expectations and reality, and people's efforts to close the gap, reminds us of the central interests of cognitive-balance theory (see Chapter 6). And its concern with comparative processes leads us into the realm of reference-group theory (see Chapter 13).

Perhaps because the relative deprivation thesis has received attention across a wide spectrum of interests, it has been embroiled in considerable controversy. Some researchers have found it a valuable explanatory tool (Geschwender, 1964; Bernstein and Crosby, 1980). Others have questioned the usefulness of the theory (Spilerman, 1970, 1971, 1976). Still others have raised doubts about its validity altogether (Miller, Bolce, and Halligan, 1977; Taylor, 1982; Gurney and Tierney, 1982). And some have questioned whether the theory is actually testable because it lacks sufficient precision in its formulation and applicability (Cook, Crosby, and Hennigan, 1977).

Resource Mobilization

Among some social scientists, efforts to link the rise and growth of social movements to a sudden increase in grievances (relative deprivation) have given way to other concerns. They focus on the contribution of social solidarity to movement strength, the ways movements recruit members, and the mobilization of resources for collective ends (McCarthy and Zald, 1977; Zald and McCarthy, 1979; Tilly, 1978; Jenkins, 1983). These social scientists view social discontent as more or less a given and thus as endemic within all modern societies. Consequently, they do not believe that an approach like relative deprivation is needed as an explanation for the forces that energize and activate collective action. Instead, they see movements forming as a result of long-term changes in group resources, organization, and opportunities for collective action.

According to resource mobilization approaches, collective action is seldom a viable option for deprived groups because they lack the resources to challenge elites. When deprived groups do mobilize, it is typically due to the infusion of outside help and the cooptation of institutional resources (garnering assistance from private foundations, social welfare and government agencies, the mass media, universities, and even business corporations). The stormy 1960s and early 1970s are seen as the product of professionals and college students with discretionary time schedules and income, liberal institutions with "slack" resources, and pervasive mass media that could be coopted by enterprising movement entrepreneurs.

Sociologists J. Craig Jenkins and Charles Perrow (1977) illustrate this thesis with historical materials dealing with farm worker insurgencies within the United States. They contrast the unsuccessful attempt to organize farm workers by the National Farm Labor Union from 1946 to 1952 with the successful organization of Mexican farm workers by the United Farm Workers from 1965 to 1972. Both groups had similar goals (union contracts), employed the same tactics (mass agricultural strikes and boycotts supported by organized labor), and encountered relatively identical obstacles. Yet the United Farm Workers prevailed and the National Farm Labor Union failed. Jenkins and Perrow claim that the United Farm Workers succeeded because internal divisions in government neutralized political elites, while the support of the liberal-labor coalition during the reform years of the 1960s and early 1970s turned the tide in favor of farm workers.

A Synthesis

The relative deprivation and resource mobilization approaches can be seen as complementary rather than competing explanations of collective action (Stark and Bainbridge, 1980; Martin, Brickman, and Murray, 1984; Muller, 1985). The resource mobilization approach is correct in emphasizing the importance of capacities for collective action based on resources and organization. But an understanding is also necessary of changes in levels of discontent (Aminzade, 1984). Although social unrest may be endemic within society, there are nevertheless cases where suddenly emerged grievances do generate organized protest. The rapid growth and development of organizations around Three Mile Island following the 1979 nuclear accident provide a good illustration of such a happening (Walsh, 1981). Much the same holds true with countermovements— protest or "anti" movements that arise in response to the social change advocated by another movement (Mottl, 1980). The antidesegregation movement in the South in the 1950s and 1960s (Vander Zanden, 1965) and the Boston antibusing movement provide examples of movements that gained support among individuals who felt threatened by impending change (Useem, 1980; Begley and Alker, 1982). Even so, unrest does not by itself produce collective action. People weigh the costs and benefits of participation. In order to participate in a social movement, they must see it as a way to obtain desired outcomes. Feelings of relative deprivation do not necessarily evoke agreement with the goals of just any movement; individuals have to perceive the goals as instrumental to the elimination of their discontent and grievances. Social networks and the resources that can be mobilized become important in this respect (Klandermans, 1984). More will be said about these matters when we consider the mobilization of participants for action.

RUMORS

In recent years, a variety of unfounded rumors have hurt the sales of some of the nation's largest corporations (Montgomery, 1979; Stevens, 1981; Blumstein, 1984). Among them have been the following: False teeth dissolve if left overnight in a glass of Coca-Cola (and by implication, think of the damage that Coke can do to natural teeth). General Foods' Pop Rocks Crackling Candy makes your stomach explode. Wearing jockey shorts makes men temporarily sterile (presumably by raising scrotal temperature and lowering sperm count). McDonald's adds worms to hamburger meat (perhaps suggested by the fact that raw hamburger looks like red worms). Bubble Yum, a bubble-gum product made by Life Savers, contains spider eggs or causes cancer. And K-Mart stores have been plagued by rumored snakes from Asia. The story goes that a poisonous Asian snake laid its eggs in a carton of Taiwan-made coats which then hatched inside the coats. When a woman at a K-Mart store tried on one of the coats, she was bitten by a snake and had to have her arm amputated.

In 1985 the Procter & Gamble Company removed the moon-and-stars trademark from its products in response to a nationwide rumor campaign that linked the logo with the devil (Salmans, 1985). The trademark had begun around 1850 as a crude cross and over the years had evolved into a cluster of stars representing the original thirteen colonies and a man-in-the-moon profile. Since 1980, rumors had circulated in various parts of the country, contending that the design was a symbol of Satanism and devil worship and urging customers to boycott Ivory Snow, Pampers, Duncan Hines, and dozens of other P&G products. By mid-1982, the firm's consumer services department was getting 15,000 queries monthly about its relationship to the devil. After trying to ignore the rumor, P&G mounted an aggressive campaign to defend itself. But the rumors persisted, and the firm decided to abandon the trademark.

These and other rumors appear to result from combinations of uncertainty and

The Growth and Spread of a Generalized Belief

We are now again in an epoch of wars of religion, but a religion is now called an ideology.

—Bertrand Russell, *Unpopular Essays,* 1950

As we have seen, structural strain and a sense of social malaise do not in themselves produce collective action. The strain must be interpreted in a meaningful manner by the people who are the potential participants. A generalized

anxiety, and from people's craving for inside information (Rosnow and Kimmel, 1979; Rosnow, 1980; Koenig, 1982). Thus rumors frequently increase when uncertainty over the economy increases. Rumors involving children's products, especially if they pose alleged hazards, have an additional dimension. By repeating such a rumor and still using the product, children can gain status as risk takers, miniature Evel Knievels.

Some research suggests that highly anxious persons spread rumors much more frequently than less anxious ones do. For instance, one investigator gave some Philadelphia high school students a standard test measuring chronic anxiety. On the basis of their scores, students were selected who were either highly anxious or relatively calm. Later, a few students of each type met with a guidance counselor to discuss the clubs to which they belonged. During the meeting, at the researcher's request, the counselor planted a rumor that budgetary limitations might force the school to curtail extracurricular activities. The counselor then left the room on an errand, leaving the students in the company of other club members. A follow-up survey revealed that students with high levels of anxiety spread the rumor much more frequently than did those with low levels of anxiety.

A choice of three strategies is available to rumor fighters. The first strategy is to ignore the rumor in hopes that with the passage of time it will die out or collapse from obvious absurdity. The problem with this approach is that the rumor may not dissipate as quickly as one might wish.

The second strategy is to tackle the rumor head-on by identifying it and ridiculing it as often as possible to the largest audiences that can be reached. However, this approach often boomerangs. Repeating a rumor merely draws attention to it, gives it credibility, and disseminates it more rapidly and more widely.

The third strategy is to outflank the rumor by rebutting it indirectly and by limiting such responses to areas where the rumor is known to be circulating. For instance, McDonald's advertises that its hamburgers contain 100 percent beef, without any additives or preservatives. In this way, the rumor is not repeated while information is provided to counteract it.

belief provides people with "answers" to their stressful circumstances. It provides (1) a diagnosis of the forces and agents that cause the strain, and (2) a response or program for coping with the strain (for easing and even erasing it).

Again, the case of the "bug epidemic" among the textile workers offers insight into this determinant. As noted earlier, the affected women were under more stress than the unaffected women. The generalized belief—an insect invasion from a shipment of English cloth—provided the women with a credible (but factually incorrect) "cause" for their symptoms. Once they possessed a credible explanation for their symptoms, the women evolved further beliefs for coping with the strain—the necessity of their staying away from the plant and seeking the assistance of a physician. As these new coping mechanisms were deemed legitimate, the probability of any given participant's use of them tended to increase as the epidemic ran its course.

Social movements commonly provide people with "answers" to their stressful circumstances in the form of an **ideology**—a set of shared definitions that provides interpretations and solutions to what is felt to be an unsatisfactory social condition. Ideology serves a number of ends (Gerlach and Hine, 1970):

□ Ideology provides *new categories* by which people interpret their sense of tension, frustration, and stress. Rather than finding themselves bogged down in the quagmire of directionless groping, people are provided with tangible enemies (communists, Yankees, Jews, atheists, oil interests, Arabs) and an indictment of existing social arrangements (capitalism, racism, male chauvinism, imperialism).

□ Ideology provides *a utopian vision* of a society in which the unsatisfactory social condition is remedied.

□ Ideology provides *a dogma*—a certainty regarding Truth—that knits people together in a consciousness of oneness, an esprit de corps.

□ Ideology provides *a conceptual filter* that permits only positive reinforcement and reinterprets negative feedback in a fashion supportive of the group's position. It is this feature that outsiders label "fanaticism." Thus of the Bible, Martin Luther could exclaim: "So tenaciously should we cling to the word revealed by the Gospel, that were I to see all the Angels of Heaven coming down to me to tell me something different, not only would I not be tempted to doubt a single syllable, but I would shut my eyes and stop my ears, for they would not deserve to be either seen or heard" (Funck-Brentano, 1939).

□ Ideology sharpens the *polarization* between outsiders and insiders, highlighting group boundaries. This is reflected in Christ's warning: "He that is not with me is against me." Moreover, the strength of a movement is frequently associated with the vividness and tangibility of its devil. When Hitler was asked whether he thought the Jew must be destroyed, he responded: "No. . . . We should have then to invent him. It is essential to have a tangible enemy, not merely an abstract one" (Hoffer, 1951).

□ Ideology provides *a sense of personal power* and control over one's destiny, transforming one's self-conception. This is accomplished through the Doctrine of the Elect: the Pentecostal notion of being a "Soldier of Christ," the communist view of the "Vanguard of the Proletariat," the Jewish belief regarding "the Chosen People."

Precipitating Factors

Conduciveness, strain, and a generalized belief merely set the stage for an episode of collective action. To occur, the behavior needs to be touched off by an event. A precipitating event creates, sharpens, and exaggerates the other factors. It provides the people who believe the ideology with concrete evidence of the evil forces at work, or of the success that awaits their action. Revolutions are usually triggered in this fashion. General Gage's 1775 march from Boston to Concord and Lexington launched the American Revolution. The seizure of the royal prison fortress by an angry French crowd in 1789 sparked the French Revolution. The March 11, 1917, tsarist decrees against Petrograd (Leningrad) strikers touched off the Russian Revolution.

In the episode of hysterical contagion at the textile mill, the epidemic was triggered by a twenty-two-year-old woman who complained of a bite and fainted soon afterward. (It is noteworthy that the woman had fainted some five times during the previous year.) A few days later the second case occurred, in a young woman who worked near the first case. She said she had been bitten a few days earlier, but had not reported to the doctor until this particular day, when she complained that she felt "like a balloon ready to burst." Shortly thereafter on the same day, four other women reported to the doctor, and by the next day the epidemic had developed with a rush.

The Mobilization of Participants for Action

Once a precipitating event has occurred, it remains only to bring the participants into action. Conversion is a central element in the mobilization process. In everyday life we explain "conversion" to social movements on purely ideological and theological grounds. In most cases, however, "the Truth" is communicated within the context of a preexisting social relationship. In his autobiography (1964), Malcolm X describes his conversion to the Black Muslims. His initial contact with the movement came through his brother, who visited him in prison, introduced him to Black Muslim ideology, and led him through the first stages of the commitment process. Indeed, some sociologists—among them, David A. Snow and his colleagues (1980)—assert that the "reasons" for joining a movement arise out of the recruitment process itself.

Similarly, converts to Pentecostal movements commonly explain that they were saved because God spoke to them. Closer examination reveals, however, that some person they already knew—someone whom they trusted and felt rapport with—took them to hear an evangelist, placed the crucial book in their hands, or listened to the broadcast with them. Recruitment flows along lines of preexisting social relationships—through relatives, neighbors, work associates, and friends (this was also true, as noted earlier, of the "bug bite" epidemic). People tend to be recruited to *specific* cells (units) in the organizational network, rather than to the movement per se. Initial recruitment is made by members at the local grass-roots level rather than by noted leaders, although the leaders may later consummate the commitment (Gerlach and Hine, 1970; Wimberly et al., 1975).

Recruitment to other religious groups, such as the Nichiren Shoshu Buddhist movement, the "Moonies," and Hare Krishna, and to political movements, such as NOW, Right to Life, and the Lesbian-Gay Alliance, reveals somewhat similar

RELIGIOUS CULTS

Over the past decade or so, Americans have been approached on street corners by young "Moonie" flower venders and solicited in airports by Krishna booksellers. However, until the 1978 mass suicide of over 900 cult members at the People's Temple settlement in Guyana, most Americans viewed the comings and goings of these various cultists with little more than curiosity. Nevertheless, a Gallup poll reveals that nearly 12 percent of the American public has at one time or another participated in some form of meditation or religious practice outside the traditional boundaries of Christianity and Judaism. Among these groups are Transcendental Meditation, the Church of Scientology, the Divine Light Mission, the Children of God, and the Unification Church of the Reverend Sun Myung Moon.

But it was the tragic developments surrounding the followers of the Reverend Jim Jones that centered public attention on religious cults. Jones had founded the People's Temple in San Francisco after he took a small, unorthodox Indiana congregation west to avoid destruction in what he believed was to be an imminent thermonuclear war. During the 1960s, Jones had come to espouse a doctrine combining Marxism and Christianity. Since he could deliver the votes of his largely young, poor, and black followers, Jones became a force in San Francisco politics. (Although claiming that he was part Cherokee Indian, Jones is thought to have been of white ancestry.) Always inclined to be somewhat paranoid, and believing that dark forces were out to victimize him, in 1977 Jones relocated his congregation in Guyana.

Because of alleged "human rights violations," relatives of church members prevailed upon a San Francisco Bay area congressman, Leo J. Ryan, to investigate the cult. Although initially a willing host to Ryan's visit, Jones's mood soon changed. He ordered the deaths of Ryan and the members of his party. This accomplished, and fearing outside retribution for the murders, Jones ordered his members to commit suicide by drinking a fruit-flavored liquid laced with cyanide. Previously, Jones had prepared his followers for the taking of their own lives through ritualistic suicide drills.

Many recent religious cults share at least some of the following characteristics:

□ The cults have a charismatic leader (see Chapter 14) who claims to have been given new exclusive revelations about God or reality. He says that those who reject his teachings are not only wrong but satanic.

□ The leader demands a total commitment from his followers. The movement consumes the entirety of the believer's daily existence. Cult members are typically isolated from outside contacts. In some cases, their mail is opened and they have limited access, if any, to telephones.

□ Although cult leaders deny that they practice brainwashing, a number of individuals who have studied cults compare their techniques with the brainwashing methods—isolation, forced confession, and sensory deprivation—practiced on American prisoners of war in Korea (Lifton, 1979). Whatever they are labeled, the groups' recruitment and indoctrination procedures seek to bring about fundamental behavioral change. Some adherents and ex-members describe constant exhortation, training to arrive at exalted spiritual states, altered consciousness, and automatic submission to directives. Some cults require long hours of prayer, chanting, meditation, marathon encounter groups, psychodrama, and guided fantasy (Singer, 1979; Siegelman and Conway, 1979). Even so, it seems that most conversions are voluntary and occur in the absence of confinement or severe stress (Robbins and Anthony, 1980; Barker, 1984).

☐ Some ex-cultists report that their critical and evaluative faculties had been held in relative abeyance while they were cult members: They listened, believed, and obeyed. Group pressures can be so powerful, as in the case of the People's Temple, that even suicide may not be an individual option but a group requirement. But the overwhelming attention that cult leaders devote to displays of commitment often boomerangs and, rather than fostering loyalty and allegiance, leads to doubt and a loss of trust. Efforts to subdue reflection do not extinguish it. And doubt and reflection often generate disaffection (Long and Hadden, 1983).

☐ Cult members commonly believe that they are an elite vanguard called out of the anonymous masses to assist the messiah. As a chosen people, they may view themselves as above

the law and as more valuable to God, to history, and to the future than other people are (Singer, 1979).

☐ Members often characterize their conversion experience as a sudden, dramatic change, sometimes termed "snapping": "Something snapped inside me" or "I don't know what happened, I just snapped" (Siegelman and Conway, 1979).

☐ Members frequently speak of guilt over defecting and fear retaliation if they try. Inner doubts about cult doctrine are attributed to one's own evil, the influence of the devil, or the spiritual pollution of the society outside (Lifton, 1979). One ex-cultist said:

> People just can't understand what the group puts into your mind. How they play on your guilts and needs. Psychological pressure is much heavier than a locked door. You can bust a locked door down in terror or anger, but chains that are mental are real hard to break. The heaviest thing I've ever done is leaving the group, breaking those real heavy bonds on my mind. (Singer, 1979: 80)

In many respects the cults have been a continuation of the protests and experiments of the 1960s. Some psychiatrists, like Robert Jay Lifton (1979), view them as a product of historical dislocations, of the loss and dishonoring of traditional family, scientific, religious, and governmental authority and moorings. They bear a resemblance to cults that have arisen under other times of stress and rapid social change, like the cargo cults of New Guinea and Melanesia, the Ghost Dance among

Box continues on next page.

Krishna Consciousness
Krishna Consciousness, a movement launched in 1961 with roots in Eastern (primarily Indian) thought, provides young people with a vehicle for expressing estrangement from mainstream culture. Signs of membership—distinctive dress and shaved heads—are viewed by the public as "weird." The movement imposes a rigid code of behavior upon its members and accepts the four divisions of the Hindu caste system as divinely ordained. (Patrick Reddy)

the American Indians of the 1870s and the 1890s, and the Church of Jesus Christ of Latter-Day Saints—the Mormons (once viewed as bizarre, and forced to migrate to the Utah wilderness, but now considered "respectable").

The recent cults have had particular appeal to youth. Many of them find that in the cults there are friends and fellowship for the friendless; a sense of belonging to something larger than oneself; the ego boost that comes to the possessor of special knowledge; ready-made decisions about careers, dating, sex, and marriage; and easy answers to complicated problems (Crewdson, 1978; Singer, 1979, Paloutzian, 1981; Levine, 1984). Psychiatrist Marc Galanter and several colleagues (1979), of the Albert Einstein College of Medicine, studied 237 members of the Unification Church (Moonies). Many joined during a period of personal crisis. Two-thirds said that they had had emotional or drug-related difficulties immediately before joining the church. About one out of three had previously sought professional help for his or her problems, and 6 percent had been hospitalized. Galanter's respondents reported a 30 percent decline in neurotic distress immediately after conversion, accompanied by a rise in religiosity as measured by a 216-item questionnaire that Galanter employed. Although membership in the church seemed to stabilize neurotic distress, the Moonies displayed

patterns (Lofland, 1966; Snow, Zurcher, and Ekland-Olson, 1980; Stark and Bainbridge, 1980). Conversion is not merely a product of prior susceptibility to a movement or its ideology. Rather, interpersonal relationships frequently play a critical part. Two factors seem particularly important. First, individuals typically have links to one or more movement members or sympathizers through a

more evidence of psychological problems than did a control group matched for age and sex.

At times, former cult members experience a good deal of psychological discomfort in reintegrating themselves into society. It may take eight to eighteen months for former cultists to become fully functional members of mainstream society. Some ex-cult members cite such problems as "floating" (the tendency to slip into altered states of consciousness), loneliness, a sense of meaninglessness, decision-making difficulties, depression, guilt and fear of retaliation associated with leaving the cult, and difficulty reentering their family and the world of work. And former members may express regret for the "lost years" during which they wandered off the main paths of everyday life, falling behind their peers in career and life pursuits (Singer, 1979). Yet only a small minority of those who join such groups actually stay for lengthy periods of time (Bird and Reimer, 1982). Accordingly, for many of these individuals departure is not a particularly disturbing event; indeed, the time they spend in the cult is often a rather benign, even therapeutic, experience, particularly if it compels them to come to terms with themselves (Galanter, 1983; Levine, 1984).

The upsurge of cults over the past two decades has produced intense hostility from established church leaders, parents of converts, disillusioned ex-converts, and some mental health workers (Robbins and Anthony, 1982). They have often sought to define cult involvement as a medical problem or illness. Supporters of a medical interpretation propose that therapeutic intervention be undertaken to "rescue cult victims" and restore them to personal autonomy. If cult involvement is a medical issue, then it cannot be a civil liberties issue, because the ill must be treated and healed.

The process of persuading cult members to relinquish their involvement with a cult has frequently involved coercive "deprogramming." The convert may be abducted from the cult, physically detained, and subjected to forcible "therapy." Supporters of a medicalization approach assert that devotees have lost their faculties for critical reasoning and consequently are incapable of leaving a cult without assistance. Opponents of the medicalization interpretation view deprogramming as a threat to religious liberty and protest the labeling of certain religious practices as bizarre and psychopathic. And on a practical level, deprogramming often does not work. It operates against the possibility that cult members will resolve their conflicts, leave the group, and rejoin the larger society on their own. Deprogramming can drive young adults back into the cult or into a pattern of later "cult-hopping" (Levine, 1984).

preexisting or emergent interpersonal bond. Second, individuals commonly lack ties to other social networks that are antagonistic to the movement and its ideology. Once individuals move into a proselytizing network, their relationships become "encapsulated" by movement members, and they are increasingly exposed to broadened socialization messages.

It is also true, however, that recruitment to a religious or social movement may occur in the absence of preestablished social ties. For instance, one study found that about 42 percent of the initial contacts between members of the Hare Krishna movement and later converts took place in public places (Rochford, 1982). Within modern societies some people actively search for "meaningful encounters," "identity change," and "creative-transformation experiences" (Richardson, 1985). For instance, Robert W. Balch (1979) found that individuals who joined a UFO cult saw themselves as "seekers" before joining. Indeed, recruitment was structured to reduce contacts between members and potential recruits. Leaders offered their message on a take-it-or-leave-it basis and did not apply social strategems to get people to join. Likewise, James V. Downton (1979), in his study of conversion to the Divine Light Mission, portrays recruits as actively seeking new ways to live and new interpretations of life. And Eileen Barker (1984), in her study of the "Moonies," concludes that most recruits are not coerced to join the movement by devious manipulations but rather are predisposed to accept the social and religious messages of the Unification Church by their traditional religious and family backgrounds. In sum, human beings are hardly passive subjects recruited and converted by external powers over which they lack control.

The Operation of Social Control

The determinant of social control "arches over" all the others. It consists of the techniques through which governing elites prevent, interrupt, deflect, or inhibit the accumulation of other determinants. Social controls fall into two broad types. First, there are controls that seek to minimize conduciveness and strain—to *prevent* discontent from arising (for instance, welfare programs designed to pacify the underclasses). Second, there are controls that aim to *repress* an episode of collective behavior *after* it has begun (for instance, police measures, imprisonment, and curfews). Social control has a critical influence on how fast, how far, and in what directions an episode will develop. At times, however, police action escalates into "police riots," such as occurred at the 1968 Democratic National Convention in Chicago (McPhail and Wohlstein, 1983).

As noted earlier in the chapter, Jenkins and Perrow (1977) cite the neutralization of political elites in the late 1960s (their inability to institute social control) as one factor in the success of the United Farm Workers. Similarly, any number of historians like Crane Brinton (1938) and sociologists like Theda Skocpol (1979) have stressed the part that the disintegration of ruling elites plays in social revolutions. The French Revolution of 1789 and the Russian and Chinese revolutions of this century began with the collapse of an autocratic monarchy, a collapse deriving from an inability to resist foreign pressures effectively. The traditional elites found their cohesiveness undermined, their ruling effectiveness impaired, and their legitimacy questioned. Each revolution was propelled at a critical stage by a mass uprising of the peasantry. And each eventuated in the creation of a new and centralized state apparatus.

---

*T*he crowd

We often mistakenly think of the crowd as a relatively spontaneous oc-currence. But this is not always true. In some nations, such as Iran and Cuba, the government organizes crowds and demonstrations, and or-chestrates their behavior for political purposes. We do not have to go very far afield, however, to find structured crowds in the United States. A good illustration of this is football and basketball games held on col-lege campuses. At Ohio State University, there is the "Bloc O" section at home football games in which students hold up colored pieces of card-board to make large designs, including an American flag and Ohio State insignia. The mascot—Brutus Buckeye—and cheerleaders orches-trate chants, fight songs, and the "wave." And they may marshal the crowd to roar and drown out the signals of the opposing team's quar-terback when the opposition is about to score. The behavior in these settings is recurrent and patterned, following a familiar script from one game to the next. This suggests that norms are prescribing what is ex-pected of students, faculty, and alumni at these events.

CROWD BEHAVIOR

Crowd behavior has long intrigued social psychologists (Ross, 1908). **Crowd** is a wide-ranging concept that refers to all sorts of human assemblages: audiences, rallies, mobs, riots, and panics. In crowds, people are in sufficiently close physical proximity that the fact of aggregation serves to influence their behavior (Milgram and Toch, 1969; Freedman and Perlick, 1979). Three types of theory are used to describe and explain the dynamics of crowd behavior: (1) contagion theory, (2) convergence theory, and (3) emergent-norm theory.

Contagion Theory

In the crowd, herd, or gang, it is a mass-mind that operates—which is to say, a mind without subtlety, a mind without compassion, a mind, finally, uncivilized.

—Robert Lindner, *Must You Conform?* 1956

No work on crowds has commanded greater attention than that of Gustave Le Bon (1895). In colorful and imaginative terms, Le Bon painted a picture of the crowd as characterized by a collective mind that overpowers and submerges the individual. His **contagion theory** assumes that the crowd assimilates its members, producing a psychic unity that alters the individual's normal emotions, thoughts, and conduct: "He [the individual] is no longer himself but has become an automaton who has ceased to be guided by his will." The sentiments and ideas of the participants all take the same direction, so that people's conscious personalities vanish. This is Le Bon's "law of the mental unity of crowds."

Although Le Bon's approach still has considerable popular appeal and acceptance, it has come under heavy criticism from social psychologists for its impressionistic portrayal of crowd behavior. And Le Bon's concept of the crowd mind as a supraindividual entity—one that is endowed with cognitive processes and a capacity for feeling and believing—is rejected by most social psychologists (Milgram and Toch, 1969). Nonetheless, Le Bon's work has had a powerful impact on social psychological thought, stimulating interest not only in crowd research, but in related behavior like deindividuation and suggestibility.

Le Bon's mob-mind view emphasized the apparent lack of differentiation in the behavior of members of a crowd. He maintained that three principal mechanisms underlie the emergence of crowd properties: anonymity, contagion, and suggestibility.

Anonymity

People immersed in a crowd lose their unique personalities and their sense of responsibility. They become engulfed in a wave of collective excitement in which the will of the collectivity is stronger than their own. Anonymity provides crowd members with a euphoric and exultant feeling of invincible power.

This formulation by Le Bon finds expression in the contemporary social psychological concept of *deindividuation* (see Chapter 11). Under some circumstances, deindividuation is thought to reduce moral restraints and to unleash a contagion of random, irrational, and destructive behavior. According to Philip G. Zimbardo, deindividuating processes lower a person's self-consciousness, which results in a "weakening of controls based upon guilt, shame, fear, and commitment" (1969: 259). Consequently, there may be an increase in behavior not normally approved by society—such as aggression, risk taking, self-enhancement, stealing, vandalism, and the uttering of obscenities (Diener, Fraser, and Beaman, 1976; Dipboye, 1977; Mann, Newton, and Innes, 1982).

Contagion

Le Bon was originally trained as a physician. Impressed with the involuntary manner in which people contract a disease from one another, he advanced the notion that a similar mechanism operates within the crowd. Excitability and the mob-mind effect spread like an infectious disease. Something of a similar sort occurs with "social coughing." James Pennebaker (1980) finds that the coughing that occurs during class lectures is contagious. It typically spreads away from the initiating person in a chain reaction. Apparently, the closer a cougher is to you, the more likely you are to pay attention to your own "cough-related sensations" and emit a cough yourself.

David Dremen (1979), president of an investment management concern, concludes that success on Wall Street lies in an understanding of crowd contagion. The enthusiastic and panicked passions of the movement provide the prevailing

Social Contagion
Social contagion operates to communicate patterns of collective behavior among students.
Here a child looks down a sewer. Other children, intrigued by his behavior, join the activity.
(Patrick Reddy)

wisdom for buying or selling various stocks. But like Le Bon, Dremen believes that current Wall Street wisdom reflects the unreliable, undiscriminating irrationality of "barbarians." Consequently, in Dremen's view investors can beat the market by putting a finger to the wind, divining the drift of the Wall Street crowd, and then heading in the opposite direction: buying when the crowd is selling and selling when the crowd is buying. This approach is known as the "contrarian" investment strategy. However, other observers of stock market history sneer at the notion. They claim that the market's movements are purely random—the so-called "random walk." According to this view an investor might as well select a stock by throwing a dart at a listing of New York Stock Exchange stocks as by guessing the psychology of the market.

Suggestibility
Within crowd settings, people come to accept uncritically the directives addressed to them. They lose their conscious personalities and commit acts that otherwise would be alien to them. Hypnotism provides the foundation for Le Bon's model of suggestibility.

Whether they label it suggestibility (Le Bon, 1895), social facilitation (Allport, 1924), or circular reaction (Blumer, 1939), most students of collective behavior note that individuals in a crowd situation are especially susceptible to the influence of others (Turner and Killian, 1972). Some shift toward collective or concerted action typically occurs in crowds (Johnson and Feinberg, 1977). However, not all researchers find that this shift necessarily leads in antisocial directions, as is implied by some formulations of the deindividuation thesis (Diener, 1976; Jorgenson and Dukes, 1976; Dipboye, 1977). This has led Norris R. Johnson (1974; Johnson, Stemler, and Hunter, 1977) to conclude that in an incipient crowd, members arrive with a variety of dispositions for action. Thorough interaction, the group polarizes, resulting in crowd action more extreme (or "risky") than the average position of the people who make it up (see Chapter 13). In some instances, the same principle may result in a shift to caution, and the crowd dissolves. In sum, it is not a foregone conclusion that a crowd will take a menacing or destructive course.

Suggestibility also occurs in other contexts. David P. Phillips (1979, 1980; Bollen and Phillips, 1981, 1982) finds that automobile fatalities increase between 30 and 40 percent after a three-day incubation period following publicized suicide stories. The more publicity the media give to the story, the greater the increase. Suicide stories about young persons are typically followed by single-vehicle crashes involving young drivers; conversely, suicide stories about older persons tend to be followed by crashes involving older drivers. Moreover, stories about murder and suicide are usually followed by multiple-vehicle crashes involving passenger deaths (whereas stories about a lone suicide tend to be linked with single-vehicle crashes). Such findings suggest that publicized suicides stimulate imitative suicidal behaviors (Wasserman, 1984). Likewise, media coverage of nuclear-power issues is closely associated with an increase in bomb threats against nuclear facilities (Mazur, 1982). The media seem to convey the message that such facilities are targets for threat hoaxes.

Convergence Theory

The spread of an infectious disease is a good analogy for the contagion theory, whereas the heart-surgery ward of a hospital can be used to illustrate **convergence theory.** The patients on the ward share a common problem, but not because they have infected one another. Rather, they select themselves out of the public at large by virtue of their common complaint and assemble on the ward with a common purpose. Contagion theorists suggest that "normal, decent people" are *transformed* under crowd influence. In contrast, convergence theorists argue that a crowd consists of a highly unrepresentative group of people who come together *because* they share certain predispositions (Milgram and Toch, 1969). According to this view, the task for social psychologists is to identify classes or categories of "crowd-prone" people.

Hostile mobs are commonly cited as cases of convergence. For angry, aggression-prone individuals, a crowd functions as an attracting magnet. It supplies them with a pretext to translate their hidden and often destructive impulses into overt behavior. Hadley Cantril (1941) notes in his study of a Leeville, Texas,

---

*C*onvergence theory of crowds

I work in a large department store. Today the store had its annual "one dollar sale" on linens. When I got to work my supervisor sent me to the linens department to help out just for today, as they expected considerable business. The store opened as usual at 9:30, and a massive tidal wave of women descended on the linens department. At the time, I was wheeling a cart of sheets past the cash register heading for the place where I was to stack them in a pile. At least twenty women suddenly bolted for the cart, shoving me out of the way. They were by no means a gentle bunch as they elbowed one another and clawed at the sheets. To be honest, they scared the hell out of me. It was a real mob scene. I just backed off and let them do as they pleased.

The crowd behavior this morning seems to me best explained by the convergence theory. The one dollar sale had selected out from the population at large a number of bargain-hungry people. Each had assembled outside the store early, determined to get some merchandise before the store sold out. Thus these individuals had converged on the store sharing similar predispositions and ready for "action."

---

lynching that poor whites and men who had police records composed the crowd of lynchers. According to Cantril, the aggravated state of relations between poor whites and blacks and the lack of commitment to lawful procedures among criminal elements provided a reservoir of people who were ready for a lynching on a minimum of provocation. Convergence also occurs among teenagers who assemble for a rock concert and among sports fans who turn out to root for the home team.

Emergent-Norm Theory

"Unanimity," "uniformity," "oneness," and "similarity" are words used by both contagion and convergence theorists to describe crowds. **Emergent-norm theory,** developed by Ralph H. Turner and Lewis M. Killian (Turner, 1964; Turner and Killian, 1972), challenges this imagery. It emphasizes the *differences* in motives, attitudes, and behaviors that characterize crowd members. It points out that crowds contain core activists, cautious activists, passive supporters, opportunistic yielders, passers-by, the curious, the unsympathetic, and dissenters. The problem, then, is not to explain the "crowd mind"; rather, it is to explain how the *illusion* of uniformity and unanimity develops (McPhail and Wohlstein, 1983).

In emergent-norm theory, Turner and Killian employ concepts derived from the study of small groups. They take their cue from the work of Muzafer Sherif (1936) with the autokinetic phenomenon and the work of Solomon Asch (1952) with distortions of judgment in group settings (both studies are described in Chapter 7). Turner and Killian stress the part norms play in crowd behavior. They argue that collective behavior typically entails an attempt to define an ambiguous situation. In ambiguous circumstances, people search for cues to appropriate and acceptable behavior. Like the participants in the Sherif experiments, who developed group norms that were different from the standards they had adopted when they were alone, crowd members evolve new standards in ill-defined settings (for instance, they might develop the norm that one should loot, burn, harass police, or whatever). In the fashioning of emergent norms, the behavior of a few conspicuous and active members becomes perceived as the dominant course of action.

Once it has been formulated, crowd members undertake to enforce the new norm, convert others to it, inhibit behavior contrary to the norm, and institute restraining action against dissenters. Although people may not necessarily share the belief or emotion themselves, because of the norm they experience social pressures against nonconformity. And when dissenters remain silent, they provide passive support for the emergent norm and contribute to the illusion of unanimity.

An emergent norm can specify the limits of behavior and define its boundaries. In the black ghetto riots of the 1960s, looting and destruction of property were common—but rioters did not indiscriminately destroy human life. Contagion theory, in contrast, fails to account for the limits on crowd excitement and action in the course of the riots. Nor did the riots release some latent "savage beast," as implied by convergence theory. Destruction was focused, and it was seemingly regulated by a clearly defined understanding of limits and permissible targets—generally, retail stores and the police (Milgram and Toch, 1969).

Although they are different, the three theories of crowd behavior are not mutually exclusive. Take crowd behavior at a homecoming football game. In the stands, an element of contagion operates through *circular reaction*—a process in which the emotions of other people elicit similar emotions in oneself, which then serve to intensify the emotions of others. (For instance, I see you getting excited, so I become excited, thus intensifying your excitement, which makes me more excited, and so on.) In the football game, convergence also operates, in that college loyalists and football enthusiasts are selected out from the public at large and come together in the stadium. In addition, an emergent norm defines appropriate behavior in reaction to a given event during the game and suppresses incongruous behavior.

SOCIAL PROBLEMS

In the popular view, a social problem is like a cancer: Society is an essentially healthy organism that is invaded by alien, destructive substances. The job of judges, legislators, police, social workers, psychiatrists, and prison officials is to act rather like social surgeons, removing the malignant tumor without basically altering the organism itself (Nisbet, 1971).

MARGARINE: THE RISE AND FALL OF A SOCIAL PROBLEM

For more than sixty years until 1950, margarine was under tight federal restriction within the United States (Ball and Lilly, 1982). Originally, margarine had been developed in Europe as a reasonably priced substitute for butter. Hence when it was introduced within the United States in 1875, the dairy industry quickly mobilized to forbid its manufacture and sale. In 1886, federal legislation was enacted placing a tax on the product and requiring annual license fees of $600 for manufacturers, $480 for wholesalers, and $48 for retailers. Without scientific evidence, margarine was branded a harmful substance and regulated much in the manner of alcohol, tobacco, and narcotics. Many states forbade the artificial coloring of the product, even though butter was also artificially colored throughout most of the year.

The impetus to the antimargarine movement came from the dairy industry, which viewed the product as a potential substitute for butter. But other factors also played a part. The fact that margarine "resembled butter but was not butter" raised suspicion as to its true qualities. Further, as one of the first processed foods, it was defined as an "artificial"—even a "counterfeit"—substance.

Sentiment favoring margarine did not appreciably shift until the 1940s. By then, researchers had begun to appreciate the nutritional value of margarine, especially when "fortified" with vitamin A and vitamin D. With the substitution of cottonseed oil for coconut oil as the base ingredient, margarine found a powerful friend within the domestic cottonseed industry. However, the butter shortage during World War II gave margarine its most powerful impetus. Soon the American Medical Association and the American Public Health Association recommended the product as the nutritional equivalent of butter. Simultaneously, articles in national magazines hammered away at the theme that the conflict between butter and margarine producers was in reality a struggle between the dairy industry and consumers. In response to these societal redefinitions, Congress removed all federal taxes and fees on margarine in 1950.

Ironically, the margarine industry was able to turn the tables on butter in the 1970s with the surfacing of the "butter problem." Medical authorities linked butter to heart disease. Indeed, margarine was hailed as a panacea by the same society that had undertaken to suppress it less than a century before.

The Nature of Social Problems

A **social problem** is a condition that a considerable number of people believe exists in their society and that they do not like. Accordingly, a social problem is a matter of social definition (see the boxed insert on margarine). People perceive certain circumstances or behaviors as deviating from an idealized standard—a norm or social value. A social problem lacks objective existence; rather, people *attribute* problem status to certain circumstances or behaviors and assign an unfavorable meaning to them. Indeed, people can even define a nonexistent condition as a social problem. In colonial times, many inhabitants of Salem, Massachusetts, believed in witches and actively hunted them down. And some 200,000 to 500,000 witches, 85 percent of whom were women, were executed in Europe between the fourteenth and seventeenth centuries (Ben-Yehuda, 1980).

No circumstances or behaviors, however unusual, constitute a social problem unless people define them as such. No matter how evil a condition may appear to an outside observer, it is not a social problem if the members of the society itself do not think it is (Blumer, 1971; Lopata, 1984). Poverty, for instance, was a conspicuous social problem in the early part of this century, but by the 1950s it had practically disappeared from public concern. Indeed, in 1958 economist John Kenneth Galbraith wrote in his influential book *The Affluent Society* that poverty in America was no longer "a massive affliction [but] more nearly an afterthought." In the past thirty years, however, the "problem" has "resurfaced."

Or consider the women's movement. Following the passage in 1920 of the Nineteenth Amendment, which gave women the right to vote, the feminist movement faded from the scene, only to be revived in the 1960s. Likewise, wife beating has recently become the object of media attention and government policy. Although wife beating has not increased in frequency, it became a public issue and problem as a result of the battered women movement (Tierney, 1982; Loseke and Cahill, 1984). Similarly, environmental pollution and ecological destruction are "social problems" of very recent vintage (see Figure 17.1).

Clashing Interests and Values

A society's norms and values are seldom neutral. They usually confer advantages on some and disadvantages on others—upper classes and lower classes, whites and blacks, men and women. Those who are better off have a stake in consolidating their power, privilege, and status through freezing the existing social arrangements. As a result, directed, conscious, deliberate social change does not simply happen. It happens because people make it happen through collective action. The notion of social intervention suggests that resistance and opposition need to be overcome. Prevailing social definitions regarding norms and roles need to be unfrozen. And elites need to be challenged in order to establish new or different social values and to redistribute power, privilege, and status.

Consider race relations, with the underlying clash of interests. Viewed from a black perspective, white racism is the problem (white-controlled institutions). Viewed from the standpoint of many white homeowners, skilled workers, and business managements, militant blacks are the problem: "The blacks want to move too fast. They're too aggressive. They're troublemakers. This country isn't ready for such radical change!" The race issue, then, ultimately becomes a test of power.

Much the same holds true for social values. Some groups—elites—are able to make their behavioral preferences the operating norms for others. After all, they

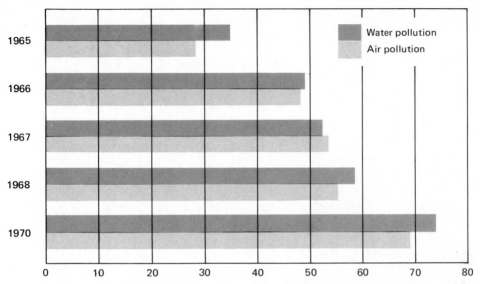

FIGURE 17.1 The Emergence of a "Social Problem"
Between 1965 and 1970, the Opinion Research Corporation surveyed Americans regarding their opinion on the seriousness of water and air pollution. In this six-year period, the perception of pollution as a problem more than doubled.
(SOURCE: H. Erskine, "The Polls: Pollution and Its Costs," *Public Opinion Quarterly,* Vol. 36 [1972], pp. 120–135.)

can control the rewards and the penalties. Since values are often invested with "gut-level" emotion, many people do not take kindly to having their behavior regulated by what they define as unacceptable—even "immoral"—standards. For example, many young people find themselves in a conflict of values with their elders about marijuana usage. As viewed by many older Americans, smoking pot is a dangerous, insidious problem; viewed from the perspective of users, it is the "uptight" standards of older Americans that are the "real" problem. Likewise, the issue of abortion involves debate over the morality of the act, the question of the origin of human life, and the specific ways in which legal abortions should be funded. Women's rights groups and their opponents wage a struggle on these questions. Whose morality shall prevail becomes a contestable matter.

Change, then, is not neutral. Generally, some groups perceive that their fortunes would be improved by a proposed change; others feel threatened. People want many different things in life. Their definitions of situations tend to vary with their places in the social order. Those whose interests are served by the existing arrangements or whose social values prevail may enter the public arena to block or curtail change that they define as imperiling "the good life" (though they may shroud their concern in the rhetoric of "God's law," "Divine will," "the sacred ways of our forefathers," "eternal Truth," or "natural law").

Legitimacy
Older people have begun to realize that they share a variety of concerns and problems, and they have sought to legitimize their concerns as a social issue worthy of attention. (Patrick Reddy)

Legitimizing Social Problems

Social definition gives birth to a social problem. But if it is not to die aborning, the problem needs to acquire **legitimacy.** While a host of social conditions are viewed as unsatisfactory and even harmful by different sets of people, exceedingly few achieve social endorsement and corrective action. Consider the following "problems": the damaging consequences of the high value that Americans place on "growth," the unearned profits that come from owning land (a problem against which Henry George campaigned nearly a century ago), the devastating social effects of the American highway system, the danger to human health from artificial food additives, and the unsavory aspects of many contemporary business and government practices. Although many conditions are pushed by various groups for societal recognition, only a few come out the end of the funnel (Blumer, 1971).

A problem must acquire a certain degree of "respectability" if it is to secure consideration in recognized public arenas: the press, television, and other media of communication; religious, educational, and civic organizations; and legislative chambers and other assemblies of officialdom. A problem is doomed unless it gains the necessary credentials of respectability. Many individuals and groups dedicate their lives—commit body and soul—to agitation that never secures a genuine public hearing. The problems they stress are viewed by decision makers as insignificant, as unworthy of consideration, as part of the established order and hence not to be tampered with, as distasteful to codes of propriety, or as merely the shouting of "crackpots" and "subversives" (Blumer, 1971).

A selective process takes place in social interaction: Many budding social problems are choked off, others are avoided, others are ignored, others have to fight their way to respectability (e.g., racism and sexism), and others are rushed along the road to legitimacy by strong and influential backing (e.g., the energy crisis). As a social problem comes to win legitimacy, its sponsors are no longer deemed simply "protest groups" but bona fide "spokespeople" for a constituency. Yet although gaining a hearing in the halls of officialdom may be regarded by protest groups as their "finest hour," it often represents the beginning of the end of their control over the issues they raise (Spector and Kitsuse, 1973).

Official Public Policy

If a social problem manages to secure social legitimacy, it enters a new stage in its career (Blumer, 1971). This consists of hammering out an official plan of action, commonly in legislative committees, legislative chambers, and executive boards. Maneuvering, manipulation, give-and-take, diplomacy, and bargaining take place in order to accommodate diverse interests and views. Compromises, concessions, trade-offs, deference to public figures high in status, responses to power, and assessments of what is "practical" and "workable" all play a part. This is a defining and redefining process, one of fashioning, reworking, and recasting the collective picture of the social problem. As a consequence, what emerges may be a far cry from the way in which its early proponents first viewed the problem. Very often the official agencies capture and monopolize the problem, neutralizing or eliminating the original protestors. This leads to anguished cries from the protest group that "We've been sold out" (Blumer, 1971; Spector and Kitsuse, 1973).

But the passage of legislation designed to remedy the problem and the creation of agencies to effect legislative goals do not end the matter. The process of collective definition is never-ending. As it is put into practical operation, a plan becomes modified, twisted, and reshaped. In sum, it takes on unforeseen accretions. Those who are in danger of losing power, privilege, or status seek to restrict the plan, bend its operation to new directions, and perhaps gain control of the administrative agency. Those who stand to benefit may strive to exploit new opportunities. And operating personnel are prone to substitute their policies and interpretations for the official policy underlying the planned program (Blumer, 1971).

The restructuring of a social problem as it passes through successive phases of the collective process may make it unrecognizable to its early sponsors. This has been the retold tale of many reform ventures—antitrust measures, pure food and drug laws, New Deal legislation, President Johnson's antipoverty program, and civil rights legislation.

Sometimes a problem is "depoliticized" by defining it as a medical condition or illness requiring professional treatment (Haines, 1979). Within our society, this has been true for some forms of "mental illness," alcoholism, hyperactivity

THE MEEK DON'T MAKE IT

The popular formula for success in American politics is to "play the game by the rules." If you have a problem, get organized and work for change, but expect to compromise along the way: "You scratch my back and I'll scratch yours" and "If you want to get along, go along."

Not all champions of change, however, play by "the rules." They get "nasty," "misbehave," and even resort to violence. Early in this century, the Tobacco Night Riders in Kentucky were such a group. They started as a secret fraternal order whose aim was to compel tobacco farmers to join the Planters Protective Association, keep tobacco off the market, and bargain collectively with the big tobacco companies. On December 1, 1906, more than 250 members swarmed into Princeton, Kentucky. They seized control of the city, disarmed the police, patrolled the streets, shot at anyone who disobeyed them, and dynamited and burned two tobacco factories. They were also active in other parts of Kentucky and in Tennessee.

Although we are told that "violence doesn't pay," by most standards the Night Riders did succeed. Within a year the Planters Protective Association handled nine-tenths of the tobacco produced in its area. The power of the tobacco trust was broken, farmers sold their tobacco at higher prices, and the state of Kentucky even passed a law providing a penalty of "triple damages" for any association member selling his tobacco "outside."

Sociologist William A. Gamson (1975) studied a sample of fifty-three reform-oriented and revolutionary groups that surfaced in the United States between 1800 and 1945. Of these, fifteen participated in some kind of violent exchange. Eight of the fifteen were "activist" groups that, whether or not they began a fight, were willing to employ violence. The other seven were passive recipients of violence. Of the eight activist groups, six (including the Night Riders) won new advantages, and five of the six were eventually accepted as part of the social scheme of things. The seven passive recipients of violence lost out completely. Gamson observes, "In the case of violence, it appears better to give than receive if you want to

in children ("hyperkinesis"), and child abuse. In the case of the Soviet Union, the ideology of mental illness has been applied to political dissidents and used to herd them into psychiatric detention centers. Such an orientation *individualizes* deviance. The relevance of social or economic conditions is downgraded, and the behavior is attributed to more or less random individual pathology. Simultaneously, medicalization depoliticizes deviance by removing it from the realm of ethical discussion. Once the labels "health" and "illness" have been successfully applied to a behavior, any discussion of desirability or tolerability becomes irrelevant and even illogical.

succeed in American politics."

Gamson finds that violence was a particularly successful strategy for groups with limited, nonrevolutionary goals (such as the Night Riders). A number of communist and revolutionary groups, however, spoke loudly but carried a small stick, advocating violence but never using it. This appeared to be the least effective strategy; such groups paid the cost of violence (becoming easy targets for repression) without gaining its benefits.

Violence was not the only high-pressure strategy associated with success. Ten of the fifty-three groups in the samples used other "unruly" strategies—strikes, boycotts, and techniques to humiliate or embarrass opponents. Eight out of the ten groups that applied such pressure won new advantages as well as acceptance; this was twice the rate of success for groups that avoided such strategies. Gamson concludes that the meek do not inherit the earth, at least in the United States. If a group wants political clout, Gamson observes, it is likely to do better when it is large, centrally organized, and ready to fight if necessary.

However, some sociologists, such as Jack A. Goldstone (1980), dispute Gamson's conclusions. Goldstone reanalyzes data for the fifty-three protest groups and concludes that tactical and organizational factors have a minimal effect on success. A major issue that divides Gamson and Goldstone has to do with whether or not a group was successful. Different criteria of success render different conclusions. Further, Goldstone suggests that the probability of a group's success is primarily a function of the incidence of national crisis. Groups that attained their ends operated during times of stress and turmoil: the Jacksonian period, the Civil War and Reconstruction period, the Progressive Era, the era of the Great Depression and World War II, and the Vietnam War years. Even so, evidence suggests that poor people's movements derive their gains largely through mass defiance (Piven and Cloward, 1977). Thus the urban riots of the 1960s and early 1970s contributed to the rise in expenditures for welfare and related social programs (Button, 1978; Jennings, 1979; Issac and Kelly, 1981; Schram and Turbett, 1983).

SOURCE: Adapted from William A. Gamson, "The Meek Don't Make It," *Psychology Today,* Vol. 8 (1975), pp. 35–41.

Second-Order Consequences

Social intervention, no matter how beneficent its purpose, has wide-ranging outcomes beyond its primary intent—**second-order consequences.** At times, this results in replacing one social problem with another. The Eighteenth Amendment destroyed saloons but drove alcoholic consumption underground and contributed to the rise of organized crime. Better street lighting in one neighborhood may decrease crime in the area by driving it into the next neighborhood. Many people who stop drinking alcohol compensate by increasing their cigarette consumption

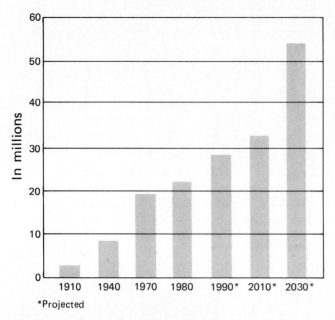

*Projected

FIGURE 17.2 Americans over Sixty-five
In solving one social problem, we often create new ones. Kingsley
Davis (1971) points out that throughout human history, life expectancy was tragically short. With advances in modern science, we
have realized a remarkable lengthening in average life expectancy.
But in so doing, we have incurred second-order consequences: En-
larging the population of older people, who are increasingly vulnerable to chronic health problems and disabilities and who live on limited retirement incomes, has resulted in higher medical and welfare
costs.
*Assuming (1) a fertility level of 2.1 children born per woman and (2) that
mortality rates decrease at a rate whereby life expectancy at birth increases
by about 0.05 year per year.*
(SOURCE: U.S. Bureau of the Census.)

(Kotler, 1973). In lengthening the human life span, medical science has created
an aged population with increased needs for medical and welfare services (see
Figure 17.2).

Revolutionary leaders often find that it is easier to attain power than it is to
govern. In an interview, Vietnamese Premier Pham Van Dong expressed the
general sense that things had not turned out as expected a decade after the
withdrawal of American units:

> Yes, we defeated the United States. But now we are plagued by problems. We do
> not have enough to eat. We are a poor, underdeveloped nation. Waging a war is
> simple, but running a country is difficult. (Ignatius, 1985: 1)

These observations are not intended as criticism of reform. They merely point up the fact that reform may not always have the consequences intended by its proponents. In solving some problems, we may create still others. This does not mean that we ought to forget about social reform. It simply means that there is often a price attached to it and that, in turn, we must attack the new "problems."

SUMMARY

1. Neil Smelser provides a "value-added" approach to collective behavior. He identifies six determinants of collective action, each shaped by those that precede it and shaping those that follow. In order of occurrence, they are: (a) structural conduciveness, (b) structural strain, (c) the growth and spread of a generalized belief, (d) precipitating factors, (e) the mobilization of participants for action, and (f) the operation of social control.

2. One type of strain underlying episodes of collective behavior is relative deprivation, which may occur under conditions of rising expectations. It may also be fostered under the condition characterized as the "rise-and-drop," or "J-curve," hypothesis.

3. Rather than focusing on the gap between expectations and achievements, other social scientists stress the view that collective behavior—especially collective violence—is a by-product of the mobilization of resources for collective ends.

4. An ideology provides new categories for interpreting sources of strain, a utopian vision of a new society, a dogma, a conceptual filter, polarization between outsiders and insiders, and a sense of personal power.

5. Three types of theories are used to describe and explain the dynamics of crowd behavior: contagion theory, convergence theory, and emergent-norm theory. Contagion theorists suggest that normal, decent people are transformed under crowd influence. Convergence theorists argue that a crowd consists of a highly unrepresentative grouping of people who come together because they share certain predispositions. Emergent-norm theory rejects the notion of unanimity and uniformity central to contagion and convergence theories; it describes how people undertake to evolve new standards for behavior in ambiguous situations and then undertake to enforce conformity to the new standards.

6. A social problem lacks objective existence. Rather, people attribute problem status to certain circumstances or behaviors to which they assign an unfavorable meaning.

7. The notion of social intervention suggests that resistance and opposition need to be overcome. Change is not neutral. Generally, some groups perceive that their fortunes would be improved by a proposed change; others feel threatened.

8. A problem must acquire a certain degree of "respectability" if it is to secure consideration in recognized public arenas. A selective process takes place in social interaction, whereby many budding social problems are choked off, others are avoided, others are ignored, others have to fight their way to

respectability, and others are rushed along the road to legitimacy by strong and influential backing.

9. If a social problem manages to secure social legitimacy, it enters the policy-making phase. The restructuring of a social problem as it passes through successive phases of this process may make it unrecognizable to its early sponsors.

GLOSSARY

Collective behavior □   Relatively spontaneous and unstructured ways of thinking, feeling, and acting that develop within a group or population as a consequence of interstimulation among the participants.

Contagion theory of crowds □   The view that a crowd assimilates its members, producing a psychic unity that alters the individual's normal emotions, thoughts, and conduct.

Convergence theory of crowds □   The view that a crowd consists of a highly unrepresentative grouping of people who come together because they share certain predispositions.

Crowd □   An assemblage in which people are in sufficiently close physical proximity that the fact of aggregation serves to influence their behavior.

Emergent-norm theory of crowds □   The view that a crowd consists of people with different motives, attitudes, and behaviors, who, faced with an ambiguous situation, evolve a group norm that gives them the illusion of uniformity and unanimity.

Ideology □   A set of shared definitions that provide interpretations and solutions to what is felt to be an unsatisfactory social condition.

Legitimacy □   That which conforms to recognized principles or accepted standards. A social problem must achieve legitimacy, or societal recognition, before action can be taken for reform.

Relative deprivation □   A state of mind in which a gap exists between what people seek and what seems attainable.

Second-order consequence □   An outcome of social intervention that goes beyond its primary intent. At times this results in replacing one social problem with another.

Social movement □   A more or less persistent and organized effort on the part of a relatively large number of people to bring about or resist social change.

Social problem □   A condition that a considerable number of people believe exists in their society and that they do not like.

Terrorism □   The use of force or violence against persons or property to intimidate or coerce a government, a formal organization, or a civilian population in furtherance of political, religious, or social objectives.

Glossary

Accommodation □ In Piaget's theory, the process in cognitive development of changing a scheme (cognitive structure) to achieve a better match to the world of reality.

Accounts □ Explanations we make for unanticipated or untoward behavior.

Affective component □ The feelings or emotions that an object, event, or situation—or its symbolic representation—evokes within an individual.

Aggression □ Behavior that is socially defined as injurious or destructive. Instrumental aggression, which has as its aim the realization of goals other than the victim's suffering, is distinguished from hostile aggression, which has as its aim the deliberate infliction of suffering or injury upon another.

Altercasting □ The process by which we undertake to shape the identity or define the role that will hold for the other person in a situation; we engage in behavior that casts another in an identity or role that will call forth from this other the responses we desire.

Altruism □ Behavior carried out to benefit another person without expectation of an external reward.

Androgyny □ A standard that allows individuals to express the full range of human emotions and role possibilities without regard to gender stereotypes.

Appearance □ Personal items that serve to identify an individual. Clothing, insignia, titles, and grooming are elements of appearance.

Assimilation □ In Piaget's theory, the process in cognitive development of taking in new information and interpreting it in such a manner that the information corresponds to a currently held scheme of the world.

Attitude □ A learned and relatively enduring tendency or predisposition to evaluate a person, event, or situation in a certain way.

Attitude consistency □ The tendency of people to organize their attitudes in a harmonious manner so that their attitudes are not in conflict.

Attribution □ The processes by which we explain and interpret events that we encounter.

Authenticity □ Behavior that is honest, sincere, and genuine, as opposed to performances that are false and artificial.

Authoritarian personality □ A set of traits characterized by rigid conventional thinking, an obsession with power, submission to authority, highly judgmental values, and cynical outlook; a "fascist" mind-set.

Authority □ Legitimate power; power used in accordance with the social values of those who are ruled, and under conditions that the ruled view as proper.

Autokinetic effect □ An optical illusion. If a small, fixed spot of light is briefly exposed in a darkened room, it will appear to move.

Backstage □ A region in which our behavior contradicts the impressions we are attempting to convey front-stage. We seek to screen the backstage region from an audience's view, because our performances there would tend to discredit our front-stage performances.

Balance theory of attitudes □ Fritz Heider's theory of attitude change, which focused on three elements: (1) the person who is the focus of attention, P; (2) some other person O; and (3) an impersonal entity X. These elements interact so as to realize attitude consistency.

Bases of power □ The resources that individuals or groups can muster in the attempt to impose their will in human affairs. The bases of power include what is used and the means to decide how it is used.

Behavior modification □ The application of the results of conditioning theory and experimental psychology to the problem of altering maladaptive behaviors.

Behavioral component □ See **conative component.**

Behaviorism □ A psychological theory that is primarily concerned with the stimuli that impinge on an organism's sense organs and the responses that these stimuli elicit.

Body language □ The nonverbal communication of meaning through physical movements and gestures.

Bonding □ A process whereby individuals or groups are linked together.

Boundaries □ Demarcation lines between discrete social units; points or zones where social interaction begins or ends.

Caretaker speech □ A systematically modified version of the language used with adults, with which parents address infants and children. Caretaker speech differs from everyday speech in its simplified vocabulary; higher pitch; exaggerated intonation; short, simple sentences; and high proportion of questions and imperatives.

Category □ An abstract representation of conceptually related information.

Catharsis □ A purging of aggressive energy through discharging it in aggressive behavior.

Causality □ Our attribution of a cause-and-effect relationship to two paired phenomena that recur in succession.

Central organizing trait □ A characteristic that has a strong effect on our overall evaluation of a person.

Choice shift □ A shift—whether toward risk or toward caution—that occurs when people make decisions in groups rather than individually.

Choking □ Under pressure we fail to perform up to our level of skills or capabilities.

Civil inattention □ Giving others enough visual notice to signal to them that we recognize their presence, but then quickly withdrawing visual contact to show that we pose no threat to them.

Classic colonialism □ Domination of an established, indigenous population by an incoming group through conquest and the imposition of a control apparatus.

Closed group □ A social unit with impermeable boundaries and therefore high or maximal barriers to entry by outsiders.

Coalition □ Two or more parties who coordinate their efforts in order to achieve their ends against the opposition of one or more competing parties.

Cognition □ All the mental processes that transform sensory input in some meaningful fashion—that code it, store it, and appropriately retrieve it.

Cognitive component □ The way we perceive an object, event, or situation; our thoughts, beliefs, and ideas about something.

Cognitive dissonance □ The theory, formulated by Leon Festinger, that there is pressure to produce consistent relations among one's attitudes or behaviors and to avoid inconsistency.

Cognitive stages in development □ Sequential periods in the growth or maturing of an individual's ability to think—to gain knowledge and awareness of the self and the environment.

Cohesiveness □ Forces that act to keep individuals within a group and prevent them from leaving it; a feeling of "we-ness."

Collective behavior □ Relatively spontaneous and unstructured ways of thinking, feeling, and acting that develop within a group or population as a consequence of interstimulation among the participants.

Commitment □ A state of being bound to or locked into a position or a course of action.

Communication □ The process by which people transmit information, ideas, attitudes, and emotions to one another.

Complementary needs □ Two different personality traits that are the counterparts of each other and that provide a sense of completeness when they are joined.

Compliance □ A behavior change without any underlying attitude change (without private acceptance).

Conative component □ The tendency or disposition to act in certain ways with reference to some object, event, or situation. The emphasis of the definition is on the tendency to act, not on the action itself.

Conditioning □ The process whereby individuals, as a result of their experience, establish an association or linkage between two events.

Conflict □ A form of interaction in which people (individually or in groups) perceive themselves as being involved in a struggle over scarce resources or social values.

Conformity □ Adherence to or behavioral change in accordance with social expectations.

Congruity theory of attitudes □ A theory of attitude change, formulated by Charles Osgood and his associates, which suggests that extreme attitudes are more resistant to change than more neutral ones.

Connotative meaning □ The emotional and evaluative associations of a word.

Conscience □ The internal operation of ethical or moral principles that control or inhibit the actions and thoughts of an individual.

Consciousness of oneness □ A sympathetic identification with others in the same group; a sense of "we-ness," so that individuals are not merely in the group but of the group.

Contagion theory of crowds □ The view that a crowd assimilates its members, producing a psychic unity that alters the individual's normal emotions, thoughts, and conduct.

Contamination □ The defilement of one party's territory by another.

Control □ Submission to the power of others; resistance is overcome not because people come to prefer a given course of action but because resistance has been made prohibitively expensive or impossible.

Convergence theory of crowds □ The view that a crowd consists of a highly unrepresentative grouping of people who come together because they share certain predispositions.

Cost-reward analysis of altruism □ The theory that whether or not a person intervenes in an emergency depends on his or her assessment of costs relative to rewards: (1) costs associated with helping, (2) costs associated with not helping, (3) rewards associated with helping, and (4) rewards associated with not helping.

Crowd □ An assemblage in which people are in sufficiently close physical proximity that the fact of aggregation serves to influence their behavior.

Crowding □ The perception that people have of themselves as receiving excessive stimulation from social sources.

Cues □ Signals, both verbal and nonverbal, that give us critical information about the nature and meaning of people's behavior.

Culture □ Shared cognitive (mental) maps that provide us with guideposts and guidelines for social life; shared recurrent definitions of given kinds of situations.

Deception □ Any intentional verbal or nonverbal act that an individual performs in order to mislead another person.

Definition of the situation □ The meaning we give to our immediate circumstances; the interpretation we make of the social factors that bear on us at a given time and in a given place.

Deindividuation □ A psychological state of diminished identity and self-awareness.

Demand characteristics □ Cues within the experimental situation that inadvertently guide and direct the responses of a subject.

Demonstration experiment □ A procedure for gathering data; the researcher introduces a "nasty surprise" or otherwise disturbs human interactions so as to reveal expectations of which we are normally unaware.

Denotative meaning □ That part of the definition of a word that "points out" an object or event—that gives certain specific properties or patterns of the object or event.

Density □ A physical condition of populations that involves spatial limitations.

Dependent variable □ The factor that is affected in an experimental setting; that which occurs or changes as a result of manipulation of another factor (the independent variable).

Diffusion of responsibility □ A process in which the obligation to help in an emergency and the potential blame for not helping are spread among observers.

Discrimination □ The arbitrary denial of power, privilege, and status to members of a minority group whose qualifications are equal to those of the dominant group.

Displacement □ The detachment of an aggressive impulse from the frustrating source and the discharge of that aggression on another person, group, or object.

Distributive question □ Who shall get what, when, and how?

Domestic colonialism □ The victimization, oppression, and subjugation by an established, indigenous population of another people, who are brought into the society against their wishes and will.

Dyad □ A two-person group.

Egocentric bias □ We overperceive ourselves as the victims or targets of events that, in reality, are not directed toward us.

Elite □ Those who rule, as opposed to those who are ruled.

Emergent-norm theory of crowds □ The view that a crowd consists of people with different motives, attitudes, and behaviors, who, faced with an ambiguous situation, evolve a group norm that gives them the illusion of uniformity and unanimity.

Equity theory □ The hypothesis that group

members will be satisfied with a distribution of rewards (outcomes) that is proportional to each member's contribution to the group (inputs).

Ethnic group ☐ A group distinguished on the basis of socially acquired lifeways.

Ethnocentrism ☐ The tendency to view one's own group as the center of everything and to rate all other people with reference to it.

Ethnomethodology ☐ The procedures (the rules and activities) that people employ in making social life and society intelligible and understandable to themselves.

Excuses ☐ Statements we provide that deny our responsibility for the negative consequences of our action and admit the behavior to be reprehensible.

Expectations ☐ The actions we can legitimately insist that others perform in relation to a role.

Experiment ☐ A study in which the investigator manipulates or varies one or more variables (termed the independent variables) and measures other variables (termed the dependent variables).

Experimenter effects ☐ The distortions in experimental outcomes that result from the behavior or characteristics of the researcher.

Expressive tie ☐ A social linkage formed when one invests oneself in and commits oneself to another person.

External causality ☐ The attribution of responsibility for events to environmental and situational circumstances that lie outside the individual.

False consensus ☐ The tendency to overestimate the extent to which other people's thinking resembles our own.

Field (also termed **life space**) ☐ The person and the environment viewed as one constellation of interdependent forces.

Field experiment ☐ An experiment in which a researcher introduces an independent variable into a natural setting to determine its impact on behavior.

Fixed territory ☐ Space that is viewed as belonging to some individual or group even when it is not being used.

Foot-in-the-door technique ☐ The idea that compliance breeds compliance. If we can induce a person to comply with an initial small request, we stand a good chance of getting him or her to comply with a larger demand later.

Force ☐ An act performed by an individual or group aimed at compelling another individual or group to follow a given course of action.

Free-rider effect ☐ One member of the group often can and will provide for the public good, making one's own contribution unnecessary.

Front ☐ The expressive equipment we intentionally or unwittingly use in presenting ourselves to others. Front consists of setting, appearance, and manner.

Front-stage ☐ Behavior that takes place in this region is intended for an audience's viewing.

Frustration ☐ Interference with or blocking of the attainment of some goal.

Frustration-aggression hypothesis ☐ The theory that frustration produces aggression.

Functionalist theory of attitudes ☐ The view that our attitudes are determined by the functions they serve for us; that people hold given attitudes because these attitudes help them achieve their basic goals.

Fundamental attribution error ☐ Our tendency to overestimate the extent to which the actions of other people derive from their underlying dispositions or personality.

Gatekeeping ☐ The decision-making process by which individuals are admitted to scarce positions and offices of power, privilege, and status within a society.

Gender identity ☐ A person's self-conception of being either male or female.

Gender roles ☐ Sets of expectations that determine the ways in which the members of each sex should behave.

Generalized other ☐ A synthesized overview of the cultural workings of our community; the attitude imputed to the entire group or society.

Gestalt ☐ A German word that suggests that the whole is greater than the sum of its parts; experience is viewed as organized and behavior as integrated.

Group ☐ Two or more people who share a feeling of unity and are bound together in relatively stable patterns of social interaction.

Groupthink ☐ A decision-making process occurring within highly cohesive groups in which the members are so preoccupied with maintaining group consensus that their critical abilities become ineffective.

Halo effect ☐ The assumption that when a person has one trait, he or she also possesses certain other traits.

Hermaphrodite ☐ An individual who has the reproductive organs of both sexes.

Homogamy ☐ The tendency of "like to marry like." People who are similar marry more often than would be expected by chance.

Homosexuality ☐ Erotic response to persons having the same sexual anatomy as oneself.

Identification ☐ See **observational learning.**

Identity ☐ Our sense of placement within the world and the meaning we attach to ourselves within the broader context of human life.

Ideology ☐ A set of shared definitions that provide interpretations and solutions to what is felt to be an unsatisfactory social condition.

Imitation ☐ See **observational learning.**

Implicit personality theories ☐ We commonly assume that a number of traits cluster to form an organized set of relationships.

Impression management ☐ The process by which we manipulate the definition of a situation, generating cues that will lead others to act in accordance with our plans.

Independent variable ☐ The factor that is manipulated in an experimental setting; the causal factor or determining condition in the relationship being studied.

Influence ☐ An authentic change in the preferences of an individual or group in accordance with the preferences of power wielders; given the same situation, an individual or group would not choose the same course of action that they favored before power was exercised.

Informal group ☐ A social organization that evolves within a formal organization although it is not defined or prescribed by the formal organization.

Ingroup ☐ A social unit that a person either belongs to or identifies with.

Institutional aggression ☐ Aggression within institutional contexts, when people commit aggressive and violent acts as part of "doing their job."

Institutional racism ☐ Those social arrangements and enduring patterns by which people of one racial group oppress and exploit the members of another racial group.

Instrumental tie ☐ A social linkage formed when one cooperates with another person to achieve a certain limited goal.

Intensity of conflict ☐ The degree to which the parties in a conflict are committed to expending resources and energy in the effort to defeat or neutralize their opponents.

Internal causality ☐ The attribution of responsibility for events to the personal qualities and traits of the individual.

Internalization ☐ The process whereby an individual incorporates within his or her personality the standards of behavior prevalent in the larger society.

Invasion ☐ Entry into a party's territory against that party's wishes.

Iron law of oligarchy ☐ The formulation by Robert Michels that large-scale organization inevitably leads to the concentration of power in the hands of a few; in turn, Michels says, the few use their positions to advance their own fortunes and selfish interests.

Justifications ☐ Statements we provide that deny responsibility for an action but reinterpret it in a more socially acceptable manner.

Just-world hypothesis ☐ The theory that people need to believe they live in a world where the deserving are rewarded and the undeserving are punished. According to the just-world hypothesis, the victim deserves to suffer.

Kinesics ☐ See **body language.**

Laboratory experiment ☐ An experiment in which specially constructed facilities are employed to facilitate determining the relationship between independent and dependent variables.

Language ☐ A socially structured system of sound patterns with standardized meanings.

Language acquisition device (lad) ☐ According to Noam Chomsky, an inborn language-generating mechanism that all human beings possess. Chomsky believes that the human organism is genetically prewired for language usage.

Language of space ☐ The different perceptions that people of different societies have regarding territorial privacy.

Learned helplessness ☐ The generalized expectancy that events are independent of what one does; the notion that one's actions and consequent events are not causally related.

Learning ☐ A more or less permanent modification in an organism's behavior or capability that results from its experience in the environment.

Legitimacy ☐ That which conforms to recognized principles or accepted standards. A social problem must achieve legitimacy, or societal recognition, before action can be taken for reform.

Life space □ See **field.**

Linguistic relativity thesis □ The theory that we adopt the view of the world that is fashioned and portrayed by our language; and since our languages differ, our world views differ.

Looking-glass self □ Our perception of ourselves as determined by the way we imagine we appear to others.

Machiavellianism □ An approach in which a person manipulates others for his or her own purposes.

Male chauvinism □ Male sexism toward women.

Manner □ Those expressions that reveal the performer's style of behavior, mood, and disposition.

Markers □ Signs that communicate to people the fact of ownership or legitimate occupancy of territory.

Matching hypothesis of mate selection □ The tendency to choose partners who have a similar degree of physical attractiveness to our own.

Material self □ An individual's experience of the stream of sensations that arise within the organism as the "bodily me."

Meaning □ The relatedness of something to all other events or objects with which it is associated in the experience of an individual or group.

Membership group □ A social unit to which an individual belongs.

Memory □ The retention of what has been experienced or learned and its activation when recollection occurs.

Minority □ Any racially or ethnically self-conscious social aggregate, with hereditary membership and a high degree of ingroup marriage, that suffers oppression at the hands of a dominant segment of a nation-state.

Modeling □ See **observational learning.**

Motherese □ A simplified, redundant, and highly grammatical form of language employed by parents in comunicating with young children.

Motivation □ Those inner states and processes that prompt, direct, and sustain activity.

Negotiated order □ A system by which we arrive at mutually shared agreements, tacit understandings, binding contracts, unhappy compromises, and coerced accommodations through processes of manipulation, persuasion, constraint, inducement, diplomacy, and bargaining.

Network □ A web of social relationships that center on a single individual and tie him or her directly to other individuals and indirectly through these other individuals to still more people.

Norm of reciprocity □ A social rule which stipulates that (1) people should help those who have helped them and (2) people should not injure those who have helped them.

Norms □ Standards for behavior that members of a social group share, to which they are expected to conform, and that are enforced by positive and negative sanctions.

Obligations □ The actions others can legitimately insist that we perform in relation to a role.

Observational learning □ The social transmission of behavior, either deliberately or inadvertently, through the examples provided by people whom we observe.

Open group □ A social unit with permeable boundaries and therefore low or minimal barriers to entry by outsiders.

Operant conditioning □ A type of learning in which behavior is altered in its strength by its consequences.

Outgroup □ A social unit that a person either does not belong to or does not identify with.

Paralanguage □ The nonsemantic aspects of speech—the stress, pitch, and volume of speech by which we communicate expressive meaning.

Participant observation □ A procedure for gathering data whereby the researcher spends a good deal of time in a natural setting, noticing, watching, and at times interacting with the people he or she is studying.

Passive resistance □ Noncooperation; the withholding of participation from an ongoing enterprise.

Perception □ The process by which we give meaning to sensations.

Person perception □ The processes by which we come to know and think about others—their characteristics, qualities, and inner states.

Personal space □ The area we actively maintain around ourselves into which others cannot intrude without arousing our discomfort.

Persuasion □ A deliberate attempt on the part of one party to influence the attitudes or behavior of another party so as to achieve some predetermined end.

Political impression management □ The achievement of power by controlling, influencing, and sustaining one party's definition of the situation; the elite induces people to share its view of reality and therefore to act in the manner it prescribes.

Positioning □ A strategy of locating oneself or one's personal effects in space so as to lay claim to a given territory.

Power □ The realization in human affairs of the will of one party (either an individual or group) over the will of another party.

Prejudice □ An attitude of aversion and hostility toward the members of a group simply because they belong to it and are therefore presumed to have the objectionable qualities ascribed to the group.

Primacy effect □ The way in which early information colors our perception of subsequent information.

Primary group □ Two or more people who relate to one another in direct, intimate, personal ways.

Primary relationship □ A social interaction that rests on expressive ties between people. In primary relationships people experience closeness; they participate as integral, committed units.

Principle of conservation □ The notion that the quantity of something stays the same despite changes in shape or position.

Privacy □ The claim of individuals or groups to determine for themselves when, how, and to what extent information about themselves is communicated to others.

Private acceptance □ A behavior change accompanied by underlying attitude change.

Privilege □ The possession or control of a portion of the surplus produced by the members of a society.

Projection □ The tendency of people to attribute to others traits that they find unacceptable in themselves.

Prosocial behavior □ Acts that benefit other people; ways of responding to other people that are sympathetic, cooperative, helpful, rescuing, comforting, and giving.

Prototype □ A category that we mentally employ to represent a loose set of features that seem to belong together.

Proximity □ Nearness in physical space.

Public territory □ An area, such as a street or playground, where an individual has freedom of access but not necessarily freedom of action. (For example, people can be arrested in public territory for nudity or drunkenness.)

Racial group □ A group distinguished on the basis of hereditary physical traits.

Reactance □ A motivational state directed toward the restoration or safeguarding of an individual's freedom with respect to some matter.

Recency effect □ The tendency to be most influenced by what we have just witnessed.

Recognition ceremonies □ Deferential gestures employed to ease the way for intrusion into another's territory.

Reference group □ The social unit with which people identify. They use the standards of their reference group to define their behavior and evaluate themselves.

Regions □ Places separating front-stage performances from backstage performances; places bounded to some degree by barriers to perception.

Reinforcer □ Any stimulus that follows a response and increases the frequency or probability of its occurrence.

Relative deprivation □ A state of mind in which a gap exists between what people seek and what seems attainable.

Release theory of the risky-shift phenomenon □ The theory that the risky shift occurs in group discussions because the discovery of another person who endorses high risk taking releases the more cautious group members from their social constraints.

Responses □ Behavior segmented into units.

Risky-shift phenomenon □ People's tendency to make more daring decisions when they are in groups than when they are alone.

Ritual □ A social act of symbolic significance that is performed on certain occasions by prescribed tradition.

Role □ The normative requirements that apply to the behavior of a specific category of people in a particular situational context. Roles specify who does what, when, and where.

Role distance □ A display of detachment from the set of norms applying to our behavior in a given situation.

Role embracement □ Commitment to given courses of action; absorption in and acceptance of the expectations and obligations defined by a set of normative rules.

Role-making □ The process of improvising new

features of action as we devise our performance and fit our line of action to that of others. In role-making we use our acts to alter the traditional expectations and obligations associated with a role.

Role strain □ Problems that individuals experience in meeting the requirements of a role.

Role-taking □ The process by which we devise our performance and fit our line of action to that of others; the translating of roles into action.

Schemata (singular **schema**) □ Abstract mental frameworks—general knowledge structures—for interpreting information from the environment.

Scheme □ In Piaget's theory, a cognitive structure that an individual evolves for dealing with a specific kind of situation in the environment.

Secondary group □ Two or more people who relate to one another in indirect, nonintimate, impersonal ways; the polar opposite of a primary group.

Secondary relationship □ A social interaction that rests on instrumental ties between people. In secondary relationships, people view themselves as independent, autonomous units, not as totally committed partners.

Second-order consequence □ An outcome of social intervention that goes beyond its primary intent. At times this results in replacing one social problem with another.

Self □ The individual as known to the individual in a socially determined frame of reference.

Self-awareness □ Attention focused inward upon the self.

Self-conception □ The overriding view one has of oneself; a sense of self through time—"the real me" or "I myself as I really am."

Self-disclosure □ The act of revealing one's "real" self to another.

Self-esteem □ The personal judgment we make of our own worth.

Self-fulfilling prophecy □ A false definition of a situation which creates conditions that make it come true.

Self-handicapping □ Any action that helps exempt us from personal responsibility for failure by constructing an impediment to our performance.

Self-image □ A mental picture or concept of oneself that is relatively temporary, subject to change from one social situation to another.

Self-indication □ The processes in which we internally note things, assess them, give them

meaning, and entertain various actions on the basis of the meaning.

Self-perception □ The processes by which we come to know and think about ourselves—the characteristics, qualities, and inner states that we attribute to ourselves.

Self-schemata (singular **schema**) □ Mental scripts or frames containing organized bodies of information in memory that we use in selecting and processing information about ourselves.

Self-serving bias □ The tendency to interpret the outcomes of behavior in ways that put ourselves in the best possible light.

Semantic differential □ A form of measurement developed by Charles Osgood for assessing the connotative meanings of words.

Setting □ The spatial and physical items of scenery (props) that we employ in staging our performance.

Sexism □ Those social arrangements and enduring patterns by which members of one gender group realize more benefits and fewer burdens than members of the other gender group.

Significant other □ A particular person who has considerable influence on another individual's self-evaluation and acceptance of given social norms.

Situation □ All the social factors that influence a person's behavior or experience at a given time and in a given place.

Situational territory □ A temporary tenancy of space while in use. Although the territory is in the public domain, it "belongs" to one individual and then to another for short periods—as when a person uses a telephone booth.

Sleeper effect □ An effect that happens because a delay occurs before the impact of a communication is felt.

Social act □ Behavior that is oriented to or influenced by another person or persons.

Social attraction □ The property by which two people are drawn together.

Social dilemmas □ Situations in which members of a group are faced with a conflict between maximizing their personal interests and maximizing the collective welfare.

Social distance □ A subjective sense of being set apart from (as opposed to being near to) certain people.

Social exchange theory □ The view that people, as they enter into relationships with one another, are engaging in a sort of mental bookkeeping that involves a ledger of rewards, costs, and profits (rewards less costs).

Social interaction □ A process directed toward, stimulated by, or influenced by another person or persons.

Socialization □ A process by which individuals develop, through interaction with other people, the ways of thinking, feeling, and acting that are essential for effective participation within society.

Social loafing □ When people work in groups, they work less hard than they do when working individually.

Social movement □ A more or less persistent and organized effort on the part of a relatively large number of people to bring about or resist social change.

Social order □ The configuration that makes human life usually appear to be organized and focused rather than haphazard and random.

Social problem □ A condition that a considerable number of people believe exists in their society and that they do not like.

Social psychology □ A scientific attempt to understand and explain how the thought, feeling, and behavior of individuals are influenced by the actual, imagined, or implied presence of others.

Social relationship □ An association that develops when social interaction continues long enough for two people to become linked together by a relatively stable set of expectations.

Social support □ The exchange of resources among individuals based on their interpersonal ties.

Social survey □ A method of research; the obtaining of quantitative data through interviews or mailed questionnaires.

Sociobiology □ A discipline that focuses on the biological basis for social behavior in species ranging from amoeba colonies to human societies.

Sociogram □ A graph or chart that shows the patterns of choice among members of a group at a given point in time.

Sociometry □ An objective method for assessing patterns of attraction, rejection, or indifference among members of a group.

Split labor market □ An economic arena in which there is a large differential in the price of labor for the same occupation; in a split labor market, conflict develops among three groups: business, higher-paid labor, and cheaper labor.

State □ An arrangement consisting of people who exercise an effective monopoly in the use of physical coercion within a given territory.

Status □ An expansive feeling of being somebody special and valuable, so that a person's self-image is positively illuminated.

Stereotype □ The unscientific and hence unreliable generalizations that we make about individuals by virtue of their membership in a group.

Stimuli □ The environment divided into units.

Sucker effect □ A situation in which other people free ride on our contributions and lead us to reduce our own contributions to the group.

Symbol □ Any object or event that has socially come to stand for something else.

Symbolic interactionism □ A social psychological school of thought based on the view that our humanness derives from the mutual impact we have upon one another. It depicts us as active agents who in the course of social interaction consciously, deliberately, and directly fashion our personal histories and the history of the world around us. It emphasizes the part that language and gestures play in the formation of the mind, self, and society.

Symbolic racism □ A set of beliefs in which the underlying racial content is disguised but nonetheless finds expression in white notions that blacks are violating cherished values and making illegitimate demands on whites for social change.

Territoriality □ Behavior in which individuals or groups maintain, mark, and defend areas against intrusion by members of their own species.

Terrorism □ The use of force or violence against persons or property to intimidate or coerce a government, a formal organization, or a civilian population in furtherance of political, religious, or social objectives.

Theory □ A way of making sense out of a confused set of data through a symbolic construction by the human mind; the net we weave to catch the world of observation.

Thinking □ A process of mental manipulation of images, symbols, and ideas.

Third-person effect in communication □ When we are exposed to a persuasive communication, we commonly think that it has a greater effect on others than on ourselves.

Traits □ Relatively enduring ways in which individuals differ; descriptive characteristics of people.

Transsexual □ An individual with normal sexual organs who psychologically feels like a member of the opposite sex.

Transvestism ☐ An overpowering urge to impersonate the opposite sex and dress in the clothes of the opposite sex.

Trust ☐ A belief by one person in the integrity of another person.

Value ☐ An ethical principle to which people feel a strong emotional commitment and which they employ in judging behavior.

Value hypothesis of the risky-shift phenomenon ☐ The theory that in social situations, people shift toward the dominant value of a given reference group.

Volition ☐ The degree of freedom individuals believe they possess in making a decision or choice.

References

Abeles, R. P. 1976. Relative deprivation, rising expectations, and Black militancy. *Journal of Social Issues,* 32:119–137.

Abelson, R. P. 1972. Are attitudes necessary? In King, B. T., and McGinnies, E. (eds.), *Attitudes, Conflict, and Social Changes.* New York: Academic Press.

———, Kinder, D. R., Peters, M. D., and Fiske, S. T. 1982. Affective and semantic components in political person perception. *Journal of Personality and Social Psychology,* 42:619–630.

Abrams, B. 1983. Advertising. *Wall Street Journal* (March 24):29.

Adair, J. G. 1984. The Hawthorne effect: A reconsideration of the methodological artifact. *Journal of Applied Psychology,* 69:334–345.

Adam, B. D. 1978. Inferiorization and "self-esteem." *Social Psychology,* 41:47–53.

Adams, J. S. 1965. Inequity in social exchange. In Berkowitz, L. (ed.), *Advances in Experimental Social Psychology.* Vol. 2. New York: Academic Press.

Adorno, T. W., Frenkel-Brunswik, E., Levinson, D. J., and Sanford, R. N. 1950. *The Authoritarian Personality.* New York: Harper and Row.

Aiello, J. R., and Cooper, R. E. 1972. Use of personal space as a function of social affect. *Proceedings, Eightieth Annual Convention, American Psychological Association:* 207–208.

Ajzen, I., and Fishbein, M. 1973. Attitudinal and normative variables as predictors of specific behaviors. *Journal of Personality and Social Psychology,* 27:41–57.

———, and ———. 1977. Attitude-behavior relations: A theoretical analysis and review of empirical research. *Psychological Bulletin,* 84:888–918.

———, and ———. 1980. *Understanding Attitudes and Predicting Social Behavior.* Englewood Cliffs, N.J.: Prentice-Hall.

Albin, R. S. 1981. How court testimony goes awry. *New York Times* (March 17):16.

Alexander, C. N., Jr., and Rudd, J. 1984. Predicting behaviors from situated identities. *Social Psychology Quarterly,* 47:172–177.

Allen, V. L., and Levine, J. M. 1971. Social support and conformity: The role of independent assessment of reality. *Journal of Experimental Social Psychology,* 7:48–58.

———, and Wilder, D. A. 1975. Categorization, belief similarity, and intergroup discrimination. *Journal of Personality and Social Psychology,* 32:971–977.

Allport, F. H. 1924. *Social Psychology.* Boston: Houghton.

Allport, G. W. 1943. The ego in contemporary psychology. *Psychological Review,* 50:451–478.

———. 1954. *The Nature of Prejudice.* Cambridge, Mass.: Addison-Wesley.

———. 1955. *Becoming.* New Haven: Yale University Press.

———. 1962. Prejudice: Is it societal or personal. *Journal of Social Issues,* 18:120–124.

———. 1968. The historical background of modern social psychology. In Lindzey, G., and Aronson, E. (eds.), *The Handbook of Social Psychology.* 2nd ed. Reading, Mass.: Addison-Wesley, 1–80.

Alper, J. 1985. The roots of morality. *Science 85* (March) 70–76.

Altman, I. 1975. *The Environment and Social Behavior: Privacy, Personal Space, Territory, and Crowding.* Monterey, Calif.: Brooks/Cole.

———. 1977. Privacy regulation: Culturally universal or culturally specific? *Journal of Social Issues,* 33:66–84.

———. 1978. Crowding: Historical and contemporary trends in crowding research. In Baum, A., and Epstein, Y. M. (eds.), *Human Responses to Crowding.* Hillsdale, N.J.: Erlbaum.

Amato, P. R. 1983. Helping behavior in urban and rural environments: Field studies based on a taxonomic organization of helping episodes. *Journal of Personality and Social Psychology,* 45:571–586.

American Psychological Association, 1982. *Ethical Principles in the Conduct of Research with Human Participants.* 2nd ed. Washington, D.C.

Aminzade, R. 1984. Capitalist industrialization and patterns of industrial protest: A comparative urban study of nineteenth-century France. *American Sociological Review,* 49:437–453.

Amir, Y. 1969. Contact hypothesis in ethnic relations. *Psychological Bulletin,* 71:319–342.

——. 1976. The role of intergroup contact in change of prejudice and ethnic relations. In Katz, P. A. (ed.), *Towards the Elimination of Racism.* New York: Pergamon Press.

Ancok, D., and Chertkoff, J. M. 1983. Effects of group membership, relative performance, and self-interest on the division of outcomes. *Journal of Personality and Social Psychology,* 45:1256–1262.

Andersen, S. M. 1984. Self-knowledge and social inference: II. The diagnosticity of cognitive/affective and behavioral data. *Journal of Personality and Social Psychology,* 46:294–307.

——, and Ross, L. 1984. Self-knowledge and social inference: 1. The impact of cognitive/affective and behavioral data. *Journal of Personality and Social Psychology,* 46:280–293.

Anderson, J. G., and Jay, S. J. 1985. The diffusion of medical technology: Social network analysis and policy research. *Sociological Quarterly,* 26:49–64.

Anderson, N. H. 1968. Application of a linear-serial model to a personality-impression task using special presentation. *Journal of Personality and Social Psychology,* 10:354–362.

Andreoli, V. A., Worchel, S., and Folger, R. 1974. Implied threat to behavioral freedom. *Journal of Personality and Social Psychology,* 30:765–771.

Andrews, L. B. 1982. Mind control in the courtroom. *Psychology Today,* 16 (March):66–73.

Ansen, D. 1980. The science of love. *Newsweek* (February 25):89–90.

Antill, J. K. 1983. Sex role complementarity versus similarity in married couples. *Journal of Personality and Social Psychology,* 45:145–155.

Apsler, R. 1975. Effects of embarrassment on behavior toward others. *Journal of Personality and Social Psychology,* 32:145–153.

——, and Friedman, H. 1975. Chance outcomes and the just world: A comparison of observers and recipients. *Journal of Personality and Social Psychology,* 31:887–894.

Archer, D., and Akert, R. M. 1977. Words and everything else: Verbal and nonverbal cues in social interpretation. *Journal of Personality and Social Psychology,* 35:443–449.

——, Iritani, B., Kimes, D. D., and Barrios, M. 1983. Face-ism: Five studies of sex differences in facial prominence. *Journal of Personality and Social Psychology,* 45:725–735.

Ardrey, R. 1961. *African Genesis.* London: Collins.

——.1966. *The Territorial Imperative.* New York: Atheneum.

Argyle, M., Alkema, F., and Gilmour, R. 1971. The communication of friendly and hostile attitudes by verbal and nonverbal signals. *European Journal of Social Psychology,* 1:385–402.

——, Furnham, A., and Graham, J. A. 1981. *Social Situations.* Cambridge: Cambridge University Press.

Arndt, W. B., Jr., Foehl, J. C., and Good, F. E. 1985. Specific sexual fantasy themes: A multidimensional study. *Journal of Personality and Social Psychology,* 48:472–480.

Aronfreed, J. 1968. *Conduct and Conscience.* New York: Academic Press.

——.1969. The concept of internalization. In Goslin, D. A. (ed.), *Handbook of Socialization Theory and Research.* Chicago: Rand McNally.

Aronson, E. 1968. Dissonance theory: Progress and problems. In Abelson, R., Aronson, E., McGuire, W., Newcomb, T., Rosenberg, M., and Tannenbaum, P. (eds.), *Theories of Cognitive Consistency: A Sourcebook.* Chicago: Rand McNally.

——. 1969. The theory of cognitive dissonance: A current perspective. In Berkowitz, L. (ed.), *Advances in Experimental Social Psychology.* New York: Academic Press.

——. 1972. *The Social Animal.* San Francisco: Freeman.

——, Brewer, M., and Carlsmith, J. M. 1985. Experimentation in social psychology. In Lindzey, G., and Aronson, E. (eds.), *Handbook of Social Psychology.* 3rd ed. Vol. 1. New York: Random House.

——, and Carlsmith, J. M. 1962. Performance expectancy as a determinant of actual performance. *Journal of Abnormal and Social Psychology,* 65:178–182.

——, and ——. 1986. Experimentation in social psychology. In Lindzey, G., and Aronson,

E. (eds.), *The Handbook of Social Psychology.* 2nd ed. Vol. 2. Reading, Mass.: Addison-Wesley.

———, and Mills, J. 1959. The effect of severity on liking for a group. *Journal of Abnormal and Social Psychology,* 59:177–181.

———, Turner, J., and Carlsmith, J. M. 1963. Communicator's credibility and communication discrepancy. *Journal of Abnormal and Social Psychology,* 67:31–36.

Asch, S. E. 1946. Forming impressions of personality. *Journal of Abnormal and Social Psychology,* 41:258–290.

———. 1952. *Social Psychology.* Englewood Cliffs, N.J.: Prentice-Hall.

———. 1956. Studies of independence and conformity: I. A minority of one against a unanimous majority. *Psychological Monographs,* 70 (9).

———, and Zukier, H. 1984. Thinking about persons. *Journal of Personality and Social Psychology,* 46:1230–1240.

Ashmore, R. D. 1981. Sex stereotypes and implicit personality theory. In Hamilton, D. (ed.), *Cognitive Processes in Stereotyping and Intergroup Behavior.* Hillsdale, N.J.: Erlbaum.

Ashton, P. T. 1975. Cross-cultural Piagetian research: An experimental perspective. *Harvard Educational Review,* 45:475–506.

Athay, M., and Darley, J. 1982. Social roles as interaction competencies. In Ickes, W., and Knowles, E. S. (eds.), *Personality, Roles, and Social Behavior.* New York: Springer-Verlag.

Austin, W., and Walster, E. 1974. Reactions to confirmations and disconfirmations of expectancies of equity and inequity. *Journal of Personality and Social Psychology,* 30:208–216.

Austin, W. T., and Bates, F. L. 1974. Ethological indicators of dominance and territory in a human captive population. *Social Forces,* 52:447–455.

Axelrod, R. 1984. *The Evolution of Cooperation.* New York: Basic Books.

Axsom, D., and Cooper, J. 1985. Cognitive dissonance and psychotherapy: The role of effort justification in inducing weight loss. *Journal of Experimental Social Psychology,* 21:149–160.

Balch, R. W. 1979. Two models of conversion and commitment in a UFO cult. Paper presented at the annual meeting of the Pacific Sociological Association, Anaheim, California.

Baldassare, M. 1978. *Residential Crowding in Urban American.* Berkeley: University of California Press.

Baldwin, D. A. 1978. Power and social exchange. *The American Political Science Review,* 72:1229–1242.

Ball, D. W. 1966. An abortion clinic ethnography. *Social Problems,* 14:293–301.

Ball, R. A., and Lilly, J. R. 1982. The menace of margarine: The rise and fall of a social problem. *Social Problems,* 29:488–498.

Bandura, A. 1965. Influence of models' reinforcement contingencies on the acquisition of imitative responses. *Journal of Personality and Social Psychology,* 1:589–595.

———. 1969. Social-learning theory of identificatory process. In Goslin, D. A. (ed.), *Handbook of Socialization Theory and Research.* Chicago: Rand McNally.

———. 1971. *Psychological Modeling: Conflicting Theories.* Chicago: Aldine-Atherton.

———. 1973a. *Aggression: A Social Learning Analysis.* Englewood Cliffs, N.J.: Prentice-Hall.

———. 1973b. Social learning theory of aggression. In Knutson, J. F. (ed.), *The Control of Aggression.* Chicago: Aldine.

———. 1977. *Social Learning Theory.* Englewood Cliffs, N.J.: Prentice-Hall.

———. 1981. Self-referent thought: The development of self-efficacy. In Flavell, J. H., and Ross, L. (eds.), *Development of Social Cognition.* New York: Cambridge University Press.

———, and Rosenthal, T. L. 1966. Vicarious classical conditioning as a function of arousal level. *Journal of Personality and Social Psychology,* 3:54–62.

———, Ross, D., and Ross, S. 1961. Transmission of aggression through imitation of aggressive models. *Journal of Abnormal and Social Psychology,* 63:575–582.

———, ———, and ———. 1963. Imitation of film-mediated aggressive models. *Journal of Abnormal and Social Psychology,* 66:3–11.

———, and Walters, R. H. 1963. *Social Learning and Personality Development.* New York: Holt, Rinehart and Winston.

Banks, W. C. 1976. White preference in blacks: A paradigm in search of a phenomenon. *Psychological Bulletin,* 83:1179–1186.

———, and Rompf, W. J. 1973. Evaluative bias and preference behavior in black and white children. *Child Development,* 44:776–783.

Baptist, B. 1984. Football makes it all happen. *Columbus Dispatch* (March 5): C-1.

Barbanel, J. 1981. A block on 42d St. in Manhattan is nether world. *New York Times* (July 6):11.

Barber, T. X. 1970. *LSD, Marihuana, Yoga and Hypnosis.* Chicago: Aldine.

Bargh, J. A., and Pietromonaco, P. 1982. Automatic information processing and social perception: The influence of trait information presented outside of conscious awareness on impression formation. *Journal of Personality and Social Psychology,* 43:437–449.

Barker, E. 1980. Free to choose? Some thoughts on the Unification Church and other religious movements. *Clergy Review,* 65:365–368 + .

———. 1984. *The Making of a Moonie.* New York: Basil Blackwell.

Barker, R. G., Dembo, T., and Lewin, K. 1941. Frustration and regression: An experiment with young children. *University of Iowa Studies in Child Welfare,* 18:1–314.

Barkow, J. H. 1978. Culture and sociobiology. *American Anthropologist,* 80:5–20.

Barnes, M. L., and Rosenthal, R. 1985. Interpersonal effects of experimenter attractiveness, attire, and gender. *Journal of Personality and Social Psychology,* 48:435–446.

Baron, R. A. 1977. *Human Aggression.* New York: Plenum Press.

———. 1981. The "Cost of deception" revisited: An openly optimistic rejoinder. *IRB: A Review of Human Subjects Research,* 3:8–10.

———, and Bell, P. A. 1976. Aggression and heat: The influence of ambient temperature, negative affect, and a cooling drink on physical aggression. *Journal of Personality and Social Psychology,* 33:245–255.

———, and ———. 1977. Sexual arousal and aggression by males: Effects of type of erotic stimuli prior to provocation. *Journal of Personality and Social Psychology,* 35:79–87.

———, and Byrne, D. 1977. *Social Psychology.* 2nd ed. Boston: Allyn and Bacon.

Baron, R. M. and Needel, S. P. 1980. Toward an understanding of the differences in the responses of humans and other animals to density. *Psychological Review,* 87:320–326.

Bart, P. B. 1981. A study of women who both were raped and avoided rape. *Journal of Social Issues,* 37:123–137.

Batson, C. D. 1983. Sociobiology and the role of religion in promoting prosocial behavior: An alternative view. *Journal of Personality and Social Psychology,* 45:1380–1385.

———, Duncan, B. D., Ackerman, P., Buckley, T., and Birch, K. 1981. Is empathic emotion a source of altruistic motivation? *Journal of Personality and Social Psychology,* 40:290–302.

———, and Gray, R. A. 1981. Religious orientation and helping behavior: Responding to one's own or to the victim's needs? *Journal of Personality and Social Psychology,* 40:511–520.

———, O'Quin, K., Fultz, J., Vanderplas, M., and Isen, A. M. 1983. Influence of self-reported distress and empathy on egoistic versus altruistic motivation to help. *Journal of Personality and Social Psychology,* 45:706–718.

———, Pate, S., Lawless, H., Sparkman, P., Lambers, S., and Worman, B. 1979. Helping under conditions of common threat: Increased "we-feeling" or ensuring reciprocity. *Social Psychology Quarterly,* 42:410–414.

Baucom, D. H., Besch, P. K., and Callahan, S. 1985. Relation between testosterone concentration, sex role identity, and personality among females. *Journal of Personality and Social Psychology,* 48:1218–1226.

Bauer, R. A. 1965. A revised model of source effect. Presidential address to the Division of Consumer Psychology, American Psychological Association annual meeting, Chicago.

Baum, A., Calesnick, L. E., Davis, G. E., and Gatchel, R. J. 1982. Individual differences in coping with crowding: Stimulus screening and social overload. *Journal of Personality and Social Psychology,* 43:821–830.

———, and Davis, G. E. 1980. Reducing the stress of high-density living: An architectural intervention. *Journal of Personality and Social Psychology,* 38:471–481.

———, Fleming, R., and Singer, J. E. 1983. Coping with victimization by technological disaster. *Journal of Social Issues,* 39:117–138.

———, and Valins, S. 1977. *Architecture and Social Behavior: Psychological Studies of Social Density.* Hillsdale, N.J.: Erlbaum.

Baumann, D. J., Cialdini, R. B., and Kenrick, D. T. 1981. Altruism as hedonism: Helping and self-gratification as equivalent responses. *Journal of Personality and Social Psychology,* 40:1039–1046.

Baumeister, R. F. 1982. A self-presentational view of social phenomena. *Psychological Bulletin,* 91:3–26.

———. 1984. Choking under pressure: Self-consciousness and paradoxical effects of incentives on skillful performance. *Journal of Personality and Social Psychology,* 46:610–620.

———, and Steinhilber, A. 1984. Paradoxical effects of supportive audiences on performance under pressure: The home field disadvantage in sports championships. *Journal of Personality and Social Psychology,* 47:85–93.

———, and Tice, D. M. 1984. Role of self-presentation and choice in cognitive dissonance under forced compliance: Necessary or sufficient causes? *Journal of Personality and Social Psychology,* 46:5–13.

Baumgardner, M. H., Leippe, M. R., Ronis, D. L., and Greenwald, A. G. 1983. In search of reliable persuasion effects: II. Associative interference and persistence of persuasion in a message-dense environment. *Journal of Personality and Social Psychology,* 45:524–537.

Baumrind, D. 1964. Some thoughts on ethics of research: After Milgram's "Behavioral study of obedience." *American Psychologist,* 19:421–423.

———. 1985. Research using intentional deception: Ethical issues revisited. *American Psychologist,* 40:165–174.

Baxter, J. C. 1970. Interpersonal spacing in natural settings. *Sociometry,* 33:444–456.

Becker, B. J. 1983. Item characteristics and sex differences on the SAT-M for mathematically able youth. Paper presented at the annual meeting of the American Education Research Association, Montreal.

Becker, F. D. 1973. Study of spatial markers. *Journal of Personality and Social Psychology,* 26:439–445.

Becker, G. 1964. The complementary needs hypothesis: Authoritarianism, dominance and other Edwards Personal Preference Schedule Scores. *Journal of Personality,* 32:45–56.

Becker, H. S. 1963. *Outsiders: Studies in the Sociology of Deviance.* New York: Free Press.

———. 1973. Labeling theory reconsidered. In *Outsiders: Studies in the Sociology of Deviance.* 2nd ed. New York: Free Press.

Beckhouse, L., Tanur, J., Weiler, J., and Weinstein, E. 1975. And some men have leadership thrust upon them. *Journal of Personality and Social Psychology,* 31:557–566.

Beckman, L. 1970. Effects of students' performance on teachers' and observers' attributions of causality. *Journal of Educational Psychology,* 61:76–82.

Begley, T. M., and Alker, H. 1982. Anti-busing protest: Attitudes and actions. *Social Psychology Quarterly,* 45:187–197.

Bell, A. P., Weinberg, M. S., and Hammersmith, S. F. 1981. *Sexual Preference: Its Development in Men and Women.* Bloomington: Indiana University Press.

Bell, D. A., Jr. 1980. A reassessment of racial balance remedies—I. *Phi Delta Kappan,* 62:177–179.

Bem, D. J. 1965. An experiment analysis of self-persuasion. *Journal of Experimental Social Psychology,* 1:199–218.

———. 1967. Self perception: An alternative interpretation of cognitive dissonance phenomena. *Psychological Review,* 74:183–200.

———. 1972. Self-perception theory. In Berkowitz, L. (ed.), *Advances in Experimental Social Psychology.* Vol. 6. New York: Academic Press.

Bem, S. L. 1975a. Androgyny vs. the tight little lives of fluffy women and chesty men. *Psychology Today,* 9:58–62.

———. 1975b. Sex role adaptability: One consequence of psychological androgyny. *Journal of Personality and Social Psychology,* 31:634–643.

———. 1979. Beyond andogyny: Some presumptuous prescriptions for a liberated sexual identity. In Sherman, J., and Denmark, F. (eds.), *Psychology of Women: Issues in Psychology.* New York: Psychological Dimensions.

———. 1981. The BSRI and gender schema theory: A reply to Spence and Helmreich. *Psychological Review,* 88:369–371.

———. 1982. Gender schema theory and self-schema theory compared: A comment on Markus, Crane, Bernstein, and Siladi's "Self-schemas and gender." *Journal of Personality and Social Psychology,* 43:1192–1194.

———. 1984. Androgyny and gender schema theory: A conceptual and empirical integration. In Sondregger, T. B. (ed.), *Nebraska Symposium on Motivation.* Lincoln: University of Nebraska Press.

Benbow, C. P., and Stanley, J. C. 1980. Sex differences in mathematical ability: Fact or artifact? *Science,* 210:1262–1264.

Benedict, R. 1938. Continuities and discontinuities in cultural conditioning. *Psychiatry,* 1:161–167.

Beniger, J. R., and Savory, L. 1981. Social exchange: Diffusion of a paradigm. *American Sociologist,* 16:240–250.

Bennett, R. P., and Carbonari, J. P. 1976. Personality patterns related to own-, joint-, and relative-gain maximizing behaviors. *Journal of Personality and Social Psychology,* 34:1127–1134.

Ben-Yehuda, N. 1980. The European witch craze of the 14th to 17th centuries: A sociologist's perspective. *American Journal of Sociology,* 86:1–31.

Berens, M. J. 1984. Crowd twice urged man to jump. *Columbus Dispatch* (June 26):1.

Berg, J. H., and Archer, R. L. 1982. Responses to self-disclosure and interaction goals. *Journal of Experimental Social Psychology,* 18:501–512.

Berglas, S., and Jones, E. E. 1978. Drug choice as a self-handicapping strategy in response to noncontingent success. *Journal of Personality and Social Psychology,* 36:405–417.

Berkman, L. F., and Breslow, L. 1983. *Health and Ways of Living: The Alameda County Study.* New York: Oxford University Press.

Berkowitz, L. 1962. *Aggression: A Social Psychological Analysis.* New York: McGraw-Hill.

———. 1965a. The concept of aggressive drives: Some additional considerations. In Berkowitz, L. (ed.), *Advances in Experimental Social Psychology.* Vol. 2. New York: Academic Press.

———. 1965b. Some aspects of observed aggression. *Journal of Personality and Social Psychology,* 2:359–369.

———. 1970a. Experimental investigations of hostility catharsis. *Journal of Consulting and Clinical Psychology,* 35: 1–7.

———. 1970b. The self, selfishness, and altruism. In Macaulay, J., and Berkowitz, L. (eds.), *Altruism and Helping Behavior.* New York: Academic Press.

———. 1973. Works and symbols as stimuli to aggressive responses. In Knutson, J. F. (ed.), *The Control of Aggression.* Chicago: Aldine.

———. 1978. Whatever happened to the frustration-aggression hypothesis? *American Behavioral Scientist,* 32:691–708.

———. 1981. How guns control us. *Psychology Today,* 15:11–12.

———. 1983. Aversively stimulated aggression. *American Psychologist,* 38:1135–1144.

———, Cochran, S. T., and Embree, M. C. 1981. Physical pain and the goal of aversively stimulated aggression. *Journal of Personality and Social Psychology,* 40:687–700.

———, and Donnerstein, E. 1982. External validity is more than skin deep. *American Psychologist,* 37:245–257.

———, and Frodi, A. 1979. Reactions to a child's mistakes as affected by her/his looks and speech. *Social Psychology Quarterly,* 42:420–425.

———, and Knurek, D. A. 1969. Label-mediated hostility generalization. *Journal of Personality and Social Psychology,* 13:200–206.

———, and Walster, E. 1976. *Equity Theory: Toward a General Theory of Social Interaction.* New York: Academic Press.

Berman, J. S., Read, S. J., and Kenny, D. A. 1983. Processing inconsistent social information. *Journal of Personality and Social Psychology,* 45:1211–1224.

Bernstein, M., and Crosby, F. 1980. An empirical examination of relative deprivation theory. *Journal of Experimental Social Psychology,* 16:442–456.

Berscheid, E. 1982. America's obsession with beautiful people. *U.S. News & World Report* (January 11):59–61.

———. 1983. Emotion. In Kelley, H. H. (ed.), *Close Relationships.* New York: W. H. Freeman.

———, Boye, D., and Darley, J. M. 1968. Effects of forced association upon voluntary choice to associate. *Journal of Personality and Social Psychology,* 8:13–19.

———, Dion, K. Walster, E., and Walster, G. W. 1971. Physical attractiveness and dating choice: A test of the matching hypothesis. *Journal of Experimental Social Psychology,* 7:173–189.

———, and Peplau, L. A. 1983. The emerging science of relationships. In Kelley, H. H. (ed.), *Close Relationships.* New York: W. H. Freeman.

———, and Walster, E. 1967. When does a harmdoer compensate a victim? *Journal of Personality and Social Psychology,* 6:435–441.

———, and ———. 1969. *Interpersonal Attraction.* Reading, Mass.: Addison-Wesley.

———, and ———. 1974a. A little bit about love. In Huston, E. L. (ed.), *Foundations of Interpersonal Attraction.* New York: Academic Press.

———, and ———. 1974b. Physical attractiveness. In Berkowitz, L. (ed.), *Advances in Experimental Social Psychology.* Vol. 7. New York: Academic Press.

Bickman, L., and Rosenbaum, D. P. 1977. Crime reporting as a function of bystander encouragement, surveillance, and credibility. *Journal of Personality and Social Psychology,* 35:577–586.

Bird, C. 1975. *The Case Against College.* New York: David McKay.

Bird, F., and Reimer, B. 1982. Participation rates in new religious movements and para-religious movements. *Journal for the Scientific Study of Religion,* 21:1–14.

Birdwhistell, R. 1952. *Introduction to Kinesics.* Louisville, Ky.: University of Louisville Press.

———. 1970. *Kinesics and Context.* Philadelphia: University of Pennsylvania Press.

Bishop, J. 1981. Experts say films can prod the disturbed. *Wall Street Journal* (April 2):1, 32.

Blanchard, F. A., Weigel, R. H., and Cook, S. W. 1975. The effect of relative competence of group members upon interpersonal attraction in cooperating interracial groups. *Journal of Personality and Social Psychology,* 32:519–530.

Blasi, A. 1980. Bridging moral cognition and

moral action: A critical review of the literature. *Psychological Bulletin,* 88:1–45.

Blau, P. M. 1964. *Exchange and Power in Social Life.* New York: Wiley.

———, and Scott, W. R. 1962. *Formal Organizations.* San Francisco: Chandler.

Blauner, R. 1972. *Racial Oppression in America.* New York: Harper and Row.

Blazer, D. G. 1982. Social support and mortality in an elderly community population. *American Journal of Epidemiology,* 115:684–694.

Bleier, R. 1979. Correspondence. *New England Journal of Medicine,* 301:839–840.

Block, J. 1981. Some enduring and consequential structures of personality. In Rubin, A. I. (ed.), *Further Explorations in Personality.* New York: Wiley.

Blood, R. O., Jr. 1969. *Marriage.* 2nd ed. New York: Free Press.

———, and Wolfe, D. M. 1960. *Husbands and Wives.* New York: Free Press.

Bloom, B. L., Asher, S. J., and White, S. W. 1978. Marital disruption as a stressor: A review and analysis. *Psychological Bulletin,* 85:867–894.

Blount, B. G. 1975. Studies in child language. *American Anthropologist,* 77:580–600.

Blum, R. H., and Funkhouser-Balbaky, M. L. 1967. Mind-altering drugs and dangerous behavior: Dangerous drugs. Annotations and Consultants' Papers, Task Force on Narcotics and Drug Abuse, President's Commission on Law Enforcement and Administration of Justice.

Blumer, H. 1939. Collective behavior. In Park, R. E. (ed.), *An Outline of the Principles of Sociology.* New York: Barnes and Noble.

———. 1961. Race prejudice as a sense of group position. In Masuoka, J., and Valien, P. (eds.), *Race Relations.* Chapel Hill: University of North Carolina Press.

———. 1962. Society as symbolic interaction. In Rose, A. M. (ed.), *Human Behavior and Social Processes.* Boston: Houghton Mifflin.

———. 1969. *Symbolic Interactionism: Perspective and Method.* Englewood Cliffs, N.J.: Prentice-Hall.

———. 1971. Social problems as collective behavior. *Social Problems,* 18:298–306.

Blumstein, M. 1984. How Wall Street rumors fly. *New York Times* (January 28):19.

Blumstein, P., and Schwartz, P. 1983. *American Couples.* New York: William Morrow.

Blumstein, P. W. 1975. Identity bargaining and self-conception. *Social Forces,* 53:476–485.

———, and Weinstein, E. A. 1969. The redress of distributive injustice. *American Journal of Sociology,* 74:408–418.

Bobo, L. 1983. Whites' opposition to busing: Symbolic racism or realistic group conflict? *Journal of Personality and Social Psychology,* 45:1196–1210.

Bodenhausen, G. V., and Wyer, R. S., Jr. 1985. Effects of stereotypes on decision making and information-processing strategies. *Journal of Personality and Social Psychology,* 48:267–282.

Boehm, L. 1962. The development of conscience. *Child Development,* 33:575–590.

Bollen, K. A., and Phillips, D. P. 1981. Suicidal motor vehicle fatalities in Detroit: A replication. *American Journal of Sociology,* 87:404–412.

———, and ———. 1982. Imitative suicides: A national study of the effects of television news stories. *American Sociological Review,* 47:802–809.

Bonacich, E. 1972. A theory of ethnic antagonism: The split labor market. *American Sociological Review,* 37:547–559.

———. 1973. A theory of middleman minorities. *American Sociological Review,* 38:583–594.

———. 1975. Abolition, the extension of slavery, and the position of free blacks: A study of split labor markets in the United States, 1830–1863. *American Journal of Sociology,* 81:601–628.

———. 1976. Advanced capitalism and black/white race relations in the United States: A split labor market interpretation. *American Sociological Review,* 41:34–51.

Bonacich, P. 1976. Secrecy and solidarity. *Sociometry,* 39:200–208.

Booth, A., and Cowell, J. 1976. Crowding and health. *Journal of Health and Social Behavior,* 17:204–220.

———, and Edwards, J. N. 1976. Crowding and family relations. *American Sociological Review,* 41:308–321.

Bornstein, M. H. 1976. Infants' recognition memory for hue. *Developmental Psychology,* 12:185–191.

———, Kessen, W., and Weiskopf, S. 1976. Color vision and hue categorization in young human infants. *Journal of Experimental Psychology: Human Perception and Performance,* 2:115–129.

———, and Marks, L. E. 1982. Color revisionism. *Psychology Today,* 16 (January):64–73.

Boulding, K. E. 1962. *Conflict and Defense.* New York: Harper and Row.

———. 1963. Towards a pure theory of threat

systems. *American Economic Review,* 53:424–434.

———. 1965. The economics of human conflict. In McNeil, E. B. (ed.), *The Nature of Human Conflict.* Englewood Cliffs, N.J.: Prentice-Hall.

Boutilier, R. G., Roed, J. C., and Svendsen, A. C. 1980. Crises in two social psychologies: A critical comparison. *Social Psychology Quarterly,* 43:5–17.

Bowerman, C. E., and Day, B. R. 1956. A test of complementary needs as applied to couples during courtship. *American Sociological Review,* 21:602–605.

Bowker, L. H. 1983. *Beating Wife-Beating.* Lexington, Mass.: Lexington Books.

Braddock, J. C. 1949. Effects of prior residence on dominance in the fish Platypoecilus maculatus. *Physiological Zoology,* 22:161–169.

Braddock, J. H., II, Crain, R. L., and McPartland, J. M. 1984. A long-term view of school desegregation: Some recent studies of graduates as adults. *Phi Delta Kappan,* 66:259–264.

Bradley, L. A., and Bradley, G. W. 1977. The academic achievement of black students in desegregated schools. A critical review: *Review of Educational Research,* 47:399–449.

Braine, M. D. S. 1963. The ontogeny of English phrase structure: The first phase. *Language,* 39:1–14.

Brainerd, C. J. 1978. The stage question in cognitive-developmental theory. *Behavioral and Brain Sciences,* 1:173–213.

———. 1979. Concept learning and development. In Klausmeir, H. J. (ed.), *Cognitive Development from an Information Processing and a Piagetian View: Results of a Longitudinal Study.* Cambridge, Mass.: Ballinger.

Bramel, D. 1968. Dissonance, expectation, and the self. In Abelson, R., Aronson, E., McGuire, W., Newcomb, T., Rosenberg, M., and Tannenbaum, P. (eds.), *Theories of Cognitive Consistency: A Sourcebook.* Chicago: Rand McNally.

Bray, R. M., Johnson, D., and Chilstrom, J. T., Jr. 1982. Social influence by group members with minority opinions: A comparison of Hollander and Moscovici. *Journal of Personality and Social Psychology,* 43:78–88.

———, Struckman-Johnson, C., Osborne, M. D., McFarlane, J. B., and Scott, J. 1978. The effects of defendant status on the decisions of student and community juries. *Social Psychology,* 41:256–260.

Breckler, S. J. 1984. Empirical validation of affect, behavior, and cognition as distinct components of attitude. *Journal of Personality and Social Psychology,* 47:1191–1205.

Bredemeir, H. C. 1977. Survey reviews. *Contemporary Sociology,* 6:646–650.

Brehm, J. W. 1966. *A Theory of Psychological Reactance.* New York: Academic Press.

———, and Cohen, A. R. 1962. *Explorations in Cognitive Dissonance.* New York: Wiley.

———, and Cole, A. 1966. Effect of a favor which reduces freedom. *Journal of Personality and Social Psychology,* 3:420–426.

Brehm, S. S., and Brehm, J. W. 1981. *Psychological Reactance: A Theory of Freedom and Control.* New York: Academic Press.

Brenner, A. 1985. Wednesday's child. *Psychology Today,* 19(May):46–50.

Brewer, M. B. 1979. In-group bias in the minimal intergroup situation: A cognitive-motivational analysis. *Psychological Bulletin,* 86:307–324.

———, and Kramer, R. M. 1985. The psychology of intergroup attitudes and behavior. *Annual Review of Psychology,* 36:219–243.

Brickman, P., Becker, L. J., and Castle, S. 1979. Making trust easier and harder through two forms of sequential interaction. *Journal of Personality and Social Psychology,* 37:515–521.

Brigham, J. C., Maass, A., Snyder, L. D., and Spaulding, K. 1982. Accuracy of eyewitness identifications in a field setting. *Journal of Personality and Social Psychology,* 42:673–681.

Brim, O. G., Jr. 1966. Socialization through the life cycle. In Brim, O. G., Jr., and Wheeler, S. (eds.), *Socialization After Childhood.* New York: Wiley.

Brinton, C. 1938. *The Anatomy of Revolution.* New York: Norton.

Brockner, J. 1980. The effects of self-esteem, success-failure, and self-consciousness on task performance. *Journal of Personality and Social Psychology,* 37:1732–1741.

———, Shaw, M. C., and Rubin, J. Z. 1979. Factors affecting withdrawal from an escalating conflict: Quitting before it's too late. *Journal of Experimental Social Psychology,* 15:492–503.

———, and Swap, W. C. 1976. Effects of repeated exposure and attitudinal similarity on self-disclosure and interpersonal attraction. *Journal of Personality and Social Psychology,* 33:531–540.

Brody, J. E. 1981. Effects of beauty found to run surprisingly deep. *New York Times* (September 1):15–16.

Broom, L., and Selznick, P. 1973. *Sociology.* 5th ed. New York: Harper and Row.

Brown, J. S. 1952. A comparative study of deviations from sexual mores. *American Sociological Review,* 17:134–146.

Brown, R. 1965. *Social Psychology.* New York: Free Press.

Brown, R. W. 1958. *Words and Things.* New York: Free Press.

Brownmiller, S. 1975. *Against Our Will: Men, Women and Rape.* New York: Simon and Schuster.

Brozan, N. 1985. Jurors in rape trials studied. *New York Times* (June 17):20.

Bruner, J. S., and Potter, M. C. 1964. Interferences in visual recognition. *Science,* 144:424–425.

Brunner, L. J. 1979. Smiles can be back channels. *Journal of Personality and Social Psychology,* 37:728–734.

Bryan, J., and Test, M. 1967. Models and helping: Naturalistic studies in aiding behavior. *Journal of Personality and Social Psychology,* 6:400–407.

Bugental, D. E., Kaswan, J. W., and Love, L. R. 1970. Perception of contradictory meanings conveyed by verbal and nonverbal channels. *Journal of Personality and Social Psychology,* 16:647–655.

Bullough, V. L. 1974. Transvestites in the middle ages. *American Journal of Sociology,* 79:1381–1394.

———. 1976. *Sexual Variance in Society and History.* New York: Wiley.

Burger, J. M., and Petty, R. E. 1981. The low-ball compliance technique: Task or person commitment. *Journal of Personality and Social Psychology,* 40:492–500.

Burgess, R. L., and Huston, T. L. 1979. *Social Exchange in Developing Relationships.* New York: Academic Press.

Burke, P. J. 1980. The self: Measurement requirements from an interactionist perspective. *Social Psychology Quarterly,* 43:18–29.

Burnkrant, R. E., and Howard, D. J. 1984. Effects of the use of introductory rhetorical questions versus statements on information processing. *Journal of Personality and Social Psychology,* 47:1218–1230.

Burt, M. R. 1980. Cultural myths and supports for rape. *Journal of Personality and Social Psychology,* 38:217–230.

Buss, A. 1961. *The Psychology of Aggression.* New York: Wiley.

———. 1963. Physical aggression in relation to different frustrations. *Journal of Abnormal and Social Psychology,* 67: 1–7.

———. 1966. Instrumentality of aggression, feedback, and frustration as determinants of physical aggression. *Journal of Personality and Social Psychology,* 3:153–162.

———. 1980. *Self-Consciousness and Social Anxiety.* San Francisco: W. H. Freeman.

Buss, A. H., and Briggs, S. R. 1984. Drama and the self in social interaction. *Journal of Personality and Social Psychology,* 47:1310–1324.

Bussey, K., and Bandura, A. 1984. Influence of gender constancy and social power on sex-linked modeling. *Journal of Personality and Social Psychology,* 47:1292–1302.

Butterfield, F. 1985. Former captives speak of reactions to captors. *New York Times* (July 2):5.

Button, J. W. 1978. *Black Violence.* Princeton, N.J.: Princeton University Press.

Byrne, D. 1971. *The Attraction Paradigm.* New York: Academic Press.

Cacioppo, J. T., Petty, R. E., and Morris, K. J. 1983. Effects of need for cognition on message evaluation, recall, and persuasion. *Journal of Personality and Social Psychology,* 45:805–818.

Calhoun, J. B. 1962. Population density and social pathology. *Scientific American,* 206:139–146.

Campbell, A., Converse, P. E., and Rodgers, W. L. 1976. *The Quality of American Life.* New York: Russell Sage Foundation.

Campbell, D. T. 1975. On the conflicts between biological and social evolution and between psychology and moral tradition. *American Psychologist,* 30:1103–1126.

Cann, A., Calhoun, L. G., Selby, J. W., and King, H. E. 1981. Rape: A contemporary overview and analysis. *Journal of Social Issues,* 37:1–4.

Cantor, N., and Mischel, W. 1979. Prototypes in person perception. In Berkowitz, L. (ed.), *Advances in Experimental Social Psychology,* 12:3–52.

Cantril, H. 1941. *The Psychology of Social Movements.* New York: Wiley.

Caplan, P. J., MacPherson, G. M., and Tobin, P. 1985. Do sex-related differences in spatial abilities exist? *American Psychologist,* 40:786–799.

Caporael, L. R. 1981. The paralanguage of caregiving: Baby talk to the institutionalized aged. *Journal of Personality and Social Psychology,* 40:876–884.

Carlopio, J., Adair, J. G., Lindsay, R. C. L., and Spinner, B. 1983. Avoiding artifact in the search for bias: The importance of assessing subjects' perceptions of the experiment. *Jour-*

nal of Personality and Social Psychology, 44:693–701.

Carlsmith, J. M., and Gross, A. E. 1969. Some effects on guilt on compliance. *Journal of Personality and Social Psychology,* 11:232–239.

Carlston, D. E., and Cohen, J. L. 1980. A closer examination of subject roles. *Journal of Personality and Social Psychology,* 38:857–870.

Carpenter, E. 1965. Comments. *Current Anthropology,* 6:55.

Carroll, J. B. 1964. *Language and Thought.* Englewood Cliffs, N.J.: Prentice-Hall.

Cartwright, D. 1968. The nature of group cohesiveness. In Cartwright, D., and Zander, A. (eds.), *Group Dynamics: Research and Theory.* 3rd ed. New York: Harper and Row.

———. 1971. Risk taking by individuals and groups: An assessment of research employing choice dilemmas. *Journal of Personality and Social Psychology,* 20:361–378.

———. 1973. Determinants of scientific progress: The case of research on risky shift. *American Psychologist,* 28:222–231.

Carver, C. S., DeGregorio, E. D., and Gillis, R. 1980. Field-study evidence of an ego-defensive bias in attribution among two categories of observers. *Personality and Social Psychology Bulletin,* 6:44–50.

———, and Humphries, C. 1981. Havana daydreaming: A study of self-consciousness and the negative reference group among Cuban Americans. *Journal of Personality and Social Psychology,* 40:545–552.

———, and Scheier, M. F. 1978. Self-focusing effects of dispositional self-consciousness, mirror presence, and audience presence. *Journal of Personality and Social Psychology,* 36:324–332.

———, and ———. 1981. *Attention and Self-Regulation: A Control-Theory Approach to Human Behavior.* New York: Springer-Verlag.

Cary, M. S. 1978*a.* The role of gaze in the initiation of conversation. *Social Psychology,* 41:269–271.

———. 1978*b.* Does civil inattention exist in pedestrian passing? *Journal of Personality and Social Psychology,* 36:1185–1193.

Cash, and Janda, L. H. 1984. The eye of the beholder. *Psychology Today,* 18(December):46–52.

———, Kehr, J., Polyson, J., and Freeman, V. 1977. Role of physical attractiveness in peer attribution of psychological disturbance. *Journal of Counseling Psychology,* 45:987–993.

Cassirer, E. 1944. *An Essay on Man.* New Haven, Conn.: Yale University Press.

Catania, A. C. 1979. *Learning.* Englewood Cliffs, N.J.: Prentice-Hall.

Certner, B. C. 1973. Exchange of self-disclosure in same-sexed groups of strangers. *Journal of Consulting and Clinical Psychology,* 40:292–297.

Chaiken, S. 1980. Heuristic versus systematic information processing and the use of source versus message cues in persuasion. *Journal of Personality and Social Psychology,* 39:752–766.

———, and Eagly, A. H. 1983. Communication modality as a determinant of persuasion: The role of communicator salience. *Journal of Personality and Social Psychology,* 45:241–256.

Chaikin, A. L., and Derlega, V. J. 1974. *Self-Disclosure.* Morristown, N.J.: General Learning Press.

Champagne, D. 1983. Social structure, revitalization movements and state building: Social change in four Native American societies. *American Sociological Review,* 48:754–763.

Charlesworth, W. R., and Kreutzer, M. A. 1973. Facial expressions of infants and children. In Ekman, P. (ed.), *Darwin and Facial Expression.* New York: Academic Press.

Check, J. V. P., and Malamuth, N. M. 1983. Sex role stereotyping and reactions to depictions of stranger versus acquaintance rape. *Journal of Personality and Social Psychology,* 45:344–356.

Cheek, J. M., and Buss, A. H. 1981. Shyness and sociability. *Journal of Personality and Social Psychology,* 41:330–339.

Cheng, L., and Bonacich, E. 1984. *Labor Immigration Under Capitalism: Asian Workers in the United States before World War II.* Berkeley: University of California Press.

Chertkoff, J. M., and Esser, J. K. 1977. A test of three theories of coalition formation when agreements can be short-term or long-term. *Journal of Personality and Social Psychology,* 35:237–249.

Chevalier-Skolnikoff, S. 1973. Facial expression of emotion in nonhuman primates. In Ekman, P. (ed.), *Darwin and Facial Expression.* New York: Academic Press.

Chomsky, N. 1968. *Language and Mind.* New York: Harcourt.

———.1975. *Reflections on Language.* New York: Pantheon.

Christian, J. J. 1963. The pathology of overpopulation. *Military Medicine,* 128:571–603.

Christie, R., and Geis, F. L. 1970. *Studies in Machiavellianism.* New York: Academic Press.

———, and Jahoda, M. 1954. *Studies in the*

Scope and Method of "The Authoritarian Personality." New York: Free Press.

Cialdini, R. B., and Richardson, K. D. 1980. Two indirect tactics of image management: Basking and blasting. *Journal of Personality and Social Psychology,* 39:406–415.

Cicone, M. V., and Ruble, D. N. 1978. Beliefs about males. *Journal of Social Issues,* 34:5–16.

Cicourel, A. V. 1975. Discourse and text. Cognitive and linguistic processes in studies of social structure. Paper read at the 1975 American Sociological Association meetings.

Claparede, E. 1924. Note sur la localisation du moi. *Archives de psychologie,* 19:173–182.

Clark, K. B. 1947. Racial identification and preference in Negro children. In Newcomb, T. M., and Hartley, E. L. (eds.), *Readings in Social Psychology.* New York: Holt.

_____. 1950. Emotional factors in racial identification and preference in Negro children. In Grossack, M. (ed.), *Mental Health and Segregation.* New York: Springer.

_____, and Clark, M. P. 1939. Development of consciousness of self and the emergence of racial identification in Negro preschool children. *Journal of Social Psychology,* 10:591–599.

Clark, M. S., Milberg, S., and Erber, R. 1984. Effects of arousal on judgments of others' emotions. *Journal of Personality and Social Psychology,* 46:551–560.

Clark, R. D., III, and Word, L. E. 1972. Why don't bystanders help? Because of ambiguity? *Journal of Personality and Social Psychology,* 24:392–400.

_____, and _____. 1974. Where is the apathetic bystander? Situational characteristics of the emergency. *Journal of Personality and Social Psychology,* 29:279–287.

Clifford, M. M., and Walster, E. 1973. The effect of physical attractiveness on teacher expectation. *Sociology of Education,* 46:248–258.

Cline, N. G. 1956. The influence of social context on the perception of faces. *Journal of Personality,* 25:142–158.

Clore, G. L., and Byrne, D. 1974. A reinforcement-affect model of attraction. In Huston, T. L. (ed.), *Foundations of Interpersonal Attraction.* New York: Academic Press.

Coates, D., and Winston, T. 1983. Counteracting the deviance of depression: Peer support groups for victims. *Journal of Social Issues,* 39:169–194.

Cockerham, W. C., and Cohen, L. E. 1980. Obedience to orders: Issues of morality and legality in combat among U.S. army paratroopers. *Social Forces,* 58:1272–1288.

Cohen, A. K. 1966. *Deviance and Control.* Englewood Cliffs, N.J.: Prentice-Hall.

Cohen, A. R. 1964. *Attitude Change and Social Influence.* New York: Basic Books.

Cohen, C. E. 1981. Person categories and social perception: Testing some boundaries of the processing effects of prior knowledge. *Journal of Personality and Social Psychology,* 40:441–452.

_____. 1983. Inferring the characteristics of other people: Categories and attribute accessibility. *Journal of Personality and Social Psychology,* 44:34–44.

Cohen, J. L., Sladen, B., and Bennett, B. 1975. The effects of situational variables on judgments of crowding. *Sociometry,* 38:273–281.

Cohen, R. 1972. Altruism: Human, cultural, or what? *Journal of Social Issues,* 28:39–57.

Cohen, S. 1978. Environmental load and the allocation of attention. In Baum, A., Singer, J., and Valines, S. (eds.), *Advances in Environmental Psychology.* Vol. 1. Hillsdale, N.J.: Erlbaum.

_____, and McKay, G. 1984. Social support, stress and the buffering hypothesis: A review of naturalistic studies. In Baum, A., Singer, J. E., and Taylor, S. E. (eds.), *Handbook of Psychology and Health.* Vol. 4. Hillsdale, N.J.: Erlbaum.

_____, and Wills, T. A. 1985. Stress, social support, and the buffering hypothesis. *Psychological Bulletin,* 98:310–357.

Coke, J. S., Baston, C. D., and McDavis, K. 1978. Empathic mediation of helping: A two-stage model. *Journal of Personality and Social Psychology,* 36:752–766.

Colby, A., Kohlberg, L., Gibbs, J., and Lieberman, M. 1983. A longitudinal study of moral judgment. *Monographs of the Society for Research in Child Development,* 48:200.

Coleman, J. S. 1966. *Equality of Educational Opportunity.* Washington, D.C.: Government Printing Office.

_____. 1975. Racial segregation in the schools: New research with new policy implications. *Phi Delta Kappan,* 57:75–82.

_____. 1976. Response to Professors Pettigrew and Green. *Harvard Educational Review,* 46:217–224.

_____, Kelley, S. D., and Moore, J. 1975. *Trends in School Segregation, 1968–1973.* Washington, D.C.: Urban Institute.

Coleman, M., and Ganong, L. H. 1985. Love and

sex role stereotypes: Do macho men and feminine women make better lovers? *Journal of Personality and Social Psychology,* 49:170–176.

Colligan, M. J., Pennebaker, J. W., and Murphy, L. R. 1982. *Mass Psychogenic Illness: A Social Psychological Analysis.* Hillsdale, N.J.: Erlbaum.

————, and Stockton, W. 1978. Assembly-line hysteria. *Psychology Today,* 12(June):93–99+.

Collins, B. E. 1969. The effect of monetary inducements on the amount of attitude change induced by forced compliance. In Elms, A. (ed.), *Role Playing, Reward, and Attitude Change.* Princeton, N.J.: Van Nostrand.

————, and Raven, B. H. 1969a. Group structure: Attraction, coalitions, communication, and power. In Lindzey, G., and Aronson, E. (eds.), *The Handbook of Social Psychology.* 2nd ed. Vol. 4. Reading, Mass.: Addison-Wesley.

————, and ————. 1969b. Psychological aspects of structure in the small group: Interpersonal attraction, coalitions, communication, and power. In Lindzey, G., and Aronson, E. (eds.), *The Handbook of Social Psychology.* 2nd ed. Vol. 4. Reading, Mass.: Addison-Wesley.

Collins, G. 1982a. Flirting: Elusive behavior. *New York Times* (February 8):24.

————. 1982b. The stress in doctors' families. *New York Times* (March 8):20.

————. 1985. A new look at intermarriage in the U.S. *New York Times* (February 11):17.

Collins, R. 1975. *Conflict Sociology.* New York: Academic Press.

Cook, K. S., and Emerson, R. M. 1978. Power, equity, and commitment in exchange networks. *American Sociological Review,* 43:721–739.

Cook, S. W. 1972. Motives in a conceptual analysis of attitude-related behavior. In Brigham, J., and Weissbach, T. (eds.), *Racial Attitudes in America: Analyses and Findings of Social Psychology.* New York: Harper and Row.

————. 1984. The 1954 Social Science Statement and school desegregation. *American Psychologist,* 39:819–832.

————. 1985. Experimenting on social issues: The case of school desegregation. *American Psychologist,* 40:452–460.

Cook, T. D., Crosby, F., and Hennigan, K. M. 1977. The construct validity of relative deprivation. In Suls, J., and Miller, R. (eds.), *Social Comparison Processes.* New York: Wiley.

————, Gruder, C. L., Hennigan, K. M., and Flay, B. R. 1979. History of the sleeper effect: Some logical pitfalls in accepting the null hypothesis. *Psychological Bulletin,* 86:662–679.

Cooke, R. A., and Rousseau, D. M. 1984. Stress and strain from family roles and work-role expectations. *Journal of Applied Psychology,* 69:252–260.

Cooley, C. H. 1902. *Human Nature and the Social Order.* New York: Scribner.

————. 1909. *Social Organization.* New York: Scribner.

Coombs, R. H. 1969. Social participation, self-concept and interpersonal valuation. *Sociometry,* 32:273–286.

Coopersmith, S. 1967. *The Antecedents of Self-Esteem.* San Francisco: W. H. Freeman.

Cordes, C. 1984. Findings debunk aggression as evolutionary inheritance. *APA Monitor* (November):17.

Coser, L. A. 1956. *The Functions of Social Conflict.* New York: Free Press.

————. 1975. Two methods in search of a substance. *American Sociological Review,* 40:691–700.

Costa, P. T., Jr., and McCrae, R. R. 1980. Still stable after all these years: Personality as a key to some issues in adulthood and old age. In Baltes, P. B., and Brim, O. G., Jr. (eds.), *Life Span Development and Behavior.* Vol. 3. New York: Academic Press.

Covington, M. V., and Omelich, C. L. 1979. Effort: The double-edged sword in school achievement. *Journal of Educational Psychology,* 71:169–182.

Cowen, E., Landes, J., and Schaet, D. E. 1959. The effects of mind frustration on the expression of prejudiced attitudes. *Journal of Abnormal and Social Psychology,* 58:33–38.

Cox, V. C., Paulus, P. B., and McCain, G. 1984. Prison crowding research. *American Psychologist,* 38:1148–1160.

Cozby, P. C. 1973. Self-disclosure: A literature review. *Psychological Bulletin,* 79:73–91.

Crain, R. L., and Mahard, R. E. 1983. The effect of research methodology on desegregation-achievement studies: A meta-analysis. *American Journal of Sociology,* 88:839–854.

Crane, M., and Markus, H. 1982. Gender identity: The benefits of a self-schema approach. *Journal of Personality and Social Psychology,* 43:1195–1197.

Crewdson, J. M. 1978. How California has become home for a plethora of cults. *New York Times* (November 30):A18.

Cronkite, R. C. 1980. Social psychological simulations: An alternative to experiments? *Social Psychology Quarterly,* 43:199–216.

Crosby, F., Bromley, S., and Saxe, L. 1980. Recent unobtrusive studies of black and white discrimination and prejudice: A literature review. *Psychological Bulletin,* 87:546–563.

Cross, K. P. 1976. *Accent on Learning.* San Francisco: Jossey-Bass.

Croyle, R. T., and Cooper, J. 1983. Dissonance arousal: Physiological evidence. *Journal of Personality and Social Psychology,* 45:782–791.

Cummings, S. 1975. An appraisal of some recent evidence dealing with the mental health of black children and adolescents, and its implications for school psychologists and guidance counselors. *Psychology in the Schools,* 12:234–238.

Cunningham, M. R. 1979. Weather, mood, and helping behavior: Quasi experiments with the sunshine Samaritan. *Journal of Personality and Social Psychology,* 37:1947–1956.

Cunningham, S. 1984*a*. Genovese: 20 years later, few heed a stranger's cries. *APA Monitor* (May):30.

———. 1984*b*. The new terrorism: Devotion or deviancy? *APA Monitor* (March):1, 14.

Curtiss, S. 1977. *Genie: A Psycholinguistic Study of a Modern Day "Wild Child."* New York: Academic Press.

Dahrendorf, R. 1959. *Class and Class Conflict in Industrial Society.* Stanford, Calif.: Stanford University Press.

Dannefer, D. 1984. Adult development and social theory: A paradigmatic reappraisal. *American Sociological Review,* 49:100–116.

Darley, J. M., and Batson, C. D. 1973. "From Jerusalem to Jericho": A study of situational and dispositional variables in helping behavior. *Journal of Personality and Social Psychology,* 27:100–108.

———, and Berscheid, E. 1967. Increasing liking as a result of anticipation of personal contact. *Human Relations,* 20:29–40.

———, and Fazio, R. H. 1980. Expectancy confirmation processes arising in the social interaction sequence. *American Psychologist,* 35:867–881.

———, and Gilbert, D. T. 1985. Social psychological aspects of environmental psychology. In Lindzey, G., and Aronson, E. (eds.), *Handbook of Social Psychology.* 3rd ed. Vol. 2. New York: Random House.

———, and Gross, P. H. 1983. A hypothesis-confirming bias in labeling effects. *Journal of Personality and Social Psychology,* 44:20–33.

———, and Latané, B. 1968. Bystander intervention in emergencies: Diffusion of responsibility. *Journal of Personality and Social Psychology,* 8:377–383.

Darwin, C. 1872. *The Expression of the Emotions in Man and Animals.* London: Murray.

Dasen, P. R. (ed.). 1977. *Piagetian Psychology: Cross-Cultural Contributions.* New York: Gardner Press.

Davidson, A. R., and Morrison, D. M. 1983. Predicting contraceptive behavior from attitudes: A comparison of within- versus across-subject procedures. *Journal of Personality and Social Psychology,* 45:997–1009.

Davidson, B. 1975. King of the iron merchants. *New York Times Magazine,* March 2, 1975.

———, Balswick, J., and Halverson, C. 1983. Affective self-disclosure and marital adjustment: A test of equity theory. *Journal of Marriage and Family,* 45:93–102.

Davies, J. C. 1962. Toward a theory of revolution. *American Sociological Review,* 27:5–19.

———. 1969. The J-curve of rising and declining satisfactions as a cause of some great revolutions and a contained revolution. In Graham, H. D., and Gurr, T. R. (eds.), *The History of Violence in America.* New York: Bantam.

———. 1974. The J-curve and power struggle theories of collective violence. *American Sociological Review,* 39:607–610.

Davis, D. E. 1958. The role of density in aggressive behavior of house mice. *Animal Behaviour,* 6:207–210.

———. 1959. Territorial rank in starlings. *Animal Behaviour,* 7:214–221.

Davis, F. 1970. The way we speak "body language." *New York Times Magazine,* May 31, 1970.

Davis, J. H., Tindale, R. S., Nagao, D. H., Hinsz, V. B., and Robertson, B. 1984. Order effects in multiple decisions by groups: A demonstration with mock juries and trial procedures. *Journal of Personality and Social Psychology,* 47:1003–1012.

Davis, K. 1949. *Human Society.* New York: Macmillan.

———. 1971. The world's population crisis. In Merton, R. K., and Nisbet, R. A. (eds.), *Contemporary Social Problems.* 3rd ed. New York: Harcourt.

Davis, K. E. 1985. Near and dear: Friendship and love compared. *Psychology Today,* 19 (February):22–30.

Davis, M., and Levine, S. 1967. Toward a sociology of public transit. *Social Problems,* 15:84–91.

Davison, W. P. 1983. The third-person effect in communication. *Public Opinion Quarterly,* 47:1–15.

Dawes, R. M., McTavish, J., and Shaklee, H. 1977. Behavior, communication, and assumptions about other people's behavior in a common dilemma situation. *Journal of Personality and Social Psychology,* 35:1–11.

Dean, L. M., Pugh, W. M., and Gunderson, E. K. E. 1975. Spatial and perceptual components of crowding: Effects on health and satisfaction. *Environment and Behavior,* 7:225–236.

Deaux, K. 1977. Sex differences. In Blass, T. (ed.), *Personality Variables in Social Behavior.* Hillsdale, N.J.: Erlbaum.

——— . 1985. Sex and gender. *Annual Review of Psychology,* 36:49–81.

——— , and Lewis, L. L. 1984. Structure of gender stereotypes: Interrelationships among components and gender labels. *Journal of Personality and Social Psychology,* 46:991–1004.

De Charms, R. 1968. *Personal Causation.* New York: Academic Press.

——— , and Wilkins, E. J. 1963. Some effects of verbal expression of hostility. *Journal of Abnormal and Social Psychology,* 66:462–470.

Deci, E. L. 1975. *Intrinsic Motivation.* New York: Plenum Press.

——— . 1980. *The Psychology of Self-Determination.* Lexington, Mass.: D. C. Heath.

DeJong, W. 1979. An examination of self-perception mediation of the foot-in-the-door effect. *Journal of Personality and Social Psychology,* 37:2221–2239.

de la Garza, R. O. 1973. *Chicanos and Native Americans.* Englewood Cliffs, N.J.: Prentice-Hall.

Della-Fave, L. R. 1980. The meek shall not inherit the earth: Self-evaluation and the legitimacy of stratification. *American Sociological Review,* 45:955–971.

Denzin, N. K. 1970. Symbolic interactionism and ethnomethodology. In Douglas, J. D. (ed.), *Understanding Everyday Life.* Chicago: Aldine.

DePaulo, B. M., Brittingham, G. L., and Kaiser, M. K. 1983. Receiving competence-relevant help: Effects on reciprocity, affect, and sensitivity to the helper's nonverbally expressed needs. *Journal of Personality and Social Psychology,* 45:1045–1060.

——— , Lanier, K., and Davis, T. 1983. Detecting the deceit of the motivated liar. *Journal of Personality and Social Psychology,* 45:1096–1103.

——— , Rosenthal, R., Eisenstat, R. A., Rogers, P. L., and Finkelstein, S. 1978. Decoding discrepant nonverbal cues. *Journal of Personality and Social Psychology,* 36:313–323.

——— , Green, C. R., and Rosenkrantz, J. 1982. Diagnosing deceptive and mixed messages from verbal and nonverbal cues. *Journal of Experimental Social Psychology,* 18:433–446.

Derlega, V. J., and Chaikin, A. L. 1977. Privacy and self-disclosure in social relationships. *Journal of Social Issues,* 33:102–115.

Dermer, M., and Thiel, D. L. 1975. When beauty may fail. *Journal of Personality and Social Psychology,* 31:1168–1176.

Desor, J. A. 1972. Toward a psychological theory of crowding. *Journal of Personality and Social Psychology,* 21:79–83.

Deutsch, M. 1968. Field theory in social psychology. In Lindzey, G., and Aronson, E. (eds.), *The Handbook of Social Psychology.* 2nd ed. Vol. 1. Reading, Mass.: Addison-Wesley.

——— . 1969. Conflicts: Productive and destructive. *Journal of Social Issues,* 25:7–41.

——— , and Collins, M. E. 1951. *Interracial Housing.* Minneapolis: University of Minnesota Press.

——— , and Krauss, R. M. 1965. *Theories in Social Psychology.* New York: Basic Books.

Devine, P. G., and Ostrom, T. M. 1985. Cognitive mediation of inconsistency discounting. *Journal of Personality and Social Psychology,* 49:5–21.

DeVito, J. A. 1970. *The Psychology of Speech and Language.* New York: Random House.

Diener, C. I., and Dweck, C. S. 1978. An analysis of learned helplessness: Continuous changes in performance, strategy, and achievement cognitions following failure. *Journal of Personality and Social Psychology,* 36:451–462.

——— , and ——— . 1980. An analysis of learned helplessness: II. The processing of success. *Journal of Personality and Social Psychology,* 39:940–952.

Diener, E. 1976. Effects of prior destructive behavior, anonymity, and group presence on deindividuation and aggression. *Journal of Personality and Social Psychology,* 33:497–507.

——— . 1979. Deindividuation, self-awareness, and disinhibition. *Journal of Personality and Social Psychology,* 37:1160–1171.

——— , Fraser, S. C., Beaman, A. L., and Kelem, R. T. 1976. Effects of deindividuation variables on stealing among Halloween trick-or-treaters. *Journal of Personality and Social Psychology,* 33:178–183.

Dion, K. 1972. Physical attractiveness and evaluations of children's transgressions. *Journal of Personality and Social Psychology,* 24:207–213.

———. 1973. Cohesiveness as a determinant of ingroup-outgroup bias. *Journal of Personality and Social Psychology,* 28:163–171.

———, and Berscheid, E. 1974. Physical attractiveness and peer perception in children. *Sociometry,* 37:1–12.

———, ———, and Walster, E. 1972. What is beautiful is good. *Journal of Personality and Social Psychology,* 24:285–290.

Dipboye, R. L. 1977. Alternative approaches to deindividuation. *Psychological Bulletin,* 84:1057–1075.

Dittmann, A. T., and Llewellyn, L. G. 1969. Body movement and speech rhythm in social conversation. *Journal of Personality and Social Psychology,* 11:98–106.

Dollard, J. 1937. *Caste and Class in a Southern Town.* New Haven: Yale University Press.

———, Miller, N., Doob, L., Mowrer, O. H., and Sears, R. R. 1939. *Frustration and Aggression.* New Haven: Yale University Press.

Donnerstein, E. 1980. Aggressive erotica and violence against women. *Journal of Personality and Social Psychology,* 39:269–277.

———, and Berkowitz, L. 1981. Victim reactions in aggressive erotic films as a factor in violence against women. *Journal of Personality and Social Psychology,* 41:710–724.

———, Donnerstein, M., Simon, S., and Ditrichs, R. 1972. Variables in interracial aggression: Anonymity, expected retaliation, and a riot. *Journal of Personality and Social Psychology,* 22:236–245.

———, ———, and Evans, R. 1975. Erotic stimuli and aggression: Facilitation or inhibition. *Journal of Personality and Social Psychology,* 32:237–244.

———, and Hallam, J. 1978. Facilitating effects of erotica on aggression against women. *Journal of Personality and Social Psychology,* 36:1270–1277.

———, and Linz, D. 1984. Sexual violence in the media: A warning. *Psychology Today,* 18:14–15.

———, and Wilson, D. W. 1976. Effects of noise and perceived control on ongoing and subsequent aggressive behavior. *Journal of Personality and Social Psychology,* 34:774–781.

Dovidio, J. F., and Ellyson, S. L. 1982. Decoding visual dominance: Attributions of power based on relative percentages of looking while speaking and looking while listening. *Social Psychology Quarterly,* 45:106–113.

Dowd, M. 1984. 20 years after Kitty Genovese's murder, experts study bad Samaritanism. *New York Times* (March 12):15.

Downton, J. V., Jr. 1979. *Sacred Journeys.* New York: Columbia University Press.

Dremen, D. 1979. *Contrarian Investment Strategy: The Psychology of Stock Market Success.* New York: Random House.

Drury, D. W. 1980. Black self-esteem and desegregated schools. *Sociology of Education,* 53:88–103.

Dubrow, M. 1984. Escorts become attackers in date rape. *USA Today* (April 4):3D.

Dullea, G. 1981. Shyness: Common affliction. *New York Times* (March 2):18.

———. 1982. On the pressures and politics of waiting in line. *New York Times* (February 11):17.

———. 1984. Homosexual couples find a quiet pride. *New York Times* (December 10):21.

Duncan, S., Jr. 1972. Some signals and rules for taking speaking turns in conversations. *Journal of Personality and Social Psychology,* 23:283–292.

Durkheim, E. 1954. *The Elementary Forms of the Religious Life.* Translated by J. W. Swain. New York: Free Press.

Dutton, D. G., and Aron, A. P. 1974. Some evidence for heightened sexual attraction under conditions of high anxiety. *Journal of Personality and Social Psychology,* 30:510–517.

Duval, S., and Wicklund, R. A. 1972. *A Theory of Objective Self-Awareness.* New York: Academic Press.

———, and ———. 1973. Effects of objective self awareness on the attribution of causality. *Journal of Experimental Social Psychology,* 9:17–31.

Dweck, C. S. 1975. The role of expectations and attributions in the alleviation of learned helplessness. *Journal of Personality and Social Psychology,* 31:674–685.

Dyson-Hudson, R., and Smith, E. A. 1978. Human territoriality: An ecological reassessment. *American Anthropologist,* 80:21–41.

Eagly, A. H., and Steffen, V. J. 1984. Gender stereotypes stem from the distribution of women and men into social roles. *Journal of Personality and Social Psychology,* 46:735–754.

Ebbesen, E. B., Kjos, G. L., and Konečni, V. J. 1976. Spatial ecology: Its effects on the choice of friends and enemies. *Journal of Experimental Social Psychology,* 12:505–518.

Eckholm, E. 1985a. Kanzi the chimp: A life in science. *New York Times* (June 25):19, 20.

———. 1985b. Pygmy chimp readily learns language skills. *New York Times* (June 24):1, 14.

Edelman, M. 1967. *The Symbolic Uses of Politics.* Urbana: University of Illinois Press.

———. 1975. Language, myths, and rhetoric. *Society,* 12:14–21.

Edinger, J. A., and Patterson, M. L. 1983. Nonverbal involvement and social control. *Psychological Bulletin,* 93:30–56.

Edney, J. J. 1975. Territoriality and control: A field experiment. *Journal of Personality and Social Psychology,* 31:1108–1115.

Edwards, J. N., Booth, A., and Edwards, P. K. 1982. Housing type, stress, and family relations. *Social Forces,* 61:241–257.

Efran, M. G. 1974. The effect of physical appearance on the judgment of guilt, interpersonal attraction, and severity of recommended punishment in a simulated jury task. *Journal of Research in Personality,* 8:45–54.

Ehrhardt, A. A., and Meyer-Bahlburg, H. F. L. 1981. Effects of prenatal sex hormones on gender-related behavior. *Science,* 211:1312–1318.

Eisenberg, L. 1972. The *human* nature of human nature. *Science,* 176:123–128.

Ekman, P. 1972. Universals in cultural differences in facial expressions of emotion. In Cole, J. K. (ed.), *Nebraska Symposium on Motivation.* Vol. 19. Lincoln: University of Nebraska Press.

———. 1980. *The Face of Man: Expressions of Universal Emotions in a New Guinea Village.* New York: Garland STPM Press.

———. 1985. *Telling Lies.* New York: Norton.

———, and Friesen, W. V. 1969. Nonverbal leakage and clues to deception. *Psychiatry,* 32:88–106.

———, and ———. 1974. Detecting deception from the body or face. *Journal of Personality and Social Psychology,* 29:288–298.

———, ———, and Bear, J. 1984. The international language of gestures. *Psychology Today,* 18:64–69.

Elias, M. 1984. Kids' gender doesn't rule behavior. *USA Today* (April 23):1D.

Elkind, D. 1968. Giant in the nursery—Jean Piaget. *New York Times Magazine* (May 26).

Elliott, G. C., and Meeker, B. F. 1984. Modifiers of the equity effect: Group outcome and causes for individual performance. *Journal of Personality and Social Psychology,* 46:586–597.

———, Rosenberg, M., and Wagner, M. 1984. Transient depersonalization in youth. *Social Psychology Quarterly,* 47:115–129.

Ellis, R. J., and Holmes, J. G. 1982. Focus of attention and self-evaluation in social interaction. *Journal of Personality and Social Psychology,* 43:67–77.

Ellyson, S. L., Dovidio, J. F., Corson, R. L., and Vinicur, D. L. 1980. Visual dominance behavior in female dyads: Situational and personality factors. *Social Psychology Quarterly,* 43:328–336.

Emerson, J. P. 1970. Nothing unusual is happening. In Shibutani, T. (ed.), *Human Nature and Collective Behavior.* Englewood Cliffs, N.J.: Prentice-Hall.

Emerson, R. M. 1962. Power-dependence relations. *American Sociological Review,* 27:31–41.

———. 1964. Power-dependence relations: Two experiments. *Sociometry,* 27:282–298.

———. 1969. Operant psychology and exchange theory. In Burgess, R., and Bushell, D. (eds.), *Behavioral Sociology.* New York: Columbia University Press.

Epstein, S., and Taylor, S. P. 1967. Instigation to aggression as a function of degree of defeat and perceived aggressive intent of the opponent. *Journal of Personality,* 35:264–289.

Epstein, Y. M., Krupat, E., and Obudho, C. 1976. Clean is beautiful: Identification and preference as a function of race and cleanliness. *Journal of Social Issues,* 32:109–118.

Erber, R., and Fiske, S. T. 1984. Outcome dependency and attention to inconsistent information. *Journal of Personality and Social Psychology,* 47:709–726.

Erickson, F. 1975. Gatekeeping and the melting pot. *Harvard Educational Review,* 45:44–70.

Erikson, E. H. 1950. *Childhood and Society.* New York: Norton.

———. 1959. Identity and the life cycle. *Psychological Issues,* 1:1–71.

Erikson, K. T. 1970. The sociology of deviance. In Stone, G. P., and Farberman, H. A. (eds.), *Social Psychology Through Symbolic Interaction.* Waltham, Mass.: Xerox.

Erskine, H. 1972. The polls: Pollution and its costs. *Public Opinion Quarterly,* 36:120–135.

———. 1973. The polls: Hopes, fears, and regrets. *Public Opinion Quarterly,* 37:132–145.

Etzioni, A. 1968. *The Active Society.* New York: Free Press.

Evans, G. W. 1978. Crowding and the developmental process. In Baum, A., and Epstein, Y. M. (eds.), *Human Responses to Crowding.* Hillsdale, N.J.: Erlbaum.

Fader, S. S. 1984. Finding "hidden jobs." *Working Women* (June):42–45.

Fanon, F. 1966. *The Wretched of the Earth.* New York: Grove Press.

———. 1967. *Black Skin; White Masks.* Translated by C. L. Markmann. New York: Grove Press.

Farley, R., Schuman, H., Bianchi, S., Colasanto, D., and Hatchett, S. 1978. Chocolate city, vanilla suburbs. *Social Science Research,* 7:319–344.

———, Wurdock, C., and Richards, T. 1980. School desegregation and white flight: An investigation of competing models and their discrepant findings. *Sociology of Education,* 53:123–139.

Fast, J. 1970. *Body Language.* New York: M. Evans.

———. 1978. Excuse me, but your eyes are talking. *Family Health,* 10 (September):22–25.

Fasteau, M. F. 1974. *The Male Machine.* New York: McGraw-Hill.

Faulkner, S. 1973. War crimes: Responsibilities of individual servicemen and of superior officers. *Guild Practitioner,* 31:131–144.

Faunce, W. A. 1984. School achievement, social status, and self-esteem. *Social Psychology Quarterly,* 47:3–14.

Fazio, R. H., Effrein, E. A., and Falender, V. J. 1981. Self-perceptions following social interaction. *Journal of Personality and Social Psychology,* 41:232–242.

———, and Zanna, M. P. 1978. Attitudinal qualities relating to the strength of the attitude-behavior relationship. *Journal of Experimental Social Psychology,* 14:398–408.

———, ———, and Cooper, J. 1977. Dissonance and self-perception: An integrative view of each theory's proper domain of application. *Journal of Experimental Social Psychology,* 13:464–479.

———, ———, and ———. 1979. On the relationship of data to theory: A reply to Ronis and Greenwald. *Journal of Experimental Social Psychology,* 15:70–76.

Featherman, D. L., and Hauser, R. M. 1976. Sexual inequalities and socioeconomic achievement in the U.S., 1962–1973. *American Sociological Review,* 41:462–483.

Feinbloom, D. H. 1977. *Transvestites and Transsexuals: Mixed Views.* New York: Delta Books.

Feld, S. L. 1981. The focused organization of social ties. *American Journal of Sociology,* 86:1015–1035.

———. 1984. The structured use of personal associates. *Social Forces,* 62:640–652.

Felson, R. B. 1980. Communication barriers and the reflected appraisal process. *Social Psychology Quarterly,* 43:223–233.

———. 1981. Social sources of information in the development of self. *Sociological Quarterly,* 22:69–80.

———. 1985. Reflected appraisal and the development of self. *Social Psychology Quarterly,* 48:71–78.

Fendrich, J. M. 1967. Perceived reference group support: Racial attitudes and overt behavior. *American Sociological Review,* 32:960–970.

Fenigstein, A. 1984. Self-consciousness and the overperception of self as a target. *Journal of Personality and Social Psychology,* 47:860–870.

Feshbach, S. 1955. The drive-reducing function of fantasy behavior. *Journal of Abnormal and Social Psychology,* 59:3–11.

———. 1971. Dynamics and morality of violence and aggression: Some psychological considerations. *American Psychologist,* 26:281–292.

———, and Malamuth, N. 1978. Sex and aggression: Proving the link. *Psychology Today,* 12 (November):111–117+.

———, and Singer, R. 1957. The effects of personal and shared threats upon social prejudice. *Journal of Abnormal and Social Psychology,* 54:411–416.

Festinger, L. 1954. A theory of social comparison processes. *Human Relations,* 7:117–140.

———. 1957. *A Theory of Cognitive Dissonance.* New York: Harper and Row.

———. 1961. The psychological effects of insufficient reward. *American Psychologist,* 16:1–11.

———, and Carlsmith, J. M. 1959. Cognitive consequences of forced compliance. *Journal of Abnormal and Social Psychology,* 58:203–210.

———, Riecken, H. W., Jr., and Schachter, S. 1956. *When Prophecy Fails.* Minneapolis: University of Minnesota Press.

———, Schachter, S., and Back, K. 1950. *Social Pressures in Informal Groups.* New York: Harper and Row.

Fields, J. M., and Schuman, H. 1976. Public beliefs about the beliefs of the public. *Public Opinion Quarterly,* 40:427–448.

Findlay, S. 1984. Mate abuse hits sexes equally hard. *USA Today* (November 2):1D.

Fine, G. A. 1979. Small groups and culture creation: The idioculture of Little League Baseball teams. *American Sociological Review,* 44:733–745.

Fischer, C. S. 1975. The myth of "territoriality"

in van den Berghe's "Bringing beasts back in." *American Sociological Review,* 40:674–676.

———, Baldassare, M., and Ofshe, R. J. 1974. *Crowding Studies and Urban Life: A Critical Review.* Working paper No. 242. Institute of Urban and Regional Development, Berkeley, California.

———, Jackson, R. M., Stueve, C. A., Gerson, K., and Jones, L. M. 1977. *Networks and Places: Social Relations in the Urban Setting.* New York: Free Press.

Fisher, A. B. 1985. Coke's brand-loyalty lesson. *Fortune* (August 5):44–46.

Fisher, J. D., and Byrne, D. 1975. Too close for comfort: Sex differences in response to invasion of personal space. *Journal of Personality and Social Psychology,* 32:15–21.

Fishman, P. M. 1978. Interaction: The work women do. *Social Problems,* 25:397–406.

Flaherty, J. F., and Dusek, J. B. 1980. An investigation of the relationship between psychological androgyny and components of self-concept. *Journal of Personality and Social Psychology,* 38:984–992.

Flavell, J. H. 1977. *Cognitive Development.* Englewood Cliffs, N.J.: Prentice-Hall.

———. 1978. Developmental stage: Explanans or explanandum? *Behavioral and Brain Sciences,* 1:187.

———. 1982. On cognitive development. *Child Development,* 53:1–10.

Fodor, E. M., and Farrow, D. L. 1979. The power motive as an influence on use of power. *Journal of Personality and Social Psychology,* 37:2091–2097.

———, and Smith, T. 1982. The power motive as an influence on group decision making. *Journal of Personality and Social Psychology,* 42:178–185.

Foley, L. A. 1976. Personality and situational influences on changes in prejudice: A replication of Cook's railroad game in a prison setting. *Journal of Personality and Social Psychology,* 34:846–856.

Folger, R., Rosenfield, D., and Robinson, T. 1983. Relative deprivation and procedural justifications. *Journal of Personality and Social Psychology,* 45:268–273.

Fontaine, G. 1974. Social comparison and some determinants of expected personal control and expected performance in a novel task situation. *Journal of Personality and Social Psychology,* 29:487–496.

Ford, C. S., and Beach, F. 1951. *Patterns of Sexual Behavior.* New York: Ace Books.

Ford, D. A. 1983. Wife battery and criminal justice: A study of victim decision-making. *Family Relations,* 32:463–475.

Forgas, J. P. Bower, G. H., and Krantz, S. E. 1984. The influence of mood on perceptions of social interactions. *Journal of Experimental Social Psychology,* 20:497–513.

Forsyth, D. R. 1980. The functions of attributions. *Social Psychology Quarterly,* 43:184–189.

———, and McMillan, J. H. 1981. Attributions, affects, and expectations. *Journal of Educational Psychology,* 73:393–403.

Forward, J., Canter, R., and Kirsch, N. 1976. Role-enactment and deception methodologies. *American Psychologist,* 31:595–604.

Foss, R. D. 1981. Structural effects in simulated jury decision-making. *Journal of Personality and Social Psychology,* 40:1055–1062.

———, and Dempsey, C. B. 1979. Blood donation and the foot-in-the-door technique: A limited case. *Journal of Personality and Social Psychology,* 37:580–590.

Fraker, S. 1984. Why women aren't getting to the top. *Fortune* (April 16):40–45.

Francese, P. 1984. Income gap may affect way women cast votes. *Columbus Dispatch* (October 10):F-1.

Frank, S. J., McLaughlin, A. M., and Crusco, A. 1984. Sex role attributes, symptom distress, and defensive style among college men and women. *Journal of Personality and Social Psychology,* 47:182–192.

Franklin, B. 1969. Operant reinforcement of prayer. *Journal of Applied Behavior Analysis,* 2:247. Submitted by B. F. Skinner.

Franklin, J. H. 1952. *From Slavery to Freedom.* New York: Knopf.

Franks, D. R., and Marolla, J. 1976. Efficacious action and social approval as interacting dimensions of self-esteem: A tentative formulation through construct validation. *Sociometry,* 39:324–341.

Franks, L. 1984. When facing the rapist: Is resistance a strategy? *New York Times* (December 27):13, 15.

Freedman, J. L. 1975. *Crowding and Behavior: The Psychology of High-Density Living.* New York: Viking.

———. 1979. Reconciling apparent differences between the responses of humans and other animals to crowding. *Psychological Review,* 86:80–85.

———, and Fraser, S. C. 1966. Compliance without pressure: The foot-in-the-door technique. *Journal of Personality and Social Psychology,* 4:195–202.

_____, Klevansky, S., and Ehrlich, P. R. 1971. The effect of crowding on human task performance. *Journal of Applied Social Psychology,* 1:7–25.

_____, and Perlick, D. 1979. Crowding, contagion, and laughter. *Journal of Experimental Social Psychology,* 15:295–303.

_____, Wallington, S. A., and Bless, E. 1967. Compliance without pressure: The effect of guilt. *Journal of Personality and Social Psychology,* 7:117–124.

Freedman, N., Blass, T., Rifkin, A., and Quitkin, F. 1973. Body movements and the verbal encoding of aggressive affect. *Journal of Personality and Social Psychology,* 26:72–85.

French, J. R. P. 1944. *Organized and Unorganized Groups Under Fear and Frustration.* Iowa City: University of Iowa Press.

_____, and Raven, B. H. 1959. The bases of social power. In Cartwright, D. (ed.), *Studies in Social Power.* Ann Arbor: University of Michigan Press.

Frey, W. H. 1979. Central city white flight: Racial and nonracial causes. *American Sociological Review,* 44:425–448.

_____. 1980. Black in-migration, white flight, and the changing economic base of the central city. *American Journal of Sociology,* 85:1395–1417.

Friedan, B. 1963. *The Feminine Mystique.* New York: Norton.

Friedkin, N. E. 1978. University social structure and social networks among scientists. *American Journal of Sociology,* 83:1444–1465.

Friedman, S. 1969. How is racism maintained? *Et Al.,* 2:19.

Friedson, E. 1960. Client control and medical practice. *American Journal of Sociology,* 65:374–382.

Fulcher, J. S. 1942. "Voluntary" facial expression in blind and seeing children. *Archives of Psychology,* 38:272.

Funck-Brentano, F. 1939. *Luther.* London: Jonathan Cape.

Fyans, L. J., Jr., and Maehr, M. L. 1979. Attributional style, task selection, and achievement. *Journal of Educational Psychology,* 781:499–507.

Gagnon, J. 1975. *Human Sexuality.* Boston: Little, Brown.

_____, and Simon, W. 1973. *Sexual Conduct.* Chicago: Aldine.

Galanter, M. 1983. Unification Church ("Moonie") dropouts: Psychological readjustment after leaving a charismatic religious group. *American Journal of Psychiatry,* 140:984–989.

_____, Rabkin, R., Rabkin, J., and Deutsch, A. 1979. The "Moonies": A psychological study of conversion and membership in a contemporary religious sect. *American Journal of Psychiatry,* 136:165–170.

Galbraith, J. K. 1958. *The Affluent Society.* Boston: Houghton Mifflin.

Galloway, J. L. 1984. How your privacy is being stripped away. *U.S. News & World Report* (April 30):46–48.

Gamson, W. A. 1961. A theory of coalition formation. *American Sociological Review,* 26:373–382.

_____. 1964. Experimental studies of coalition formation. In Berkowitz, L. (ed.), *Advances in Experimental Social Psychology.* Vol. 1. New York: Academic Press.

_____. 1968. *Power and Discontent.* Homewood, Ill.: Dorsey.

_____. 1974. Power and probability. In Tedeschi, J. T. (ed.), *Perspectives on Social Power.* Chicago: Aldine.

_____. 1975. *The Strategy of Social Protest.* Homewood, Ill.: Dorsey.

Garber, J., and Seligman, M. E. P. 1980. *Human Helplessness: Theory and Applications.* New York: Academic Press.

Gardner, B. T., and Gardner, R. A. 1971. Two-way communication and an infant chimpanzee. In Schrier, A., and Stollnitz, F. (eds.), *Behavior of Non-Human Primates.* Vol. 4. New York: Academic Press.

Garfield, R. 1985. Researchers put us under microscope. *USA Today* (January 8):B-1.

Garfinkel, H. 1964. Studies of the routine grounds of everyday activities. *Social Problems,* 11:225–250.

_____. 1967. *Studies in Ethnomethodology.* Englewood Cliffs, N.J.: Prentice-Hall.

_____. 1974. The origins of the term "ethnomethodology." In Turner, R. (ed.), *Ethnomethodology.* Middlesex, England: Penguin Books.

Gecas, V. 1982. The self concept. In Turner, R. H., and Short, J. F. (eds.), *Annual Review of Sociology,* 8:1–33.

_____, and Schwalbe, M. L. 1983. Beyond the looking-glass self: Social structure and efficacy-based self-esteem. *Social Psychology Quarterly,* 46:77–88.

Geen, R. G. 1968. Effects of frustration, attack, and prior training in aggressiveness upon aggressive behavior. *Journal of Personality and Social Psychology,* 9:316–321.

_____, and Berkowitz, L. 1967. Some conditions

facilitating the occurrence of aggression after the observation of violence. *Journal of Personality,* 35:666–676.

———, Stonner, D., and Shope, G. L. 1975. The facilitation of aggression by aggression: Evidence against the catharsis hypothesis. *Journal of Personality and Social Psychology,* 31:721–726.

Geertz, C. 1963. The integrative revolution. In Geertz, C. (ed.), *Old Societies and New States.* New York: Free Press.

Geis, F. L., and Moon, T. H. 1981. Machiavellianism and deception. *Journal of Personality and Social Psychology,* 41:766–775.

Geiselman, R. E., Haight, N. A., and Kimata, L. G. 1984. Context effects on the perceived physical attractiveness of faces. *Journal of Experimental Social Psychology,* 20:409–424.

Geller, D. M. 1978. Involvement in role-playing simulations: A demonstration with studies on obedience. *Journal of Personality and Social Psychology,* 36:219–235.

Gelles, R. J. 1980. Violence in the family: A review of research in the seventies. *Journal of Marriage and the Family,* 42:873–885.

———. 1983. Violence in the family. In Olson, D. H., and Miller, B. C. (eds.), *Family Studies Review Yearbook.* Vol. 1. Beverly Hills, Calif.: Sage.

Genovese, E. D. 1974. *Roll, Jordan, Roll: The World the Slaves Made.* New York: Pantheon.

Gentry, W. D. 1970. Effects of frustration, attack, and prior aggressive training on overt aggression and vascular processes. *Journal of Personality and Social Psychology,* 16:718–725.

Gerard, H. B. 1983. School desegregation. *American Psychologist,* 38:869–877.

———, and Hoyt, M. F. 1974. Distinctiveness of social categorization and attitude toward ingroup members. *Journal of Personality and Social Psychology,* 29:836–842.

———, and Miller, N. 1975. *School Desegregation.* New York: Plenum Press.

———, Wilhelmy, R. A., and Conolley, E. S. 1968. Conformity and group size. *Journal of Personality and Social Psychology,* 8:79–82.

Gerbasi, K. C., Zuckerman, M., and Reis, H. T. 1977. Justice needs a new blindfold: A review of mock jury research. *Psychological Bulletin,* 84:323–345.

Gergen, K. J. 1965. Interaction goals and personalistic feedback as factors affecting the presentation of self. *Journal of Personality and Social Psychology,* 1:413–424.

———. 1971. *The Concept of Self.* New York: Holt, Rinehart and Winston.

———. 1972. Multiple identity. *Psychology Today,* 5(May):31–35, 64–66.

———, Ellsworth, P., Maslach, C., and Seipel, M. 1975. Obligation, donor resources, and reactions to aid in three cultures. *Journal of Personality and Social Psychology,* 31:390–400.

———, and Gergen, M. 1971. International assistance in psychological perspective. *Yearbook of World Affairs,* 25:87–103.

———, ———, and Barton, W. H. 1973. Deviance in the dark, *Psychology Today,* 7:129–130.

———, and Wishnov, B. 1965. Others' self-evaluations and interaction anticipation as determinants of self-presentation. *Journal of Personality and Social Psychology,* 2:348–358.

Gerlach, L. P., and Hine, V. H. 1970. *People, Power, Change Movements of Social Transformation.* Indianapolis: Bobbs-Merrill.

Geschwender, J. A. 1964. Social structure and the Negro revolt: An examination of some hypotheses. *Social Forces,* 43:248–256.

Giesen, M., and McClaren, H. A. 1976. Discussion, distance and sex: Changes in impressions and attraction during small group interaction. *Sociometry,* 39:60–70.

Giles, M. W. 1978. White enrollment stability and school desegregation: A two-level analysis. *American Sociological Review,* 43:848–864.

Gilligan, C. 1982a. *In a Different Voice: Psychological Theory and Women's Development.* Cambridge, Mass.: Harvard University Press.

———. 1982b. Why should a woman be more like a man? *Psychology Today,* 16 (June):68–77.

Gitlin, T. 1971. The price men pay for supremacy. *New York Times* (December 11):31.

Givens, D. 1983. *Love Signals: How to Attract a Mate.* New York: Crown.

Glazer, N. 1984. The structure of ethnicity. *Public Opinion,* 7 (October/November):2–5.

Gluckman, M. 1955. *Custom and Conflict in Africa.* Oxford, England: Blackwell.

Goethals, G. R., Cooper, J., and Naficy, A. 1979. Role of foreseen, foreseeable, and unforeseeable behavioral consequences in the arousal of cognitive dissonance. *Journal of Personality and Social Psychology,* 37:1179–1185.

Goff, R. 1949. *Problems and Emotional Difficulties in Negro Children.* New York: Columbia University Press.

Goffman, E. 1959. *The Presentation of Self in Everyday Life.* Garden City, N.Y.: Doubleday.

———. 1961a. *Asylums: Essays on the Social Situation of Mental Patients and Other Inmates.* Chicago: Aldine.

_____ . 1961*b*. *Encounters*. Indianapolis: Bobbs-Merrill.

_____ . 1963. *Behavior in Public Places*. New York: Free Press.

_____ . 1967. *Interaction Ritual*. Garden City, N.Y.: Doubleday.

_____ . 1971. *Relations in Public*. New York: Basic Books.

_____ . 1974. *Frame Analysis: An Essay on the Organization of Experience*. Cambridge, Mass.: Harvard University Press.

_____ . 1981. *Forms of Talk*. Philadelphia: University of Pennsylvania Press.

_____ . 1983. The interaction order. *American Sociological Review*, 48:1–17.

Goldberg, L. R. 1978. Differential attribution of trait-descriptive terms to oneself as compared to well-liked, neutral, and disliked others: A psychometric analysis. *Journal of Personality and Social Psychology*, 36:1012–1028.

Goldin-Meadows, S., and Feldman, H. 1977. The development of languagelike communication without a language model. *Science*, 197:401–403.

_____ , and Mylander, C. 1983. Gestural communication in deaf children: Noneffect of parental input on language development. *Science*, 221:372–373.

Goldstone, J. A. 1980. The weakness of organization: A new look at Gamson's *The Strategy of Social Protest*. *American Journal of Sociology*, 85:1017–1042.

Goleman, D. 1984*a*. A bias puts self at center of events. *New York Times* (June 12):19.

_____ , 1984*b*. Psychologists starting to take measure of love. *New York Times* (November 20):17, 20.

_____ . 1985*a*. Great altruists: Science ponders soul of goodness. *New York Times* (March 5):19, 22.

_____ . 1985*b*. Political forces come under new scrutiny of psychology. *New York Times* (April 2):17.

_____ . 1985*c*. Researchers identify true clues to lying. *New York Times* (February 12):17, 18.

_____ . 1985*d*. "Social chameleon" may pay emotional price. *New York Times* (March 12):15, 16.

_____ . 1985*e*. Study lists ways to deter rapists. *New York Times* (May 5):15.

_____ . 1985*f*. *Vital Lies, Simple Truths: The Psychology of Self-Deception*. New York: Simon and Schuster.

Gonzales, M. H., Davis, J. M., Loney, G. L., KuKens, C. K., and Junghans, C. M. 1983. Interactional approach to interpersonal attraction. *Journal of Personality and Social Psychology*, 44:1192–1197.

Goode, E. 1969. Multiple drug use among marijuana smokers. *Social Problems*, 17:49–64.

_____ . 1975. On behalf of labeling theory. *Social Problems*, 22:570–583.

Goode, W. J. 1960. A theory of role strain. *American Sociological Review*. 25:483–496.

_____ . 1972. The place of force in human society. *American Sociological Review*, 37:507–519.

Goodman, W. 1984. Faiths rely on Bible for views on homosexuality. *New York Times* (July 14):8.

Goodstadt, B. E., and Hjelle, L. A. 1973. Power to the powerless: Locus of control and the use of power. *Journal of Personality and Social Psychology*, 27:190–196.

_____ , and Kipnis, D. 1970. Situational influences on the use of power. *Journal of Applied Psychology*, 54:201–207.

Goodstein, L. D., and Reinecker, V. M. 1974. Factors affecting self-disclosure: A review of the literature. In Maher, B. A. (ed.), *Progress in Experimental Personality Research*. Vol. 7. New York: Academic Press.

Goodstein, R. K., and Page, A. W. 1981. Battered wife syndrome: Overview of dynamics and treatment. *American Journal of Psychiatry*, 138:1036–1044.

Gordon, L. 1970. Functions of the family. In Tanner, L. B. (ed.), *Voices from Women's Liberation*. New York: New American Library.

Gottlieb, J., and Carver, C. S. 1980. Anticipation of future interaction and the bystander effect. *Journal of Experimental Social Psychology*, 16:253–260.

Gould, C. G. 1983. Out of the mouths of beasts. *Science 83*, 4:69–72.

Gould, R. L. 1972. The phases of adult life: A study in developmental psychology. *American Journal of Psychiatry*, 129:33–43.

_____ . 1978. *Transformations*. New York: Simon and Schuster.

Gouldner, A. W. 1955. Metaphysical pathos and the theory of bureaucracy. *American Political Science Review*, 49:496–507.

_____ . 1960. The norm of reciprocity: A preliminary statement. *American Sociological Review*, 25:161–178.

Gove, W. R. 1970. Societal reaction as an explanation of mental illness: An evaluation. *American Sociological Review*, 35:873–884.

_____ , and Howell, P. 1974. Individual resources and mental hospitalization: A comparison and evaluation of the societal reaction and psychiatric perspectives. *American Sociological Review,* 39:86–100.

——— , and Hughes, M. 1980. Reexamining the ecological fallacy. *Social Forces,* 58:1157–1177.

——— , and ——— . 1983. *Overcrowding in the Household: An Analysis of Determinants and Effects.* New York: Academic Press.

——— , ——— , and Galle, O. R. 1979. Overcrowding in the home: An empirical investigation of its possible pathological consequences. *American Sociological Review,* 44:59–80.

Granovetter, M. S. 1973. The strength of weak ties. *American Journal of Sociology,* 78:1360–1380.

——— . 1976. Network sampling: Some first steps. *American Journal of Sociology,* 81:1287–1303.

Greeley, A. M. 1974. *Ethnicity in the United States.* New York: Wiley.

Green, R. 1985. Gender identity in childhood and later sexual orientation: Follow-up of 78 males. *American Journal of Psychiatry,* 142:339–341.

Greenberg, J. 1978. Effects of reward value and retaliative power on allocation decisions: Justice, generosity, or greed? *Journal of Personality and Social Psychology,* 36:367–379.

——— . 1980. Attentional focus and locus of performance causality as determinants of equity behavior. *Journal of Personality and Social Psychology,* 38:579–585.

——— . 1983. Self-image versus impression management in adherence to distributive justice standards: The influence of self-awareness and self-consciousness. *Journal of Personality and Social Psychology,* 44:5–19.

——— , and Pyszczynski, T. 1985. The effect of an overheard ethnic slur on evaluations of the target: How to spread a social disease. *Journal of Experimental Social Psychology,* 21:61–72.

——— , ——— , and Paisley, C. 1985. Effect of extrinsic incentives on use of test anxiety as an anticipatory attributional defense: Playing it cool when the stakes are high. *Journal of Personality and Social Psychology,* 47:1136–1145.

Greenblatt, M., Becerra, R. M., and Serafetinides, E. A. 1982. Social networks and mental health: An overview. *American Journal of Psychiatry,* 139:977–984.

Greene, D., and Lepper, M. R. 1974. How to turn play into work. *Psychology Today,* 8 (September):49–54.

Greenwald, A. G. 1975. On the inconclusiveness of "crucial" cognitive tests of dissonance vs. self-perception theories. *Journal of Experimental Social Psychology,* 11:490–499.

——— . 1980. The totalitarian ego: Fabrication and revision of personal history. *American Psychologist,* 35:608–616.

——— . 1982. Is anyone in charge? Person-analysis versus the principle of personal unity. In Suls, J. (ed.), *Psychological Perspectives on the Self.* Hillsdale, N.J.: Erlbaum.

——— , and Pratkanis, A. R. 1984. The self. In Wyer, R. S., and Srull, T. K. (eds.), *Handbook of Social Cognition.* Hillsdale, N.J.: Erlbaum.

Greenwald, J. 1985. Coca-Cola's big fizzle. *Time* (July 22):48–52.

Greenwell, J., and Dengerink, H. A. 1973. The role of perceived versus actual attack in human physical aggression. *Journal of Personality and Social Psychology,* 26:66–71.

Greer, D. L. 1983. Spectator booing and the home advantage: A study of social influence in the basketball arena. *Social Psychological Quarterly,* 46:252–261.

Griffitt, W., and Veitch, R. 1971. Hot and crowded: Influence of population density and temperature on interpersonal affective behavior. *Journal of Personality and Social Psychology,* 17:92–98.

Grimm, J., and Stern, R. 1974. Sex roles and internal labor market structures: The female semi-professions. *Social Problems,* 21:690–705.

Gross, A. E., and Crofton, C. 1977. What is good is beautiful. *Sociometry,* 40:80–90.

Gross, E. 1968. The sexual structure of occupations over time. *Social Problems,* 16:198–208.

Gross, N., Mason, W. S., and McEachern, A. W. 1958. *Explorations in Role Analysis.* New York: Wiley.

Guimond, S., and Dubé-Simard, L. 1983. Relative deprivation theory and the Quebec Nationalist Movement: The cognition-emotion distinction and the personal-group deprivation issue. *Journal of Personality and Social Psychology,* 44:526–535.

Gurin, G., Veroff, J., and Feld, S. 1960. *Americans View Their Mental Health.* New York: Basic Books.

Gurney, J. N., and Tierney, K. J. 1982. Relative deprivation and social movements: A critical look at twenty years of theory and research. *The Sociological Quarterly,* 23:33–47.

Gurr, T. R. 1970. *Why Men Rebel.* Princeton: Princeton University Press.

Guthrie, E. R. 1935. *The Psychology of Learning.* New York: Harper and Row.

Haber, G. M. 1982. Spatial relations between dominants and marginals. *Social Psychology Quarterly,* 45:219–228.

Haga, W. J., Graen, G., and Dansereau, F., Jr. 1974. Professionalism and role making in a service organization. *American Sociological Review,* 39:122–133.

Hagan, J. 1977. Review. *American Journal of Sociology,* 83:240–242.

Haines, H. H. 1979. Cognitive claims-making, enclosure, and the depoliticization of social problems. *The Sociological Quarterly,* 20:119–130.

Hall, E. T. 1966. *The Hidden Dimension.* Garden City, N.Y.: Doubleday.

Hall, J. A. 1978. Gender effects in decoding nonverbal cues. *Psychological Bulletin,* 85:845–857.

Hall, P. M. 1972. A symbolic interactionist analysis of politics. *Sociological Inquiry,* 42:35–75.

Halloran, R. 1982. Army special forces try to rebuild image by combining brains and brawn. *New York Times* (August 21):7.

Hamblin, R., Buckholdt, D., Ferritor, D., Kozloff, M., and Blackwell, L. 1971. *The Humanization Process.* New York: Wiley.

Hamilton, D. L. 1979. A cognitive-attributional analysis of stereotyping. In Berkowitz, L. (ed.), *Advances in Experimental Social Psychology.* Vol. 12. New York: Academic Press.

———, Dugan, P. M., and Trolier, T. K. 1985. The formation of stereotypic beliefs: Further evidence for distinctiveness-based illusory correlations. *Journal of Personality and Social Psychology,* 48:5–17.

Hamilton, V. L. 1978. Obedience and responsibility: A jury simulation. *Journal of Personality and Social Psychology,* 36:126–146.

Hampson, R. B. 1984. Adolescent prosocial behavior: Peer-group and situational factors associated with helping. *Journal of Personality and Social Psychology,* 46:153–162.

Haney, C., Banks, C., and Zimbardo, P. G. 1973. Interpersonal dynamics in a simulated prison. *International Journal of Crime and Penology,* 1:69–97.

Harden, M. 1984. Is this youth or brutality? *Columbus Dispatch* (September 12):B1.

Hardin, G. 1974. *Mandatory Motherhood: The True Meaning of "Right to Life."* Boston: Beacon Press.

Hardin, G. J. 1968. The tragedy of the commons. *Science,* 162:1243–1248.

Harkins, S. G., and Petty, R. E. 1981. Effects of source magnification of cognitive effort on attitudes: An information-processing view. *Journal of Personality and Social Psychology,* 40:401–413.

———, and ———. 1982. Effects of task difficulty and task uniqueness on social loafing. *Journal of Personality and Social Psychology,* 43:1214–1229.

Harris, M. J., and Rosenthal, R. 1985. Mediation of interpersonal expectancy effects: 31 metaanalyses, *Psychological Bulletin,* 97:363–386.

Harry, J. 1982. *Gay Children Grown Up.* New York: Praeger.

———. 1984. *Gay Couples.* New York: Praeger.

Hartnett, J. J., Bailey, K. G., and Gibson, F. W. 1970. Personal space as influenced by sex and type of movement. *Journal of Psychology,* 76:139–144.

Hartshorne, H., and May, M. A. 1928. *Studies in the Nature of Character.* Vol. I: Studies in Deceit. New York: Macmillan.

———, ———, and Maller, J. B. 1929. *Studies in the Nature of Character.* Vol. II: Studies in Self-Control. New York: Macmillan, 1929.

———, ———, and Shuttleworth, F. K. 1930. *Studies in the Nature of Character.* Vol. III: Studies in the Organization of Character. New York: Macmillan.

Hass, R. G. 1984. Perspective taking and self-awareness: Drawing an E on your forehead. *Journal of Personality and Social Psychology,* 46:788–798.

Hastie, R. 1984. Causes and effects of causal attribution. *Journal of Personality and Social Psychology,* 46:44–56.

———, Penrod, S. D., and Pennington, N. 1983. *Inside the Jury.* Cambridge, Mass.: Harvard University Press.

Haug, M. R., and Lavin, B. 1981. Practitioner or patient—Who's in charge? *Journal of Health and Social Behavior,* 22:212–229.

Hawley, A. H. 1963. Power as an attribute of social system. *American Journal of Sociology,* 68:422–431.

Hawley, W. D. 1979. Getting the facts straight about the effects of school desegregation. *Educational Leadership,* 36:314–321.

Hayano, D. 1979. Poker lies and tells. *Human Behavior,* 8 (March):18–22.

Hayduk, L. A. 1978. Personal space: An evaluative and orienting overview. *Psychological Bulletin,* 85:117–134.

———, and Mainprize, S. 1980. Personal space of the blind. *Social Psychology Quarterly,* 43:216–223.

Hayes, C., and Hayes, K. 1951. *The Ape in Our House.* New York: Harper and Row.

Hays, R. B. 1985. A longitudinal study of friendship development. *Journal of Personality and Social Psychology,* 48:909–924.

Hediger, H. 1950. *Wild Animals in Captivity.* London: Butterworth.

Heider, F. 1946. Attitudes and cognitive organization. *Psychology,* 21:107–122.

———. 1958. *The Psychology of Interpersonal Relations.* New York: Wiley.

Heilbrun, A. B., Jr. 1981. Gender differences in the functional linkage between androgyny, social cognition, and competency. *Journal of Personality and Social Psychology,* 41:1106–1118.

———. 1984. Sex-based models of androgyny: A further cognitive elaboration of competence differences. *Journal of Personality and Social Psychology,* 46:216–229.

Heiss, J., and Owens, S. 1972. Self-evaluations of blacks and whites. *American Journal of Sociology,* 78:360–370.

Heller, J. F., Groff, B. D., and Solomon, S. H. 1977. Toward an understanding of crowding: The role of physical interaction. *Journal of Personality and Social Psychology,* 35:183–190.

Hendrick, C. 1972. Effects of salience of inconsistency on impression formation. *Journal of Personality and Social Psychology,* 22:219–222.

Hendrick, S. S. 1981. Self-disclosure and marital satisfaction. *Journal of Personality and Social Psychology,* 40:1150–1159.

Henshel, R. L. 1980. The purposes of laboratory experimentation and the virtues of deliberate artificiality. *Journal of Experimental Social Psychology,* 16:466–478.

Hepburn, C., and Locksley, A. 1983. Subject awareness of stereotyping: Do we know when our judgments are prejudiced? *Social Psychology Quarterly,* 46:311–318.

Herbers, J. 1978. Black-white split persists a decade after warning. *New York Times* (February 26):1ff.

Hernton, C. C. 1965. *Sex and Racism in America.* Garden City, N.Y.: Doubleday.

Heussenstamm, F. K. 1971. Bumper stickers and the cops. *Trans-action,* 8:32–33.

Hewitt, J. P. 1976. *Self and Society: A Symbolic Interactionist Social Psychology.* Boston: Allyn and Bacon.

Higbee, K. L. 1977. *Your Memory.* Englewood Cliffs, N.J.: Prentice-Hall.

Hilberman, E. 1980. Overview: The "wife-beater's wife" reconsidered. *American Journal of Psychiatry,* 137:1336–1347.

Hilgard, E. R., Atkinson, R. L., and Atkinson, R.

C. 1979. *Introduction to Psychology.* New York: Harcourt Brace Jovanovich.

Hill, C. T., Rubin, Z., and Peplau, L. A. 1976. Breakups before marriage: The end of 103 affairs. *Journal of Social Issues,* 32:147–167.

Hiller, E. T. 1933. *Principles of Sociology.* New York: Harper and Row.

Hinde, R. A. 1974. *Biological Bases of Human Social Behavior.* New York: McGraw-Hill.

Hockett, C. F. 1954. Chinese vs. English: An exploration of the Whorfian thesis. In Hoizer, H. (ed.), *Language in Culture.* Chicago: University of Chicago Press.

Hoelter, J. W. 1982. Race differences in selective credulity and self-esteem. *Sociological Quarterly,* 23:527–537.

———. 1983. Factorial invariance and self-esteem: Reassessing race and sex differences. *Social Forces,* 61:834–846.

———. 1984. Relative effects of significant others on self-evaluation. *Social Psychology Quarterly,* 47:255–262.

Hoffer, E. 1951. *The True Believer.* New York: Harper and Row.

Holahan, C. J. 1977. Effects of urban size and heterogeneity on judged appropriateness of altruistic responses: Situational vs. subject variables. *Sociometry,* 40:378–382.

Hollander, E. P. 1964. *Leaders, Groups, and Influence.* New York: Oxford University Press.

———, and Hunt, R. G. (eds.). 1971. *Current Perspectives in Social Psychology.* 3rd ed. New York: Oxford University Press.

Holt, L. E. 1970. Resistance to persuasion on explicit beliefs as a function of commitment to and desirability of logically related beliefs. *Journal of Personality and Social Psychology,* 16:583–591.

Holtz, R., and Miller, N. 1985. Assumed similarity and opinion certainty. *Journal of Personality and Social Psychology,* 48:890–898.

Homans, G. C. 1950. *The Human Group.* New York: Harcourt.

———. 1963/1974. *Social Behavior: Its Elementary Forms.* Rev. ed. New York: Harcourt. (First published in 1961.)

Hong, L. K. 1978. Risky shift and cautious shift: Some direct evidence on the culture-value theory. *Social Psychology,* 41:342–346.

Horai, J., Naccari, N., and Fatoullah, E. 1974. The effects of expertise and physical attractiveness upon opinion, agreement, and liking. *Sociometry,* 37:601–606.

Horn, J. 1978. The Gombe chimps—A slight case of murder. *Psychology Today,* 12 (July):18.

House, J. S. 1981. *Work Stress and Social Sup-*

port. Reading, Mass.: Addison-Wesley.

———, Robbins, C., and Metzner, H. L. 1982. The association of social relationships and activities with mortality: Prospective evidence from the Tecumseh Community Health Study. *American Journal of Epidemiology,* 116:123–140.

———, and Wolf, S. 1978. Effects of urban residence on interpersonal trust and helping behavior. *Journal of Personality and Social Psychology,* 36:1029–1043.

Houston, J. P. 1976. *Fundamentals of Learning.* New York: Academic Press.

Howard, J. A. 1984. Societal influences on attribution: Blaming some victims more than others. *Journal of Personality and Social Psychology,* 47:494–505.

Howard, W., and Crano, W. D. 1974. Effects of sex, conversation, location, and size of observer group on bystander intervention in a high risk situation. *Sociometry,* 37:491–507.

Hughes, G. 1979. American terror. *New York Review of Books* (January 25):3–4.

Hull, C. L. 1943. *Principles of Behavior.* New York: Appleton-Century-Crofts.

———. 1952. *A Behavior System.* New Haven: Yale University Press.

Hull, J. B. 1982. Female bosses say biggest barriers are insecurity and being a woman. *Wall Street Journal* (November 2):29.

Hunt, M. 1973. Man and beast. In Montagu, A. (ed.), *Man and Aggression.* 2nd ed. New York: Oxford University Press.

———. 1982a. How the mind works. *New York Times Magazine* (January 24):30–33+.

———. 1982b. Putting juries on the couch. *New York Times Magazine* (November 28):70–88.

———. 1982c. Research through deception. *New York Times Magazine* (September 12):66+.

Huston, T. L. 1983. Power. In Kelley, H. H. (ed.), *Close Relationships.* New York: Freeman.

———, Geis, G., and Wright, R. 1976. The angry Samaritans. *Psychology Today,* 10 (June):61–64+.

———, and Korte, C. 1976. The responsive bystander: Why he helps. In Lickona, T. (ed.), *Moral Development and Behavior.* New York: Holt, Rinehart and Winston.

———, Ruggiero, M., Conner, R., and Geis, G. 1981. Bystander intervention into crime: A study based on naturally occurring episodes. *Social Psychology Quarterly,* 44:14–23.

Hyde, J. S. 1981. How large are cognitive gender differences? *American Psychologist,* 36:892–901.

———. 1984. How large are gender differences in aggression? A developmental meta-analysis. *Developmental Psychology,* 20:722–736.

———, and Rosenberg, B. G. 1976. *Half of the Human Experience.* Lexington, Mass.: D. C. Heath.

Hyman, H. H., and Singer, E. 1968. Introduction. In Hyman, H. H., and Singer, E. (eds.), *Readings in Reference Group Theory and Research.* New York: Free Press.

Ickes, W. 1984. Compositions in black and white: Determinants of interaction in interracial dyads. *Journal of Personality and Social Psychology,* 47:330–341.

———, and Barnes, R. D. 1977. The role of sex and self-monitoring in unstructured dyadic interactions *Journal of Personality and Social Psychology,* 35:315–330.

———, and ———. 1978. Boys and girls together—and alienated: On enacting stereotyped sex roles in mixed-sex dyads. *Journal of Personality and Social Psychology,* 36:669–683.

Ignatius, D. 1985. Vietnam's legacy. *Wall Street Journal* (January 14):1, 10.

Imperato-McGinley, J., Peterson, R. E., Gautier, E., and Sturla, N. 1979. Androgens and the evolution of male-gender identity among male pseudohermaphrodites with 5a-reductase deficiency. *New England Journal of Medicine,* 300:1233–1237.

Inbau, F., and Reid, J. 1962. *Criminal Interrogation and Confessions.* Baltimore: Williams and Wilkins.

Ingham, A. G., Levinger, G., Graves, J., and Peckham, V. 1974. The Ringelmann effect: Studies of group size and group performance. *Journal of Experimental Social Psychology,* 10:371–384.

Insko, C. A., Drenan, S., Smith, R., and Wade, T. J. 1983. Conformity as a function of the consistency of positive self-evaluation with being liked and being right. *Journal of Experimental Social Psychology,* 19:341–358.

———, and Wilson, M. 1977. Interpersonal attraction as a function of social interaction. *Journal of Personality and Social Psychology,* 35:903–911.

Isen, A. M., Clark, M., Shalker, T. E., and Karp, L. 1978. Affect, accessibility of material in memory, and behavior: A cognitive loop? *Journal of Personality and Social Psychology,* 36:1–12.

Issac, L., and Kelly, W. R. 1981. Racial insurgency,

the state and welfare expansion. *American Journal of Sociology,* 86:1348–1386.

Jaccard, J. 1981. Toward theories of persuasion and belief change. *Journal of Personality and Social Psychology,* 40:260–269.

Jackson, M. R., and Muha, M. J. 1984. Education and intergroup attitudes: Moral enlightenment, superficial democratic commitment, or ideological refinement? *American Sociological Review,* 49:751–769.

Jacobson, M. B. 1981. Jurors go easy on handsome rapists with homely victims. *Psychology Today,* 15 (October):27.

James, R. 1959. Status and competence of jurors. *American Journal of Sociology,* 64:563–570.

James, W. 1890. *Principles of Psychology.* 2 vols. New York: Holt.

Janis, I. L. 1971. Groupthink. *Psychology Today,* 5:43–46, 74–76.

———. 1972. *Victims of Groupthink.* Boston: Houghton Mifflin.

———, and Feshbach, S. 1953. Effects of fear-arousing communications. *Journal of Abnormal and Social Psychology,* 48:78–92.

Janoff-Bulman, R., and Frieze, I. H. 1983. A theoretical perspective for understanding reactions to victimization. *Social Issues,* 39:1–17.

Jenkins, J. C. 1983. Resource mobilization theory and the study of social movements. *Annual Review of Sociology,* 9:527–553.

———, and Perrow, C. 1977. Insurgency of the powerless: Farm worker movements (1946–1972). *American Sociological Review,* 42:249–268.

Jennings, E. T. 1979. Urban riots and welfare policy change. In Ingram, H., and Mann, D. (eds.), *Why Politics Succeed or Fail.* Beverly Hills, Calif.: Sage.

Johnson, N. R. 1974. Collective behavior as group-induced shift. *Sociological Inquiry,* 44:105–110.

———, and Feinberg, W. E. 1977. A computer simulation of the emergence of consensus in crowds. *American Sociological Review,* 42:505–521.

———, Stemler, J. G., and Hunter, D. 1977. Crowd behavior as "risky shift": A laboratory experiment. *Sociometry,* 40:183–187.

Johnson, R. D., and Downing, L. L. 1979. Deindividuation and valence of cues: Effects on prosocial and antisocial behavior. *Journal of Personality and Social Psychology,* 37:1532–1538.

Johnson, T. J., Feigenbaum, R., and Weiby, M. 1964. Some determinants and consequences of the teachers perception of causation. *Journal of Educational Psychology,* 55:237–246.

Jones, E. E. 1985. Major developments in social psychology during the past five decades. In Lindzey, G., and Aronson, E. (eds.), *Handbook of Social Psychology.* 3rd ed. Vol. 1. New York: Random House.

———, and Goethals, G. R. 1971. *Order Effects in Impression Formation: Attribution Context and the Nature of the Entity.* Morristown, N.J.: General Learning Press.

———, and Nisbett, R. E. 1971. *The Actor and the Observer: Divergent Perceptions of the Causes of Behavior.* Morristown, N.J.: General Learning Press.

———, Rock, L., Shaver, K. G., Goethals, G. R., and Ward, L. M. 1968. Patterns of performance and ability attribution. *Journal of Personality and Social Psychology,* 10:317–340.

Jones, R. A. 1970. Volunteering to help: The effects of choice, dependence, and anticipated dependence. *Journal of Personality and Social Psychology,* 14:121–129.

Jones, R. G., and Welsh, J. B. 1971. Ability attribution and impression formation in a strategic game: A limiting case of the primacy effect. *Journal of Personality and Social Psychology,* 20:166–175.

Jorgenson, D. O., and Dukes, F. O. 1976. Deindividuation as a function of density and group membership. *Journal of Personality and Social Psychology,* 34:24–29.

Jorgensen, S. R., and Gaudy, J. C. 1980. Self-disclosure and satisfaction in marriage: The relation examined. *Family Relations,* 29:281–287.

Joseph, N. 1981. Campus couples and violence. *New York Times* (June 23):22.

Julia, P. 1983. *Explanatory Models in Linguistics: A Behavioral Perspective.* Princeton, N.J.: Princeton University Press.

Kagan, J. 1971. *Change and Continuity in Infancy.* New York: Wiley.

———. 1985. On love and violence. *Science 85,* 6 (March):28–32.

Kahle, L. R., and Berman, J. J. 1979. Attitudes cause behaviors: A cross-lagged panel analysis. *Journal of Personality and Social Psychology,* 37:315–321.

Kahn, A., O'Leary, V., Krulewitz, J. E., and Lamm, H. 1980. Equity and equality: Male and female means to a just end. *Basic and Applied Social Psychology,* 1:173–197.

Kalmuss, D. S. 1984. The intergenerational transmission of marital aggression. *Journal of Marriage and the Family,* 46:11–19.

———, and Straus, M. A. 1982. Wife's marital dependency and wife abuse. *Journal of Marriage and the Family,* 44:277–286.

Kaplan, A. 1964. *The Conduct of Inquiry: Methodology for Behavioral Science.* San Francisco: Chandler.

Kaplowitz, S. A. 1978. Towards a systematic theory of power attribution. *Social Psychology,* 41:131–148.

Karlin, R. A., Epstein, Y. M., and Aiello, J. R. 1978. A setting-specific analysis of crowding. In Baum, A., and Epstein, Y. M. (eds.), *Human Responses to Crowding.* Hillsdale, N.J.: Erlbaum.

Katcher, A. 1955. The discrimination of sex differences by young children. *Journal of Genetic Psychology,* 87:131–143.

Katz, D. 1960. The functional approach to the study of attitudes. *Public Opinion Quarterly,* 24:163–204.

Katz, P. A., and Zalk, S. R. 1974. Doll preferences: An index of racial attitudes? *Journal of Educational Psychology,* 66:663–668.

Keating, C. F., Mazur, A., Segall, M. H., Cysneiros, P. G., Divale, W. T., Kilbridge, J. E., Komin, S., Leahy, P., Thurman, B., and Wirsing, R. 1981. Culture and the perception of social dominance from facial expression. *Journal of Personality and Social Psychology,* 40:615–626.

Keen, S. J. 1979. Correspondence. *New England Journal of Medicine,* 301:840.

Keller, H. 1904. *The Story of My Life.* New York: Grosset and Dunlap.

———. 1938. *The World I Live In.* New York: Appleton-Century-Crofts.

Kelley, H. H. 1952. Two functions of reference groups. In Swanson, G. E., Newcomb, T. M., and Hartley, E. L. (eds.), *Readings in Social Psychology.* New York: Holt, Rinehart and Winston.

———. 1967. Attribution theory in social psychology. In Levine, D. (ed.), *Nebraska Symposium on Motivation.* Lincoln: University of Nebraska Press.

———. 1971. Attribution theory in social interaction. In Jones, E. E. (ed.), *Attribution: Perceiving the Causes of Behavior.* New York: General Learning Press.

———. 1983. Love and commitment. In Kelley, H. H. (ed.), *Close Relationships.* New York: Freeman.

Kellogg, L. A., and Kellogg, W. N. 1933. *The Ape and the Child.* New York: McGraw-Hill.

Kelman, H. C. 1967. Humans' use of human subjects: The problem of deception in social psychological experiments. *Psychological Bulletin,* 67:1–11.

———, and Lawrence, L. H. 1972. Assignment of responsibility in the case of Lt. Calley: Preliminary report on a national survey. *Journal of Social Issues,* 28:177–212.

Kenny, D. T. 1952. An experimental test of the catharsis hypothesis of aggression. Unpublished doctoral dissertation, University of Washington.

Kerckhoff, A. C. 1964. Meaning. In Gould, J., and Kolb, W. L. (eds.), *A Dictionary of the Social Sciences.* New York: Free Press.

———, and Back, K. W. 1968. *The June Bug: A Case of Hysterical Contagion.* New York: Appleton-Century-Crofts.

———, and Davis, K. E. 1962. Value consensus and need complementarity in mate selection. *American Sociological Review,* 27:295–303.

Kerner Commission. 1968. *Report of the National Advisory Commission on Civil Disorders.* New York: Bantam.

Kerr, N. L. 1983. Motivation losses in small groups: A social dilemma analysis. *Journal of Personality and Social Psychology,* 45:819–828.

———, and Bruun, S. E. 1983. Dispensability of member effort and group motivation losses: Free-rider effects. *Journal of Personality and Social Psychology,* 44:78–94.

———, and MacCoun, R. J. 1985. The effects of jury size and polling method on the process and product of jury deliberation. *Journal of Personality and Social Psychology,* 48:349–363.

Kessler, S. J., and McKenna, W. 1978. *Gender: An Ethnomethodological Approach.* New York: Wiley.

Kiesler, C. 1969. Group pressure and conformity. In Miles, J. (ed.), *Experimental Social Psychology.* New York: Macmillan.

———. 1971. *The Psychology of Commitment.* New York: Academic Press.

———, and Pallak, M. S. 1976. Arousal properties of dissonance manipulations. *Psychological Bulletin,* 83:1014–1025.

Killian, L. M. 1952. The effects of Southern white workers on race relations in Northern plants. *American Sociological Review,* 17:327–331.

———. 1953. The adjustment of Southern white migrants to Northern urban norms. *Social Forces,* 33:66–69.

———. 1981. The sociologists look at the cuckoo's nest: The misuse of ideal types. *American Sociologist,* 16:230–239.

Killworth, P. D., and Bernard, H. R. 1979. A pseudo-model of the small world problem. *Social Forces,* 58:477–505.

Kilpatrick, D. G., Resick, P. A., and Veronen, L. J. 1981. Effects of a rape experience: A longitudinal study. *Journal of Social Issues,* 37:105–122.

Kinder, D. R., and Sears, D. O. 1981. Prejudice and politics: Symbolic racism versus racial threats to the good life. *Journal of Personality and Social Psychology,* 40:414–431.

King, H. E., and Webb, C. 1981. Rape crisis centers: Progress and problems. *Journal of Social Issues,* 37:93–104.

King, W. 1985. Church members go on with sanctuary drive. *New York Times* (January 23):6.

Kipnis, D. 1974. The powerholder. In Tedeschi, J. T. (ed.), *Perspectives on Social Power.* Chicago: Aldine.

———. 1976. *The Powerholders.* Chicago: University of Chicago Press.

———. 1984. The view from the top. *Psychology Today,* 18 (December):30–36.

———, and Consentino, J. 1979. Use of leadership powers in industry. *Journal of Applied Psychology,* 53:460–466.

———, and Lane, W. 1962. Self-confidence and leadership. *Journal of Applied Psychology,* 46:291–295.

———, and Schmidt, S. 1985. The language of persuasion. *Psychology Today,* 19 (April):40–46.

Kitsuse, J. I. 1962. Societal reaction to deviant behavior: Problems of theory and method. *Social Problems,* 9:247–256.

Klandermans, B. 1984. Mobilization and participation: Social-psychological expansions of resource mobilization theory. *American Sociological Review,* 49:583–600.

Klapp, O. E. 1969. *Collective Search for Identity.* New York: Holt, Rinehart and Winston.

Kleinke, C. 1981. How not to pick up a woman. *Psychology Today,* 15 (August):16, 19.

Klinger, E. 1977. *Meaning and Void: Inner Experience and the Incentives in People's Lives.* Minneapolis: University of Minnesota Press.

Kluckhorn, C., and Leighton, D. 1946. *The Navaho.* Cambridge, Mass.: Harvard University Press.

Knowles, E. S. 1973. Boundaries around group interaction: The effect of group size and member status on boundary permeability. *Journal of Personality and Social Psychology,* 26:327–331.

———, Kreuser, B., Haas, S., Hyde, M., and Schuchart, G. E. 1976. Group size and the extension of social space boundaries. *Journal of Personality and Social Psychology,* 33:647–654.

Koenig, F. 1982. Today's conditions make U.S. "ripe for the rumor mill." *U.S. News & World Report* (December 6):41.

Kohlberg, L. 1963. The development of children's orientations toward a moral order. I: Sequence in the development of human thought. *Vita Humana,* 6:11–33.

———. 1966. A cognitive-developmental analysis of children's sex-role concepts and attitudes. In Maccoby, E. E. (ed.), *The Development of Sex Differences.* Stanford, Calif.: Stanford University Press.

———. 1969a. *Stages in the Development of Moral Thought and Action.* New York: Holt, Rinehart and Winston.

———. 1969b. Stage and sequence: The cognitive developmental approach to socialization. In Goslin, D. (ed.), *Handbook of Socialization Theory and Practice.* Chicago: Rand McNally.

———. 1973. Continuities in childhood and adult moral development revisited. In Kohlberg, L. (ed.), *Collected Papers on Moral Development and Moral Education.* Mimeographed.

———. 1976. Moral stages and moralization. In Lickona, T. (ed.), *Moral Development and Behavior: Theory, Research, and Social Issues.* New York: Holt, Rinehart and Winston.

———. 1978. Revisions in the theory and practice of moral development. *New Directions for Child Development,* 2:83–87.

———. 1980. Moral education. *Educational Leadership,* 38:19–23.

———. 1981. *The Philosophy of Moral Development.* New York: Harper and Row.

———, and Doob, A. N. 1972. Catharsis through displacement of aggression. *Journal of Personality and Social Psychology,* 23:379–387.

———, and Gilligan, C. F. 1971. The adolescent as philosopher: The discovery of the self in a postconventional world. *Daedalus,* 100:1051–1086.

———, and Ullian, D. Z. 1974. Stages in the development of psychosexual concepts and attitudes. In Friedman, R. C., Richart, R. N., and Vande Wiele, R. L. (eds.), *Sex Differences in Behavior.* New York: Wiley.

Kolditz, T. A., and Arkin, R. M. 1982. An impression management interpretation of the self-handicapping strategy. *Journal of Personality and Social Psychology,* 43:492–502.

Kollock, P., Blumstein, P., and Schwartz, P. 1985. Sex and power in interaction: Conversational privileges and duties. *American Sociological Review,* 50:34–46.

Komarovsky, M. 1976. *Dilemmas of Masculinity: A Study of College Youth.* New York: Norton.

Komorita, S. S. 1974. A weighted probability model of coalition formation. *Psychological Review,* 81:242–256.

———, and Barth, J. M. 1985. Components of reward in social dilemmas. *Journal of Personality and Social Psychology,* 48:364–373.

———, and Chertkoff, J. M. 1973. A bargaining theory of coalition formation. *Psychological Review,* 80:149–162.

———, Hamilton, T. P., and Kravitz, D. A. 1984. Effects of alternatives in coalition bargaining. *Journal of Experimental Social Psychology,* 20:116–136.

———, and Kravitz, D. A. 1981. Effects of prior experience on coalition bargaining. *Journal of Personality and Social Psychology,* 40:675–686.

———, and Meek, D. D. 1978. Generality and validity of some theories of coalition formation. *Journal of Personality and Social Psychology,* 36:392–404.

———, and Moore, D. 1976. Theories and processes of coalition formation. *Journal of Personality and Social Psychology,* 33:371–381.

———, and Tumonis, T. M. 1980. Extensions and tests of some descriptive theories of coalition formation. *Journal of Personality and Social Psychology,* 39:256–268.

Kopel, S. A., and Arkowitz, H. S. 1974. Role playing as a source of self-observation and behavior change. *Journal of Personality and Social Psychology,* 29:677–686.

Korte, C. 1971. Effects of individual responsibility and group communication on help-giving in an emergency. *Human Relations,* 24:149–159.

———, and Milgram, S. 1970. Acquaintance networks between racial groups. *Journal of Personality and Social Psychology,* 15:101–108.

Koten, J., and Kilman, S. 1985. How Coke's decision to offer 2 colas undid 4½ years of planning. *Wall Street Journal* (July 15):1, 13.

Kotler, P. 1973. The elements of social action. In Zaltman, G. (ed.), *Processes and Phenomena of Social Change.* New York: Wiley.

Kramer, B. M. 1949. Dimensions of prejudice. *The Journal of Psychology,* 27:389–451.

Krantz, S. E., and Rude, S. 1984. Depressive attributions: Selection of different causes or assignment of dimensional meanings? *Journal of Personality and Social Psychology,* 47:193–203.

Krause, N. 1983. The racial context of black self-esteem. *Social Psychology Quarterly,* 46:98–107.

Krauss, R. M., Apple, W., Morency, N., Wenzel, C., and Winston, W. 1981. Verbal, vocal, and visible factors in judgments of another's affect. *Journal of Personality and Social Psychology,* 40:312–320.

Kraut, R. E., Lewis, S. H., and Swezey, L. W. 1982. Listener responsiveness and the coordination of conversation. *Journal of Personality and Social Psychology,* 43:718–731.

———, and Poe, D. 1980. Behavioral roots of person perception: The deception judgments of customs inspectors and laymen. *Journal of Personality and Social Psychology,* 39:784–798.

Kravitz, D. A. 1981. Effects of resources and alternatives on coalition formation. *Journal of Personality and Social Psychology,* 41:87–98.

———, and Iwaniszek, J. 1984. Number of coalitions and resources as sources of power in coalition bargaining. *Journal of Personality and Social Psychology,* 47:534–548.

Kreithen, M. L., and Eisner, T. 1978. Ultraviolet light detection by the homing pigeon. *Nature,* 272:347–348.

Kriesberg, L. 1973. *The Sociology of Social Conflicts.* Englewood Cliffs, N.J.: Prentice-Hall.

Kuhlman, D. M., and Wimberley, D. L. 1976. Expectations of choice behavior held by cooperators, competitors, and individualists across four classes of experimental games. *Journal of Personality and Social Psychology,* 34:69–81.

Kuhn, M. H. 1960. Self-attitudes by age, sex, and professional training. *Sociological Quarterly,* 1:39–55.

Kulik, J. A., and Brown, R. 1978. Frustration, attribution of blame, and aggression. *Journal of Experimental Social Psychology,* 15:183–194.

Kurth, S. B. 1970. Friendship and friendly relations: In McCall, G. (ed.), *Social Relationships.* Chicago: Aldine.

La France, M., and Carmen, B. 1980. The nonverbal display of psychological androgyny. *Journal of Personality and Social Psychology,* 38:36–49.

Laird, J. D. 1974. Self-attribution of emotion: The effects of expressive behavior on the quality of emotional experience. *Journal of Personality and Social Psychology,* 29:475–486.

Lamm, H., and Schwinger, T. 1980. Norms concerning distributive justice: Are needs taken into consideration in allocation decisions? *Social Psychology Quarterly,* 43:425–429.

Landy, D., and Sigall, H. 1974. Beauty is talent: Task evaluation as a function of the performer's physical attractiveness. *Journal of Personality and Social Psychology,* 29:299–304.

Langley, M. 1984. AT&T has call for a new corporate culture. *Wall Street Journal* (February 28):32.

LaPiere, R. T. 1934. Attitudes versus actions. *Social Forces,* 13:230–237.

Larzelere, R. E., and Huston, T. L. 1980. The dyadic trust scale. *Journal of Marriage and the Family,* 42:595–604.

Lasswell, H. 1936. *Politics: Who Gets What, When, How.* New York: McGraw-Hill.

Latané, B., and Darley, J. M. 1968. Group inhibition of bystander intervention in emergencies. *Journal of Personality and Social Psychology,* 10:215–221.

————, and ————. 1970. *The Unresponsive Bystander.* New York: Appleton-Century-Crofts.

————, and Nida, S. 1981. Ten years of research on group size and helping. *Psychological Bulletin,* 89:308–324.

————, and Rodin, J. 1969. A lady in distress: Inhibiting effects of friends and strangers on bystander intervention. *Journal of Experimental Social Psychology,* 5:189–202.

————, Williams, K., and Harkins, S. 1979a. Many hands make light the work: The causes and consequences of social loafing. *Journal of Personality and Social Psychology,* 37:822–832.

————, ————, and ————. 1979b. Social loafing. *Psychology Today,* 13 (October):104–110.

Lau, R. R. 1984. Dynamics of the attribution process. *Journal of Personality and Social Psychology,* 46:1017–1028.

Lauderdale, P. 1976. Deviance and moral boundaries. *American Sociological Review,* 41:660–676.

————, Parker, J., Smith-Cunnien, P., and Inverarity, J. 1984. External threat and the definition of deviance. *Journal of Personality and Social Psychology,* 46:1058–1068.

Lauer, J., and Lauer, R. 1985. Marriages made to last. *Psychology Today,* 19 (June):22–26.

Leakey, R. 1982. Discarding the concept of man as "killer ape." *U.S. News & World Report* (January 18):62.

Leary, R. W., and Moroney, R. J. 1962. The effects of home-cage environments on the social dominance of monkeys. *Journal of Comparative and Physiological Psychology,* 55:256–259.

Le Bon, G. 1895. *Psychologie des Foules.* Trans. *The Crowd: A Study of the Popular Mind.* London: Ernest Benn, 1896.

Lee, F. 1984. Housework and men still don't mix. *USA Today* (August 31):1D.

Leffler, A., Gillespie, D. L., and Conaty, J. C. 1982. The effects of status differentiation on nonverbal behavior. *Social Psychology Quarterly,* 45:153–161.

LeGrand, C. E. 1973. Rape and rape laws: Sexism in society and law. *California Law Review,* 61:919–941.

Leipold, W. D. 1963. Psychological distance in a dyadic interview. Unpublished doctoral dissertation, University of North Dakota.

Lenneberg, E. H. 1967. *Biological Foundations of Language.* New York: Wiley.

————. 1969. On explaining language. *Science,* 164:635–643.

Lenski, G. E. 1966. *Power and Privilege.* New York: McGraw-Hill.

Lepper, M. R., and Greene, D. 1975. Turning play into work: Effects of adult surveillance and extrinsic rewards on children's intrinsic motivations. *Journal of Personality and Social Psychology,* 31:479–486.

————, ————, and Nisbett, R. E. 1973. Undermining children's intrinsic interest with extrinsic reward. *Journal of Personality and Social Psychology,* 28:129–137.

Lerner, M. J. 1965. Evaluation of performance as a function of performer's reward and attractiveness. *Journal of Personality and Social Psychology,* 1:355–360.

————. 1970. The desire for justice and reaction to victim. In Macaulay, J., and Berkowitz, L. (eds.), *Altruism and Helping Behavior.* New York: Academic Press.

————. 1971. Observer's evaluation of a victim: Justice, guilt, and veridical perception. *Journal of Personality and Social Psychology,* 20:127–135.

————. 1974. Social psychology of justice and interpersonal attraction. In Houston, T. L. (ed.), *Foundations of Interpersonal Attraction.* New York: Academic Press.

————. 1975. The justice motive in social behavior: Introduction. *Journal of Social Issues,* 31:1–19.

————. 1980. *The Belief in a Just World: A Fundamental Delusion.* New York: Plenum Press.

————, and Simmons, C. 1966. Observer's reaction to the "innocent victim." Compassion or rejection? *Journal of Personality and Social Psychology,* 4:203–210.

Lester, M. 1980. Generating newsworthiness: The interpretive construction of public events. *American Sociological Review,* 45:984–994.

Leung, K., and Bond, M. H. 1984. The impact of

cultural collectivism on reward allocation. *Journal of Personality and Social Psychology,* 47:793–804.

Leventhal, G. S. 1976. The distribution of rewards and resources in groups and organizations. In Berkowitz, L., and Walster, E. (eds.), *Advances in Experimental Social Psychology.* Vol. 9. New York: Academic Press.

———, and Lane, D. W. 1970. Sex, age, and equity behavior. *Journal of Personality and Social Psychology,* 15:312–316.

———, and Michaels, J. W. 1971. Locus of cause and equity motivation as determinants of reward allocation. *Journal of Personality and Social Psychology,* 17:229–235.

———, and Weiss, T. 1971. Perceived need and the response to inequitable distribution of reward. Unpublished manuscript, Wayne State University.

Leventhal, H. 1967. Fear—For your health. *Psychology Today,* 1 (June):54–58.

———. 1970. Findings and theory in the study of fear communications. In Berkowitz, L. (ed.), *Advances in Experimental Social Psychology.* Vol. 5. New York: Academic Press.

Levine, C. 1984. Making city spaces lovable places. *Psychology Today,* 18 (June):56–63.

Levine, D. U., and Meyer, J. K. 1977. Level and rate of desegregation and white enrollment decline in a big city school district. *Social Problems,* 24:451–462.

Levine, F. M. (ed.). 1975. *Theoretical Readings in Motivation.* Chicago: Rand McNally.

Levine, J., Vinson, A., and Wood, D. 1973. Subway behavior. In Birenbaum, A., and Sagarin, E. (eds.), *People in Places.* New York: Praeger.

Levine, S. V. 1984. Radical departures. *Psychology Today,* 18 (August):21–27.

Levinger, G. 1964. Note on need complementarity in marriage. *Psychological Bulletin,* 61:153–157.

———, Senn, D. J., and Jorgensen, B. W. 1970. Progress toward permanence in courtship: A test of the Kerckhoff-Davis hypothesis. *Sociometry,* 33:427–443.

Levinson, D. J., Carrow, C. M., Klein, E. B., Levinson, M. H., and McKee, B. 1974. The psychosocial development of men in nearly adulthood and the midlife transition. In Ricks, D. F., Thomas, A., and Roff, M. (eds.), *Life History Research in Psychotherapy.* Vol. 3. Minneapolis: University of Minnesota Press.

———, ———, ———, ———, and ———. 1976. Periods in the adult development of men: Ages 18 to 45. *Counseling Psychologist,* 6:21–25.

———, ———, ———, ———, and ———. 1978. *The Seasons of Man's Life.* New York: Knopf.

Lewicki, P. 1983. Self-image bias in person perception. *Journal of Personality and Social Psychology,* 45:384–393.

———. 1984. Self-schema and social information processing. *Journal of Personality and Social Psychology,* 47:1177–1190.

Lewin, K. 1939. Field theory and experiment in social psychology: Concepts and methods. *American Journal of Sociology,* 44:868–896.

———. 1948. *Resolving Social Conflicts.* New York: Harper and Row.

———. 1951. *Field Theory in Social Science.* New York: Harper and Row.

———, Lippitt, R., and White, R. K. 1939. Patterns of aggressive behavior in experimentally created "social climates." *Journal of Social Psychology,* 10:271–299.

Lewin, R. 1968. *Rommel as Military Commander.* New York: Random House.

Lieberson, S. 1961. A societal theory of race and ethnic relations. *American Sociological Review,* 26:902–910.

———. 1970. Stratification and ethnic groups. *Sociological Inquiry,* 40:172–181.

Liebman, M. 1970. The effects of sex and race norms on personal space. *Environment and Behavior,* 2:208–246.

Liebow, E. 1967. *Tally's Corner: A Study of Negro Streetcorner Men.* Boston: Little Brown.

Liebowitz, M. R. 1983. *The Chemistry of Love.* Boston: Little, Brown.

Lifton, R. J. 1979. The appeal of the death trap. *New York Times Magazine* (January 7):26–31.

Limber, J. 1977. Language in child and chimp? *American Psychologist,* 32:280–295.

Lincoln, A., and Levinger, G. 1972. Observers' evaluations of the victim and the attacker in an aggressive incident. *Journal of Personality and Social Psychology,* 22:202–210.

Linden, F. 1984. *The Working Woman: A Progress Report.* New York: The Conference Board.

Lindzey, G. 1950. Differences between the high and low in prejudice and their implications for a theory of prejudice. *Journal of Personality,* 19:16–40.

Linn, L. S. 1965. Verbal attitudes and overt behavior: A study of racial discrimination. *Social Forces,* 43:353–364.

Linton, R. 1936. *The Study of Man.* New York: Appleton-Century-Crofts.

Linville, P. W., and Jones, E. E. 1980. Polarized appraisals of out-group members. *Journal of*

Personality and Social Psychology, 38:689–703.

Lipman, A. 1968. Building designs and social interaction. *Architects Journal,* 147:23–30.

Lippa, R., and Beauvais, C. 1983. Gender jeopardy: The effects of gender, assessed femininity and masculinity, and false success/failure feedback on performance in an experimental quiz game. *Journal of Personality and Social Psychology,* 44:344–353.

Lippmann, W. 1922. *Public Opinion.* New York: Harcourt.

Lipset, S. M., Trow, M. A., and Coleman, J. S. 1956. *Union Democracy.* Garden City, N.Y.: Doubleday.

Liska, A. E. 1974. Emergent issues in the attitude-behavior consistency controversy. *American Sociological Review,* 39:261–272.

Livingstone, F. B. 1962. On the non-existence of human races. *Current Anthropology,* 3:279–281.

Locksley, A., Ortiz, V., and Hepburn, C. 1980. Social categorization and discriminatory behavior. Extinguishing the minimal intergroup discrimination effect. *Journal of Personality and Social Psychology,* 39:773–783.

Lofland, J. 1966. *Doomsday Cult.* Englewood Cliffs, N.J.: Prentice-Hall.

———. 1967. Role management. Mimeographed paper No. 30 of the Center for Research in Social Organization. University of Michigan, June 1967.

———. 1981. Collective behavior: The elementary forms. In Rosenberg, M., and Turner, R. H. (eds.), *Social Psychology.* New York: Basic Books.

Loftin, C., and Ward, S. K. 1983. A spatial autocorrelation model of the effects of population density on fertility. *American Sociological Review,* 48:121–128.

Loftus, E. F. 1979. *Eyewitness Testimony.* Cambridge, Mass.: Harvard University Press.

———. 1984. Eyewitnesses: Essential but unreliable. *Psychology Today,* 18 (February):22–26.

London, P. 1970. The rescuers: Motivational hypotheses about Christians who saved Jews from the Nazis. In Macaulay, J., and Berkowitz, L. (eds.), *Altruism and Helping Behavior.* New York: Academic Press.

Long, T. E., and Hadden, J. K. 1983. Religious conversion and the concept of socialization: Integrating brainwashing and drift models. *Journal for the Scientific Study of Religion,* 22:1–14.

Loo, C. 1972. The effects of spatial density on the social behavior of children. *Journal of Applied Social Psychology,* 2:372–381.

Lopata, H. Z. 1984. Social construction of social problems over time. *Social Problems,* 31:249–272.

Lord, C. G., Lepper, M. R., and Mackie, D. 1984. Attitude prototypes as determinants of attitude-behavior consistency. *Journal of Personality and Social Psychology,* 46:1254–1266.

———, Ross, L., and Lepper, M. R. 1979. Biased assimilation and attitude polarization: The effects of prior theories on subsequently considered evidence. *Journal of Personality and Social Psychology,* 37:2098–2109.

Lorenz, K. 1966. *On Aggression.* New York: Harcourt.

Loseke, D. R., and Cahill, S. E. 1984. The social construction of deviance: Experts on battered women. *Social Problems,* 31:296–310.

Lothstein, L. M. 1982. Sex reassignment surgery: Historical, bioethical, and theoretical issues. *American Journal of Psychiatry,* 139:417–426.

Lott, A., and Lott, B. 1974. The role of reward in the formation of positive interpersonal attitudes. In Huston, T. L. (ed.), *Foundations of Interpersonal Attraction.* New York: Academic Press.

Love, R. E. 1972. Utility of inadvertent nonverbal responses on measures of attitudes. Unpublished doctoral dissertation, Ohio State University.

Lubinski, D., Tellegen, A., and Butcher, J. N. 1981. The relationship between androgyny and subjective indicators of emotional well-being. *Journal of Personality and Social Psychology,* 40:722–730.

———, ———, and ———. 1983. Masculinity, femininity, and androgyny viewed and assessed as distinct concepts. *Journal of Personality and Social Psychology,* 44:428–439.

Luce, R. D., and Raiffa, H. 1957. *Games and Decisions: Introduction and Critical Survey.* New York: Wiley.

Luchins, A. S. 1957a. Experimental attempts to minimize the impact of first impressions. In Hovland, C. I., et al. (eds.), *The Order of Presentation in Persuasion.* New Haven: Yale University Press.

———. 1957b. Primacy-recency in impression formation. In Hovland, C. I., et al. (eds.), *The Order of Presentation in Persuasion.* New Haven: Yale University Press.

Luginbuhl, J. E. R., Crowe, D. H., and Kahan, J. P. 1975. Causal attributions for success and failure. *Journal of Personality and Social Psychology,* 31:86–93.

Lyman, S. M., and Scott, M. B. 1967. Territoriality. *Social Problems,* 15:236–249.

Lynn, S. J. 1978. Three theories of self-disclosure exchange. *Journal of Experimental Social Psychology,* 14:466–479.

Maass, A., and Clark, R. D., III. 1984. Hidden impact of minorities: Fifteen years of minority influence research. *Psychological Bulletin,* 95:428–450.

Macaulay, J. 1970. A shill for charity. In Macaulay, J., and Berkowitz, L. (eds.), *Altruism and Helping Behavior.* New York: Academic Press.

———, and Berkowitz, L. 1970. Overview. In Macaulay, J. R., and Berkowitz, L. (eds.), *Altruism and Helping Behavior.* New York: Academic Press.

McCain, G., Cox, V., and Paulus, P. 1976. The relationship between illness complaints and degree of crowding in a prison environment. *Environment and Behavior,* 8:289–291.

McCall, G. J., and Simmons, J. L. 1966. *Identities and Interaction.* New York: Free Press.

McCallum, R., Rusbult, C. E., Hong, G. K. Walden, T. A., and Schopler, J. 1979. Effects of resource availability and importance of behavior on the experience of crowding. *Journal of Personality and Social Psychology,* 37:1304–1313.

McCarthy, J. D., and Yancey, W. L. 1971. Uncle Tom and Mr. Charlie: Metaphysical pathos in the study of racism and personal disorganization. *American Journal of Sociology,* 76:648–672.

———, and Zald, M. 1977. Resource mobilization and social movements: A partial theory. *American Journal of Sociology,* 82:1212–1241.

McClosky, H., and Dahlgren, H. E. 1959. Primary group influence on party loyalty. *American Political Science Review,* 53:757–776.

Maccoby, E. E., and Jacklin, C. N. 1975. *The Psychology of Sex Differences.* Stanford, Calif.: Stanford University Press.

McConahay, J. B., Hardee, B. B., and Batts, V. 1981. Has racism declined in America? It depends on who is asking and what is asked. *Journal of Conflict Resolution,* 25:563–579.

———, and Hough, J. C., Jr. 1976. Symbolic racism. *Journal of Social Issues,* 32:23–45.

MacCrone, I. D. 1937. *Race Attitudes in South Africa.* London: Oxford University Press.

McDougall, W. 1908. *An Introduction to Social Psychology.* London: Methuen.

McFarland, C., Ross, M., and Conway, M. 1984. Self-persuasion and self-presentation as mediators of anticipatory attitude change. *Journal of Personality and Social Psychology,* 46:529–540.

McGinley, H., LeFevre, R., and McGinley, P. 1975. The influence of a communicator's body position on opinion change in others. *Journal of Social Psychology,* 31:686–690.

McGinnies, E. 1966. Studies in persuasion: III. Reactions of Japanese students to one-sided and two-sided communications. *Journal of Social Psychology,* 70:87–93.

McGrath, J. E. 1984. *Groups: Interaction and Performance.* Englewood Cliffs, N.J.: Prentice-Hall.

McGuire, W. J. 1964. Introducing resistance to persuasion. In Berkowitz, L. (ed.), *Advances in Experimental Social Psychology.* Vol. I. New York: Academic Press.

———. 1969. The nature of attitudes and attitude change. In Lindzey, G., and Aronson, E. (eds.), *The Handbook of Social Psychology.* Reading, Mass.: Addison-Wesley.

———. 1976. The concept of attitudes and their relations to behaviors. In Sinaiko, H. W., and Broedling, L. A. (eds.), *Perspectives on Attitude Assessment: Surveys and Their Alternatives.* Champaign, Ill.: Pendleton.

———. 1985. Attitudes and attitude change. In Lindzey, G., and Aronson, E. (eds.), *Handbook of Social Psychology.* 3rd ed. Vol. 2. New York: Random House.

———, and Papageorgis, D. 1962. Effectiveness of forewarning in developing resistance to persuasion. *Public Opinion Quarterly,* 26:24–34.

Machlowitz, M. 1981. In dating, men remain the more troubled sex. *New York Times* (April 28):13.

MacIver, R. M. 1948. *The More Perfect Union.* New York: Macmillan.

———. 1954. Foreword. In Berger, M. *Equality by Statute.* New York: Columbia University Press.

Mackie, D., and Cooper, J. 1984. Attitude polarization: Effects of group membership. *Journal of Personality and Social Psychology,* 46:575–585.

McKinlay, J. B. 1973. Social networks, lay consultation, and help-seeking behavior. *Social Forces,* 51:275–292.

McMahan, I. D. 1973. Relationships between causal attributions and expectancy of success. *Journal of Personality and Social Psychology,* 28:108–114.

McMillen, D. L. 1971. Transgression, self-image, and compliant behavior. *Journal of Personality and Social Psychology,* 20:176–179.

————, and Wohlstein, R. T. 1983. Individual and collective behaviors within gatherings, demonstrations, and riots. *Annual Review of Sociology,* 9:579–600.

McWhirter, R. M., and Jecker, J. D. 1967. Attitude similarity and inferred attraction. *Psychonomic Science,* 7:225–226.

Maddux, J. E., and Rogers, R. W. 1980. Effects of source expertness, physical attractiveness, and supporting arguments on persuasion: A case of brains over beauty. *Journal of Personality and Social Psychology,* 39:235–244.

————, and ————, 1983. Protection motivation and self-efficacy: A revised theory of fear appeals and attitude change. *Journal of Experimental Social Psychology,* 19:469–479.

Major, B., and Adams, J. B. 1983. Role of gender, interpersonal orientation, and self-presentation in distributive-justice behavior. *Journal of Personality and Social Psychology,* 45:598–608.

————, Carnevale, P. J. D., and Deaux, K. 1981. A different perspective on androgyny: Evaluations of masculine and feminine personality characteristics. *Journal of Personality and Social Psychology,* 41:988–1001.

————, and Deaux, K. 1982. Individual differences in justice behavior: In Greenberg, J., and Cohen, R. L. (eds.), *Equity and Justice in Social Behavior.* New York: Academic Press.

Malamuth, N. M. 1981. Rape proclivity among males. *Journal of Social Issues,* 37:138–157.

————. 1983. Factors associated with rape predictors of laboratory aggression against women. *Journal of Personality and Social Psychology,* 45:432–442.

————, Heim, M., and Feshbach, S. 1980. Sexual responsiveness of college students to rape depictions: Inhibitory and disinhibitory effects. *Journal of Personality and Social Psychology,* 38:399–408.

Malcolm X. 1964. *The Autobiography of Malcolm X.* New York: Grove Press.

Mann, J. H. 1959. The relationship between cognitive, affective, and behavioral aspects of racial prejudice. *Journal of Social Psychology,* 49:223–228.

Mann, L. 1981. The baiting crowd in episodes of threatened suicide. *Journal of Personality and Social Psychology,* 41:703–709.

————, and Janis, I. L. 1968. A follow-up study on the long-term effects of emotional role playing. *Journal of Personality and Social Psychology,* 8:339–342.

————, Newton, J. W., and Innes, J. M. 1982. A test between deindividuation and emergent norm theories of crowd aggression. *Journal of Personality and Social Psychology,* 42:260–272.

Manning, S. A., and Taylor, D. A. 1975. Effects of viewed violence and aggression: Stimulation and catharsis. *Journal of Personality and Social Psychology,* 31:180–188.

Manucia, G. K., Baumann, D. J., and Cialdini, R. B. 1984. Mood influences on helping: Direct effects or side effects. *Journal of Personality and Social Psychology,* 46:357–364.

Marecek, J., and Mettee, D. R. 1972. Avoidance of continued success as a function of self-esteem, level of esteem certainty, and responsibility for success. *Journal of Personality and Social Psychology,* 22:98–107.

Margulis, S. T. 1977a. Introduction. *Journal of Social Issues,* 33:1–4.

————. 1977b. Conceptions of privacy: Current status and next steps. *Journal of Social Issues,* 33:5–21.

Mark, M. M. 1985. Expectations, procedural justice, and alternative reactions to being deprived of a desired outcome. *Journal of Experimental Social Psychology,* 21:114–137.

Markides, K. C., and Cohn, S. F. 1982. External conflict/internal cohesion: A reevaluation of an old theory. *American Sociological Review,* 47:88–89.

Marks, G., Miller, N., and Maruyama, G. 1981. Effect of targets' physical attractiveness on assumptions of similarity. *Journal of Personality and Social Psychology,* 41:198–206.

Markus, H. 1977. Self-schemata and processing information about the self. *Journal of Personality and Social Psychology,* 35:63–78.

————, and Zajonc, R. B. 1985. The cognitive perspective in social psychology. In Lindzey, G., and Aronson, E. (eds.), *Handbook of Social Psychology.* 3rd ed. Vol. 1. New York: Random House.

Marlatt, G. A., and Rohsenow, D. J. 1981. The think-drink effect. *Psychology Today,* 15 (December):60–69 + .

Marler, P. 1976. On animal aggression: The roles of strangeness and familiarity. *American Psychologist,* 31:239–246.

Martin, D. 1976. *Battered Wives.* San Francisco: Glide.

Martin, J., Brickman, P., and Murray, A. 1984. Moral outrage and pragmatism: Explanations for collective action. *Journal of Experimental Social Psychology,* 20:484–496.

Marx, G. T., and Wood, J. L. 1975. Strands of theory and research in collective behavior. *Annual Review of Sociology,* 1:363–428.

Maselli, M. D., and Altrocchi, J. 1969. Attribution of intent. *Psychological Bulletin,* 71:445–454.

Maslow, A. H. 1967. Self-actualization and beyond. In Bugental, J. F. T. (ed.), *Challenges of Humanistic Psychology.* New York: McGraw-Hill.

———. 1970. *Motivation and Personality.* 2nd ed. New York: Harper and Row.

Mayer, P. 1961. *Townsmen or Tribesmen.* Cape Town, South Africa: Oxford University Press.

Mazis, M. B. 1975. Antipollution measures and psychological reactance theory: A field experiment. *Journal of Personality and Social Psychology,* 31:654–660.

Mazur, A. 1973. A cross-species comparison of status in small established groups. *American Sociological Review,* 38:513–530.

———. 1975. Cross-species comparisons of aggression. *American Sociological Review,* 40:667–678.

———. 1982. Bomb threats and the mass media: Evidence for a theory of suggestion. *American Sociological Review,* 47:407–411.

———, Rosa, E., Faupel, M., Heller, J., Leen, R., and Thurman, B. 1980. Physiological aspects of communications via mutual gaze. *American Journal of Sociology,* 86:50–74.

Mead, G. H. 1932. *The Philosophy of the Present.* Chicago: Open Court.

———. 1934. *Mind, Self, and Other.* Chicago: University of Chicago Press.

———. 1938. *The Philosophy of the Act.* Chicago: University of Chicago Press.

Mead, M. 1935. *Sex and Temperament in Three Primitive Societies.* New York: Morrow.

———. 1949. *Male and Female.* New York: Morrow.

Mehan, H., and Wood, H. 1975. *The Reality of Ethnomethodology.* New York: Wiley.

———, and ———. 1976. De-secting ethnomethodology. *American Sociologist,* 11:13–21.

Mehrabian, A. 1968. Communication without words. *Psychology Today* (September):53–55.

———. 1972. *Nonverbal Communication.* New York: Aldine-Atherton.

———, and Diamond, S. G. 1971. Seating arrangement and conversation. *Sociometry,* 34:281–289.

Meindl, J. R., and Lerner, M. J. 1984. Exacerbation of extreme responses to an out-group. *Journal of Personality and Social Psychology,* 47:71–84.

Merton, R. K. 1968. *Social Theory and Social Structure.* Enlarged ed. New York: Free Press.

———, and Kitt, A. S. 1950. Contributions to the theory of reference group behavior. In Merton, R. K., and Lazarsfeld, P. F. (eds.), *Continuities in Social Research: Studies in the Scope and Method of "The American Soldier."* New York: Free Press.

Messé, L. A., Stollak, G. E., Larson, R. W., and Michaels, G. Y. 1979. Interpersonal consequences of person perception process in two social contexts. *Journal of Personality and Social Psychology,* 37:369–379.

Meyer, J., and Reter, C. 1979. Sex reassignment: Follow-up. *Archives of General Psychiatry,* 36:1010–1015.

Meyer, J. P., and Pepper, S. 1977. Need compatibility and marital adjustment in young married couples. *Journal of Personality and Social Psychology,* 35:331–342.

Meyer, T. P. 1972. The effects of sexually arousing and violent films on aggressive behavior. *Journal of Sex Research,* 8:324–333.

Meyers, B. 1984. Minority group: An ideological formulation. *Social Problems,* 32:1–15.

Michels, R. 1966. *Political Parties.* New York: Free Press. (First published in 1911.)

Michener, H. A., and Burt, M. R. 1975. Components of "authority" as determinants of compliance. *Journal of Personality and Social Psychology,* 31:606–614.

———, Fleishman, J. A., and Vaske, J. J. 1976. A test of the bargaining theory of coalition formation in four-person groups. *Journal of Personality and Social Psychology,* 34:1114–1126.

———, Lawler, E. J., and Bacharach, S. B. 1973. Perception of power in conflict situations. *Journal of Personality and Social Psychology,* 28:155–162.

Middleton, D. 1983. Departing army chief's goal: Professionalism through loyalty to unit. *New York Times* (June 23):10.

Milgram, S. 1965. Some conditions of obedience and disobedience to authority. *Human Relations,* 18:57–76.

———. 1967. The small-world problem. *Psychology Today,* 1:61–67.

———. 1974. *Obedience to Authority.* New York: Harper and Row.

———. 1977. *The Individual in a Social World.* Reading, Mass.: Addison-Wesley.

———, and Toch, H. 1969. Collective behavior: Crowds and social movements. In Lindzey, G., and Aronson, E. (eds.), *The Handbook of Social Psychology.* 2nd ed. Vol. 4. Reading, Mass.: Addison-Wesley.

Miller, A., Bolce, L., and Halligan, M. 1977. The J-curve theory and the black urban riots.

American Political Science Review, 71:967–982.

Miller, C. E. 1980a. A test of four theories of coalition formation: Effects of payoffs and resources. *Journal of Personality and Social Psychology,* 38:153–164.

———. 1980b. Effects of payoffs and resources on coalition formation: A test of three theories. *Social Psychology Quarterly,* 43:154–164.

———. 1980c. Coalition formation in characteristic function games: Competitive tests of three theories. *Journal of Experimental Social Psychology,* 16:61–76.

Miller, C. T. 1982. The role of performance-related similarity in social comparison of abilities: A test of the related attributes hypothesis. *Journal of Experimental Social Psychology,* 18:513–523.

Miller, D. T., and Porter, C. A. 1983. Self-blame in victims of violence. *Journal of Social Issues,* 39:139–152.

Miller, G. A., and Chomsky, N. 1963. Finitary models of language users. In Luce, R. D., Bush, R. R., and Galanter, E. (eds.), *Handbook of Mathematical Psychology.* Vol. 2. New York: Wiley.

Miller, N., and Brewer, M. 1984. *Groups in Contact: The Psychology of Desegregation.* New York: Academic Press.

———, Maruyama, G., Beaber, R. J., and Valone, K. 1976. Speed of speech and persuasion. *Journal of Personality and Social Psychology,* 34:615–624.

Miller, N. E. 1941. The frustration-aggression hypothesis. *Psychological Review,* 48:337–342.

Mills, C. J., and Tyrrell, D. J. 1983. Sex-stereotypic encoding and release from proactive interference. *Journal of Personality and Social Psychology,* 45:772–781.

Mills, J. 1969. The experimental method. In Mills, J. (ed.), *Experimental Social Psychology.* New York: Macmillan.

Milmoe, S., and Liebert, R. M. 1966. Effects of discrepancies between deserved and imposed reward criteria on their acquisition and transmission. *Journal of Personality and Social Psychology,* 3:45–53.

———, Rosenthal, R., Blane, H. T., Chafetz, M. E., and Wolf, I. 1967. The doctor's voice: Postdictor of successful referral of alcoholic patients. *Journal of Abnormal Psychology,* 72:78–84.

Mischel, W. 1968. *Personality and Assessment.* New York: Wiley.

———. 1969. Continuity and change in personality. *American Psychologist,* 24:1012–1018.

———. 1971. *Introduction to Personality.* New York: Holt, Rinehart and Winston.

———. 1973. Toward a cognitive social learning reconceptualization of personality. *Psychological Review,* 80:252–283.

———. 1977. On the future of personality measurement. *American Psychologist,* 32:246–254.

———. 1984. Convergences and challenges in the search for consistency. *American Psychologist,* 39:351–364.

———, and Mischel, H. N. 1976. A cognitive social-learning approach to morality and self-regulation. In Lickona, T. (ed.), *Moral Development and Behavior: Theory, Research, and Social Issues.* New York: Holt, Rinehart and Winston.

Mitchell, C. 1984. USA family earnings rise 7.6%. *USA Today* (February 1):1A.

Mitchell, R. E. 1971. Some social implications of high density housing. *American Sociological Review,* 36:18–29.

———, Billings, A. G., and Moos, R. H. 1983. Social support and well-being: Implications for prevention programs. *Journal of Primary Prevention,* 3:77–98.

Miyamoto, S. F., and Dornbusch, S. M. 1956. A test of interactionist hypotheses of self-conception. *American Journal of Sociology,* 61:399–403.

Mogul, K. M. 1979. Women in midlife: Decisions, rewards, and conflicts related to work and careers. *American Journal of Psychiatry,* 136:1139–1143.

Moine, D. J. 1982. To trust, perchance to buy. *Psychology Today,* 16 (August):51–54.

Molm, L. D. 1981a. Power use in the dyad: The effects of structure, knowledge, and interaction history. *Social Psychology Quarterly,* 44:42–48.

———. 1981b. The conversion of power imbalance to power use. *Social Psychology Quarterly,* 44:151–163.

Molotch, H., and Lester, M. 1975. Accidental news: The great oil spill as a local occurrence and national event. *American Journal of Sociology,* 81:235–260.

Money, J. 1977. Destereotyping sex roles. *Society,* 14: (July/August):25–28.

———. 1980. *Love and Love Sickness: The Science of Sex, Gender Difference, and Pair-Bonding.* Baltimore: Johns Hopkins University Press.

———, and Ehrhardt, A. 1972. *Man & Woman, Boy & Girl: The Differentiation and Dimorphism of Gender Identity from Conception to*

Maturity. Baltimore: Johns Hopkins University Press.

———, and Primrose, C. 1969. Sexual dimorphism and dissociation in the psychology of male transsexuals. In Green, R., and Money, J. (eds.), *Transsexualism and Sex Reassignment.* Baltimore: Johns Hopkins University Press.

———, and Tucker, P. 1975. *Sexual Signatures: On Being a Man or a Woman.* Boston: Little, Brown.

Montagu, A. 1963. What is remarkable about varieties of man is likenesses, not differences. *Current Anthropology,* 4:361–364.

———. 1964. *The Concept of Race.* New York: Free Press.

——— (ed.). 1973. *Man and Aggression.* 2nd ed. New York: Oxford University Press.

Montgomery, J. 1979. Rumor-plagued firms use various strategies to keep damage low. *Wall Street Journal* (February 6):1, 15.

Mooney, J. 1973. *The Ghost Dance Religion and Wounded Knee.* New York: Dover.

Moreland, R. L. 1985. Social categorization and the assimilation of "new" group members. *Journal of Personality and Social Psychology,* 48:1173–1190.

Morgan, C. P., and Aram, J. D. 1975. The preponderance of arguments in the risky shift phenomenon. *Journal of Experimental Social Psychology,* 11:25–34.

Morgan, W. R., and Sawyer, J. 1979. Equality, equity, and procedural justice in social exchange. *Social Psychology Quarterly,* 42:71–75.

Moriarty, T. 1975. Crime, commitment, and the responsive bystander: Two field experiments. *Journal of Personality and Social Psychology,* 31:370–376.

Morland, J. K. 1962. Racial acceptance and preference of nursery school children in a southern city. *Merrill-Palmer Quarterly of Behavior and Development,* 8:271–280.

Morris, D. 1968. *The Naked Ape.* New York: McGraw-Hill.

Morris, J. 1974. *Conundrum.* New York: Harcourt.

Morse, N. C., and Allport, F. H. 1953. The causation of anti-Semitism: An investigation of seven hypotheses. *Journal of Psychology,* 34:197–233.

Mortimer, J. T., and Simmons, R. G. 1978. Adult socialization. *Annual Review of Sociology,* 4:421–454.

Moscovici, S. 1976. *Social Influence and Social Change.* London: Academic Press.

———, and Faucheux, C. 1972. Social influences, conformity bias, and the study of active minorities. In Berkowitz, L. (ed.), *Advances in Experimental Social Psychology.* Vol. 6. New York: Academic Press.

———, and Personnaz, B. 1980. Studies in social influence: V. Minority influences and conversion behavior in a perceptual task. *Journal of Experimental Social Psychology,* 16:270–282.

Moskos, C. C., Jr. 1969. Why men fight. *Transaction,* 7:13–23.

———. 1984. The sociology of combat. *Contemporary Sociology,* 13:420–422.

Moss, R., and Van Dort, B. 1976. Student physical symptoms and the social climate of college living groups. Unpublished manuscript. Social Ecology Laboratory, Department of Psychiatry and Behavioral Sciences, Stanford University.

Mott, F. L. 1982. *The Employment Revolution: Young American Women of the 1970s.* Cambridge: MIT Press.

Mottl, T. L. 1980. The analysis of countermovements. *Social Problems,* 27:620–635.

Muehleman, J. T., Bruker, C., and Ingram, C. M. 1976. The generosity shift. *Journal of Personality and Social Psychology,* 34:344–351.

Mulford, H. A., and Salisbury, W. W., II. 1964. Self-conceptions in a general population. *Sociological Quarterly,* 3:115–121.

Muller, E. N. 1985. Income inequality, regime repressiveness, and political violence. *American Sociological Review,* 50:47–61.

Murdock, G. P. 1935. Comparative data on the division of labor by sex. *Social Forces,* 15:551–553.

Murphy, G. 1947. *Personality: A Biosocial Approach to Origins and Structure.* New York: Harper and Row.

Murphy-Berman, V., Berman, J. J., Singh, P., Pachauri, A., and Kumar, P. 1984. Factors affecting allocation to needy and meritorious recipients: A cross-cultural comparison. *Journal of Personality and Social Psychology,* 46:1267–1272.

Murstein, B. I. 1967. Empirical tests of role, complementary needs, and homogamy theories of marital choice. *Journal of Marriage and the Family,* 29:689–696.

———. 1972. Physical attractiveness and marital choice. *Journal of Personality and Social Psychology,* 22:8–12.

———. 1976. *Who Will Marry Whom?* New York: Springer.

Muson, H. 1979. Moral thinking: Can it be taught? *Psychology Today,* 12 (February):48–68+.

Myers, A. M., and Gonda, G. 1982. Utility of the

masculinity-femininity construct: Comparison of traditional and androgyny approaches. *Journal of Personality and Social Psychology,* 43:514–522.

Myers, D. G., and Lamm, H. 1976. The group polarization phenomenon. *Psychological Bulletin,* 83:602–627.

Mynatt, C., and Sherman, S. J. 1975. Responsibility attribution in groups and individuals: A direct test of the diffusion of responsibility hypothesis. *Journal of Personality and Social Psychology,* 32:1111–1118.

Nadel, S. F. 1957. *The Theory of Social Structure.* New York: Free Press.

Nadelson, C. C., Notman, M. T., Zackson, H., and Gornick, J. 1982. A follow-up study of rape victims. *American Journal of Psychiatry,* 139:1266–1270.

Nagel, J. 1975. *The Descriptive Analysis of Power.* New Haven: Yale University Press.

Nahemow, L., and Lawton, M. P. 1975. Similarity and propinquity in friendship formation. *Journal of Personality and Social Psychology,* 32:205–213.

National Commission on the Causes and Prevention of Violence. 1969. *To Establish Justice, to Insure Domestic Tranquility, Final Report.* Washington, D.C.: Government Printing Office.

Nel, E., Helmreich, R., and Aronson, E. 1969. Opinion change in the advocate as a function of the persuasibility of his audience. A clarification of the meaning of dissonance. *Journal of Personality and Social Psychology,* 12:117–124.

Nelson, E. A. 1969. Social reinforcement for expression versus suppression of aggression. *Merrill-Palmer Quarterly,* 15:259–278.

Nelson, K. 1972. The relation of form recognition to concept development. *Child Development,* 43:67–74.

—— . 1977. Facilitating children's syntax acquisition. *Developmental Psychology,* 13:101–107.

Nemeth, C. 1972. A critical analysis of research utilizing the Prisoner's Dilemma paradigm for the study of bargaining. In Berkowitz, L. (ed.), *Advances in Experimental Social Psychology.* Vol. 6. New York: Academic Press.

—— , Endicott, J., and Wachtler, J. 1976. From the '50s to the '70s: Women in jury deliberations. *Sociometry,* 39:293–304.

Neugarten, B. L. 1979. Time, age, and the life cycle. *American Journal of Psychiatry,* 136:887–894.

Newcomb, T. M. 1950. *Social Psychology.* New York: Holt, Rinehart and Winston.

—— . 1956. The prediction of interpersonal attraction. *American Psychologist,* 11:575–586.

—— . 1961. *The Acquaintance Process.* New York: Holt, Rinehart and Winston.

—— . 1963. Stabilities underlying changes in interpersonal attraction. *Journal of Abnormal and Social Psychology,* 66:376–386.

Nicholls, J. G. 1979. Quality and equality in intellectual development. *American Psychologist,* 34:1071–1084.

Nielsen, F. 1985. Toward a theory of ethnic solidarity in modern societies. *American Sociological Review,* 50:133–149.

Nisan, M., and Kohlberg, L. 1982. Universality and variation in moral development: A longitudinal and cross-sectional study in Turkey. *Child Development,* 53:865–876.

Nisbet, R. 1971. Introduction. In Merton, R. K., and Nisbet, R. (eds.), *Contemporary Social Problems.* 3rd. ed. New York: Harcourt.

Nisbett, R. E., Caputo, C., Legant, P., and Marecek, J. 1973. Behavior as seen by the actor and as seen by the observer. *Journal of Personality and Social Psychology,* 27:154–164.

—— , and Wilson, T. D. 1977a. The halo effect: Evidence for unconscious alteration of judgments. *Journal of Personality and Social Psychology,* 35:250–256.

—— , and —— . 1977b. Telling more than we can know: Verbal reports on mental processes. *Psychological Review,* 84:231–259.

Norvell, N., and Worchel, S. 1981. A reexamination of the relation between equal status contact and intergroup attraction. *Journal of Personality and Social Psychology,* 41:902–908.

Nye, F. I. 1978. Is choice and exchange theory the key? *Journal of Marriage and the Family,* 40:219–233.

Oberschall, A. 1973. *Social Conflict and Social Movements.* Englewood Cliffs, N.J.: Prentice-Hall.

Olsen, M. E. 1968. *The Process of Social Organization.* New York: Holt, Rinehart and Winston.

—— . 1970. *Power in Societies.* New York: Macmillan.

Olson, J. M., and Zanna, M. P. 1979. A new look at selective exposure. *Journal of Experimental Social Psychology,* 15:1–15.

Olson, M. 1965. *The Logic of Collective Action: Public Goods and the Theory of Groups.* New York: Schocken.

O'Reilly, J. 1983. Wife beating: The silent crime. *Time* (September 5):23–25.

Orne, M. 1962. On the social psychology of the psychological experiment. *American Psychologist,* 17:776–783.

Osgood, C. E. 1962. Studies on the generality of affect meaning systems. *American Psychologist,* 17:10–18.

———. 1967. Semantic differential technique in the comparative study of cultures. In Jakobovits, L. S., and Miron, M. S. (eds.), *Readings in the Psychology of Language.* Englewood Cliffs, N.J.: Prentice-Hall.

———, May, W. H., and Miron, M. S. 1975. *Cross-Cultural Universality of Affective Meaning Systems.* Urbana: University of Illinois Press.

———, Suci, G., and Tannenbaum, P. 1957. *The Measurement of Meaning.* Urbana: University of Illinois Press.

———, and Tannenbaum, P. H. 1955. The principle of congruity in the prediction of attitude change. *Psychological Review,* 62:42–55.

Ostrom, T. M., and Davis, D. 1979. Idiosyncratic weighting of trait information in impression formation. *Journal of Personality and Social Psychology,* 37:2025–2043.

O'Sullivan, M., Ekman, P., Friesen, W., and Scherer, K. 1985. What you say and how you say it: The contribution of speech content and voice quality to judgments of others. *Journal of Personality and Social Psychology,* 48:54–62.

Padgett, V. R., and Wolosin, R. J. 1980. Cognitive similarity in dyadic communication. *Journal of Personality and Social Psychology,* 39:654–659.

Paloutzian, R. F. 1981. Purpose in life and value changes following conversion. *Journal of Personality and Social Psychology,* 41:1153–1160.

Parke, R. D. 1967. Nurturance, nurturance withdrawal, and resistance to deviation. *Child Development,* 38:1101–1110.

———. 1970. The role of punishment in the socialization process. In Hoppe, R. A., Milton, G. A., and Simmel, E. C. (eds.), *Early Experiences and the Processes of Socialization.* New York: Academic Press.

Pascale, R. 1984. Fitting new employees into the company culture. *Fortune* (May 28):28–41.

Patchen, M. 1982. *Black-White Contact in Schools: Its Social and Academic Effects.* West Lafayette, Ind.: Purdue University Press.

———, Hofmann, G., and Brown, W. R. 1980. Academic performance of black high school students under different conditions of contact with white peers. *Sociology of Education,* 53:33–51.

Pate, G. S. 1981. Research on prejudice reduction. *Educational Leadership,* 38:288–291.

Paton, S. M., Walberg, H. J., and Yeh, E. G. 1973. Ethnicity, environmental control, and academic self-concept in Chicago. *American Educational Research Journal,* 10:85–99.

Patterson, F. P. 1985. Talking with apes. *USA Today* (March 1):11A.

Patterson, M. L., Kelly, C. E., Kondracki, B. A., and Wulf, L. J. 1979. Effects of seating arrangement on small-group behavior. *Social Psychology Quarterly,* 42:180–185.

Paulus, P. B., Annis, A. B., Seta, J. J., Schkade, J. K., and Matthews, R. W. 1976. Density does affect task performance. *Journal of Personality and Social Psychology,* 34:248–253.

Pearce, D. M. 1979. Gatekeepers and home-seekers: Institutional patterns in racial steering. *Social Problems,* 26:325–342.

Pearlin, L. I. 1954. Shifting group attachments and attitudes toward Negroes. *Social Forces,* 33:47–50.

Pennebaker, J. 1980. Social coughs. *Psychology Today,* 14 (August):25–26.

Pennebaker, J. W., Burnam, M. A., Schaeffer, M. A., and Harper, D. C. 1977. Lack of control as a determinant of perceived physical symptoms. *Journal of Personality and Social Psychology,* 35:167–174.

Pepitone, A. 1981. Lessons from the history of social psychology. *American Psychologist,* 36:972–985.

Perinbanayagam, R. S. 1974. The definition of the situation. *Sociological Quarterly,* 15:531–537.

Perry, D. G., and Bussey, K. 1979. The social learning theory of sex differences: Imitation is alive and well. *Journal of Personality and Social Psychology,* 37:1699–1712.

———, White, A. J., and Perry, L. C. 1984. Does early sex typing result from children's attempts to match their behavior to sex role stereotypes? *Child Development,* 55:2114–2121.

Person, E. S., and Ovesey, L. 1974. The psychodynamics of male transsexualism. In Friedman, R. C., Richart, R. M., and Vande Wiele, R. L. (eds.), *Sex Differences in Behavior.* New York: Wiley.

Pervin, L. A. 1976. A free-response description approach to the analysis of person-situation interaction. *Journal of Personality and Social Psychology,* 34:465–474.

Petersen, K. K., and Dutton, J. E. 1975. Central-ity, extremity, intensity: Neglected variables in research on attitude-behavior consistency. *Social Forces,* 54:393–414.

Peterson, I. 1979. Stress can cause work "epidemics." *New York Times* (May 29):C1–2.

Pettigrew, T. F., and Green, R. L. 1976. School desegregation in large cities: A critique of the Coleman "white flight" thesis. *Harvard Educational Review,* 46:1–53.

Petty, R. E., and Cacioppo, J. T. 1977. Forewarning, cognitive responding, and resistance to persuasion. *Journal of Personality and Social Psychology,* 35:645–655.

———, and ———. 1981. *Attitudes and Persuasion: Classic and Contemporary Approaches.* Dubuque, Iowa: Wm. C. Brown.

———, and ———. 1984. The effects of involvement on responses to argument quantity and quality: Central and peripheral routes to persuasion. *Journal of Personality and Social Psychology,* 46:69–81.

———, ———, and Goldman, R. 1981. Personal involvement as a determinant of argument-based persuasion. *Journal of Personality and Social Psychology,* 41:847–855.

Pfeiffer, J. 1985. Girl talk, boy talk. *Science 85,* 6 (February):58–63.

Phillips, D. A., and Zigler, E. 1980. Children's self-image disparity: Effects of age, socioeconomic status, ethnicity, and gender. *Journal of Personality and Social Psychology,* 39:689–700.

Phillips, D. P. 1979. Suicide, motor vehicle fatalities, and the mass media: Evidence toward a theory of suggestion. *American Journal of Sociology,* 84:1150–1174.

———. 1980. Airplane accidents, murder, and the mass media: Towards a theory of imitation and suggestion. *Social Forces,* 58:1001–1024.

———, and Conviser, R. H. 1972. Measuring the structure and boundary properties of groups: Some uses of information theory. *Sociometry,* 35:235–254.

———, and Feldman, K. A. 1973. A dip in deaths before ceremonial occasions: Some new relationships between social integration and mortality. *American Sociological Review,* 38:678–696.

Phoenix, C. H., Goy, R. W., and Resko, J. A. 1969. Psychosexual differentiation as a function of androgenic stimulation. In Diamond, M. (ed.), *Reproduction and Sexual Behavior.* Bloomington: Indiana University Press.

Piaget, J. 1948. *The Moral Judgment of the Child.* New York: Free Press.

———. 1960. The general problems of the psychobiological development of the child. In Tanner, J. M., and Inhelder, B. (eds.), *Discussions on Child Development: Proceedings of the World Health Organization Study Group on the Psychobiological Development of the Child.* Vol. 4. New York: International Universities Press, 3–27.

Piliavin, I. M., and Piliavin, J. A. 1972. Effects of blood on reactions to a victim. *Journal of Personality and Social Psychology,* 23:353–361.

———, ———, and Rodin, J. 1975. Costs, diffusion, and the stigmatized victim. *Journal of Personality and Social Psychology,* 32:429–438.

———, Rodin, J., and Piliavin, J. A. 1969. Good Samaritanism: An underground phenomenon? *Journal of Personality and Social Psychology,* 13:289–299.

Pineo, P. C. 1961. Disenchantment in the later years of marriage. *Marriage and Family Living,* 23:3–11.

Pines, M. 1978. Is sociobiology all wet? *Psychology Today,* 11 (May):23–24.

———. 1981. The civilizing of Genie. *Psychology Today,* 15 (September):28–34.

———. 1983. Can a rock walk? *Psychology Today,* 17 (November):46–54.

Pittman, T. S., and Pittman, N. L. 1980. Deprivation of control and the attribution process. *Journal of Personality and Social Psychology,* 39:377–389.

Pitt-Rivers, J. 1967. Race, color, and class in Central America and the Andes. *Daedalus,* 96:542–559.

Piven, F., and Cloward, R. 1977. *Poor People's Movements.* New York: Pantheon.

Plummer, K. 1975. *Sexual Stigma: An Interactionist Account.* London: Routledge.

Podsakoff, P. M., and Schriesheim, C. A. 1985. Field studies of French and Raven's bases of power: Critique, reanalysis, and suggestions for future research. *Psychological Bulletin,* 97:387–411.

Pope, K. S. 1980. Defining and studying romantic love. In Pope, K. S. (ed.), *On Love and Loving.* San Francisco: Jossey-Bass.

Porter, J. 1971. *Black Child, White Child: The Development of Racial Attitudes.* Cambridge, Mass.: Harvard University Press.

Premack, D. 1971. Language in chimpanzee? *Science,* 172:808–822.

Prentice-Dunn, S., and Rogers, R. W. 1980. Effects of deindividuating situational cues and aggressive models on subjective deindividuation and aggression. *Journal of Personality and Social Psychology,* 39:104–113.

———, and ———. 1982. Effects of public and

private self-awareness on deindividuation and aggression. *Journal of Personality and Social Psychology,* 43:503–513.

Presidential Commission on Obscenity and Pornography. 1971. *Technical Report.* Washington, D.C.: Government Printing Office.

Prewitt, K., and Stone, A. 1973. *The Ruling Elites.* New York: Harper and Row.

Priest, R. F., and Sawyer, J. 1967. Proximity and peership: Bases of balance in interpersonal attraction. *American Journal of Sociology,* 72:633–649.

Proshansky, H. M. 1976. Environmental psychology and the real world. *American Psychologist,* 31:303–310.

———, Ittleson, W. H., and Rivlin, L. G. 1970. Freedom of choice and behavior in a physical setting. In Proshansky, H. M., Ittleson, W. H., and Rivlin, L. G. (eds.), *Environmental Psychology.* New York: Holt, Rinehart and Winston.

Pruitt, D. G. 1971a. Choice shifts in group discussion: An introductory review. *Journal of Personality and Social Psychology,* 20:339–360.

———. 1971b. Conclusions: Toward an understanding of choice shifts in group discussion. *Journal of Personality and Social Psychology,* 20:495–510.

———, and Gahagan, J. P. 1974. Campus crisis: The search for power. In Tedeschi, J. T. (ed.), *Perspectives on Social Power.* Chicago: Aldine.

Pryor, J. B., Ostrom, T. M., Dukerich, J. M., Mitchell, M. L., and Herstein, J. A. 1983. Preintegrative categorization of social information: The role of persons as organizing categories. *Journal of Personality and Social Psychology,* 44:923–932.

Quadagno, D. M., Briscoe, R., and Quadagno, J. S. 1977. Effect of perinatal gonadal hormones on selected nonsexual behavior patterns: A critical assessment of the nonhuman and human literature. *Psychological Bulletin,* 84:62–80.

Quarantelli, E. L., and Cooper, J. 1966. Self-conceptions and others: A further test of Meadian hypotheses. *Sociological Quarterly,* 7:281–297.

Rabbie, J. M., and Horowitz, M. 1969. Arousal of ingroup-outgroup bias by a chance win or loss. *Journal of Personality and Social Psychology,* 13:269–277.

Ramirez, J., Bryant, J., and Zillmann, D. 1982. Effects of erotica on retaliatory behavior as a function of prior provocation. *Journal of Personality and Social Psychology,* 43:971–978.

Rapaport, K., and Burkhart, B. R. 1984. Personality and attitudinal characteristics of sexually coercive college men. *Journal of Abnormal Psychology,* 93:216–221.

Rapoport, A., and Kahan, J. P. 1976. When three is not always two against one: Coalitions in experimental three-person cooperative games. *Journal of Experimental Social Psychology,* 12:253–273.

Raven, B. H. 1974. The comparative analysis of power and power preference. In Tedeschi, J. T. (ed.), *Perspectives on Social Power.* Chicago: Aldine.

———, and Kruglanski, A. W. 1970. Conflict and power. In Swingle, P. (ed.), *The Structure of Conflict.* New York: Academic Press.

Ravitch, D. 1978. The "white flight" controversy. *The Public Interest,* 51:135–149.

Razran, G. 1950. Ethnic dislike and stereotypes: A laboratory study. *Journal of Abnormal and Social Psychology,* 45:7–27.

Reed, R. 1985. Little Rock a symbol again: The resegregation of schools. *New York Times* (March 27):1, 7.

Regan, D. T. 1971. Effects of a favor and liking on compliance. *Journal of Experimental Social Psychology,* 7:627–639.

———, Williams, M., and Sparling, S. 1972. Voluntary expiation of guilt: A field experiment. *Journal of Personality and Social Psychology,* 24:42–45.

Reinisch, J. M. 1981. Prenatal exposure to synthetic progestins increases potential for aggression in humans. *Science,* 211 (March 13):1171–1173.

Reis, H. T., and Burns, L. B. 1982. The salience of the self in responses to inequity. *Journal of Experimental Social Psychology,* 18:464–475.

———, Nezlek, J., and Wheeler, L. 1980. Physical attractiveness in social interaction. *Journal of Personality and Social Psychology,* 38:604–617.

———, Wheeler, L., Kernis, M. H., Speigel, N., and Nezlek, J. 1985. On specificity in the impact of social participation on physical and psychological health. *Journal of Personality and Social Psychology,* 48:456–471.

———, ———, Speigel, N., Kernis, M. H., Nezlek, J., and Perri, M. 1982. Physical attractiveness in social interaction: II. Why does appearance affect social experience? *Journal of Personality and Social Psychology,* 43:979–996.

Ricateau, P. 1971. Processus de catégorisation d'autrui et les mécanismes d'influence. *Bulletin de Psychologie,* 24:909–919.

Richardson, J. T. 1985. The active vs. passive convert: Paradigm conflict in conversion/recruitment research. *Journal for the Scientific Study of Religion,* 24:163–179.

Riche, M. F. 1980. Women at work. *American Demographics,* 2 (September):44–47.

Riegel, K. F. 1975a. Adult life crises: A dialectical interpretation of development. In Datan, N., and Ginsberg, L. H. (eds.), *Life-span Developmental Psychology: Normative Life Crises.* New York: Academic Press.

———. 1975b. Toward a dialectical theory of development. *Human Development,* 18:50–64.

———. 1976. The dialectics of human development. *American Psychologist,* 31:689–700.

———. 1978. *Psychology, Mon Amour: A Countertext.* Boston: Houghton Mifflin.

Riemer, B. S. 1975. Influence of causal beliefs on affect and expectancy. *Journal of Personality and Social Psychology,* 31:1163–1167.

Riess, M., Rosenfeld, P., Melburg, V., and Tedeschi, J. T. 1981. Self-serving attributions: Biased private perceptions and distorted public descriptions. *Journal of Personality and Social Psychology,* 41:224–231.

Riger, S., and Gordon, M. T. 1981. The fear of rape: A study in social control. *Journal of Social Issues,* 37:71–92.

Riggio, R. E., and Friedman, H. S. 1983. Individual differences and cues to deception. *Journal of Personality and Social Psychology,* 45:899–915.

Riordan, C., and Ruggiero, J. 1980. Producing equal-status interracial interaction: A replication. *Social Psychology Quarterly,* 43:131–136.

Riordan, C. A., Marlin, N. A., and Kellogg, R. T. 1983. The effectiveness of accounts following transgression. *Social Psychology Quarterly,* 46:213–219.

Robbins, T., and Anthony, D. 1980. The limits of "coercive persuasion" as an explanation for conversion to authoritarian sects. *Political Psychology,* 2:22–37.

———, and ———. 1982. Deprogramming, brainwashing, and the medicalization of deviant religious groups. *Social Problems,* 29:283–297.

Robinson, I. E., Balkwell, J. W., and Ward, D. M. 1980. Meaning and behavior: An empirical study in sociolinguistics. *Social Psychology Quarterly,* 43:253–258.

Rochford, E. B., Jr. 1982. Recruitment strategies: Ideology and organization in the Hare Krishna movement. *Social Problems,* 29:399–410.

Rodin, J., Solomon, S. K., and Metcalf, J. 1978. Role of control in mediating perceptions of density. *Journal of Personality and Social Psychology,* 36:988–999.

Roger, D. B., and Schumacher, A. 1983. Effects of individual differences on dyadic conversational strategies. *Journal of Personality and Social Psychology,* 45:700–705.

Rogers, C. R. 1970. *On Becoming a Person: A Therapist's View of Psychotherapy.* Boston: Houghton Mifflin.

Rogers, L. 1976. Male hormones and behavior. In Lloyd, B., and Archer, J. (eds.), *Exploring Sex Differences.* New York: Academic Press.

Rogers, M., Miller, N., Mayer, F. S., and Duval, S. 1982. Personal responsibility and salience of the request for help: Determinants of the relation between negative affect and helping behavior. *Journal of Personality and Social Psychology,* 43:956–970.

Rogers, M. F. 1974. Instrumental and infra-resources: The basis of power. *American Journal of Sociology,* 79:1418–1433.

Rogers, R. W. 1983. Cognitive and physiological processes in fear appeals and attitude change: A revised theory of protection motivation. In Cacioppo, J., and Petty, R. (eds.), *Social Psychophysiology.* New York: Guilford Press.

———, and Deckner, C. W. 1975. Effects of fear appeals and physiological arousal upon emotion, attitudes, and cigarette smoking. *Journal of Personality and Social Psychology,* 32:222–230.

Rokeach, M. 1968. *Beliefs, Attitudes, and Values.* San Francisco: Jossey-Bass.

Romer, D. 1979. Internalization versus identification in the laboratory: A causal analysis of attitude change. *Journal of Personality and Social Psychology,* 37:2171–2180.

Rook, K. S., and Dooley, D. 1985. Applying social support research: Theoretical problems and future directions. *Journal of Social Issues,* 41:5–28.

Rosa, E., and Mazur, A. 1979. Incipient status in small groups. *Social Forces,* 58:18–37.

Rose, J. D. 1974. *Introduction to Sociology.* 2nd ed. Chicago: Rand McNally.

Rose, P. I. 1979. *Socialization and the Life Cycle.* New York: St. Martin's Press.

Rosenberg, B. G., and Sutton-Smith, B. 1972. *Sex and Identity.* New York: Holt, Rinehart and Winston.

Rosenberg, M. 1979. *Conceiving the Self.* New York: Basic Books.

_____ , and Simmons, R. G. 1972. *Black and White Self-esteem: The Urban School Child.* Washington, D.C.: American Sociological Association.

Rosenberg, S., and Olshan, K. 1970. Evaluative and descriptive aspects in personality perception. *Journal of Personality and Social Psychology,* 16:619–626.

Rosenblatt, P. C., and Miller, N. 1972. Problems and anxieties in research design and analysis. In McClintock, C. G. (ed.), *Experimental Social Psychology.* New York: Holt, Rinehart and Winston.

Rosenhan, D. L., Salovey, P., and Hargis, K. 1981. The joys of helping: Focus of attention mediates the impact of positive affect on altruism. *Journal of Personality and Social Psychology,* 40:899–905.

_____ , Underwood, B., and Moore, B. 1974. Affect moderates self-gratification and altruism. *Journal of Personality and Social Psychology,* 30:546–552.

Rosenthal, R. 1966. *Experimenter Effects in Behavioral Research.* New York: Appleton-Century-Crofts.

_____ , and Jacobson, L. 1968. *Pygmalion in the Classroom.* New York: Holt, Rinehart and Winston.

_____ , and Rubin, D. B. 1978. Interpersonal expectancy effects: The first 345 studies. *Behavioral and Brain Sciences,* 3:377–415.

Rosenthal, T. L., and Zimmerman, B. J. 1978. *Social Learning and Cognition.* New York: Academic Press.

Rosnow, R. L. 1980. Psychology of rumor reconsidered. *Psychological Bulletin,* 87:578–591.

_____ , and Kimmel, A. J. 1979. Lives of a rumor. *Psychology Today,* 13 (June):88–92.

Rosow, I. 1957. Issues in the concept of need-complementarity. *Sociometry,* 20:216–233.

_____ . 1974. *Socialization to Old Age.* Berkeley: University of California Press.

Ross, E. A. 1908. *Social Psychology: An Outline and Source Book.* New York: Macmillan.

Ross, J. M., Vanneman, R. D., and Pettigrew, T. F. 1976. Patterns of support for George Wallace: Implications for racial change. *Journal of Social Issues,* 32:69–91.

Ross, L. 1977. The intuitive psychologist and his shortcomings: Distortions in the attribution process. In Berkowitz, L. (ed.), *Advances in Experimental Social Psychology.* Vol. 10. New York: Academic Press.

_____ , Greene, D., and House, P. 1977. The "false consensus" effect: An egocentric bias in social perception and attribution processes. *Journal of Experimental Social Psychology,* 13:279–301.

Ross, M., McGarland, C., Conway, M., and Zanna, M. P. 1983. Reciprocal relation between attitudes and behavior recall: Committing people to newly formed attitudes. *Journal of Personality and Social Psychology,* 45:257–267.

_____ , and Sicoly, F. 1979. Egocentric biases in availability and attribution. *Journal of Personality and Social Psychology,* 37:322–336.

Rossell, C. 1976. School desegregation and white flight. *Political Science Quarterly,* 90:675–698.

Rossi, A. S. 1984. Gender and parenthood. *American Sociological Review,* 49:1–19.

Rothbaum, F., Weisz, J. R., and Snyder, S. S. 1982. Changing the world and changing the self: A two-process model of perceived control. *Journal of Personality and Social Psychology,* 42:5–37.

Rubenstein, H. 1973. Some problems of meaning in natural languages. In Pool, I., et al. (eds.), *Handbook of Communication.* Chicago: Rand McNally.

Ruberman, W., Weinblatt, E., Goldberg, J. D., and Chaudhary, B. S. 1984. Psychosocial influences on mortality after myocardial infarction. *New England Journal of Medicine,* 311:552–559.

Rubin, L. 1980. Women of a certain age. *Society,* 17 (March/April):68–76.

Rubin, R. T., Reinisch, J. M., and Haskett, R. F. 1981. Postnatal gonadal steroid effects on human behavior. *Science,* 211 (March 20):1318–1324.

Rubin, Z. 1973. *Liking and Loving.* New York: Holt, Rinehart and Winston.

_____ . 1974. From liking to loving: Patterns of attraction in dating relationships. In Huston, T. L. (ed.), *Foundations of Interpersonal Attraction.* New York: Academic Press.

_____ . 1975. Disclosing oneself to a stranger: Reciprocity and its limits. *Journal of Experimental Social Psychology,* 11:233–260.

_____ . 1977. The love research. *Human Behavior,* 6 (February):56–59.

Rubovits, P. C., and Maehr, M. L. 1973. Pygmalion black and white. *Journal of Personality and Social Psychology,* 25:210–218.

Rusbult, C. E. 1983. A longitudinal test of the investment model: The development (and deterioration) of satisfaction and commitment in heterosexual involvements. *Journal of Personality and Social Psychology,* 45:101–117.

———, and Zembrodt, I. M. 1983. Responses to dissatisfaction in romantic involvements: A multidimensional scaling analysis. *Journal of Experimental Social Psychology,* 19:274–293.

———, ———, and Gunn, L. K. 1982. Exit, voice, loyalty, and neglect: Responses to dissatisfaction in romantic involvements. *Journal of Personality and Social Psychology,* 43:1230–1242.

Russell, C. 1980. Portrait of women. *American Demographics,* 2 (September):40–41.

Russell, D. E. H. 1982. *Rape in Marriage.* New York: Macmillan.

Russo, N. F. 1976. The motherhood mandate. *Journal of Social Issues,* 32:143–153.

Rutkowski, G. K., Gruder, C. L., and Romer, D. 1983. Group cohesiveness, social norms, and bystander intervention. *Journal of Personality and Social Psychology,* 44:545–552.

Rychlak, J. F. 1965. The similarity, compatibility, or incompatibility of needs in interpersonal selection. *Journal of Personality and Social Psychology,* 2:334–340.

Ryen, A. H., and Kahn, A. 1975. Effects of intergroup orientation on group attitudes and proxemic behavior. *Journal of Personality and Social Psychology,* 31:302–310.

Saegert, S. 1978. High-intensity environments: Their personal and social consequences. In Baum, A., and Epstein, Y. M. (eds.), *Human Responses to Crowding.* Hillsdale, N.J.: Erlbaum.

———, Swap, W., and Zajonc, R. B. 1973. Exposure, context, and interpersonal attraction. *Journal of Personality and Social Psychology,* 25:234–242.

Saenger, G., and Gilbert, E. 1950. Customer reactions to the integration of Negro sales personnel. *International Journal of Opinion and Attitude Research,* 4:57–76.

Safire, W. 1975a. Secrets of "American English" may yield to dialect geography. *New York Times* (September 28):8E.

———. 1975b. Big week for gays. *New York Times* (September 29):31.

Sage, W. 1978. Social scientists have some answers about the busing controversy. What are they? To find out you just pay your money and take your choice. *Human Behavior,* 7:18–23.

St. John, N. 1975. *School Desegregation: Outcomes for Children.* New York: Wiley.

Saks, M. J. 1977. *Jury Verdicts: The Role of Group Size and Social Decision Rule.* Lexington, Mass.: Lexington Books.

Salmans, S. 1985. Man in the moon loses job at P&G. *New York Times* (April 25):31, 36.

Salzinger, K. 1979. Language behavior. In Catania, A. C., and Brigham, T. A. (eds.), *Handbook of Applied Behavior Analysis.* New York: Irvington.

Sampson, E. E. 1975. On justice as equality. *Journal of Social Issues,* 31:45–64.

Sanday, P. R. 1981. The socio-cultural context of rape: A cross-cultural study. *Journal of Social Issues,* 37:5–27.

Sanders, W. B. 1974. *The Sociologist as Detective.* New York: Praeger.

Sapir, E. 1949. *Selected Writings in Language, Culture, and Personality.* Berkeley: University of California Press.

Sarty, M. 1975. *The "Pretty Girl" as a Sexual and Reproductive Stereotype.* Department of Human Behavior, University of Southern California School of Medicine.

Savage-Rumbaugh, E. S. 1979. Symbolic communication—Its origins and early development in the chimpanzee. *New Directions for Child Development,* 3:1–15.

———, Rumbaugh, D. M., Smith, S. T., and Lawson, J. 1980. Reference: The linguistic essential. *Science,* 210:922–924.

Scarr, S. 1985. Constructing psychology. *American Psychologist,* 40:499–512.

Schachter, S. 1959. *The Psychology of Affiliation.* Stanford, Calif.: Stanford University Press.

Schaeffer, G. H., and Patterson, M. L. 1980. Intimacy, arousal, and small group crowding. *Journal of Personality and Social Psychology,* 38:283–290.

Schafer, A. T., and Gray, M. W. 1981. Sex and mathematics. *Science,* 211:231.

Schafer, R. B., and Keith, P. M. 1985. A causal model approach to the symbolic interactionist view of the self-concept. *Journal of Personality and Social Psychology,* 48:963–969.

Schank, R. C., and Abelson, R. P. 1977. *Scripts, Plans, Goals, and Understanding.* Hillsdale, N.J.: Erlbaum.

Schattschneider, E. E. 1960. *The Semi-Sovereign People.* New York: Holt, Rinehart and Winston.

Scheflen, A. E. 1965. Quasi-courtship behavior in psychotherapy. *Psychiatry,* 28:245–257.

Scheier, M. F., and Carver, C. S. 1977. Self-focused attention and the experience of emotion: Attraction, repulsion, elation, and depression. *Journal of Personality and Social Psychology,* 35:625–636.

Schein, E. H., Schneier, I., and Barker, C. H. 1961. *Coercive Pressure.* New York: Norton.

Scherer, K. R., Abeles, R. P., and Fischer, C. S.

1975. *Human Aggression and Conflict: Interdisciplinary Perspectives*. Englewood Cliffs, N.J.: Prentice-Hall.

Schiffenbauer, A. 1974. Effect of observer's emotional state on judgments of the emotional state of others. *Journal of Personality and Social Psychology,* 30:31–35.

Schlenker, B. R. 1980. *Impression Management: The Self-Concept, Social Identity, and Interpersonal Relations*. Monterey, Calif.: Brooks/Cole.

———, Brown, R. C., Jr., and Tedeschi, J. T. 1975. Attraction and expectations of harm and benefits. *Journal of Personality and Social Psychology,* 32:664–670.

———, and Leary, M. R. 1982. Social anxiety and self-presentation: A conceptualization and model. *Psychological Bulletin,* 92:641–669.

Schlesinger, A., Jr. 1965. *A Thousand Days*. Boston: Houghton Mifflin.

Schmidt, D. E., and Keating, J. P. 1979. Human crowding and personal control: An integration of the research. *Psychological Bulletin,* 86:680–700.

Schmidt, D. F., and Sherman, R. C. 1984. Memory for persuasive messages: A test of a schema-copy-plus-tag model. *Journal of Personality and Social Psychology,* 47:17–25.

Schmidt, W. E. 1985. Jim Crow is gone, but white resistance remains. *New York Times* (April 6):1, 7.

Schneider, D. J. 1973. Implicit personality theory: A review. *Psychological Bulletin,* 79:294–319.

———, and Blankmeyer, B. L. 1983. Prototype salience and implicit personality theories. *Journal of Personality and Social Psychology,* 44:712–722.

Schneider, W., and Lewis, I. A. 1984. The straight story on homosexuality and gay rights. *Public Opinion,* 7 (February/March):16–20+.

Schofield, J. W. 1975. Effects of norms, public disclosure, and need for approval on volunteering behavior consistent with attitudes. *Journal of Personality and Social Psychology,* 31:1126–1133.

———. 1982. *Black and White in School: Trust, Tension, or Tolerance?* New York: Praeger.

Schopler, J., and Layton, B. 1972. Determinants of the self-attribution of having influenced another person. *Journal of Personality and Social Psychology,* 22:326–332.

———, and ———. 1974. Attributions of interpersonal power. In Tedeschi, J. T. (ed.), *Perspectives on Social Power*. Chicago: Aldine.

Schram, S. F., and Turbett, J. P. 1983. Civil disorder and the welfare explosion: A two-step process. *American Sociological Review,* 48:408–414.

Schulman, G. I. 1974. Race, sex, and violence: A laboratory test of the sexual threat of the black male hypothesis. *American Journal of Sociology,* 79:1260–1277.

Schutte, J. G., and Light, J. M. 1978. The relative importance of proximity and status of friendship choices in social hierarchies. *Social Psychology,* 41:260–264.

Schutz, A. 1964. *Collected Papers*. Edited by A. Bodersen. The Hague: Martin Nijhoff.

———. 1971. *Collected Papers*. The Hague: Martin Nijhoff.

Schwartz, B., and Barsky, S. F. 1977. The home advantage. *Social Forces,* 55:641–661.

———, Tesser, A., and Powell, E. 1982. Dominance cues in nonverbal behavior. *Social Psychology Quarterly,* 45:114–120.

Schwartz, M. F., and Masters, W. H. 1984. The Masters and Johnson treatment program for dissatisfied homosexual men. *American Journal of Psychiatry,* 141:173–181.

Schwartz, S., and David, A. B. 1976. Responsibility and helping in an emergency: Effects of blame, ability and denial of responsibility. *Sociometry,* 39:406–415.

———, and Fleishman, J. A. 1978. Personal norms and the mediation of legitimacy effects on helping. *Social Psychology,* 41:306–315.

Schwartz, S. H., and Gottlieb, A. 1980a. Bystander anonymity and reactions to emergencies. *Journal of Personality and Social Psychology,* 39:418–430.

———, and ———. 1980b. Participation in a bystander intervention experiment and subsequent everyday helping: Ethical considerations. *Journal of Experimental Social Psychology,* 16:161–171.

———, and ———. 1981. Participants' post-experimental reactions and the ethics of bystander research. *Journal of Experimental Social Psychology,* 17:396–407

Schwarz, L. M., Foa, U. G., and Foa, E. B. 1983. Multichannel nonverbal communication: Evidence for combinatory rules. *Journal of Personality and Social Psychology,* 45:274–281.

Schwarz, N., and Clore, G. L. 1983. Mood, misattribution, and judgment of well-being: Informative and directive functions of affective states. *Journal of Personality and Social Psychology,* 45:513–523.

Scott, J. W. 1982. The mechanization of women's work. *Scientific American,* 247:167–187.

Scott, M. B., and Lyman, S. M. 1968. Accounts. *American Sociological Review,* 33:46–62.

Scott, W. A., and Scott, R. 1981. Intercorrelations among structural properties of primary groups. *Journal of Personality and Social Psychology,* 41:279–292.

Scruton, R. 1984. Public space and the classical vernacular. *Public Interest,* 74:5–16.

Scully, D., and Marolla, J. 1984. Convicted rapists' vocabulary of motive: Excuses and justifications. *Social Problems,* 31:530–544.

Sears, D. O., and Kinder, D. R. 1985. Whites' opposition to busing: On conceptualizing and operationalizing group conflict. *Journal of Personality and Social Psychology,* 48:1141–1147.

Sears, R. R., Rau, L., and Alpert, R. 1965. *Identification and Child Rearing.* Stanford, Calif.: Stanford University Press.

Sebeok, T. A., and Umiker-Sebeok, J. 1980. *Speaking of Apes: A Critical Anthology of Two-Way Communication with Man.* New York: Plenum Press.

Seeman, M., Seeman, T., and Sayles, M. 1985. Social networks and health status: A longitudinal analysis. *Social Psychology Quarterly,* 48:237–248.

Segal, M. W. 1974. Alphabet and attraction: An unobtrusive measure of the effect of propinquity in a field setting. *Journal of Personality and Social Psychology,* 30:654–657.

Seligman, C., Bush, M., and Kirsch, K. 1976. Relationship between compliance in the foot-in-the-door paradigm and size of first request. *Journal of Personality and Social Psychology,* 33:517–520.

Seligman, M. E. P. 1975. *Helplessness.* San Francisco: Freeman.

Seligmann, J. 1984. The date who rapes. *Newsweek* (April 9):91–92.

Selznick, G. J., and Steinberg, S. 1969. *The Tenacity of Prejudice.* New York: Harper and Row.

Selznick, P. 1952. *The Organizational Weapon.* New York: McGraw-Hill.

Sensenig, J., and Brehm, J. W. 1968. Attitude change from an implied threat to attitudinal freedom. *Journal of Personality and Social Psychology,* 8:324–330.

Serbin, L. A., O'Leary, K. D., Kent, R. N., and Tonick, I. J. 1973. A comparison of teacher response to the pre-academic and problem behavior of boys and girls. *Child Development,* 44:796–804.

Serrin, W. 1984. Experts say job bias against women persists. *New York Times* (November 25):1, 18.

Shaffer, D. R. 1975. Some effects of consonant and dissonant attitudinal advocacy on initial attitude salience and attitude change. *Journal of Personality and Social Psychology,* 32:160–168.

———, and Sadowski, C. 1975. This table is mine: Respect for marked barroom tables as a function of gender of spatial marker and desirability of locale. *Sociometry,* 38:408–419.

Shanteau, J., and Nagy, G. F. 1979. Probability of acceptance in dating choice. *Journal of Personality and Social Psychology,* 37:522–533.

Shapley, L. S., and Shubik, M. 1954. A method of evaluating the distribution of power in a committee system. *American Political Science Review,* 48:787–792.

Shaw, M. E. 1971. *Group Dynamics: The Psychology of Small Groups.* New York: McGraw-Hill.

———, and Costanzo, P. R. 1982. *Theories of Social Psychology.* 2nd ed. New York: McGraw-Hill.

Sheehy, G. 1976. *Passages.* New York: Dutton.

Shellenberg, J. A., and Bee, L. S. 1960. A reexamination of the theory of complementary needs in mate selection. *Marriage and Family Living,* 22: 227–232.

Sheppard, B. H., and Vidmar, N. 1980. Adversary pretrial procedures and testimonial evidence: Effects of lawyer's role and Machiavellianism. *Journal of Personality and Social Psychology,* 39:320–332.

Sherif, C. W. 1980. Comment on ethic issues in Malamuth, Heim, and Feshbach's "Sexual responsiveness of college students to rape depictions: Inhibitory and disinhibitory effects." *Journal of Personality and Social Psychology,* 38:409–412.

Sherif, M. 1936. *The Psychology of Social Norms.* New York: Harper and Row.

———, Harvey, O. J., White, B. J., Hood, W. R., and Sherif, C. W. 1961. *Intergroup Conflict and Cooperation: The Robbers Cave Experiment.* Norman: Institute of Group Relations, University of Oklahoma.

———, and Sherif, C. W. 1969. *Social Psychology.* New York: Harper and Row.

Sherman, J. 1978. *Sex-Related Cognitive Differences.* Springfield, Ill.: Charles C. Thomas.

———. 1980. Mathematics, spatial visualization, and related factors: Changes in girls and boys, grades 8–11. *Journal of Educational Psychology,* 72:476–482.

Sherman, L. W., and Berk, R. A. 1984. The specific deterrent effects of arrest for domestic assault. *American Sociological Review,* 49:261–272.

———, and Bouza, A. V. 1984. The need to police domestic violence. *Wall Street Journal* (May 22):30.

Sherwood, J. J., Barron, J. W., and Fitch, H. G. 1969. Cognitive dissonance: Theory and research. In Wagner, R. V., and Sherwood, J. J. (eds.), *The Study of Attitude Change.* Belmont, Calif.: Brooks/Cole.

Shibutani, T. 1961. *Society and Personality.* Englewood Cliffs, N.J.: Prentice-Hall.

———, and Kwan, K. M. 1965. *Ethnic Stratification.* New York: Macmillan.

Shiflett, S. 1979. Toward a general model of small group productivity. *Psychological Bulletin,* 86:67–79.

Shils, E. A. 1950. Primary groups in the American army. In Merton, R. K., and Lazarsfeld, P. F. (eds.), *Continuities in Social Research.* New York: Free Press.

———, and Janowitz, M. 1948. Cohesion and disintegration in the Wehrmacht in World War II. *Public Opinion Quarterly,* 12:280–315.

Shinn, M., Lehmann, S., and Wong, N. W. 1984. Social interaction and social support. *Journal of Social Issues,* 40:55–76.

Shipp, E. R. 1985. Racism lingers in Mississippi despite gains. *New York Times* (April 2):1, 12.

Shortell, J., Epstein, S., and Taylor, S. P. 1970. Instigation to aggression as a function of degree of defeat and perceived aggressive intent of the opponent. *Journal of Personality,* 38:313–328.

Shotland, R. L. 1985. When bystanders just stand by. *Psychology Today,* 19 (June):50–55.

———, and Huston, T. L. 1979. Emergencies: What are they and do they influence bystanders to intervene? *Journal of Personality and Social Psychology,* 37:1822–1834.

Shrauger, J. S., and Schoeneman, T. J. 1979. Symbolic interactionist view of self-concept: Through the looking glass darkly. *Psychological Bulletin,* 86:549–573.

Shumaker, S. A., and Brownell, A. 1984. Toward a theory of social support: Closing conceptual gaps. *Journal of Social Issues,* 40:11–36.

———, and Jackson, J. S. 1979. The aversive effects of nonreciprocated benefits. *Social Psychology Quarterly,* 42:148–158.

Sieber, J. E. 1983. Deception in social research III: The nature and limits of debriefing. *IRB: A Review of Human Subjects Research,* 5:1–4.

Siegelman, J., and Conway, F. 1979. Snapping: Welcome to the eighties. *Playboy,* 26 (March):59+.

Sigall, H., and Ostrove, N. 1975. Beautiful but dangerous: Effects of offender attractiveness and nature of the crime on juridic judgment. *Journal of Personality and Social Psychology,* 31:410–414.

Simkus, A. A. 1978. Residential segregation by occupation and race in ten urbanized areas, 1950–1970. *American Sociological Review,* 43:81–93.

Simmel, G. 1902. The number of members as determining the sociological form of the group. *American Journal of Sociology,* 8:1–46, 158–196.

———. 1955. *Conflict.* Translated by K. H. Wolff. New York: Free Press.

———. 1971. *On Individuality and Social Forms.* Edited by D. Levine. Chicago: University of Chicago Press.

Simmons, R. G., Brown, L., Bush, D. M., and Blyth, D. A. 1978. Self-esteem and achievement of black and white adolescents. *Social Problems,* 26:86–96.

Simons, C. W., and Piliavin, J. A. 1972. Effects of deception on reactions to a victim. *Journal of Personality and Social Psychology,* 21:56–60.

Simpson, D. D., and Ostrom, T. M. 1976. Contrast effects in impression formation. *Journal of Personality and Social Psychology,* 34:625–629.

Singer, E. 1981. Reference groups and social evaluations. In Rosenberg, M., and Turner, R. H. (eds.), *Social Psychology: Sociological Perspectives.* New York: Basic Books.

Singer, M. T. 1979. Coming out of the cults. *Psychology Today,* 12 (January):72–82+.

Skinner, B. F. 1948. *Walden Two.* New York: Macmillan.

———. 1953. *Science and Human Behavior.* New York: Macmillan.

———. 1957. *Verbal Behavior.* New York: Appleton-Century-Crofts.

———. 1974. *About Behaviorism.* New York: Vintage Books.

Skocpol, T. 1979. *States and Social Revolutions: A Comparative Analysis of France, Russia, and China.* New York: Cambridge University Press.

Skrypnek, B. J., and Snyder, M. 1982. On the self-perpetuating nature of stereotypes about men and women. *Journal of Experimental Social Psychology,* 18:277–291.

Smelser, N. 1963. *Theory of Collective Behavior.* New York: Free Press.

Smith, E. R. 1984. Attributions and other inferences: Processing information about the self versus others. *Journal of Experimental Social Psychology,* 20:97–115.

Smith, G. F., and Dorfman, D. D. 1975. The effect of stimulus uncertainty on the relationship between frequency of exposure and liking. *Journal of Personality and Social Psychology,* 31:150–155.

Smith, H. W. 1981. Territorial spacing on a beach revisited: A cross-national exploration. *Social Psychology Quarterly,* 44:132–137.

Smith, M. 1978. Perspectives on selfhood. *American Psychologist,* 33:1053–1063.

Smith, M. D., Zingale, S. A., and Coleman, J. M. 1978. The influence of adult expectancy/child performance discrepancies upon children's self-concepts. *American Eductional Research Journal,* 15:259–265.

Smith, M. J. 1982. *Persuasion and Human Action: A Review and Critique of Social Influence Theories.* Belmont, Calif.: Wadsworth.

Smith, S. S., and Richardson, D. 1983. Amelioration of deception and harm in psychological research: The important role of debriefing. *Journal of Personality and Social Psychology,* 44:1075–1082.

Smith, T. W., and Sheatsley, P. B. 1984. American attitudes toward race relations. *Public Opinion,* 7 (October/November):14–15, 50–53.

Snow, C. E. 1977. The development of conversation between mothers and babies. *Journal of Child Language,* 4:1–22.

Snow, D. A., Zurcher, L. A., Jr., and Ekland-Olson, S. 1980. Social networks and social movements: A microstructural approach to differential recruitment. *American Sociological Review,* 45:787–801.

Snyder, C. R. and Fromkin, H. L. 1980. *Uniqueness: The Human Pursuit of Difference.* New York: Plenum Press.

⸺ , Higgins, R., and Stucky, R. J. 1983. *Excuses: Masquerades in Search of Grace.* New York: Wiley.

⸺ , and Smith, T. W. 1982. Symptoms as self-handicapping strategies: The virtues of old wine in a new bottle. In Weary, G., and Mirels, H. L. (eds.), *Integrations of Clinical and Social Psychology.* New York: Oxford University Press.

⸺ , ⸺ , Augelli, R. W., and Ingram, R. E. 1985. On the self-serving function of social anxiety: Shyness as a self-handicapping strategy. *Journal of Personality and Social Psychology,* 48:970–980.

Snyder, D., and Tilly, C. 1972. Hardship and collective violence in France, 1820 to 1960. *American Sociological Review,* 37:520–532.

Snyder, M. 1974. Self-monitoring of expressive behavior. *Journal of Personality and Social Psychology,* 30:526–537.

⸺ . 1980. The many me's of the self-monitor. *Psychology Today,* 13 (March):33–40 + .

⸺ , and Cantor, N. 1980. Thinking about ourselves and others: Self-monitoring and social knowledge. *Journal of Personality and Social Psychology,* 39:222–234.

⸺ , and Cunningham, M. R. 1975. To comply or not comply: Testing the self-perception explanation of the "foot-in-the-door" phenomenon. *Journal of Personality and Social Psychology,* 31:64–67.

⸺ , Gangestad, S., and Simpson, J. A. 1983. Choosing friends as activity partners: The role of self-monitoring. *Journal of Personality and Social Psychology,* 45:1061–1072.

⸺ , and Kendzierski, D. 1982. Acting on one's attitudes: Procedures for linking attitude and behavior. *Journal of Experimental Social Psychology,* 18:165–183.

⸺ , and Simpson, J. A. 1984. Self-monitoring and dating relationships. *Journal of Personality and Social Psychology,* 47:1281–1291.

⸺ , and Uranowitz, S. W. 1978. Reconstructing the past: Some cognitive consequences of person perception. *Journal of Personality and Social Psychology,* 36:941–950.

Snyder, M. L., Stephan, W. G., and Rosenfield, D. 1976. Egotism and attribution. *Journal of Personality and Social Psychology,* 33:435–441.

Sobel, D. 1980. In pursuit of love: Three current studies. *New York Times* (January 22):C1, C5.

⸺ . 1981. For some people, studies find, "one true self" isn't enough. *New York Times* (November 24):19.

Sommer, R. 1961. Leadership and group geography. *Sociometry,* 24:99–110.

⸺ . 1966. Man's proximate environment. *Journal of Social Issues,* 22:59–70.

⸺ . 1967. Small group ecology. *Psychological Bulletin,* 67:145–152.

⸺ . 1969. *Personal Space: The Behavioral Basis of Design.* Englewood Cliffs, N.J.: Prentice-Hall.

Sorrentino, R. M., King, G., and Leo, G. 1980. The influence of the minority on perception: A note on a possible alternative explanation. *Journal of Experimental Social Psychology,* 16:293–301.

Spector, M., and Kitsuse, J. I. 1973. Social problems: A re-formulation. *Social Problems,* 21:145–159.

Speier, H. 1941. The social types of war. *American Journal of Sociology,* 46:445–454.

Spence, J. T., and Helmreich, R. L. 1978. *Masculinity and Femininity: Their Psychological Dimensions, Correlates, and Antecedents.* Austin: University of Texas Press.

Spilerman, S. 1970. The causes of racial disturbances: A comparison of alternate explanations. *American Sociological Review,* 35:627–649.

———. 1971. The causes of racial disturbances: Tests of explanations. *American Sociological Review,* 36:427–442.

———. 1976. Structural characteristics of cities and the severity of racial disorders. *American Sociological Review,* 41:771–793.

Spinetta, J. J., and Rigler, D. 1975. The child-abusing parent: A psychological review. *Psychological Bulletin,* 77:296–304.

Stagner, R., and Congdon, C. S. 1955. Another failure to demonstrate displacement of aggression. *Journal of Abnormal and Social Psychology,* 51:659–696.

Stahl, S. M., and Lebedun, M. 1974. Mystery gas: An analysis of mass hysteria. *Journal of Health and Social Behavior,* 15:44–50.

Stake, J. E. 1983. Factors in reward distribution: Allocator motive, gender, and Protestant Ethic endorsement. *Journal of Personality and Social Psychology,* 44:410–418.

———, 1985. Exploring the basis of sex differences in third-party allocations. *Journal of Personality and Social Psychology,* 48:1621–1629.

———, and Katz, J. F. 1982. Teacher-pupil relationships in the elementary school classroom: Teacher-gender and pupil-gender differences. *American Educational Research Journal,* 19:465–471.

Stannard, U. 1972. The mask of beauty. In Gornick, V., and Moran, B. K. (eds.), *Woman in Sexist Society.* New York: New American Library.

Stark, R. S., and Bainbridge, W. S. 1980. Networks of faith: Interpersonal bonds and recruitment to cults and sects. *American Journal of Sociology,* 85:1376–1395.

Staub, E. 1978. *Positive Social Behavior and Morality: Social and Personal Influences.* Vol. 1. New York: Academic Press.

Steele, B. G., and Pollock, C. B. 1968. A psychiatric study of parents who abuse infants and small children. In Helfer, R. E., and Kempe, C. H. (eds.), *The Battered Child.* Chicago: University of Chicago Press.

Steele, C. M., and Liu, T. J. 1983. Dissonance processes as self-affirmation. *Journal of Personality and Social Psychology,* 45:5–19.

———, Southwick, L. L., and Critchlow, B. 1981. Dissonance and alcohol: Drinking your troubles away. *Journal of Personality and Social Psychology,* 41:831–846.

Stember, C. H. 1976. *Sexual Racism.* New York: Elsevier.

Stephan, C. W., and Langlois, J. H. 1984. Baby beautiful: Adult attributions of infant competence as a function of infant attractiveness. *Child Development,* 55:576–585.

Stephan, W. G., and Rosenfield, D. 1978. Effects of desegregation on race relations and self-esteem. *Journal of Educational Psychology,* 70:670–679.

Stephenson, B., and Wicklund, R. A. 1983. Self-directed attention and taking the other's perspective. *Journal of Experimental Social Psychology,* 19:58–77.

———, and ———. 1984. The contagion of self-focus within a dyad. *Journal of Personality and Social Psychology,* 46:163–168.

Sternberg, R. J., and Grajek, S. 1984. The nature of love. *Journal of Personality and Social Psychology,* 47:312–319.

Sternthal, B., Phillips, L. W., and Dholakia, R. 1978. The persuasive effect of source credibility: A situational analysis. *Public Opinion Quarterly,* 42:285–314.

Stevens, C. W. 1981. K-Mart has a little trouble killing those phantom snakes from Asia. *Wall Street Journal* (October 20):31.

Stewart, S. A. 1984. Pay for women up, but unequal. *USA Today* (October 31):1D.

———. 1985. Intermarriage: Keeping the faith. *USA Today* (May 22):4D.

Stiles, W. B., Orth, J. E., Scherwitz, L., Hennrikus, D., and Vallbona, C. 1984. Role behaviors in routine medical interviews with hypertensive patients: A repertoire of verbal exchanges. *Social Psychology Quarterly,* 47:244–254.

Stokols, D. 1972. On the distinction between density and crowding: Some implications for future research. *Psychology Review,* 79:275–277.

———. 1978. A typology of crowding experiences. In Baum, A., and Epstein, Y. M. (eds.), *Human Responses to Crowding.* Hillsdale, N.J.: Erlbaum.

Stoller, R. J. 1975. *Sex and Gender.* Vol. 2: The Transsexual Experiment. New York: Aronson.

Stone, G. P. 1970. Appearance and the self. In Stone, G. P., and Faberman, H. A. (eds.), *Social Psychology through Symbolic Interaction.* Waltham, Mass.: Xerox.

Stoner, J. A. F. 1961. A comparison of individual and group decisions involving risk. Unpublished master's thesis, School of Industrial Management, Massachusetts Institute of Technology.

Storms, M. D. 1973. Videotape and the attribution process: Reversing actors' and observers' points of view. *Journal of Personality and Social Psychology,* 27:165–175.

———. 1979. Sex role identity and its relationships to sex role attributes and sex role stereotypes. *Journal of Personality and Social Psychology,* 37:1779–1789.

———. 1980. Theories of sexual orientation. *Journal of Personality and Social Psychology,* 38:783–792.

———, and Thomas, G. C. 1977. Reactions to physical closeness. *Journal of Personality and Social Psychology,* 35:412–418.

Straus, M. A., Gelles, R. J., and Steinmetz, S. K. 1980. *Behind Closed Doors: Violence in the American Family.* New York: Anchor Books.

Strauss, A. 1964. *Psychiatric Ideologies and Institutions.* New York: Free Press.

Streufert, S., and Streufert, S. C. 1969. Effects of conceptual structure, failure, and success on attribution of causality and interpersonal attitudes. *Journal of Personality and Social Psychology,* 11:138–147.

Stricker, G. 1963. Scapegoating: An experimental investigation. *Journal of Abnormal and Social Psychology,* 67:125–131.

Strodtbeck, F. L., and Hook, L. H. 1961. The social dimensions of a twelve-man jury table. *Sociometry,* 24:397–415.

———, James, R., and Hawkins, C. 1957. Social status in jury deliberations. *American Sociological Review,* 22:713–718.

———, and Mann, R. 1956. Sex role differentiation in jury deliberations. *Sociometry,* 19:3–11.

Strube, M. J., and Barbour, L. S. 1983. The decision to leave an abusive relationship: Economic dependence and psychological commitment. *Journal of Marriage and the Family,* 45:785–803.

———, and ———. 1984. Factors related to the decision to leave an abusive relationship. *Journal of Marriage and the Family,* 46:837–844.

Stryker, S. 1977. Developments in "two social psychologies": Toward an appreciation of mutual relevance. *Sociometry,* 40:145–160.

———. 1980. *Symbolic Interactionism: A Social Structural Version.* Menlo Park, Calif.: Benjamin/Cummings.

———, and Statham, A. 1985. Symbolic interaction and role theory. In Lindzey, G., and

Aronson, E. (eds.), *Handbook of Social Psychology.* 3rd ed. Vol. 1. New York: Random House.

Sullivan, H. S. 1947. *Conceptions of Modern Psychiatry.* Washington, D.C.: William A. White Psychiatric Foundation.

———. 1953. *The Interpersonal Theory of Psychiatry.* New York: Norton.

Sumner, W. G. 1906. *Folkways.* Boston: Ginn.

Sundstrom, E. 1975. An experimental study of crowding: Effects of room size, intrusion, and goal blocking on nonverbal behavior, self-disclosure, and self-reported stress. *Journal of Personality and Social Psychology,* 32:645–654.

———. 1978. Crowding as a sequential process: Review of research on the effects of population density on humans. In Baum, A., and Epstein, Y. M. (eds.), *Human Responses to Crowding.* Hillsdale, N.J.: Erlbaum.

———, and Altman, I. 1974. Field study of territorial behavior and dominance. *Journal of Personality and Social Psychology,* 30:115–124.

Sussman, N. M., and Rosenfeld, H. M. 1982. Influence of culture, language, and sex on conversational distance. *Journal of Personality and Social Psychology,* 42:66–74.

Suttles, G. D. 1968. *The Social Order of the Slum.* Chicago: University of Chicago Press.

Swann, W. B., Jr., and Ely, R. J. 1984. A battle of wills: Self-verification versus behavioral confirmation. *Journal of Personality and Social Psychology,* 46:1287–1302.

———, and Hill, C. A. 1982. When our identities are mistaken: Reaffirming self-conceptions through social interaction. *Journal of Personality and Social Psychology,* 43:59–66.

———, and Read. S. J. 1981a. Acquiring self-knowledge: The search for feedback that fits. *Journal of Personality and Social Psychology,* 41:1119–1128.

———, and ———. 1981b. Self-verification processes: How we sustain our self-conceptions. *Journal of Experimental Social Psychology,* 17:351–372.

Tagiuri, R. 1969. Person perception. In Lindzey, G., and Aronson, E. (eds.), *The Handbook of Social Psychology.* 2nd ed. Vol. 3. Reading, Mass.: Addison-Wesley.

Tajfel, H. 1981. *Human Groups and Social Categories.* New York: Cambridge University Press.

———, and Billig, M. 1974. Familiarity and categorization in intergroup behavior. *Journal of Experimental Social Psychology,* 10:159–170.

Takooshian, H., Haber, S., and Lucido, D. J. 1977. Who wouldn't help a lost child? You, maybe. *Psychology Today,* 10 (February):67–68+.

Tanford, S., and Penrod, S. 1983. Computer modeling of influence in the jury: The role of the consistent juror. *Social Psychology Quarterly,* 46:200–212.

Tannenbaum, A. S. 1965. Unions. In March, J. G. (ed.), *Handbook of Organizations.* Chicago: Rand McNally.

Tavris, C. 1983. *Anger: The Misunderstood Emotion.* New York: Simon and Schuster.

Taylor, D. G., Sheatsley, P. B., and Greeley, A. M. 1978. Attitudes toward racial integration. *Scientific American,* 238 (June):42–49.

Taylor, M. C. 1982. Improved conditions, rising expectations, and dissatisfaction: A test of the past/present relative deprivation hypothesis. *Social Psychology Quarterly,* 45:24–33.

———, and Hall, J. A. 1982. Psychological androgyny: Theories, methods, and conclusions. *Psychological Bulletin,* 92:347–366.

Taylor, R. B., and Lanni, J. C. 1981. Territorial dominance: The influence of the resident advantage in triadic decision making. *Journal of Personality and Social Psychology,* 41:909–915.

Taylor, S. E. 1975. On inferring one's attitudes from one's behavior: Some delimiting conditions. *Journal of Personality and Social Psychology,* 31:126–131.

———, Wood, J. V., and Lichtman, R. R. 1983. It could be worse: Selective evaluation as a response to victimization. *Journal of Social Issues,* 39:19–40.

Tedeschi, J. T., Schlenker, B., and Bonoma, T. 1973. *Conflict, Power, and Games.* Chicago: Aldine.

Tennov, D. 1979. *Love and Limerence.* New York: Stein & Day.

Terborg, J. R., Castore, C., and DeNinno, J. A. 1976. A longitudinal field investigation of the impact of group composition on group performance and cohesion. *Journal of Personality and Social Psychology,* 34:782–790.

Terrace, H. S. 1979. How Nim Chimpsky changed my mind. *Psychology Today,* 13 (November):65–76.

Tetlock, P. E. 1979. Identifying victims of groupthink from public statements of decision makers. *Journal of Personality and Social Psychology,* 37:1314–1324.

———. 1983. Accountability and the persever-

ance of first impressions. *Social Psychology Quarterly,* 46:285–292.

Theodorson, G. A., and Theodorson, A. G. 1969. *Modern Dictionary of Sociology.* New York: Crowell.

Thibaut, J. W. 1950. An experimental study of the cohesiveness of underprivileged groups. *Human Relations,* 3:251–278.

———, and Coules, J. 1952. The role of communication in the reduction of interpersonal hostility. *Journal of Abnormal and Social Psychology,* 46:770–777.

———, Friedland, N., and Walker, L. 1974. Compliance with rules: Some social determinants. *Journal of Personality and Social Psychology,* 30:792–801.

———, and Kelley, H. H. 1959. *The Social Psychology of Groups.* New York: Wiley.

———, and Riecken, H. W. 1955. Some determinants and consequences of the perception of social causality. *Journal of Personality,* 24:113–133.

Thiessen, D., and Rice, M. 1976. Mammalian scent gland marking and social behavior. *Psychological Bulletin,* 83:505–539.

Thistlethwaite, D. L., and Kamenetzky, J. 1955. Attitude change through refutation and elaboration of audience counterarguments. *Journal of Abnormal and Social Psychology,* 51:3–9.

Thoits, P. A. 1983. Multiple identities and psychological well-being: A reformulation and test of the social isolation hypothesis. *American Sociological Review,* 48:174–187.

Thomas, W. I. 1931. The relation of research to the social process. In *Essays on Research in the Social Sciences.* Washington, D.C.: The Brookings Institution.

———. 1937. *The Unadjusted Girl.* Boston: Little, Brown.

Thompson, S. C., and Kelley, H. H. 1981. Judgments of responsibility for activities in close relationships. *Journal of Personality and Social Psychology,* 41:469–477.

Thorndike, E. L. 1907. *The Elements of Psychology.* New York: A. G. Seiler.

———. 1931. *Human Learning.* New York: Appleton.

Thornton, B. 1984. Defensive attribution of responsibility: Evidence for an arousal-based motivational bias. *Journal of Personality and Social Psychology,* 46:721–734.

Thornton, R. 1981. Demographic antecedents of a revitalization movement: Population change, population size, and the 1890 Ghost Dance. *American Sociological Review,* 46:88–96.

Thurow, L. C. 1981. Why women are paid less than men. *New York Times* (March 8):41.

Tierney, K. J. 1982. The battered women movement and the creation of the wife beating problem. *Social Problems,* 29:207–220.

Tilly, C. 1978. *From Mobilization to Revolution.* Reading, Mass.: Addison-Wesley.

Timnick, L. 1983. When women rape men. *Psychology Today,* 17:74–75.

Tinbergen, N. 1939. The behavior of the snow bunting. *Transactions of the Linnaean Society,* 5:1–95.

Tobias, S. 1982. Sexist equations. *Psychology Today,* 16 (January):14–17.

Toi, M., and Batson, C. D. 1982. More evidence that empathy is a source of altruistic motivation. *Journal of Personality and Social Psychology,* 43:281–292.

Tolman, E. C. 1932. *Purposive Behavior in Animals and Men.* New York: Appleton-Century-Crofts.

Tolstoy, L. 1869/1957. *War and Peace.* Middlesex, England: Penguin.

Townsend, B. 1985. Working women. *American Demographics,* 7 (January):4–7.

Traugott, M. 1978. Reconceiving social movements. *Social Problems,* 26:38–49.

Travers, J., and Milgram, S. 1969. An experimental study of the small-world problem. *Sociometry,* 32:425–443.

Triandis, H. C. 1971. *Attitude and Attitude Change.* New York: Wiley.

Trimboli, C., and Walker, M. B. 1982. Smooth transitions in conversational turn-taking: Implications for theory. *Journal of Social Psychology,* 117:305–306.

———, and ———. 1984. Switching pauses in cooperative and competitive conversations. *Journal of Experimental Social Psychology,* 20:297–311.

Truninger, E. 1971. Marital violence. The legal solutions. *The Hastings Law Journal,* 23:259–276.

Tuddenham, R. D., and Macbride, P. 1959. The yielding experiment from the subject's point of view. *Journal of Personality,* 27:259–271.

Turnbull, C. M. 1972. *The Mountain People.* New York: Simon and Schuster.

Turner, R. H. 1962. Role-taking: Process versus conformity. In Rose, A. M. (ed.), *Human Behavior and Social Processes.* Boston: Houghton Mifflin.

———. 1964. Collective behavior. In Faris, R. E. L. (ed.), *Handbook of Modern Sociology.* Chicago: Rand McNally.

———. 1968a. Role. In Sills, D. (ed.), *International Encyclopedia of the Social Sciences.* New York: Macmillan.

———. 1968b. The self-conception in social interaction. In Gordon, C., and Gergen, K. J. (eds.), *The Self in Social Interaction.* New York: Wiley.

———. 1978. The role and the person. *American Journal of Sociology,* 84:1–23.

———, and Killian, L. M. 1972. *Collective Behavior.* 2nd ed. Englewood Cliffs, N.J.: Prentice-Hall.

Underwood, B., and Moore, B. 1982. Perspective-taking and altruism. *Psychological Bulletin,* 91:143–173.

U.S. Bureau of the Census. 1972. *Census of the Population: 1970.* Vol. 1. Characteristics of the Population. Washington, D.C.: Government Printing Office.

Urdy, R. 1965. Structural correlates of feminine beauty preference in Britain and the United States. *Sociology and Social Research,* 49:330–342.

Urruti, G., and Miller, C. E. 1984. Test of the bargaining and equal excess theories of coalition formation: Effects of experience, information about payoffs, and monetary stakes. *Journal of Personality and Social Psychology,* 46:825–836.

Useem, B. 1980. Solidarity model, breakdown model, and the Boston anti-busing movement. *American Sociological Review,* 45:357–369.

Vaillant, G. E., and Vaillant, C. O. 1981. Natural history of male psychological health. X: Work as a predictor of positive mental health. *American Journal of Psychiatry,* 138:1433–1440.

Valins, S. 1966. Cognitive effects of false heart-rate feedback. *Journal of Personality and Social Psychology,* 4:400–408.

Van Creveld, M. 1982. *Fighting Power: German and U.S. Army Performance, 1939–1945.* Westport, Conn.: Greenwood Press.

van den Berghe, P. L. 1967. *Race and Racism.* New York: Wiley.

———. 1974. Bringing beasts back in. *American Sociological Review,* 39:777–788.

———. 1975. Reply to Fischer, Moberg, and Mazur. *American Sociological Review,* 40:678–682.

van der Pligt, J. 1984. Attributions, false consensus, and valence: Two field studies. *Journal of Personality and Social Psychology,* 46:57–68.

Vander Zanden, J. W. 1965. *Race Relations in Transition*. New York: Random House.

———. 1972. *American Minority Relations*. 3rd ed. New York: Ronald.

———. 1983. *American Minority Relations*. New York: Knopf.

———. 1985. *Human Development*. 3rd ed. New York: Knopf.

Varca, P. 1980. An analysis of home and away game performance of male college basketball teams. *Journal of Sport Psychology*, 2:245–257.

Vinsel, A., Brown, B. B., Altman, I., and Foss, C. 1980. Privacy regulation, territorial displays, and effectiveness of individual functioning. *Journal of Personality and Social Psychology*, 39:1104–1115.

von Baeyer, C. L., Sherk, D. L., and Zanna, M. P. 1981. Impression management in the job interview: When the female applicant meets the male "chauvinist" interviewer. *Personality and Social Psychology Bulletin*, 7:45–51.

Wagley, C., and Harris, M. 1964. *Minorities in the New World*. New York: Columbia University Press.

Wagner, R. V. 1975. Complementary needs, role expectations, interpersonal attraction, and the stability of working relationships. *Journal of Personality and Social Psychology*, 32:116–124.

Walker, L. J. 1982. The sequentiality of Kohlberg's stages of moral development. *Child Development*, 53:1330–1336.

Walsh, E. J. 1981. Resource mobilization and citizen protest in communities around Three Mile Island. *Social Problems*, 29:1–21.

———, and Warland, R. H. 1983. Social movement involvement in the wake of a nuclear accident: Activists and free riders in the TMI area. *American Sociological Review*, 48:764–780

Walster, E., Aronson, E., and Abrahams, D. 1966. On increasing the persuasiveness of a low prestige communicator. *Journal of Experimental Social Psychology*, 2:325–342.

———, Aronson, V., Abrahams, D., and Rottman, L. 1966. Importance of physical attractiveness in dating behavior. *Journal of Personality and Social Psychology*, 5:508–516.

———, Berscheid, E., and Walster, G. W. 1973. New directions in equity research. *Journal of Personality and Social Psychology*, 25:151–176.

———, and Walster, G. W. 1963. Effect of expecting to be liked on choice associates. *Journal of Abnormal and Social Psychology*, 67:402–404.

———, and ———. 1970. The matching hypothesis. Unpublished manuscript, University of Wisconsin.

———, and ———. 1975. Equity and social justice. *Journal of Social Issues*, 31:21–43.

Walters, R. H., and Karol, P. 1960. Social deprivation and verbal behavior. *Journal of Personality*, 28:89–107.

Warner, K. E. 1981. Cigarette smoking in the 1970s: The impact of the antismoking campaign on consumption. *Science*, 211 (February 13):729–730.

Warner, L. G., and DeFleur, M. L. 1969. Attitude as an interactional concept: Social constraint and social distance as intervening variables between attitudes and action. *American Sociological Review*, 34:153–169.

Warr, M. 1985. Fear of rape among urban women. *Social Problems*, 32:238–250.

Warr, P., and Knapper, C. 1968. *The Perception of People and Events*. New York: Wiley.

Warren, C., and Laslett, B. 1977. Privacy and secrecy: A conceptual comparison. *Journal of Social Issues*, 33:43–51.

Wasserman, I. M. 1984. Imitation and suicide: A reexamination of the Werther effect. *American Sociological Review*, 49:427–436.

Watson, D. 1982. The actor and the observer: How are their perceptions of causality divergent? *Psychological Bulletin*, 92:682–700.

———, and Clark, L. A. 1984. Negative affectivity: The disposition to experience aversive emotional states. *Psychological Bulletin*, 96:465–490.

Watson, J. B. 1914. *Behavior: An Introduction to Comparative Psychology*. New York: Holt, Rinehart and Winston.

———. 1919. *Psychology from the Standpoint of a Behaviorist*. Philadelphia: Lippincott.

———. 1925. *Behaviorism*. New York: People's Institute.

Watts, W. A., and Holt, L. E. 1979. Persistence of opinion change induced under conditions of forewarning and distraction. *Journal of Personality and Social Psychology*, 37:778–789.

Weary, G. 1980. Examination of affect and egotism as mediators of bias in causal attributions. *Journal of Personality and Social Psychology*, 38:348–357.

Weatherley, D. 1961. Anti-Semitism and the expression of fantasy aggression. *Journal of Abnormal and Social Psychology*, 62:454–457.

Weber, S. J., and Cook, T. D. 1972. Subject effects in laboratory research: An examination of subject roles, demand characteristics, and valid inference. *Psychological Bulletin,* 77:273–295.

Webster, B. 1978. A pigeon's-eye view may aid scientists. *New York Times* (May 14):15.

———. 1980. Mystery of birds' migration unravels. *New York Times* (April 15):C1–C2.

Webster, M., Jr., and Driskell, J. E., Jr. 1983. Beauty as status. *American Journal of Sociology,* 89:140–165.

Wegner, D. M., and Vallacher, R. R. 1980. *The Self in Social Psychology.* New York: Oxford University Press.

Weinberg, M. S. 1965. Sexual modesty, social meanings, and the nudist camp. *Social Problems,* 12:314–318.

Weinberg, S. K. 1974. *Deviant Behavior and Social Control.* Dubuque, Iowa: Wm. C. Brown.

Weiner, B. 1972. *Theories of Motivation: From Mechanism to Cognition.* Chicago: Markham.

———. 1979. A theory of motivation for some classroom experiences. *Journal of Educational Psychology,* 71:3–25.

———. 1980. A cognitive (attribution)-emotion-action model of behavior: An analysis of judgments of help-giving. *Journal of Personality and Social Psychology,* 39:186–200.

———, Heckhausen, H., Meyer, W. U., and Cook, R. E. 1972. Causal ascriptions and achievement motivation: A conceptual analysis of effort and reanalysis of locus of control. *Journal of Personality and Social Psychology,* 21:239–248.

———, and Kukla, A. 1970. An attributional analysis of achievement motivation. *Journal of Personality and Social Psychology,* 15:1–20.

Weiner, F. H. 1976. Altruism, ambiance, and action: The effects of rural and urban rearing on helping behavior. *Journal of Personality and Social Psychology,* 34:112–124.

Weinstein, E. A., and Deutschberger, P. 1963. Some dimensions of altercasting. *Sociometry,* 26:454–466.

Weinstein, N. D. 1980. Unrealistic optimism about future life events. *Journal of Personality and Social Psychology,* 39:806–820.

Weisz, J. 1981. Learned helplessness in black and white children identified by their schools as retarded and nonretarded: Performance deterioration in response to failure. *Developmental Psychology,* 17:246–255.

Wellman, B. 1971. Social identities in black and white. *Sociological Inquiry,* 41:57–66.

Werner, C. M., Brown, B. B., and Damron, G.

1981. Territorial marking in a game arcade. *Journal of Personality and Social Psychology,* 41:1094–1104.

West, S. G., and Gunn, S. P. 1978. Some issues of ethics and social psychology. *American Psychologist,* 33:30–38.

———, ———, and Chernicky, P. 1975. Ubiquitous Watergate: An attributional analysis. *Journal of Personality and Social Psychology,* 32:55–65.

Westie, F. R. 1964. Race and ethnic relations. In Faris, R. E. L. (ed.), *Handbook of Modern Sociology.* Chicago: Rand McNally.

Westin, A. 1967. *Privacy and Freedom.* New York: Atheneum.

Wetzel, C. G., and Insko, C. A. 1982. The similarity-attraction relationship: Is there an ideal one? *Journal of Experimental Social Psychology,* 18:253–276.

Weyant, J. M. 1978. Effects of mood states, costs, and benefits on helping. *Journal of Personality and Social Psychology,* 36:1169–1176.

Wheaton, B. 1974. Interpersonal conflict and cohesiveness in dyadic relationships. *Sociometry,* 37:328–348.

Wheeler, L. 1974. Social comparison and selective affiliation. In Huston, T. L. (ed.), *Foundations of Interpersonal Attraction.* New York: Academic Press.

White, G. L. 1980. Physical attractiveness and courtship progress. *Journal of Personality and Social Psychology,* 39:660–668.

———, Fishbein, S., and Rutstein, J. 1981. Passionate love and the misattribution of arousal. *Journal of Personality and Social Psychology,* 41:56–62.

White, H. C., Boorman, S. A., and Breiger, R. L. 1976. Social structure for multiple networks. I. Blockmodels of roles and positions. *American Journal of Sociology,* 81:730–780.

White, L. A. 1949. *The Science of Culture, A Study of Man and Civilization.* New York: Farrar, Straus.

White, R. W. 1965. The experience of efficacy in schizophrenia. *Psychiatry,* 28:199–211.

White, T. H. 1961. *The Making of the President 1960.* New York: Atheneum.

Whitley, B. E., Jr. 1983. Sex role orientation and self-esteem: A critical meta-analytic review. *Journal of Personality and Social Psychology,* 44:765–778.

Whorf, B. L. 1956. *Language, Thought, and Reality.* Cambridge, Mass.: MIT Press.

Whyte, W. F. 1943. *Street Corner Society.* Chicago: University of Chicago Press.

———. 1946. When workers and customers

meet. In Whyte, W. F. (ed.), *Industry and Society*. New York: McGraw-Hill.

Whyte, W. H., Jr. 1956. *The Organization Man*. New York: Simon and Schuster.

Wichman, H. 1972. Effects of communication on cooperation in a 2-person game. In Wrightsman, L., O'Connor, J., and Baker, N. (eds.), *Cooperation and Competition*. Belmont, Calif.: Brooks/Cole.

Wicker, A. W. 1969. Attitudes versus actions: The relationship of verbal and overt behavioral responses to attitude objects. *Journal of Social Issues*, 25:41–78.

———. 1971. An examination of the "other variables" explanation of attitude-behavior inconsistency. *Journal of Personality and Social Psychology*, 19:18–30.

Wicker, T. 1968. Introduction. *Report of the National Advisory Commission on Civil Disorders*. New York: Bantam.

Wicklund, R. A. 1979. The influence of self on human behavior. *American Scientist*, 67:187–193.

———, and Brehm, J. W. 1968. Attitude change as a function of felt competence and threat to attitudinal freedom. *Journal of Experimental Social Psychology*, 4:64–75.

———, and Hormuth, S. E. 1981. On the functions of the self: A reply to Hull and Levy. *Journal of Personality and Social Psychology*, 40:1029–1037.

Wilder, D. A. 1978a. Perceiving persons as a group: Effects on attributions of causality and beliefs. *Social Psychology*, 41:13–23.

———. 1978b. Reduction of intergroup discrimination through individuation of the out-group. *Journal of Personality and Social Psychology*, 36:1361–1374.

———. 1984. Intergroup contact: The typical member and the exception to the rule. *Journal of Experimental Social Psychology*, 20:177–194.

———, and Shapiro, P. N. 1984. Role of out-group cues in determining social identity. *Journal of Personality and Social Psychology*, 47:342–348.

———, and Thompson, J. E. 1980. Intergroup contact with independent manipulations of ingroup and out-group interaction. *Journal of Personality and Social Psychology*, 38:589–603.

Williams, A. W., Ware, J. E., and McDonald, C. A. 1981. A model of mental health, life events, and social supports applicable to general populations. *Journal of Health and Social Behavior*, 22:324–336.

Williams, J. E., Tucker, R. D., and Dunham, F. Y. 1971. Changes in the connotations of color names among Negroes and Caucasians: 1963–1969. *Journal of Personality and Social Psychology*, 19:222–228.

Williams, J. L. 1963. Personal space and its relation to extroversion-introversion. Unpublished master's thesis, University of Alberta.

Williams, K. Harkins, S., and Latané, B. 1981. Identifiability as a deterrent to social loafing: Two cheering experiments. *Journal of Personality and Social Psychology*, 40:303–311.

Williams, L. S. 1984. The classic rape: When do victims report? *Social Problems*, 31:459–467.

Williams, R. M., Jr. 1964. *Strangers Next Door*. Englewood Cliffs, N.J.: Prentice-Hall.

Willie, C. V. 1984. *School Desegregation Plans That Work*. Westport, Conn.: Greenwood Press.

Willis, F. N. 1966. Initial speaking distance as a function of the speaker's relationship. *Psychonomic Science*, 5:221–222.

Wilson, E. O. 1975. *Sociobiology: The New Synthesis*. Cambridge, Mass.: Belknap Press.

———. 1978a. *On Human Nature*. Cambridge: Harvard University Press.

———. 1978b. What is sociobiology? *Society*, 15:(September/October):10–14.

Wilson, J. D., George, F. W., and Griffin, J. E. 1981. The hormonal control of sexual development. *Science*, 211:1278–1284.

Wilson, J. P. 1976. Motivation, modeling, and altruism: A person X situation analysis. *Journal of Personality and Social Psychology*, 34:1078–1086.

Wimberly, R. C., Hood, T. C., Lipsey, C. M., Clelland, D., and Hay, M. 1975. Conversion in a Billy Graham crusade: Spontaneous event or ritual performance? *Sociological Quarterly*, 16:162–170.

Winch, R. F. 1958. *Mate Selection: A Study of Complementary Needs*. New York: Harper and Row.

Winokur, S. 1976. *A Primer of Verbal Behavior: An Operant View*. Englewood Cliffs, N.J.: Prentice-Hall.

Winter, L., and Uleman, J. S. 1984. When are social judgments made? Evidence for the spontaneousness of trait inferences. *Journal of Personality and Social Psychology*, 47:237–252.

Wishman, S. 1981. A lawyer's guilty secrets. *Newsweek* (November 9):25.

Wishner, J. 1960. Reanalysis of "impressions of personality." *Psychological Review*, 67:96–112.

Wispé, L. G. 1972. Positive forms of social behavior: An overview. *Journal of Social Issues,* 28:1–19.

Wolfe, D. A. 1985. Child-abusive parents: An empirical review and analysis. *Psychological Bulletin,* 97:462–482.

Wolfe, M., and Laufer, R. S. 1974. The concept of privacy in childhood and adolescence. In Carson, D. H. (ed.), *Man-Environment Interactions: Evaluation and Applications.* Washington, D.C.: Environmental Design Research Associates.

Wolff, M. 1973. Notes on the behavior of pedestrians. In Birenbaum, A., and Sagarin, E. (eds.), *People in Places.* New York: Praeger.

Wood, W., Kallgren, C. A., and Preisler, R. M. 1985. Access to attitude-relevant information in memory as a determinant of persuasion: The role of message attributes. *Journal of Experimental Social Psychology,* 21:73–85.

Worchel, S., and Brehm, J. W. 1970. Effect of threats to attitudinal freedom as a function of agreement with the communicator. *Journal of Personality and Social Psychology,* 14:18–22.

———, and ———. 1971. Direct and implied social restoration of freedom. *Journal of Personality and Social Psychology,* 18:294–304.

———, and Brown, E. H. 1984. The role of plausibility in influencing environmental attributions. *Journal of Experimental Social Psychology,* 20:86–96.

Worthy, M., Gary, A. L., and Kahn, G. M. 1969. Self-disclosure as an exchange process. *Journal of Personality and Social Psychology,* 13:59–63.

Wortman, C. B., Costanzo, P. R., and Witt, T. R. 1973. Effect of anticipated performance on the attributions of causality to self and others. *Journal of Personality and Social Psychology,* 27:372–381.

Wrightsman, L. S. 1978. The American trial jury on trial: Empirical evidence and procedural modifications. *Journal of Social Issues,* 34:137–164.

Wrong, D. H. 1961. The oversocialized conception of man in modern sociology. *American Sociological Review,* 26:183–193.

———. 1968. Some problems in defining social power. *American Journal of Sociology,* 73:673–681.

———. 1976. *Postscript 1975: Skeptical Sociology.* New York: Columbia University Press.

Wyer, R. S., Bodenhausen, G. V., and Gorman, T. F. 1985. Cognitive mediators of reactions to rape. *Journal of Personality and Social Psychology,* 48:324–338.

Wylie, R. 1979. *The Self-Concept.* Rev. ed. Lincoln: University of Nebraska Press.

Yakimovich, D., and Saltz, E. 1971. Helping behavior: The cry for help. *Psychonomic Science,* 23:427–428.

Yancey, W. L., Rigsby, L., and McCarthy, J. D. 1972. Social position and self-evaluation: The relative importance of race. *American Journal of Sociology,* 78:338–359.

Yarmey, A. D. 1979. *The Psychology of Eyewitness Testimony.* New York: Free Press.

Yinger, J. M. 1965. *Toward a Field Theory of Behavior.* New York: McGraw-Hill.

Yllo, K., and Straus, M. A. 1981. Interpersonal violence among married and cohabiting couples. *Family Relations,* 30:339–347.

Zachry, W. 1978. Ordinality and interdependence of representation and language development in infancy. *Child Development,* 49:681–687.

Zajonc, R. B. 1960. The concepts of balance, congruity, and dissonance. *Public Opinion Quarterly,* 24:280–296.

———. 1967. *Social Psychology: An Experimental Approach.* Belmont, Calif.: Brooks-Cole.

———. 1980. Feeling and thinking: Preferences need no inferences. *American Psychologist,* 35:151–175.

———. 1984. On the primacy of affect. *American Psychologist,* 39:117–123.

Zald, M., and McCarthy, J. 1979. *The Dynamics of Social Movements.* Cambridge, Mass.: Winthrop.

Zanna, M. P., Olson, J. M., and Fazio, R. H. 1980. Attitude-behavior consistency: An individual difference perspective. *Journal of Personality and Social Psychology,* 38:432–440.

———, and Pack, S. J. 1975. On the self-fulfilling nature of apparent sex differences in behavior. *Journal of Experimental Social Psychology,* 11:583–591.

Zawadzki, B. 1948. Limitations of the scapegoat theory of prejudice. *Journal of Abnormal and Social Psychology,* 43:127–141.

Zeldow, P. B., Clark, D., and Daugherty, S. R. 1985. Masculinity, femininity, Type A behavior, and psychosocial adjustment in medical students. *Journal of Personality and Social Psychology,* 48:481–492.

Zetterberg, H. L. 1966. The secret ranking. *Journal of Marriage and Family Life,* 28:134–142.

Zillmann, D. 1984. *Connections Between Sex and Aggression.* Hillsdale, N.J.: Erlbaum.

———, Hoyt, J. L., and Day, K. D. 1974. Strength and duration of the effect of aggressive, violent, and erotic communications on subsequent aggressive behavior. *Communication Research,* 1:286–306.

——, Katcher, A. H., and Milavsky, B. 1972. Excitation transfer from physical exercise to subsequent aggressive behavior. *Journal of Experimental Social Psychology,* 8:247–259.

——, and Sapolsky, B. S. 1977. What mediates the effect of mild erotica on annoyance and hostile behavior in males? *Journal of Personality and Social Psychology,* 35:587–596.

Zimbardo, P. C. 1969. The human choice: Individuation, reason, and order versus deindividuation, impulse, and chaos. In Arnold, W., and Levine, D. (eds.), *Nebraska Symposium on Motivation,* 17:237–307.

——. 1974. On the ethics of intervention in human psychological research: With special reference to the Stanford prison experiment. *Cognition,* 2:243–256.

——. 1977. *Shyness: What It Is, What to Do About It.* Reading, Mass.: Addison-Wesley.

——. 1978. Misunderstanding shyness: The counterattack. *Psychology Today,* 12 (June):17–18 + .

——, Haney, C., and Banks, W. C. 1973. A Pirandellian prison. *New York Times Magazine* (April 8).

Zimmerman, D. 1985. "Talking" gorilla mourns dead pet. *USA Today* (January 10):D1.

Zimmerman, D. H. 1976. A reply to Professor Coser. *American Sociologist,* 11:4–13.

——, and West, C. 1975. Sex roles, interruptions and silences in conversation. In Thorne, B., and Henley, N. (eds.), *Language and Sex Difference and Dominance.* Rowley, Mass.: Newbury House.

Zirkel, P. A. 1971. Self-concept and the "disadvantage" of ethnic group membership and mixture. *Review of Educational Research,* 41:211–225.

Zuckerman, D. 1985. Can genes help helping? *Psychology Today,* 19 (March):80.

Zuckerman, M., Depaulo, B. M., and Rosenthal, R. 1981. The verbal and nonverbal communication of deception. In Berkowitz, L. (ed.), *Advances in Experimental Social Psychology.* Vol. 14. New York: Academic Press.

——, Kernis, M. R., Driver, R., and Koestner, R. 1984. Segmentation of behavior: Effects of actual deception and expected deception. *Journal of Personality and Social Psychology,* 46:1173–1182.

——, ——, Guarnera, S. M., Murphy, J. F., and Rappoport, L. 1983. The egocentric bias: Seeing oneself as cause and target of others' behavior. *Journal of Personality,* 51:621–630.

——, Larrance, D. T., Spiegel, N. H., and Klorman, R. 1981. Controlling nonverbal displays: Facial expressions and tone of voice. *Journal of Experimental Social Psychology,* 17:506–524.

——, Lipets, M. S., Koivumaki, J. H., and Rosenthal, R. 1975. Encoding and decoding nonverbal cues of emotion. *Journal of Personality and Social Psychology,* 32:1068–1076.

Author Index

Abeles, R. P., 354, 534
Abelson, R. P., 53–54, 178, 466
Abrams, B., 198
Adair, J. G., 25
Adam, B. D., 485
Adams, J. B., 325
Adams, J. S., 319
Adorno, T. W., 490
Aiello, J. R., 381, 385
Ajzen, I., 181
Akert, R. M., 82
Albin, R. S., 53
Alexander, C. N., Jr., 61
Alkema, F., 82
Alker, H., 537
Allen, V. L., 222, 405
Allport, F. H., 337–338, 549–550
Allport, G. W., 2–3, 145, 146, 178, 465, 470
Alper, J., 301
Alpert, R., 128
Altman, I., 290, 368, 378, 379, 384
Altrocchi, J., 341
Amato, P. R., 307
Aminzade, R., 537
Amir, Y., 468–470
Ancok, D., 321
Andersen, S. M., 154. 157
Anderson, J. G., 269
Anderson, N. H., 45
Andreoli, V. A., 190
Andrews, L. B., 427, 428
Ansen, D., 284
Anthony, D., 543, 545
Antill, J. K., 288
Apsler, R., 232, 318
Aram, J. D., 420–421
Archer, D., 82, 498–499
Archer, R. L., 290
Ardrey, R., 333, 334, 335, 369
Argyle, M., 61, 82
Arkin, R. M., 171
Arkowitz, H. S., 156

Arndt, W. B., Jr., 514
Aron, A. R., 281
Aronfreed, J., 127
Aronson, E., 21–24, 29–30, 31, 168, 189, 192, 194, 322
Asch, S. E., 43–44, 45, 46–47, 219–221, 233, 551–552
Asher, S. J., 264
Ashmore, R. D., 43
Ashton, P. T., 127
Athay, M., 239
Austin, W., 320
Austin, W. T., 384
Axelrod, R., 364
Axsom, D., 189–190

Bacharach, S. B. 441, 442
Back, K. W., 272–273, 528, 532
Bailey, K. G., 375
Bainbridge, W. S., 537, 541–544
Balch, R. W., 546
Baldassare, M., 376, 380
Baldwin, D. A., 436
Balkwell, J. W., 76
Ball, D. W., 250, 252
Ball, R. A., 553
Balswick, J., 290–291
Bandura, A., 120–122, 128, 157, 329, 339, 508–509
Banks, W. C., 28, 343–345, 446, 485
Baptist, B., 412
Barbanel, J., 342
Barber, T. X., 514
Barbour, L. S., 331
Barker, C. H., 230
Barker, E., 543, 546
Barker, R. G., 336
Barkow, J. H., 304
Barnes, M. L., 24–25
Barnes, R. D., 258–259
Baron, R. A., 29, 313–315, 346
Baron, R. M., 377

Barron, J. W., 191
Barsky, S. F., 370
Bart, P. B., 350, 352–353
Barth, J. M., 426, 427
Bates, F. L., 384
Batson, C. D., 300, 301, 304, 308, 322
Batts, V., 471
Baucom, D. H., 502
Bauer, R. A., 195
Baum, A., 377, 380, 381
Baumann, D. J., 300, 309
Baumeister, R. F., 170, 192
Baumgardner, M. H., 201
Baumrind, D., 28
Baxter, J. C., 374–375
Beach, F., 494, 506
Beaman, A. L., 548
Bear, J., 76
Beauvais, C., 517
Becerra, R. M., 264, 267
Becker, B. J., 511
Becker, F. D., 375, 391
Becker, G., 288
Becker, L. J., 364
Beckhouse, L., 440
Beckman, L., 57
Bee, L. S., 288
Beech, P. K., 502
Begley, T. M., 537
Bell, A. P., 506–507
Bell, D. A., Jr., 484
Bell, P. A., 346
Bem, D. J., 156, 163–164, 187, 230
Bem, S. L., 515–516
Benbow, C. P., 510–511
Benedict, R., 132
Beniger, J. R., 10
Bennett, B., 377
Bennett, R. P., 363
Ben-Yehuda, N., 554
Berens, M. J., 298
Berg, J. H., 290

Berglas, S., 171
Berk, R. A., 331
Berkman, L. F., 400
Berkowitz, L., 24, 48, 300, 320, 329, 336, 337–338, 339–341, 346, 347
Berman, J. J., 178
Berman, J. S., 50
Bernard, H. R., 270
Bernstein, M., 536
Berscheid, E., 48, 264, 275, 278, 279, 280, 281, 290–291, 320, 321, 497
Bickman, L., 313, 325
Billig, M., 408
Billings, A. G., 399
Bird, C., 371–372
Bird, F., 545
Birdwhistell, R. L., 82, 89
Blanchard, F. A., 483
Blankmeyer, B. L., 42–43
Blasi, A., 128
Blau, P. M., 10, 288, 290–291, 292, 417, 436
Blauner, R., 473
Blazer, D. G., 400
Bleier, R., 502
Bless, E., 230
Block, J., 158–159
Bloom, B. L., 264
Blount, B. G., 97
Blum, R. H., 514
Blumer, H., 13, 67, 146, 150, 153, 241, 265, 404, 465, 549–550, 554, 556–557
Blumstein, M., 538
Blumstein, P., 137, 434, 507, 518–519
Blumstein, P. W., 146, 321, 439
Bobo, L., 465
Bodenhausen, G. V., 318, 465–466
Boehm, L., 128
Bolce, L., 536
Bollen, K. A., 450
Bonacich, E., 364, 480, 481
Bond, M. H., 324
Bonoma, T., 445
Boorman, S. A., 266
Booth, A., 380
Bornstein, M. H., 102–103
Boulding, K. E., 355, 436
Boutilier, R. G., 3
Bouza, A. V., 331
Bower, G. H., 59
Bowerman, C. E., 288

Bowker, L. H., 330, 331
Braddock, J. C., 369
Braddock, J. H., 485
Bradley, G. W., 484
Bradley, L. A., 484
Braine, M. D. S., 96
Brainerd, C. J., 127
Bramel, D., 192
Bray, R. M., 223, 423
Breckler, S. J., 174
Bredemeier, H. C., 12
Brehm, J. W., 190, 323
Brehm, S. S., 190
Breiger, R. L., 266
Brenner, A., 332
Breslow, L., 400
Brewer, M. B., 21, 408, 468, 471
Brickman, P., 364, 537
Briggs, S. R., 251, 256
Brigham, J. C., 52
Brim, O. G., 133
Brinton, C., 546
Briscoe, R., 502
Brittingham, G. L., 324
Brockner, J., 168, 360
Brody, J. E., 275
Bromley, S., 471
Broom, L., 416
Brown, B. B., 392
Brown, E. H., 377
Brown R., 341, 364, 420–421
Brown, R. C., Jr., 286
Brown, R. W., 97, 99
Brownell, A., 400
Brownmiller, S., 350
Brozan, N., 348–349
Bruker, C., 420–421
Bryant, J., 346
Buckhout, R., 53
Bugental, D. E., 82
Bullough, V. L., 506
Burger, J. M., 231
Burgess, R. L., 290–291
Burke, P. J., 142
Burkhart, B. R., 349
Burns, L. B., 320
Burt, M. R., 348, 445
Bush, M., 231
Buss, A. H., 142, 145, 158, 251, 256, 337
Bussey, K., 508, 509
Butcher, J. N., 515, 517
Butterfield, F., 391
Button, J. W., 559
Byrne, D., 285–286, 313–315, 375

Cacioppo, J. T., 201–202, 203
Cahill, S. E., 554
Calhoun, J. B., 375
Callahan, S., 502
Campbell, A., 264
Campbell, D. T., 300
Cann, A., 348
Canter, R., 30
Cantor, N., 42, 258
Cantril, H., 342, 550–551
Caplan, P. J., 510
Caporael, L. R., 79
Carbonari, J. P., 363
Carlopio, J., 25
Carlsmith, J. M., 21, 24, 29–30, 31, 168, 192, 196, 231, 232
Carlston, D. E., 25
Carmen, B., 516
Carnevale, P. J. D., 516
Carpenter, E., 414
Carroll, J. B., 78, 98, 99
Cartwright, D., 405, 420
Carver, C. S., 60, 148–149, 313, 419
Cary, M. S., 85, 86
Cash, T. F., 48–49
Cassirer, E., 77
Castle, S., 364
Castore, C., 405
Catania, A. C., 93–94
Certner, B. C., 290
Chaiken, S., 197, 202
Chaikin, A. L., 290
Champagne, D., 533
Charlesworth, W. R., 89
Check, J. V. P., 349
Cheek, J. M., 158
Cheng, L., 481
Chernicky, P., 28, 29
Chertkoff, J. M., 321, 365
Chevalier-Skolnikoff, S., 89
Chilstrom, J. T., Jr., 223
Chomsky, N., 94–95, 96
Christian, J. J., 375
Christie, R., 442, 490
Cialdini, R. B., 252, 300, 309
Cicone, M. V., 498
Cicourel, A. W., 210, 211
Claparède, E., 146
Clark, D., 517
Clark, K. B., 485
Clark, L. A., 155
Clark, M. P., 485
Clark, M. S., 59
Clark, R. D., III, 32, 223, 315
Clifford, M. M., 48

Cline, N. G., 61
Clore, G. L., 59, 285–286
Cloward, R., 559
Coates, D., 353
Cochran, S. T., 337–338
Cockerham, W. C., 229
Cohen, A. K., 209
Cohen, A. R., 178, 190
Cohen, C. E., 52
Cohen, J. L., 25, 377
Cohen, L. E., 229
Cohen, R., 300, 301
Cohen, S., 381, 400, 401
Cohn, S. F., 405
Colby, A., 129–131
Cole, A., 323
Coleman, J. S., 449, 484, 487
Coleman, M., 516
Colligan, M. J., 529, 532
Collins, B. E., 192, 405, 444
Collins, G., 137, 464
Collins, M. E., 470
Collins, R., 443, 449, 450
Conaty, J. C., 87
Congdon, C. S., 337–338
Conolley, E. S., 233
Consentino, J., 446, 447
Converse, P. E., 264
Conviser, R. H., 401
Conway, F., 543
Conway, M., 202
Cook, K. S., 436
Cook, S. W., 468–470, 483, 484
Cook, T. D., 25, 203, 536
Cooke, R. A., 245
Cooley, C. H., 5, 13, 145–146,
    147, 148, 161, 414–415
Coombs, R. H., 168
Cooper, J., 19, 162–163, 187,
    189–190, 191, 421
Cooper, R. E., 385
Coopersmith, S., 143, 165
Cordes, C., 335
Coser, L. A., 213, 215, 354
Costa, P. T., Jr., 158–159
Costanzo, P. R., 5, 57
Coules, J., 338–339
Covington, M. V., 59
Cowell, J., 380
Cowen, E., 337–338
Cox, V. C., 380–381
Cozby, P. C., 290
Crain, R. L., 485
Crane, M., 515
Crano, W. D., 310
Crewdson, J. M., 544

Critchlow, B., 189
Cronkite, R. C., 31
Crosby, F., 471, 536
Cross, K. P., 123
Crowe, D. H., 57
Croyle, R. T., 187
Crusco, A., 515
Cummings, S., 485–486
Cunningham, M. R., 230, 309
Cunningham, S., 298, 313, 314,
    535
Curtiss, S., 114

Dahlgren, H. E., 416
Dahrendorf, R., 360
Damron, G., 392
Dannefer, D., 138
Dansereau, F., Jr., 243
Darley, J. M., 239, 308, 310–311,
    312, 381, 483
Darwin, C., 89
Dasen, P. R., 127
Daugherty, S. R., 517
David, A. B., 305
Davidson, A. R., 180
Davidson, B., 253, 290–291
Davies, J. C., 535–536
Davis, D., 45
Davis, D. E., 370–371
Davis, F., 86
Davis, G. E., 377
Davis, J. H., 430
Davis, K., 107, 113–114, 412,
    413–414, 560
Davis, K. E., 279, 280, 288
Davis, T., 55
Davison, W. P., 198, 199
Dawes, R. M., 363–364
Day, B. R., 288
Day, K. D., 346
Dean, L. M., 380
Deaux, K., 48, 325, 494, 497, 511,
    516, 517
De Charms, R., 338–339, 343
DeFleur, M. L., 180
DeGregorio, E. D., 60
DeJong, W., 231
Della-Fave, L. R., 451, 452
De la Garza, R. O., 482
Dembo, T., 336
Dempsey, C. B., 231
Dengerink, H. A., 341
DeNinno, J. A., 405
Denzin, N. K., 67
DePaulo, B. M., 54, 55, 82, 324

Derlega, V. J., 290
Dermer, M., 48
Desor, J. A., 377
Deutsch, M., 5, 9, 470
Deutschberger, P., 255–256, 440
Devine, P. G., 16
DeVito, J. A., 75, 76–77
Dewey, J., 13
Dholakia, R., 194, 196
Diamond, S. G., 385
Diener, C. I., 119
Diener, E., 343, 548, 550
Dion, K., 48, 275, 408, 497
Dipboye, R. L., 548, 550
Dittmann, A. T., 89
Dollard, J., 489
Donnerstein, E., 346, 347
Donnerstein, M., 24, 338, 346
Dooley, D., 401
Dornbusch, S. M., 19, 162
Dovidio, J. F., 434
Dowd, M., 298
Downton, J. V., 546
Dremen, D., 548–549
Driskell, J. E., Jr., 48, 50, 497
Drury, D. W., 486–487
Dubé-Simard, L., 535
Dubrow, M., 350
Dugan, P. M., 466
Dukes, F. O., 550
Dullea, G., 159, 214, 507
Duncan, S., Jr., 80
Dunham, F. Y., 75
Durkheim, E., 5, 410, 412
Dusek, J. B., 516
Dutton, D. G., 281
Dutton, J. E., 180
Duval, S., 55, 148
Dweck, C. S., 119
Dyson-Hudson, R., 371

Eagly, A. H., 197, 495
Eckholm, E., 112
Edelman, M., 455
Edinger, J. A., 86
Edney, J. J., 370, 371, 380
Edwards, J. N., 380
Edwards, P. K., 380
Effrein,, E. A., 165
Efran, M. G., 48
Ehrhardt, A. A., 500
Eisenberg, L., 335
Eisner, T., 37
Ekland-Olson, S., 269, 541–544
Ekman, P., 54, 55, 76, 89–91

Elias, M., 512
Elkind, D., 124
Elliott, G. C., 143, 325
Ellis, R. J., 146
Ellyson, S. L., 434
Ely, R. J., 165
Embree, M. C., 337–338
Emerson, J. P., 530
Emerson, R. M., 233, 292, 434–435, 436, 439
Endicott, J., 428
Epstein, S., 341
Epstein, Y. M., 381, 485
Erber, R., 47, 50, 59
Erickson, F., 476, 477–479
Erikson, E. H., 143
Erikson, K. T., 214–215, 402
Esser, J. K., 365
Etzioni, A., 452
Evans, G. W., 375, 381
Evans, R., 346

Fader, S. S., 269
Falender, V. J., 165
Fanon, F., 446, 489
Farley, R., 471, 487
Farrow, D. L., 446
Fast, J., 80, 85, 86, 256–257, 384
Fasteau, M. F., 499
Fatoullah, E., 445
Faucheux, C., 223
Faulkner, S., 228
Fazio, R. H., 165, 180, 187, 483
Featherman, D. L., 523
Feigenbaum, R., 57
Feinberg, W. E., 550
Feinbloom, D. H., 503–504
Feld, S. L., 264–265
Feldman, H., 113
Felson, R. B., 163–164
Fendrich, J. M., 482
Fenigstein, A., 155
Feshbach, S., 28, 198, 329, 337–339, 346, 347
Festinger, L., 26, 186–190, 192, 203, 272–273, 286
Fields, J. M., 60
Findlay, S., 330
Fine, G. A., 415
Fischer, C. S., 266, 354, 371, 376
Fishbein, M., 181
Fisher, J. D., 375
Fishman, P., 90–92
Fiske, S. T., 47, 50
Fitch, H. G., 191

Flaherty, J. F., 516
Flavell, J. H., 124, 127
Fleishman, J. A., 301, 365
Foa, E. B., 82
Foa, U. G., 82
Fodor, E. M., 424, 446
Foehl, J. C., 514
Foley, L. A., 468–470
Folger, R., 190, 533
Fontaine, G., 58
Ford, C. S., 494, 506
Ford, D. A., 331
Forgas, J. P., 59
Forsyth, D. R., 59, 60
Forward, J., 30
Foss, R. D., 231, 430
Fouts, R., 110
Fraker, S., 137
Francese, P., 523–524
Frank, S. J., 515
Franklin, B., 7
Franklin, J. H., 435
Franks, D. R., 165
Franks, L., 350
Fraser, S. C., 230, 548
Freedman, J. L., 230, 232, 334, 375, 376, 380, 547
Freedman, N., 89
French, J. R. P., 10, 444, 445
Frey, W. H., 487
Friedkin, N. E., 266
Friedland, N., 233
Friedman, H. S., 54, 318
Friedman, S., 473
Friedson, E., 267–269
Friesen, W. V., 55, 76, 89
Frieze, I. H., 352
Frodi, A., 48
Fromkin, H. L., 142
Fulcher, J. S., 89
Funck-Brentano, F., 540
Funkhouser-Balbaky, M. L., 514
Furnham, A., 61
Fyans, L. J., Jr., 59

Gagnon, J., 514
Gahagan, J. P., 358, 433–434
Galanter, M., 544, 545
Galbraith, J. K., 554
Galle, O. R., 380
Galloway, J. L., 378
Gamson, W. A., 364, 433–434, 444, 558–559
Gangestad, S., 258
Ganong, L. H., 516

Garber, J., 118
Gardner, B. T., 109–110
Gardner, R. A., 109–110
Garfield, R., 378
Garfinkel, H., 16, 26–27, 212, 504
Gary, A. L., 290
Gaudy, J. C., 290
Gecas, V., 165
Geen, R. L., 337, 338–339
Geertz, C., 460
Geis, F. L., 442, 443
Geis, G., 306
Geiselman, R. E., 61
Geller, D. M., 30
Gelles, R. J., 330–331, 332
Genovese, E. D., 435
Gentry, W. D., 337
George, F. W., 500
Gerard, H. B., 233, 408, 484, 487
Gerbasi, K. C., 428, 429, 430
Gergen, K. J., 143, 165–167, 322, 323–324, 343
Gergen, M., 322
Gerlach, L. P., 540, 541
Geschwender, J. A., 534, 536
Gibson, F. W., 375
Giesen, M., 375
Gilbert, D. T., 381
Gilbert, E., 179–180
Giles, M. W., 487
Gillespie, D. L., 87
Gilligan, C. F., 123, 131, 325
Gillis, R., 60
Gilmour, R., 82
Gitlin, T., 498
Givens, D., 86, 88
Glazer, N., 464
Gluckman, M., 279
Goethals, G. R., 47, 191
Goff, R., 485
Goffman, E., 84, 108, 164, 237, 240, 243, 246–247, 249, 251–252, 254, 256, 374, 375, 384, 387, 389, 392, 439
Goldberg, L. R., 55
Goldin-Meadows, S., 113
Goldman, R., 202
Goldstone, J. A., 559
Goleman, D., 42, 54, 155, 258, 283, 306, 351, 441
Gonda, G., 517
Gonzales, M. H., 284
Good, F. E., 514
Goode, E., 514
Goode, W. J., 244, 434, 440
Goodman, W., 503

Goodstadt, B. E., 446, 447
Goodstein, L. D., 290
Goodstein, R. K., 330
Gordon, L., 518
Gordon, M. T., 352
Gorman, T. F., 318
Gottlieb, A., 30, 311
Gottlieb, J., 313
Gould, C. G., 77, 113
Gould, R. L., 135
Gouldner, A. W., 321–322, 449
Gove, W. R., 380
Goy, R. W., 511
Graen, G., 243
Graham, J. A., 61
Grajek, S., 281, 283
Granovetter, M. S., 267, 269
Gray, M. W., 511
Gray, R. A., 301
Greeley, A. M., 459, 479
Green, R., 508
Green, R. L., 487
Greenberg, J., 171, 321, 324, 325, 482
Greenblatt, M., 264, 267
Greene, D., 60
Greenwald, A. G., 155, 157, 187
Greenwell, J., 341
Greer, D. L., 370
Griffin, J. E., 500
Griffitt, W., 346
Grimm, J., 522
Groff, B. D., 380
Gross, A. E., 229, 230
Gross, E., 522
Gross, N., 244
Gross, P. H., 483
Gruder, C. L., 312
Guimond, S., 535
Gunderson, E. K. E., 380
Gunn, L. K., 294
Gunn, S. P., 24, 28, 29, 31
Gurney, J. N., 536
Gurr, T. R., 533
Guthrie, E. R., 6
Guttman, L., 177

Haber, G. M., 384
Haber, S., 307
Hadden, J. K., 543
Haga, W. J., 243
Haight, N. A., 61
Haines, H. H., 557
Hall, E. T., 91, 369, 374–375, 382, 392–393

Hall, J. A., 515, 517
Hall, P. M., 455, 456
Hallam, J., 346
Halligan, M., 536
Halloran, R., 534
Halverson, C., 290–291
Hamblin, R., 13
Hamilton, D. L., 43, 466
Hamilton, T. P., 361
Hamilton, V. L., 229
Hammersmith, S. F., 507
Hampson, R. B., 308
Haney, C., 28, 343–345, 446
Hardee, B. B., 471
Harden, M., 343
Hardin, G. J., 426, 427, 518
Hargis, K., 309
Harkins, S. G., 197, 424, 425
Harris, M., 460
Harry, J., 507, 508
Hartnett, J. J., 375
Hartshorne, H., 308
Haskett, R. F., 502, 503
Hass, R. G., 146, 147
Hastie, R., 53–54, 429
Hatfield, E., 281, 285, 321
Haug, M. R., 243
Hauser, R. M., 523
Hawkins, C., 428
Hawley, A. H., 434
Hawley, W. D., 485, 487–488
Hayano, D., 250–251
Hayduk, L. A., 374
Hayes, C., 109
Hayes, K., 109
Hays, R. B., 269, 270, 292
Hediger, H., 369
Heider, F., 53–54, 183–185, 285
Heilbrun, A. B., Jr., 515, 517
Heim, M., 28, 347
Heiss, J., 487
Heller, J. F., 380
Helmreich, R. L., 192, 498, 516–517
Hendrick, C., 50
Hendrick, S. S., 290
Hennigan, K. M., 536
Henshel, R. L., 24
Hepburn, C., 408, 467
Herbers, J., 473
Hernton, C. C., 489
Heussenstamm, F. K., 24
Hewitt, J. P., 61, 211, 237–238, 241
Higbee, K. L., 51
Higgins, R., 215–216

Hilberman, E., 330, 335
Hill, C. A., 158
Hill, C. T., 283
Hiller, E. T., 75
Hinde, R. A., 89
Hine, V. H., 540, 541
Hjelle, L. A., 447
Hockett, C. F., 102
Hoelter, J. W., 165, 486, 487
Hoffer, E., 357, 540
Holahan, C. J., 307
Hollander, E. P., 5, 223
Holmes, J. G., 146
Holt, L. E., 202, 203
Holtz, R., 408
Homans, G. C., 10, 233, 288, 319, 400
Hong, L. K., 420–421
Hook, L. H., 384
Horai, J., 445
Hormuth, S. E., 148
Horn, J., 335
Horowitz, M., 357, 408
Hough, J. C., Jr., 471
House, J. S., 307, 399, 400
House, P., 60
Houston, J. P., 52
Howard, J. A., 60
Howard, W., 310
Hoyt, J. L., 346
Hoyt, M. F., 408
Hughes, G., 329
Hughes, M., 380
Hull, C. L., 6
Hull, J. B., 137
Humphries, C., 419
Hunt, M., 29, 31, 40, 334, 335, 427, 430
Hunt, R. G., 5
Hunter, D., 421, 550
Huston, T. L., 290–291, 306, 307, 308–309, 315, 434, 445
Hyde, J. S., 509–512
Hyman, H. H., 418

Ickes, W., 258–259, 471
Ignatius, D., 560
Imperato-McGinley, J., 502
Inbau, F., 370
Ingham, A. G., 424–425
Ingram, C. M., 420–421
Innes, J. M., 342, 343, 548
Insko, C. A., 222, 274, 286
Isen, A. M., 309
Issac, L., 559

Ittleson, W. H., 373
Iwaniszek, J., 365

Jaccard, J., 202
Jacklin, C. N., 510, 512
Jackson, J. S., 324
Jackson, M. R., 465
Jacobson, L., 488
Jacobson, M. B., 48
Jahoda, M., 490
James, R., 428
James, W., 13, 143
Janda, L. H., 48–49
Janis, I. L., 198, 422–424
Janoff-Bulman, R., 352
Janowitz, M., 416–417
Jay, S. J., 269
Jecker, J. D., 285
Jenkins, J. C., 530, 536, 537, 546
Jennings, E. T., 559
Jensen, A. R., 303–304
Johnson, D., 223
Johnson, N. R., 421, 550
Johnson, T. J., 57
Jones, E. E., 3, 8, 47, 54, 57, 171, 405
Jones, R. A., 190
Jones, R. G., 47
Jorgensen, B. W., 288
Jorgensen, S. R., 290
Jorgenson, D. O., 550
Joseph, N., 330
Julia, P., 93–94

Kagan, J., 127, 334
Kahan, J. P., 57, 361
Kahle, L. R., 178
Kahn, A., 325, 405
Kahn, G. M., 290
Kaiser, M. K., 324
Kallgren, C. A., 202
Kalmuss, D. S., 331
Kamenetzky, J., 201
Kaplan, A., 5
Kaplowitz, S. A., 434, 441
Karlin, R. A., 381
Karol, P., 233
Kaswan, J. W., 82
Katcher, A. H., 346, 509
Katz, D., 175–178
Katz, J. F., 325
Katz, P. A., 485
Keating, C. F., 89
Keating, J. P., 381

Keen, S. J., 502
Keith, P. M., 163
Keller, H., 72–73, 74–75, 98–99
Kelley, H. H., 10, 60, 156, 280, 281, 288, 321, 418
Kelley, S. D., 487
Kellogg, L. A., 108–109
Kellogg, R. T., 215
Kellogg, W. N., 108–109
Kelly, W. R., 559
Kelman, H. C., 28, 229
Kenny, D. A., 50
Kenny, D. T., 338–339
Kenrick, D. T., 300
Kerckhoff, A. C., 78, 288, 528, 532
Kerr, N. L., 426, 429
Kessen, W., 102
Kessler, S. J., 505
Kiesler, C., 187, 202, 221
Killian, L. M., 470, 483, 549–550, 551–552
Killworth, P. D., 270
Kilman, S., 20
Kimata, L. G., 61
Kimmel, A. J., 538–539
Kinder, D. R., 471
King, G., 219
King, H. E., 354
King, W., 322
Kipnis, D., 343, 439, 446, 447–449
Kirsch, K., 231
Kirsch, N., 30
Kitsuse, J. I., 557
Kitt, A. S., 533
Klandermans, B., 537
Klapp, O. E., 142
Klinger, E., 264
Kluckhohn, C., 100
Knapper, C., 45
Knowles, E. S., 401
Knurek, D. A., 340–341
Koenig, F., 538–539
Koffka, K., 9
Kohlberg, L., 123, 128–131, 509
Köhler, W., 8
Kolditz, T. A., 171
Kollock, P., 434
Komarovsky, M., 498
Komorita, S. S., 361, 365, 426, 427
Kopel, S. A., 156
Korte, C., 270, 307, 308–309
Koten, J., 20
Kotler, P., 559–560

Kramer, B. M., 465
Kramer, R. M., 471
Krantz, S. E., 59
Krause, N., 487
Krauss, R. M., 5, 55
Kravitz, D. A., 361, 365
Kreithen, M. L., 40
Kreutzer, M. A., 89
Kriesberg, L., 354
Kruglanski, A. W., 446, 449
Krupat, E., 485
Kuhlman, D. M., 363
Kuhn, M. H., 18–19·
Kukla, A., 58
Kulik, J. A., 341
Kurth, S. B., 265
Kwan, K. M., 405, 409

La France, M., 516
Lamm, H., 325, 421
Landes, J., 337–338
Landy, D., 48, 497
Lane, D. W., 321
Lane, W., 447
Langlois, J. H., 48
Lanier, K., 55
Lanni, J. C., 370
LaPiere, R. T., 179
Larzelere, R. E., 290
Laslett, B., 378
Lasswell, H., 437
Latané, B., 308, 310–311, 312, 424–425
Lau, R. R., 59
Lauderdale, P., 215, 405
Lauer, J., 282
Lauer, R., 282
Laufer, R. S., 378
Lavin, B., 243
Lawler, E. J., 441, 442
Lawrence, L. H., 229
Lawson, J., 111
Lawton, M. P., 273–274
Layton, B., 57, 436
Leakey, R., 335
Leary, M. R., 170, 249
Leary, R. W., 369
Lebedun, M., 529
Le Bon, G., 342, 547–550
Lee, F., 519
LeFevre, R., 83
Leffler, A., 87
LeGrand, C. E., 520
Lehmann, S., 401
Leighton, D., 100

Leipold, W. D., 374–375
Lenneberg, E. H., 95, 96–97, 103
Lenski, G. E., 355–356, 438, 450, 453
Leo, G., 219
Lepper, M. R., 43, 203
Lerner, M. J., 317, 318, 319, 405
Lester, M., 456
Leung, K., 324
Leventhal, G. S., 58, 321, 324, 325
Leventhal, H., 198
Levine, C., 388
Levine, D. U., 487
Leviine, F. M., 300
Levine, J., 84
Levine, J. M., 222
Levine, S. V., 544, 545
Levinger, G., 288, 318
Levinson, D. J., 133–138
Lewicki, P., 60, 160
Lewin, K., 5, 9–10, 336
Lewin, R., 441
Lewis, I. A., 503
Lewis, L. L., 48, 494, 497
Lichtman, R. R., 352
Lieberson, S., 460, 481
Liebman, M., 375
Liebowitz, M. R., 283–284
Lifton, R. J., 542–543
Light, J. M., 274
Likert, R., 176
Lilly, J. R., 553
Limber, J., 113
Lincoln, A., 318
Linden, F., 523, 524
Lindzey, G., 337–338
Linn, L. S., 179
Linville, P. W., 405
Linz, D., 347
Lipman, A., 375
Lippa, R., 517
Lippitt, R., 10
Lippmann, W., 174
Lipset, S. M., 449
Liska, A. E., 180
Liu, T. J., 192
Livingstone, F. B., 463
Llewellyn, L. G., 89
Locksley, A., 408, 467
Lofland, J., 238, 530, 541–544
Loftus, E. F., 52
London, P., 305–307
Long, T. E., 543
Loo, C., 376
Lopata, H. Z., 554

Lord, C. G., 43, 203
Lorenz, K., 333, 335, 369
Loseke, D. R., 554
Lothstein, L. M., 506
Lott, A., 285–286, 290–291
Lott, B., 285–286, 290–291
Love, L. R., 82
Love, R. E., 89
Lowie, R., 355
Lubinski, D., 515, 517
Luce, R. D., 361, 362
Luchins, A. S., 47
Lucido, D. J., 307
Luginbuhl, J. E. R., 57
Lyman, S. M., 215, 375, 387, 389
Lynn, S. J., 290, 291

Maass, A., 223
Macaulay, J., 300
McCain, G., 380–381
McCall, G. J., 401–402
McCallum, R., 380
McCarthy, J. D., 485–486, 487, 536
McClaren, H. A., 375
McClosky, H., 416
Maccoby, E. E., 510, 512
McConahay, J. B., 471
MacCoun, R. J., 429
McCrae, R. R., 158–159
MacCrone, I. D., 489
McDonald, C. A., 399
McEachern, A. W., 244
McFarland, C., 202
McGinley, H., 83
McGinley, P., 83
McGinnies, E., 201
McGrath, J. E., 412
McGuire, W. J., 47, 178, 195, 196, 197, 200–201, 202, 203
Maddux, J. E., 196, 200
MacIver, R. M., 468, 470
McKay, G., 400
McKenna, W., 505
Mackie, D., 43, 421
McKinlay, J. B., 267–269
McLaughlin, A. M., 515
McMahan, I. D., 58
McMiillan, J. H., 59
McMillen, D. L., 232
McPartland, J. M., 485
McPhail, C., 546, 551
MacPherson, G. M., 510
McTavish, J., 363–364
McWhirter, R. M., 285

Maehr, M. L., 59, 488
Mahard, R. E., 485
Mainardi, P., 519
Mainprize, S., 374
Major, B., 325, 516
Malamuth, N. M., 28, 346, 347, 349
Malcolm X, 541
Maller, J. B., 308
Mann, J. H., 465
Mann, L., 342, 343, 346, 548
Mann, R., 428
Mann, T., 76
Manning, S. A., 338–339
Manucia, G. K., 309
Marecek, J., 168
Margulis, S. T., 378
Mark, M. M., 336
Markides, K. C., 405
Marks, G., 275
Marks, L. E., 102–103
Markus, H., 8–9, 159, 161, 515
Marlatt, G. A., 63
Marler, P., 334
Marlin, N. A., 215
Marolla, J., 165, 349
Martin, D., 330, 332
Martin, J., 537
Maruyama, G., 275
Marx, G. T., 531
Maselli, M. D., 341
Maslow, A. S., 133, 144–145
Mason, W. S., 244
Masters, W. H., 514
May, M. A., 308
May, W. H., 78
Mayer, P., 401
Mazis, M. B., 191
Mazur, A., 84, 86, 371, 550
Mead, G. H., 13, 145–146, 147, 152, 161
Mead, M., 494
Meek, D. D., 365
Meeker, B. F., 325
Mehan, H., 212
Mehrabian, A., 82, 83, 385
Meindl, J. R., 405
Merton, R. K., 410–411, 466–467, 483, 533
Messé, L. A., 61
Metcalf, J., 381
Mettee, D. R., 168
Metzner, H. L., 400
Meyer, J., 506
Meyer, J. P., 288
Meyer, T. P., 346

Meyer-Bahlburg, H. F. L., 500
Meyers, B., 460
Meyers, D. G., 421
Michaels, J. W., 58
Michels, R., 449
Michener, H. A., 365, 441, 442, 445
Middleton, D., 416
Milavsky, B., 346
Milgram, S., 28, 30, 59, 224–227, 233, 266, 270, 343, 402–403, 531, 547, 548, 550, 552
Miller, A., 536
Miller, C. E., 361, 365
Miller, C. T., 286
Miller, D. T., 353
Miller, G. A., 94
Miller, N., 30, 196, 275, 408, 468, 487
Miller, N. E., 336
Mills, C. J., 515
Mills, J., 21
Milmoe, S., 79
Miron, M. S., 78
Mischel, H. N., 128
Mischel, W., 42, 120, 128, 308
Mitchell, C., 473
Mitchell, R. E., 376, 399
Miyamoto, S. F., 19, 162
Mogul, K. M., 137–138
Moine, D. J., 195
Molm, L. D., 434
Money, J., 284, 500, 501–502, 503, 506, 508
Montagu, A., 334, 463
Montgomery, J., 538
Moon, T. H., 443
Mooney, J., 533
Moore, B., 304, 309
Moore, D., 365
Moore, J., 487
Moos, R. H., 399
Moreland, R. L., 408
Morgan, C. P., 420–421
Morgan, W. R., 325
Moriarty, T., 312–313
Morland, J. K., 485
Moroney, R. J., 369
Morris, D., 333, 335
Morris, J., 504
Morris, K. J., 202
Morrison, D. M., 180
Morse, N. C., 337–338
Mortimer, J. T., 131, 133
Moscovici, S., 219, 223
Moskos, C. C., Jr., 416, 417

Mott, F. L., 521
Mottl, T. L., 537
Muehleman, J. T., 420–421
Muha, M. J., 465
Mulford, H. A., 19, 496–497
Murdock, G. P., 494
Murphy, G., 143
Murphy, L. R., 529, 532
Murphy-Berman, V., 324
Murray, A., 537
Murstein, B. I., 278, 288, 293
Muson, H., 131
Myer, J. K., 487
Myers, A. M., 517
Mylander, C., 113
Mynattt, C., 311

Naccari, N., 445
Nadel, S. F., 401
Naficy, A., 191
Nagy, G. F., 278
Nahemow, L., 273–274
Needel, S. P., 377
Nel, E., 192
Nelson, E. A., 338–339
Nelson, K., 97, 103
Nemeth, C., 364, 428
Neugarten, B. L., 138
Newcomb, T. M., 143, 285
Newton, J. W., 342, 343, 548
Nezlek, J., 275
Nicholls, J. G., 58–59
Nida, S., 310, 311
Nielsen, F., 460
Nisan, M., 129–131
Nisbet, R., 552
Nisbett, R. E., 31, 45–46, 54, 56, 57
Norvell, N., 470

Oberschall, A., 356
Obudho, C., 485
Ofshe, R. J., 376
Olsen, M. E., 211, 265, 434, 449
Olshan, K., 45
Olson, J. M., 180, 203
Omelich, C. L., 59
O'Reilly, J., 330
Orne, M., 24–25
Ortiz, V., 408
Osgood, C. E., 45, 78, 177, 185–186
Ostrom, T. M., 16, 45, 61
Ostrove, N., 48, 428

O'Sullivan, M., 82–83, 89
Ovesey, L., 508
Owens, S., 487

Pack, S. J., 496
Padgett, V. R., 285
Page, A. W., 330
Paisley, C., 171
Pallak, M. S., 187
Paloutzian, R. F., 544
Papageorgis, D., 203
Patchen, M., 484, 485
Pate, G. S., 468
Paton, S. M., 485–486
Patterson, M. L., 86, 381, 385
Patterson, P., 110
Paulus, P. B., 380–381
Pearce, D. M., 479
Pearlin, L. I., 482
Pennebaker, J. W., 381, 529, 532, 548
Pennington, N., 429
Penrod, S. D., 429
Peplau, L. A., 264, 283
Pepper, S., 288
Perinbanayagam, R. S., 257
Perlick, D., 380, 547
Perrow, C., 537, 546
Perry, D. G., 508, 509
Perry, L. C., 508
Person, E. S., 508
Personnaz, B., 219
Petersen, K. K., 180
Peterson, I., 529, 532
Pettigrew, T. F., 487
Petty, R. E., 197, 201–202, 203, 231, 425
Phillips, D. A., 485–486
Phillips, D. P., 401, 450
Phillips, L. W., 194, 196
Phoenix, C. H., 511
Piaget, J., 122–127, 128–129
Piliavin, I. M., 315–316
Piliavin, J. A., 315–316, 318
Pines, M., 53, 115, 304
Piscale, R., 108
Pittman, N. L., 60
Pittman, T. S., 60
Pitt-Rivers, J., 463
Piven, F., 559
Plummer, K., 514
Podsakoff, P. M., 444–445, 449
Pollock, C. B., 332
Pope, K. S., 279
Porter, C. A., 353

Porter, J., 485
Powell, E., 384
Pratkanis, A. R., 155
Preisler, R. M., 202
Premack, A., 110
Premack, D., 110
Prentice-Dunn, S., 343
Prewitt, K., 438, 451
Priest, R. F., 273–274
Primrose, C., 508
Proshansky, H. M., 368, 373
Pruitt, D. G., 358, 420, 421, 433–434
Pugh, W. M., 380
Pyszczynski, T., 171, 482

Quadagno, D. M., 502
Quadagno, J. S., 502
Quarantelli, E. L., 21, 162–163

Rabbie, J. M., 357, 408
Raiffa, H., 361, 362
Ramirez, J., 346
Rapaport, K., 349
Rapoport, A., 361
Rau, L., 128
Raven, B. H., 405, 444, 445–446, 449
Ravitch, D., 487
Razran, G., 50–51
Read, S. J., 50, 165
Reed, R., 473
Regan, D. T., 232–234
Reid, J., 370
Reimer, B., 545
Reinecker, V. M., 290
Reinisch, J. M., 502, 503, 511
Reis, H. T., 48, 49, 275, 320, 400, 428, 429, 430
Resko, J. A., 511
Reter, C., 506
Ricateau, P., 223
Rice, M., 391
Richards, T., 487
Richardson, D., 23
Richardson, J. T., 546
Richardson, K. D., 252
Riche, M. F., 518
Riecken, H. W., Jr., 26, 188
Riemer, B. S., 58
Riess, M., 61
Riger, S., 352
Riggio, R. E., 54

Rigler, D., 332
Rigsby, L., 485–486
Riordan, C., 470
Riordan, C. A., 215
Rivlin, L. G., 373
Robbins, C., 400
Robbins, T., 543, 545
Robinson, I. E., 76
Robinson, T., 533
Rochford, E. B., Jr., 546
Rodgers, W. L., 264
Rodin, J., 310, 315–316, 381
Roed, R. C., 3
Roger, D. B., 92
Rogers, C. R., 145, 146
Rogers, M., 309
Rogers, M. F., 444
Rogers, R. W., 196, 198, 200,.343
Rohsenow, D. J., 63
Rokeach, M., 170
Romer, D., 196, 312
Rompf, W. J., 485
Rook, K. S., 401
Rosa, E., 86
Rose, J. D., 267–269
Rose, P. I., 107
Rosenbaum, D. P., 313, 325
Rosenberg, B. G., 509–512
Rosenberg, M., 143, 146, 163, 485–486
Rosenberg, S., 45
Rosenblatt, P. C., 30
Rosenfeld, H. M., 394
Rosenfield, D., 60, 487, 533
Rosenhan, D. L., 309
Rosenthal, R., 24–25, 54, 122, 483, 488
Rosenthal, T. L., 122
Rosnow, R. L., 538–539
Rosow, I., 133, 288
Ross, D., 121, 339
Ross, E. A., 547
Ross, J. M., 471
Ross, L., 55, 60, 154, 157, 203
Ross, M., 202, 321
Ross, S., 121, 339
Rossell, C., 487
Rossi, A. S., 115
Rothbaum, F., 60
Rousseau, D. M., 245
Rubenstein, H., 78
Ruberman, W., 400
Rubin, D. B., 24
Rubin, J. Z., 360
Rubin, L., 137
Rubin, R. T., 502, 503

Rubin, Z., 5, 281, 283, 291
Ruble, D. N., 498
Rubovits, P. C., 488
Rudd, J., 61
Rude, S., 59
Ruggiero, J., 470
Rumbaugh, D. M., 110, 111
Rusbult, C. E., 292, 294
Russell, D. E. H., 348
Russo, N. F., 518
Rutkowski, G. K., 312
Rychlak, J. F., 288
Ryen, A. H., 405

Sacks, H., 212
Sadowski, C., 391
Saegert, S., 381
Saenger, G., 179–180
Sage, W., 486–487, 488
St. John, N., 485, 486–487, 488
Saks, M. J., 429
Salisbury, W. W., II, 19, 496–497
Salmans, S., 538
Salovey, P., 309
Saltz, E., 308
Salzinger, K., 93–94
Sanday, P. R., 349
Sanders, W. B., 19–20
Sapir, E., 100
Sapolsky, B. S., 346
Savage-Rumbaugh, E. S., 111
Savory, L., 10
Sawyer, J., 273–274, 325
Saxe, L., 471
Sayles, M., 401
Scarr, S., 5
Schachter, S., 26, 188, 233, 272–273
Schaeffer, G. H., 381
Schaet, D. E., 337–338
Schafer, A. T., 511
Schafer, P. M., 163
Schank, R. C., 53–54
Schattschneider, E. E., 360
Scheflen, A. E., 86
Scheier, M. F., 148–149
Schein, E. H., 230
Scherer, K. R., 354
Schiffenbauer, A., 59
Schlenker, B. R., 170, 249, 252, 286, 445
Schlesinger, A., Jr., 422–424, 449
Schmidt, D. E., 381
Schmidt, D. F., 202
Schmidt, S., 447–449

Schmidt, W. E., 473
Schneider, D. J., 42–43
Schneider, W., 503
Schneier, I., 230
Schoeneman, T. J., 163, 164
Schofield, J. W., 219, 485
Schopler, J., 57, 436
Schram, S. F., 559
Schriesheim, C. A., 444–445, 449
Schulman, G. I., 490
Schumacher, A., 92
Schuman, H., 60
Schutte, J. G., 274
Schutz, A., 38–39, 238, 241–242
Schwalbe, M. L., 165
Schwartz, B., 370, 384
Schwartz, M. F., 514
Schwartz, P., 137, 434, 507, 518–519
Schwartz, S., 301, 305
Schwartz, S. H., 30, 311
Schwarz, L. M., 82
Schwarz, N., 59
Schwinger, T., 325
Scott, J. W., 522
Scott, M. B., 215, 375, 387, 389
Scott, R., 405
Scott, W. A., 405
Scott, W. R., 417
Scruton, R., 388
Scully, D., 349
Sears, D. O., 471
Sears, R. R., 128
Sebeok, T., 102
Seeman, M., 401
Seeman, T., 401
Segal, M. W., 272
Seligman, C., 231
Seligman, M. E. P., 118–119
Seligmann, J., 348
Selznick, G. J., 468
Selznick, P., 416, 449
Sen, D. J., 288
Sensenig, J., 190
Serafetinides, E. A., 264, 267
Serrin, W., 521, 524
Shaffer, D. R., 391
Shaklee, H., 363–364
Shanteau, J., 278
Shapiro, P. N., 405
Shapley, L. S., 365
Shaw, M. C., 360
Shaw, M. E., 5, 405
Sheatsley, P. B., 471, 472, 479
Sheehy, G., 133

Shellenberg, J. A., 288
Sheppard, B. H., 443
Sherif, C. W., 219
Sherif, M., 28, 219, 405, 406–407, 468, 551–552
Sherk, D. L., 496
Sherman, J., 510
Sherman, L. W., 331
Sherman, R. C., 202
Sherman, S. J., 311
Sherwood, J. J., 191
Shibutani, T., 214, 405, 409
Shiflett, S., 405
Shils, E. A., 416–417
Shinn, M., 401
Shipp, E. R., 473
Shockley, W., 303–304
Shope, G. L., 338–339
Shortell, J., 341
Shotland, R. L., 309, 314, 315
Shrauger, J. S., 163, 164
Shubik, M., 365
Shumaker, S. A., 324, 400
Sicoly, F., 321
Sieber, J. E., 23
Siegelman, J., 543
Sigall, H., 48, 428, 497
Simkus, A. A., 479
Simmel, G., 5, 238, 354, 361
Simmons, C., 318
Simmons, J. L., 401–402
Simmons, R. G., 131, 133, 485–487
Simon, W., 514
Simpson, D. D., 61
Simpson, J. A., 258, 259
Singer, E., 418
Singer, M. T., 543, 544, 545
Singer, R., 337–338
Skinner, B. F., 6, 12–13, 92–93, 94, 96, 117–118, 144–145
Skocpol, T., 546
Skrypnek, B. J., 495
Sladen, B., 377
Smelser, N., 530–531
Smith, E. A., 371
Smith, E. R., 159
Smith, H. W., 394
Smith, M. D., 161–162
Smith, M. J., 175
Smith, S. S., 23
Smith, S. T., 111
Smith, T. W., 171, 424, 471, 472
Snow, C. E., 94
Snow, D. A., 269, 541–544
Snyder, C. R., 142, 171, 215–216

Snyder, M., 41, 230, 257, 258–259, 495
Snyder, S. S., 60
Sobel, D., 161, 257, 258, 284
Solomon, S. H., 380
Solomon, S. K., 381
Sommer, R., 369, 370, 372, 373–374, 381–384, 385, 389, 390–391
Sorrentino, R. M., 219
Southwick, L. L., 189
Sparling, S., 232
Spector, M., 557
Speier, H., 409
Spence, J. T., 498, 516–517
Spilerman, S., 536
Spinetta, J. J., 332
Stagner, R., 337–338
Stahl, S. M., 529
Stake, J. E., 325–326
Stanley, J. C., 510–511
Stannard, U., 497
Stark, R. S., 537, 541–544
Statham, A., 3, 14
Staub, E., 299, 301, 305, 308–309, 311, 324
Steele, B. G., 332
Steele, C. M., 189, 192
Steffen, V. J., 495
Steinberg, S., 468
Steinhilber, A., 170
Steinmetz, S. K., 330, 332
Stember, C. H., 490
Stemler, J. G., 421, 550
Stephan, C. W., 48
Stephan, W. G., 60, 487
Stephenson, B., 146, 148
Stern, R., 522
Sternberg, R. J., 281, 283
Sternthal, B., 192, 194
Stevens, C. W., 538
Stewart, S. A., 523
Stiles, W. B., 239
Stockton, W., 529, 532
Stokols, D., 376–377, 380
Stoller, R. J., 503–504
Stone, A., 438, 451
Stone, G. P., 254, 439
Stoner, J. A. F., 420
Stonner, D., 338–339
Storms, M. D., 55, 385, 506, 508
Straus, M. A., 330, 331, 332
Strauss, A., 216–218
Streufert, S., 57
Streufert, S. C., 57
Stricker, G., 337–338

Strodtbeck, F. L., 384, 428
Strube, M. J., 331
Stryker, S., 3, 14, 15, 146
Stucky, R. J., 215–216
Suci, G., 45
Sullivan, H. S., 161
Sumner, W. G., 409
Sundstrom, E., 376, 377, 380, 384
Sussman, N. M., 394
Suttles, G. D., 373
Sutton-Smith, B., 512
Svendsen, A. C., 3
Swann, W. B., Jr., 158, 165

Tajfel, H., 408, 465–466
Takooshian, H., 307
Tanford, S., 429
Tannenbaum, A. S., 449
Tannenbaum, P., 45, 185
Tavris, C., 339
Taylor, D. A., 338–339
Taylor, D. G., 479
Taylor, M. C., 515, 517, 536
Taylor, M. G., 167
Taylor, R. B., 370
Taylor, S. E., 156, 352
Taylor, S. P., 341
Tedeschi, J. T., 286, 445
Tellegen, A., 515, 517
Tennov, D., 280
Terborg, J. R., 405
Terrace, H. S., 112
Tesser, A., 384
Tetlock, P. E., 50, 424
Theodorson, A. G., 61, 65
Theodorson, G. A., 61, 65
Thibaut,, J. W., 10, 233, 288, 338–339
Thiel, D. L., 48
Thiessen, D., 391
Thistlethwaite, D. L., 201
Thoits, P. A., 141
Thomas, G. C., 385
Thomas, W. I., 13, 62, 63
Thompson, J. E., 470
Thompson, S. C., 321
Thorndike, E. L., 6
Thornton, B., 319
Thornton, R., 533
Thurow, L. C., 137, 523
Thurstone, L., 176
Tice, D. M., 192
Tierney, K. J., 536, 554
Tilly, C., 536
Timnick, L., 354

Tinbergen, N., 369
Tobias, S., 511
Tobin, P., 510
Toch, H., 402–403, 547, 548, 550, 552
Toi, M., 304
Tolman, E. C., 6
Tolstoy, L., 369
Townsend, B., 518, 519, 524
Traugott, M., 530
Travers, J., 270
Triandis, H. C., 174
Trimboli, C., 80
Trolier, T. K., 466
Trow, M. A., 449
Truninger, E., 331
Tucker, P., 500, 501, 502, 503, 506
Tucker, R. D., 75
Tumonis, T. M., 361
Turbett, J. P., 559
Turner, J., 196
Turner, R. H., 154, 155, 158, 241, 247, 549–550, 551–552
Tyrrell, D. J., 515

Uleman, J. S., 43
Ullian, D. Z., 509
Umiker-Sebeok, D. J., 112
Underwood, B., 304, 309
Uranowitz, S. W., 41
Urruti, G., 365
Useem, B., 537

Vaillant, C. O., 135
Vaillant, G. E., 135
Valins, S., 380
Vallacher, R. R., 145
Van Creveld, M., 416
van den Berghe, P. L., 371, 481
van der Pligt, J., 60
Vander Zanden, J. W., 405, 435, 463, 468–470, 509, 537
Varca, P., 370
Vaske, J. J., 365
Veitch,, R., 346
Vidmar, N., 443
Vinsel, A., 379
Vinson, A., 84
von Baeyer, C. L., 496

Wachtler, J., 428
Wagley, C., 460
Wagner, M., 143

Wagner, R. V., 288
Walberg, H. J., 485–486
Walker, L., 233
Walker, M. B., 80, 129–131
Wallington, S. A., 232
Walsh, E. J., 427, 537
Walster, E., 48, 196, 275, 277, 278, 281, 285, 290–291, 320, 321, 450, 497
Walster, G. W., 278, 285, 290–291, 320, 321, 450
Walters, R. H., 120, 233
Ward, D. M., 76
Ware, J. E., 399
Warland, R. H., 427
Warner, K. E., 199
Warner, L. G., 180
Warr, M., 352
Warr, P., 45
Warren, C., 378
Wasserman, I. M., 550
Watson, D., 55, 155
Watson, J. B., 6, 144–145
Watts, W. A., 203
Weary, G., 57, 61
Weatherley, D., 337–338
Webb, C., 354
Weber, M., 5
Weber, S. J., 25
Webster, B., 40
Webster, M., Jr., 48, 50, 497
Wegner, D. M., 145
Weiby, M., 57
Weigel, R. H., 483
Weinberg, M. S., 506–507
Weinberg, S. K., 506
Weiner, B., 58, 316
Weiner, F. H., 307
Weinstein, E. A., 255–256, 321, 440
Weiskopf, S., 102
Weiss, T., 325
Weisz, J., 119
Weisz, J. R., 60
Wellman, B., 19
Welsh, J. B., 47
Werner, C. M., 392
Wertheimer, M., 9
West, S. G., 24, 28, 29, 31
Westie, F. R., 366–337
Westin, A., 378
Wetzel, C. G., 286
Weyant, J. M., 309
Wheaton, B., 354
Wheeler, L., 275
White, A. J., 508
White, G. L., 278, 279, 282

White, H. C., 266
White, L. A., 76
White, R. K., 10
White, S. W., 264
White, T. H., 381
Whitely, B. E., Jr., 517
Whorf, B. L., 100–102
Whyte, W. F., 26, 250
Whyte, W. H., Jr., 419
Wichman, H., 363
Wicker, A. W., 179, 180
Wicker, T., 472–473
Wicklund, R. A., 55, 145, 146, 148, 190
Wilder, D. A., 405, 408, 470
Wilhelmy, R. A., 233
Wilkins, E. J., 338–339
Willliams, A. W., 399
Williams, J. E., 75
Williams, J. L., 374–375
Williams, K., 424
Williams, L. S., 348
Williams, M., 232
Williams, R. M., Jr., 462, 465
Willie, C. V., 487
Willis, F. N., 374–375
Willis, T. A., 401
Wilson, D. W., 346
Wilson, E. O., 300, 302–304
Wilson, J. D., 500
Wilson, J. P., 305, 308
Wilson, M., 274

Wilson, T. D., 31, 45–46
Wimberley, D. L., 363
Wimberly, R. C., 541
Winch, R. F., 287
Winston, T., 353
Winter, L., 43
Wishman, S., 250–251
Wishner, J., 45
Wishnov, B., 166
Wispé, L. G., 300
Witt, R. R., 57
Wohlstein, R. T., 546, 551
Wolf, S., 307
Wolfe, D. A., 332
Wolfe, M., 378
Wolosin, R. J., 285
Wong, N. W., 401
Wood, D., 84
Wood, H., 212
Wood, J. L., 531
Wood, J. V., 352
Wood, W., 202
Worchel, S., 190, 377, 470
Word, L. E., 30, 315
Worthy, M., 290
Wortman, C. B., 57
Wright, R., 306
Wrightsman, L. S., 429, 430
Wrong, D. H., 165, 209, 441
Wurdock, C., 487
Wyer, R. S., Jr., 318, 465–466
Wylie, R., 164–165, 485–486

Yakimovich, D., 308
Yancey, W. L., 485–486, 487
Yarmey, A. D., 52
Yeh, E. G., 485–486
Yinger, J. M., 144, 161
Yllo, K., 330

Zachry, W., 103
Zajonc, R. B., 3, 8–9, 53–54, 59, 182
Zald, M., 536
Zalk, S. R., 485
Zanna, M. P., 180, 187, 203, 496
Zawadzki, B., 337–338
Zeldow, P. B., 517
Zembrodt, I. M., 294
Zetterberg, H. L., 497–498
Zigler, E., 485–486
Zillmann, D., 346
Zimbardo, P., 28, 30, 157, 158–159, 342, 344–345, 405, 446, 548
Zimmerman, B. J., 122
Zimmerman, D., 110
Zimmerman, D. H., 212
Zirkel, P. A., 485
Zuckerman, D., 300
Zuckerman, M., 54, 55, 89, 155, 428, 429, 430
Zukier, H., 47
Zurcher, L. A., Jr., 269, 541–544

Subject Index

abused children, 332
abused wives, 330–332
accommodation, 123
acts, social, 65, 66, 153–154
advertising, effectiveness of, 198–199
age thirty transition stage, 134
aggression, 328–354; anonymity in, 342–343; as cathartic act, 338–339; definition of, 329; displacement of, 337–338; erotic materials and, 345–348; in families, 330–332; frustration as cause of, 336–339; as 'imitated behavior, 121; as instinct, 333–335; institutionalized, 343–345; in prisons, 343–345; ritualization of, 333; sexual, 345–354; social factors as influence on, 339–341, 370–373; victims of, 352–353

aid, 300
altercasting, 255–256, 440
altruism, 297–327; cost-reward analysis of, 315; motivations for, 299–305; sociobiological definition of, 302–304
androgyny, 514–517
anonymity, 548
anticipatory socialization, 131–132, 418, 420
appearance, 253

assimilation, 123
association principle, 252
attempt-suppressing signals, 81–82
attitudes, 173–205; behavior related to, 178–182; change of, 83, 178, 194–203; components of, 174–175; definition of, 173–174; functions of, 175–178; measurement of, 176–177; organization of, 182–193
attraction, social, 269–293; to complements, 287–288; definition of, 272; love and, 279–284; to physical beauty, 275–279; proximity as influence in, 272–274; to rewards, 288–293; to similar attitudes and beliefs, 284–287
attribution, 39, 53–61, 230; bias in, 59–60; of causality, 53–59; in deceptiveness, 54–55; definition of, 53; function of, 60–61; of motivation, 58–59; to other people, 53–61; to self, 156; in success and failure, 57–59; Weiner's approach to, 58–59
attribution theory, 8, 156
authentic behavior, 256–257
authentic identity, 133
authoritarian personality, 490
authority: force transformed into, 452–453; types of, 452
autokinetic effect, 219
averaging models, 45

back-channel communication, 82
backstage, 254–255
balance theory, 183–185
bargaining theory of coalition formation, 365
behavioral theory, 6–7, 115–116
behavior modification, 119
biases: in attribution processes, 59–60; egocentric, 155, 321; in experimentation, 24–25; mood, 59; self-serving, 60; societal, 60
blaming the victim, 60
body language, 79–91, 389, 390; attitude change indicated by, 83; in courtship behavior, 86, 88; difficulties in deciphering of, 89; facial expressions as, 89–91; liking indicated by, 83; preening as, 87; status and, 86–87
bonding, 264
boundaries of groups, 401–403

bystander effect, 312–313

caretaker speech, 94
caste systems, 481
categories, schematic processing and, 41–42
catharsis, 338–339
causality: internal vs. external, 53–57; motivation and, 58–59
central organizing traits, 43–45
charismatic authority, 452
child abuse, 332
chimpanzee studies, 108–113
choice shifts, 421
choking, 170–171
civil inattention, eye contact and, 84–86
coalitions, 360–365
coercive power, 444–445
cognition, 8, 187
cognitive consistency, 285
cognitive development, 122–127; stages of, 124–127
cognitive dissonance, 24, 186–193
cognitive scripts, 159–161
cognitive structures, 8–9
cognitive theory, 8–9
cohesiveness, 404–405
collective behavior, 528–562; definition of, 529–530; elements of, 529–546; growth and spread of, 538–540; participants mobilized in, 541–546; precipitating factors for, 540–541; social movements vs., 530; structural conduciveness as determinant for, 531–532; structural strain as determinant for, 532–537
colonialism, 481–482
commitment, 190–191
communication, 71–73; body language as, 79–91; civil inattention as, 84–86; definitions of, 73, 74; eye contact as, 84–86; gender and, 91–92; gestures as, 75–76; language as, 13–14, 74–92; multiple channels of, 82–83, 90; one-sided vs. two-sided, 201; persuasiveness in, 194–203; process of, 74, 75; selfhood and, 152–154; speech as, 76–79; third-person effect in, 198–199. *See also* language
communicators, 194–197
comparison function, 418
compartmentalization, 246
competition, 480–481; cooperation vs., 362–364
complementary needs, 287–288
compliance, 227–234; effects of

guilt on, 231–232; foot-in-the-door technique for, 227–231
concrete operations, 124–126
conditioning, 115–119, 121–122
conflict, 354–365; aggressor-defender view of, 358; coalitions formed for, 360–365; conflict-spiral view of, 358–359; definition of, 354; intensity of, 359–360; between interest groups, 354–356; model approaches to, 358–359; prisoner's dilemma game as, 362–364; structural-change view of, 359; in values, 356–358
conformity, 233; Asch's experiments on, 219–221; definition of, 219; to false group judgments, 219–222; in group settings, 218–227; social support as deterrent to, 222–223
congruity theory, 185–186
connotative meaning, 78
consciousness of oneness, 404–410
conservation, principle of, 126
constraints, 444
constructed reality, 210
contagion, 549–550
contamination, social, 387–389
control, 451–452; over information flow, 455
conventional level, 129–131
convergence theory, 550–551
conversation: arranging speaking turns in, 80–82; distancing in, 383, 392–394; gender and, 91–92
cooperation, 300; competition vs., 362–364
cost-reward analysis, 315
courtship behavior, body language in, 86, 88
crowd behavior, 547–552; contagion theory of, 547–550; convergence theory of, 550–551; emergent-norm theory of, 551–552
crowding, 375–381; crime and, 376; density vs., 376–381; overload in, 381
cues, 249
cults, religious, 542–545
culture, 67, 415

debriefing, 23
deception, 54–55
deindividuation, 342–343, 548
denotative meaning, 78
density, 266–267; crowding vs., 376–381

determinism, 60
development, cognitive, 122–127
deviance, 224
diffusion of responsibility, 311–313
discrimination, 467–471
displacement, 337–338
dissonance, cognitive, 24, 186–193
distributive justice, 319
distributive question, 437
donating, 300
duty-to-rescue laws, 314
dyad, attraction in, 269–293

early adult transition stage, 134
egocentric bias, 155, 321
elites, 450–451; information flow controlled by, 455; social control as technique of, 546; symbolic mobilization of support by, 455–456
emergent-norm theory, 551–552
empathy, 304–305
entering adult world, 134
equality, 319–326; of opportunity, 319; of results, 319
equity theory, 319–321, 364
erotic materials, 345–348
ethics in research, 28–31
ethnocentrism, 409
ethnomethodology, 16–17, 212–213, 504–505
exclusion movements, 481
excuses, 215–216
expectations, 240–241, 534
experimenter effects, 24–25
experiments, 19–31; conditions for, 23–24; debriefing for, 23; demand characteristics of, 24–25; demonstration, 26–27; dependent variables in, 19–20, 23; ethics of, 28–31; experimenter effects on, 24–25; in field, 24–25; independent variables in, 19–20, 23; in laboratory, 20–24; problems of, 24–25
expert power, 445
expertness, 196
expressive-instrumental continuum, 265
expressive ties, 264–265
eye contact, civil inattention and, 84–86

facial expressions, 89–91
facial prominence, 498–499
false consensus, 60
family violence, 330–332
fear appeals, 198–200
female intuition, 91

female-labeled professions, 496
field experiments, 24
field theory, 9–10
fixed-role theory, 243
force, 449–456; definition of, 449–450; as foundation of state, 450–456; transformations of, 452–456
foreign aid, 322–323
formal operations, 126–127
free-rider effect, 426–428
friendship. *See* relationships, social
front-stage, 254–255
fronts, 252–254
frustration-aggression hypothesis, 336–339, 489
functionalist theory of attitudes, 175, 178
fundamental attribution error, 55

gatekeeping, 473–479; definition of, 474; ethnicity and, 476–478; nature of, 473–476; race and, 478–479
gender identities, 494, 496–512; acquisition of, 508–512; anatomical determination of, 500–502; definition of, 496; ethnomethodological view of, 504–505; of hermaphrodites, 501; of homosexuals, 503–508; of transsexuals, 503–508; of transvestites, 503–508
gender roles, 494–496; as androgynous, 514–517; communication processes and, 91–92; definition of, 494; psychology of, 510–512
generalized other, 150, 151
Gestalt theory, 9
gestures, 75–76, 152–153, 389
good Samaritan laws, 314
groups, 399–431; boundaries of, 401–403; characteristics of, 400–412; closed, 403; conformity in, 218–227; consciousness of oneness in, 404–410; culture creation by, 415; decisions made by, 422–424; definition of, 400; deliberations by, 425–430; ethnic, 409, 462–463; false judgments made by, 219–222; goals of, 406–407; informal, 417; membership, 418–430; minority, 460–465; minority vs. majority in, 223, 233; open, 403; polarization effects in, 419–422; primary, 412–417; as products of social definitions, 403–404; ra-

cial, 462–463; reference, 418–430, 482–483; risky shift effect in, 420–422; rituals of, 410–412; secondary, 412–417; social distance vs., 408–410
groupthink, 422–424
guilt, compliance effected by, 231–232
Guttman scales, 177

habituation, 102
halo effects, 45–46, 48–49
health, support networks and, 400–401
helping behavior. *See* altruism
hermaphrodites, 501, 504
hierarchy of obligations, 246
home-cage effect, 369–370
homicide, 329, 330
homogamy, 284–285
homosexuality, 86, 164, 503–508
hostages, 390–391
hypotheses, 21–24
hysterical contagion, 529

identity, 141–142, 160. *See also* self
ideologies, 540
idiocultures, 415
implicit personality theories, 42–43
impression formation, 41–53
impression management, 249–256; fronts projected in, 252–254; political, 453–456; power achieved through, 439–440; regions manipulated in, 254–255
inducements, 444
influence, 452; force transformed into, 453–456
informal groups, 417
informational power, 445
ingroups, 404–405
institutional aggression, 343–345
institutional racism, 472–473
institutionalized roles, 14
instrumental ties, 265
interest groups, clashing of, 354–356
intergroup relations, 460–480; gatekeeping in, 473–479; institutional racism in, 472–473; of minorities, 460–465; prejudice in, 465–472
internalization, 127–131, 221
interpersonal behavior: physical environment and, 368–396. *See also* relationships, social; spatial distance; territoriality
introspection, 6
iron law of oligarchy, 449

jury research, 425–430
just-world hypothesis, 317–326
justifications, 215–216

kinesics, 79–81
knowledge structures, 8–9

laboratory experiments, 21–24
language, 74–103; acquisition of, 92–98; as container of thought, 102–103; definition of, 76; levels of, 77; motor development and, 96–98; nature of, 71–92; properties of, 77; significance of, 72–73; symbols and, 13–14, 74–92; thought and, 98–103
language acquisition device, 94
language-generating mechanism, 94
language of space, 392–394
leadership, 63
learned helplessness, 118–119
learning, 115–131; by conditioning, 115–119; definition of, 115; observational, 120–122; symbols employed in, 122, 124
learning theory of language acquisition, 92–94, 96
legal-rational authority, 452
legitimate power, 445, 452
legitimization of roles, 240
life space, 9–10
Likert scales, 176–177
liking, 196–197
linguistic relativity thesis, 99–102
loafing, 424–425
looking-glass self, 147, 151
love, 279–284; as brain chemistry, 283–284; as labeling, 281–283; nature of, 279–281
lying, 54–55

Machiavellianism, 442–443
male chauvinism, 493, 519
manner, 254
markers, 391–392
marriage, 282–283; ingroup, 464–465; intergroup, 464
masochists, 167–168
matching hypothesis of mate selection, 277, 278–279
mate attraction, 88, 277, 278–279
meaning, definition of, 77–78
membership groups, 418–430
memory, 50–53; alteration and distortion of, 52–53; nature of, 51–52

mental illness, 143
messages, 197–202
mid-life transition stage, 134–135
middle adulthood restabilization stage, 135
minimal resource theory, 364
minority groups, 460–465; ascribed membership of, 463–464; definition of, 465; high social visibility of, 462–463; ingroup marriages of, 464–465; oppression and disabilities suffered by, 460–461; as self-conscious social units, 463
mood states, 309–310
moral development, 128–131
morality, obedience and, 228–229
motherese, 94
motivations: causality and, 58–59; for prosocial behavior, 299–305
movements, social, 528–562; collective behavior vs., 530; elements of, 529–546; ideologies of, 540; resource mobilization for, 536–537; social control vs., 546

nativist theory of language acquisition, 94–95, 96
naturalistic observation, 26–27
need, 324–326
negotiated order, 216–218
networks, 265–269; for support, 400–401
normative function, 418
norms, 417; definition of, 213; formation of, 219; of reciprocity, 232–234, 321–324; of social order, 213–215; of social responsibility, 305, 312
nudist camps, 68

obedience, 224–229
object permanence, 124, 125
obligations, 232–234, 240–241; hierarchy of, 246; in reciprocal behavior, 322–324
observation, 26–27, 120–122
operant conditioning, 115, 116; definition of, 117; reinforcers in, 118–119
order, social, 210–218
outgroups, 404–405

paralanguage, 78–79
participant observation, 26

perception, 36–68; averaging models for, 45; categorizing for, 41–42; of central traits, 43–45; definition of, 37–38; distortion of, 221; halo effects in, 45–46, 48–49; inconsistency in, 47–50; memory processes in, 50–53; of physical attractiveness, 48–50; primacy effect of, 46–47; prototyping for, 42–43; recency effect of, 46–47; selective, 2; of self, 154–157, 163–164, 230–231; sensation and, 37, 40; of situation, 61–68; stereotyping for, 43; summation models for, 45; superstition and, 43
person perception, 41
personal space, 373–375
personality variables, 489–490
persuasion, 83, 178, 194–203, 444
phi phenomenon, 9
physical attractiveness, 274–278
physical environment, interpersonal behavior and, 368–396
pivotal power theory, 364–365
poker, 250–251
polarization effects, 420–422
political impression management, 453–456
positioning, 390–391
postconventional level of moral development, 129–131
power, 433–458; altercasting and, 440; assessment of, 440–443; attributions of, 436–437; bases of, 444–445; control and, 447; definition of, 433–434; displays of, 435; of elites, 450–451; force as instrument of, 449–456; impression management and, 439–440; for gain, 437–439; legitimate, 445, 452; nature of, 433–439; passive resistance to, 435; preference, 445–449; as process, 439–449; sources of, 446–449; of state, 450; as two-way street, 434–436; unequal, 481–482; use of, 448
preconventional level of moral development, 129–131
preening, 87
prejudice, 465–472; definition of, 465; discrimination vs., 467–471; negative feelings as component of, 466–467; stereotyping as component of, 465–467; symbolic racism as, 471–472

preoperational thought, 124
primacy effect, 46–47
primary groups, 412–417; definition of, 412; importance of, 413–416; within secondary groups, 416–417
primary relationships, 264–265
prisoner's dilemma game, 362–364
privacy, 378–379, 394; captivity and loss of, 390–391
privilege, 438
projection, 175, 489–490
property, redefinition of, 450, 451
prosocial behavior, 298–327; altruistic motives for, 299–305; in ambiguous situations, 310–313; definition of, 298; diffusion of responsibility vs., 311–313; equity theory of, 319–321; just-world hypothesis of, 317–319; mood states contributing to, 309–310; personality traits contributing to, 305–309; as reciprocal, 321–324; in unambiguous situations, 313–317
prototypes, for impression formation, 42–43
proximity, 272–274
public territory, 375

questionnaires, 18–19

racism, 459–492; competition as source of, 480–481; examples of, 467; institutional, 471–472; in intergroup relations, 460–480; personality variables as sources of, 489–490; reference groups as sources of, 482–483; remedies for, 468–470; self-fulfilling prophecy as source of, 483–488; sources of, 480–490; symbolic, 471–472; unequal power as source of, 481–482
rape, 348–354; precautions taken against, 350–351; victims of, 352–354
reactance, 190–191
recency effect, 46–47
reciprocal reinforcement, 117
reciprocity: norm of, 232–234, 321–324; of roles, 239–241
recognition ceremonies, 389
reference groups, 418–430, 482–483
referent power, 445
regions, 254–255

reinforcement, 7, 118–119, 285–286
reinforcers, 118–119
relationships, social, 2, 262–269; definition of, 264; dissatisfaction in, 294; networks of, 265–269; primary, 264–265; quality of, 258–259; secondary, 265; types of ties in, 264–269
relative deprivation, 418, 533–536, 537
release theory, 421–422
responses, 6–7
reward power, 444–445
rewards: dissonance and, 192; distribution of, 324–326
rise-and-drop hypothesis, 535–536
risky shift effect, 420–422
ritualization, 333
rituals, 410–412
role-making, 242–244
role-person merger, 247–249
role-taking, 241–242
role theory, 14–15
role transitions, socialization and, 131–132
roles, 237–261; ambiguity of, 246; conflicts in, 244–246; definition of, 238; distance from, 246–248; influencing others with, 249–259; legitimization of, 240; nature of, 238–249; as reciprocal, 239–241; strain caused by, 244–246
rumors, 538–539

schemata, 42, 159–161
school desegregation, effects of, 484–488
second-order consequences, 559–561
secondary groups, 412–417; definition of, 413; primary groups within, 416–417
secondary relationships, 265
selective perception, 2
self, 141–171; attribution to, 156; behavioral view of, 144–145; cognitive scripts for, 159–161; as communicative process, 152–154; conceptions of, 2, 19, 26, 157–169; controversial nature of, 144–146; definition of, 142–143; material, 146; overperceptions of, 155; perception of, 154–157, 163–164, 230–231; psychoanalytic view of, 144;

social, 147–151; symbolic interactionist view of, 146–154
self-actualization, 133, 144–145
self-appraisals, 162–165
self-attribution, 156
self-awareness, 148–149
self-conceptions, 2, 19, 26, 157–169; behavior and, 167–169; dissonance and, 192; sources of, 161–165
self-disclosure, 290–291
self-esteem, 165–167, 232, 485–486
self-fulfilling prophecy, 59, 483–488
self-handicapping, 171
self-image, 158–159
self-indication, 150
self-interest, 324–326
self-knowledge, 157
self-monitoring, 257–259
self-presentation, 249–259; fronts employed in, 252–254; monitoring of, 257–259
self-schemata, 159–160
self-socialization, 509
semantic differential, 78, 177
semantic differential scales, 177
sensation, 37, 40
sensitivity training, 10
sensorimotor stage of cognitive development, 124
setting, 252–253
settling down, 134
sexism, 518–524; definition of, 493; in home, 518–521; in wage economy, 521–524
sexuality, 493–527; symbols and meanings of, 512–514
shyness, 158–159
significant other, 147
situational territory, 375
situations: definitions of, 61, 62–68, 377, 439–440; perception of, 61–68; shared definitions of, 64–68
sleeper effect, 203
slum life, 372–373
small world studies, 266, 270–271
social acts, 65, 66, 153–154
social comparison processes, 286–287, 311
social constructs, 39
social control, 546
social dilemmas, 426–427
social distance, 408–410
social exchange theory, 10–13, 288–293
social inequality, 319–326
social interaction. See relationships, social
social learning theory, 120

social loafing, 424–425

social order, 210–218; accounting for negative behavior and, 215–216; construction of, 211–212; definition of, 211; ethnomethodological view of, 212–213; negotiation of, 216–218; norms of, 213–215

social problems, 409–410, 552–561; as interest group and value clashes, 554–555; legitimacy of, 556–557; nature of, 553–554; public policy formulated for, 557–558; rise and fall of, 553; second-order consequences of, 559–561

social psychology, 2–27; definition of, 2–3; methods of, 17–27; origins of, 3–5; psychology and, 3–5; sociology and, 3–5; subject matter of, 4; theories of, 5–17

social relationships, 51

social support, 400–401

socialization, 14, 106–115; of adults vs. children, 133; appropriate environment presumed by, 107, 113–115; definition of, 106–107; of employees, 108–109; genetic endowment presupposed by, 107, 108–113; internalization as process of, 127–131; across life span, 131–138; life stage approach to, 133–139; preconditions for, 107–115; role transitions and, 131–133. *See also* learning

sociobiology, 302–304

sociogram, 268

sociometry, 266, 268

spatial distance, 381–394; architecture and, 388; interpersonal dynamics of, 381–385; language of, 392–394; social significance of, 382. *See also* territoriality

speech, 76–77; caretaker vs. everyday, 94; in conversations, 80–82; paralanguage in, 78–79. *See also* language

split labor market, 480

status, 233, 439; body language and, 86–87; craving for, 355–356; spatial distance and, 384

stereotypes, 43, 174, 465–467

stimuli, 6–7

Stockholm Syndrome, 390

structural conduciveness, 531–532

structural strain, 532–537

sucker effect, 427

suggestibility, 549–550

summation models, 45

superstitions, 43

surveys, 18–19; misreading of, 20–21

symbolic interactionism, 3–5; meaning in, 14; role theory and, 14–15; self and, 146–154; self–appraisal and, 162; varieties of, 13

symbols, 75–76, 77; as critical to learning, 122, 124; language and, 13–14, 74–92

sympathy, 300

targets, 202–203

territoriality, 368–381; defense in, 389–392; definition of, 369; expressions of, 373–375; hierarchy in, 370–371; invasions in, 385–389; in ordering slum life, 372–373; privacy in, 378–379; social roots of, 370–373. *See also* spatial distance

terrorism, 534–535

testosterone, 502

T-groups, 10

theories: definition of, 5–6; evaluation of, 17

thought, language and, 98–103

Thurstone scales, 176

traditional authority, 452

traits, 305–309

transformational grammar, 94

transsexuals, 503–508

transvestites, 503–508

trust, 290–291

trustworthiness, 194–196

turn-yielding signals, 80

Twenty-Statements Test (TST), 18–19, 496

value hypothesis, 420–421

values: clashing of, 356–358; definition of, 356–357

variables in experiments, 19–20

vicarious conditioning, 121–122

victimization, 352–353

violence, 330–332, 558–559

volition, 191

weapons effect, 340

weighted probability theory, 365

white flight, 487–488

Whorfian hypothesis, 100–102

wife abuse, 330–332

writing. *See* language

About the Author

James W. Vander Zanden is a professor in the College of Social and Behavioral Sciences at Ohio State University and previously taught at Duke University. His Ph.D. degree is from the University of North Carolina. Professor Vander Zanden's published works include more than twenty professional articles and eight other books.